AF207894

MARITIME PAINTING
LES MAÎTRES DE LA PEINTURE MARINE
MARITIME MALEREI
MARINAS

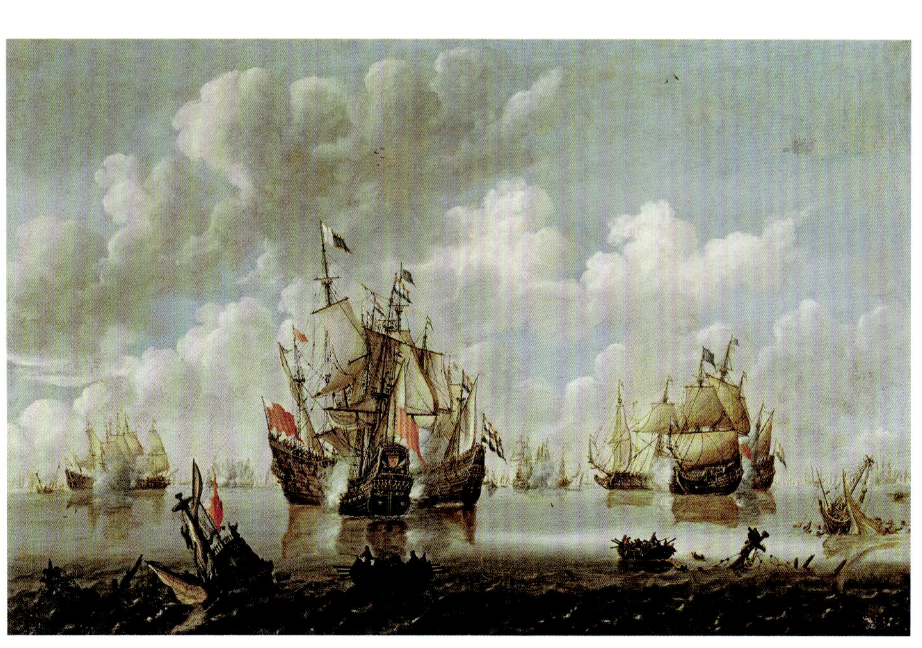

DANIEL KIECOL

MARITIME PAINTING
LES MAÎTRES DE LA PEINTURE MARINE
MARITIME MALEREI
MARINAS

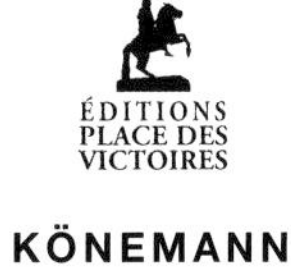

ÉDITIONS
PLACE DES
VICTOIRES

KÖNEMANN

p. 2

Willem van de Velde d. J. (1633–1707)

Battle at Sea

Bataille navale

Seeschlacht

Batalla naval

Batalha naval

Zeeslag*l*

1675–1699, Oil on canvas/Huile sur toile, 110 × 171,2 cm, Musée des Beaux-Arts, Orléans

KÖNEMANN

© 2019 koenemann.com GmbH

www.koenemann.com

© Éditions Place des Victoires

6, rue du Mail – 75002 Paris

www.victoires.com

ISBN: 978-2-8099-1758-1

Dépôt légal: 4ᵉ trimestre 2019

Concept, Project Management: koenemann.com GmbH

Text: Daniel Kiecol

Editing: Jenny Tiesler

Translation into English, French, Spanish, Portuguese, Dutch:

TEXTCASE
Translation Agency

info@textcase.nl

textcase.de   textcase.eu

Layout: Regine Ermert

Picture credits: Bridgeman Images, except akg-images gmbh: pp 197, 270

ISBN: 978-3-7419-2493-4

Printed in China by Shyft Publishing/Hunan Tianwen Xinhua Printing Co., Ltd

Contents   Sommaire   Inhalt   Índice   Inhoud

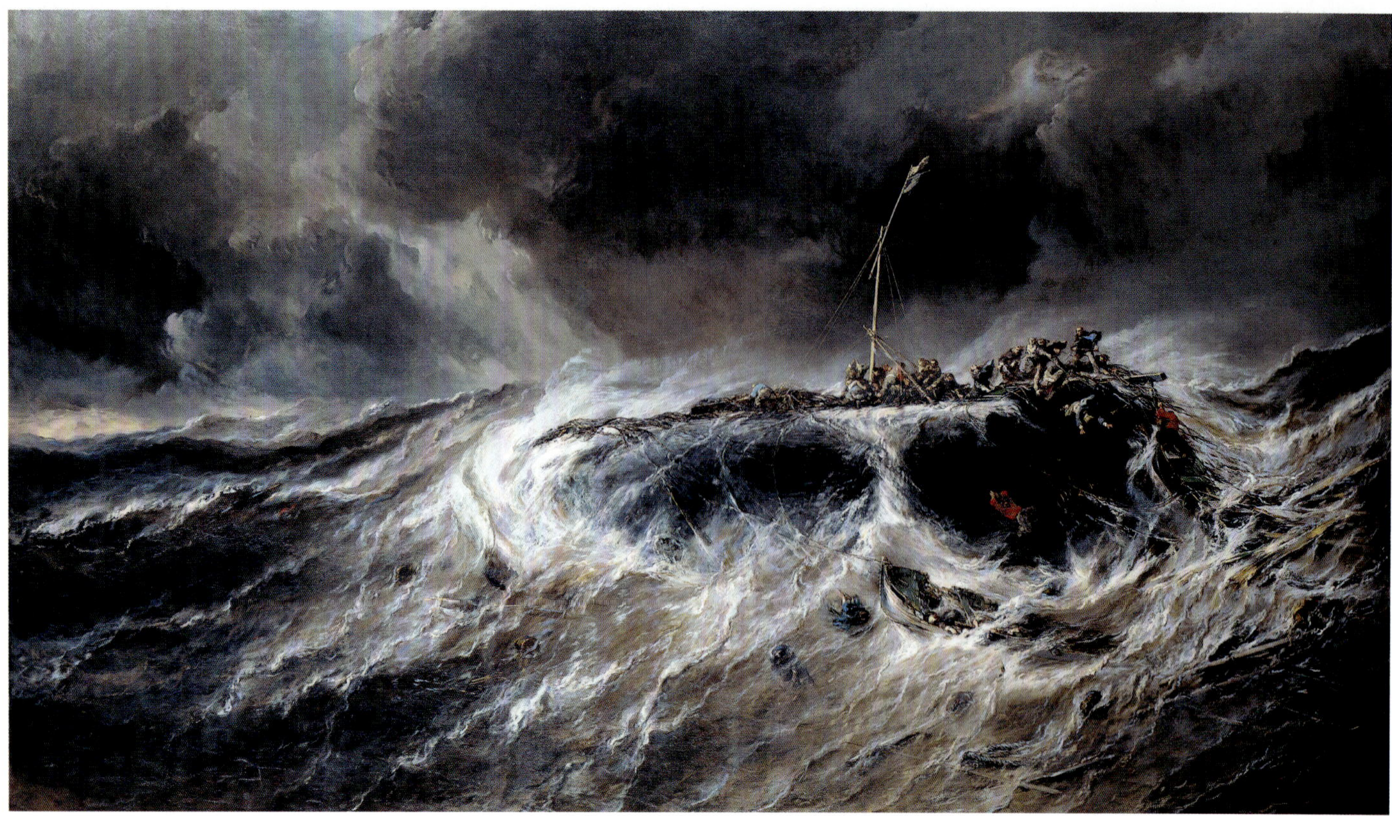

If one attempts to investigate the differences and similarities when it comes to how the subject of ships and the sea are treated in the different countries of the world, one soon discovers a linguistic phenomenon that reflects the core of these differences. The difficulty of appropriately transferring the English term "seascape", used in the title of so many images from the English-speaking world, into another language points to a fundamentally different perception of the sea: where the sea is a special kind of landscape, which also makes every painting of the sea a kind of landscape painting. And it was not the romantic 19th century paintings of a Turner and a Constable showing the sea as a vast expanse of color in contrast to the sky that first allowed the English to make the same transition to abstraction and the dissolving of the natural and the objective that the French made with their images of wheat fields and hills.

From the very beginning, the painting of the sea has always been marked by the tension between the human and nature. After all, in earlier cultures the sea was not only a place associated with great danger in the transport of people and goods, but it was even thought to represent the very ends of the world

Si l'on tente d'étudier les différences et les similitudes sur la manière dont les navires et la mer sont traités dans les différents pays du monde, on découvre rapidement un phénomène linguistique qui reflète le cœur de ces différences. La difficulté de transférer correctement dans une autre langue l'expression « paysage marin », utilisé dans le titre d'un si grand nombre d'images du monde anglophone, montre une perception fondamentalement différente de la mer : la mer est un paysage particulier, ce qui fait de toutes les peintures de la mer une sorte de peinture de paysage. Et ce ne sont pas les peintures romantiques du XIXᵉ siècle d'un Turner et d'un Constable qui présentent la mer comme une vaste étendue de couleur en contraste avec le ciel qui ont permis aux Anglais de faire la même transition vers l'abstraction et la dissolution du côté naturel et objectif que les Français créaient avec leurs images de champs de blé et de collines.

Dès le début, la peinture de la mer a toujours été marquée par la tension entre l'homme et la nature. Après tout, dans les cultures antérieures, la mer n'était pas seulement un lieu associé à un grand danger pour le transport des personnes et des marchandises ; on pensait qu'elle représentait les extrémités du monde lui-même. Il n'est donc pas surprenant que les premières

Versucht man die Unterschiede und Gemeinsamkeiten zu ergründen, die das Thema Schiffe und Meer in verschiedenen Ländern der Welt betreffen, stößt man schon bald auf ein sprachliches Phänomen, das den Kern dieser Unterschiede widerspiegelt. Die Schwierigkeit, den englischen Begriff *seascape,* der sich in zahlreichen Titeln angelsächsischer Bilder findet, angemessen in andere Sprachen zu übertragen, verweist auf eine grundlegend andere Wahrnehmung. Das Meer als eine besondere Art der Landschaft, die auch ein jedes Seegemälde zu einem Landschaftsgemälde macht. Nicht erst im romantisch geprägten 19. Jahrhundert eines Turner und eines Constable ermöglichte diese Vorstellung des Meeres als weite, farbige, mit dem Himmel kontrastierende Fläche den Engländern, den Übergang zur Abstraktion zu finden, die Auflösung des Natürlich-Gegenständlichen, der sich bei den Franzosen eher in Bildern von Weizenfeldern und Hügeln vollzog.

Von Beginn an befand sich die Seemalerei immer im Spannungsfeld zwischen Mensch und Natur, besonders ausgeprägt dadurch, dass das Meer vor allem für die frühen Kulturen nicht nur mit viel größeren Gefahren beim Transport von Menschen und Waren verbunden war, sondern lange Zeit auch die Vorstellung vom Ende der

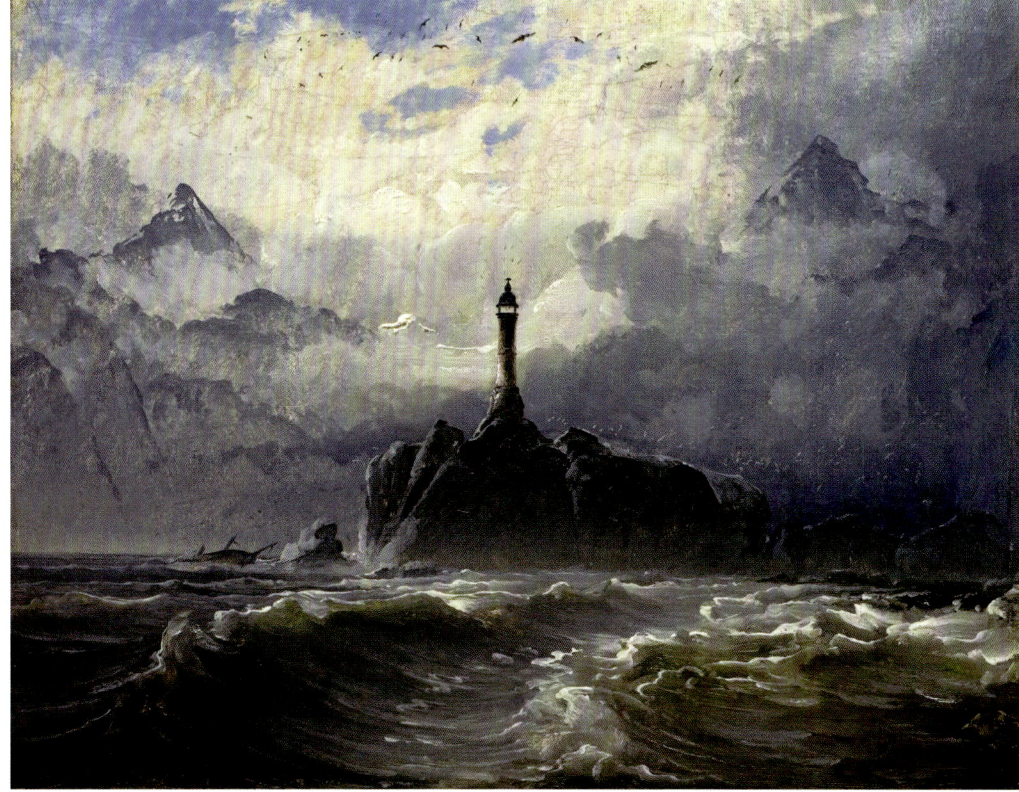

Si uno trata de averiguar las diferencias y similitudes en relación con el tema de los barcos y el mar en diferentes países del mundo, se llega pronto a un fenómeno lingüístico que refleja la esencia de estas diferencias. La dificultad para transmitir adecuadamente a otros idiomas el término inglés *seascape*, que se encuentra en numerosos títulos de cuadros anglosajones, ya nos muestra que existe una percepción fundamentalmente diferente. El mar como un tipo especial de paisaje que hace de cada marina un cuadro de paisaje. Esta representación del mar amplia, colorista, con el cielo en contraste con las superficies inglesas, que no se hace por primera vez en el siglo XIX con el carácter romántico de Turner y Constable, permite encontrar la transición a la abstracción, la disolución de la representación figurativa, que para los franceses se llevó a cabo más bien en las imágenes de los campos de trigo y las colinas.

Desde el principio, la pintura marítima siempre se encontraba en el campo de tensión entre el hombre y la naturaleza, sobre todo caracterizada por el hecho de que el mar, especialmente para las primeras culturas, estaba conectado no sólo con grandes peligros en el transporte de personas y mercancías, sino que durante mucho tiempo estuvo incluida la representación del

Sempre que nós tentamos analisar as diferenças e semelhanças relacionadas ao tema navios e mar, em diferentes países do mundo, nos deparamos imediatamente com um fenômeno lingüístico que reflete a essência dessas diferenças. A dificuldade de tradução adequada, para outras línguas, do termo inglês *seascape*, que pode ser encontrado em inúmeros títulos de quadros anglo-saxões, indica uma percepção fundamentalmente distinta. O mar como um tipo especial de paisagem, que faz que cada pintura marinha seja igualmente uma pintura de paisagem. Não somente no século XIX, marcado pelo romantismo de um Turner ou um Constable, essa conceção de mar como uma superfície ampla, cheia de cor, contrastando com o céu, permitiu aos pintores ingleses encontrarem a transição para a abstração, a dissolução do concreto-natural, que no caso dos pintores franceses se consumou em representações de campos de trigo e colinas.

Desde o início que a pintura de marinhas esteve sempre no campo de tensão entre o homem e a natureza, particularmente marcado pelo fato de que, para as primeiras culturas, o mar estava principalmente associado não só a riscos muito maiores no transporte de pessoas e mercadorias, mas, por um longo período, também a uma idéia de fim de mundo. Por isso, não

Wie met betrekking tot het thema "zee en schepen" verschillen en overeenkomsten tussen diverse regionale stijlen probeert te vinden, stuit al snel op de Engelse term *seascape*, waarmee de zee in talrijke schilderijtitels als een afzonderlijk type landschap wordt aangeduid en de maritieme schilderkunst als een bijzondere vorm van landschapsschilderkunst wordt beschouwd. Pas in de romantische negentiende eeuw van Turner en Constable was het voor de Britse landschapsschilderkunst mogelijk om met de uitbeelding van de zee als een weids en kleurrijk beeldvlak dat met de luchten erboven contrasteerde, tot een vervaging van het naturalistische en figuratieve en te komen en daarmee tot de abstractie, terwijl deze overgang in de Franse schilderkunst zich veeleer in uitbeeldingen van korenvelden en heuvellandschappen voltrok.

Vanaf het eerste begin heeft de maritieme schilderkunst zich altijd in het spanningsveld tussen mens en natuur bevonden, een spanningsveld dat werd versterkt door het feit dat de zee vooral in vroege culturen niet alleen met de gevaren van het vervoer van mensen en goederen was verbonden, maar lange tijd ook met de voorstelling van het einde der wereld. Het zal dus niet verbazen dat de eerste bewaard gebleven uitbeeldingen van de scheepvaart, bijvoorbeeld in wandschilderingen

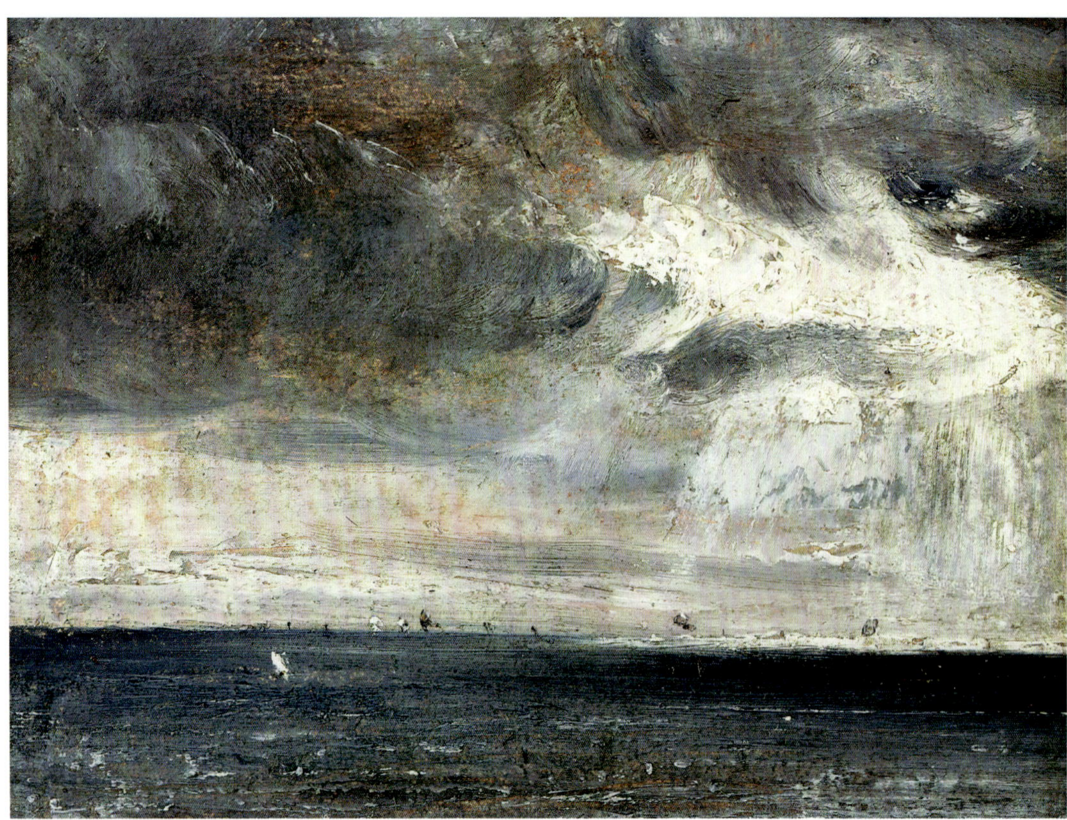

John Constable (1776–1837)
Study of Sea and Sky
Étude de la mer et du ciel
Studie mit Meer und Himmel
Estudio de mar y cielo
Estudo de mar e céu
Studie met zee en luchten
n. d., Oil on canvas/Huile sur toile,
Private collection

itself. It should therefore not be surprising that the earliest portrayals of seafaring, such as the murals of ancient Egypt, Santorini, and Pompeii, mostly show a mythological place populated with gods and heroes.

European painting of the sea really got its start with the Dutch Golden Age of the 17th century. Previously, the sea had usually only served as a backdrop for solemn occasions, royal receptions, and ship demonstrations, in other words, painters restricted themselves to painting events at the seaside. But from the 17th century, the seascape itself gradually became its own more firmly defined genre. Given the particular geographic location and the unique national identity of the Dutch, it seems only natural that Holland was the country where this genre was first created. Painters like Hendrick Vroom (c. 1563–1640), Simon de Vlieger (1601–1653), and Jan Porcellis (c. 1582–1632) are often mentioned in order to emphasize the variety of styles and themes used.

Interestingly, one can date the advent of continental seascapes on the British Isles with the arrival Willem van de Velde Senior and Junior came from Leiden to England in the winter of 1672–73. These members of a respecting painting family soon received commissions from the highest ranks of society. They were given the

représentations de la mer, telles que les peintures murales de l'Égypte ancienne, de Santorin et de Pompéi, montrent surtout un lieu mythologique peuplé de dieux et de héros.

La peinture européenne de la mer a vraiment commencé avec l'âge d'or néerlandais du XVIIᵉ siècle. Auparavant, la mer avait uniquement servi de toile de fond aux occasions solennelles, aux réceptions royales et aux manifestations navales. Autrement dit, les peintres se limitaient à peindre des événements en bord de mer. Mais à partir du XVIIᵉ siècle, le paysage marin lui-même est devenu progressivement un genre propre bien défini. Compte tenu de la situation géographique particulière et de l'identité nationale unique des Hollandais, il semble tout naturel que la Hollande ait été le pays de création de ce genre de peinture. Des peintres comme Hendrick Vroom (c. 1563–1640), Simon de Vlieger (1601–1653) et Jan Porcellis (c. 1582–1632) sont souvent mentionnés afin de souligner la variété des styles et des thèmes utilisés.

Fait intéressant, on peut remonter à l'avènement des paysages marins continentaux sur les îles britanniques avec l'arrivée de Willem van de Velde Senior et Junior, depuis Leyde jusqu'en Angleterre au cours de l'hiver 1672–73. Ces membres d'une famille de peintres

Welt mit einbezog. So kann es nicht überraschen, dass die frühesten uns erhaltenen Darstellungen der Seefahrt, etwa auf Wandgemälden des alten Ägypten, aus Santorin oder aus Pompeji, meist mythologischer Natur sind und das Meer zur Bühne für den Auftritt der Götter und Helden machen.

Die europäische Marinemalerei begann, im niederländischen Goldenen Zeitalter, dem 17. Jahrhundert. Vorher bildete das Meer als solches meist eine bloße Kulisse für feierliche Aktionen, Empfänge und Schiffsvorführungen – maritimes Ereignisbild ist der Begriff, unter dem diese Darstellungen zusammengefasst werden. Ab dem 17. Jahrhundert etablierte sich das Seestück langsam zu einem fester umrissenen Genre. Angesichts der besonderen geographischen Lage und der Besonderheiten der nationalen Identität erscheint es nur natürlich, dass die Niederlande geradezu prädestiniert waren, diesem Genre zum Durchbruch zu verhelfen. Maler wie Hendrick Vroom (circa 1563–1640), Simon de Vlieger (1601–1653) und Jan Porcellis (circa 1582–1632) werden meist genannt, um auch die Vielfalt der verwendeten Stile und Themen zu betonen.

Recht genau lässt sich der Zeitpunkt bestimmen, an dem die kontinentaleuropäische Marinemalerei auch

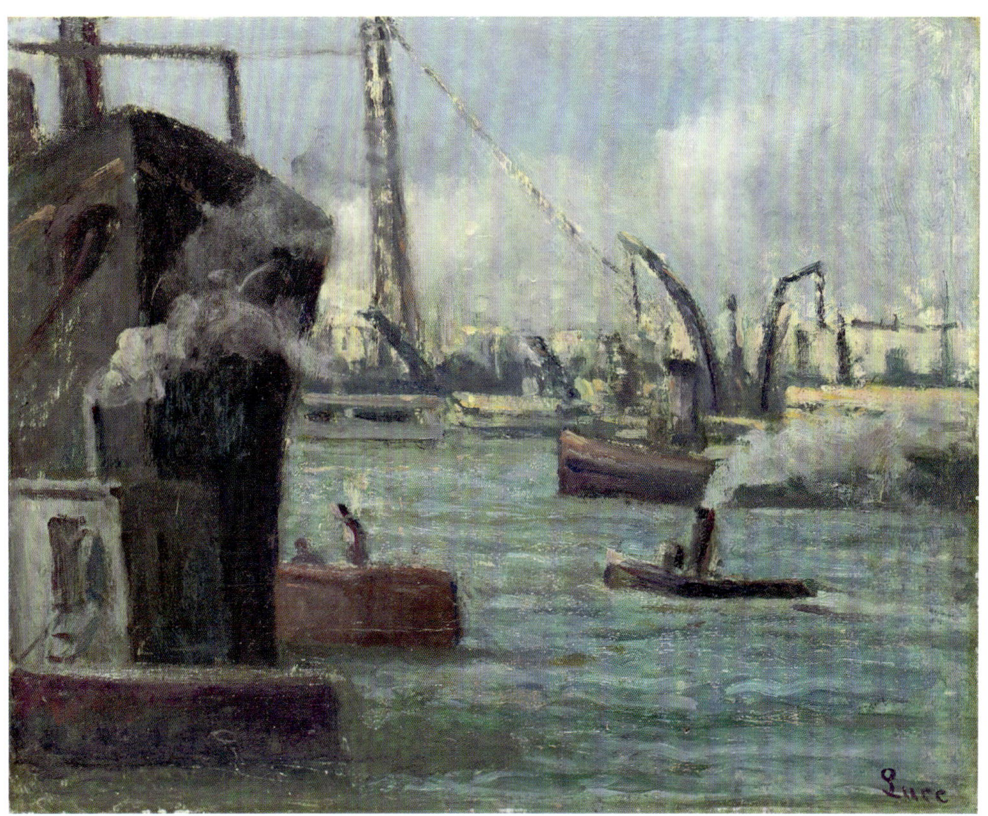

Maximilien Luce (1858–1941)
Rouen Port
Le Port de Rouen
Der Hafen von Rouen
El puerto de Rouen
O porto de Rouen
De haven van Rouen
n. d., Oil on canvas/Huile sur toile,
33,7 × 40,6 cm, Private collection

fin del mundo. Por lo tanto, no es sorprendente que las primeras representaciones marítimas que se conservan, como las pinturas murales del antiguo Egipto, en Santorini o en Pompeya, por lo general sean de naturaleza mitológica y que el mar se utilice de escenario para la salida a escena de dioses y héroes.

En Europa, la pintura de marinas comenzó en el Siglo de Oro holandés, el siglo XVII. Anteriormente, el mar se constituía por lo general como un mero telón de fondo para las acciones de celebración, recepciones y exhibiciones de navíos – imagen de acontecimiento marítimo es el término por el cual se resumen estas representaciones. A partir del siglo XVII, el paisaje marino se estableció lentamente como un género sólidamente determinado. Dada la especial ubicación geográfica y las particularidades de la identidad nacional, parece natural que los Países Bajos estuvieran predestinados para que este género hiciera su aparición. Podemos nombrar a pintores como Hendrick Vroom (aprox. 1563–1640), Simon de Vlieger (1601–1653) y Jan Porcellis (aprox. 1582–1632) para poner de relieve la diversidad de estilos y temas usados.

Podemos determinar con bastante precisión el momento en que la pintura de marinas de la Europa

é surpreendente que as primeiras representações que sobreviveram da navegação, por exemplo em murais do Antigo Egito, de Santorini ou de Pompéia, sejam na sua maioria de caráter mitológico, fazendo do mar um palco para o aparecimento dos deuses e heróis.

A pintura marinha europeia teve seu início na Idade de Ouro dos Países Baixos, o século XVII. Anteriormente, o mar em si mesmo conformava um mero pano de fundo para atos comemorativos, recepções e exibições de navios – quadro de cenas marítimas é o termo sob o qual essas representações são resumidas. A partir do século XVII, a marinha se estabeleceu gradualmente até um gênero com um perfil sólido. Dada sua localização geográfica especial, e as especificidades da identidade nacional, parece bastante natural que os Países Baixos tenham sido predestinados a ajudar no avanço deste gênero. Pintores como Hendrick Vroom (cerca de 1563–1640), Simon de Vlieger (1601–1653) e Jan Porcellis (cerca de 1582–1632) são geralmente nomeados para enfatizar também a diversidade de estilos e temas utilizados.

É possível determinar de forma bastante precisa o momento em que a pintura marinha europeia continental também alcançou as Ilhas Britânicas, pois isso ocorreu na figura de uma distinta família

uit het oude Egypte, Santorini of Pompeï, vooral van mythologische aard zijn, waarin de zee als schouwtoneel voor de handelingen van goden en helden werd uitgebeeld.

De maritieme schilderkunst van Europa heeft zijn oorsprong in de Nederlandse zeventiende eeuw, de Gouden Eeuw. Vóór die tijd was de zee weinig meer dan een decor voor plechtige handelingen, ontvangsten en scheepsschouwen, in een genre dat als 'maritieme gedenkschilderkunst' deel uitmaakte van de historieschilderkunst. Maar in de zeventiende eeuw ontwikkelde het zeegezicht zich geleidelijk aan tot een vastomlijnd en zelfstandig genre. Gezien de bijzondere geografische ligging en de geheel eigen nationale identiteit van de Lage Landen is het niet meer dan logisch dat het juist de Nederlanden waren die dit genre een voorname plaats in de kunstgeschiedenis gaven. Schilders als Hendrick Vroom (circa 1563–1640), Simon de Vlieger (1601–1653) en Jan Porcellis (circa 1582–1632) worden in dit verband vaak genoemd om de diversiteit van toegepaste stijlen en motieven te illustreren.

Het tijdstip waarop de maritieme schilderkunst zich van het continent naar de Britse Eilanden verspreidde, is niet precies te bepalen, maar wel dat deze overstap het werk was van één vooraanstaand schildersgeslacht, de uit Leiden afkomstige familie Van de Velde. In de winter van

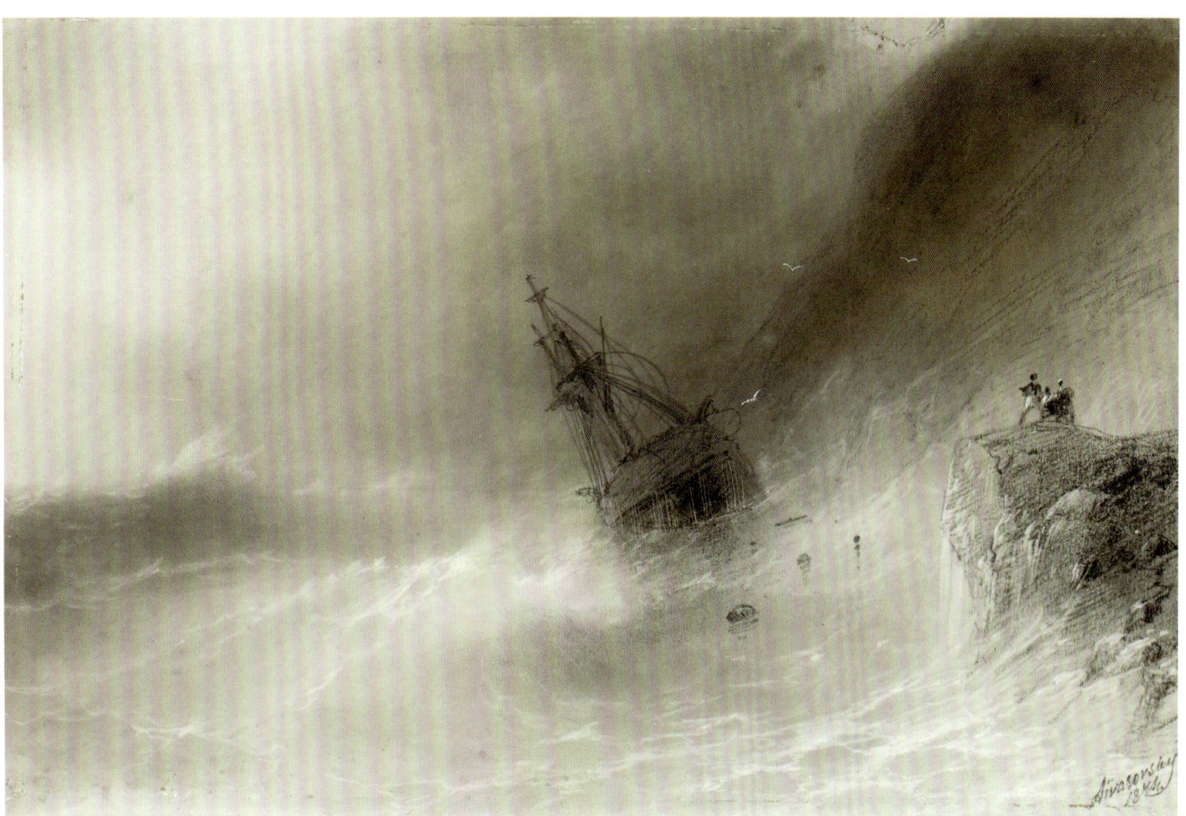

*Ivan Aivazovsky
(1817–1900)*

Shipwreck

Naufrage

Schiffswrack

Naufragio

Naufrágio

Scheepswrak

1874, Pencil and
gouache on paper/
Crayon et gouache sur
papier, 23 × 32,7 cm,
Private collection

important task of glorifying the emerging British Navy
in a way similar to what they had done for the Dutch.

The wars of the 18th century certainly offered
plenty of fodder for scenes at sea, especially when
it came to glorifying the home nation's war fleet.
This applied in particular to the English-Dutch wars,
the American War of Independence, and later the
Napoleonic wars with the Battle of Trafalgar. Painters
now focused on painting events, which included not
only the many naval battles, but also sinkings and
dramatic rescue operations. New printing technologies
allowed these works to become enormously popular,
for example, the engravings by Frenchman Claude
Joseph Vernet.

It was not until the Romantics, such as Turner,
Caspar David Friedrich, and Andreas Achenbach,
that the depiction of the sea itself as a natural force
would be emancipated from shipping scenes that
focused on the transport of people and goods or
war at sea. On the other hand, the sea often became
loaded with a strong symbolic content: the seeming
endlessness and expanse of the sea came to be seen
as a metaphor for the human soul and life, while the
struggle of the ships with the storms and waves as
symbolic of the eternal human struggle with nature.

respectueuse reçurent rapidement des commandes
des plus hauts rangs de la société. Ils furent chargés de
la tâche importante qui consistait à glorifier la marine
britannique émergente d'une manière similaire à ce
qu'ils avaient fait pour les Hollandais.

Les guerres du XVIIIe siècle ont certainement offert
beaucoup de fourrage pour des scènes en mer, surtout
quand il s'agissait de glorifier la flotte de guerre de
la nation. Cela s'appliquait en particulier aux guerres
anglais-hollandaises, à la guerre d'indépendance
américaine et plus tard aux guerres napoléoniennes
avec la bataille de Trafalgar. Les peintres se
concentraient maintenant sur la peinture d'événements,
dont les nombreuses batailles navales, mais aussi les
naufrages et les opérations de sauvetage dramatiques.
Les nouvelles technologies d'impression permirent à ces
œuvres de devenir extrêmement connues, par exemple
les gravures du français Claude Joseph Vernet.

Ce n'est qu'à partir des Romantiques, tels que Turner,
Caspar David Friedrich et Andreas Achenbach, que la
représentation de la mer elle-même en tant que force
naturelle est libérée des scènes d'expédition axées sur
le transport de personnes et de marchandises ou sur la
guerre sur mer. D'autre part, la mer était souvent chargée
d'un fort contenu symbolique : l'apparente infinitude et

die britischen Inseln erreichte, geschah dies doch in
Gestalt einer angesehenen Familie von Malern, den aus
Leiden stammenden van de Veldes. Im Winter 1672/73
emigrierten Vater und Sohn Willem van de Velde nach
England, wo sie schnell Aufträge von höchster Stelle
erhielten. Eine wichtige Aufgabe etwa bestand für sie
darin, die aufstrebende britische Flotte in ähnliche Weise
zu glorifizieren, wie dies zuvor in den Niederlanden
geschehen war.

Die kriegerischen Auseinandersetzungen des 18.
Jahrhundert boten der marinen Kunst eine Fülle an
Anschauungsmaterial und Stoff zur Verherrlichung der
jeweils eigenen Kriegsflotte. Vor allem waren das die
Englisch-Niederländischen Kriege, der Amerikanische
Unabhängigkeitskrieg und später die Napoleonischen
Kriege mit der Schlacht von Trafalgar. In der Malerei
dominierten nun die Ereignisbilder, zu denen man nicht
nur die vielen Seeschlachten zählen kann, sondern auch
Schiffsuntergänge und dramatische Rettungsaktionen.
Durch neue Techniken erlangten diese Bilder als Drucke
eine enorme Popularität. Als Beispiel mag hier der
Franzose Claude Joseph Vernet gelten, dessen Stiche
eine große Verbreitung fanden.

Erst bei den Romantikern, wie J. M. W. Turner,
Caspar David Friedrich oder dem Düsseldorfer Andreas

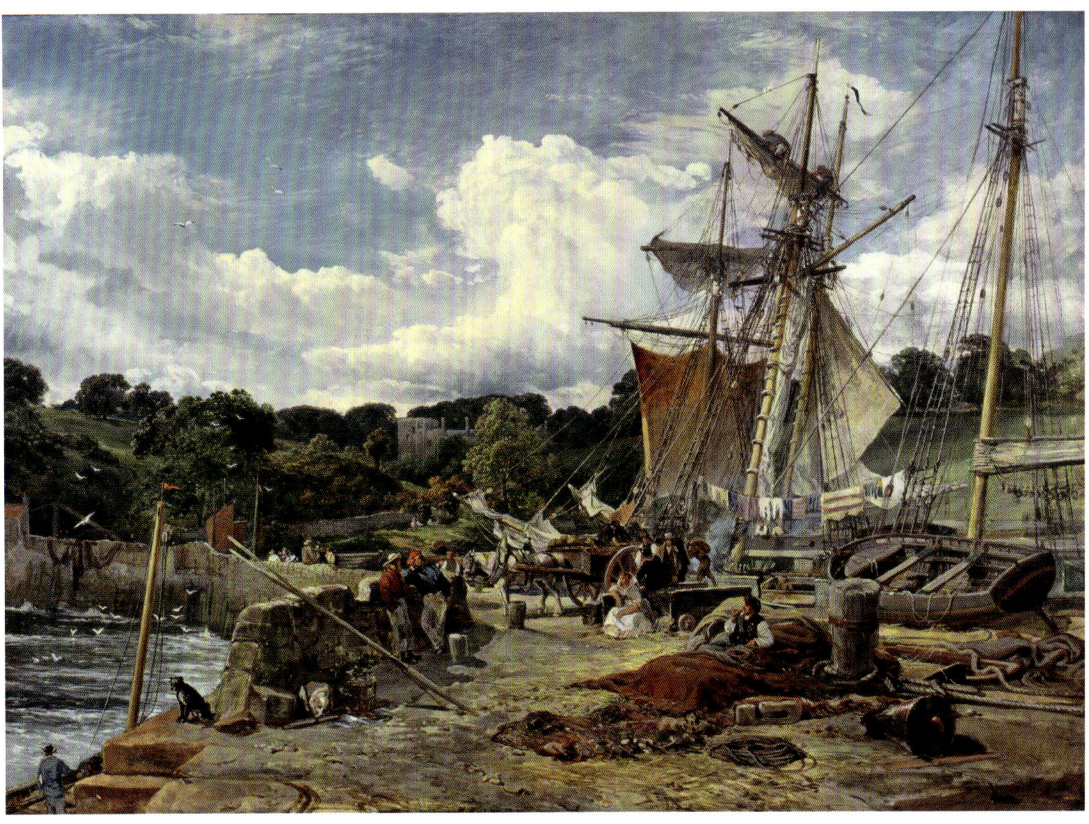

continental llegó a las Islas Británicas, a través de una distinguida familia de pintores natural de Leiden, los van de Velde. En el invierno de 1672–1673 los dos Willem van de Velde, padre e hijo, emigraron a Inglaterra, donde recibieron rápidamente encargos de la autoridad más alta. Una tarea importante estaba preparada para ellos, glorificar a la emergente flota británica de una manera similar a como se había hecho anteriormente en los Países Bajos.

Los conflictos bélicos del siglo XVIII ofrecen al arte una gran cantidad de recursos visuales y materiales para la gloria de su propia flota de combate. Sobre todo hablamos de la guerra entre Países Bajos en Inglaterra, la Guerra de Independencia americana y posteriormente, las guerras napoleónicas con la Batalla de Trafalgar. En la pintura, dominaban ahora las imágenes de acontecimientos, entre las que se incluyen no sólo las muchas batallas navales, sino también los naufragios y las dramáticas operaciones de rescate. Gracias a las nuevas técnicas, estas imágenes a modo de grabados obtuvieron una enorme popularidad. A modo de ejemplo podemos considerar al francés Claude Joseph Vernet, cuyos grabados obtuvieron una gran difusión.

Por primera vez con los románticos como J. M. W. Turner, Caspar David Friedrich o Andreas Achenbach,

de pintores, os van de Velde, originários de Leiden. No inverno de 1672–1673, pai e filho Willem van de Velde emigraram para a Inglaterra, onde rapidamente receberam encomendas das mais altas autoridades. Talvez uma tarefa importante para eles consistisse de glorificar a frota britânica em ascensão, da mesma forma que haviam feito anteriormente nos Países Baixos.

Os conflitos armados do século XVIII ofereceram para a arte marinha uma panóplia de material visual, e matéria para exaltação das respetivas frotas de guerra. Foram sobretudo as guerras anglo-holandesa, a Guerra Revolucionária Americana, e mais tarde, as guerras napoleônicas, com a batalha de Trafalgar. Na pintura dominariam os quadros de cenas marítimas, entre os quais se incluem não somente as muitas batalhas navais, mas também naufrágios e operações dramáticas de salvamento. Graças a novas técnicas, esses quadros se tornaram bastante populares sob a forma de estampas. Um exemplo disso é o francês Claude Joseph Vernet, cujas gravuras tiveram ampla divulgação.

Somente com românticos como J. M. W. Turner, Caspar David Friedrich, ou Andreas Achenbach, de Düsseldorf, a natureza se emancipou. Por um lado, da navegação, pois com esses pintores o foco já não

1672/1673 emigreerden vader en zoon Willem van de Velde naar Engeland, waar ze al snel opdrachten uit de hoogste kringen ontvingen. Een belangrijke opgave voor de beide schilders was het uitbeelden van de groeiende rol van de Engelse vloot, zoals ze dat eerder met de Nederlandse vloot hadden gedaan.

De oorlogen van de achttiende eeuw boden de maritieme schilderkunst een veelheid van motieven en onderwerpen ter verheerlijking van oorlogsvloten. Het waren vooral de Engels-Nederlandse oorlogen, de Amerikaanse Onafhankelijkheidsoorlog en later de Napoleontische Oorlogen met de beroemde Zeeslag bij Trafalgar die dit genre domineerden. De maritieme schilderkunst werd nu beheerst door gedenkstukken, waarmee niet alleen talloze zeeslagen werden herdacht, maar ook de ondergang van schepen en dramatische reddingsacties. Met behulp van nieuwe technieken wisten deze stukken als prenten een enorme populariteit te bereiken. Een goed voorbeeld is het werk van de Fransman Claude Joseph Vernet, wiens etsen een grote oplage bereikten.

Pas bij romantici als J. M. W. Turner, Caspar David Friedrich en de Düsseldorfse schilder Andreas Achenbach werd het zelfstandige zeelandschap geëmancipeerd ten opzichte van het zeetransport

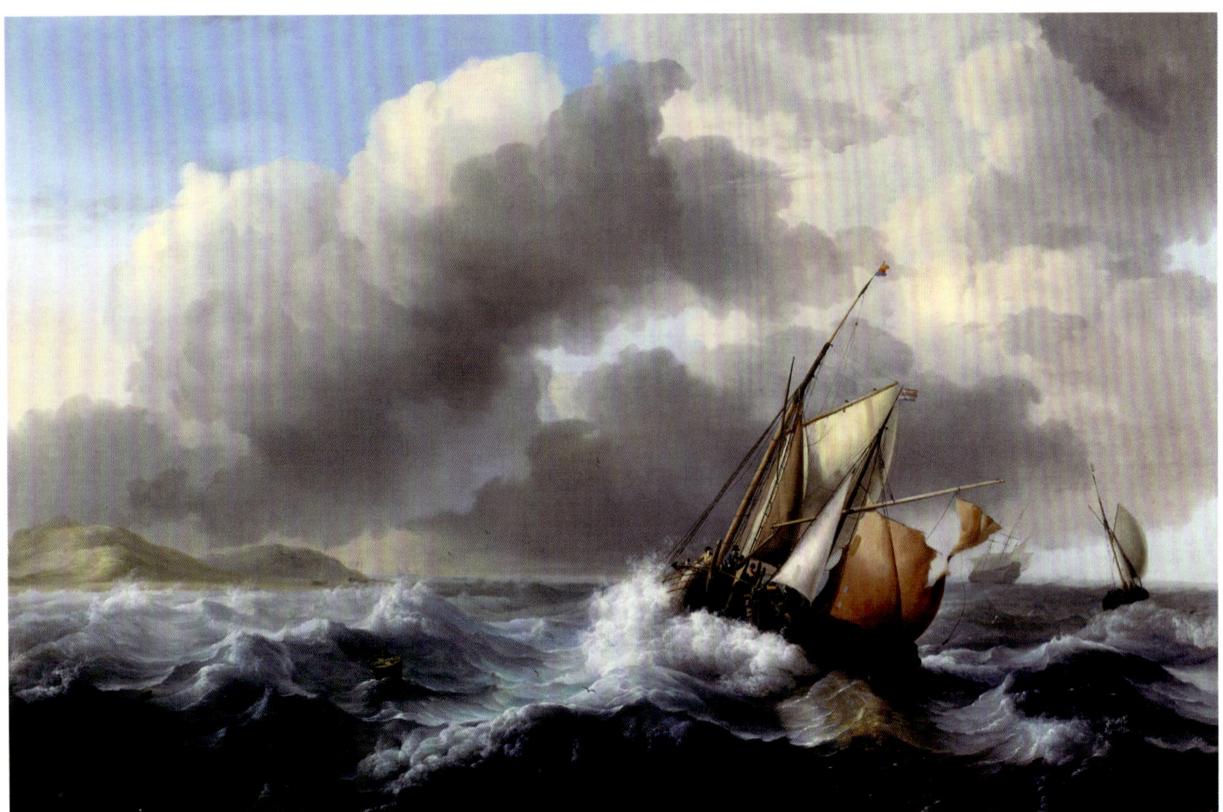

Dramatic shipwrecks also allowed all sorts of emotions in the face of approaching death to be depicted.

It was only from the mid-19th century that maritime painting set a new course, when many painters began to paint the seas mainly as nature studies and ships often played a less important role. For instance, Victorian painter John Brett began as a pre-Raphaelite, but soon realized that the group's love of detail was not compatible with his natural panoramas. In several respects, the career of Danish painter Anton Melbye is typical of a maritime painter. He came from a family of painters also active in this genre and also came into contact with high-ranking people who commissioned works from him. In his case, these included the Ottoman sultan in Constantinople and also French Emperor Napoleon III.

If the Romantics had already been fascinated by the effects of expanse, light, and the horizon, these were all aspects that the Impressionists would take to the next level. For them, it was the landscape along the English Channel that attracted them. Even the painters of the Barbizon and the Realist Courbet practiced their art of sea painting. Later, artists such as Claude Monet, Paul Signac, Georges Seurat, and many others would depict the coast of the English Channel with the bizarre

étendue de la mer devinrent considérées comme une métaphore de l'âme et de la vie humaine, alors que la lutte des navires avec les orages et les vagues comme une symbolique de la lutte éternelle de l'homme avec la nature. Les naufrages spectaculaires permirent aussi de représenter toutes sortes d'émotions face à la mort prochaine.

Ce n'est qu'à partir du milieu du XIXᵉ siècle que la peinture maritime ouvrit une nouvelle voie, lorsque de nombreux peintres commencèrent à peindre la mer principalement comme des études de la nature, et que les navires jouaient un rôle moins important. Par exemple, le peintre victorien John Brett, en tant que préraphaélite, se rendit vite compte que l'amour du groupe pour les détails n'était pas compatible avec ses panoramas naturels. À plusieurs égards, la carrière du peintre danois Anton Melbye est typique de celle d'un peintre maritime. Né d'une famille de peintres également actifs dans ce genre, il entra en contact avec des personnes de haut rang qui lui commandèrent des œuvres. Dans son cas, il s'agissait du sultan ottoman de Constantinople et de l'empereur français Napoléon III.

Si les romantiques avaient déjà été fascinés par les effets de l'étendue, de la lumière et de l'horizon, ce sont tous des aspects que les impressionnistes reprirent.

Achenbach, emanzipierte sich die Natur einerseits von der Schifffahrt, indem der Transport von Menschen und Waren und auch der Krieg zur See bei ihnen nicht mehr im Fokus stand. Andererseits wurde das Meer nun oft mit einem starken symbolischen Gehalt aufgeladen – die scheinbare Endlosigkeit und Weite der See als Metapher für die menschliche Seele und das Leben; der Kampf der Schiffe mit Stürmen und Wellenbergen als Sinnbild des ewigen Kampfes des Menschen mit der Natur. Dramatische Schiffbrüche erlaubten es, alle nur denkbaren menschlichen Gefühle im Angesicht des nahenden Todes abzubilden.

Erst ab der Mitte des 19. Jahrhunderts nahm die maritime Malerei einen neuen Kurs, als viele Maler die Seestücke vor allem zu Zwecken des Naturstudiums nutzten und Schiffe häufig eine weniger wichtige Rolle spielten. So begann etwa der viktorianische Maler John Brett als Präraffaelit, erkannte aber bald, dass sich die Detailverliebtheit dieser Künstlergruppe nicht für seine Naturpanoramen vertrug. In mehrfacher Hinsicht typisch für einen Marinemaler ist auch die Karriere des Dänen Anton Melbye. Zum einen stammte er aus einer ebenfalls in diesem Genre tätigen Malerfamilie, zum anderen kam er durch seine Kunst in Kontakt zu hochgestellten Persönlichkeiten, bei denen er Anstellung fand. In seinem

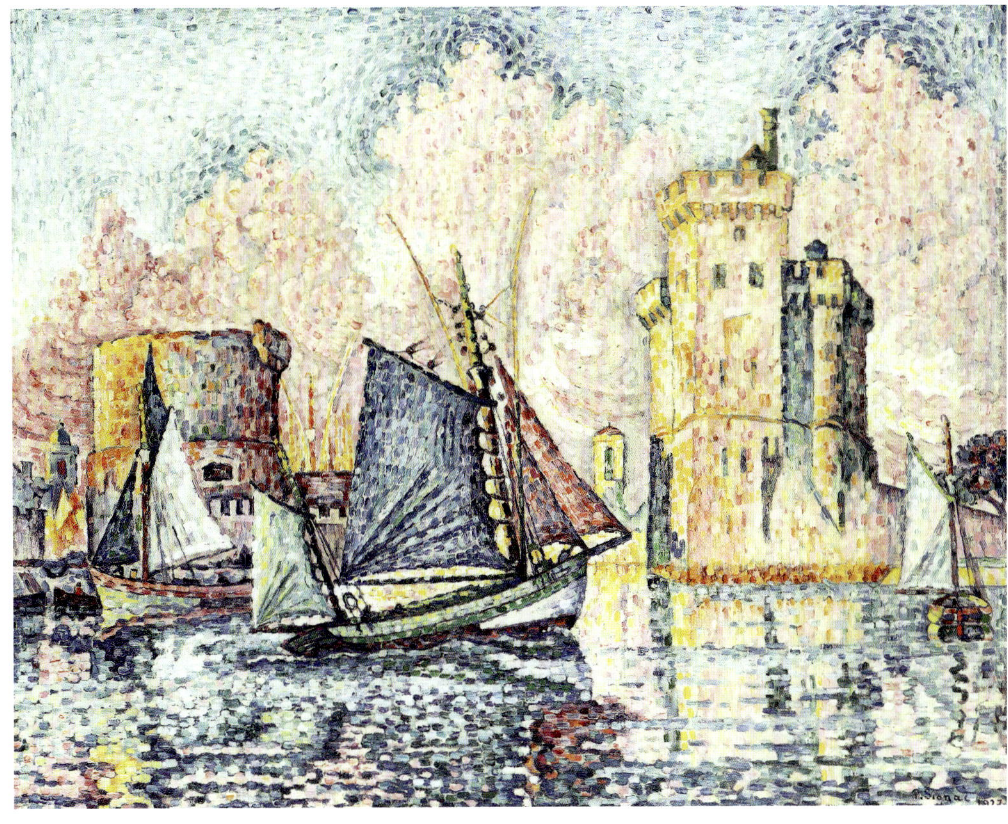

de Düsseldorf, por un lado se emancipó la naturaleza de la navegación, de manera que el transporte de personas y mercancías así como la guerra en el mar ya no estaba en el foco de atención para ellos. Y por otro lado, a menudo el mar se llenaba de un fuerte significado simbólico – la infinitud aparente y la vastedad del mar como metáfora para el alma humana y la vida; la batalla de los barcos con tormentas y las crestas de las olas como símbolo de la eterna lucha entre el hombre y la naturaleza. Los dramáticos naufragios permitieron reproducir cada emoción humana imaginable a la vista de la inminente muerte.

No fue hasta mediados del siglo XIX que la pintura de marinas tomó un nuevo curso, ya que muchos pintores utilizaban los paisajes marinos principalmente con fines de estudio de la naturaleza y los barcos empezaron a jugar un papel menos importante. Por ejemplo, el pintor victoriano John Brett comenzó como un prerrafaelista, pero pronto se dio cuenta de que la minuciosidad de este grupo de artistas no podía ser compatible con sus panoramas naturales. La carrera del danés Anton Melbye es, en muchas maneras, muy típica de un pintor de marinas. En primer lugar, provenía también de una familia que trabajaba en pinturas de género, por otra parte, entraba en contacto a través de su arte con

era mais o transporte de pessoas e mercadorias, nem a guerra no mar. Por outro lado, o mar assumia agora frequentemente um valor marcadamente simbólico – a aparente infinidade e vastidão do mar como uma metáfora para a alma humana e a vida; a batalha dos navios com tempestades e cristas das ondas, enquanto um símbolo da eterna luta entre o homem e a natureza. Naufrágios dramáticos tornavam possível retratar todas as emoções humanas somente concebíveis perante a aproximação da morte.

Só a partir de meados do século XIX a pintura marinha tomou um novo rumo, com muitos pintores usando as marinhas principalmente para fins de estudo da natureza, e os navios desempenhando muitas vezes um papel de menor importância. Por exemplo, o pintor vitoriano John Brett se iniciou como um pré-rafaelita, mas logo percebeu que a atenção ao detalhe deste grupo de artistas não era conciliável com suas panorâmicas da natureza. Em muitos aspectos, a carreira do dinamarquês Anton Melbye é igualmente característica de um pintor de marinhas. De um lado, também ele cresceu no seio de uma família de pintores que se dedicavam a este gênero. De outro lado, através de sua arte, ele contatou com distintas personalidades, junto das quais ele encontrou trabalho. No seu caso,

van mensen en goederen en van de oorlog op zee. Anderzijds kreeg de zee nu vaak een sterk symbolische lading: de schier eindeloze weidsheid van de zee als metafoor van de menselijke ziel en de menselijke ervaring, en de strijd van schepen tegen wind en golven als zinnebeeld van de eeuwige strijd tussen mens en natuur. In dramatische schipbreuken konden alle mogelijke menselijke emoties in het aangezicht van de dood worden verkend en uitgebeeld.

Pas vanaf halverwege de negentiende eeuw zette de maritieme schilderkunst een nieuwe koers uit, toen talloze schilders het zeestuk vooral als natuurstudie gingen gebruiken en schepen een steeds minder prominente rol speelden. Zo begon de Victoriaanse schilder John Brett als Pre-Rafaëliet, maar moest al snel erkennen dat de gedetailleerde schilderstijl van deze kunstenaarsgroep niet goed viel te rijmen met zijn weidse natuurlandschappen. In meerdere opzichten kenmerkend voor de maritieme schilderkunst is ook de loopbaan van de Deen Anton Melbye. Niet alleen was hij afkomstig uit een maritieme schildersfamilie, hij kwam door zijn werk ook in contact met vooraanstaande personen die hem opdrachten gaven. In zijn geval waren dat naast de sultan in Constantinopel ook de Franse keizer Napoleon III.

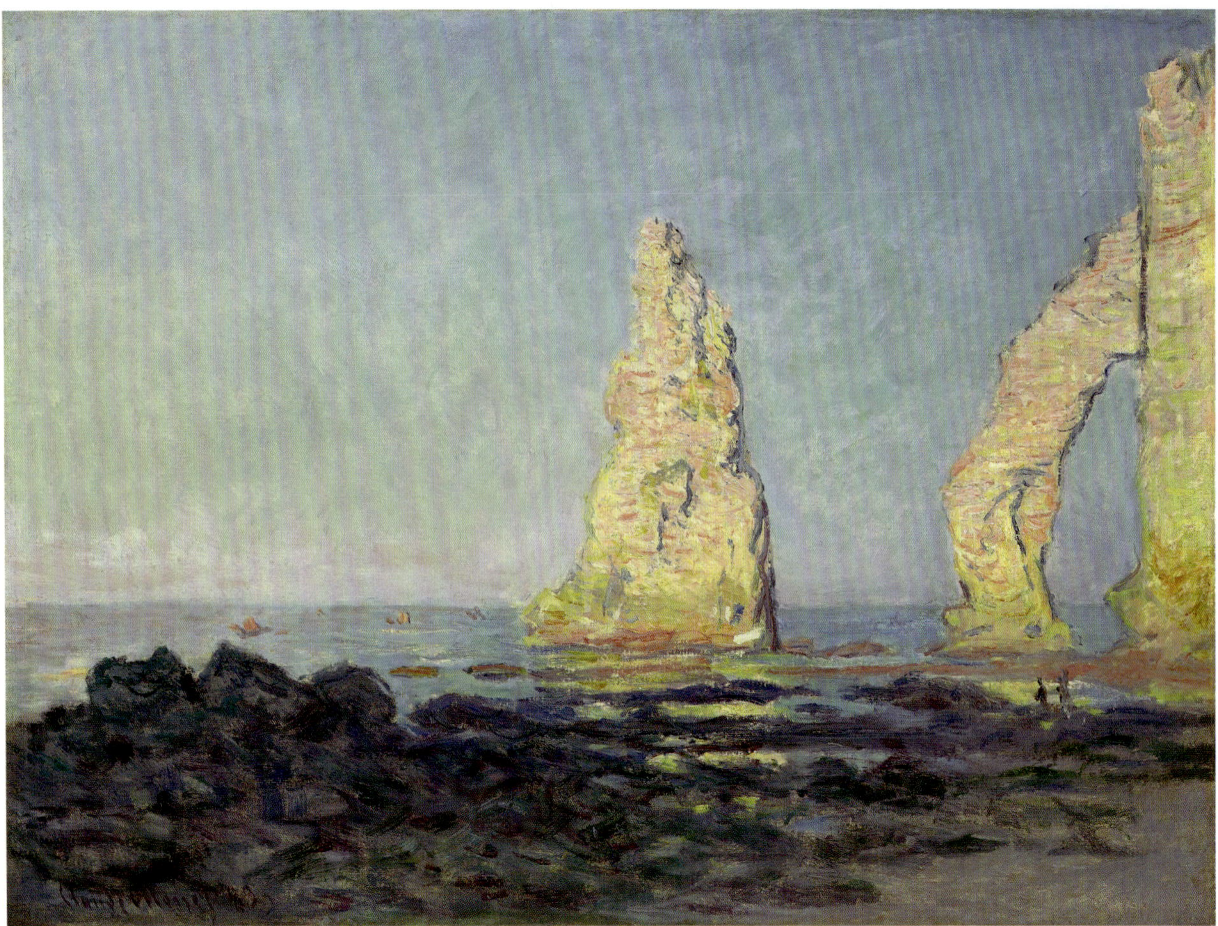

rock formations at Étretat or the Seine estuary near Honfleur. Pictures of ships themselves became rarer and virtually no Impressionist depicted naval battles, with the exception of Édouard Manet, who in 1864 had inadvertently witnessed a scuffle between ships from the two sides of the American Civil War in Cherbourg.

En ce qui les concerne, c'était le paysage bordant la Manche qui les attirait. Même les peintres de Barbizon et le réaliste Courbet pratiquèrent l'art de la peinture de la mer. Plus tard, des artistes tels que Claude Monet, Paul Signac, Georges Seurat et de nombreux autres représentèrent la côte de la Manche avec les formations rocheuses bizarres à Étretat ou l'estuaire de la Seine près d'Honfleur. Les images des navires eux-mêmes devinrent plus rares et presqu'aucun impressionniste ne représenta de batailles navales, à l'exception d'Édouard Manet, qui, en 1864, fut témoin par inadvertance d'un conflit entre les navires des deux côtés de la guerre civile américaine à Cherbourg.

Fall waren das neben dem Sultan in Konstantinopel auch der französische Kaiser Napoleon III.

Wenn es schon bei den Romantikern sehr um die Wirkung der Weite, das Licht und den Horizont ging, so waren dies alles Effekte, die von den Impressionisten noch stärker in den Vordergrund gerückt werden sollten. Für sie spielt vor allem die Landschaft der Kanalküste eine große Rolle. Schon die Maler von Barbizon oder der Realist Courbet übten sich hier in der Kunst der Seemalerei. Auch später bei Künstlern wie Claude Monet, Paul Signac, Georges Seurat und vielen anderen prägt die französische Kanalküste zum Beispiel mit den bizarren Felsformationen von Étretat oder der Seinemündung bei Honfleur die Werke der Impressionisten. Bilder von Schiffen selbst wurden seltener, und von Seeschlachten war auf den Bildern der Impressionisten kaum noch etwas zu sehen. Eine Ausnahme bildet hier jedoch ein Werk Édouard Manets, der 1864 in Cherbourg zufällig Augenzeuge einer Auseinandersetzung zwischen zwei Schiffen der amerikanischen Kriegsparteien im Bürgerkrieg wurde.

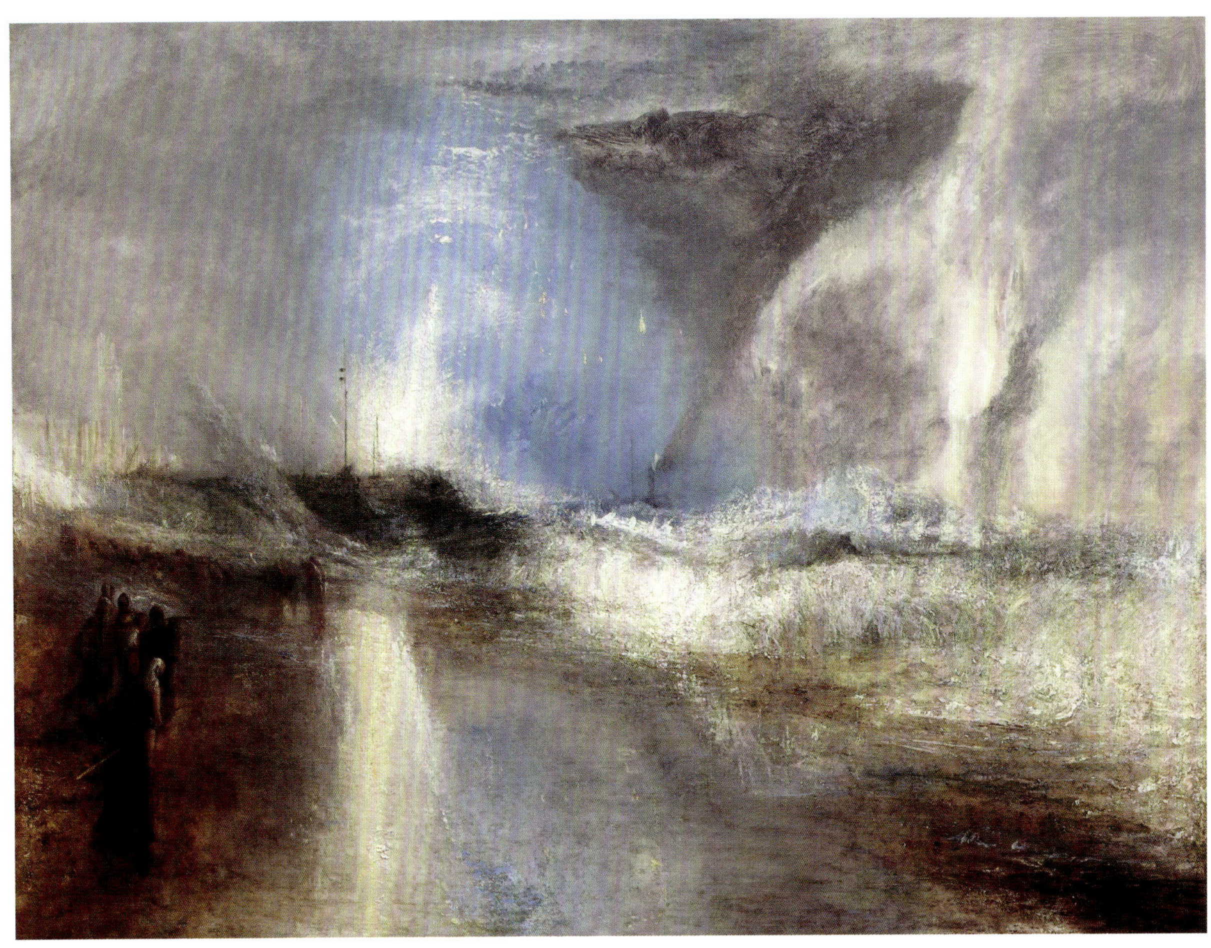

personalidades de alto rango, donde encontró empleo. En su caso, el sultán de Constantinopla y el emperador francés Napoleón III.

Si bien para los románticos el efecto de amplitud, la luz y el horizonte eran más secundarios, todos estos efectos debían retornar al primer plano para los impresionistas. Para ellos, jugaba un papel importante sobre todo el paisaje de la costa. Ya los pintores de Barbizon o el realista Courbet se ejercitaron aquí en el arte de la marina. Incluso artistas posteriores como Claude Monet, Paul Signac, Georges Seurat y muchos otros, caracterizaron sus obras impresionistas con la costa francesa, por ejemplo, con las extrañas formaciones rocosas de Étretat o el estuario del Sena en Honfleur. Las representaciones de barcos eran poco frecuentes, y las batallas navales apenas se podían ver en los cuadros de los impresionistas. Una excepción, sin embargo, la constituye aquí una obra de Édouard Manet, en 1864, Cherburgo fue testigo accidental de un altercado entre dos barcos de las facciones americanas en la guerra civil.

além do sultão de Constantinopla, o Imperador francês Napoleão III.

Se já os românticos procuravam muito o efeito da distância, a luz e o horizonte, tudo isso eram efeitos que os impressionistas trariam com ainda maior intensidade para primeiro plano. Para eles, é principalmente a paisagem da costa do Canal da Mancha que desempenha um papel importante. Já os pintores de Barbizon, ou o realista Courbet, praticaram ali a arte da pintura de marinhas. Mesmo mais tarde, em artistas como Claude Monet, Paul Signac, Georges Seurat, e muitos outros, a costa francesa do Canal caracteriza, por exemplo, com as bizarras formações rochosas de Étretat, ou o estuário do Sena, em Honfleur, as obras dos impressionistas. Quadros de navios, propriamente, se tornaram mais raros, e os quadros dos impressionistas praticamente não mostravam nenhuma batalha naval. Uma exceção, porém, é uma obra de Édouard Manet, que testemunhou acidentalmente em 1864, em Cherbourg, um confronto entre dois navios das facções americanas na guerra civil.

Terwijl het in de maritieme schilderkunst van de romantici al duidelijk om het effect van weidsheid, licht en horizon ging, werden deze aspecten door de impressionisten nog sterker op de voorgrond geplaatst. In hun werk speelde vooral het landschap van de Kanaalkust een belangrijke rol. Zo oefenden de schilders van de School van Barbizon en de realist Gustave Courbet zich daar in de kunst van het zeegezicht. Ook in het werk van latere kunstenaars als Claude Monet, Paul Signac, Georges Seurat en anderen was de Franse Kanaalkust – vooral de bizarre rotsformaties bij Étretat – alom aanwezig. In het werk van de impressionisten dook ook de monding van de Seine bij Honfleur vaak op. Schilderijen van schepen waren bij de impressionisten zeldzaam, terwijl zeeslagen eigenlijk niet meer werden uitgebeeld. Een uitzondering daarop was het werk van Édouard Manet, die in 1864 in Cherbourg bij toeval ooggetuige was van een treffen in de Amerikaanse Burgeroorlog, tussen een schip van de Unie en een van de Confederatie.

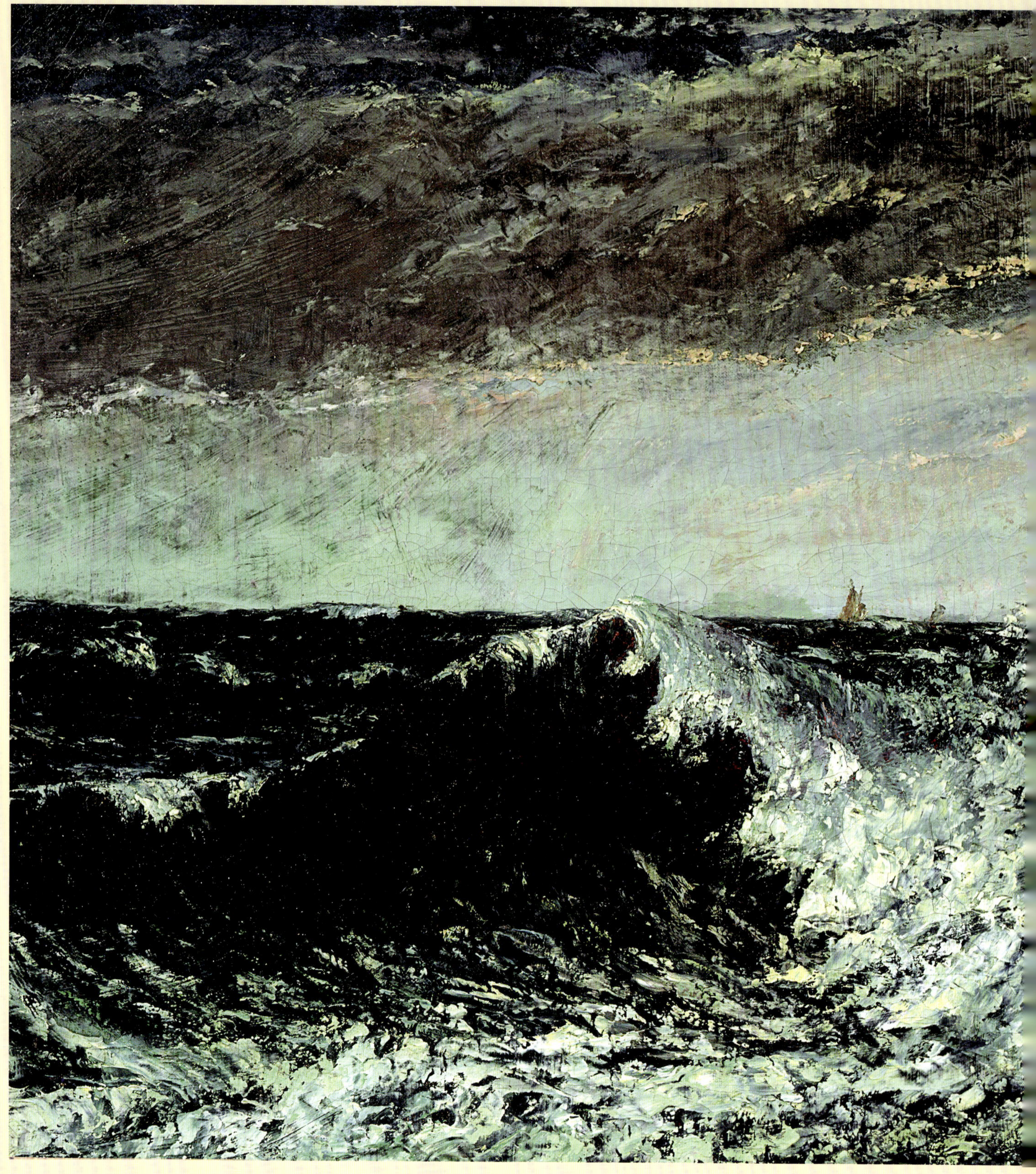

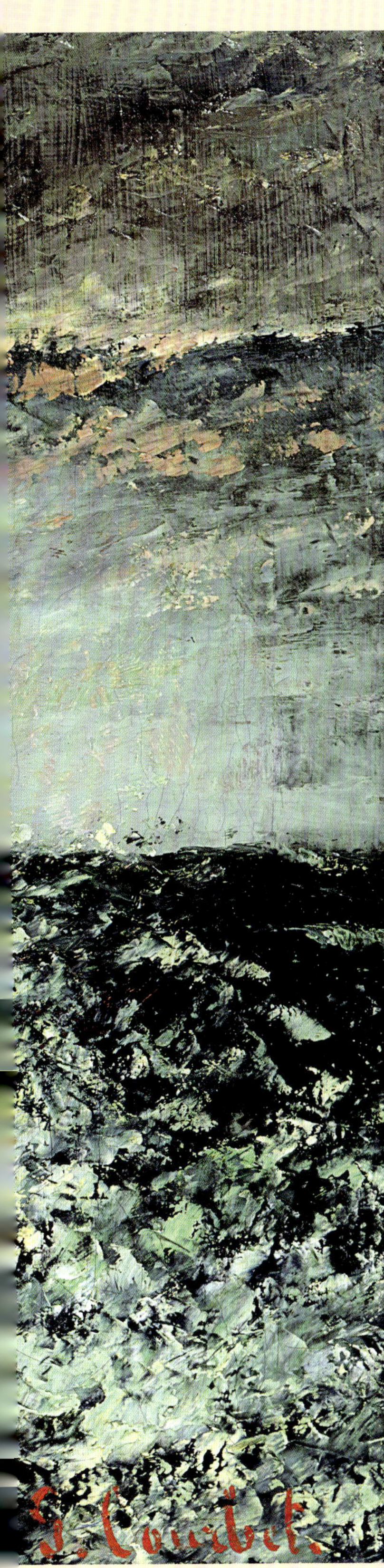

Gustave Courbet (1819–77)
The Wave
La Vague
Die Welle
La ola
A onda
De golf
n. d., Oil on canvas/Huile sur toile, Private collection

The sea and the sky

La mer et le ciel

Das Meer und der Himmel

El mar y el cielo

O mar e o céu

Zee en luchten

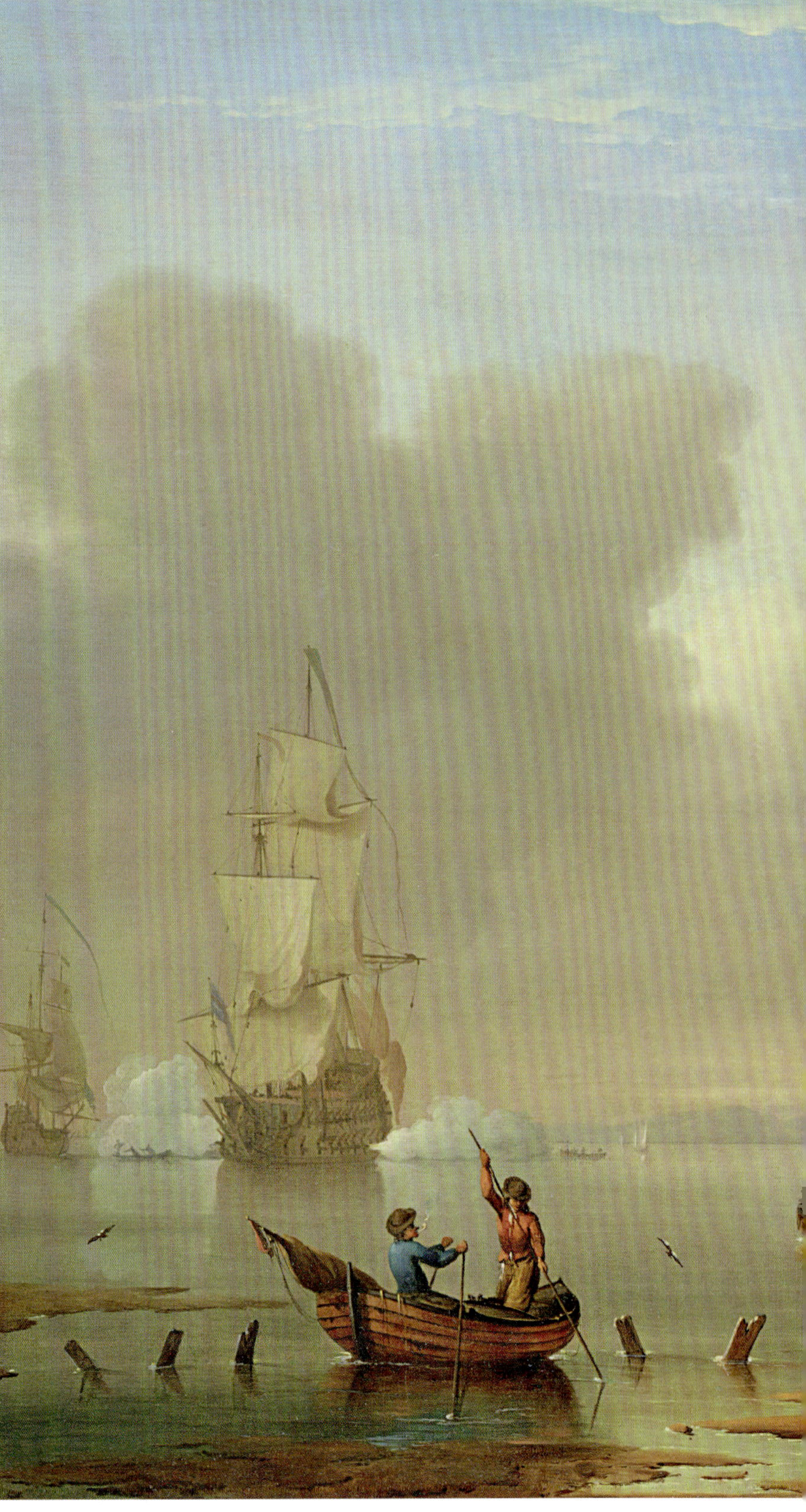

London-born Peter Monamy became one of the most important English painters of the sea in the 18th century. His preference to depict ships in calm, shallow waters. He also liked to depict solemn ceremonies such as the shooting of salutes with cannons.

Peter Monamy, originaire de Londres, est devenu l'un des peintres de mer anglais les plus importants au XVIIIᵉ siècle. Il préférait représenter les navires dans des eaux calmes et peu profondes. Il aimait également représenter des cérémonies solennelles telles que le tir de salut avec des canons.

Der in London geborene Peter Monamy gehörte zu den wichtigsten Marinemalern im England des 18. Jahrhunderts. Seine Vorliebe galt ruhigen Schiffsszenen in seichten Gewässern, vorzugsweise bei Windstille. Auch stellte er gern feierliche Zeremonien dar wie das Abfeuern von Salutschüssen.

Peter Monamy, nacido en Londres, fue uno de los pintores de marinas más importantes del siglo XVIII en Inglaterra. Su predilección la constituían escenas tranquilas de barcos en aguas poco profundas, preferentemente sin viento. También le gustaban las solemnes ceremonias como el disparo de salvas.

O londrino Peter Monamy foi um dos pintores de marinhas mais importantes na Inglaterra do século XVIII. Sua preferência eram cenas tranquilas de navios em águas rasas, de preferência, sem vento. Ele também gostava de pintar cerimónias festivas, como o disparo de salvas de tiros.

De in Londen geboren Peter Monamy behoorde tot de belangrijkste maritieme schilders van het achttiende-eeuwse Engeland. Zijn favoriete motief was het kalme scheepstafereel in rustig water, bij voorkeur bij windstilte. Ook beeldde hij graag plechtige ceremoniën uit, zoals het afvuren van saluutschoten.

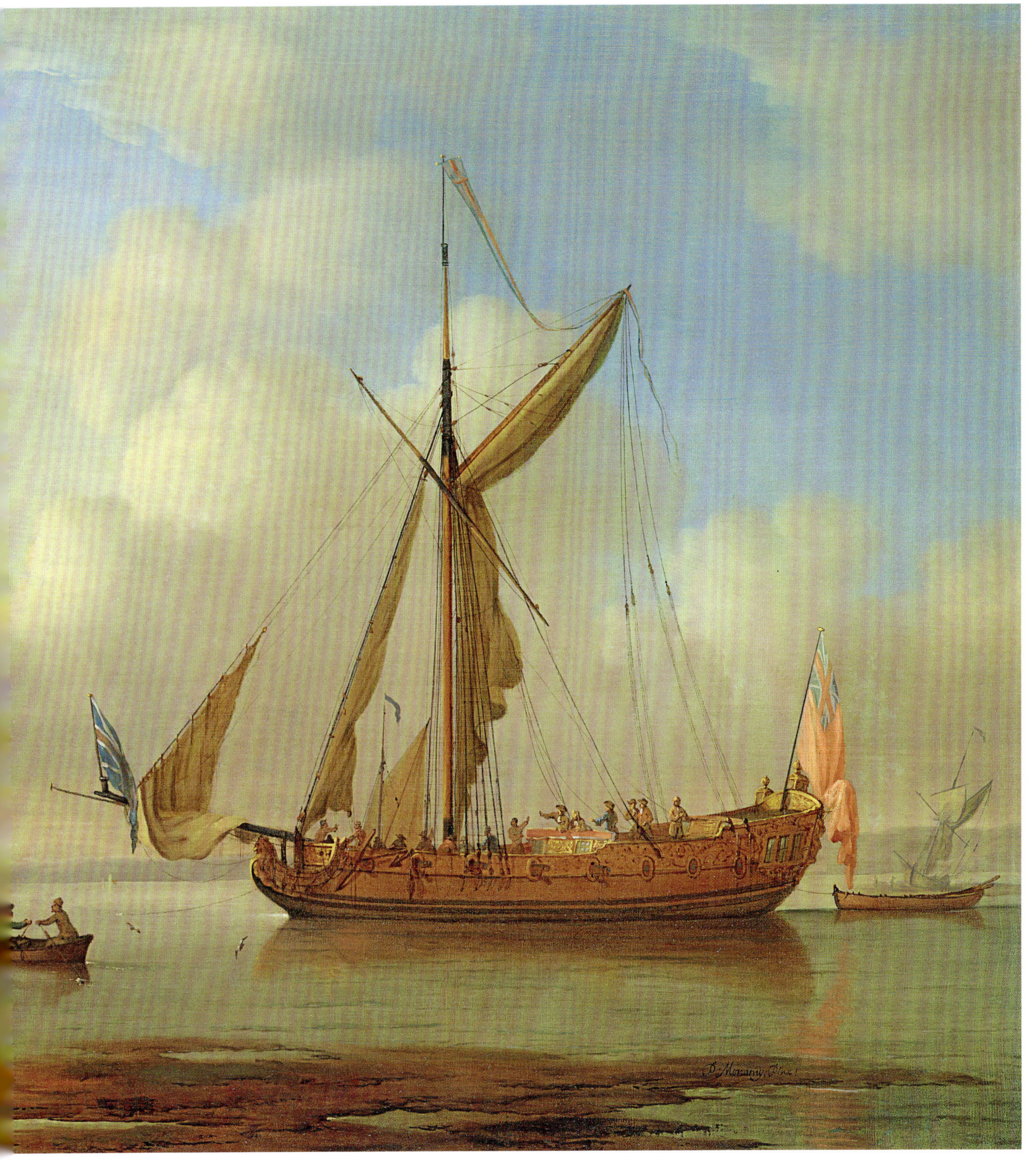

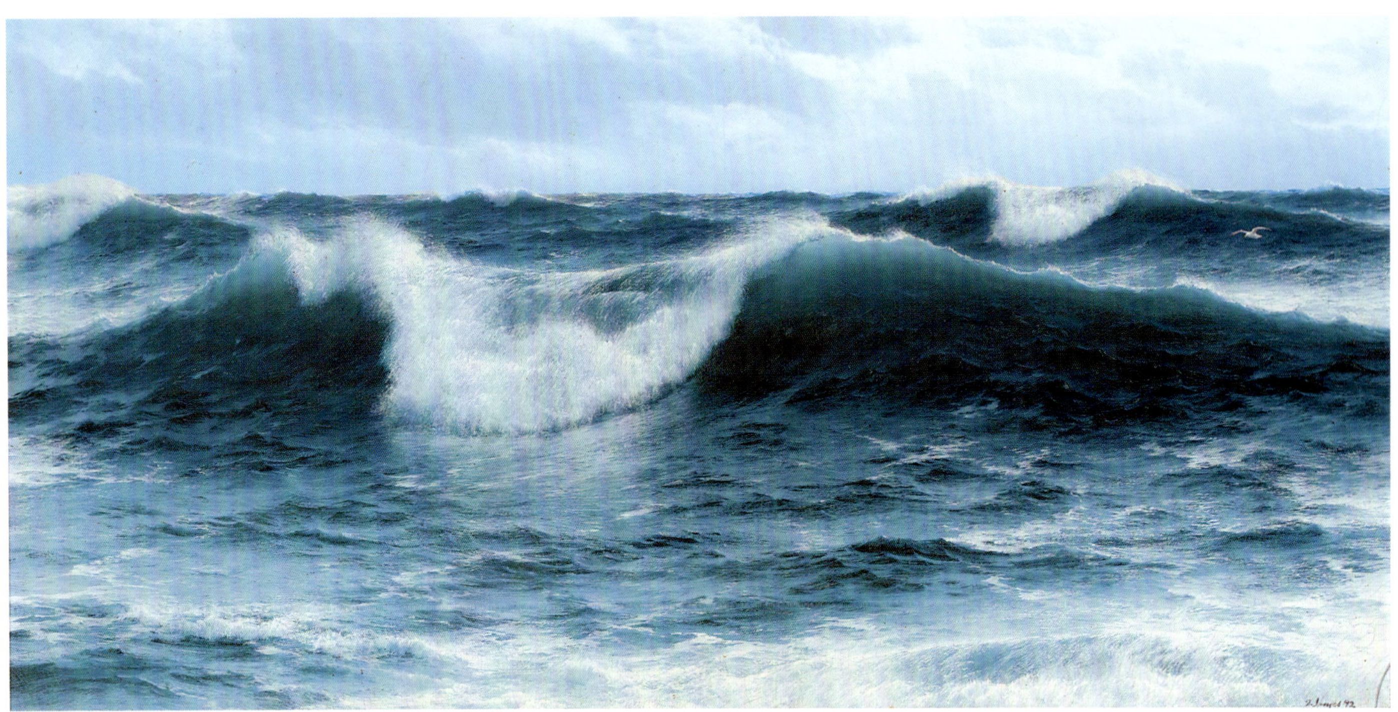

David James (1853–1904)

Crashing Waves

Vagues qui se brisent

Brandung

Olas rompiendo

Rebentação

Branding

1892, Oil on canvas/Huile sur toile, 62,2 × 125,7 cm, Private collection

David James (1853–1904)

Atlantic Roll

Rouleau de l'Atlantique

Wellen im Atlantik

Olas en el Atlántico

Ondas no Atlântico

Golven in de Atlantische Oceaan

1895, Oil on canvas/Huile sur toile, 62,8 × 127 cm, Private collection

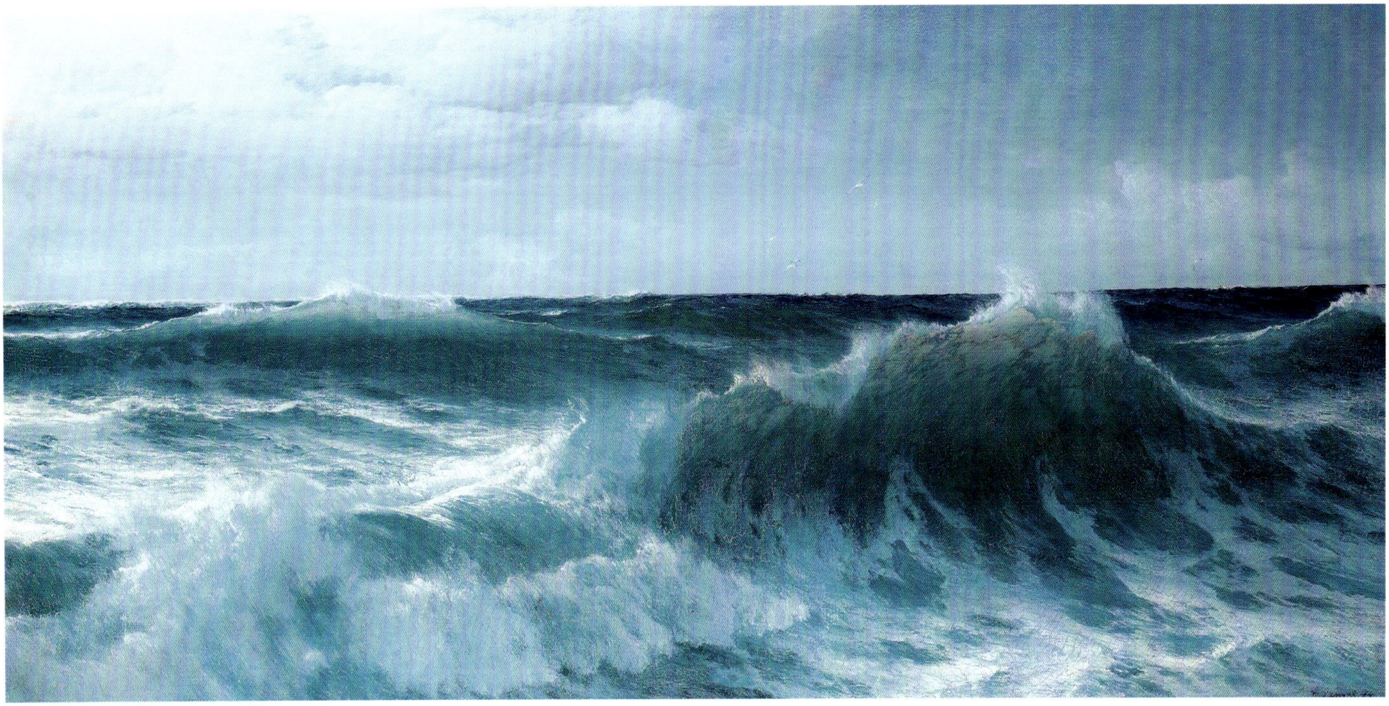

David James (1853–1904)

A Breaking Wave | Brechende Welle | Onda quebrando
Déferlante | Una ola rompiendo | Brekende golven

1894, Oil on canvas/Huile sur toile, 63,5 × 127 cm, Private collection

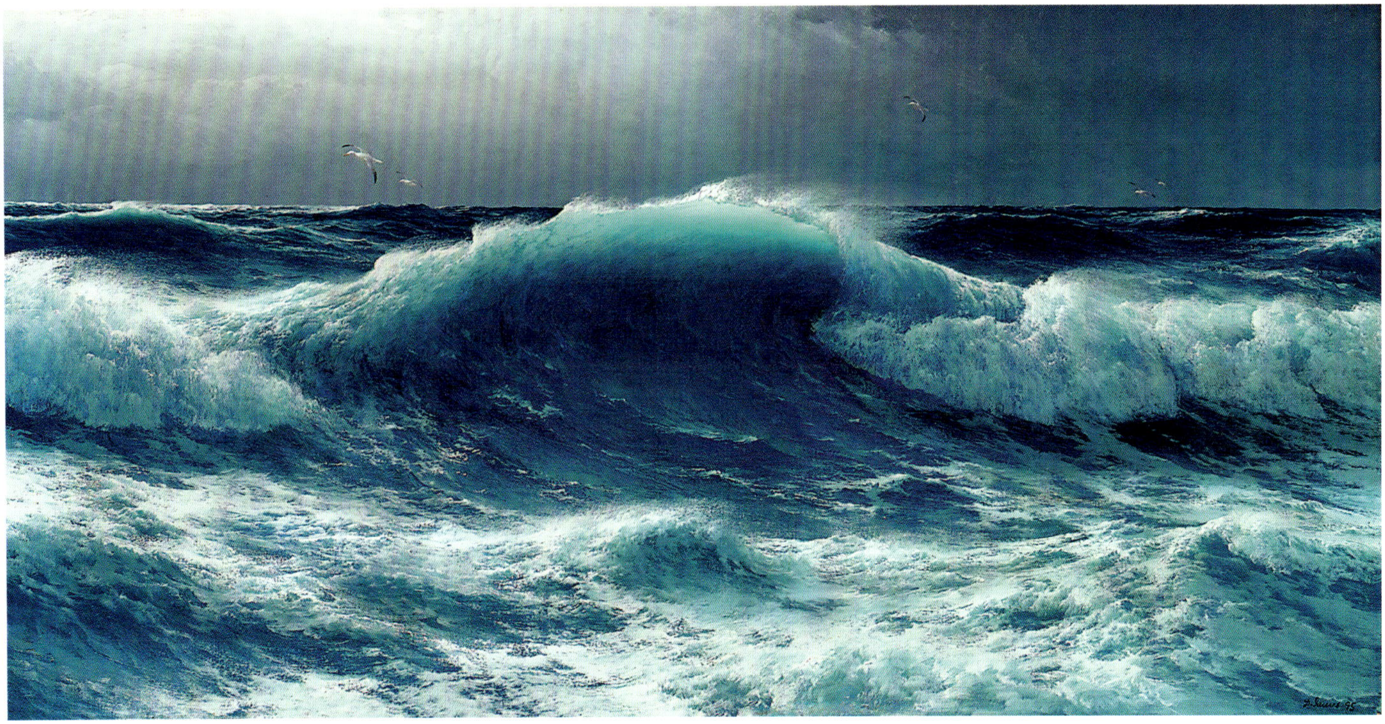

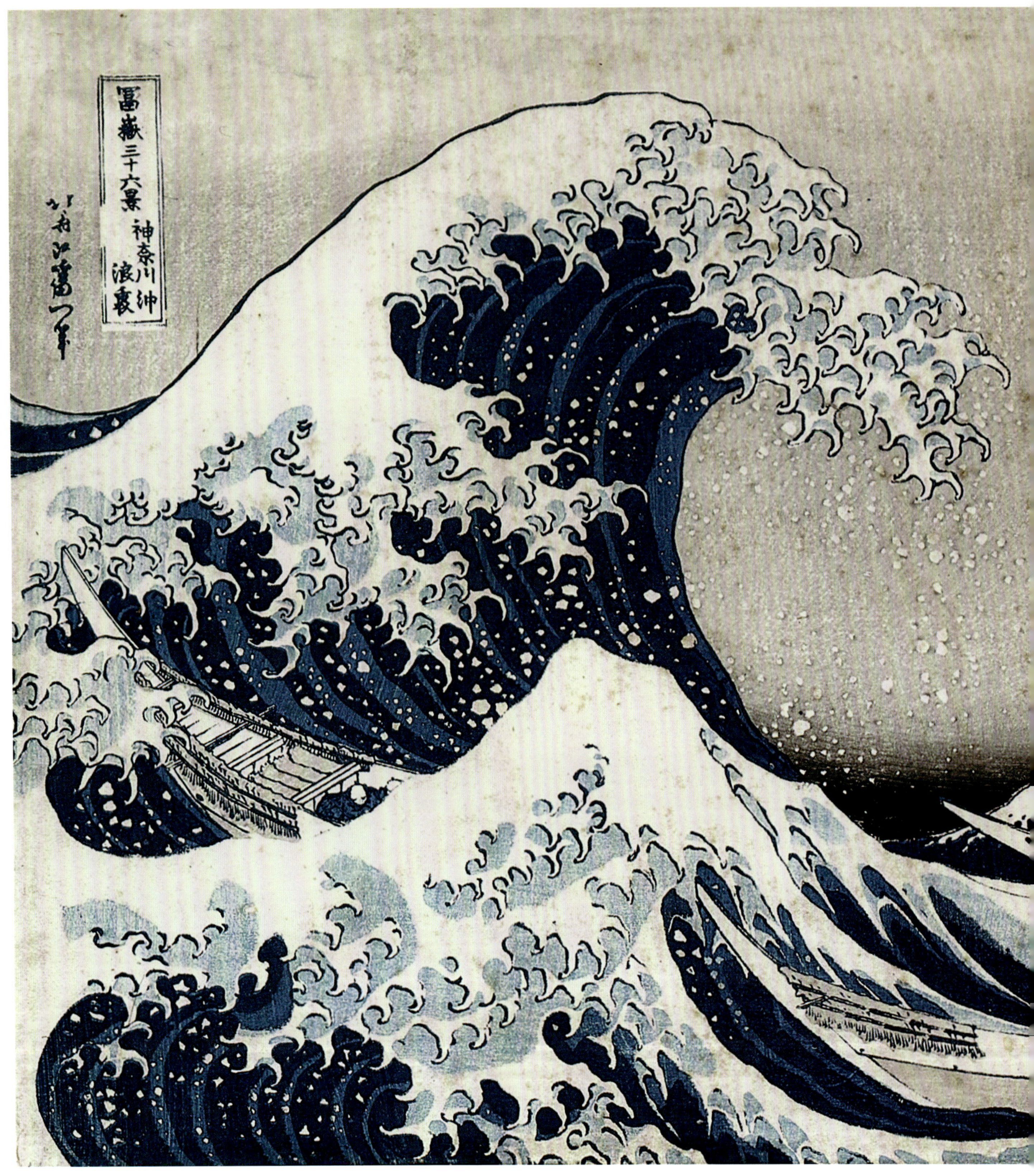

冨嶽三十六景 神奈川沖
浪裏
北斎 前北斎為一筆

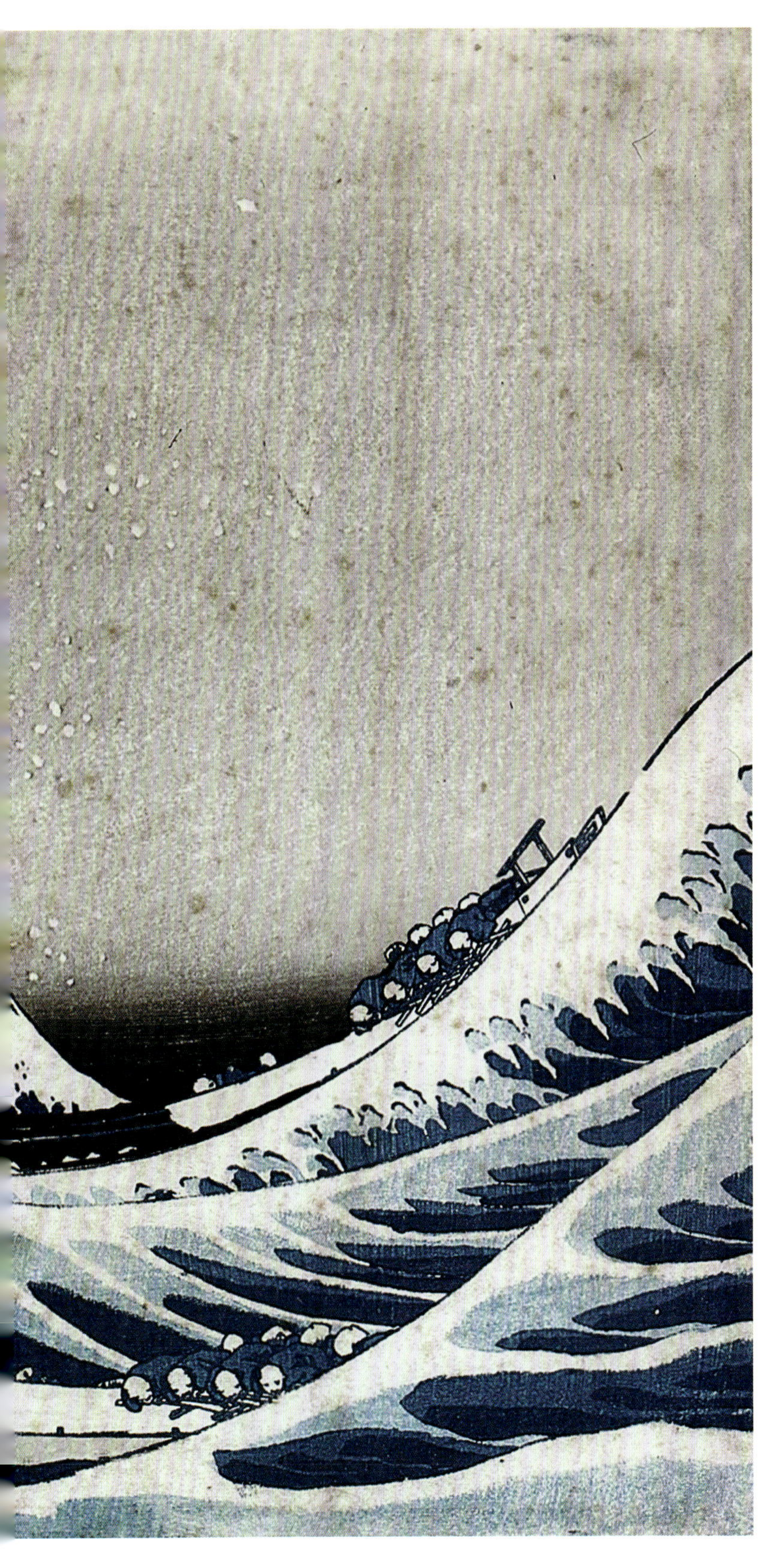

Katsushika Hokusai (1760–1849)

The Great Wave off Kanagawa

La Grande Vague de Kanagawa

Die große Welle vor Kanagawa

La gran ola delante de Kanagawa

A Grande Onda de Kanagawa

De grote golf voor de kust van Kanagawa

c. 1830, Color woodcut/Gravure en couleur, 24,6 × 37,5 cm, Private collection

Hardly any Japanese work of art has proved to be as popular as this color woodcut by Tokyo-born Katsushika Hokusai. Even if from a series entitled 36 Views of Mount Fuji, it has become famous for its almost emblematic portrayal of a ferocious sea.

Presqu'aucune œuvre d'art japonaise ne s'est avérée aussi populaire que cette sculpture sur bois de Katsushika Hokusai, originaire de Tokyo. Même si elle provenait d'une série intitulée 36 Vues du Mont Fuji, elle est devenue célèbre pour sa représentation presque emblématique d'une mer féroce.

Kaum ein japanisches Kunstwerk dürfte eine solche Popularität genießen wie dieser Farbholzschnitt des in Tokio geborenen Katsushika Hokusai. Auch wenn er aus einer Serie mit 36 Ansichten des Berges Fuji stammt, ist er doch allein zu einer fast emblematischen Darstellung des aufgepeitschten Meeres geworden.

Casi ninguna otra obra de arte japonés debería gozar de tanta popularidad como este grabado en madera de color del artista de Tokio, Katsushika Hokusai. A pesar de que proviene de su Serie de 36 vistas del monte Fuji, puede constituir por sí sola una representación casi emblemática de la furia del mar.

Dificilmente uma obra de arte japonesa apreciaria tanta popularidade como esta xilogravura de Katsushika Hokusai, nascido em Tóquio. Mesmo fazendo parte de uma série de Trinta e seis vistas do Monte Fuji, a obra se tornou isoladamente uma representação quase emblemática do mar revolto.

Er is waarschijnlijk geen Japans kunstwerk dat zó beroemd is als deze kleurenhoutsnede van de in Tokio geboren Katsushika Hokusai. Hoewel de prent tot de serie 36 gezichten op de berg Fuji behoort, is hij als zelfstandig kunstwerk bijna tot symbool van de uitbeelding van de wrede zee geworden.

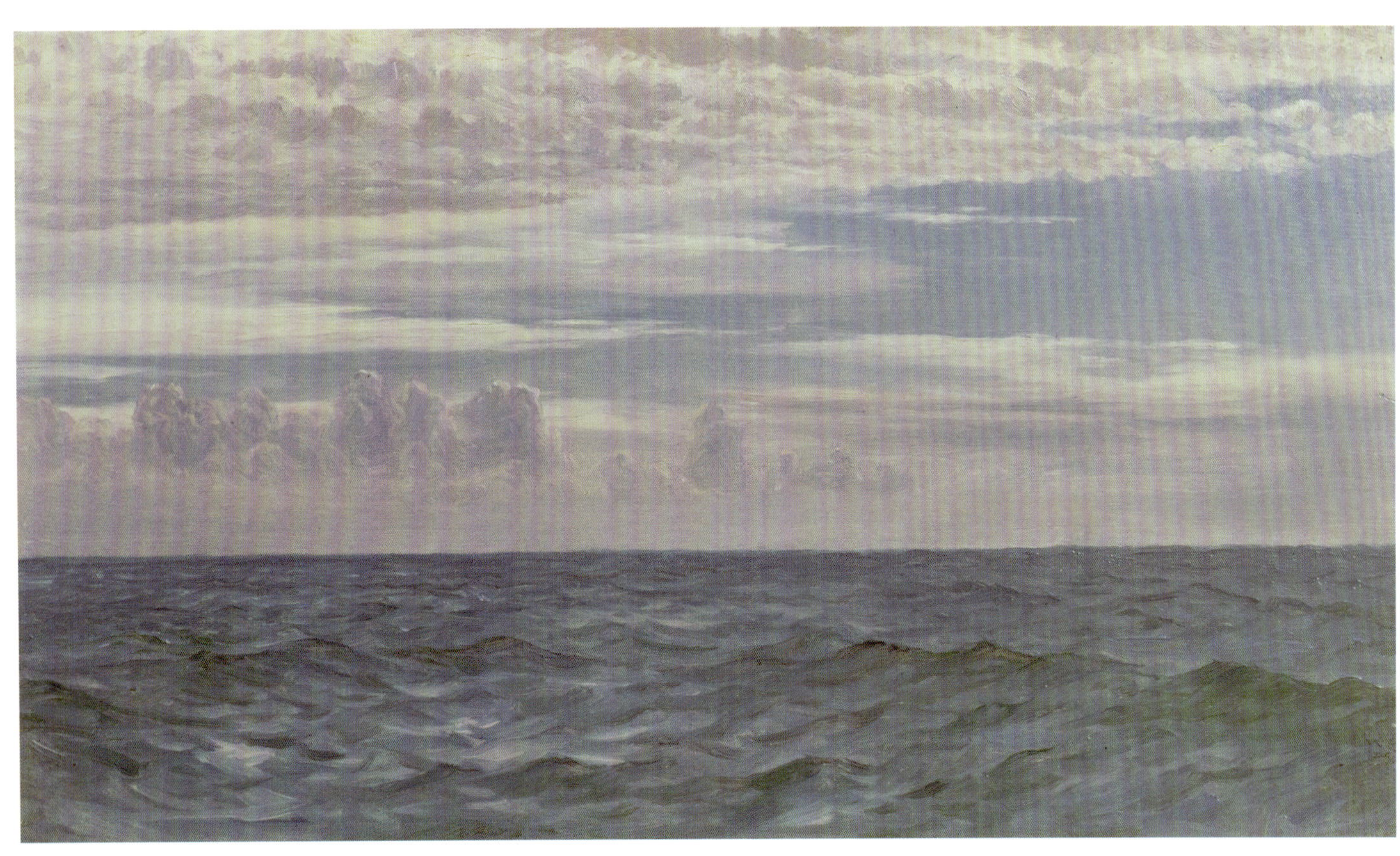

Charles Parsons Knight (1829–97)

Seascape

Paysage marin

Meerespanorama

Paisaje marino

Paisagem marinha

Zeegezicht

n. d., Oil on canvas/Huile sur toile, 23,2 × 40 cm, Private collection

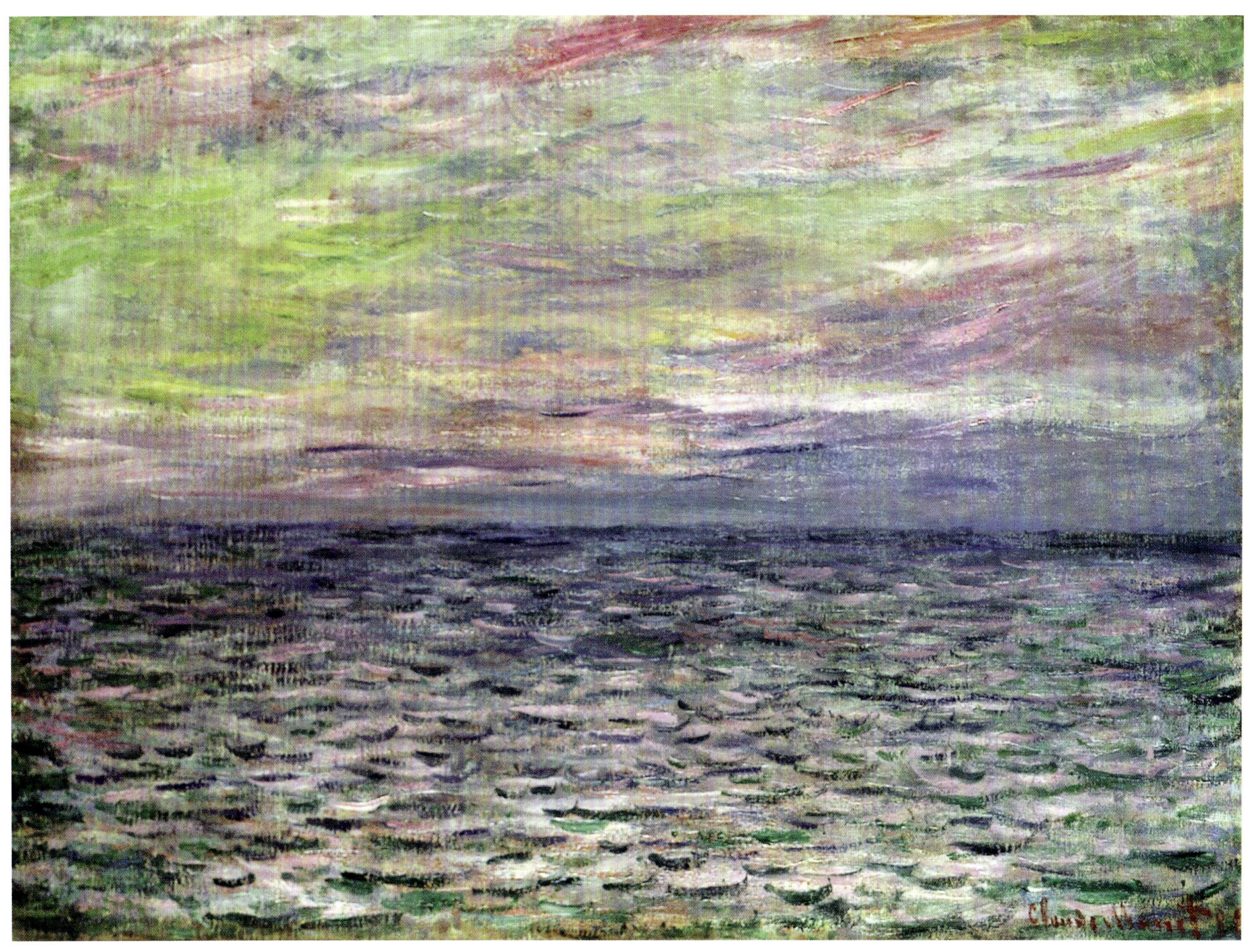

Claude Monet (1840–1926)

Sunset at Pourville

Coucher de soleil à Pourville

Sonnenuntergang bei Pourville

Puesta de sol en Pourville

Pôr do sol em Pourville

Zonsondergang bij Pourville

1882, Oil on canvas/Huile sur toile, 54 × 73 cm, Private collection

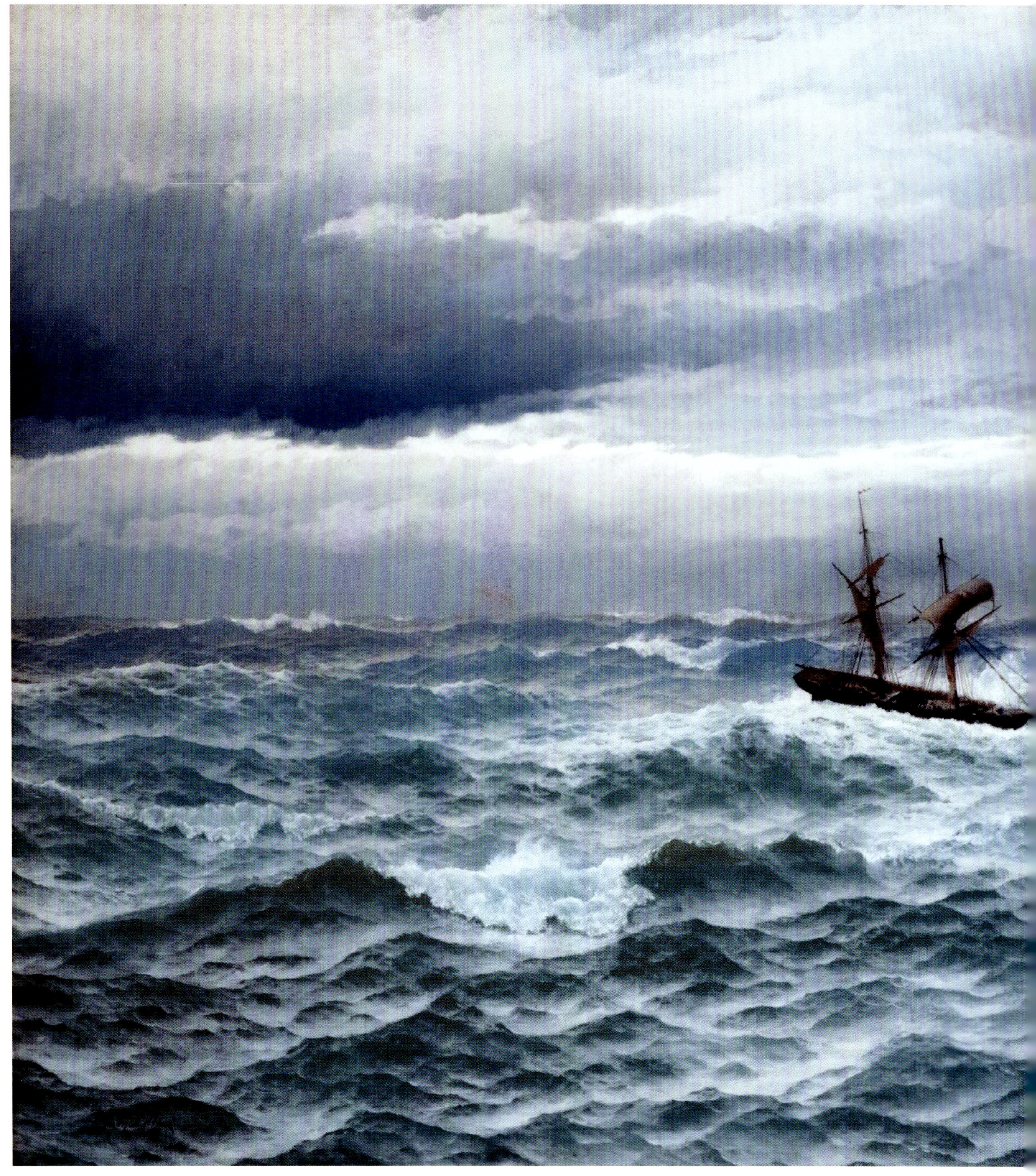

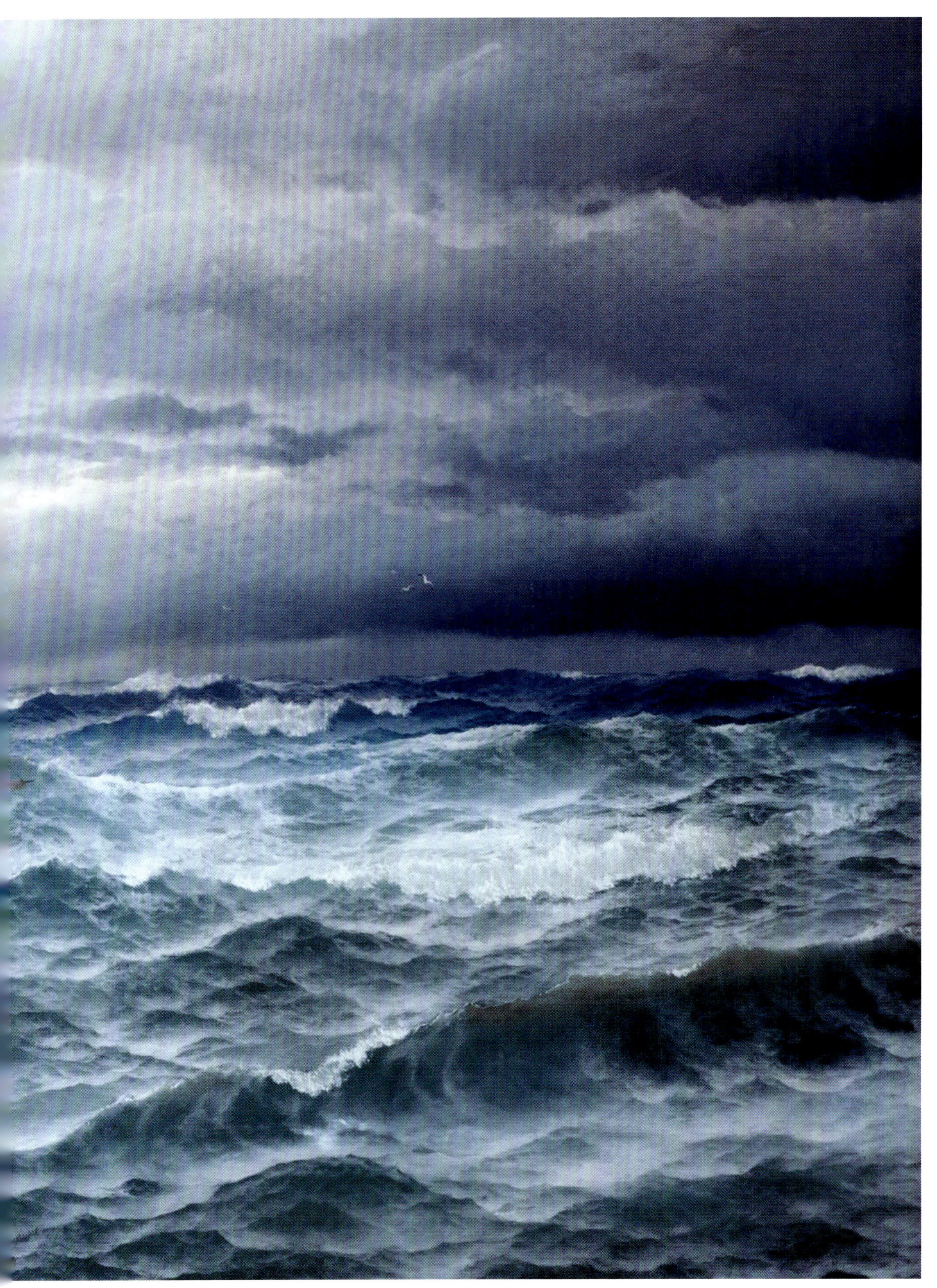

James David (1853−1904)

Sea Piece

Œuvre maritime

Seestück

Pieza marina

Marinha

Zeegezicht

1882, Oil on canvas/Huile sur
toile, 76,5 × 127 cm, Shipley
Art Gallery, Gateshead

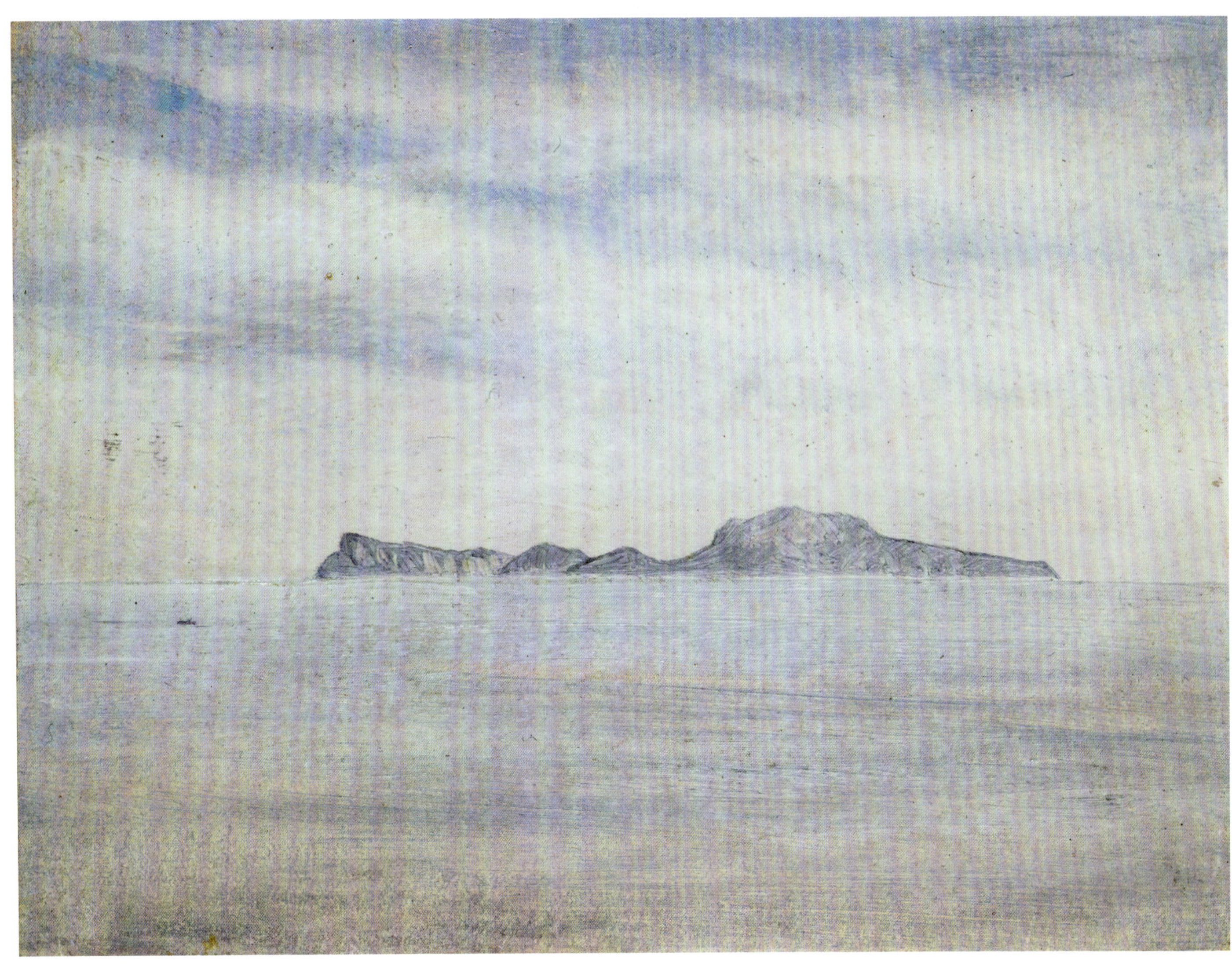

Karl Gustav Carus (1789–1869)

Island in the Sea (Capri)

Île dans la mer

Insel im Meer

Isla en el mar

Ilha no mar

Eiland in zee

1828, Oil on panel/Huile sur bois, Kupferstichkabinett, Dresden

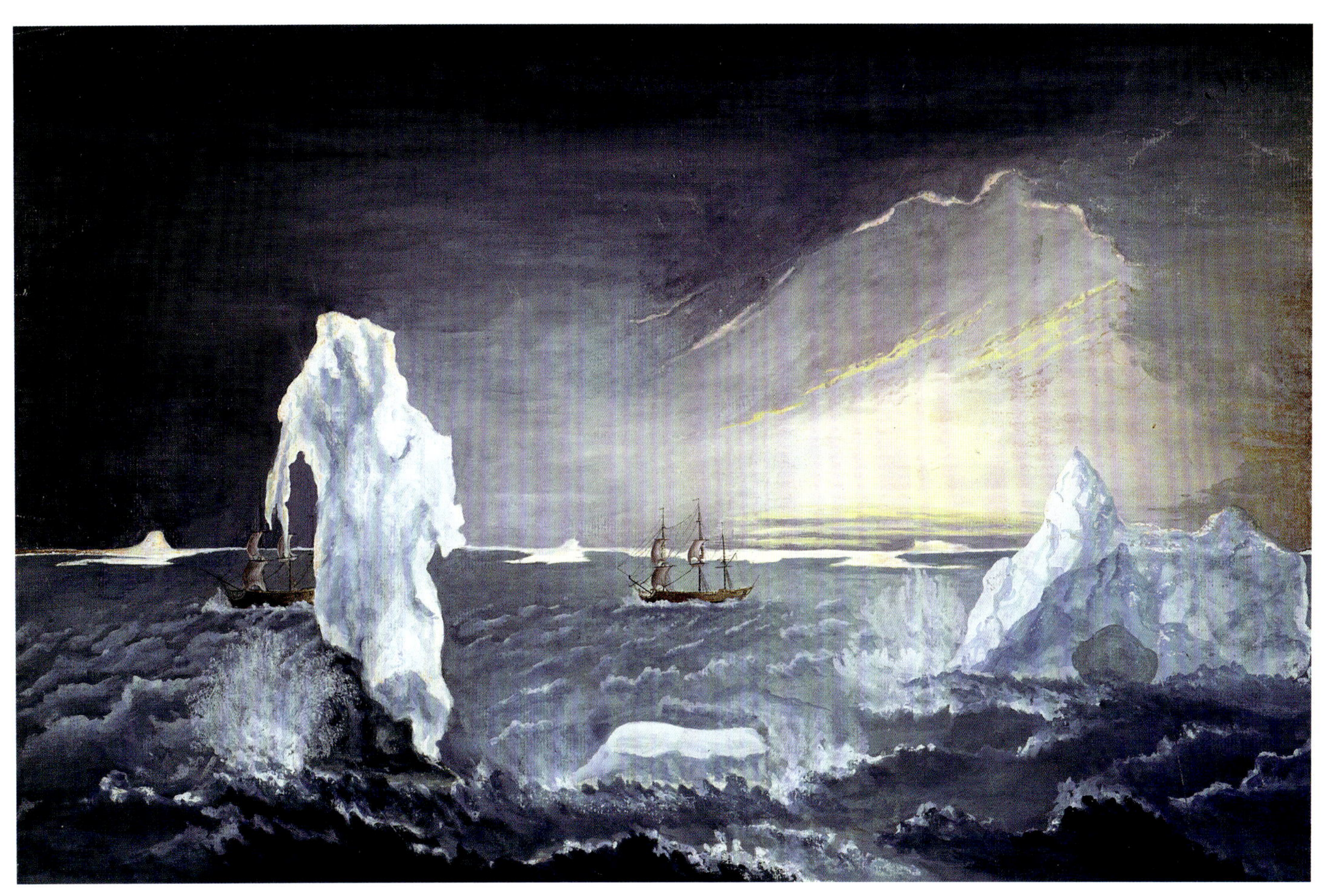

George E. Forster (1817–96)

Arctic Sea Glow

Lueur en Arctique

Eismeerleuchten

Luz del Mar Ártico

Luzes do Ártico

Lichtschijnsel van de IJszee

n. d., Gouache on paper/Gouache sur papier, State Library of New South Wales, Sydney

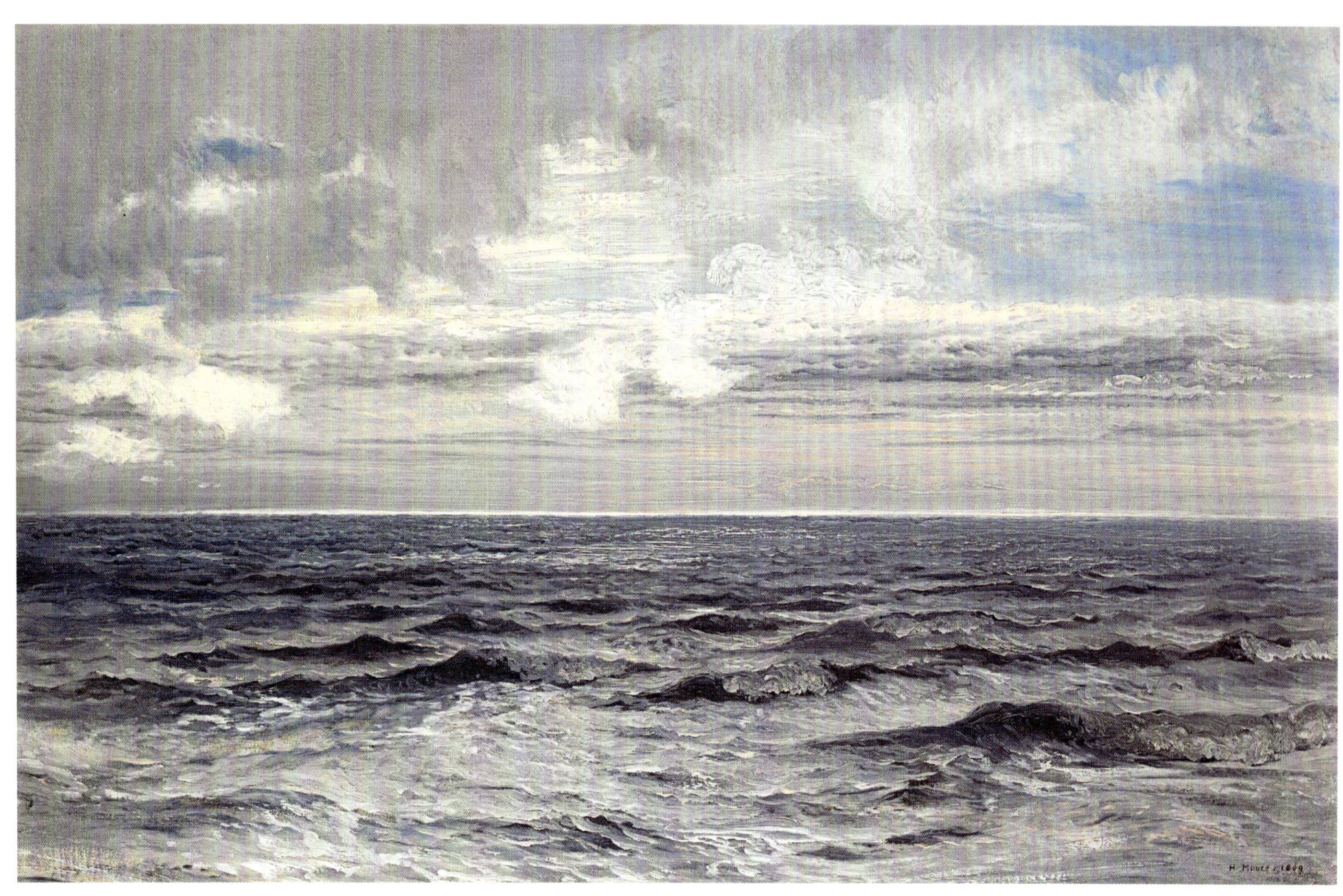

Henry Moore (1831–95)

Silver Sea

Mer argentée

Silbernes Meer

Mar de plata

Mar de prata

Zilveren zee

1869, Oil on canvas/Huile sur toile, 15,5 × 25,3 cm, Private collection

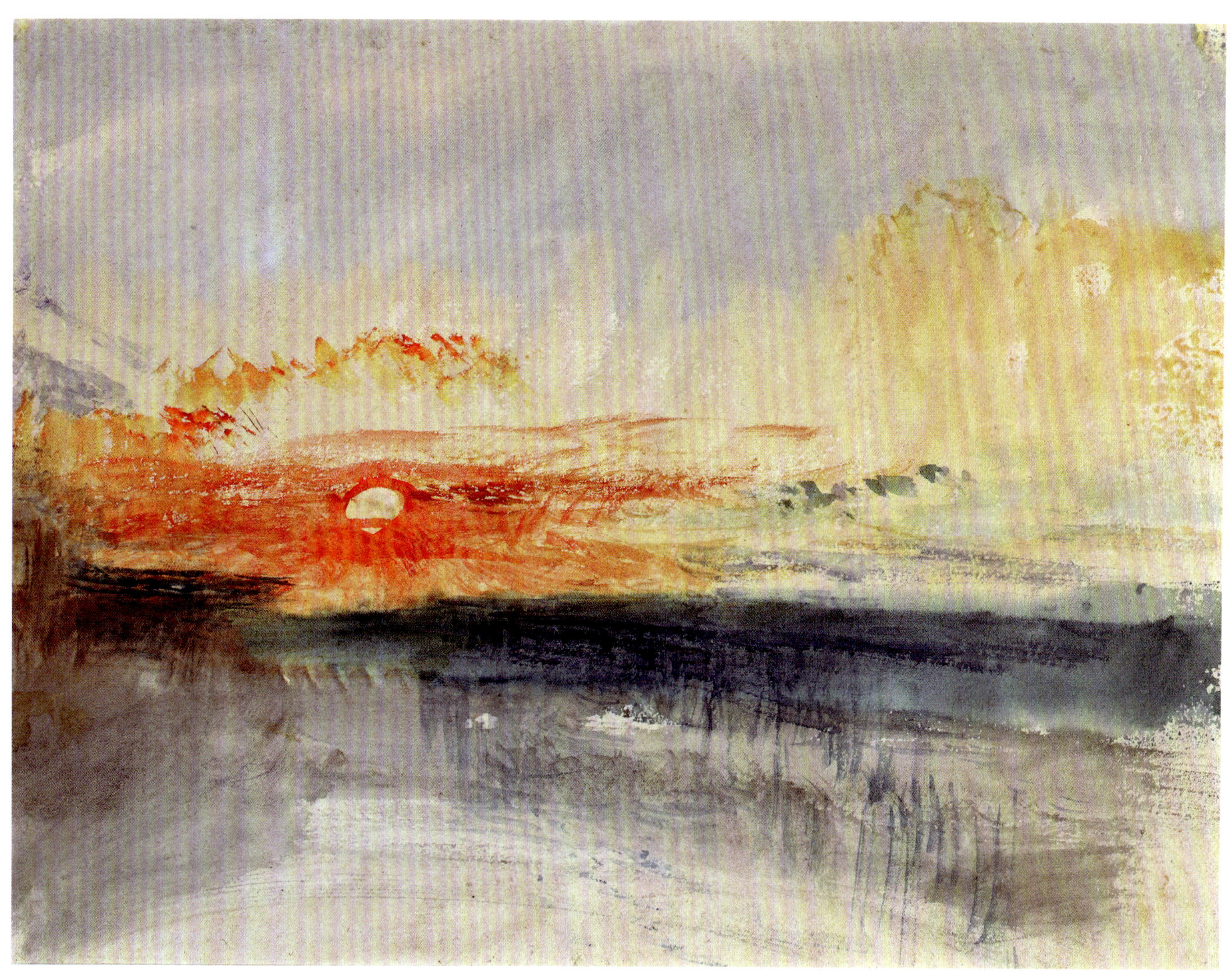

Joseph Mallord William Turner (1775–1851)

Sunset

Coucher de soleil

Sonnenuntergang

Puesta de sol

Pôr do sol

Zonsondergang

c. 1845, Watercolor on paper/Aquarelle sur papier, 23 × 29,7 cm, Manchester Art Gallery, Manchester

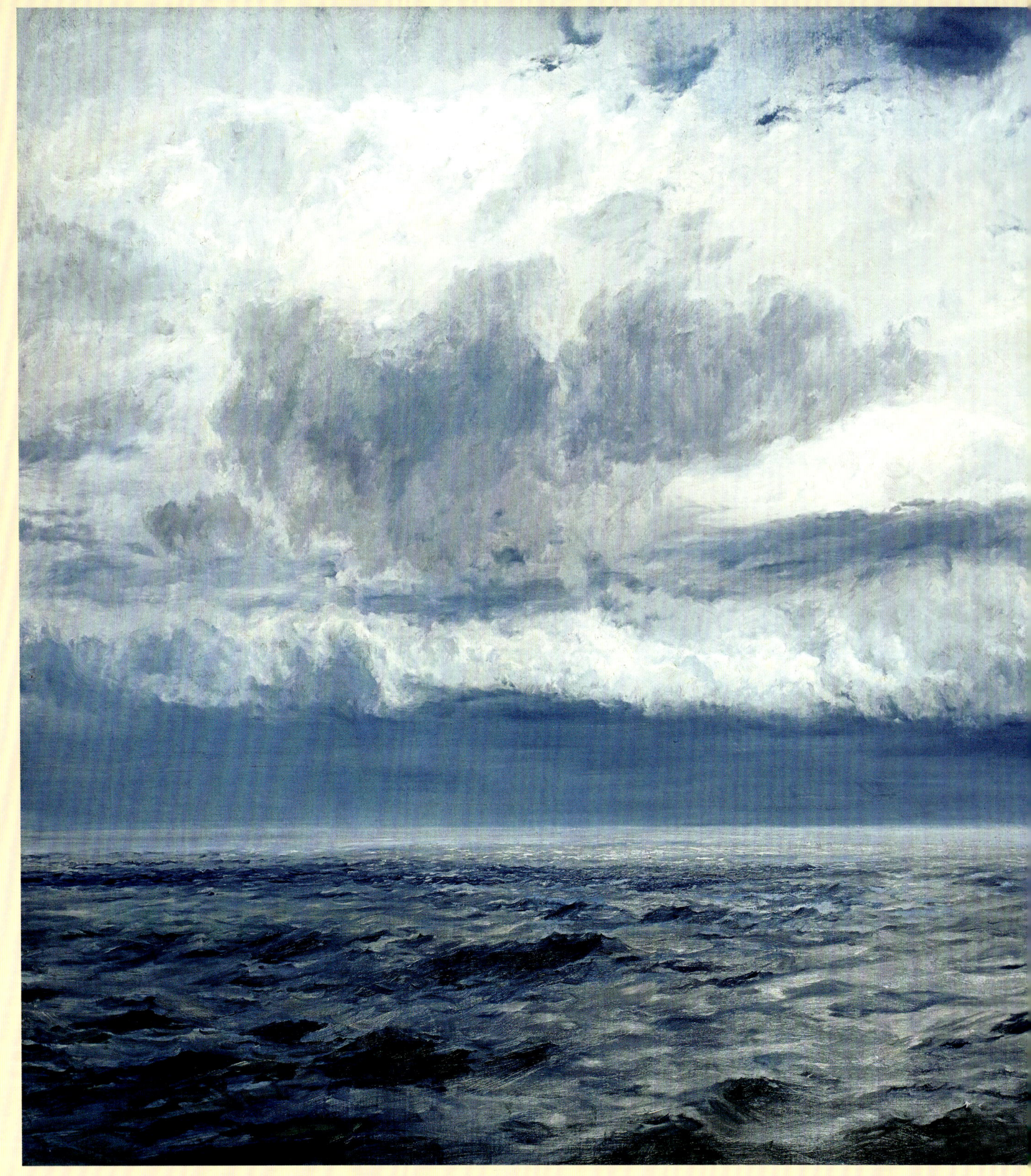

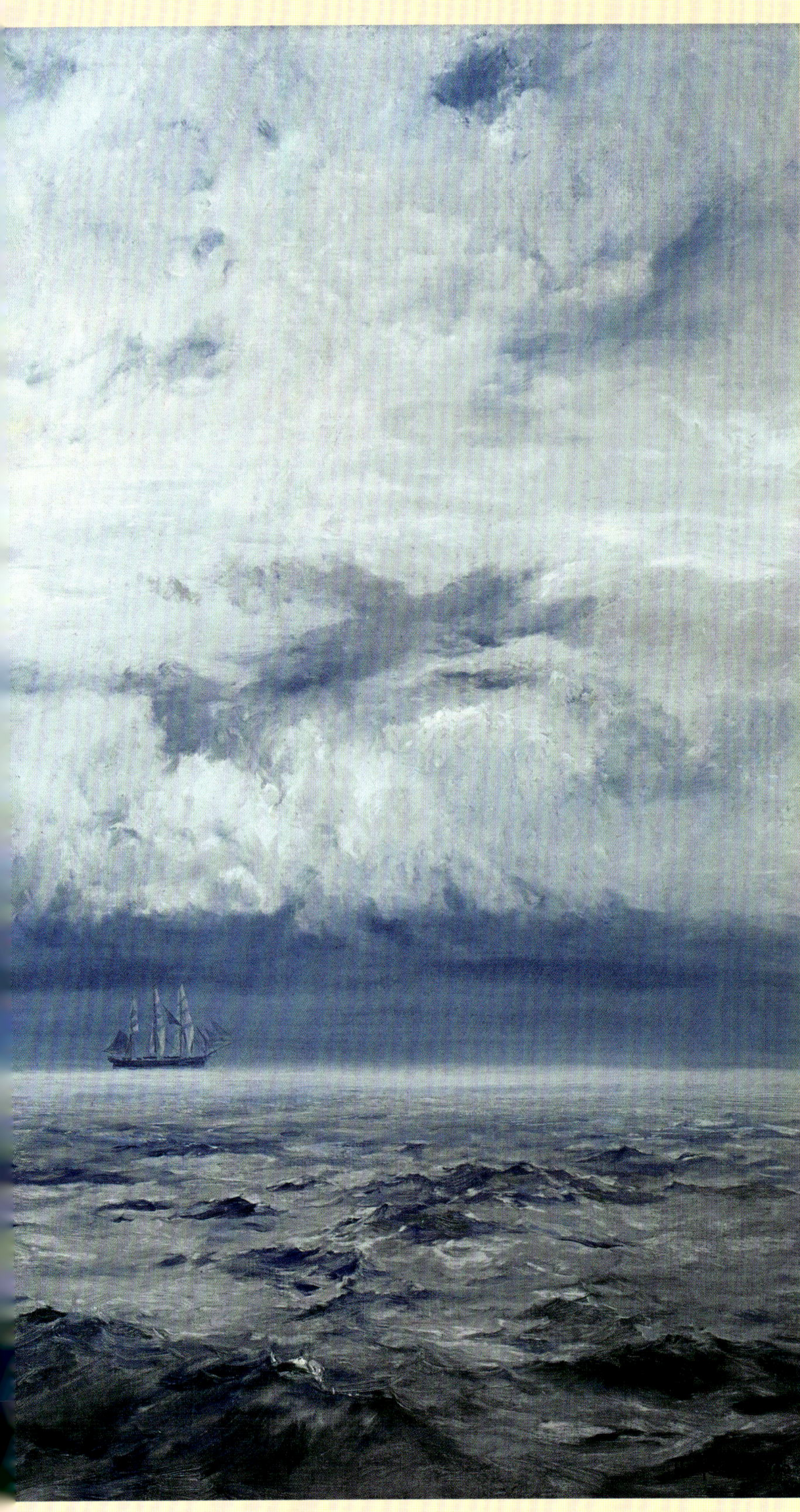

Storm

Tempête

Sturm

Tormenta

Tempestade

Storm

Henry Moore (1831–95)
Storm Brewing
L'Orage se prépare
Sturm braut sich zusammen
Tormenta avecinándose
Tempestade se formando
Opkomende storm
1890, Oil on canvas/Huile sur toile, 119,4 × 180,3 cm, Private collection

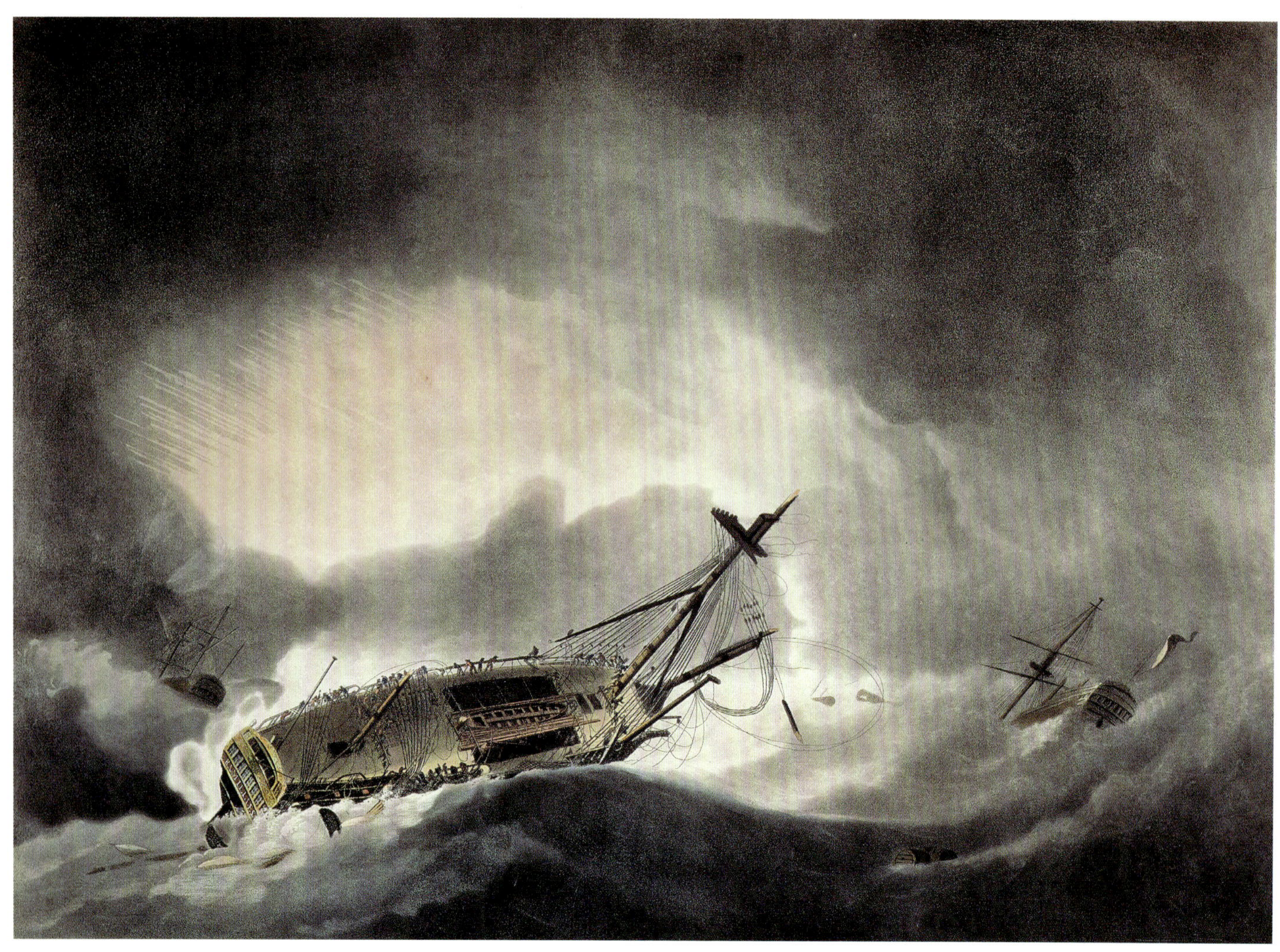

Robert Dodd (1748−1815)

The Storm Increased

L'Orage s'intensifie

Zunehmender Sturm

La tormenta empeora

Tempestade aumentando

Aanwakkerende storm

1795, Aquatint/Aquatinte, Royal Navy Museum, Portsmouth

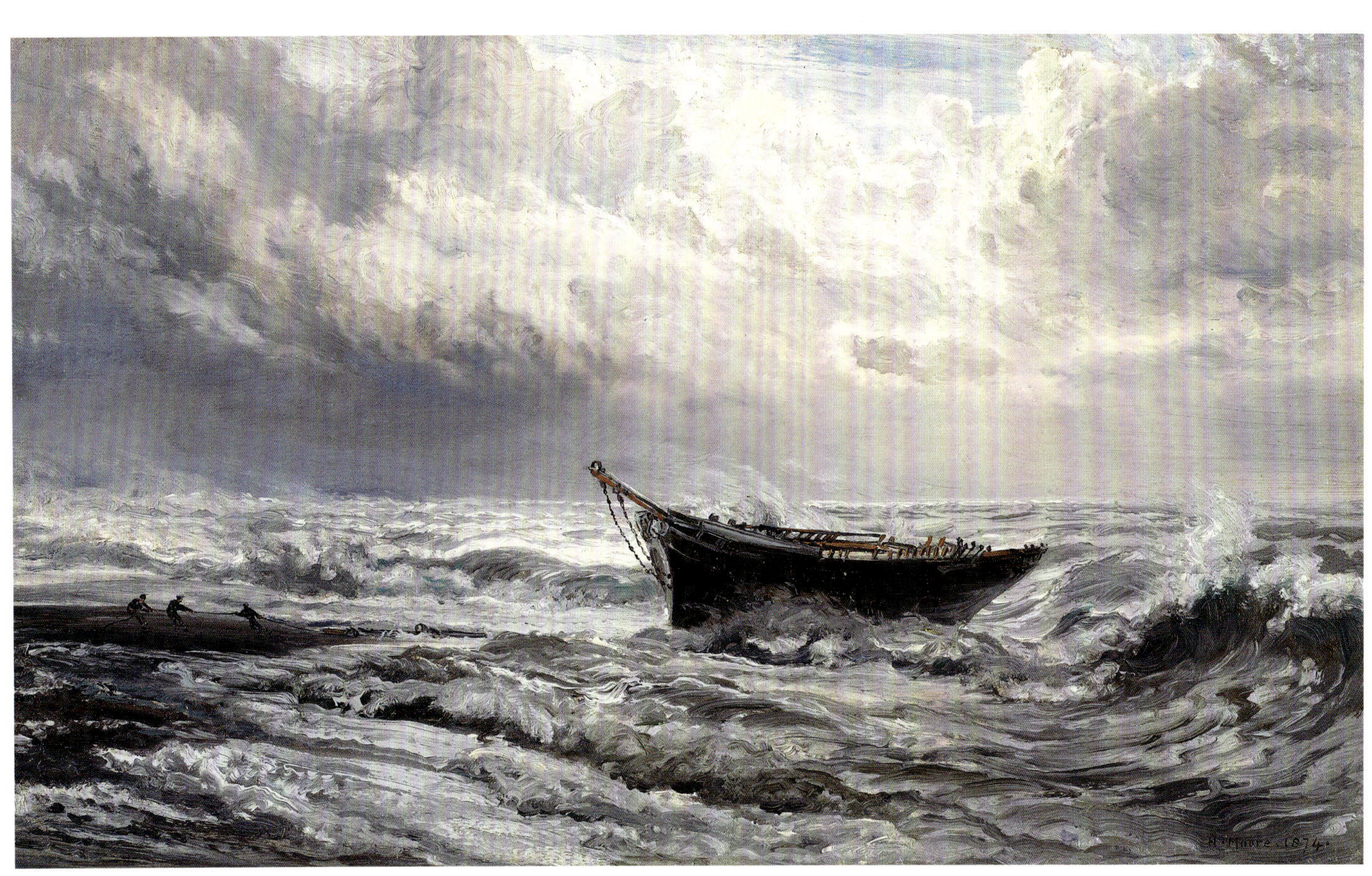

Henry Moore (1831–95)

Stormy Seas

Mer agitée

Stürmische See

Mar de tormenta

Mar bravo

Stormachtige zee

1874, Oil on canvas/Huile sur toile, 30,5 × 50,2 cm, Private collection

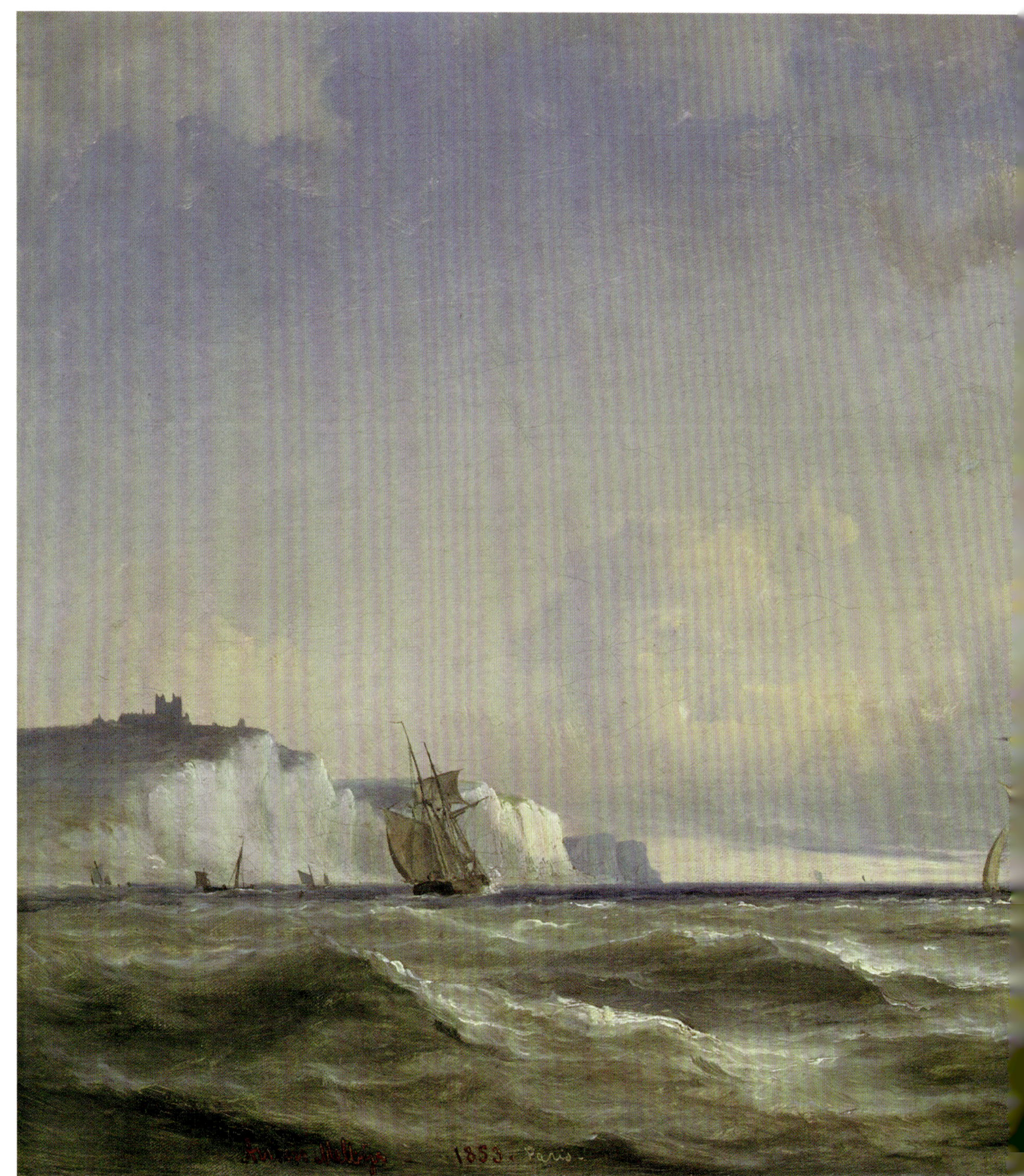

Anton Melbye
(1818–75)

The Gathering Storm

Orage menaçant

Der Sturm braut
sich zusammen

Tormenta
avecinándose

A tempestade
se forma

De opkomende storm

1853, Oil on canvas/
Huile sur toile,
40,5 × 78 cm,
Kunsthalle, Hamburg

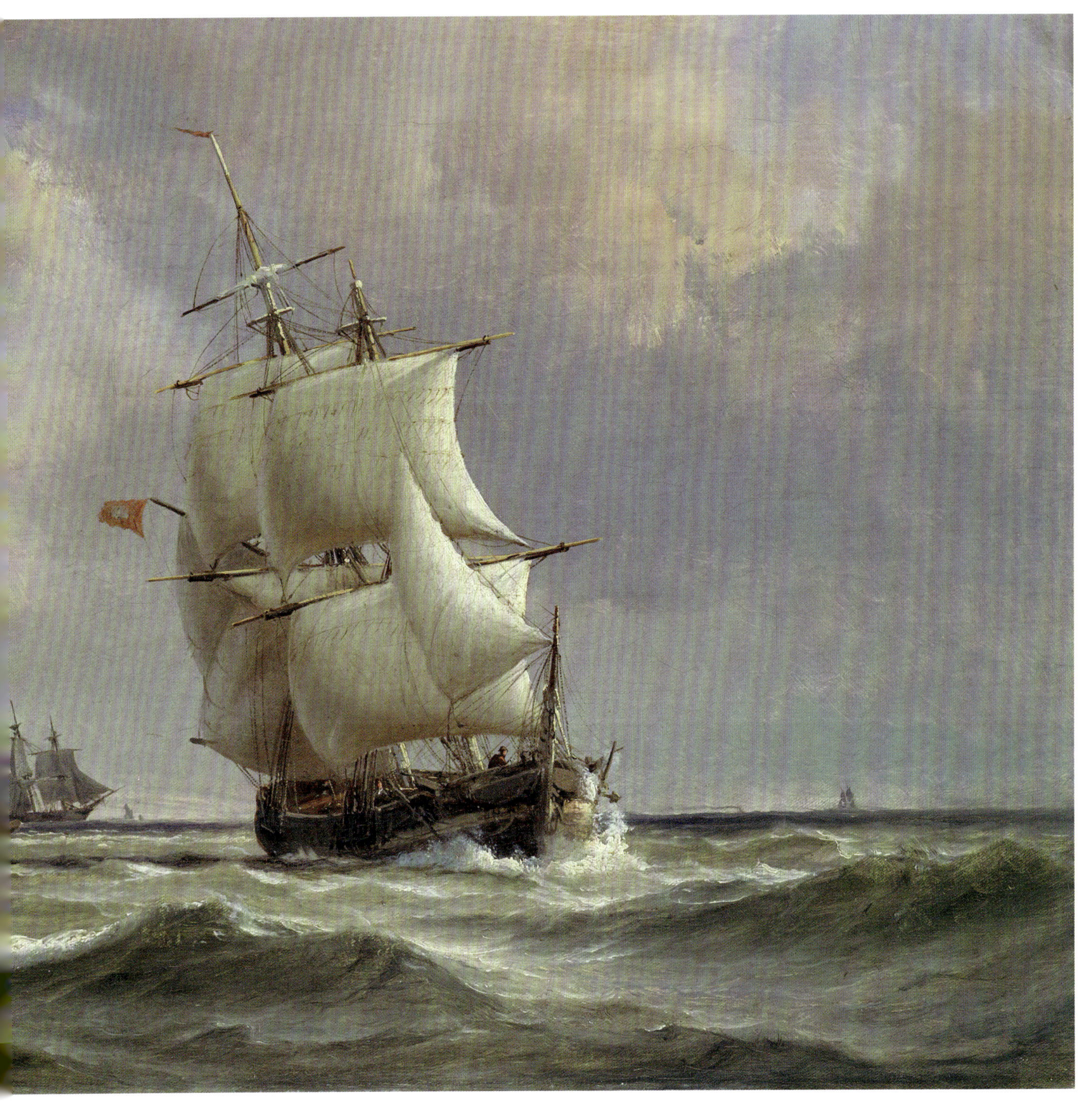

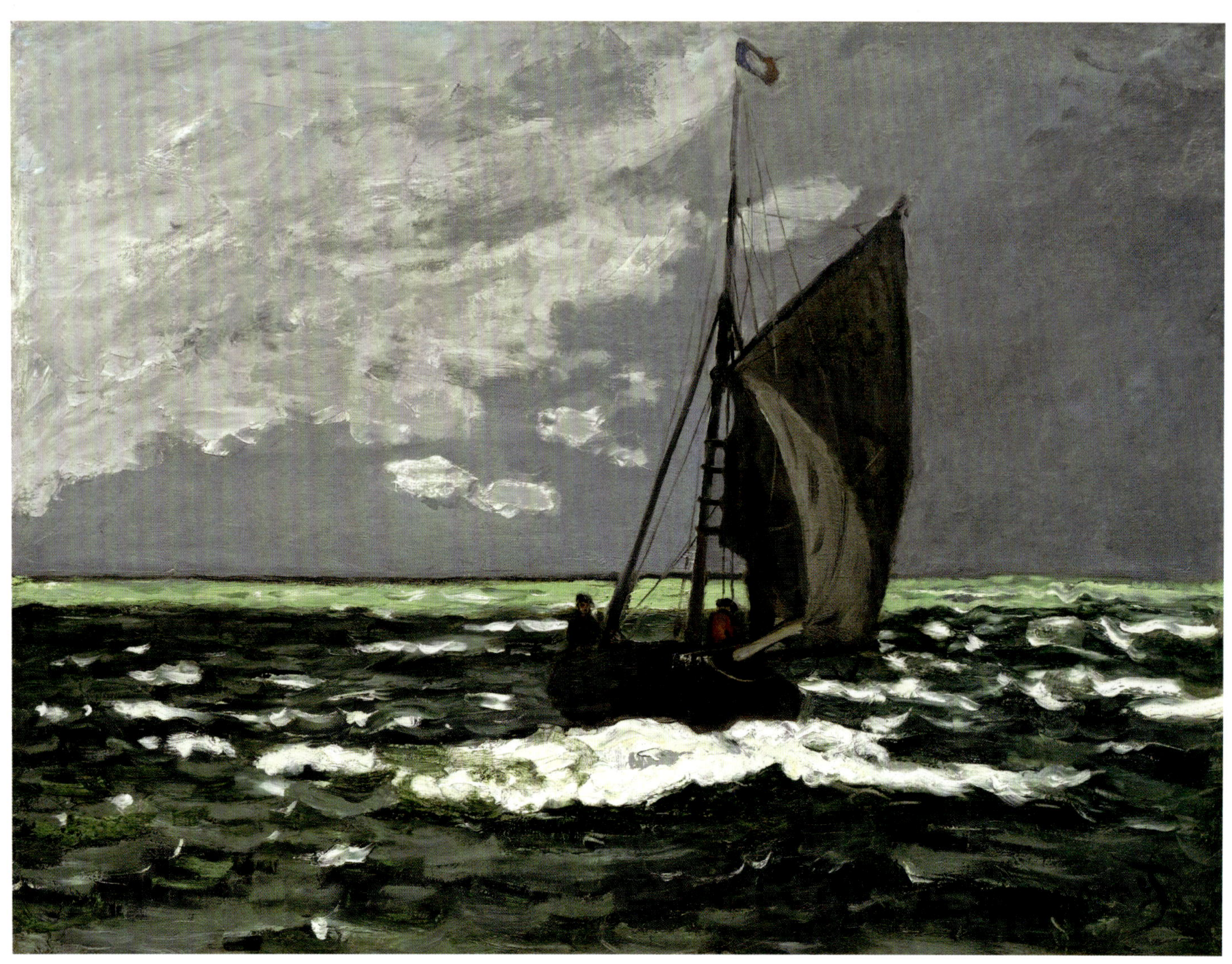

Claude Monet (1840–1926)

Seascape - Storm   Meerespanorama mit Sturm   Paisagem marinha com tempestade

Paysage de mer – l'orage   Paisaje marino con tormenta   Zeegezicht bij storm

1866, Oil on canvas/Huile sur toile, 48,7 × 64,6 cm, Clark Art Institute, Williamstown

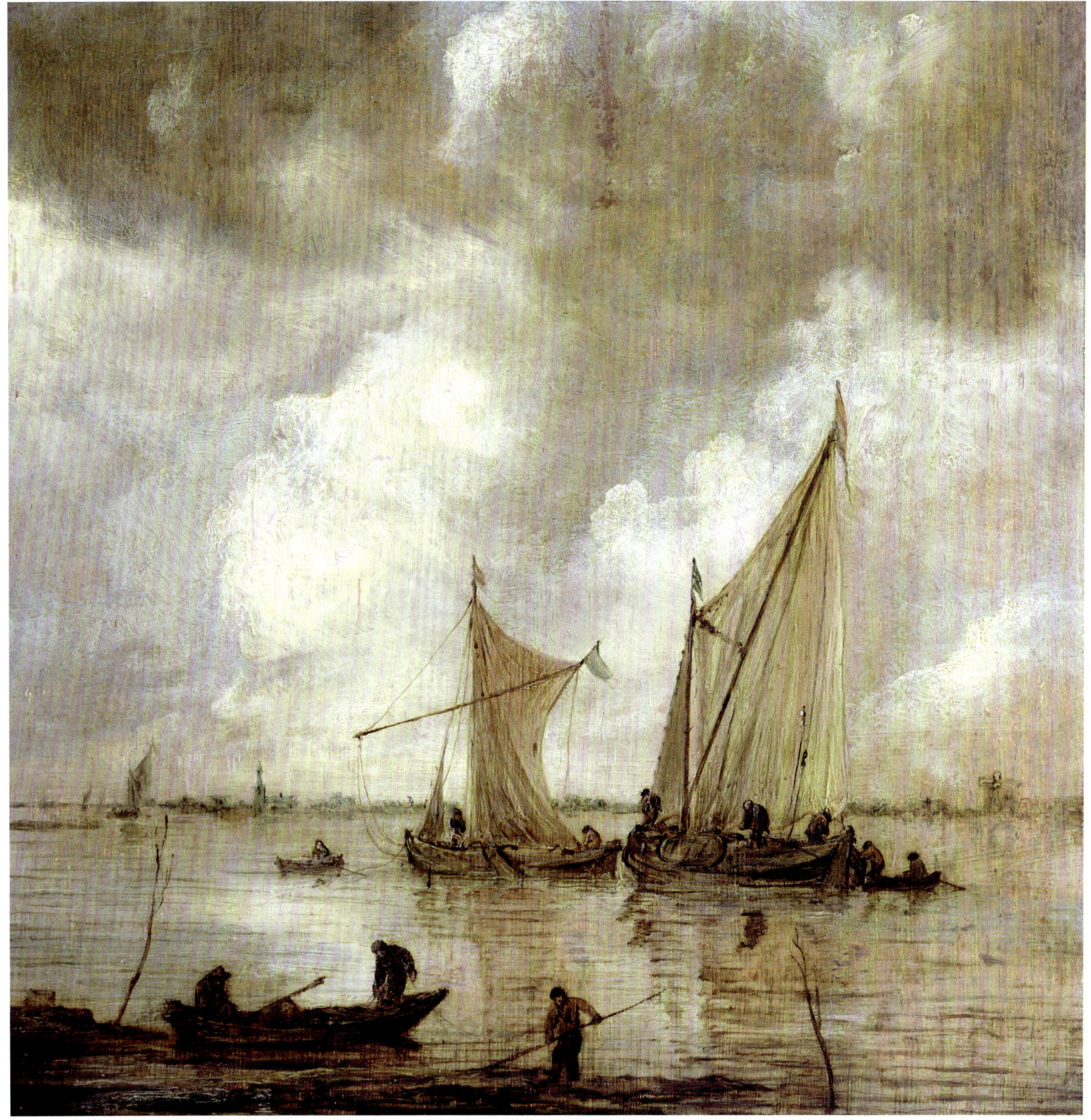

Jan van Goyen (1596–1656)

Stormy Seascape	Stürmisches Meerespanorama	Paisagem marinha tempestuosa
Paysage de mer orageux	Paisaje de mar tormentoso	Zeegezicht, storm

1655, Oil on canvas/Huile sur toile, 32,5 × 32 cm, Musée des Beaux-Arts, Rouen

1856, Pencil and gouache on paper/Crayon et gouache sur papier, 23 × 32,7 cm, Private collection

Ivan Konstantinovich Aivazovski, a Russian painter of Armenian descent, holds a special place among international maritime painters. Not only was the sea the most frequent subject of his approx. 20,000 works, it is also extraordinary that he painted all of them from memory, far from the sea.

Peintre russe d'origine arménienne, Ivan Konstantinovich Aivazovski occupe une place privilégiée parmi les peintres de mer internationaux. Non seulement la mer était le sujet le plus fréquent de ses quelques 20 000 œuvres, mais c'est également extraordinaire qu'il ait réalisé toutes ses peintures de mémoire, loin de la mer.

Ivan Konstantinovitsch Aivasovski, russischer Maler armenischer Abstammung, nimmt unter den internationalen Marinemalern sicher einen besonderen Rang ein. Im Werk kaum eines anderen Künstlers seiner Zeit hatten das Meer und die Seefahrt eine solch große Bedeutung wie bei ihm. So war das Meer nicht nur Aivasovskis wichtigstes Sujet seiner bis zu 20 000 Bilder – außergewöhnlich ist auch, dass er diese alle aus der Erinnerung, weit entfernt von der See angefertigt haben soll.

Ivan Konstantinovich Aivasovski, pintor ruso de origen armenio, ocupa sin duda un lugar especial entre los pintores internacionales de marinas. Casi en ninguna obra de cualquier otro artista de su época, el mar y la navegación han tenido una importancia tan grande como en la suya. No sólo el mar era para Aivasovski el tema principal de sus 20 000 cuadros – sino que también es extraordinario que lo haya hecho de memoria pues vivía lejos del mar.

Ivan Konstantinovich Aivasovski, pintor russo de ascendência armênia, ocupa certamente entre os pintores internacionais de marinhas uma posição especial. Na obra de praticamente nenhum outro artista de sua época o mar e a navegação assumiram uma importância tão grande como no caso deste pintor. Assim, o mar não foi somente o principal tema de Aivasovski, que pintou até 20.000 quadros – é igualmente extraordinário que ele tenha pintado todos eles memória, bem longe do mar.

Ivan Konstantinovitsj Ajvasovski, een Russische schilder van Armeense afkomst, neemt onder de maritieme schilders een bijzondere plaats in. Bij weinig andere kunstenaars van zijn tijd speelde de scheepvaart een zo belangrijke rol. Zo was de zee niet alleen het belangrijkste motief in het 20 000 doeken tellende oeuvre van Ajvasovski, maar zou hij al deze werken ook op grote afstand van enige zee en uit pure verbeeldingskracht hebben geschilderd.

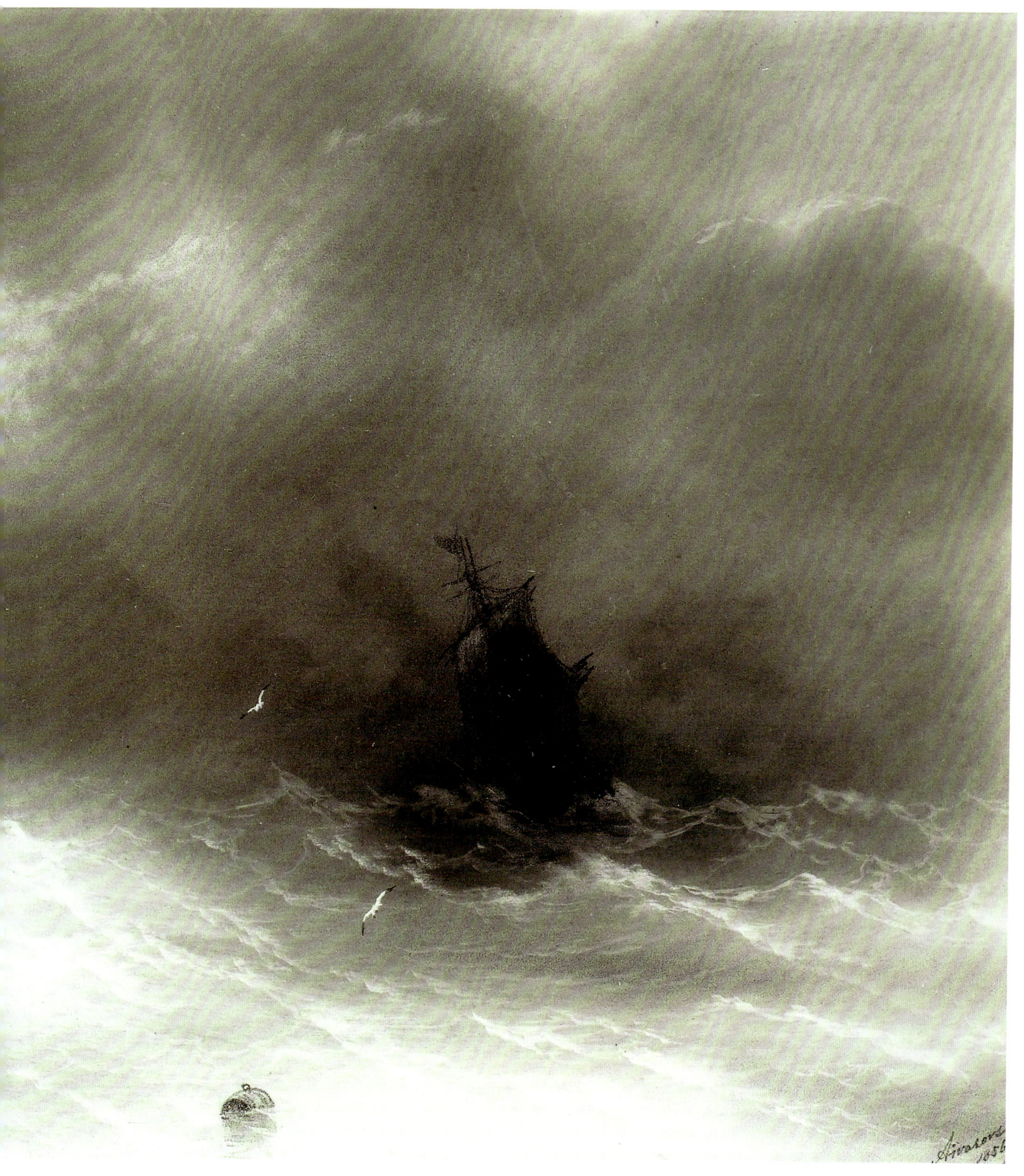

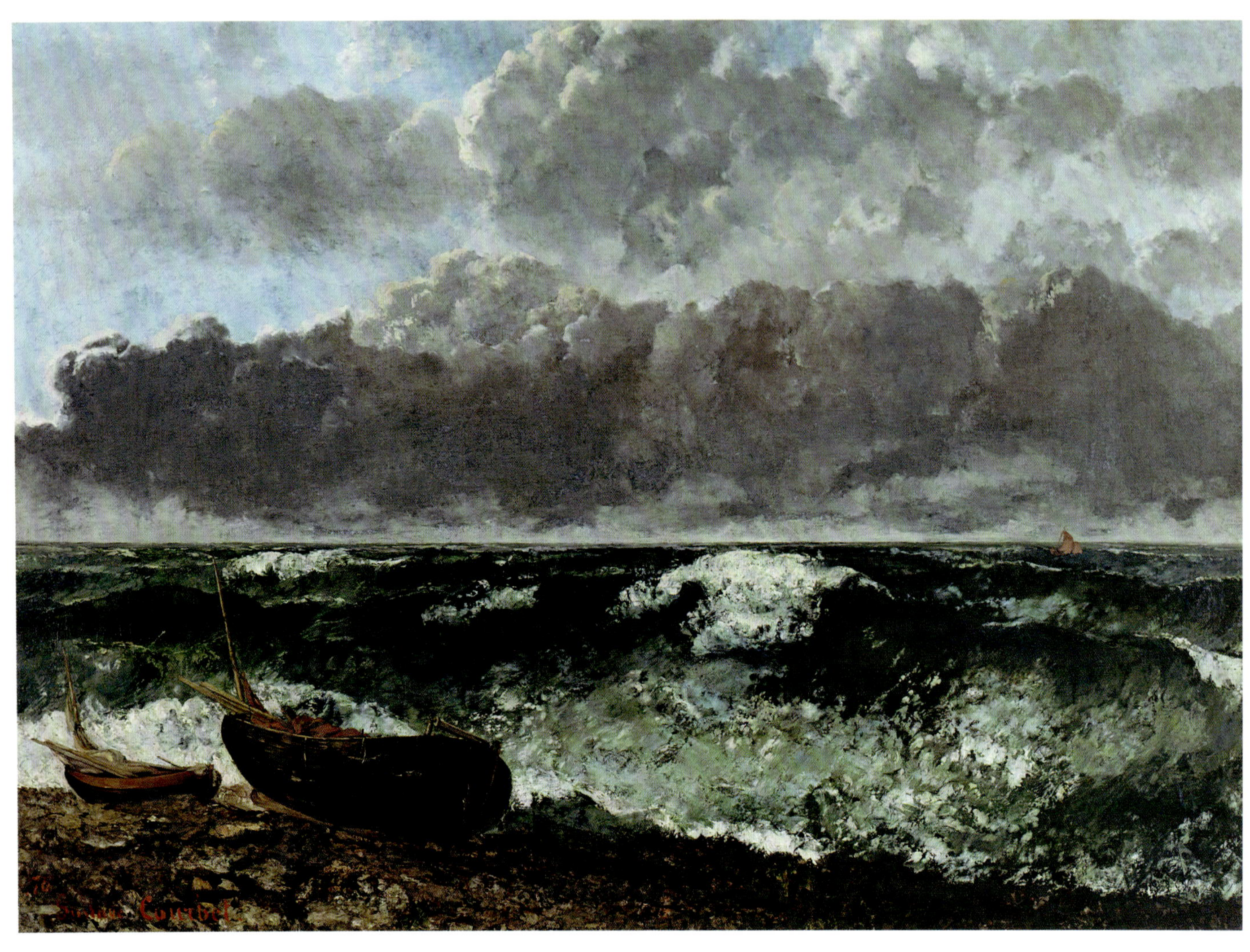

Gustave Courbet (1819–77)

The Stormy Sea *or* The Wave

Mer agitée *ou* La Vague

Das Stürmische Meer *oder* Die Welle

Mar de tormenta *o* La ola

O Mar Tempestuoso *ou* A Onda

De stormachtige zee *of* De golf

1870, Oil on canvas/Huile sur toile, 117 × 160,5 cm, Musée d'Orsay, Paris

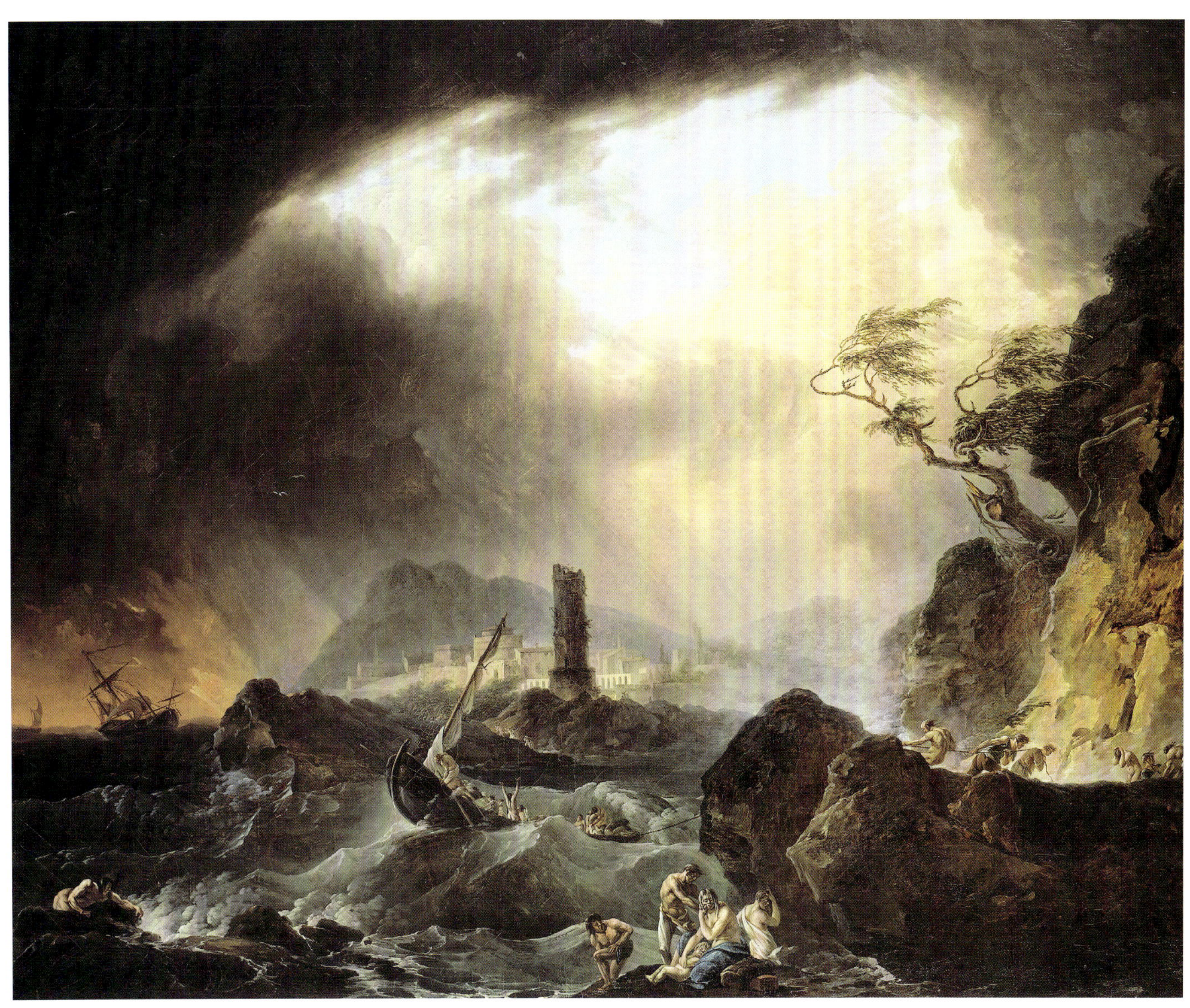

François-Valentin Gazard (c. 1750–1817)

The Storm

Une Tempête

Der Sturm

La tormenta

A Tormenta

De storm

c. 1800, Oil on canvas/Huile sur toile, 126 × 156 cm, Musée des Augustins, Toulouse

Eugène Boudin was one of those maritime painters who discovered their love for the sea, coast, and ships early on in life. Born in Honfleur, Normandy where the Seine empties into the English Channel, he became a ship's boy at the age of ten and began to draw his experiences. His travels led Boudin to many places, but never inland. He spent his life almost exclusively on the coast, which he painted throughout his life with an enthusiasm that never seemed to abate.

Eugène Boudin était l'un de ces peintres de mer qui découvrirent précocement leur amour pour la mer, la côte et les navires. Né à Honfleur, en Normandie, où la Seine se déverse dans la Manche, il devint mousse d'un navire à l'âge de dix ans et commença à dessiner ses expériences. Ses voyages conduisirent Boudin en de nombreux lieux, mais jamais à l'intérieur des terres. Il passa sa vie presque exclusivement sur la côte, qu'il a peinte avec un enthousiasme qui ne s'atténua à priori jamais.

Eugène Boudin gehörte zu jenen Marinemalern, die ihre Liebe zum Meer, zur Küste und den Schiffen früh entdeckten. Im normannischen Honfleur an der Mündung der Seine geboren, arbeitete er schon mit zehn Jahren als Schiffsjunge und begann zu zeichnen. Seine Reisen führten Boudin an viele Orte, aber nie landeinwärts. Sein Leben verbrachte er fast ausschließlich an der Küste, die er zeit seines Lebens mit kaum nachlassender Begeisterung malte.

Eugène Boudin fue uno de los pintores de marinas que descubrieron a una edad temprana su amor por el mar, la costa y los barcos. Nació en Honfleur, Normandía, en la desembocadura del Sena, y ya con diez años trabajó como grumete y comenzó a dibujar. Sus viajes le llevaron a muchos sitios, pero nunca hacia el interior. Pasó su vida casi exclusivamente en la costa, a la que dedicó su pintura durante toda su vida con un entusiasmo apenas decreciente.

Eugène Boudin foi um daqueles pintores de marinhas que descobriram bem cedo seu amor pelo mar, a costa e os navios. Nascido em Honfleur, na Normandia, na foz do rio Sena, com dez anos ele já trabalhava como grumete, e começou a desenhar. Suas viagens levaram Boudin para muitos lugares, mas nunca para o interior. Ele passou sua vida quase que exclusivamente na costa, que ele pintou durante toda sua vida com um entusiasmo praticamente inesgotável.

Eugène Boudin behoorde tot de maritieme schilders die al vroeg hun liefde voor de zee, het kustlandschap en de scheepvaart ontdekten. Hij werd geboren in het Normandische Honfleur aan de monding van de Seine, werkte als 10-jarige als scheepsjongen en begon al vroeg te tekenen. Zijn reizen voerden hem naar talloze oorden, maar nooit landinwaarts. Hij bracht zijn hele leven aan de kust door, die hij met niet aflatend enthousiasme bleef schilderen.

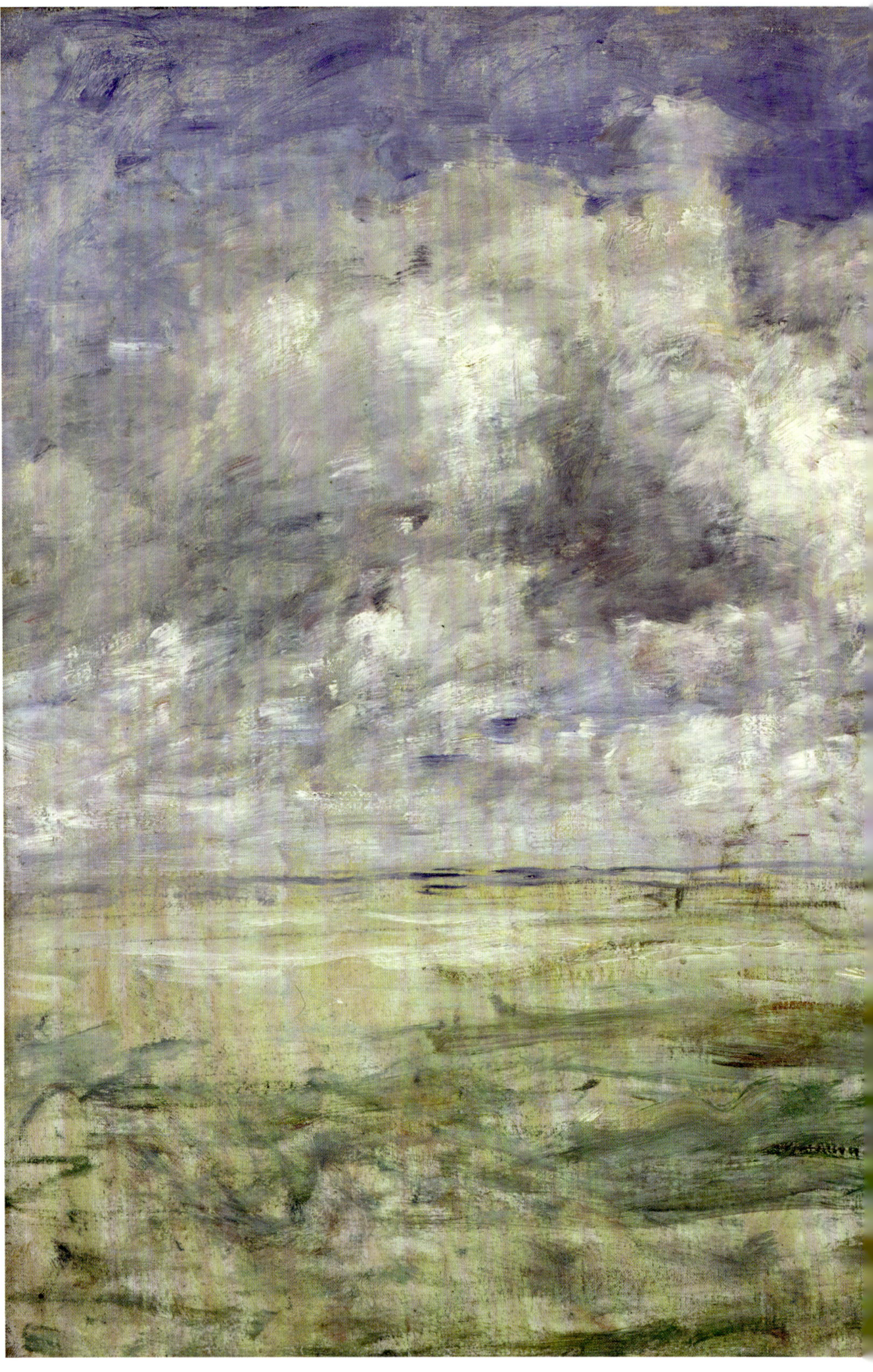

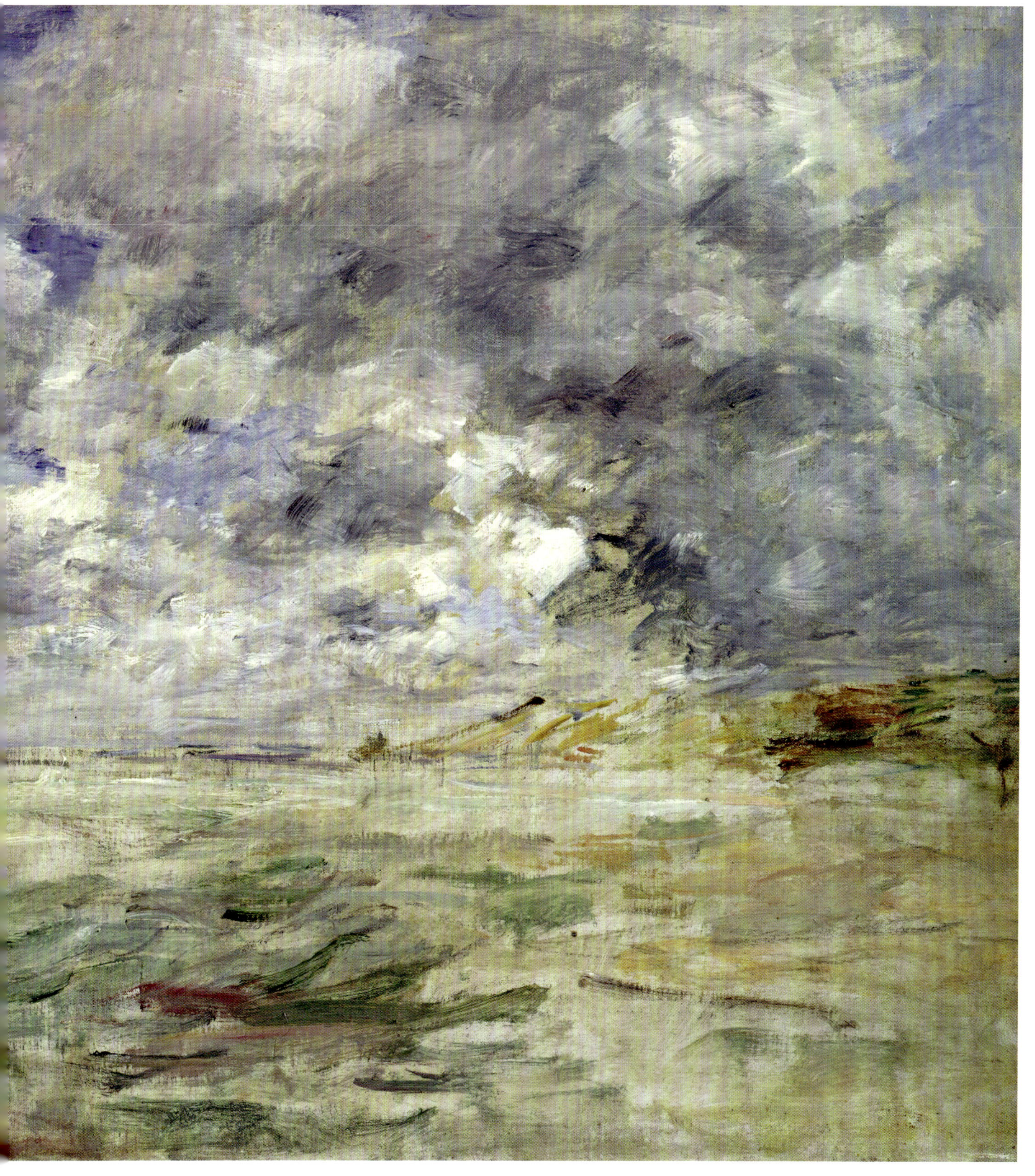

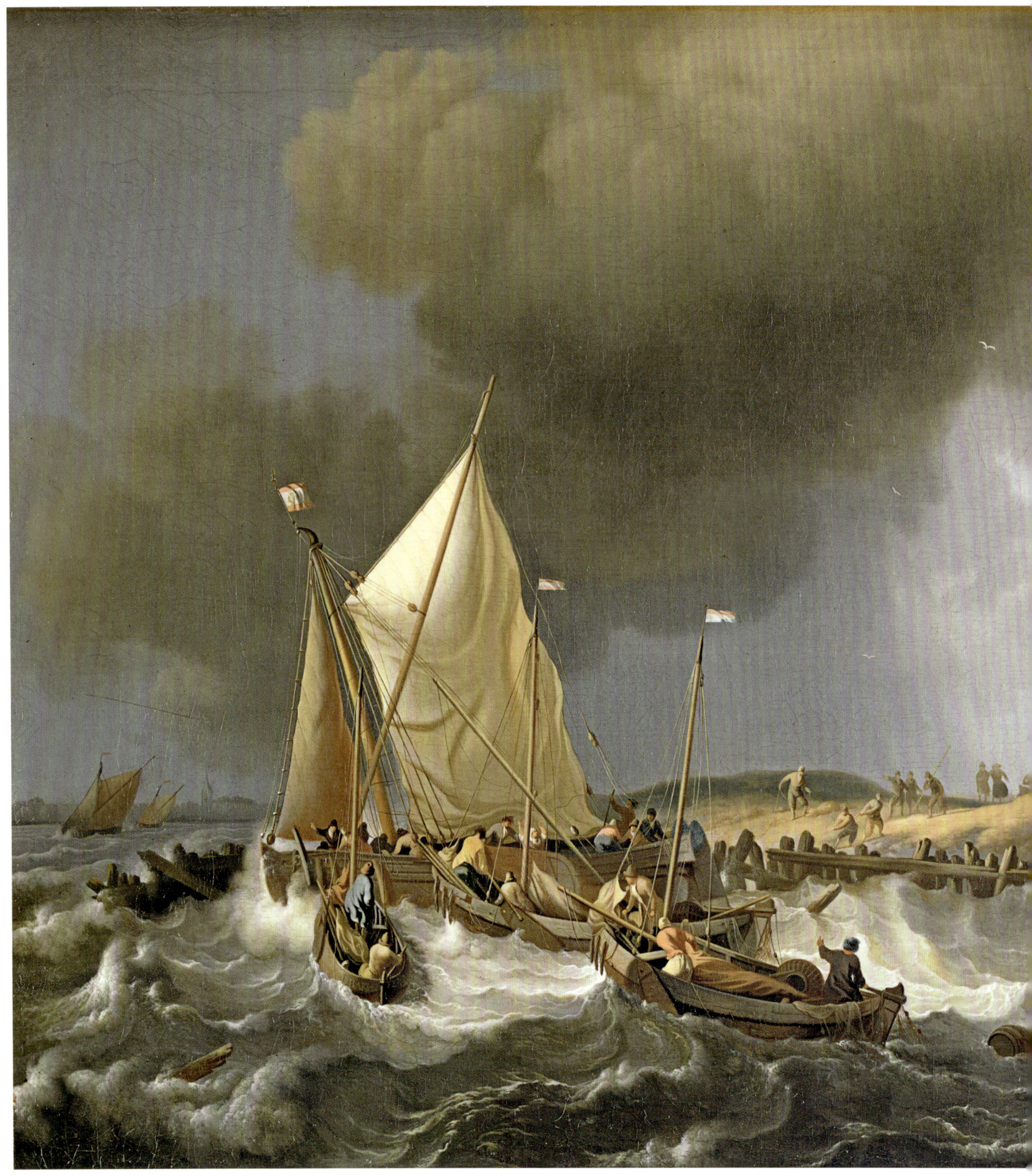

In addition to Willem van de Velde the Younger, Ludolf Backhuysen was the most important representative of Dutch sea painting in the late 17th century. He specialized in portraying ships in stormy seas, as can be seen in this late work. He became internationally famous for his works and his naval pictures adorned the salons of Europe long after his death.

En plus de Willem van de Velde le Jeune, Ludolf Backhuysen était le plus important représentant de la peinture maritime hollandaise à la fin du XVIIe siècle. Il se spécialisa dans la représentation de navires sur des mers orageuses, comme on peut le voir dans ce travail tardif. Il devint célèbre dans le monde entier pour ses œuvres, et ses images navales ornèrent les salons d'Europe bien après sa mort.

Neben Willem van de Velde d. J. gilt vor allem Ludolf Backhuysen als bedeutendster Vertreter der holländischen Marinemalerei des späten 17. Jahrhunderts. Spezialisiert hat er sich auf Darstellungen von Schiffen in stürmischer See, wie es auch in diesem Spätwerk zu sehen ist. Er brachte es zu internationaler Bekanntheit und auch lange nach seinem Tod schmückten seine Marinebilder die Salons Europas.

Ludolf Backhuysen, junto a Willem van de Velde el Joven, está considerado el representante por excelencia de la pintura marina holandesa de finales del siglo XVII. Estaba especializado en representaciones de barcos en mares tormentosos, como se puede ver en esta obra tardía. Llegó a ser reconocido internacionalmente e incluso mucho tiempo después de su muerte, sus imágenes de marinas adornaban los salones de Europa.

Além de Willem van de Velde, o Jovem, principalmente Ludolf Backhuysen é considerado o representante mais destacado da pintura marinha holandesa do final do século XVII. Ele se especializou em representações de navios em mares tempestuosos, como também pode ser visto nesta sua obra tardia. A ela se deve seu reconhecimento internacional e, mesmo muito tempo após a sua morte, suas pinturas marinhas decoraram os salões da Europa.

Naast Willem van de Velde de Jongere wordt vooral Ludolf Backhuysen als de belangrijkste vertegenwoordiger beschouwd van de Hollandse maritieme schilderkunst van de late zeventiende eeuw. Hij was gespecialiseerd in uitbeeldingen van schepen in zware zee, zoals ook in dit late werk te zien is. Hij maakte internationaal naam en na zijn dood sierden zijn zeegezichten de salons van de machtigen van Europa.

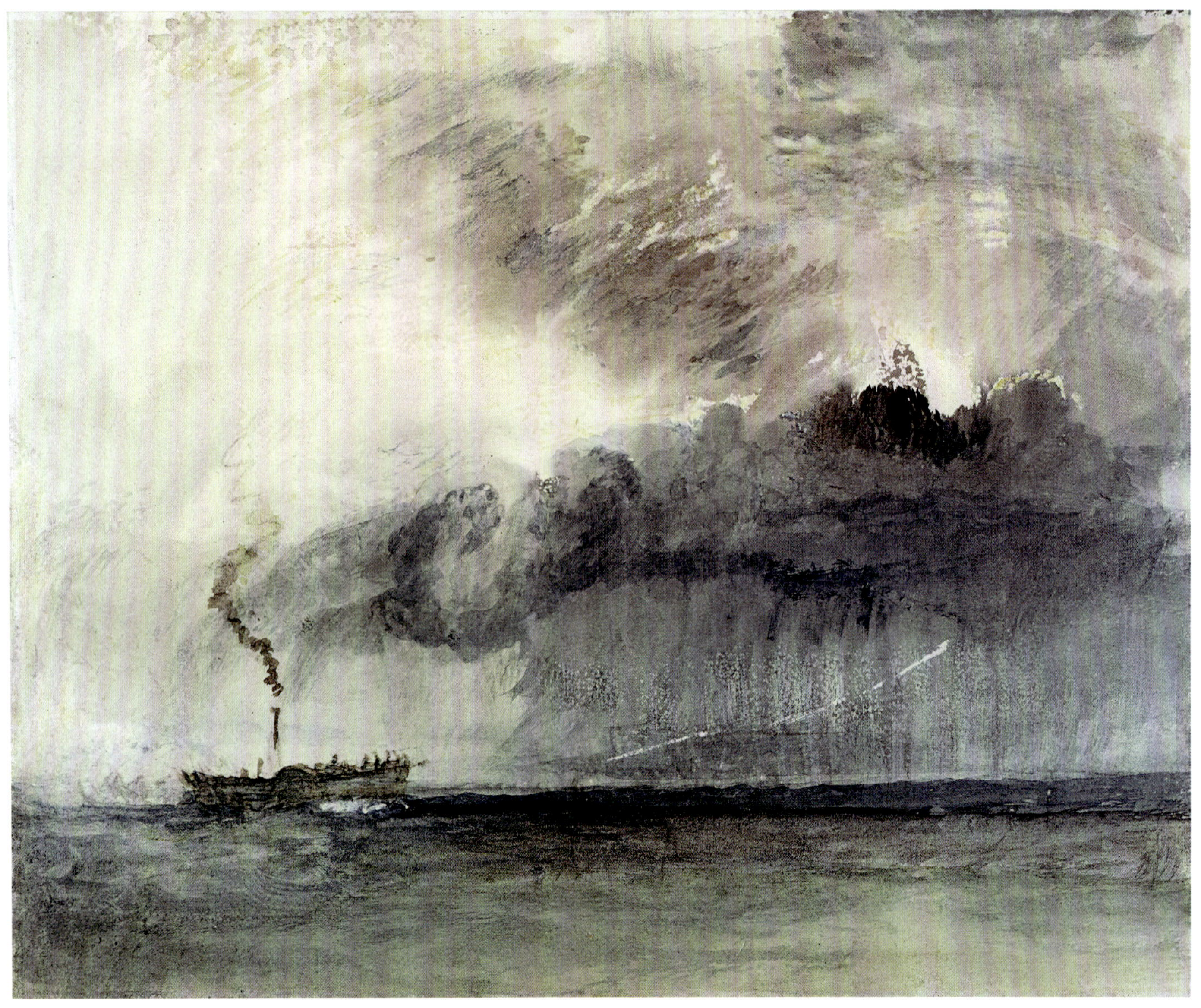

Joseph Mallord William Turner (1775–1851)

Steamboat in a Storm

Bateau-vapeur pris dans la tempête

Dampfschiff in einem Sturm

Barco de vapor en una tormenta

Navio a vapor em uma tempestade

Stoomboot in een storm

c. 1841, Watercolor and pencil on paper/Aquarelle et crayon sur papier, 23 × 30,2 cm, Yale Center for British Art, New Haven

Samuel Scott (c. 1702–72)

Shipping in a Choppy Sea

Navigation par mer agitée

Schiffe in unruhiger See

Barcos en mar agitado

Navios em um mar tempestuoso

Schepen in zware zee

1753, Oil on canvas/Huile sur toile, Yale Center for British Art, New Haven

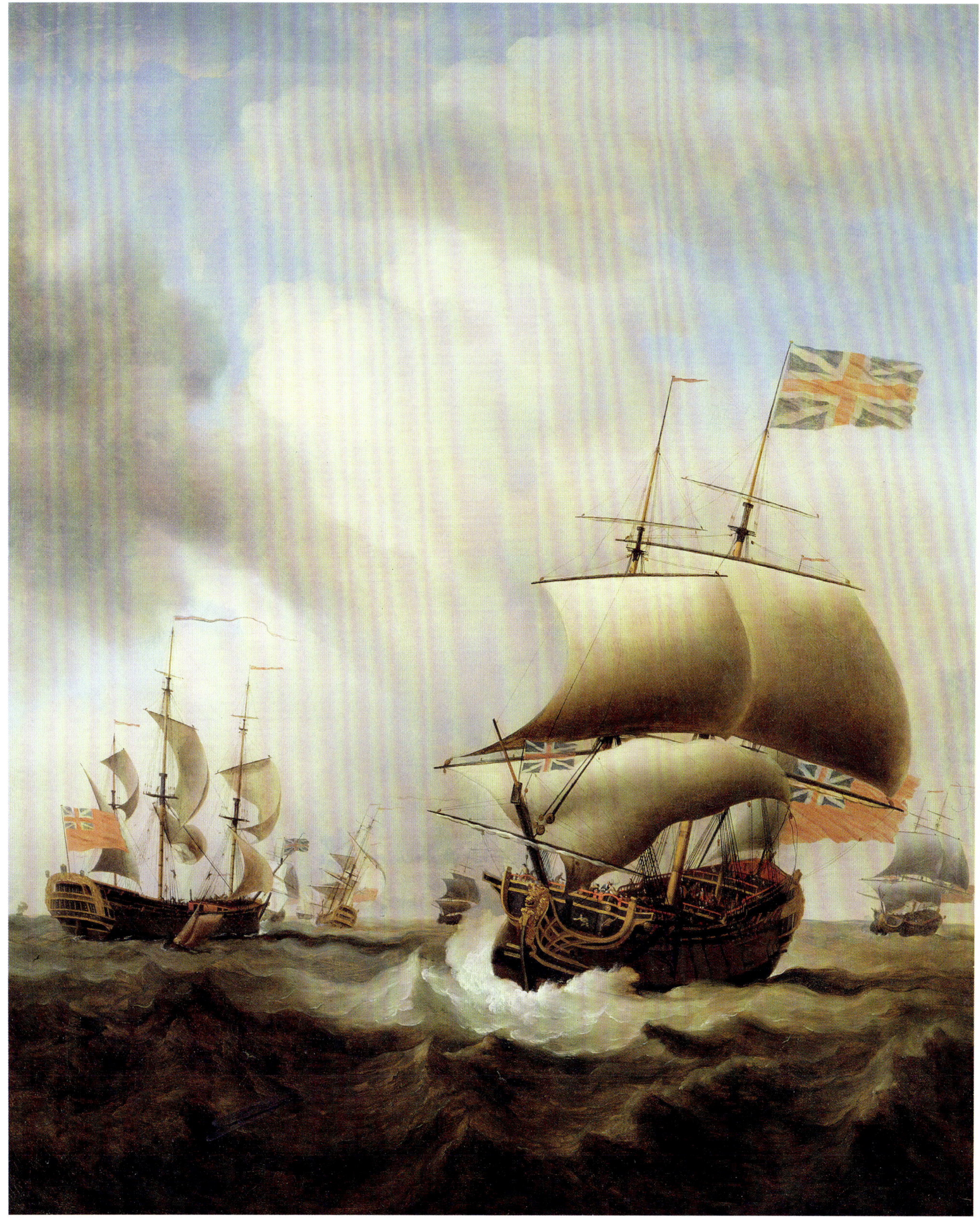

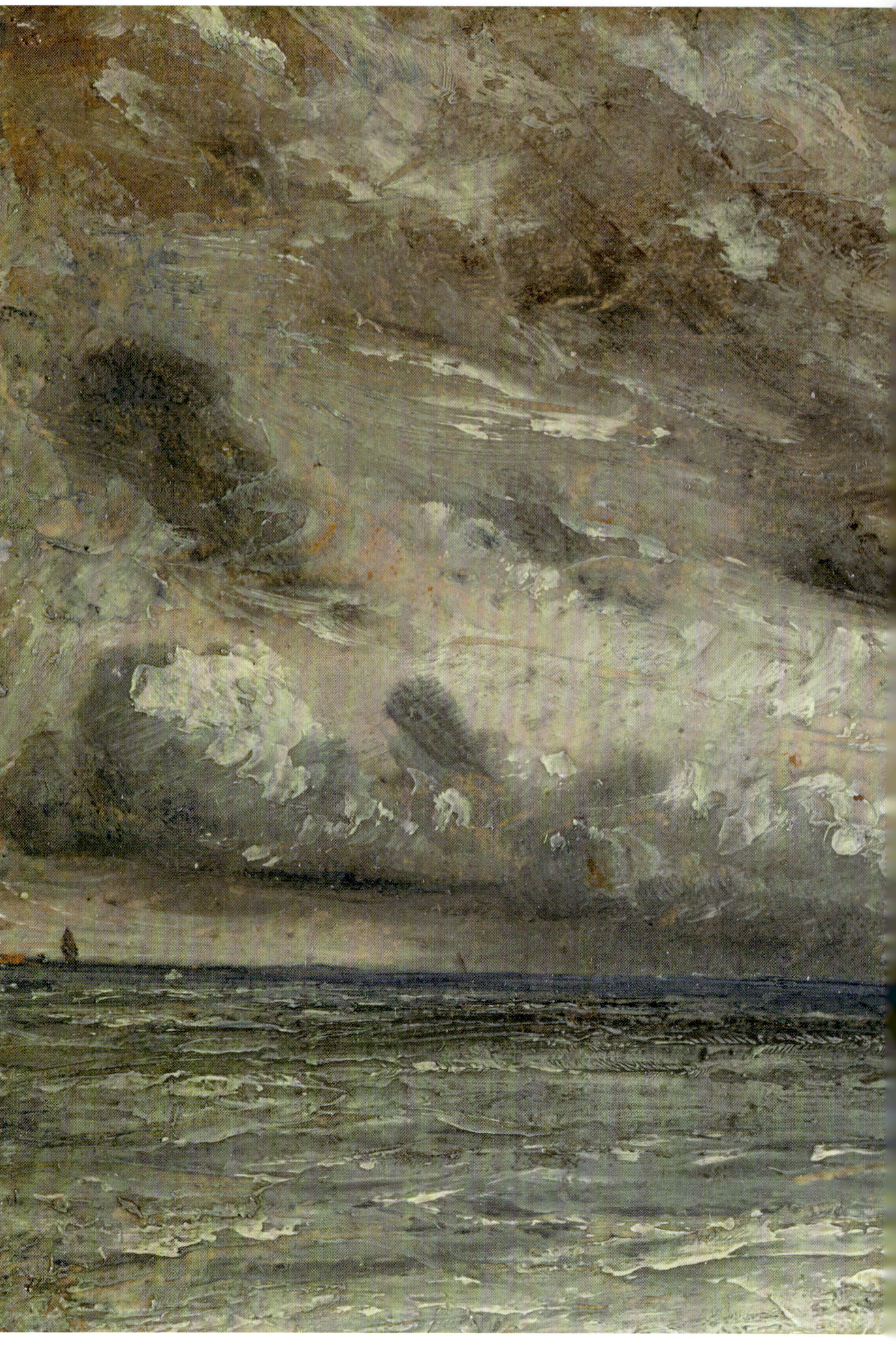

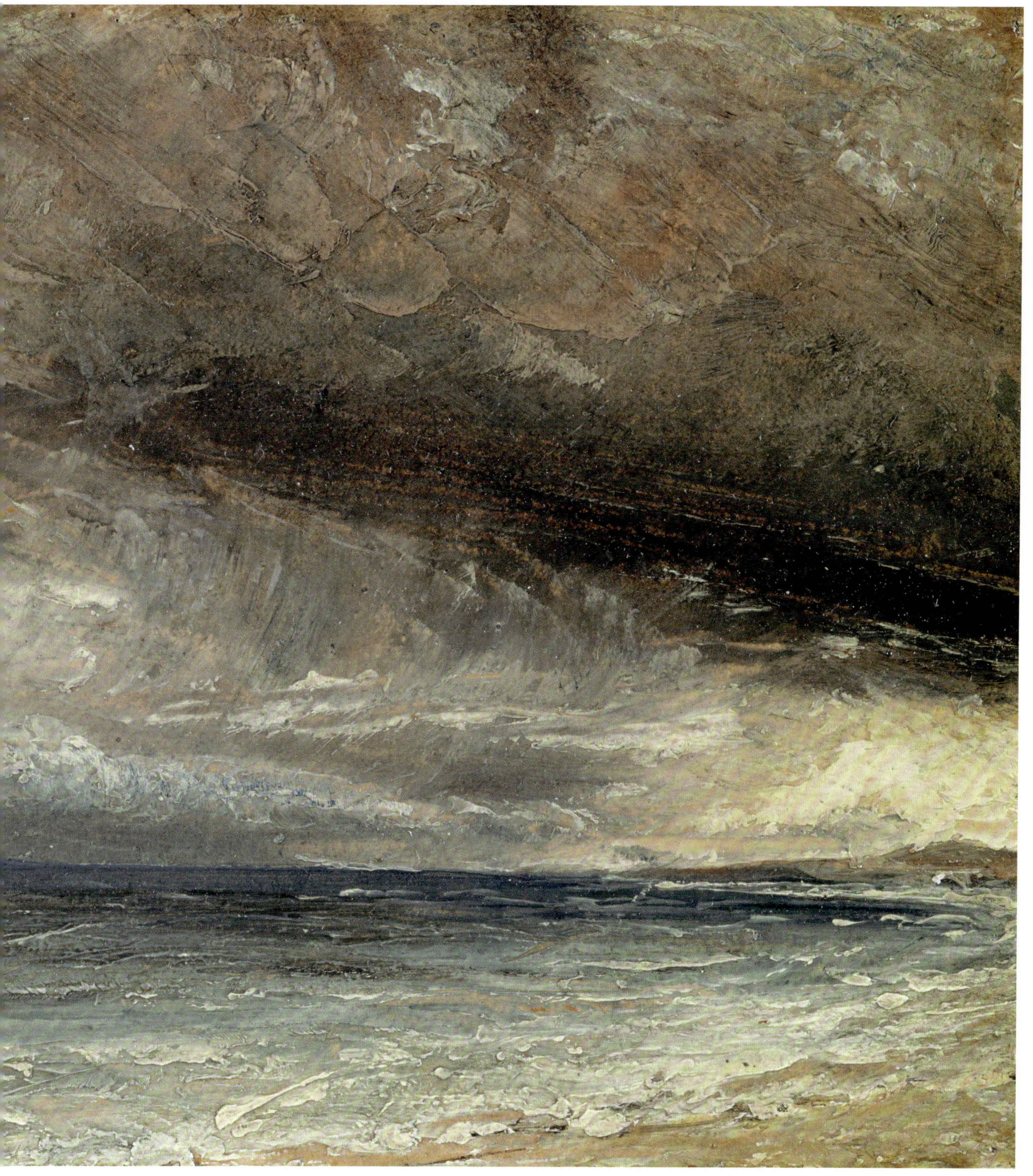

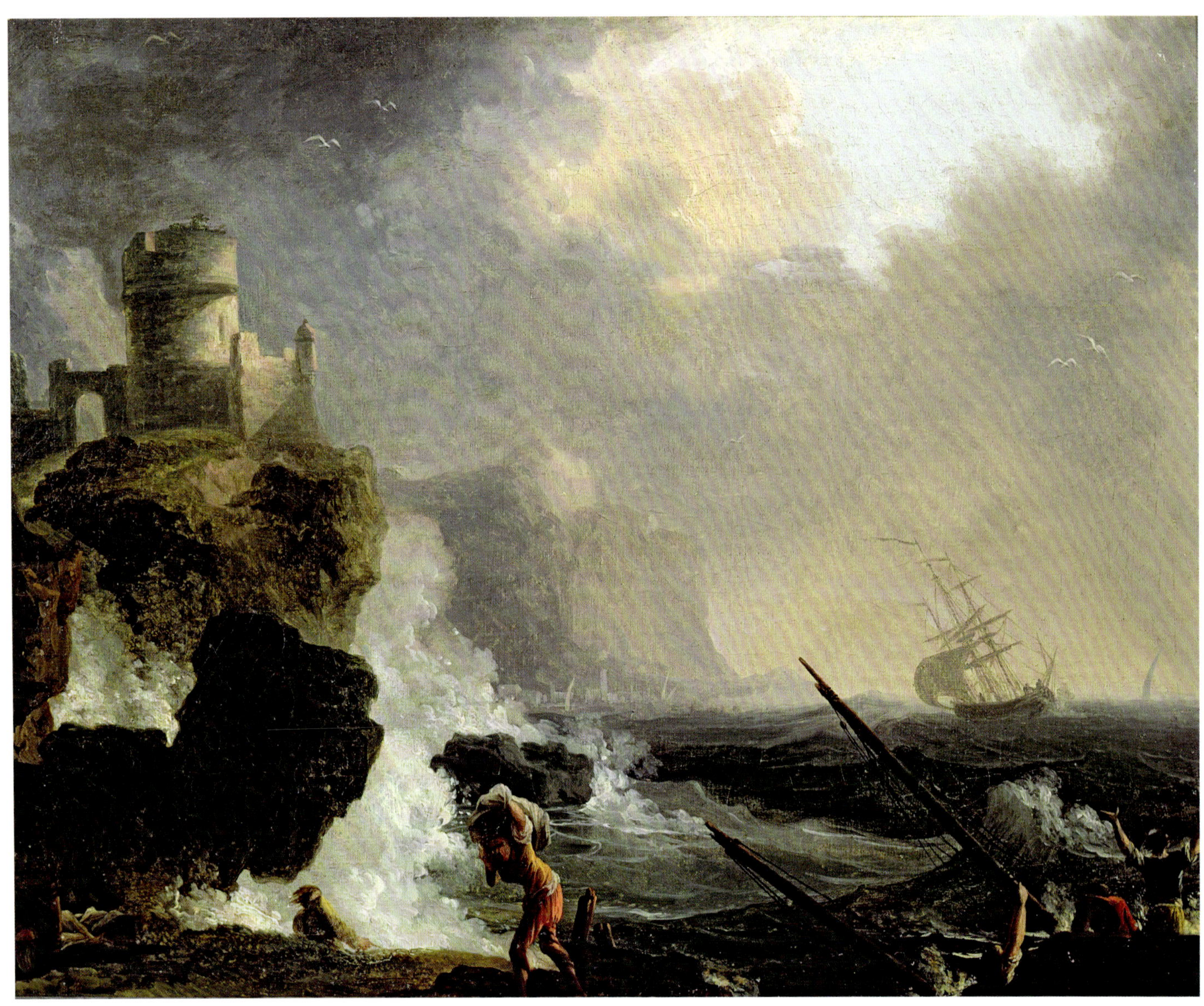

Charles François Lacroix de Marseille (c. 1700–82)

Storm

Tempête

Sturm

Tormenta

Tempestade

Storm

n.d., Oil on canvas/Huile sur toile, 35 × 45 cm, Musée des Augustins, Toulouse

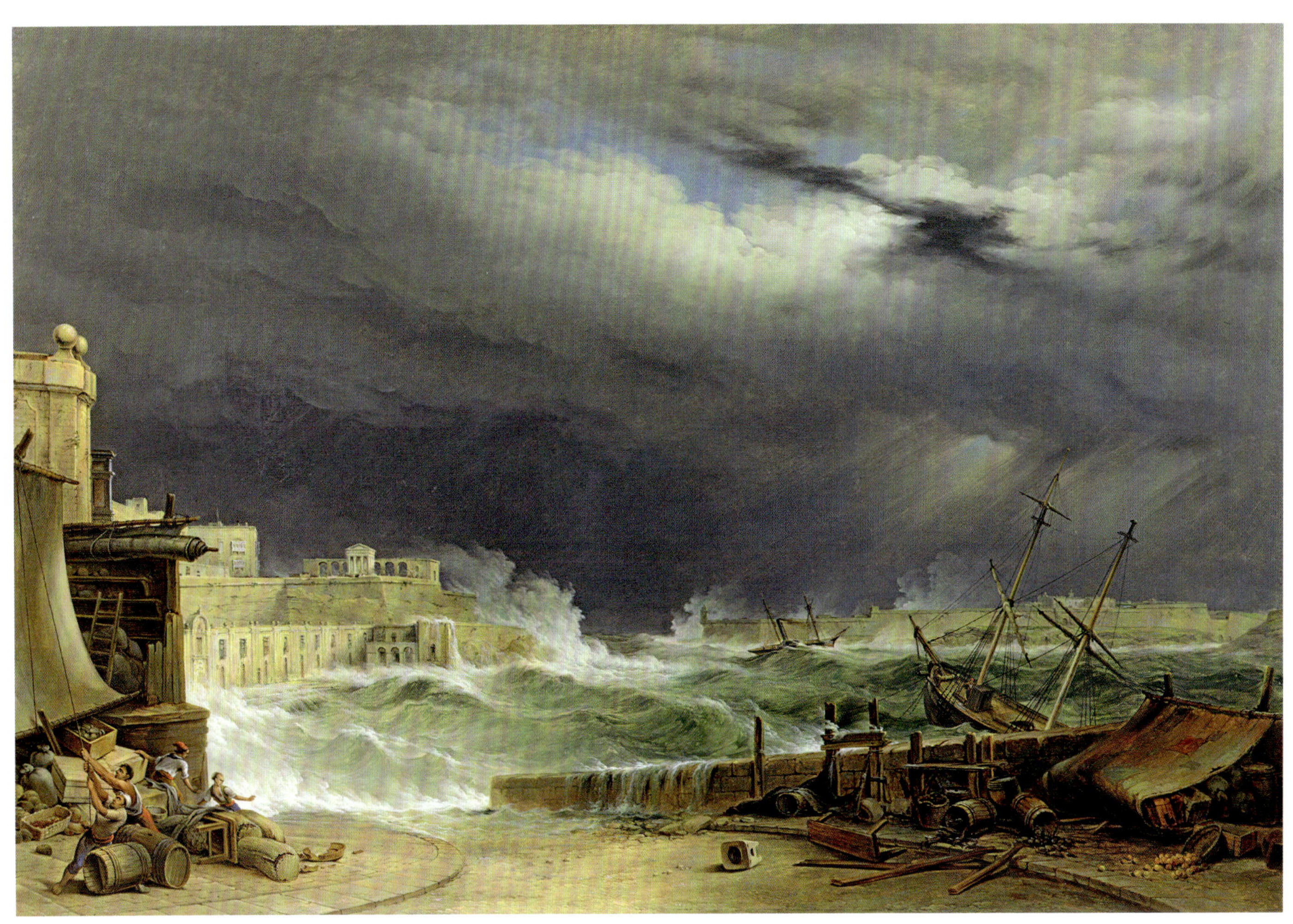

John Schranz (1794–1882)

Storm, Malta

Orage, Malte

Sturm, Malta

Tormenta, Malta

Tempestade, Malta

Storm, Malta

1850, Oil on canvas/Huile sur toile, Private collection

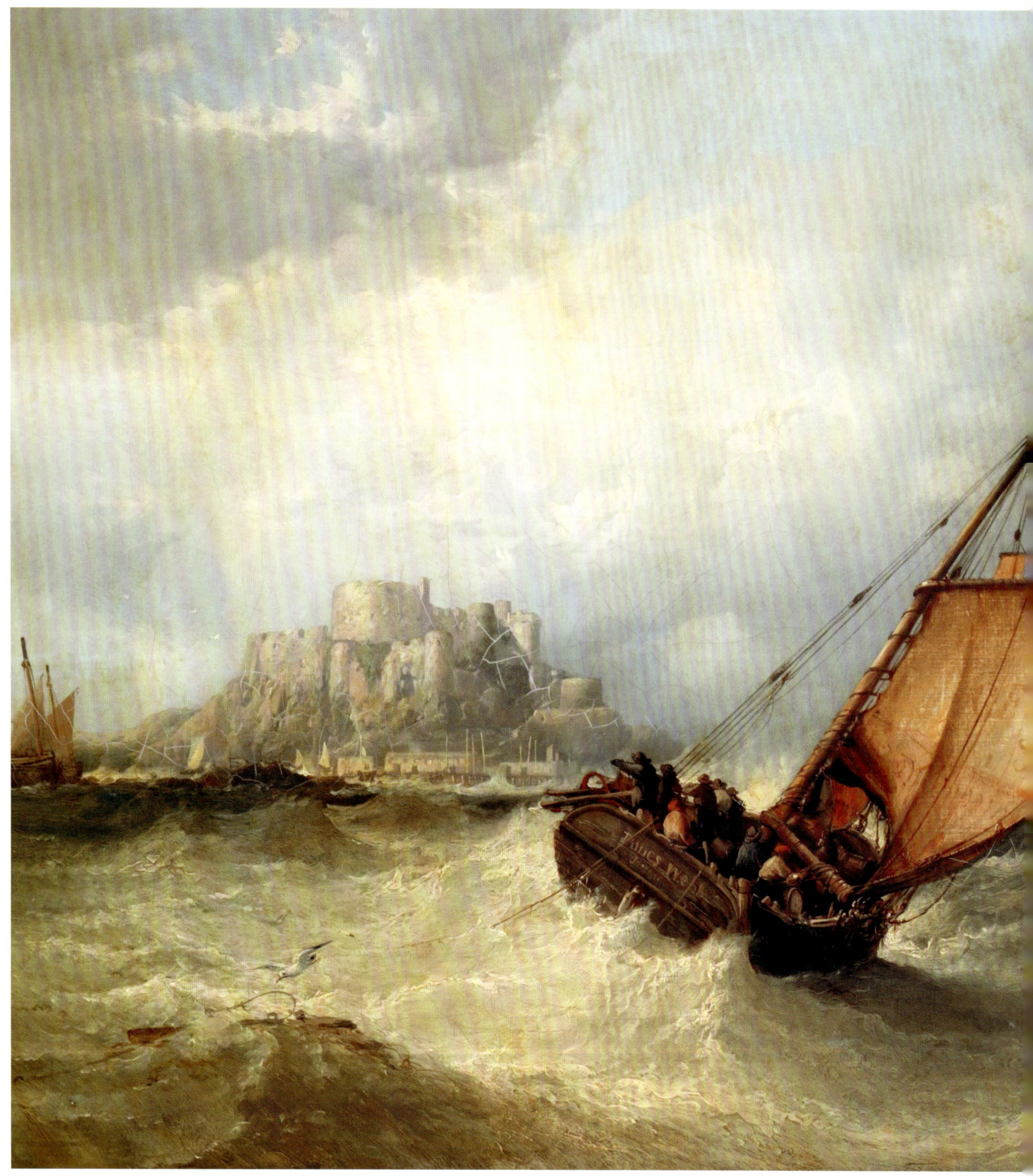

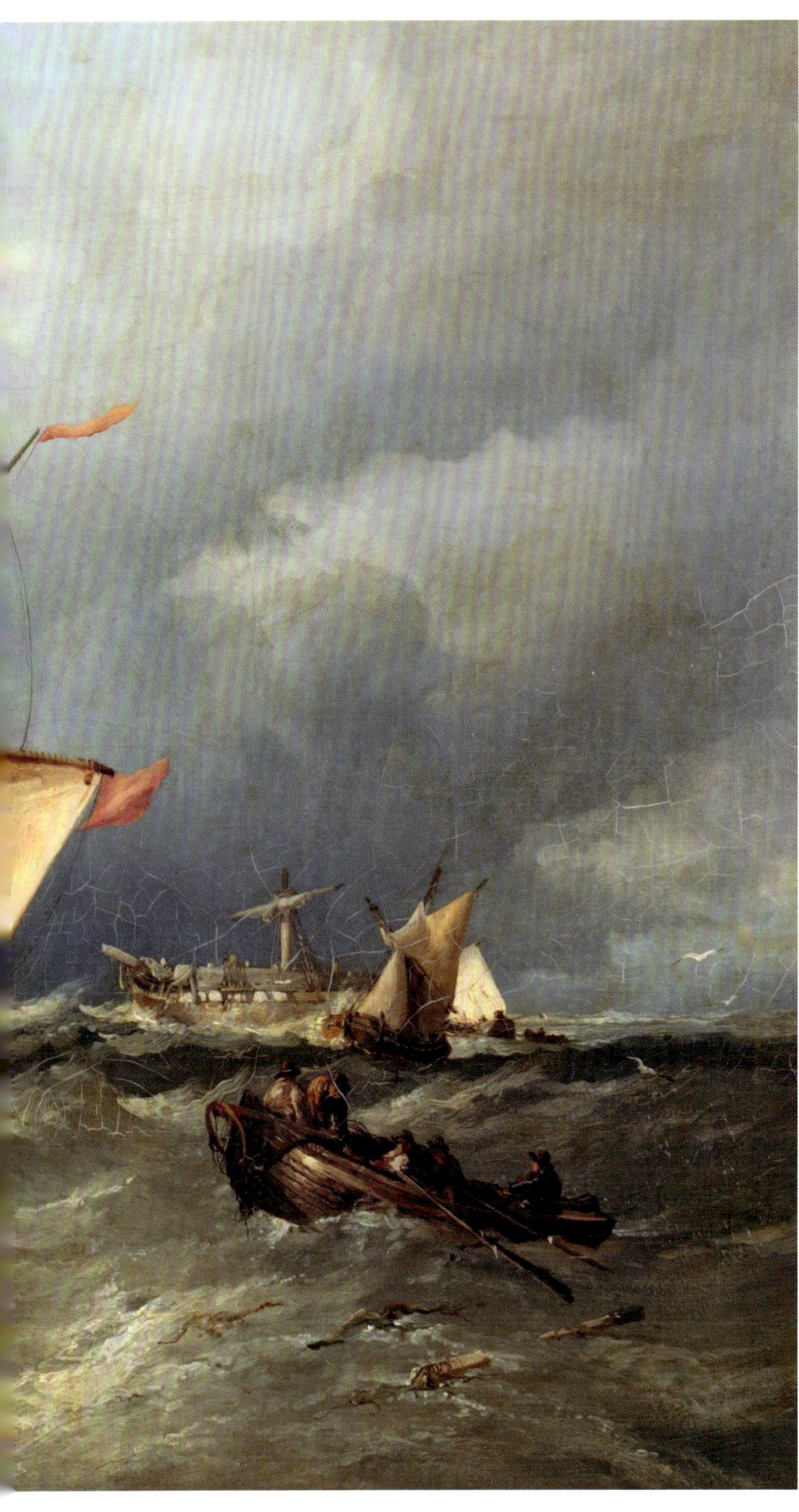

James Webb (1825–95)

After the Storm

Après l'orage

Nach dem Sturm

Tras la tormenta

Depois da tempestade

Na de storm

n. d., Oil on canvas/Huile sur toile, 77 × 115 cm,
Manchester Art Gallery, Manchester

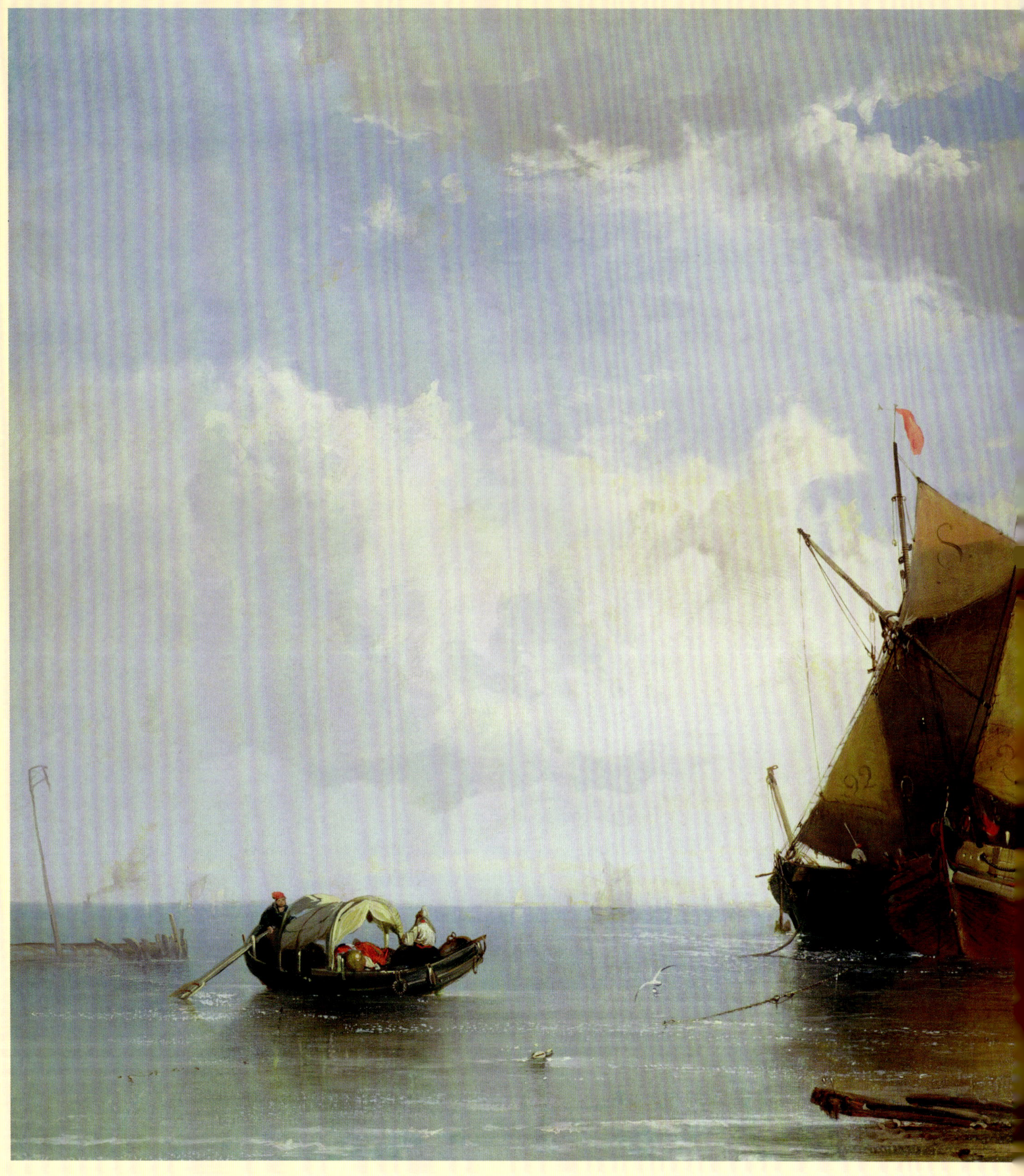

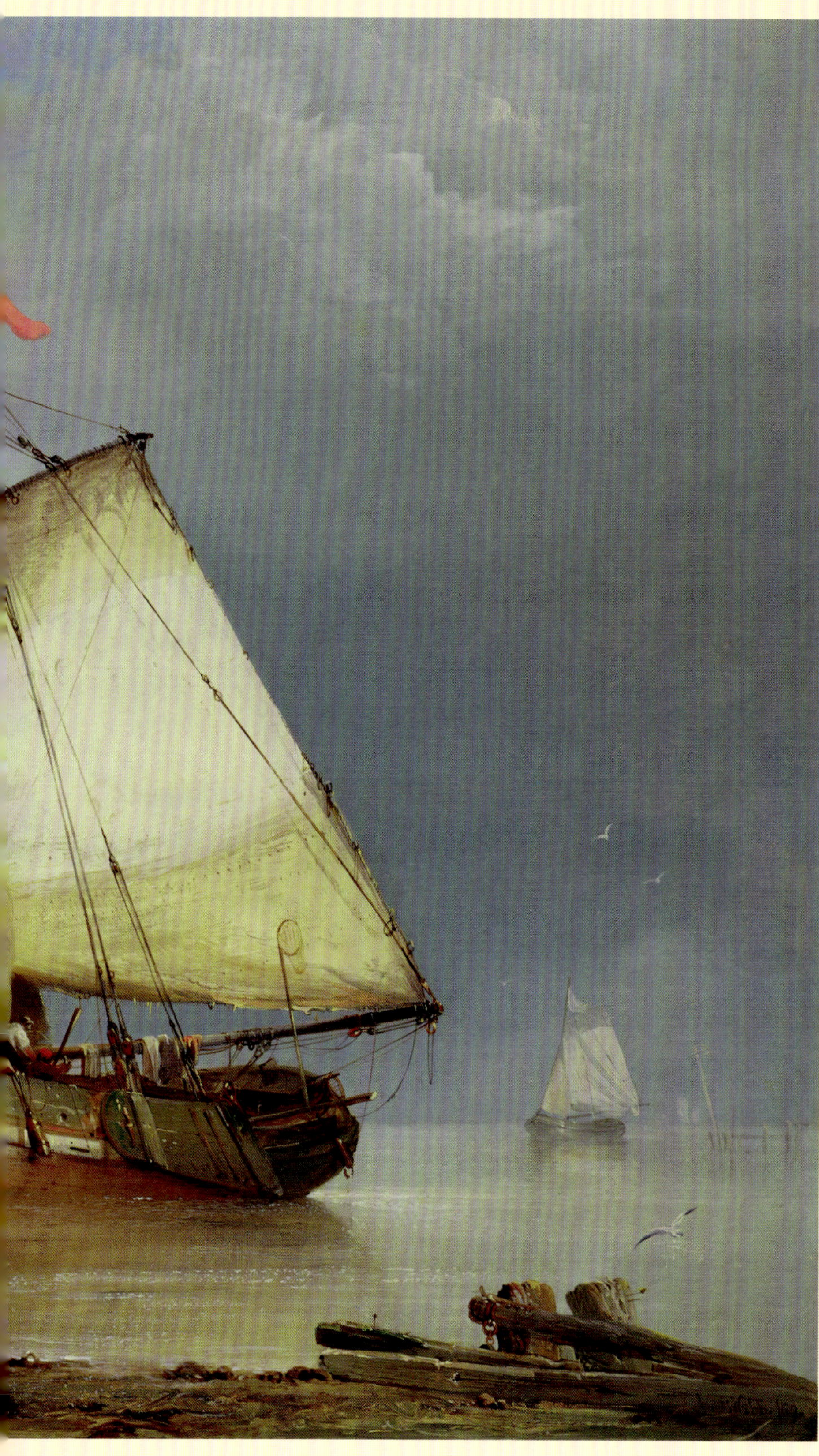

James Webb (1825–95)
Shipping in a Calm
Navigation sur mer calme
Schiffe in der Flaute
Pescando en mar en calma
Navios na calmaria
Schepen bij windstilte
1869, Oil on canvas/Huile sur toile, 78,7 × 119,4 cm, Private collection

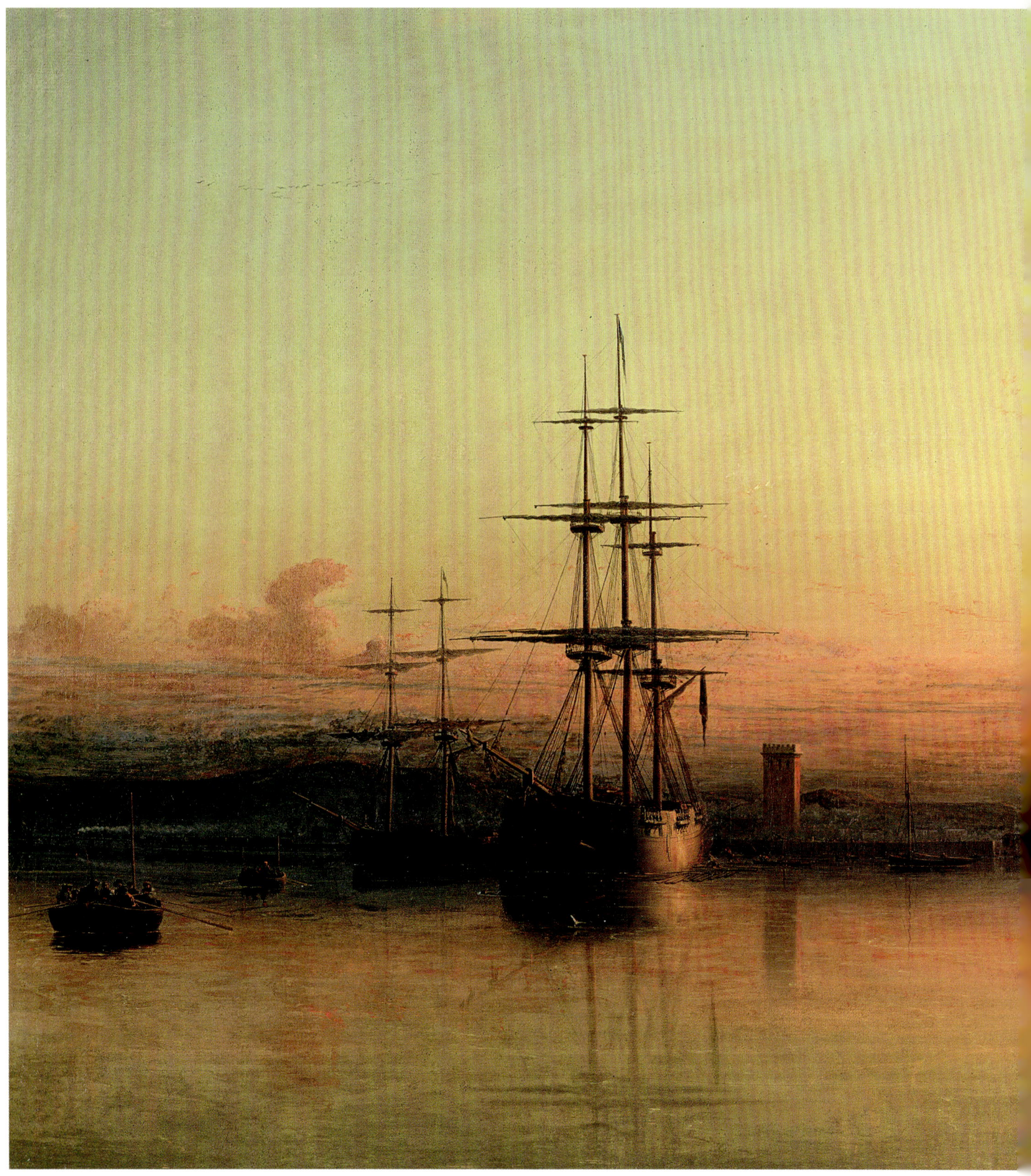

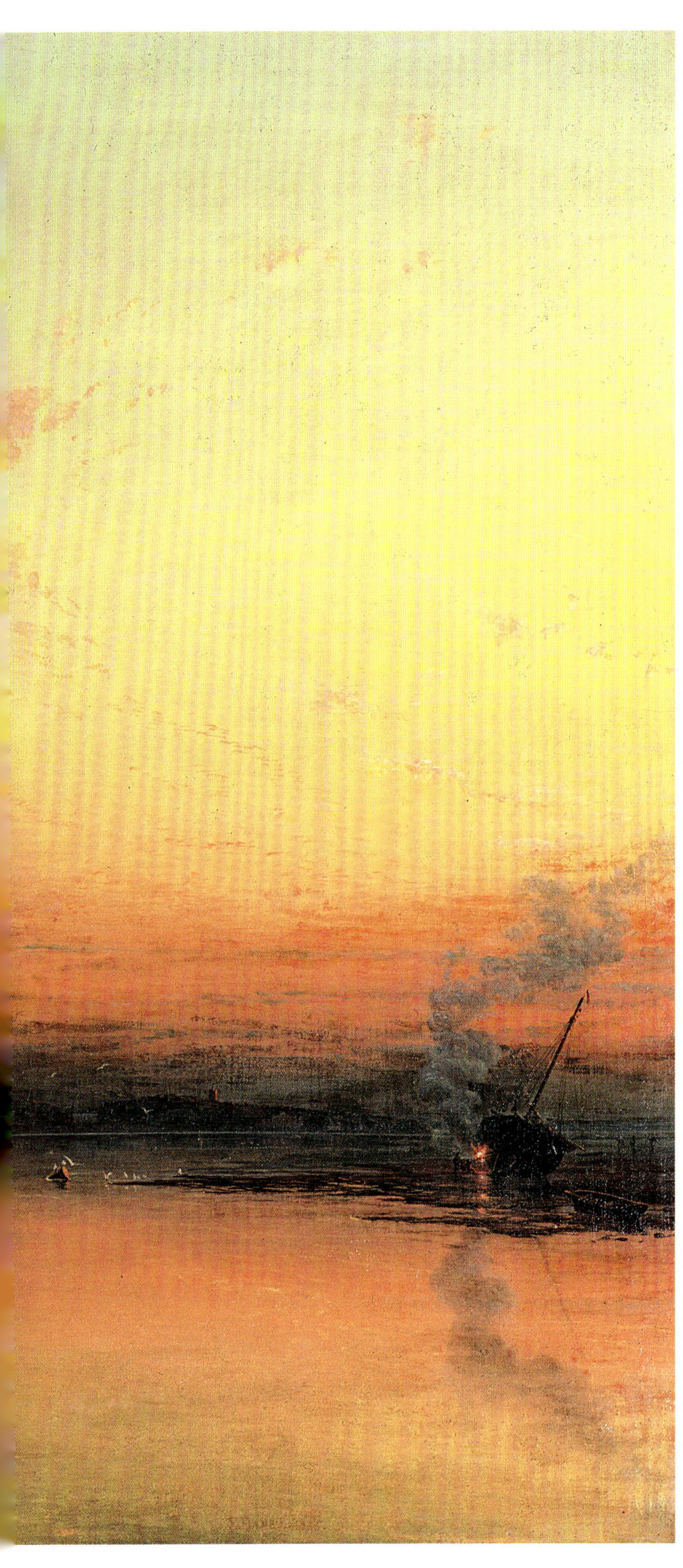

This painting by Irish painter Francis Danby illustrates his predilection for the special effects of nature and the poetic mood of coastal landscapes. In addition, it documents a curiosity of Victorian engineering: the tower which can be seen in the background is a pumping station for the short-lived railway by technology pioneer Isambard Brunel.

Cette peinture du peintre irlandais Francis Danby illustre sa prédilection pour les effets spéciaux de la nature et l'ambiance poétique des paysages côtiers. Il présente de plus une curiosité de l'ingénierie victorienne : la tour qui peut être vue en arrière-plan est une station de pompage pour le chemin de fer provisoire du pionnier de la technologie Isambard Brunel.

Dieses Bild des irischen Malers Francis Danby veranschaulicht seine Vorliebe für die besonderen Effekte der Natur und die poetische Stimmung von Küstenlandschaften. Außerdem aber dokumentiert es noch eine Kuriosität der viktorianischen Ingenieurskunst: Der mittig im Hintergrund zu erkennende Turm ist eine Pumpstation der kurzlebigen Atmosphärischen Eisenbahn des Technik-Pioniers Isambard Brunel.

Esta imagen del pintor irlandés Francis Danby ilustra su preferencia por los efectos especiales de la naturaleza y la atmósfera poética de los paisajes costeros. Además, documentó más de una curiosidad de la ingeniería victoriana: la torre que se reconoce en el centro del fondo de la imagen es una estación de bombeo del ferrocarril atmosférico, que no duró mucho, del pionero de la técnica, Isambard Brunel.

Este quadro do pintor irlandês Francis Danby é exemplificativo de sua preferência pelos efeitos especiais da natureza, e a atmosfera poética de paisagens costeiras. Mas ele documenta, além disso, mais uma curiosidade da engenharia vitoriana: a torre que reconhecemos ao centro, no fundo, é uma estação de bombeamento da ferrovia atmosférica, que teve curta duração, do pioneiro da técnica, Isambard Brunel.

Dit werk van de Ierse schilder Francis Danby toont zijn voorliefde voor bijzondere natuurlijke effecten en de poëzie van het kustlandschap. Daarnaast legt het een curieus voorbeeld van Victoriaanse ingenieurskunst vast: de amper op de achtergrond te herkennen toren is een pompstation van een sfeervolle spoorlijn, die geen lang leven was beschoren maar door de technologische pionier Isambard Brunel was ontworpen.

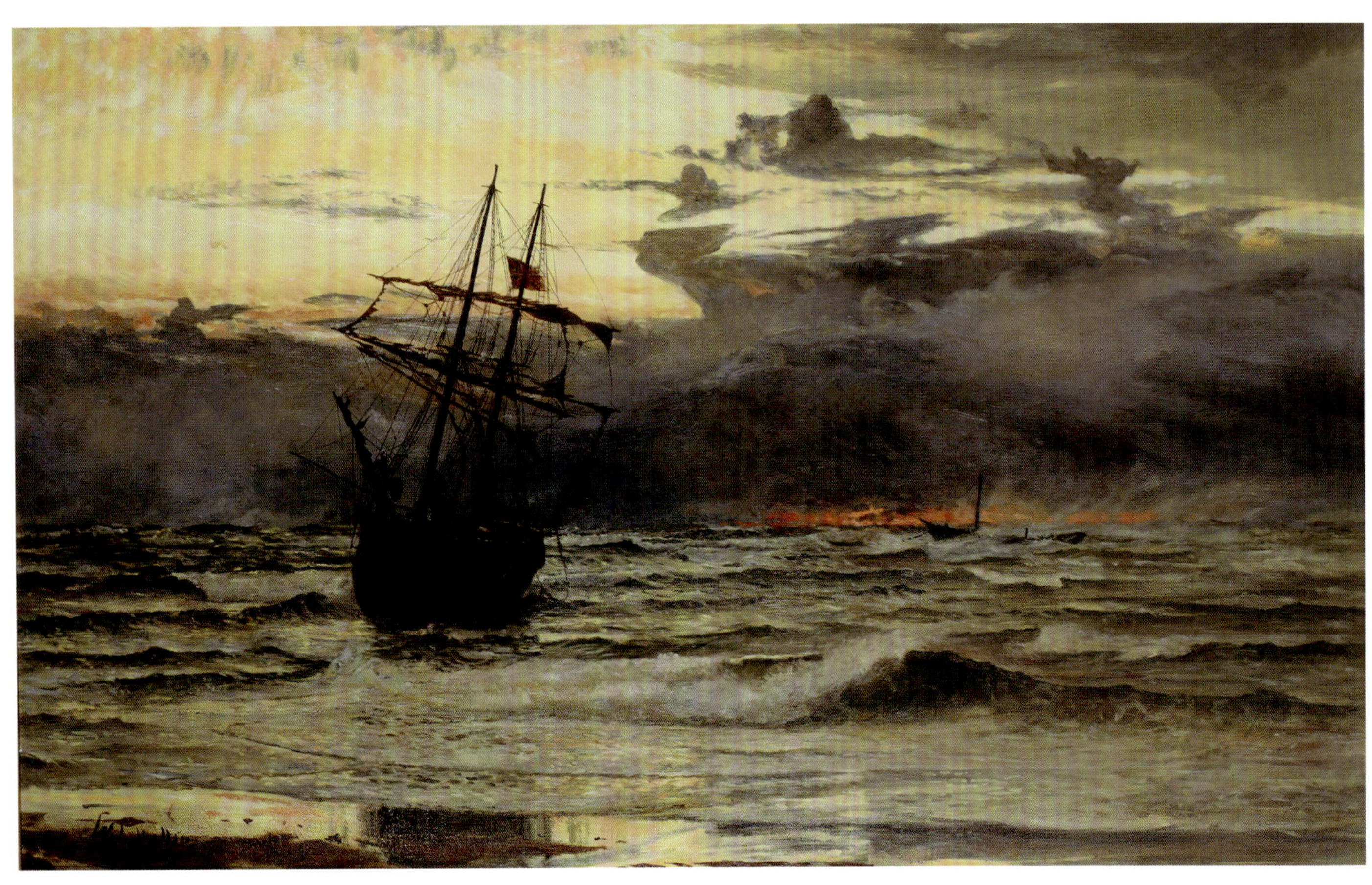

William Lionel Wyllie (1851–1931)

Dawn after the Storm

Levée du jour après l'orage

Dämmerung nach dem Sturm

Amanecer tras la tormenta

Crepúsculo após a tempestade

Ochtendgloren na de storm

n. d., Oil on canvas/Huile sur toile, 76,2 × 127 cm, Private collection

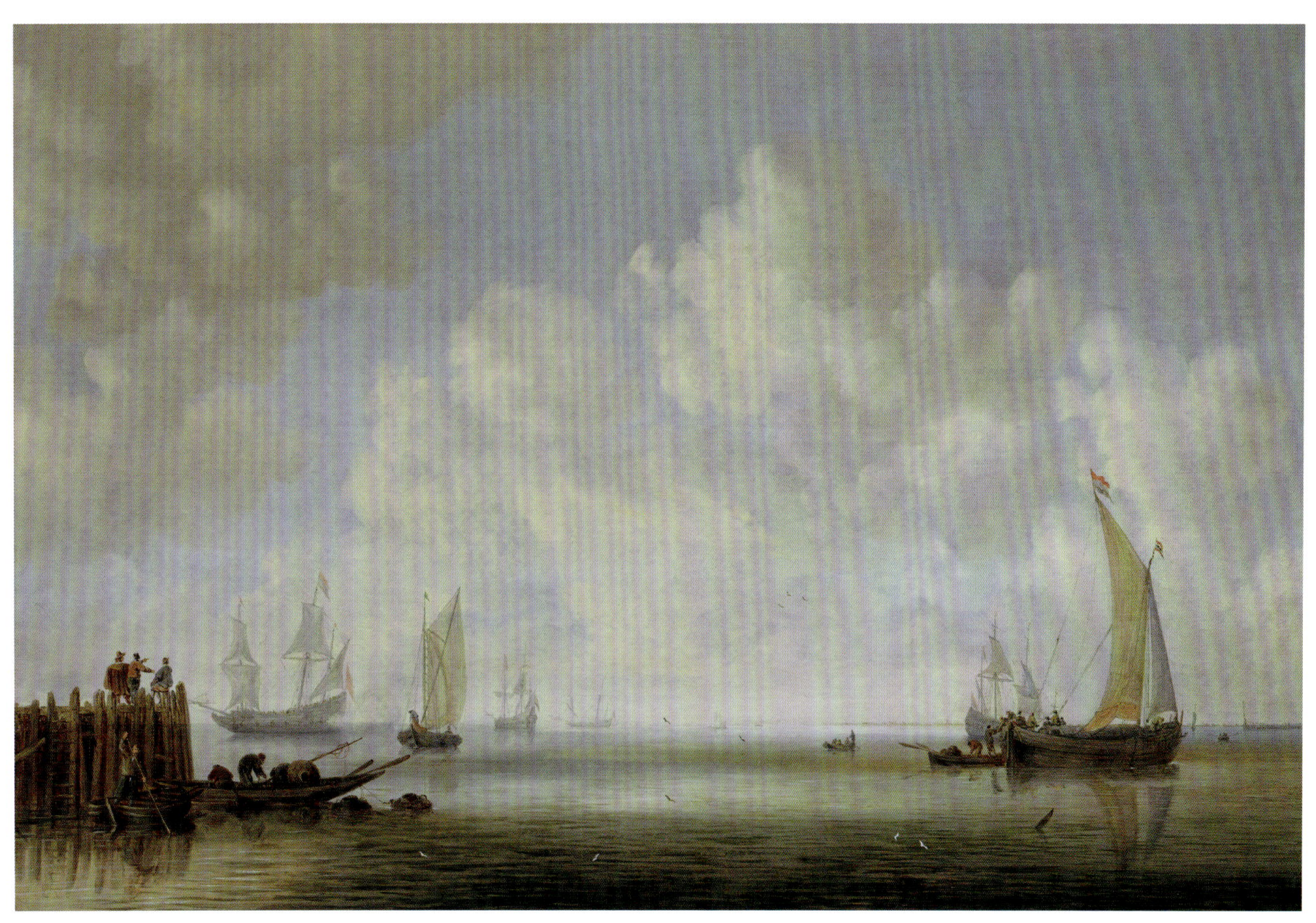

Willem van Diest (c. 1610–78)

Ships Offshore in a Calm with Figures on a Jetty

Navires au large sur mer calme, personnages sur une jetée

Schiffe nahe der Küste und Menschen auf dem Anleger

Embarcaciones cerca de la costa y figuras en el embarcadero

Navios perto da costa e pessoas no cais

Schepen voor de kust en mensen op een steiger

n. d., Oil on panel/Huile sur bois, 66 × 98 cm, Private collection

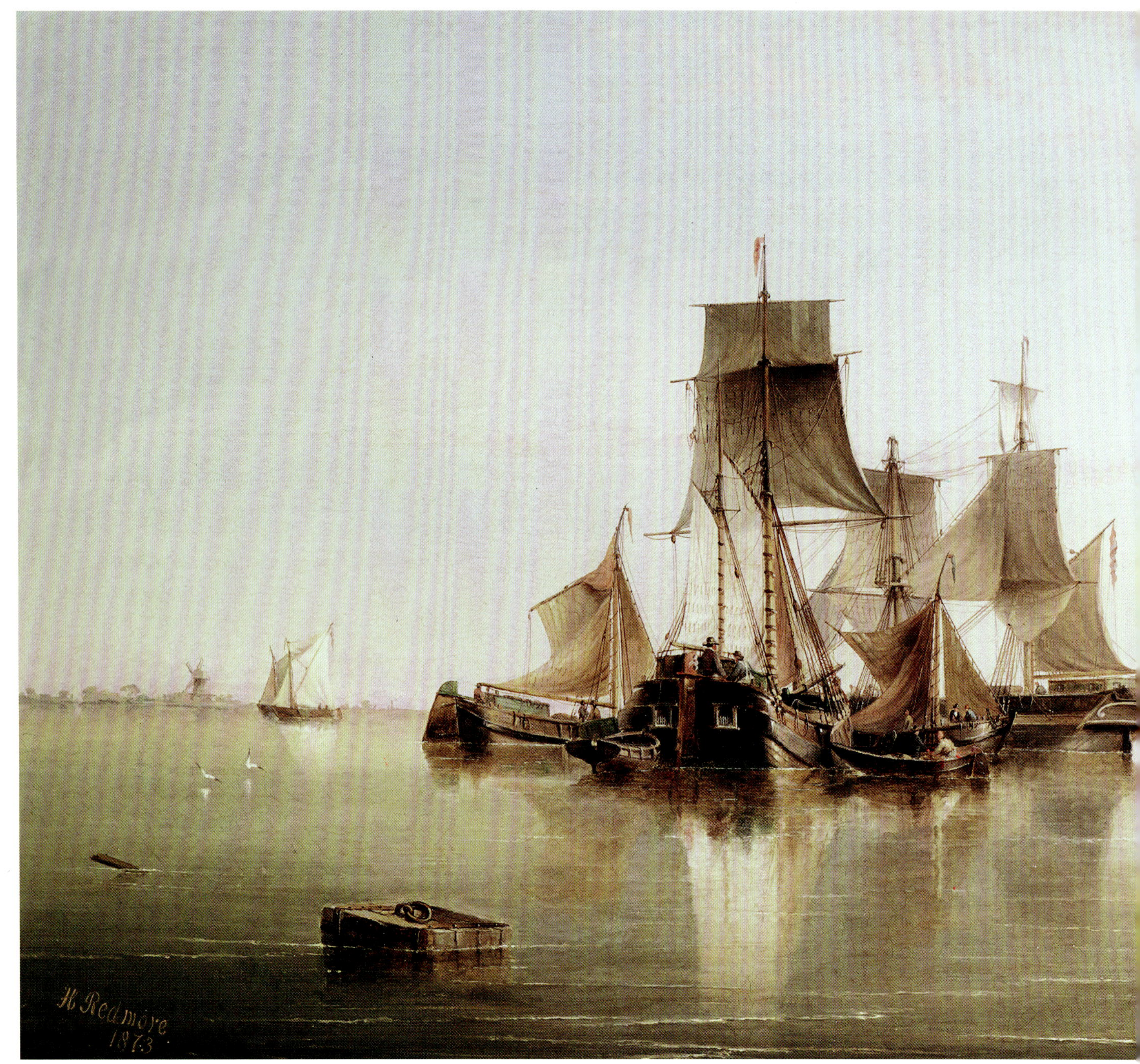

Henry Redmore (1820–87)

Ships in a Calm

Bateaux sur mer calme

Schiffe in einer Flaute

Barcos en mar en calma

Navios na calmaria

Schepen bij windstilte

1873, Oil on canvas/Huile sur toile, Private collection

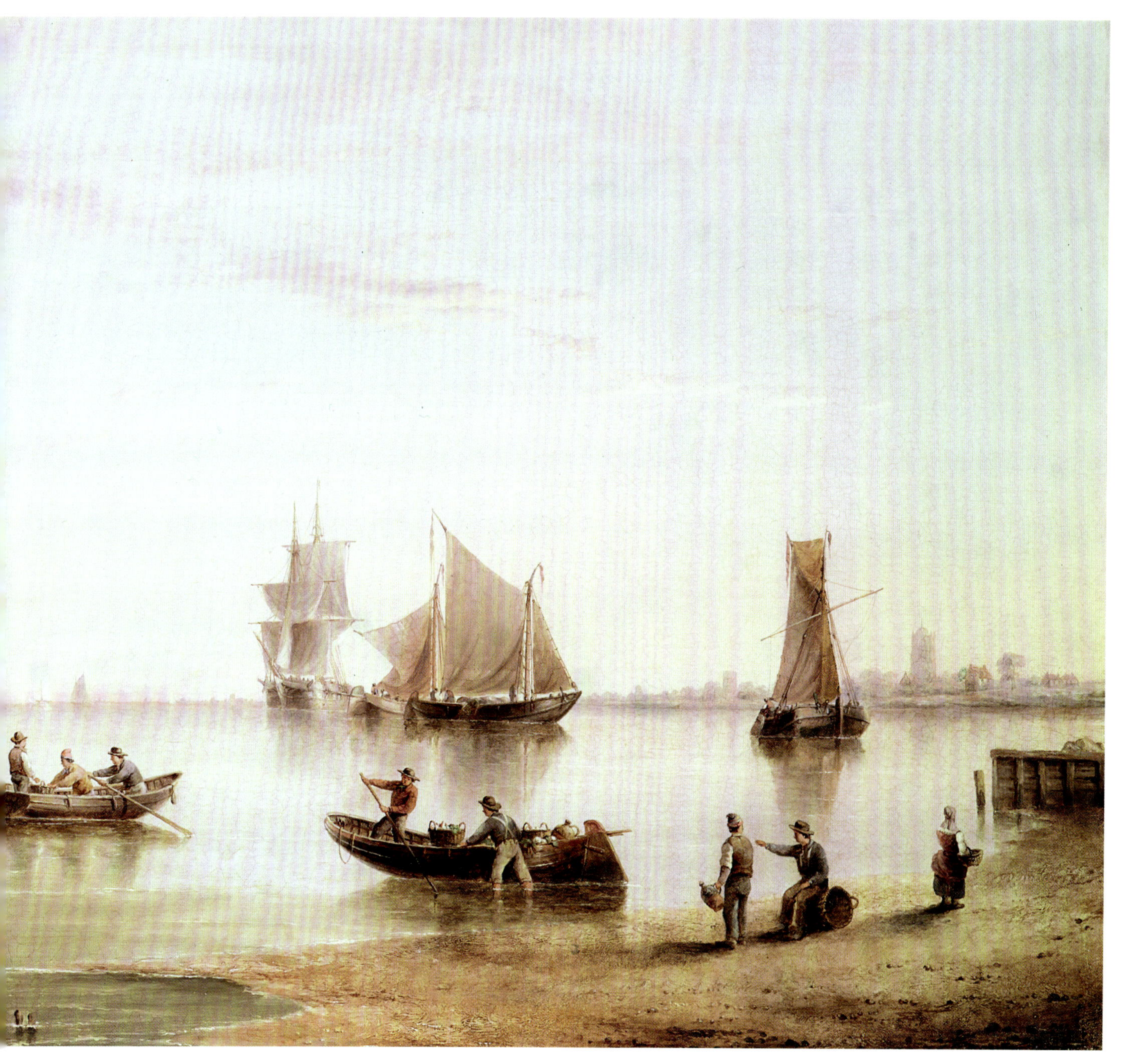

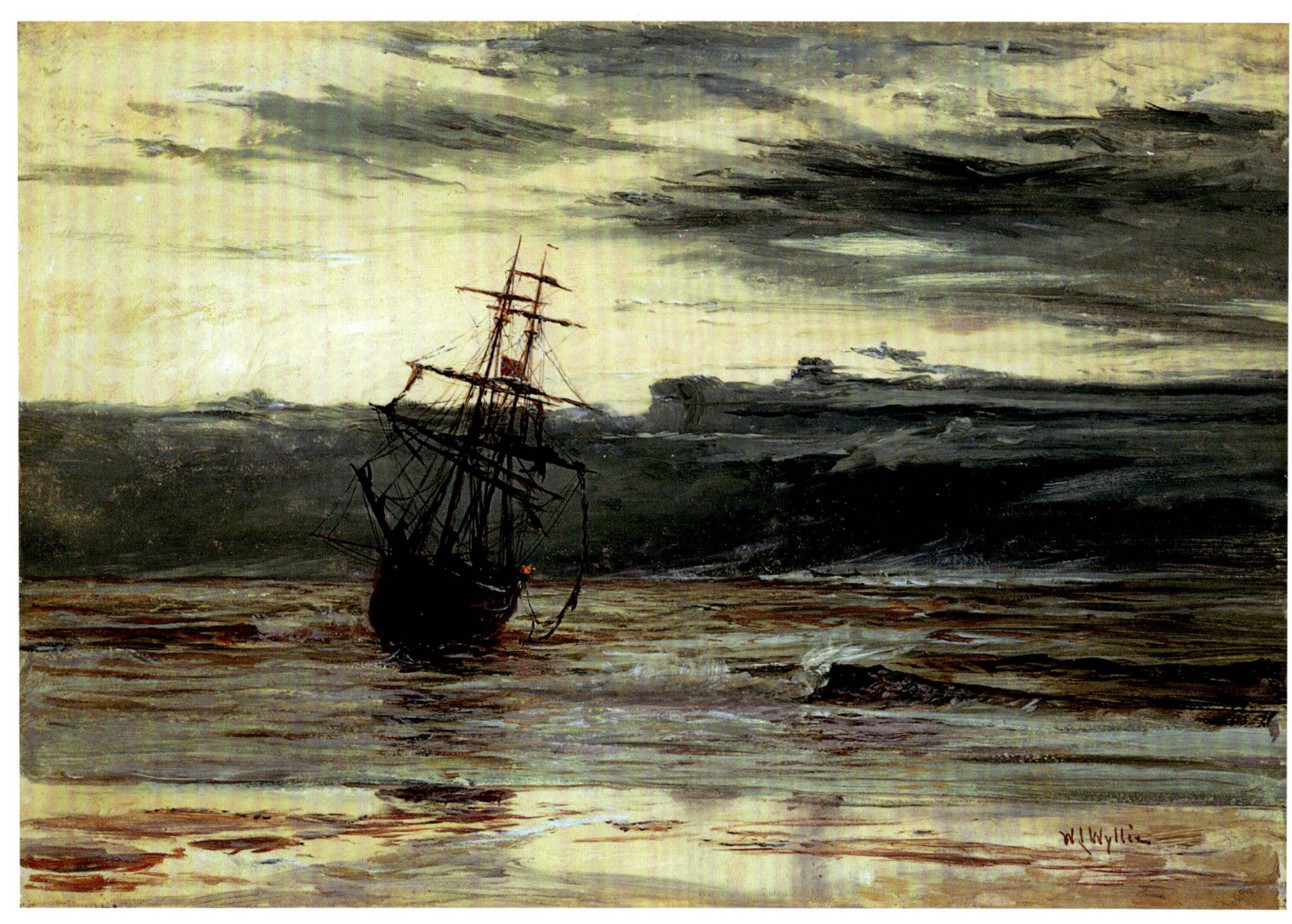

William Lionel Wyllie (1851–1931)

Dawn after a Storm

Levée du jour après un orage

Dämmerung nach einem Sturm

Amanecer tras la tormenta

Crepúsculo após uma tempestade

Ochtendgloren na een storm

n. d., Oil on panel/Huile sur bois, 24 × 36 cm, Private collection

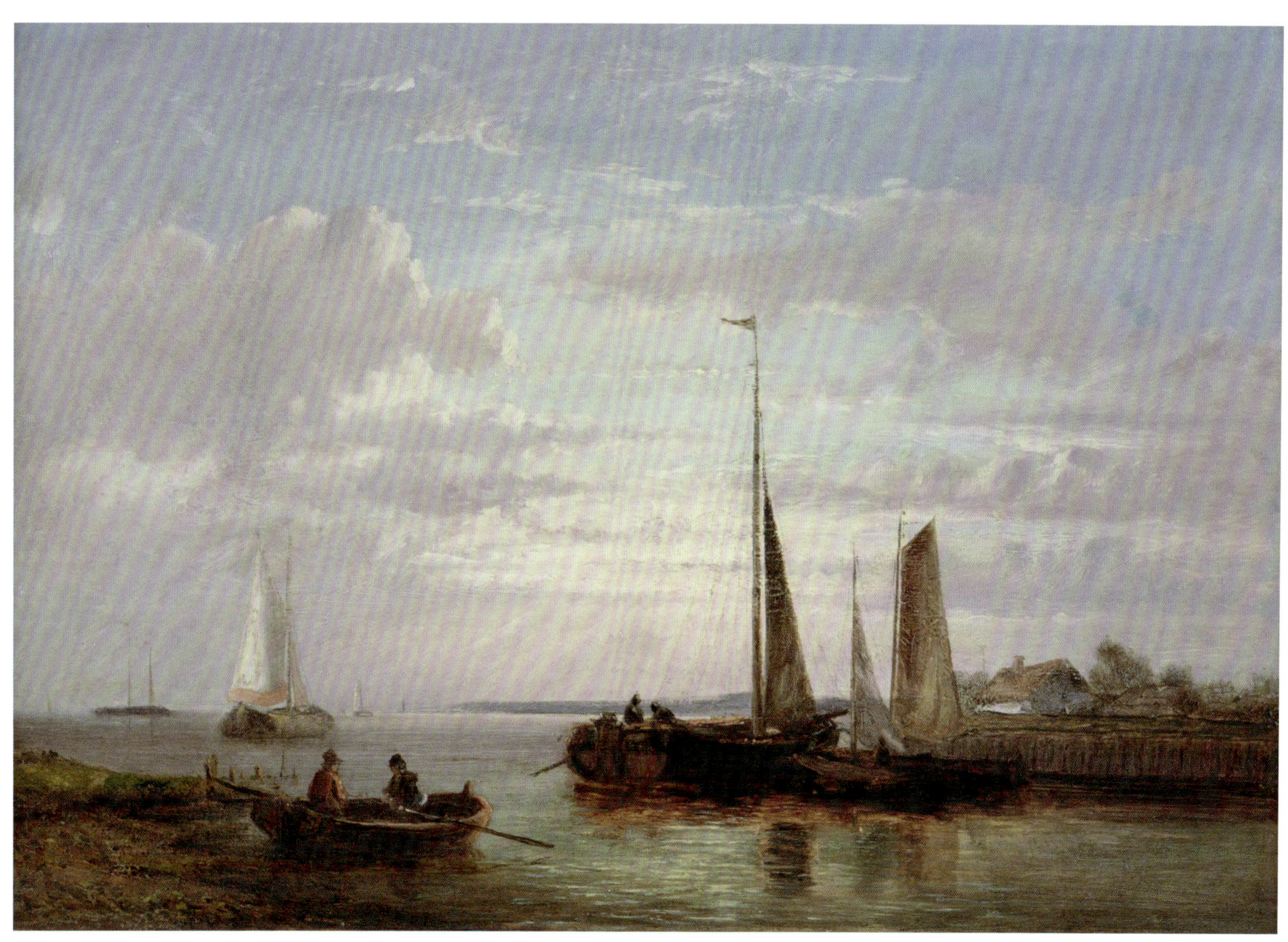

Abraham Hulk (1813–97)

Shipping in a Calm

Navigation sur mer calme

Schiffe bei Windstille

Barcos en calma

Navios na bonança

Schepen bij windstilte

n. d., Oil on panel/Huile sur bois, Private collection

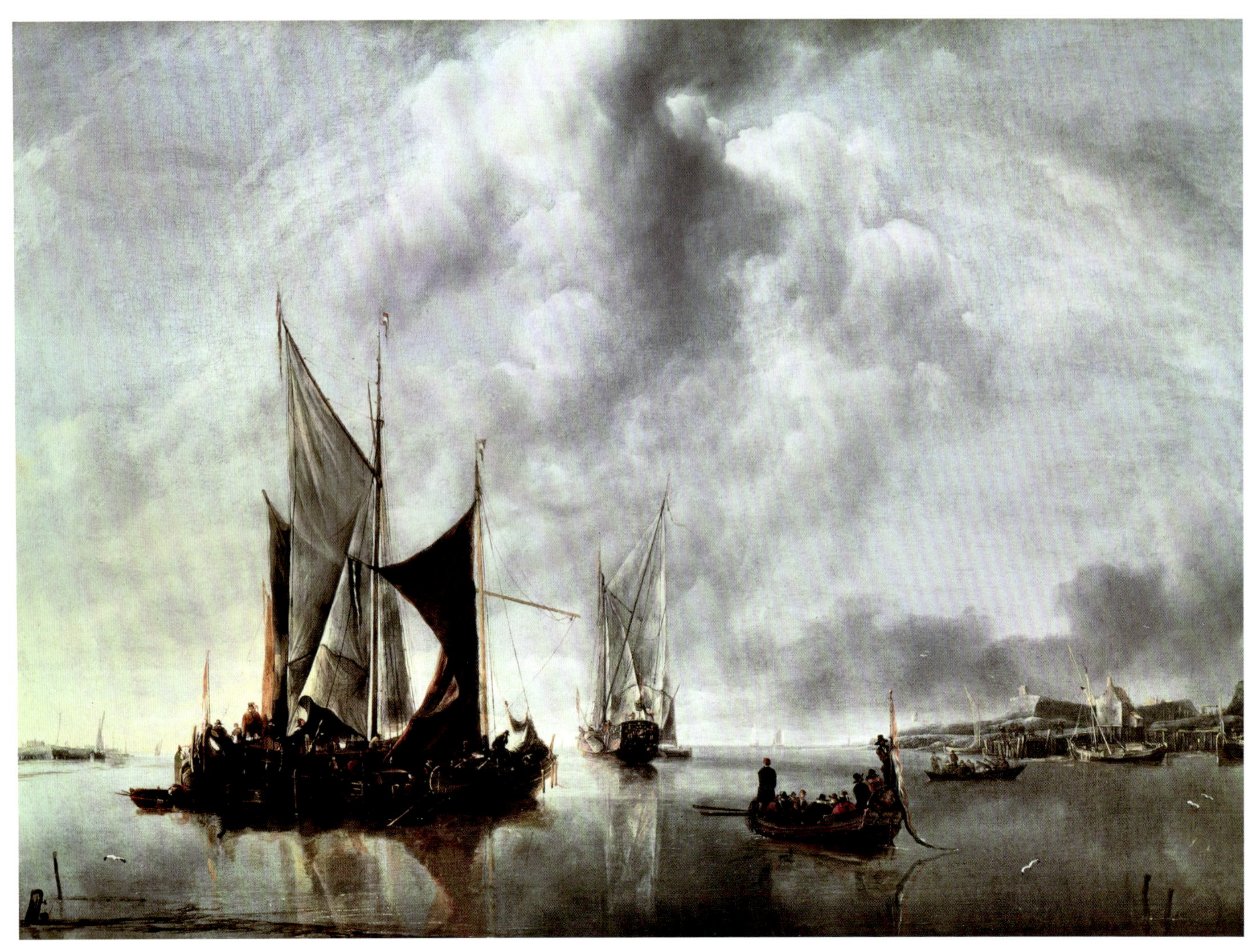

Jan van de Capelle (1624–79)

Calm *or* Boats near the Coast

Mer calme *ou* Bateaux près de la côte

Windstille *oder* Boote nahe der Küste

Calma *o* Barcos en la costa

Bonança *ou* barcos perto da costa

Windstilte *of* Boten voor de kust

after 1651, Oil on canvas/Huile sur toile, 61 × 84 cm, Toledo Museum of Art, Toledo OH

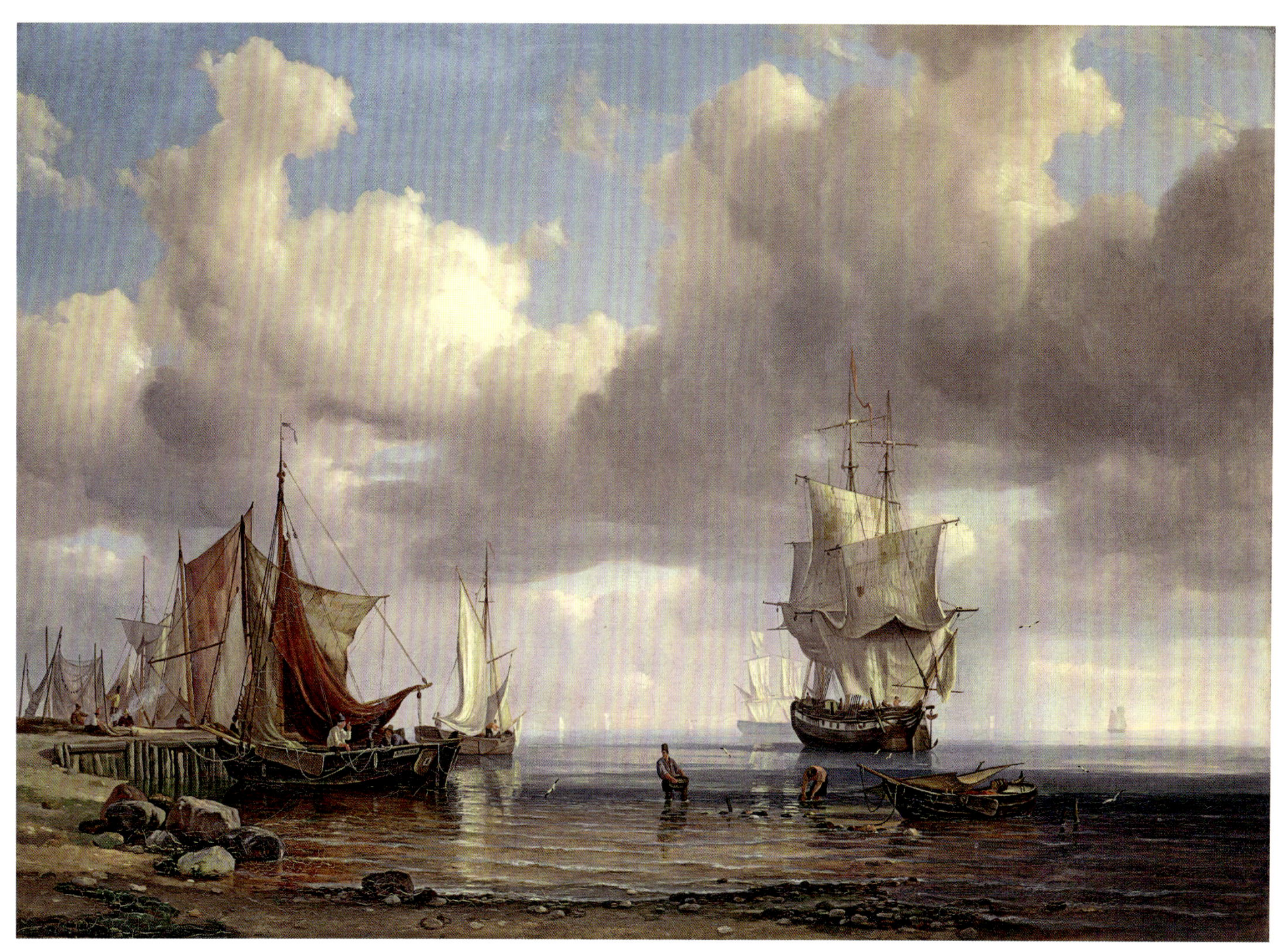

Adolf Vollmer (1806–75)

Calm Sea

Mer calme

Stille See

Mar en calma

Mar calmo

Kalme zee

1863, Oil on canvas/Huile sur toile, 63,5 × 89,2 cm, Kunsthalle, Hamburg

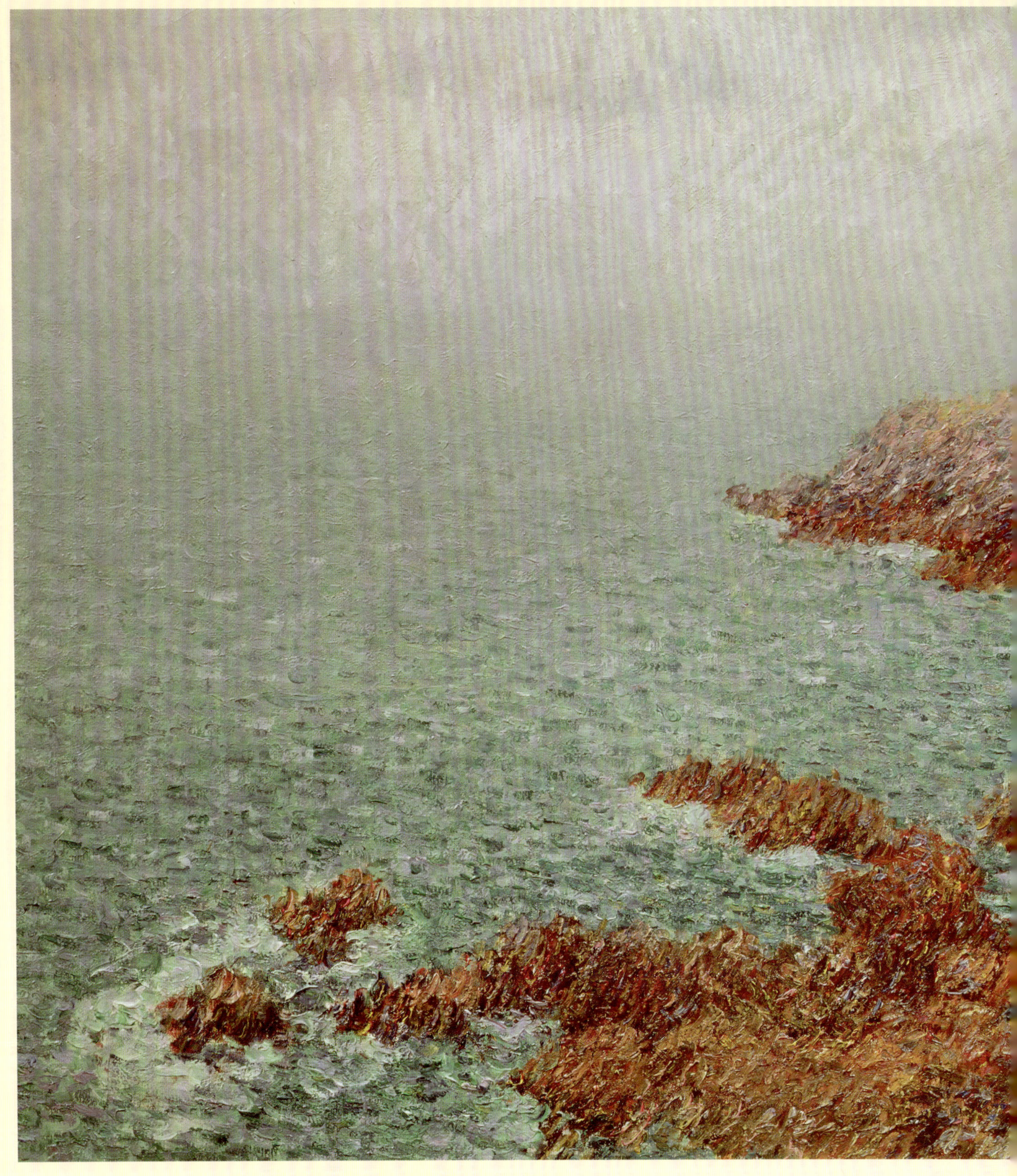

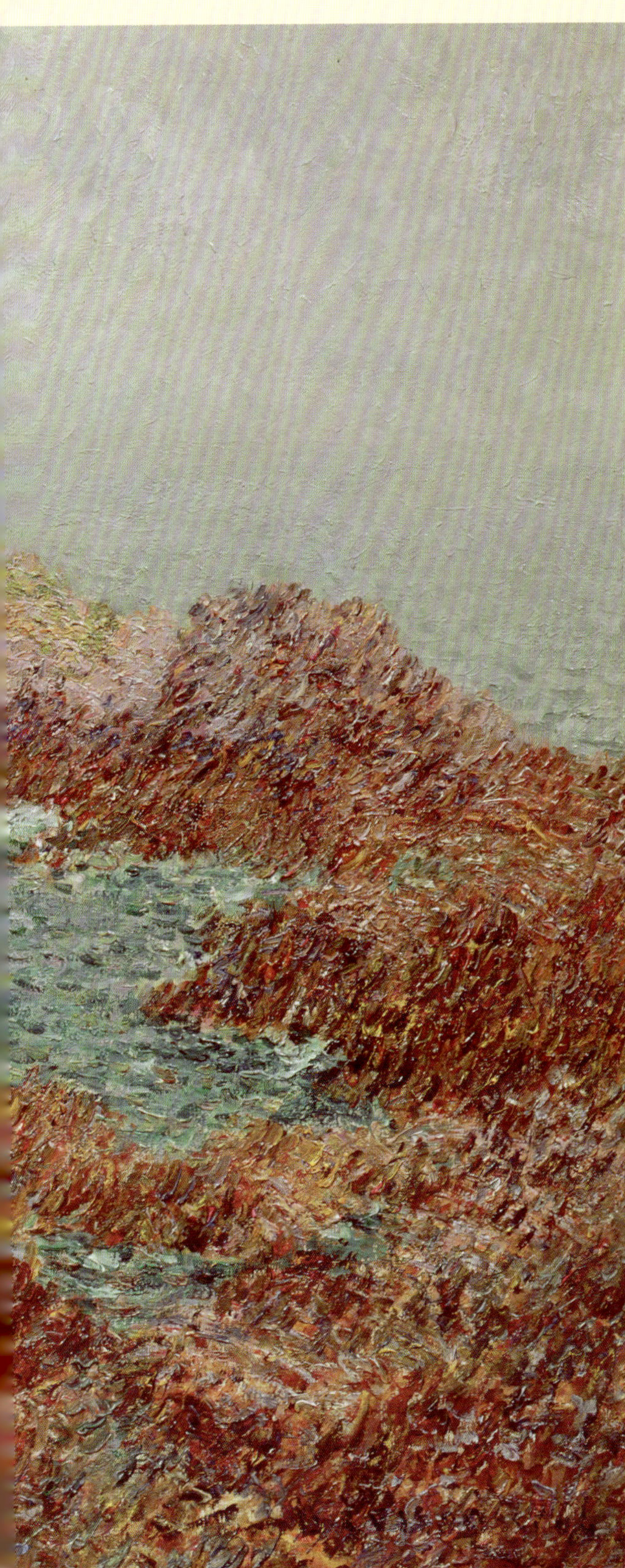

Côte

Küste

Costa

Costa

Kusten

Gustave Loiseau (1865–1935)
The Red Cliffs
Les Falaises rouges
Die roten Felsen: Belle-Île
Las rocas rojas: Belle-Île
Os rochedos vermelhos: Belle-Île
De rode rotsen: Belle-Île

1904, Oil on canvas/Huile sur toile, 61 × 82 cm, Private collection

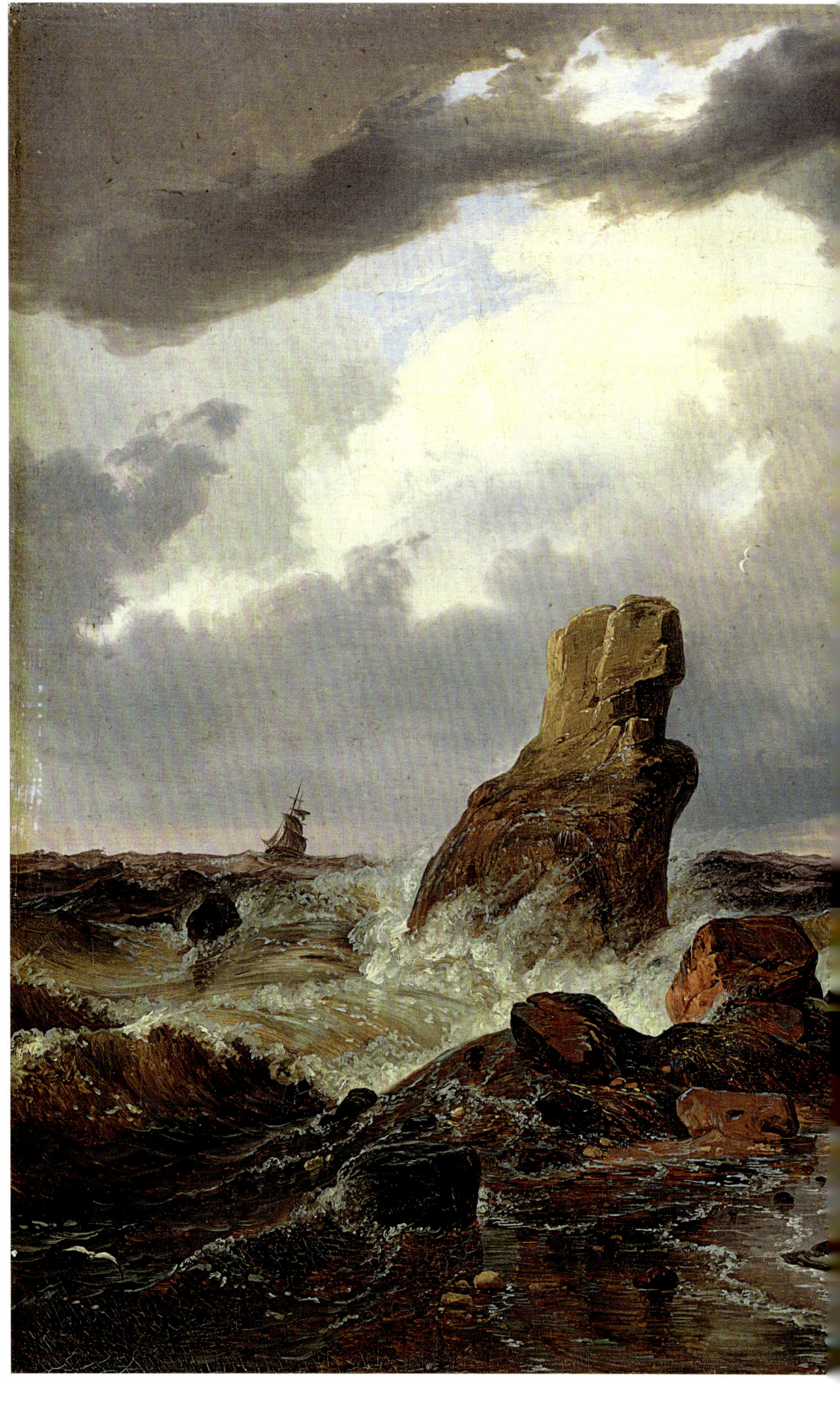

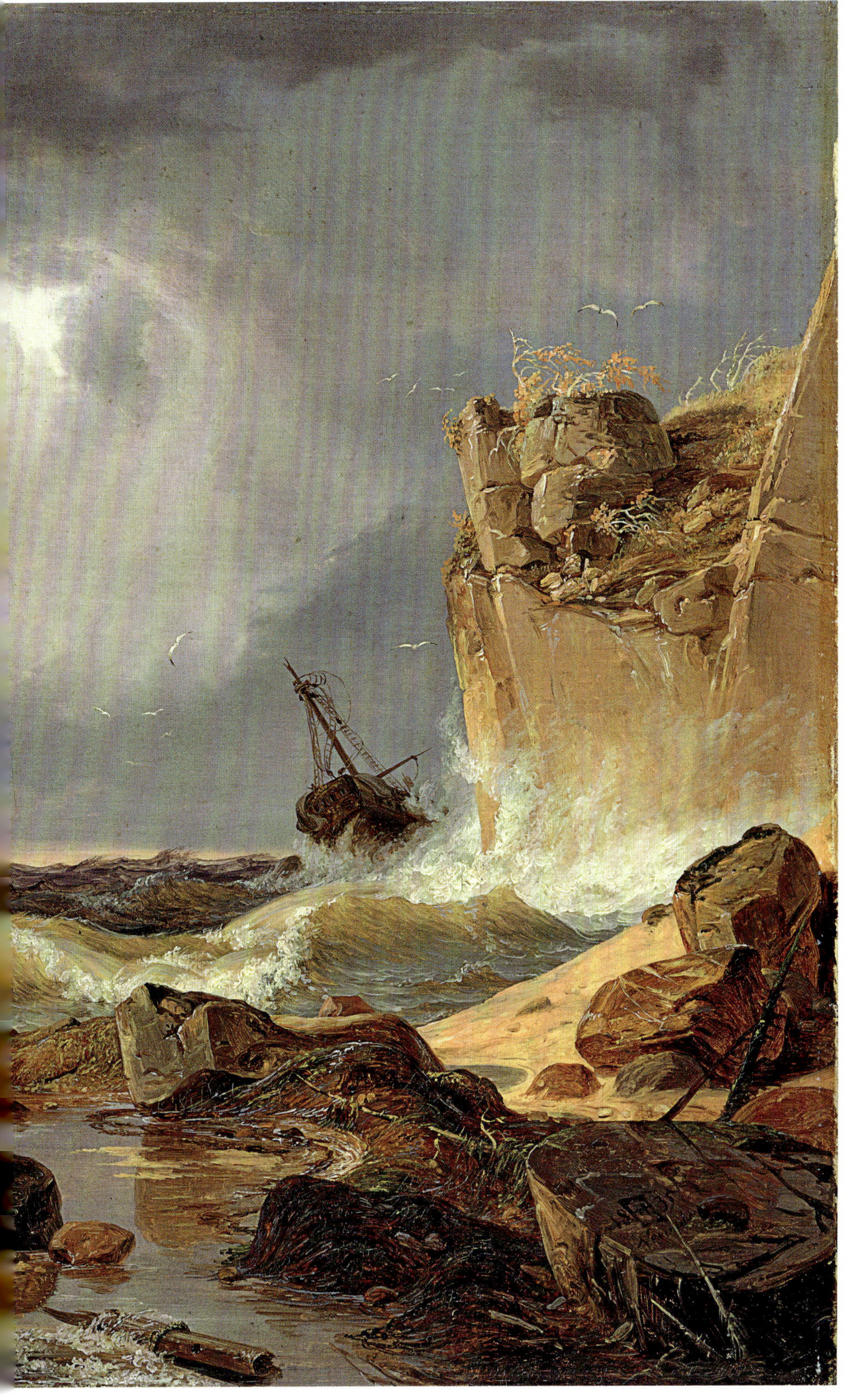

Prince Andreas Achenbach of Düsseldorf dominated the upscale salon painting market of his era. His works are known for their stirring presentation of movement. With waves whipped up by storms and breaking on the rocks, threatening clouds in the sky, and mountainous waves crowned with foamy spray, his work made him one of the most popular painters of his era.

Le prince Andreas Achenbach de Düsseldorf domina le marché haut de gamme de la peinture de salon de son époque. Ses œuvres sont connues pour leur présentation animée du mouvement. Avec des vagues agitées par des orages et se brisant sur les rochers, des nuages menaçants et des vagues gigantesques couronnées de mousse, ses travaux le transformèrent en l'un des peintres les plus populaires de son époque.

Der Düsseldorfer Malerfürst Andreas Achenbach beherrschte den Markt der gehobenen Salonmalerei zu seiner Zeit fast nach Belieben. Typisch für seine Bilder war vor allem die mitreißende Darstellung der Bewegung. Vom Sturm aufgepeitschte Wellen, die sich an Felsen brechen; bedrohliche Wolken am Himmel; von schäumender Gischt gekrönte Wellenberge – all das machte ihn europaweit zu einem der beliebtesten Maler seiner Zeit.

El príncipe pintor de Düsseldorf, Andreas Achenbach, dominó el mercado de los salones de pintura de lujo en su tiempo casi a voluntad. La convincente ilustración del movimiento fue especialmente típica en sus pinturas. Olas de mar agitado por la tormenta, que rompen contra las rocas; amenazantes nubes en el cielo; crestas de olas coronadas de espuma – todo esto le convirtió en uno de los pintores más populares en la Europa de su tiempo.

O pintor e Príncipe Andreas Achenbach de Düsseldorf dominou o mercado da pintura requintada de salão em sua época, quase à sua vontade. Típica em suas pinturas foi sobretudo a representação arrebatadora do movimento. Ondas fustigadas pela tempestade, quebrando em rochas; nuvens ameaçadoras no céu; cristas de ondas coroadas de espuma – tudo isso fez dele um dos pintores mais populares de sua época, na Europa toda.

De Düsseldorfse schildersvorst Andreas Achenbach beheerste in zijn tijd vrijwel in zijn eentje de markt voor verheven salonstukken. Typisch voor zijn doeken was de meeslepende uitbeelding van beweging: van stormen en een opgezweepte zee die op de rotsen breekt, wolkenpartijen en dreigende luchten, en torenhoge golven met schuimkoppen. Dat alles maakte hem in heel Europa tot een van de bekendste schilders van zijn tijd.

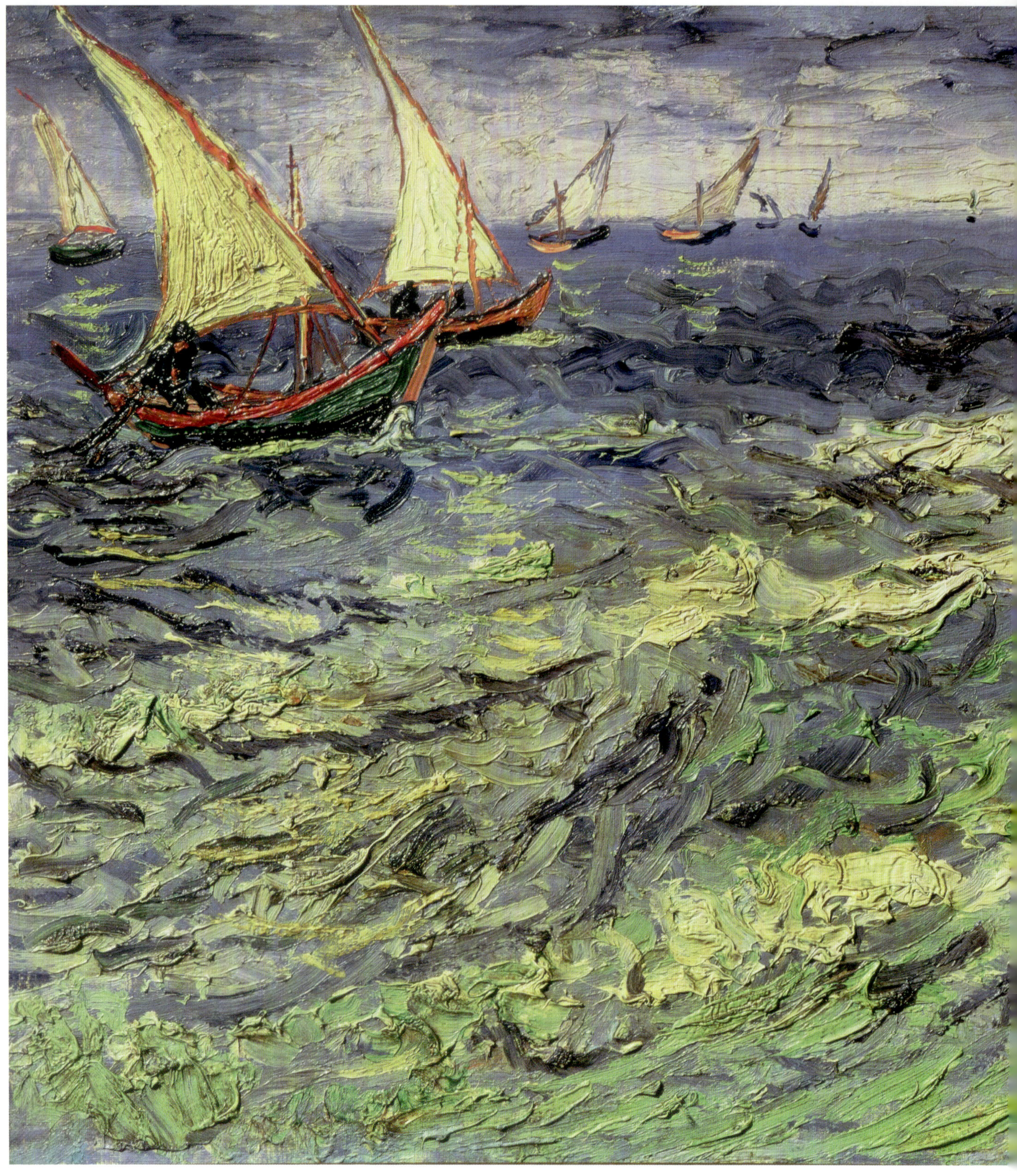

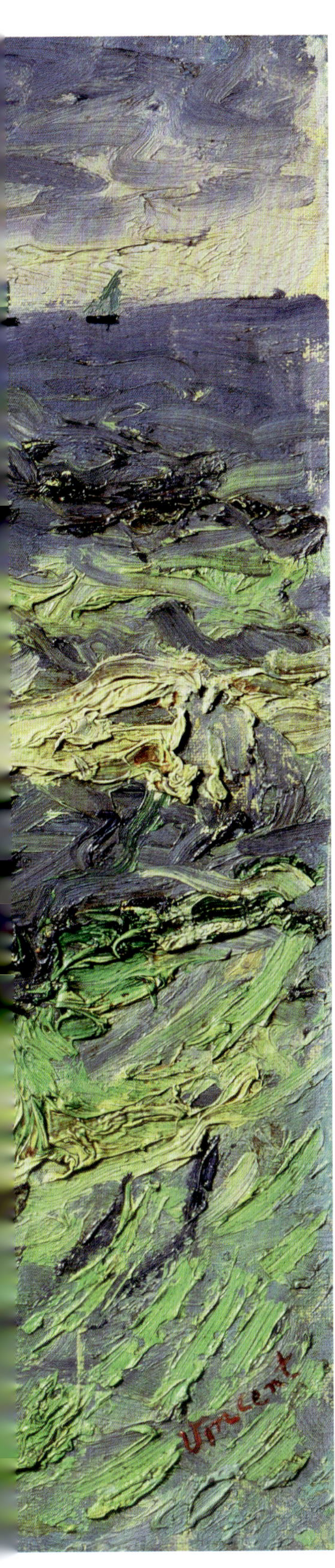

Vincent van Gogh (1853–90)

Seascape at Saintes-Maries-de-la-Mer

Petite marine aux Saintes-Maries-de-la-Mer

Meerespanorama bei Saintes-Maries-de-la-Mer

Paisaje marino en Saintes-Maries-de-la-Mer

Paisagem marinha em Saintes-Maries-de-la-Mer

Zeegezicht bij Saintes-Maries-de-la-Mer

1888, Oil on canvas/Huile sur toile, 44 × 53 cm, Pushkin Museum, Moscow

Vincent van Gogh's Seascape at Saintes-Maries-de-la-Mer *is part of a series of
pictures done in different techniques that he made in Saintes-Maries-de-la-Mer, the
capital of the Camargue, where he was staying for health reasons in 1888.*

L'œuvre Petite marine aux Saintes-Maries-de-la-Mer-de-la-Mer, *de Vincent van Gogh,
fait partie d'une série d'images réalisées avec différentes techniques aux Saintes-Maries-de-
la-Mer, capitale de la Camargue, où il séjourna en 1888 pour des raisons de santé.*

Vincent van Goghs Meerespanorama bei Saintes-Maries-de-la-Mer *gehört zu einer ganzen Serie von
Bildern unterschiedlicher Techniken, die er 1888 während eines Aufenthaltes in Saintes-Maries-de-la-
Mer anfertigte, der Hauptstadt der Camargue, wo er sich aus gesundheitlichen Gründen aufhielt.*

Paisaje marino en Saintes-Maries-de-la-Mer *de Van Gogh pertenece a una serie numerosa
de imágenes hechas con diferentes técnicas que realizó en 1888 durante una estancia en
Saintes-Maries-de-la-Mer, capital de La Camarga, donde fue por razones de salud.*

Paisagem marinha em Saintes-Maries-de-la-Mer, *de Vincent van Gogh, faz parte de toda uma
série de quadros de diferentes técnicas que ele pintou em 1888, durante sua estada em Saintes-
Maries-de-la-Mer, capital da Camargue, onde o pintor permaneceu por motivo de saúde.*

Vincent van Goghs Zeegezicht bij Saintes-Maries-de-la-Mer *behoort tot een reeks schilderijen
in diverse technieken die hij in 1888 tijdens zijn verblijf in Saintes-Maries-de-la-Mer creëerde.
Van Gogh verbleef om gezondheidsredenen in de hoofdstad van de Camargue.*

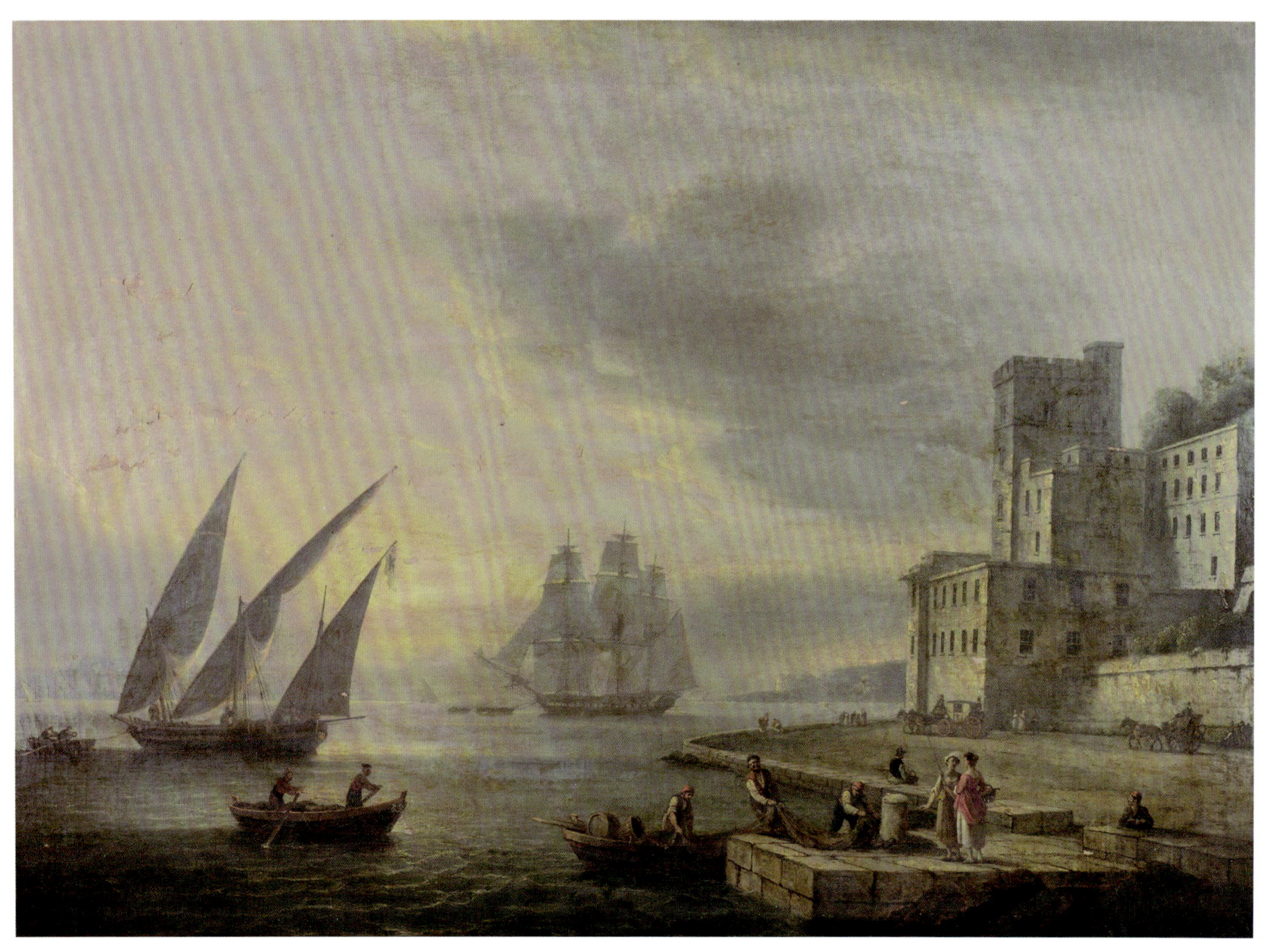

Thomas Luny (1759–1837)

The Bay of Naples from Posilippo

La Baie de Naples de Posilippo

Die Bucht von Neapel, von Posilippo aus

La bahía de Nápoles desde Posillippo

A baía de Nápoles, vista de Posillipo

De Baai van Napels gezien vanuit Posilippo

c. 1829, Oil on canvas/Huile sur toile, 95,2 × 132 cm, Private collection

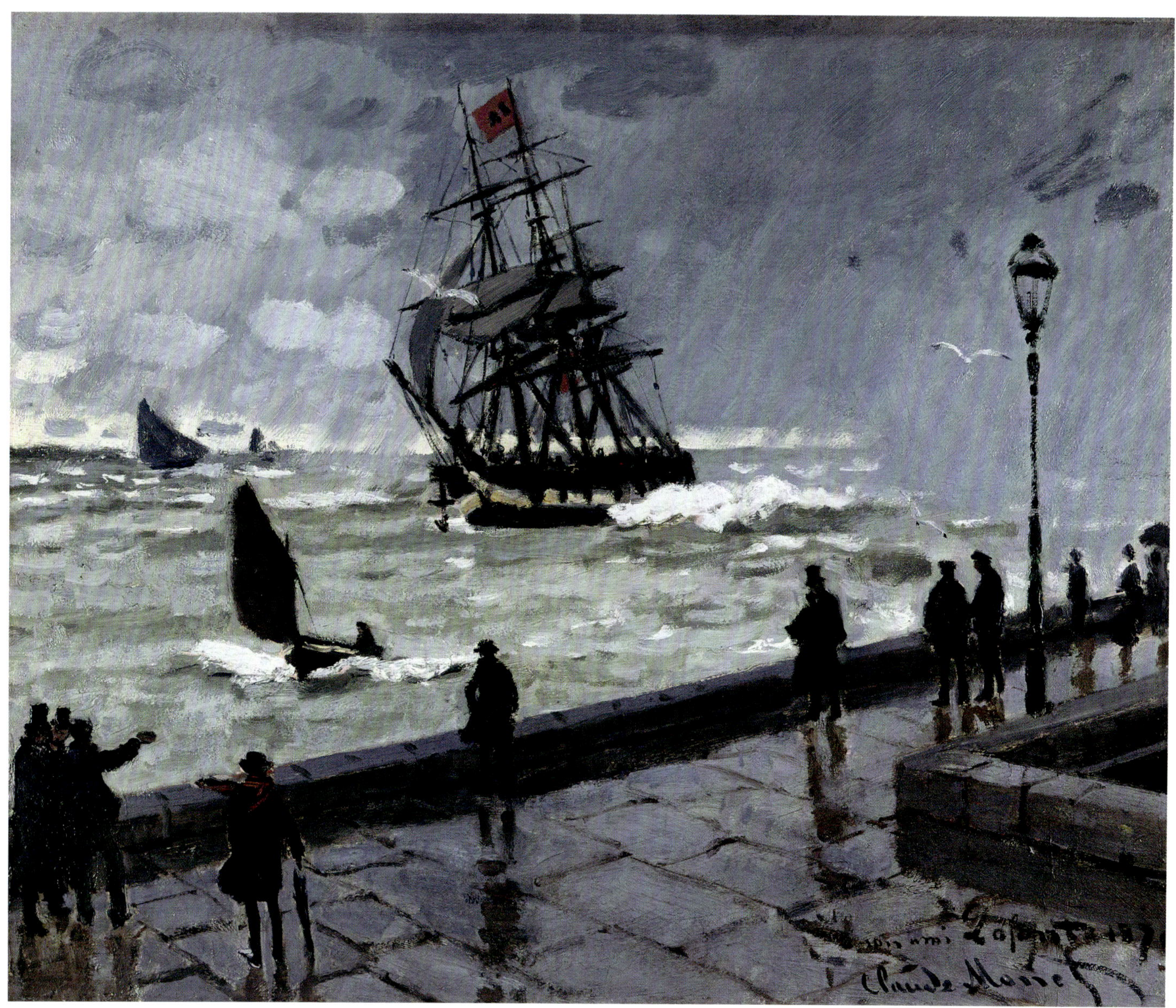

Claude Monet (1840–1926)

The Jetty at Le Havre, Bad Weather

La Jetée du Havre par mauvais temps

Anleger in Le Havre, schlechtes Wetter

Embarcadero de Le Havre, mal tiempo

Cais em Le Havre, mau tempo

De kade van Le Havre bij slecht weer

1870, Oil on canvas/Huile sur toile, 50 × 60 cm, Private collection

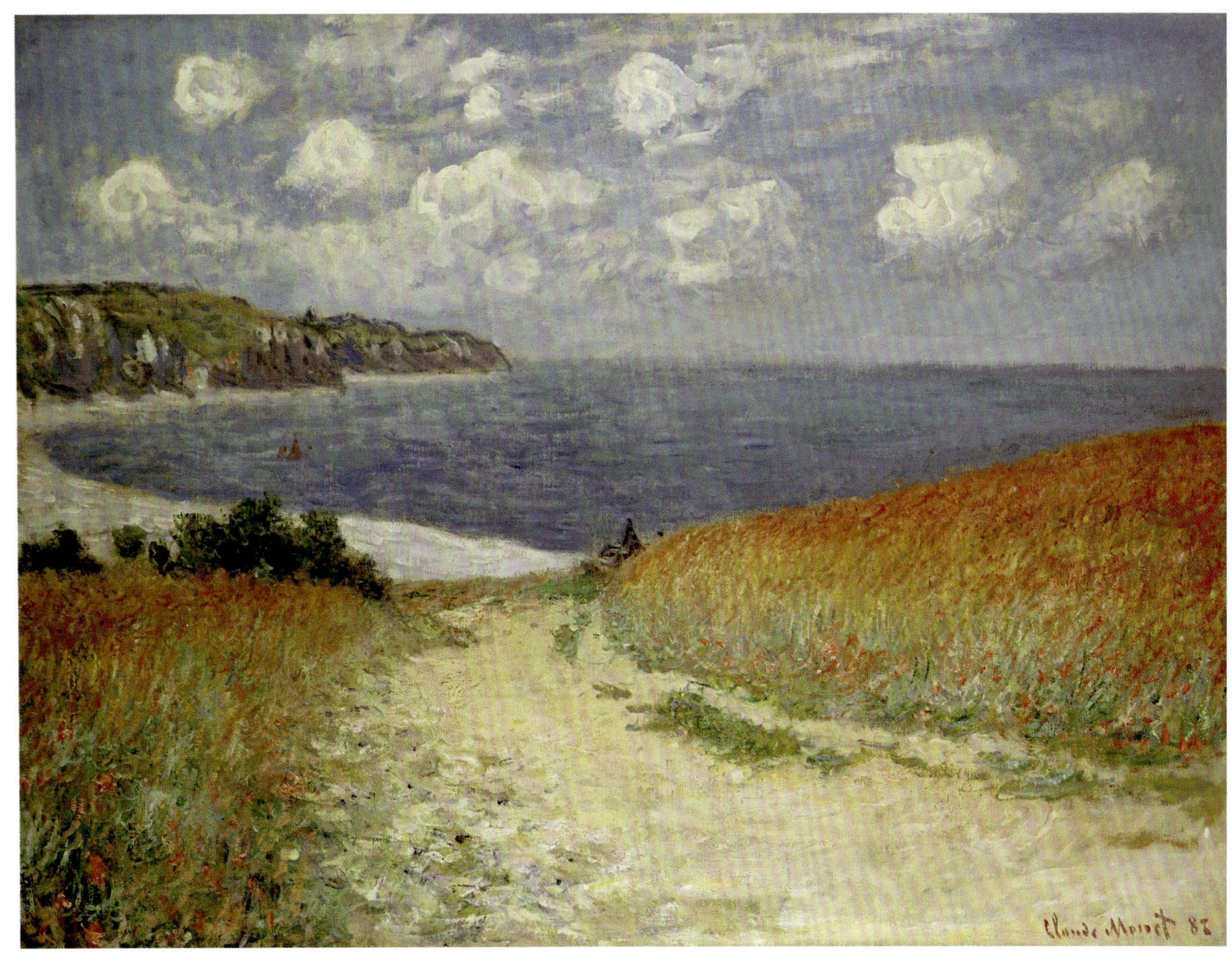

Claude Monet (1840–1926)

Path in the Wheat at Pourville

Chemin dans les blés à Pourville

Pfad im Weizen bei Pourville

Camino entre los campos de trigo en Pourville

Caminho no trigo em Pourville

Pad door het koren bij Pourville

1882, Oil on canvas/Huile sur toile, 58,2 × 78 cm, Private collection

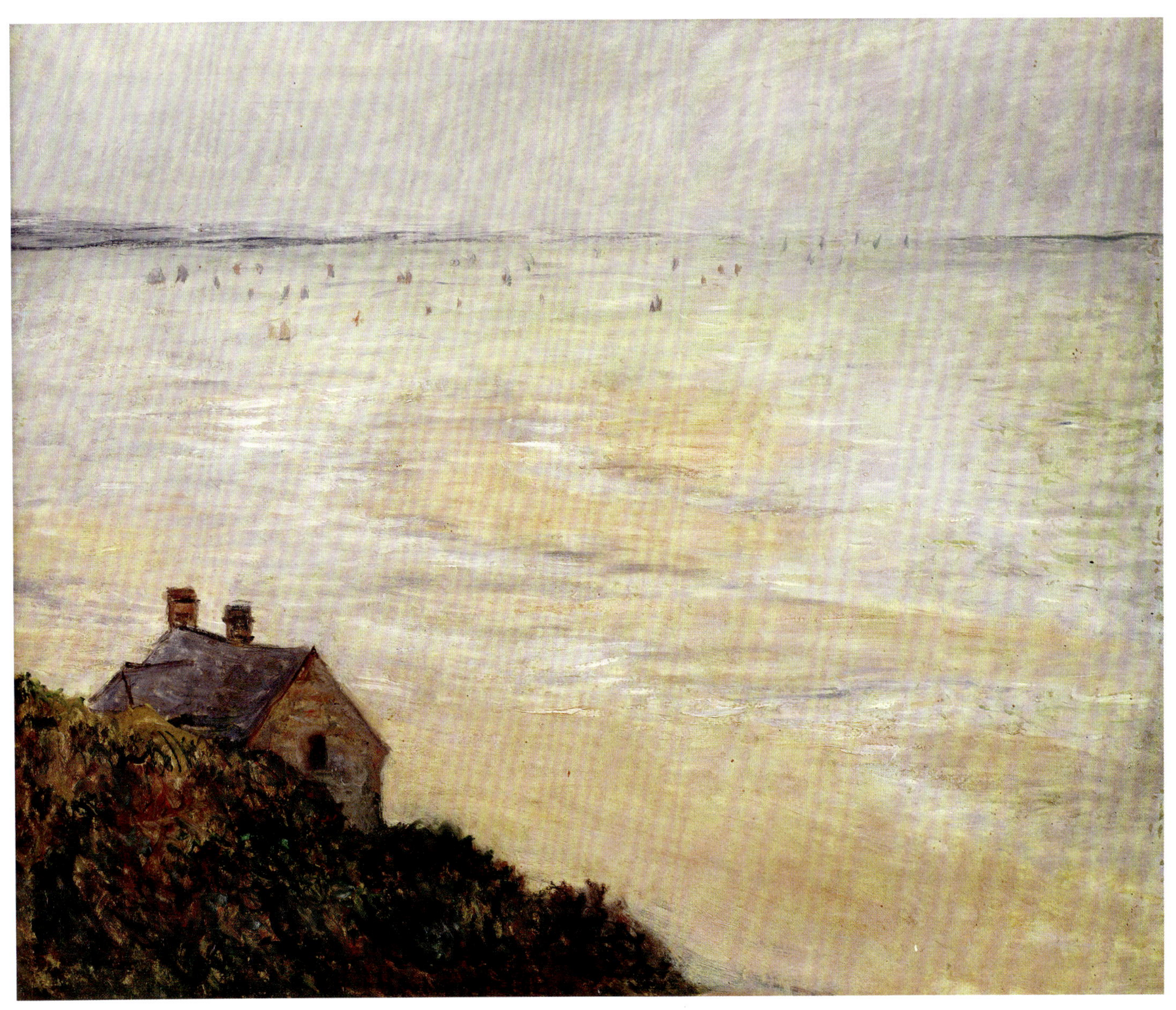

Claude Monet (1840–1926)

The Hut at Trouville, Low Tide

La Cabane à Trouville

Die Hütte in Trouville bei Ebbe

La cabaña en Trouville, marea baja

A cabana em Trouville na maré baixa

De hut in Trouville bij eb

1881, Oil on canvas/Huile sur toile, Private collection

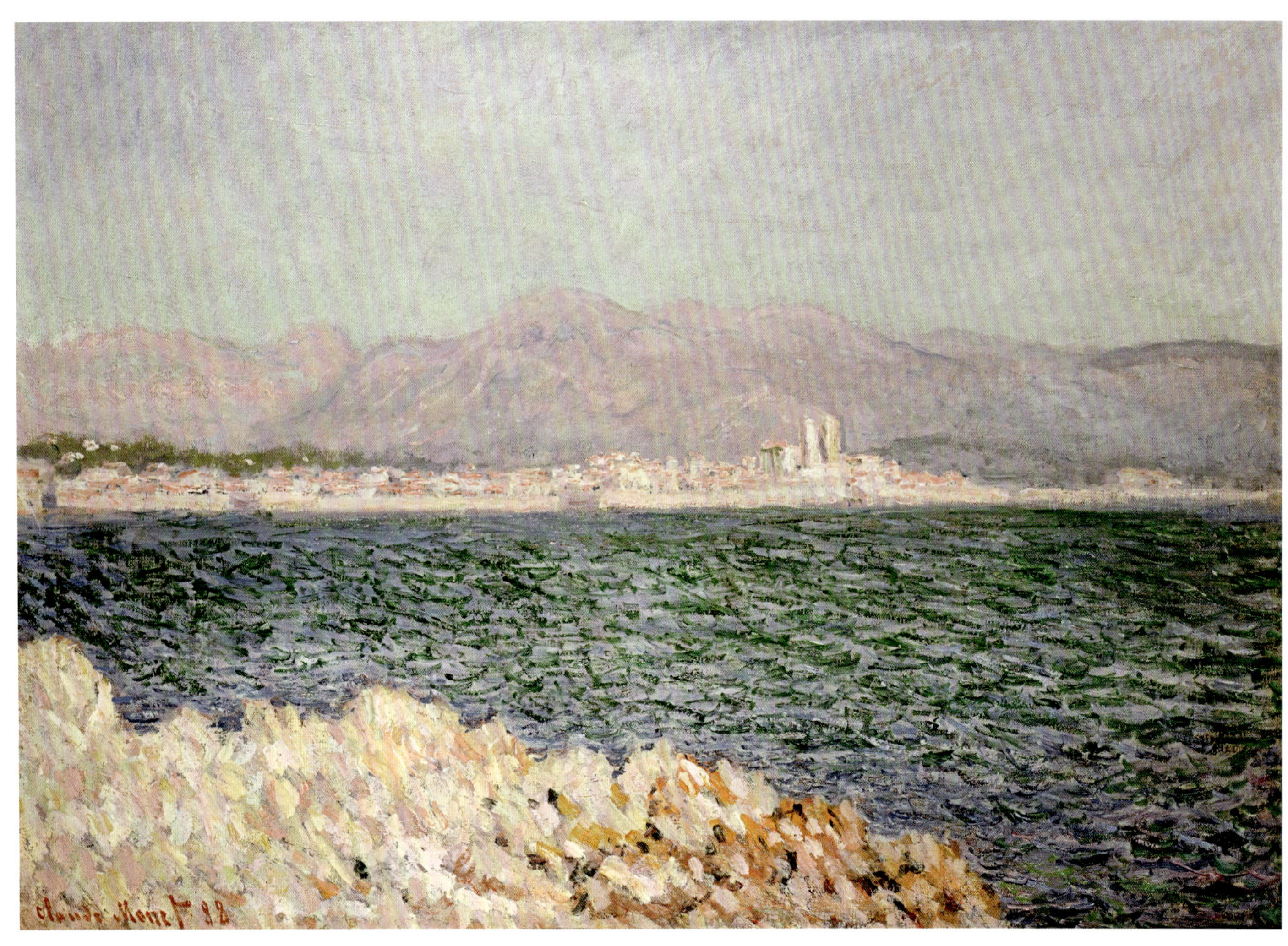

Claude Monet (1840–1926)

The Gulf of Antibes

Golf d'Antibes

Golf von Antibes

El Golfo de Antibes

Golfo de Antibes

De baai van Antibes

1888, Oil on canvas/Huile sur toile, 65 × 92 cm, Private collection

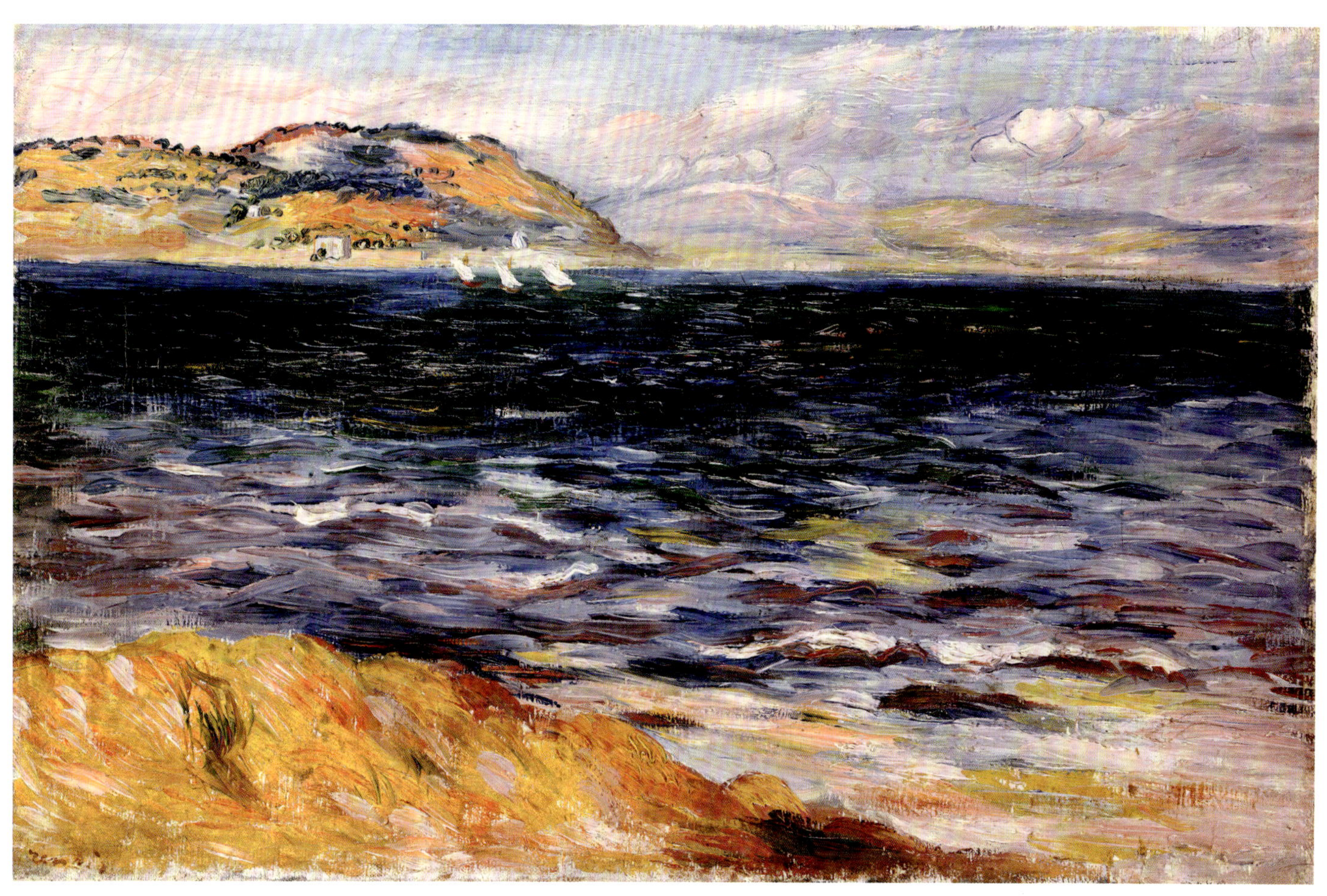

Pierre Auguste Renoir (1841–1919)

Bordighera

c. 1888, Oil on canvas/Huile sur toile, Private collection

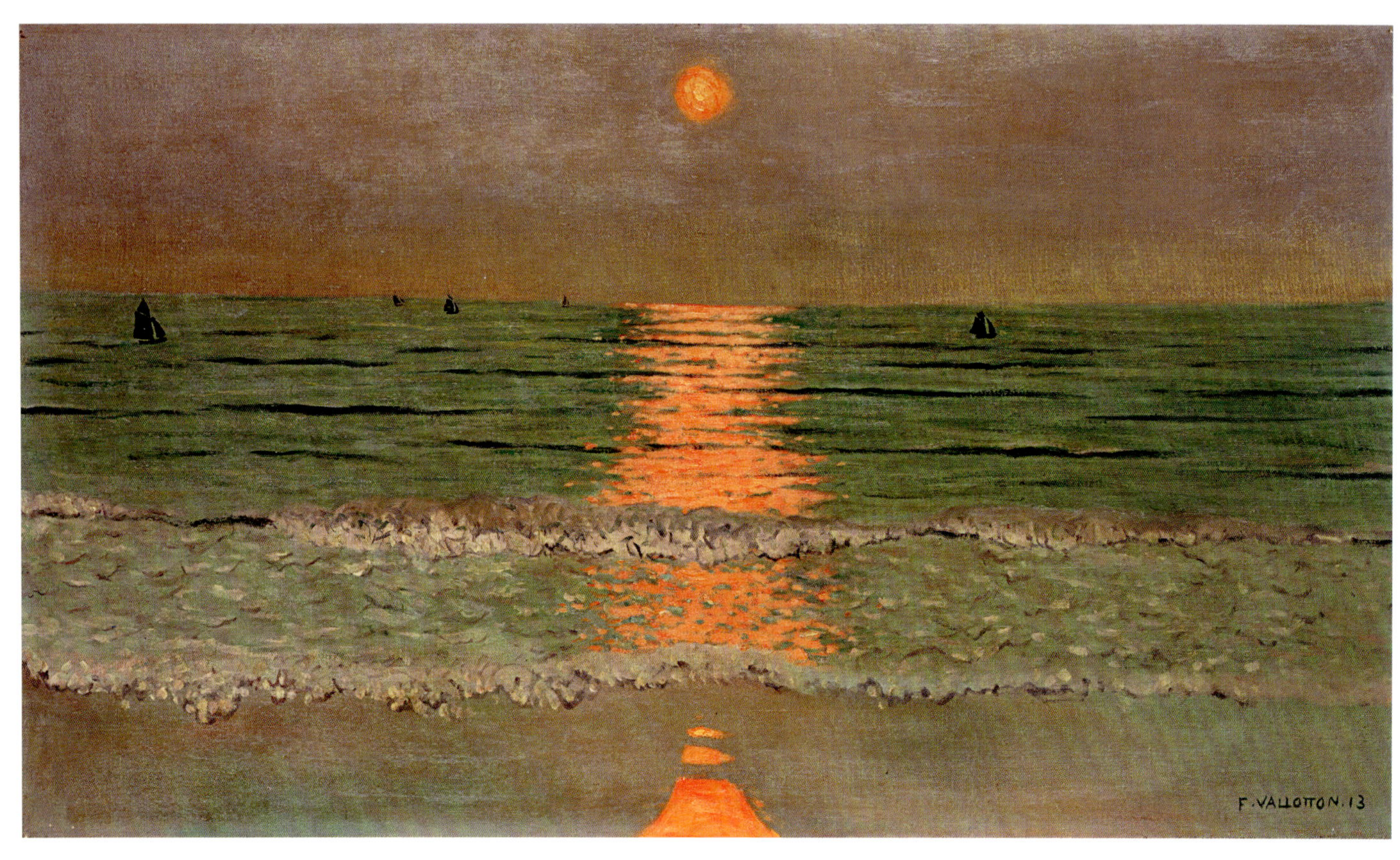

Félix Édouard Valloton (1865–1925)

Sunset

Coucher de soleil

Sonnenuntergang

Puesta de sol

Pôr do sol

Zonsondergang

1913, Oil on canvas/Huile sur toile, Private collection

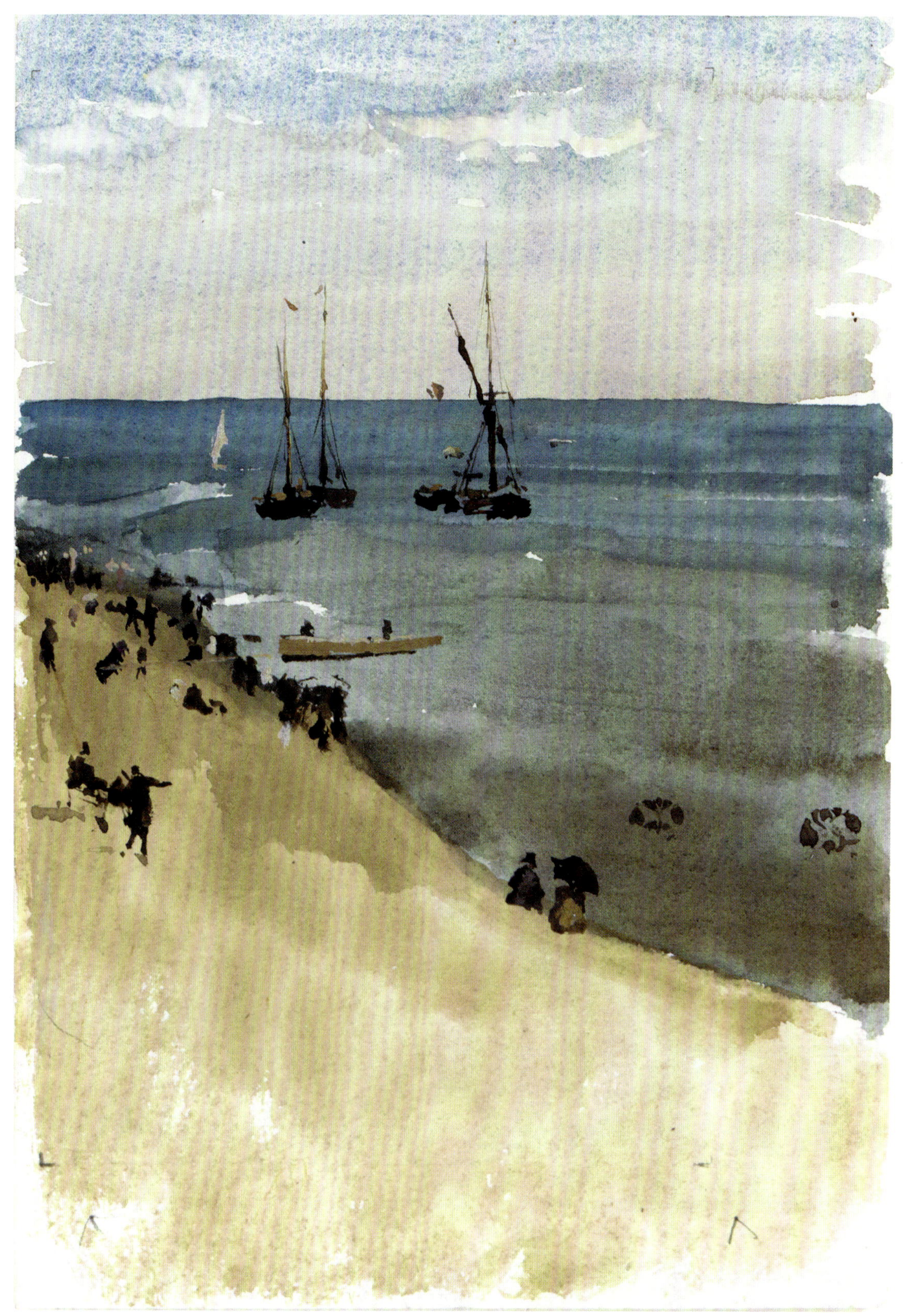

James Abbott McNeil Whistler
(1834–1903)

Green and Silver –
The Bright Sea, Dieppe

Vert et argent, la brillante mer

Grün und Silber – Das helle Meer

Verde y plata – El mar brillante

Verde e prata – O Mar Claro

Groen en zilver – De heldere zee

c. 1883–85, Watercolor and gouache
on paper/Aquarelle et gouache sur
papier, 25,4 × 18 cm, Private collection

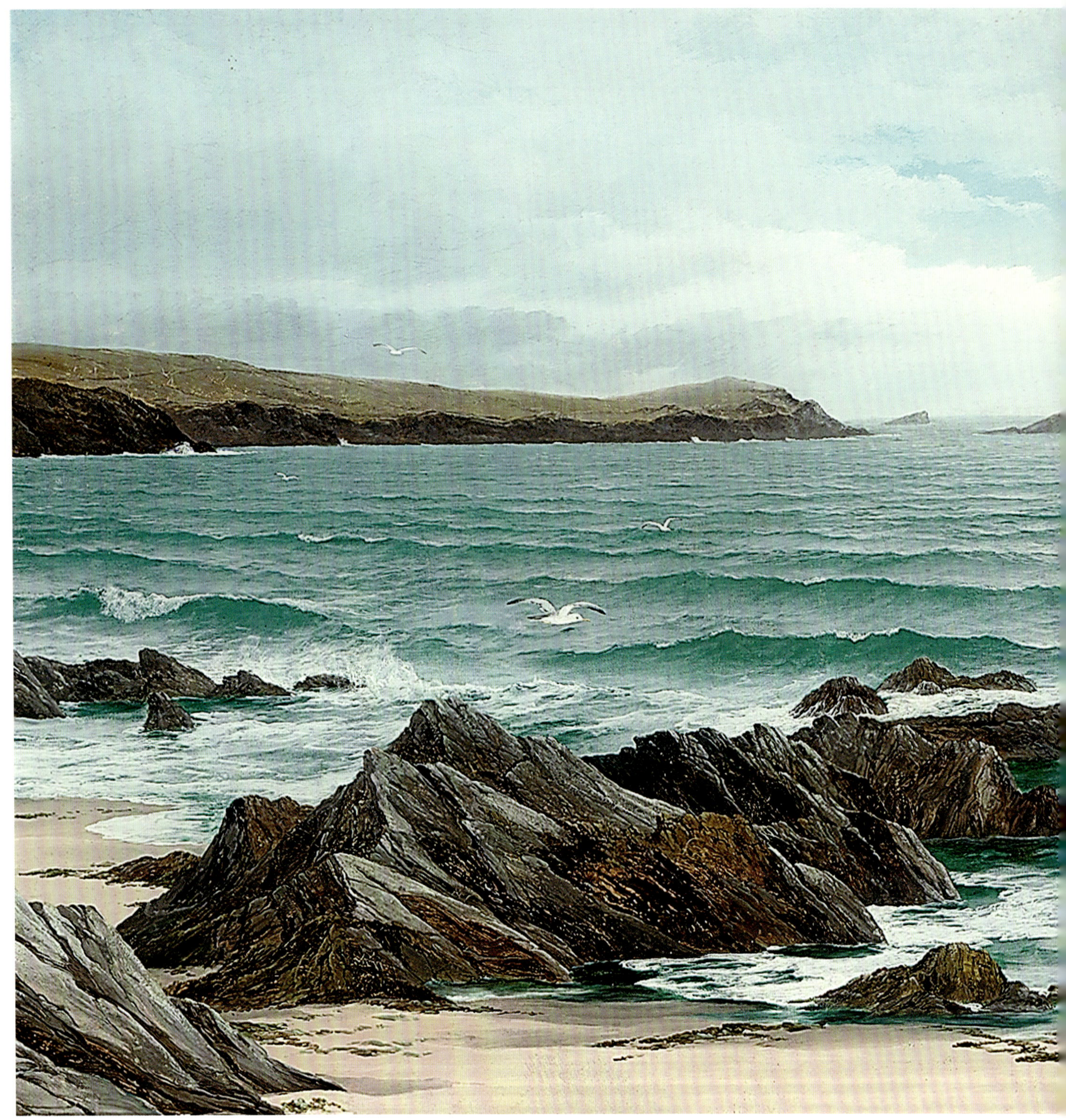

David James (1853–1904)

A Rocky Coastline   Côte rocheuse   Eine felsige Küste   Costa rocosa   A costa rochosa   Een rotskust

n. d., Oil on canvas/Huile sur toile, 30,5 × 50,8 cm, Private collection

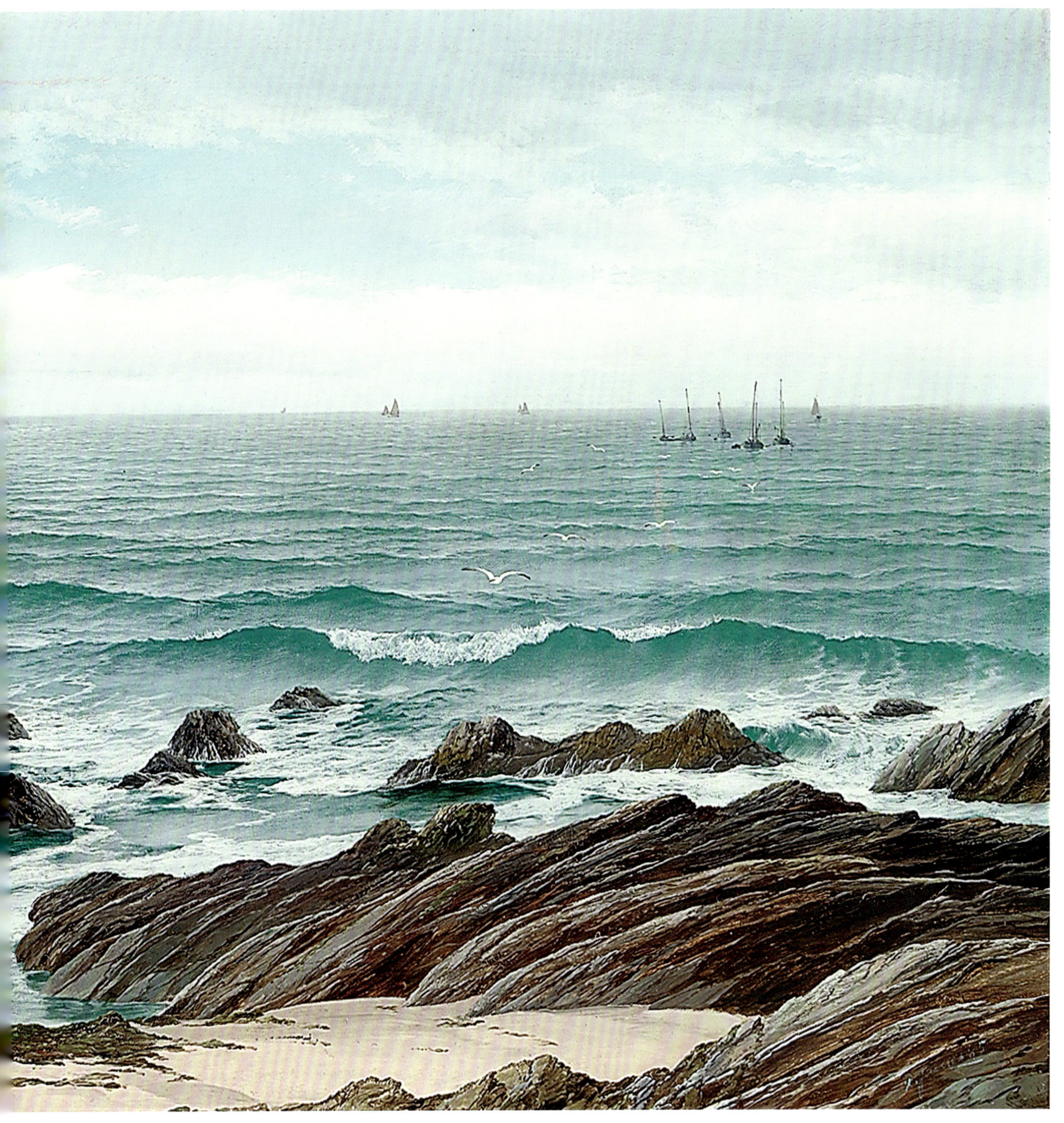

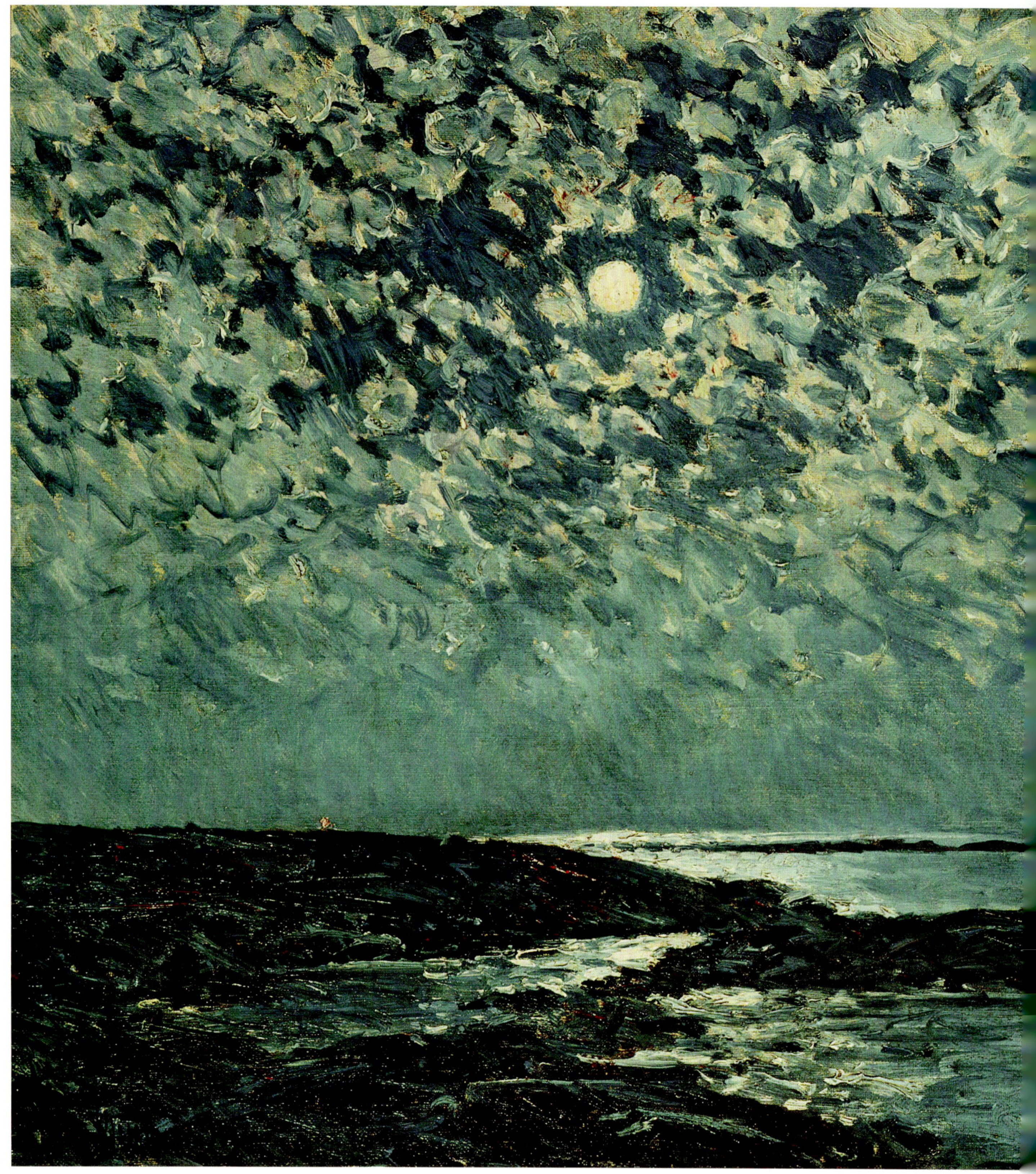

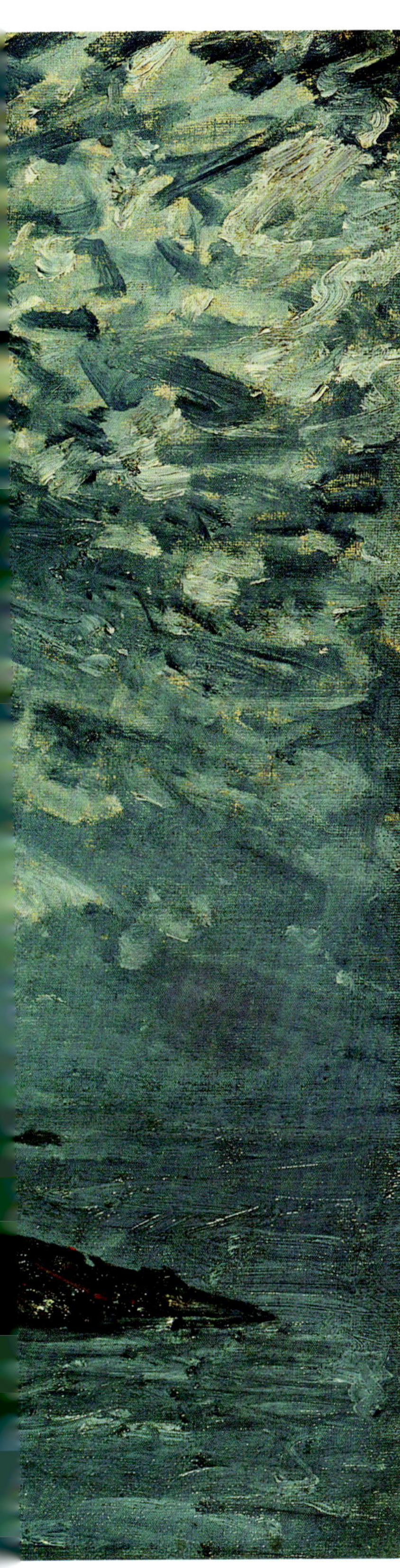

Moonlight, Isle of Shoals

Clair de lune, Île de Shoals

Mondlicht, Isle of Shoals

Luz de luna, Isla de Shoals

Luar, Isle of Shoals

Maneschijn, Isle of Shoals

1892, Oil on canvas/Huile sur toile, Private collection

*This fantastic image by American Impressionist Childe Hassam is representative of an entire branch of
maritime painting that focuses on the effects of the moonlight reflected by the water. Here, the moon is shown
over the Isles of Shoals, which run along the Atlantic coasts of Maine and New Hampshire.*

*Cette image fantastique de l'impressionniste américain Childe Hassam représente une branche entière
de la peinture de mer, et qui met l'accent sur les effets des reflets de la lune sur l'eau. Ici, la lune se reflète
sur les îles Shoals, qui s'étendent sur la côte atlantique du Maine et du New Hampshire.*

*Dieses fantastische Bild des US-amerikanischen Impressionisten Childe Hassam kann für einen ganzen Zweig der maritimen
Malerei stehen, den, der auf die Effekte des vom Wasser reflektierten Mondlicht setzt. Hier ist es der Mond über der
Inselgruppe der Isles of Shoals, die sich über die amerikanischen Bundesstaat Maine und New Hampshire erstreckt.*

*Esta increíble imagen del impresionista estadounidense Childe Hassam puede representar a toda una rama de la pintura
marítima, la que se basa en los efectos de la luz de la luna reflejada en el agua. Aquí está la luna sobre el archipiélago
de las Islas de Shoals, que se extiende por todo el estado estadounidense de Maine y New Hampshire.*

*Este fantástico quadro do impressionista americano Childe Hassam pode ser representativo de todo um ramo
da pintura marinha, que assenta nos efeitos do luar refletido na água. Aqui nós vemos a lua sobre o arquipélago
de Isles of Shoals, que se estende por todo o estado norte-americano do Maine e New Hampshire.*

*Dit fantasievolle schilderij van de Amerikaanse impressionist Childe Hassam zou voor een aparte tak van maritieme
schilderkunst kunnen staan, namelijk die waarin het effect van het maanlicht op het water wordt behandeld. Hier staat
de maan boven de Isles of Shoals, die voor de kunst van de Amerikaanse staten Maine en New Hampshire liggen.*

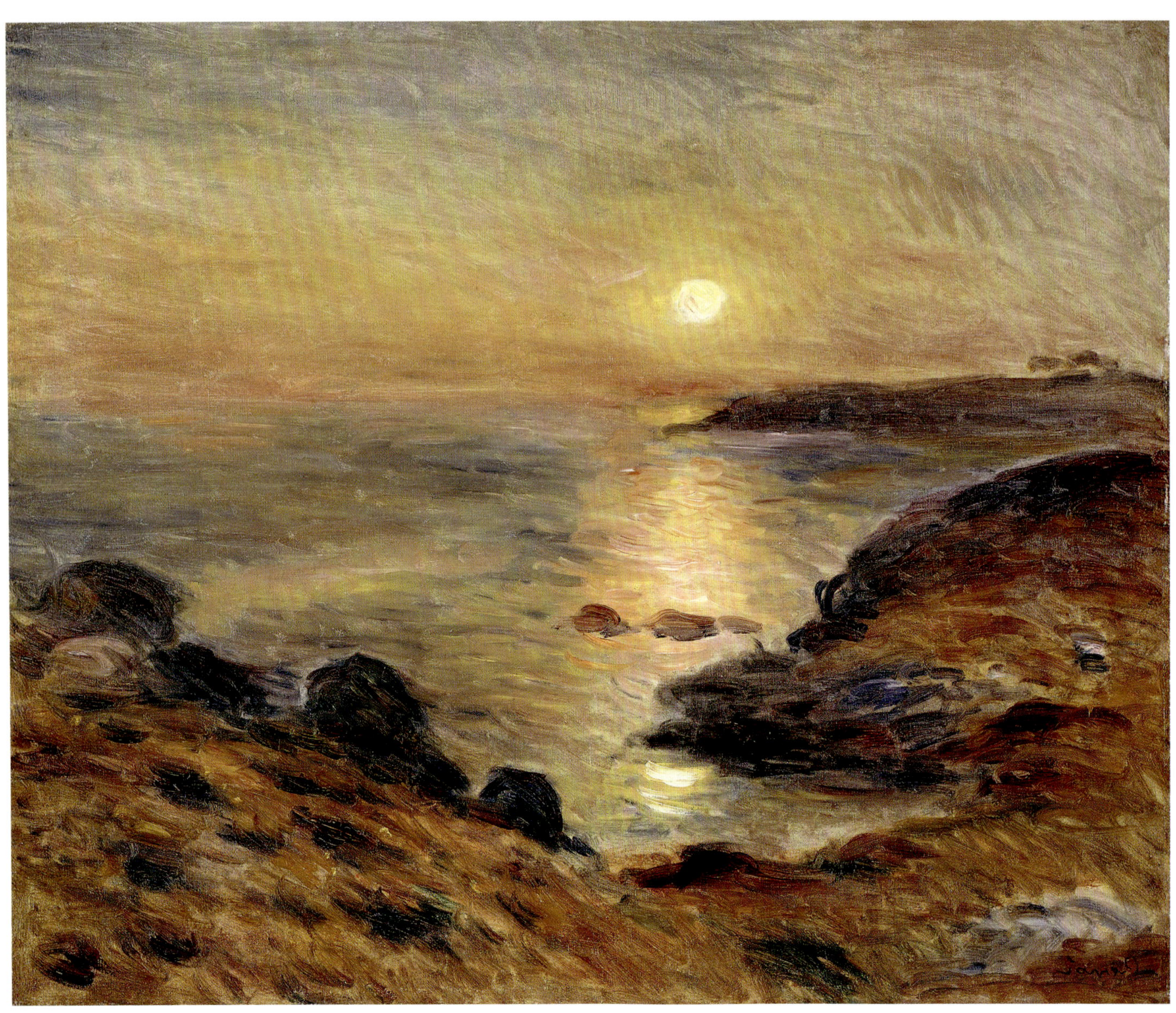

Pierre Auguste Renoir (1841–1919)

The Setting of the Sun at Douarnenez

Coucher de soleil à Douarnenez

Sonnenuntergang in Douarnenez

Puesta de sol en Douarnenez

Pôr do sol em Douarnenez

Zonsondergang in Douarnenez

1883, Oil on canvas/Huile sur toile, 54,3 × 66,1 cm, Private collection

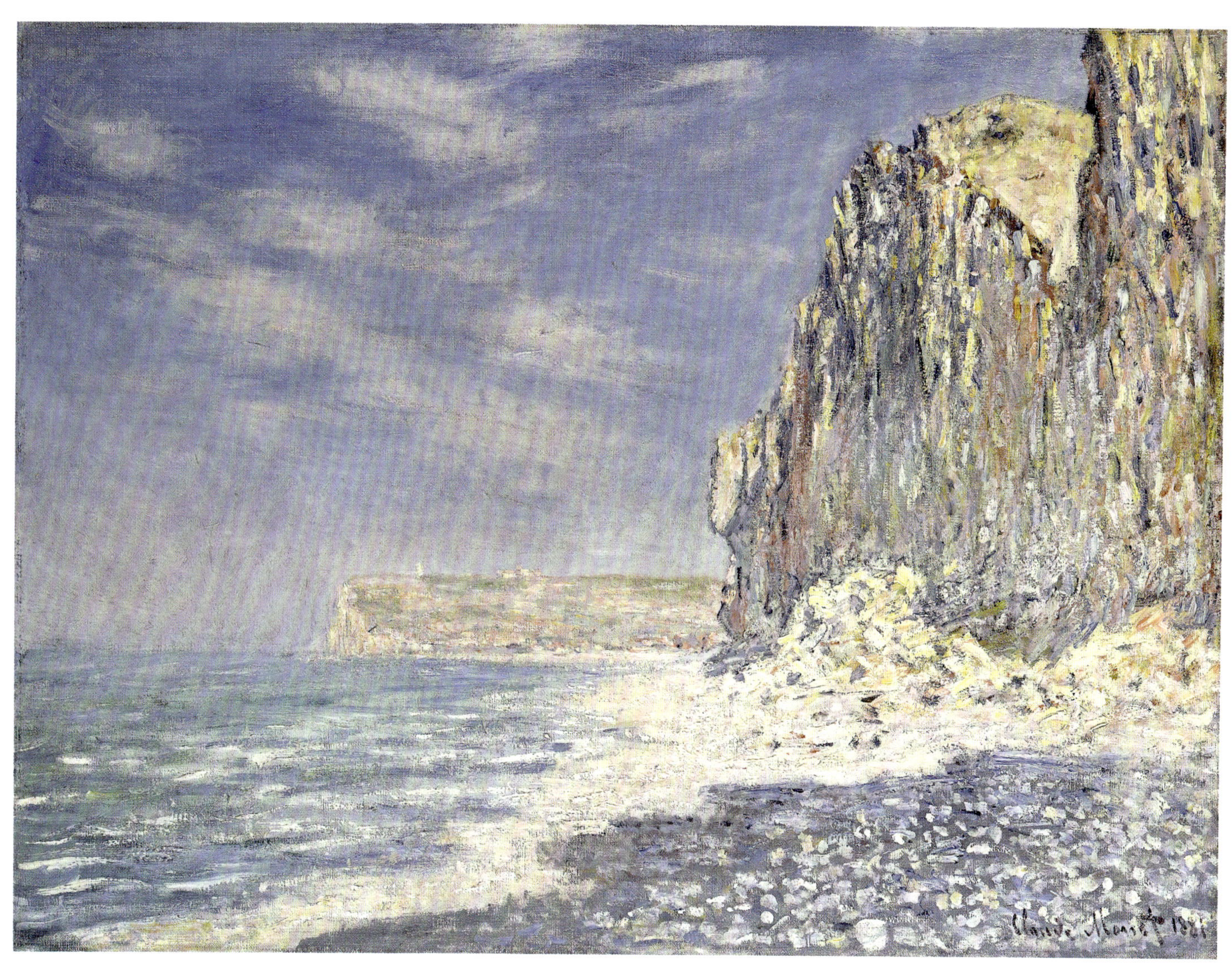

Claude Monet (1840–1926)

Cliffs near Fécamp

Falaise de Fécamp

Steilküste bei Fécamp

Acantilados en Fécamp

Penhascos de Fécamp

Klippen bij Fécamp

1881, Oil on canvas/Huile sur toile, 61 × 79 cm, Private collection

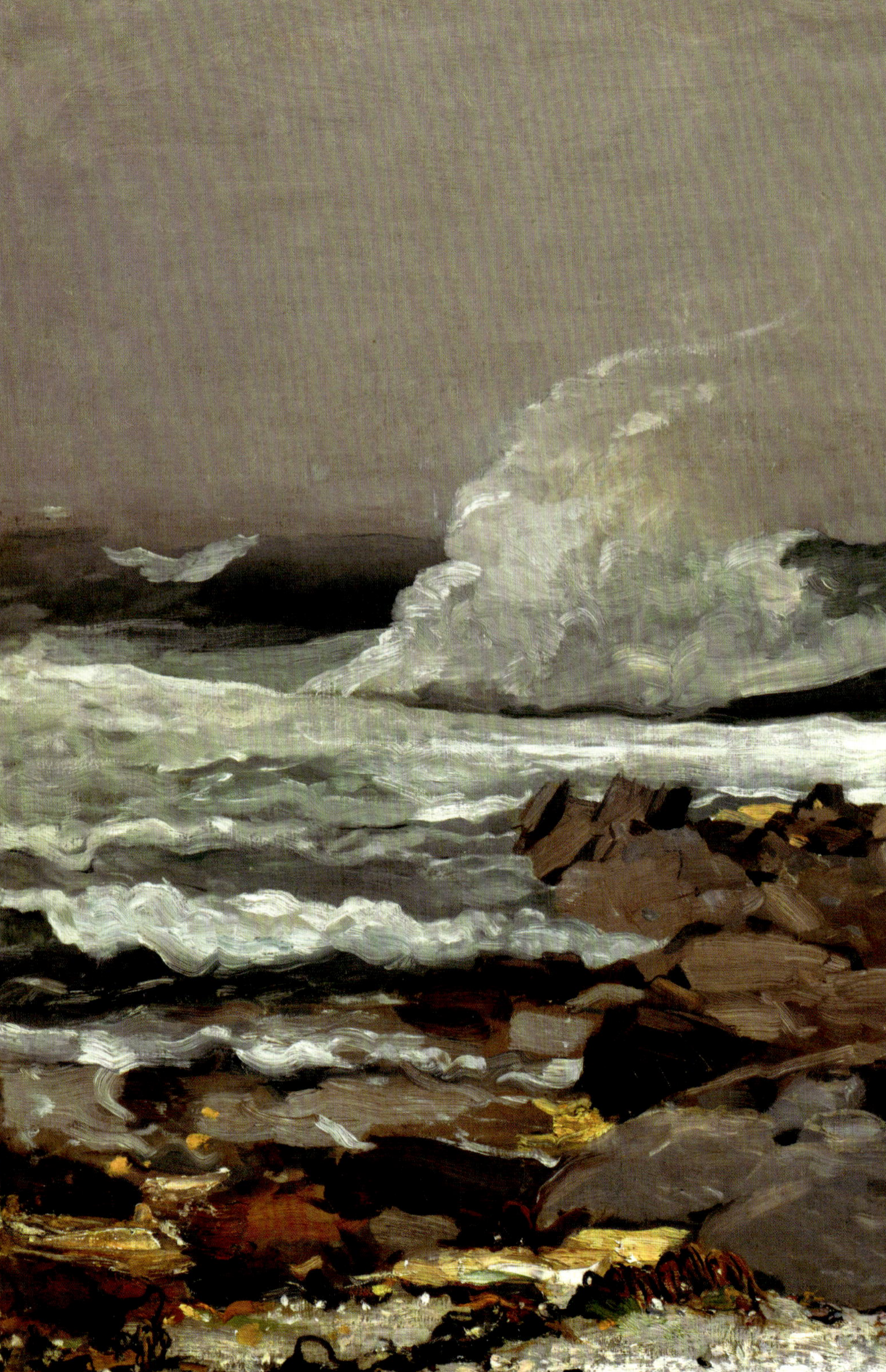

*The work of American painter Winslow Homer
is as extensive as it is diverse. Maritime pictures
occupy a special place, although he discovered his
love for the sea very late in life, when he settled near
the northern town of Tynemouth, England in 1881.
The year and a half he spent there forever changed
Homer's style, as can be seen in this image of the
coast of Eastern Point peninsula in Massachusetts.*

*Le travail du peintre américain Winslow Homer
est aussi large que varié. Les images maritimes
occupent un endroit spécial, bien qu'il ait découvert
très tard son amour pour la mer, lorsqu'il
s'installa en 1881 près de la ville de Tynemouth,
au nord de l'Angleterre. L'année et demie passé
là-bas changea pour toujours le style d'Homère,
comme on peut le voir sur cette représentation
du point Est de la péninsule Massachusetts.*

*Das Werk des US-Amerikaners Winslow Homer
ist so umfangreich wie vielfältig. Maritime Bilder
nehmen darin einen besonderen Platz ein, obwohl
er erst recht spät seine Liebe zum Meer entdeckt,
als er sich 1881 für anderthalb Jahre nahe der
nordenglischen Stadt Tynemouth niederließ. Dieser
Aufenthalt veränderte seinen Stil nachhaltig,
was sich auch in diesem Bild von der Küste der
Halbinsel Eastern Point in Massachusetts zeigt.*

*La obra del artista estadounidense Winslow Homer
es tan amplia como variada. Las marinas ocupan
un lugar muy especial, pese a que descubrió muy
tarde su amor por el mar, cuando se estableció en
1881 durante dieciocho meses cerca de la ciudad de
Tynemouth, al norte de Inglaterra. Esta estancia
cambió su estilo de manera permanente, lo que
también se refleja en esta imagen de la costa de
la península Eastern Point en Massachusetts.*

*A obra do norte-americano Winslow Homer é
tão vasta quanto variada. Quadros de marinhas
ocupam aí um lugar especial, apesar de que ele
somente descobriu seu amor pelo mar muito tarde,
quando se estabeleceu, em 1881, por um ano e meio,
perto de Tynemouth, cidade inglesa do norte da
Inglaterra. Essa estadia mudou seu estilo de forma
duradoura, como demonstra este quadro da costa
da península de Eastern Point, em Massachusetts.*

*Het oeuvre van de Amerikaan Winslow Homer
is evenzo omvangrijk als veelzijdig. Maritieme
schilderijen nemen daarin een bijzondere plaats
in, hoewel hij vrij laat zijn liefde voor de zee
ontdekte, toen hij in 1881 anderhalf jaar lang
in het Noord-Engelse Tynemouth verbleef. Dit
bezoek veranderde zijn stijl definitief, wat ook
te zien is in dit schilderij van de kust van het
schiereilandje Eastern Point in Massachusetts.*

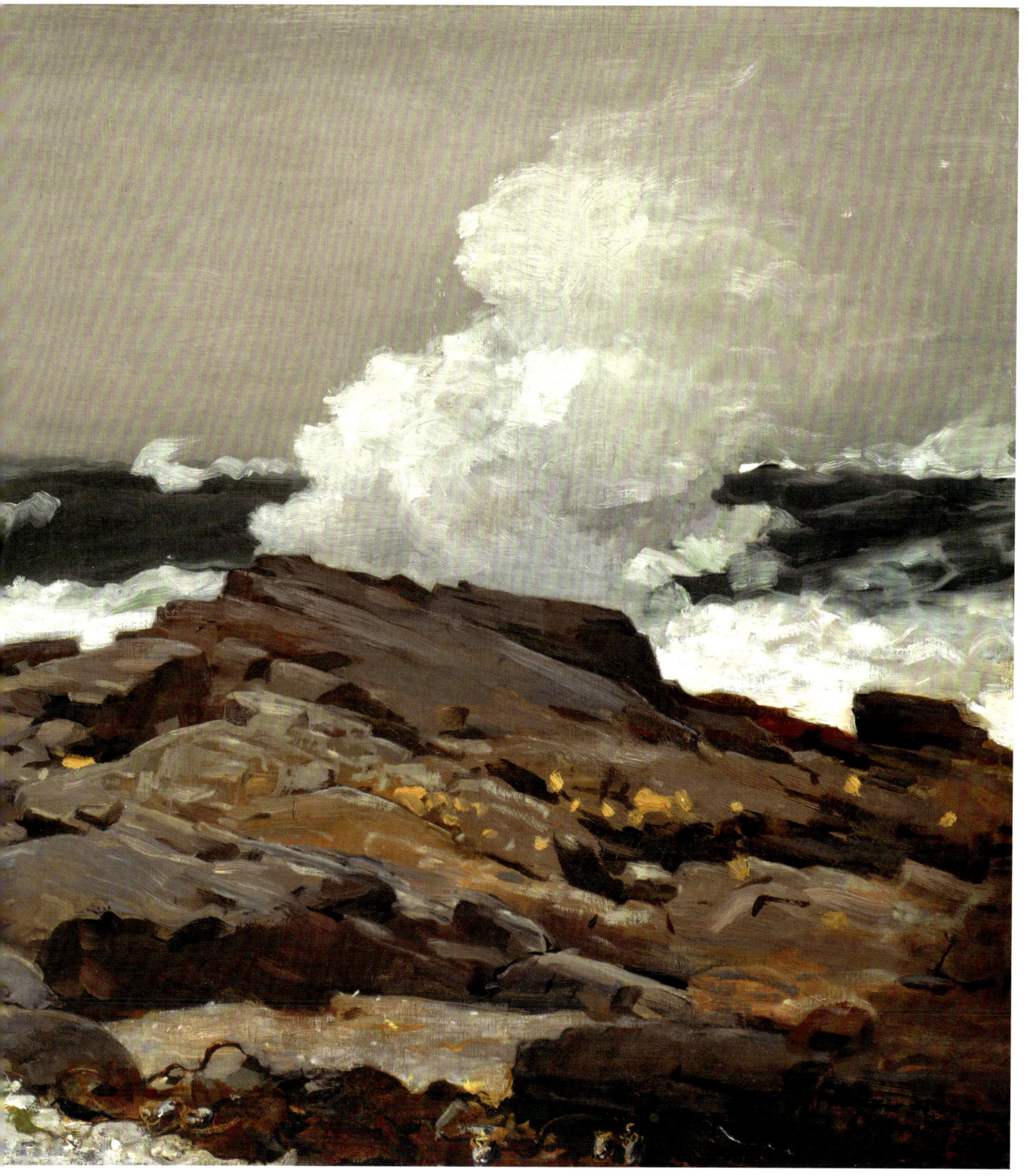

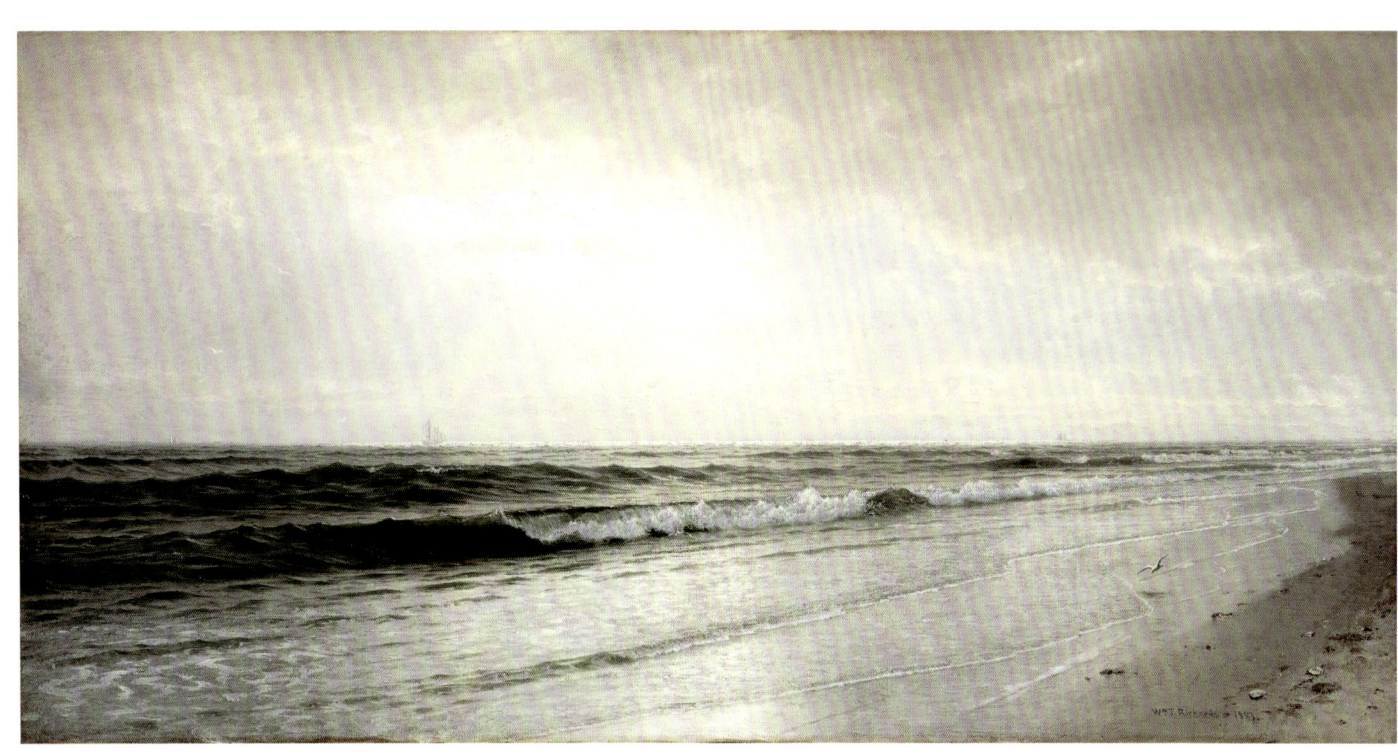

William Trost Richards (1833–1905)

Quiet Seascape

Paysage de mer silencieux

Ruhiges Meerespanorama

Paisaje marino en calma

Paisagem marinha calma

Gezicht op een kalme zee

1883, Oil on canvas/Huile sur toile, 51,1 × 101,6 cm, Minneapolis Institute of Arts, Minneapolis

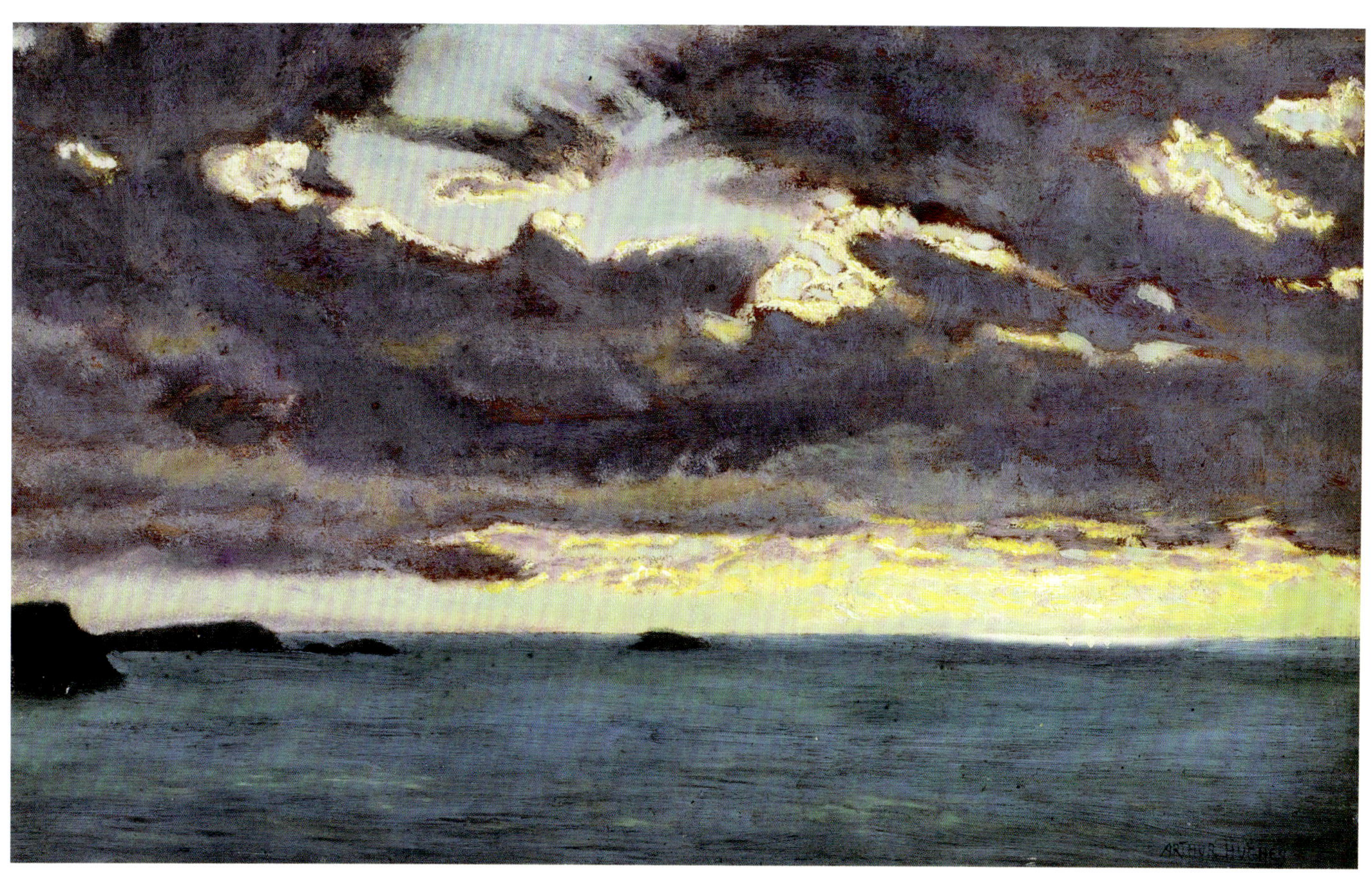

Arthur Hughes (1832–1915)

From Pentire Point

Vue de Pentire Point

Blick von Pentire Point

Vista de Pentire Point

Vista de Pentire Point

Gezicht vanaf Pentire Point

n. d., Oil on panel/Huile sur bois, 22,2 × 38,1 cm, Private collection

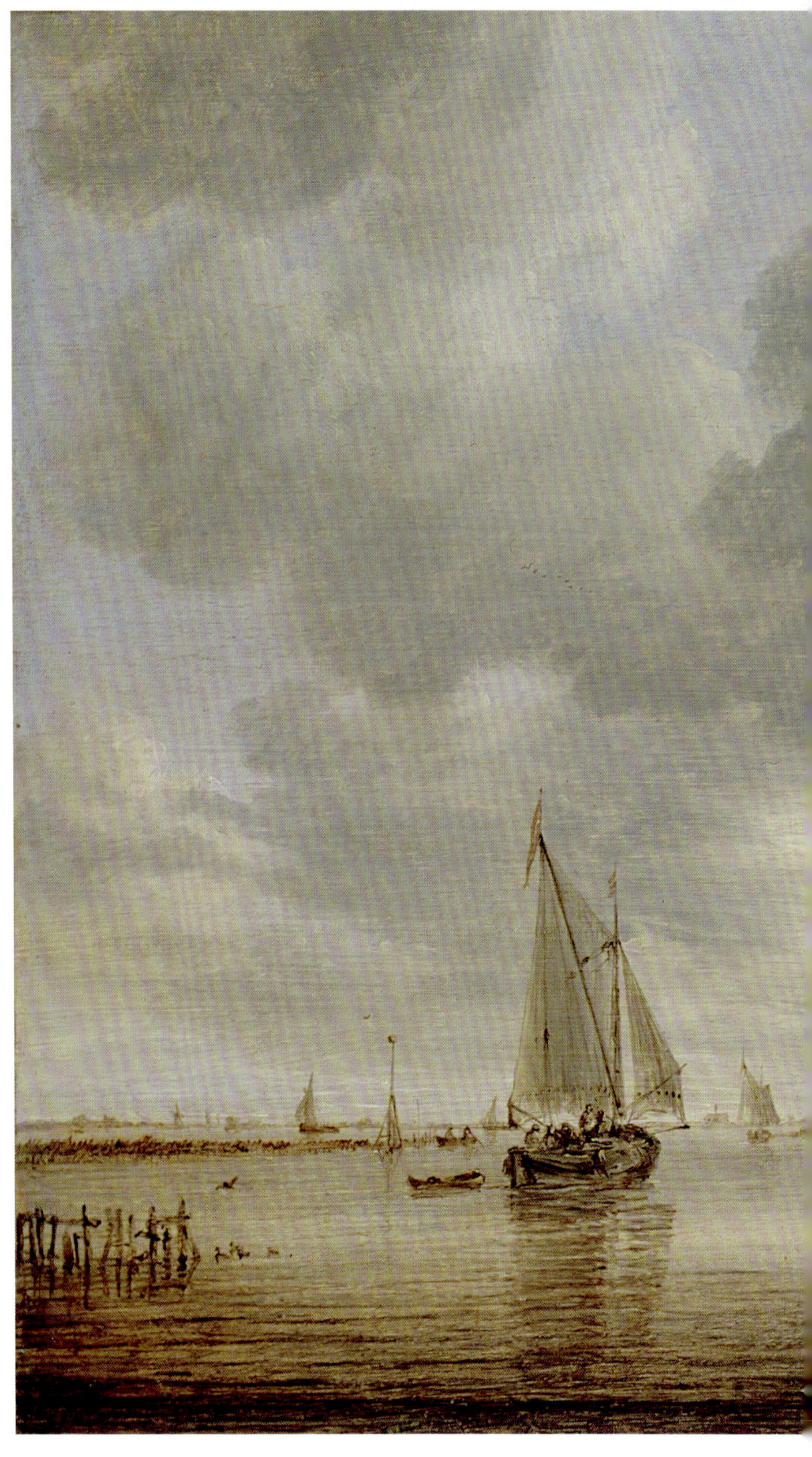

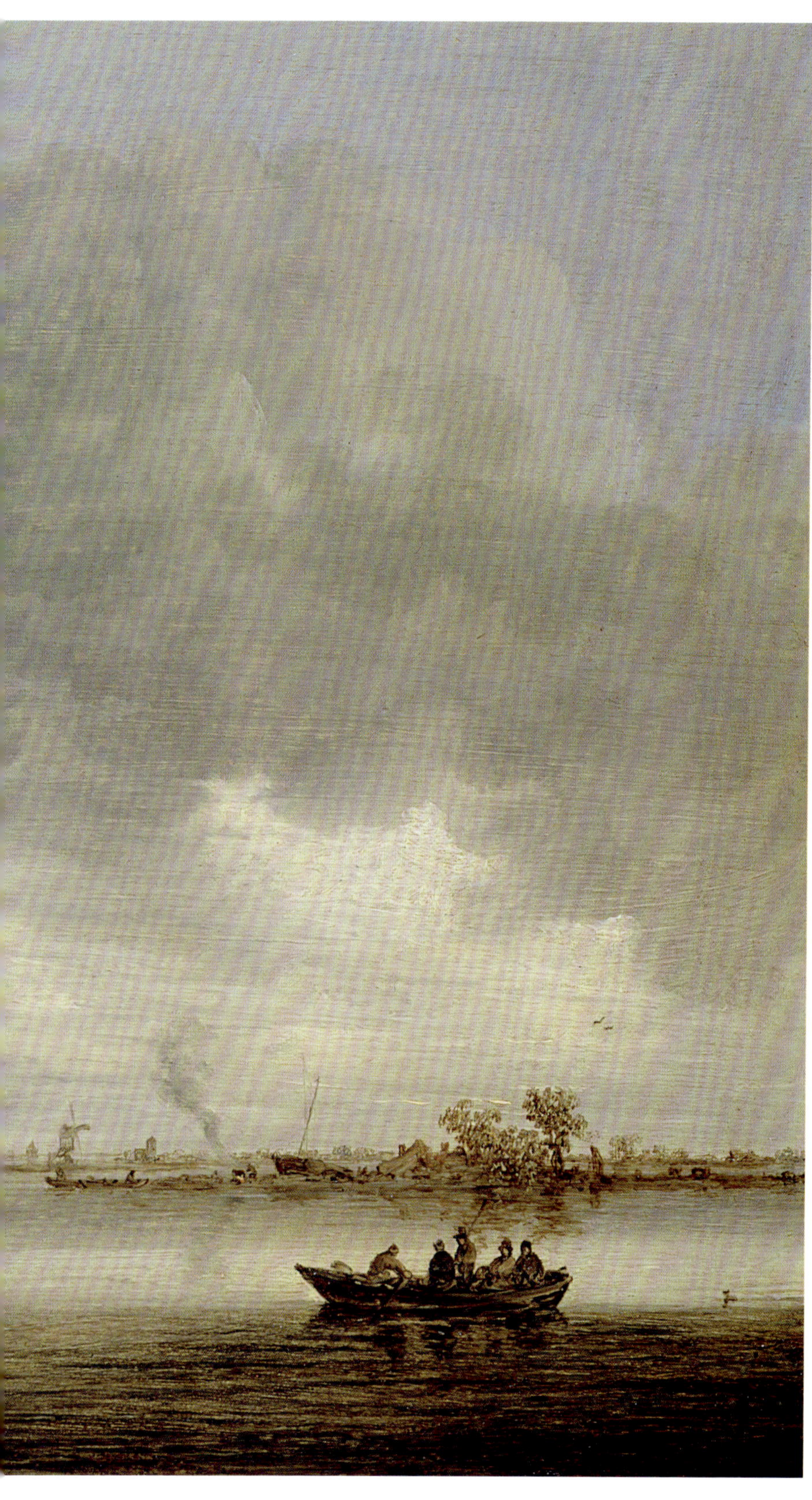

Even if seascapes were the exception in oeuvre of Leiden's master painter Jan van Goyen, ships appear in many of his works, as can be seen here in this fine late work, which shows us boats at the mouth of a river.

Même si les paysages marins étaient l'exception dans l'œuvre du grand peintre Jan van Goyen de Leyde, les navires apparaissent dans un grand nombre de ses œuvres, comme on peut le voir ici dans ce travail tardif présentant des bateaux à l'embouchure d'une rivière.

Auch wenn Seestücke im eigentlichen Sinn eher eine Ausnahme im Œuvre des Leidener Meisters Jan van Goyen bilden, so finden sich Schiffe doch in zahlreichen seiner Werke. So auch hier in diesem feinen Spätwerk, das uns Boote in einer Flussmündung zeigt.

Aunque las marinas realmente son una excepción en la obra del maestro de Leiden Jan van Goyen, los barcos son elementos que se pueden encontrar en muchas de sus obras. Al igual que aquí, en esta delicada obra tardía, que muestra los barcos en un estuario.

Embora as marinhas propriamente sejam uma exceção na obra do mestre de Leiden Jan van Goyen, podemos encontrar navios em muitas de suas obras. Tal como aqui nesta refinada obra tardia, representando barcos em um estuário.

Ook al maken zeegezichten in de eigenlijke zin van het woord geen deel uit van het oeuvre van de Leidse meester Jan van Goyen, zijn toch op veel van zijn doeken schepen te zien. Zo ook in dit late werk, dat boten in de monding van een rivier toont.

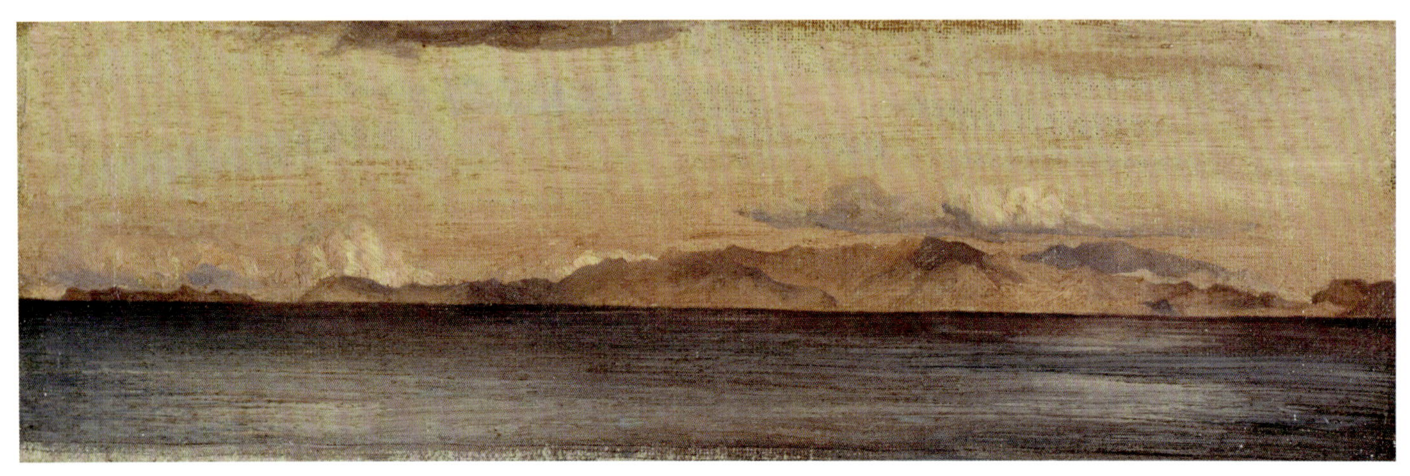

Frederic Leighton (1830–96)

Distant View of Mountains in the Aegean Sea

Vue éloignée des montagnes depuis la mer Égée

Entfernte Berge in der Ägäis

Vista lejana de montañas en el Mar Egeo

Montanhas distantes no Mar Egeu

Vergezicht op bergen aan de Egeïsche Zee

1867, Oil on canvas/Huile sur toile, 8 × 27 cm, National Museum Cardiff, Cardiff

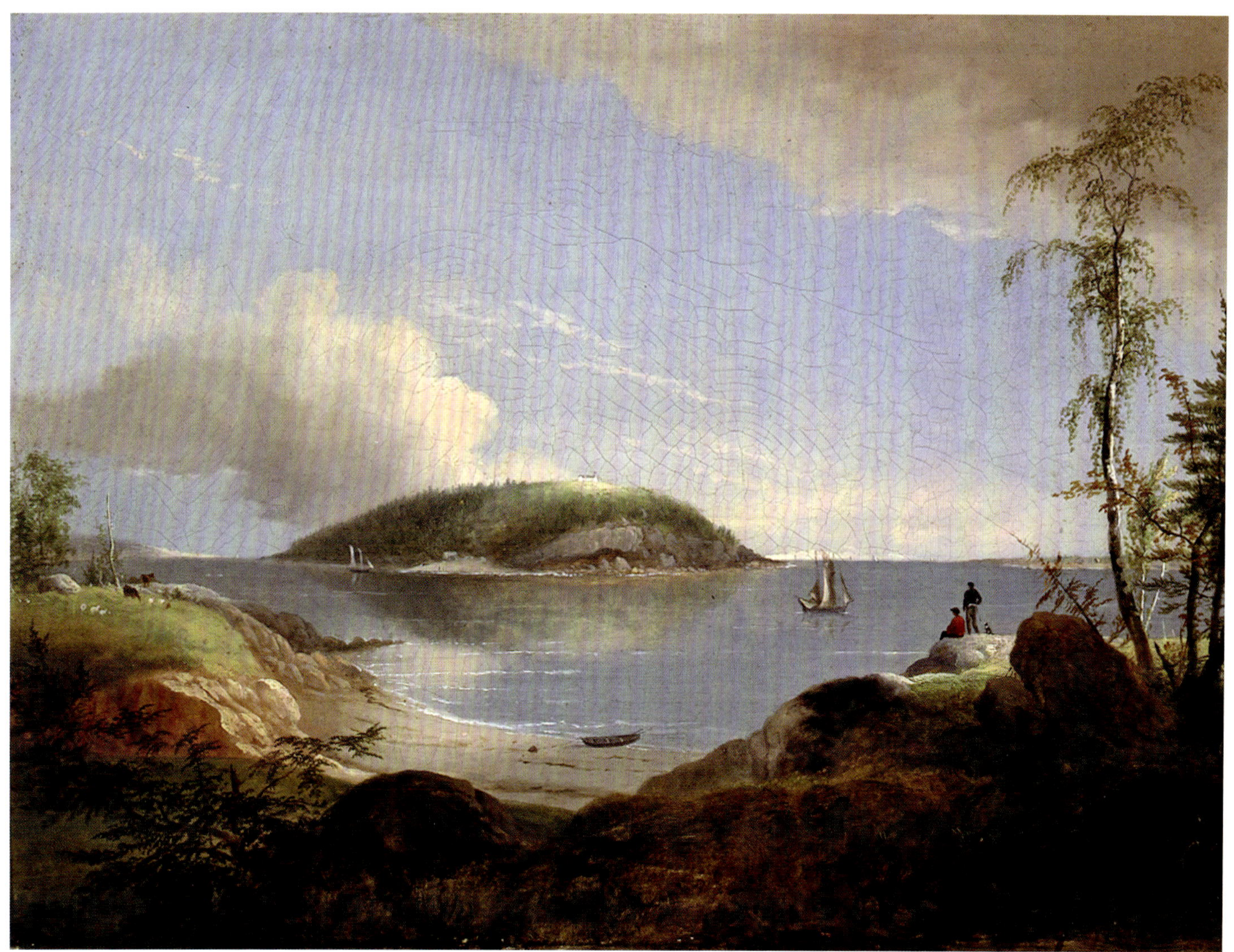

Alvan Fisher (1792–1863)
Souvenir of Bear Island, Maine
Souvenir de l'Île aux ours, Maine
Erinnerung an Bear Island, Maine
Recuerdo de Bear Island, Maine
Memória de Bear Island, Maine
Herinnering aan Bear Island, Maine
1850, Oil on canvas/Huile sur toile, 45,2 × 60,5 cm, Shelburne Museum, Shelburne

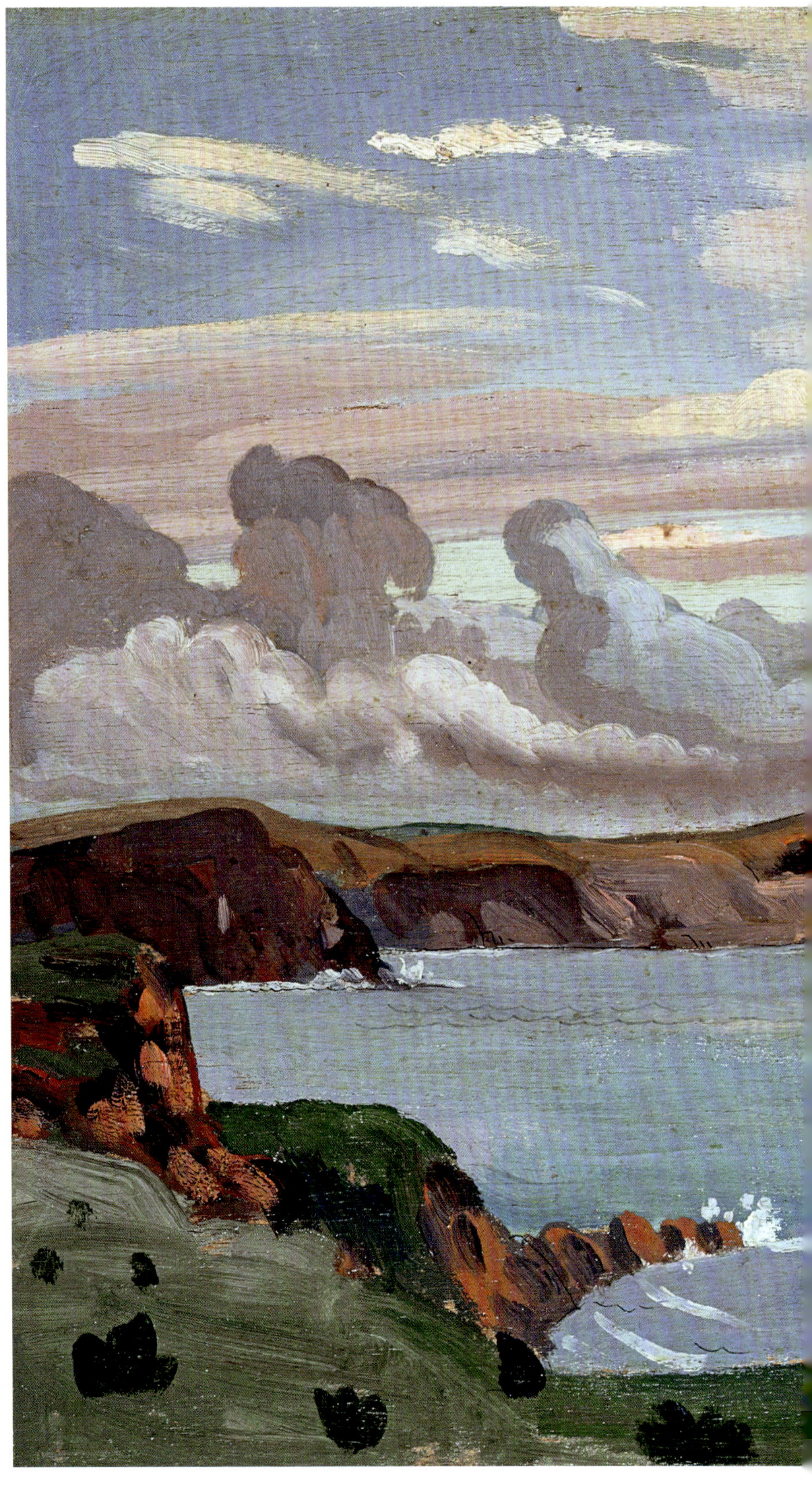

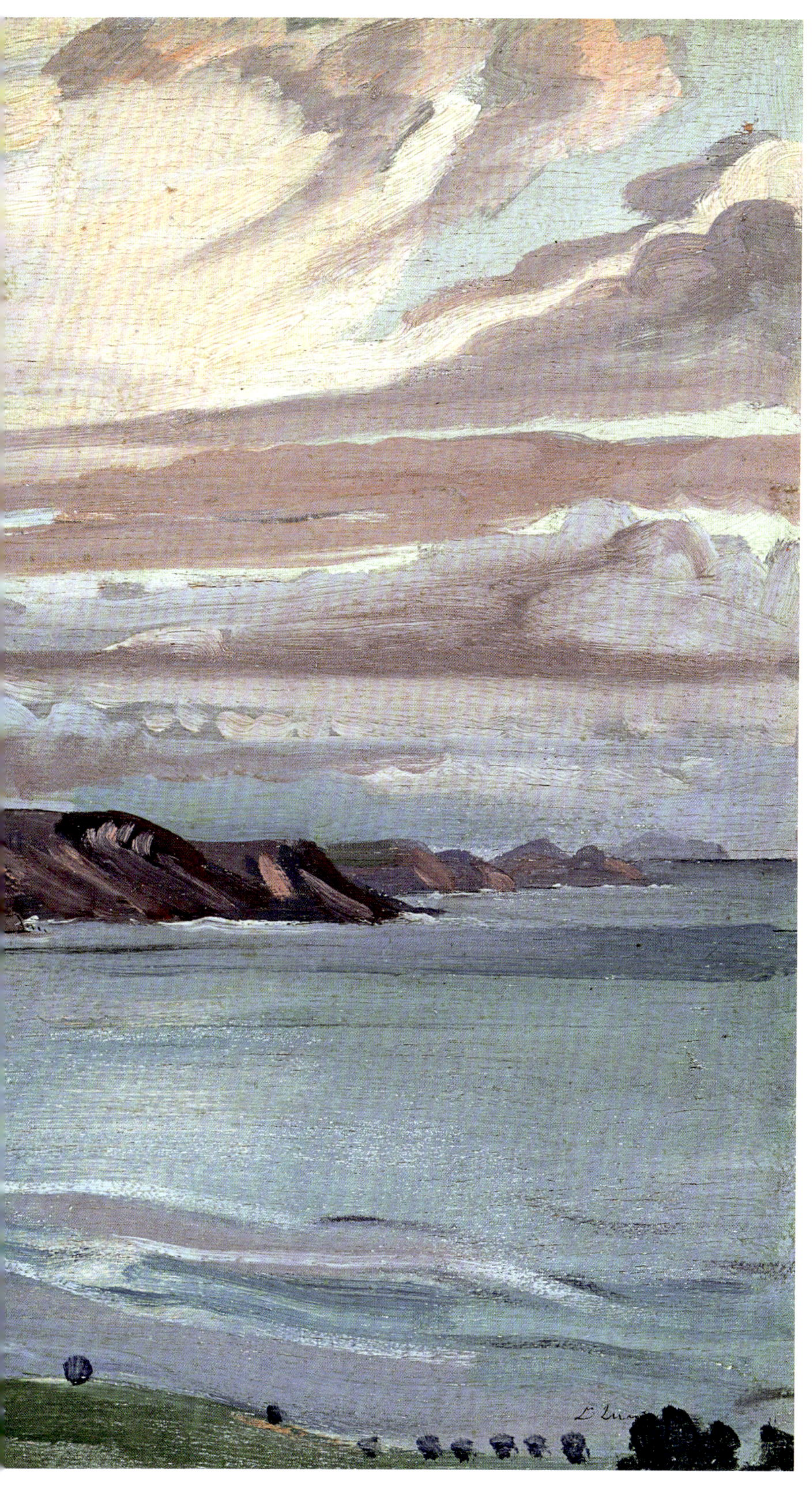

James Dickson Innes (1887–1914)

Pembroke Coast

Côte de Pembroke

Küste in Pembrokeshire

Costa de Pembrokeshire

Costa em Pembrokeshire

De kust van Pembrokeshire

n. d., Oil on panel/Huile sur bois, 33,2 × 40,2 cm,
National Museum Cardiff, Cardiff

*This landscape by Welsh painter James Dickson Innes shows
the South Wales coast from the time just before the First World
War. During this time, Innes often painted with his friend
Augustus John, a fact reflected in the style of this image.*

*Ce paysage du peintre gallois James Dickson Innes présente la côte
du pays de Galles du Sud juste avant la Première Guerre mondiale.
Au cours de cette période, Innes peignait souvent avec son ami
Augustus John, un fait qui se reflète dans le style de cette image.*

*Dieses Landschaftsbild des Walisers James Dickson Innes aus der
Zeit kurz vor dem Ersten Weltkrieg zeigt die südwalisische Küste.
In dieser Zeit malte Innes oft mit seinem Freund Augustus John
zusammen, was sich auch im Stil dieses Bildes widerspiegelt.*

*Este paisaje del galés James Dickson Innes, de la época previa a la
Primera Guerra Mundial, muestra la costa del sur de Gales. En
aquella época, Innes pintó a menudo junto a su amigo Augustus
John, lo que también se refleja en el estilo de esta imagen.*

*Esta paisagem do galês James Dickson Innes, datando de pouco
antes da Primeira Guerra Mundial, exibe a costa sul de Gales.
Nessa época, Innes pintava frequentemente com seu amigo
Augustus John, o que também se reflete no estilo desse quadro.*

*Dit landschap van de schilder James Dickson Innes uit Wales,
dat kort voor de Eerste Wereldoorlog ontstond, toont de kust van
Zuid-Wales. In deze tijd schilderde Innes vaak samen met zijn
vriend Augustus John, wat zich ook in de stijl van dit werk uit.*

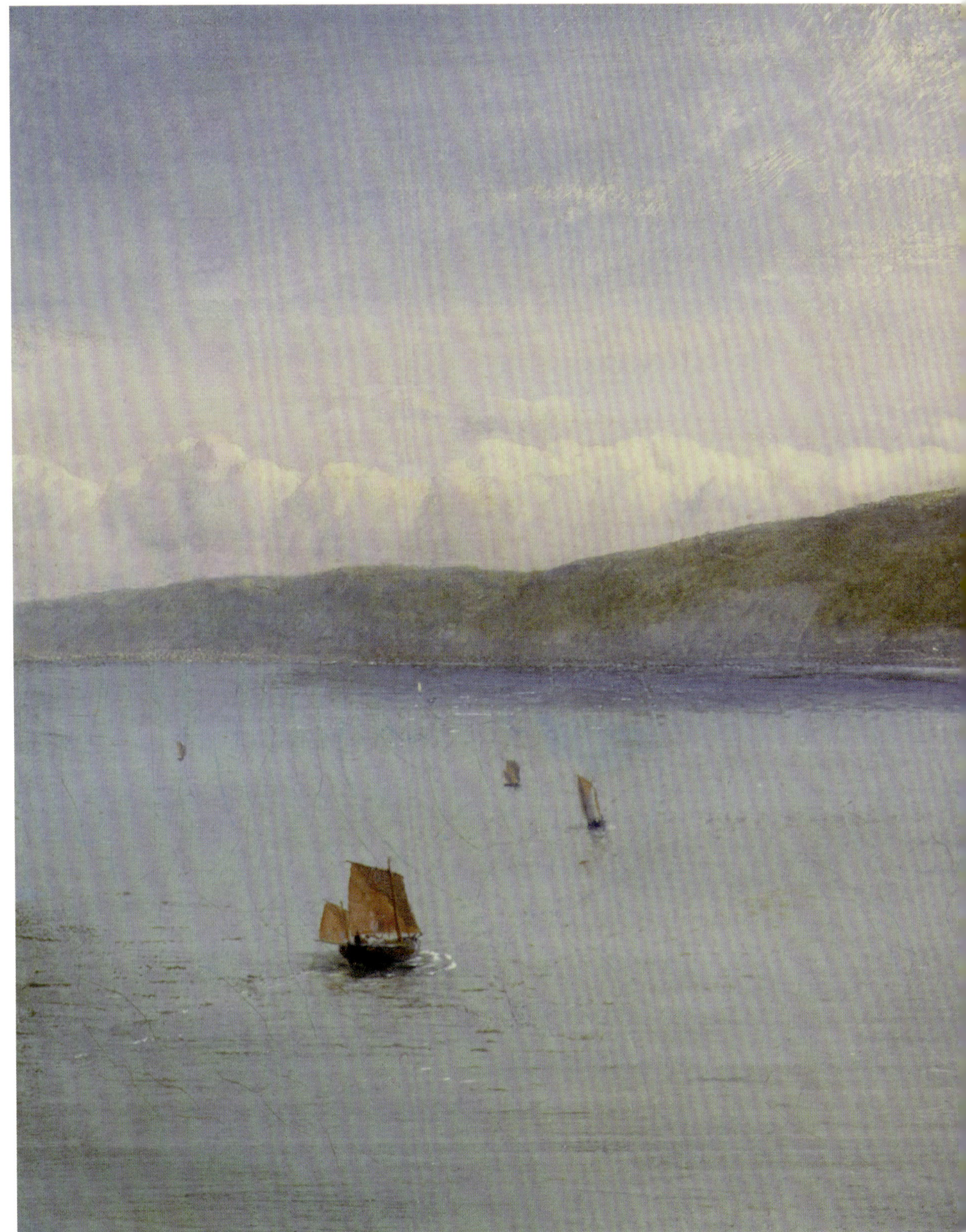

Charles Napier Hemy
(1841–1917)

The Sun-Lit Ocean

Océan éclairé
par le soleil

Sonnenbestrahltes
Meer

Mar con luz del sol

Mar raiado pelo sol

De door de zon
beschenen zee

1864, Oil on
canvas/Huile sur
toile, 28 × 48 cm,
Private collection

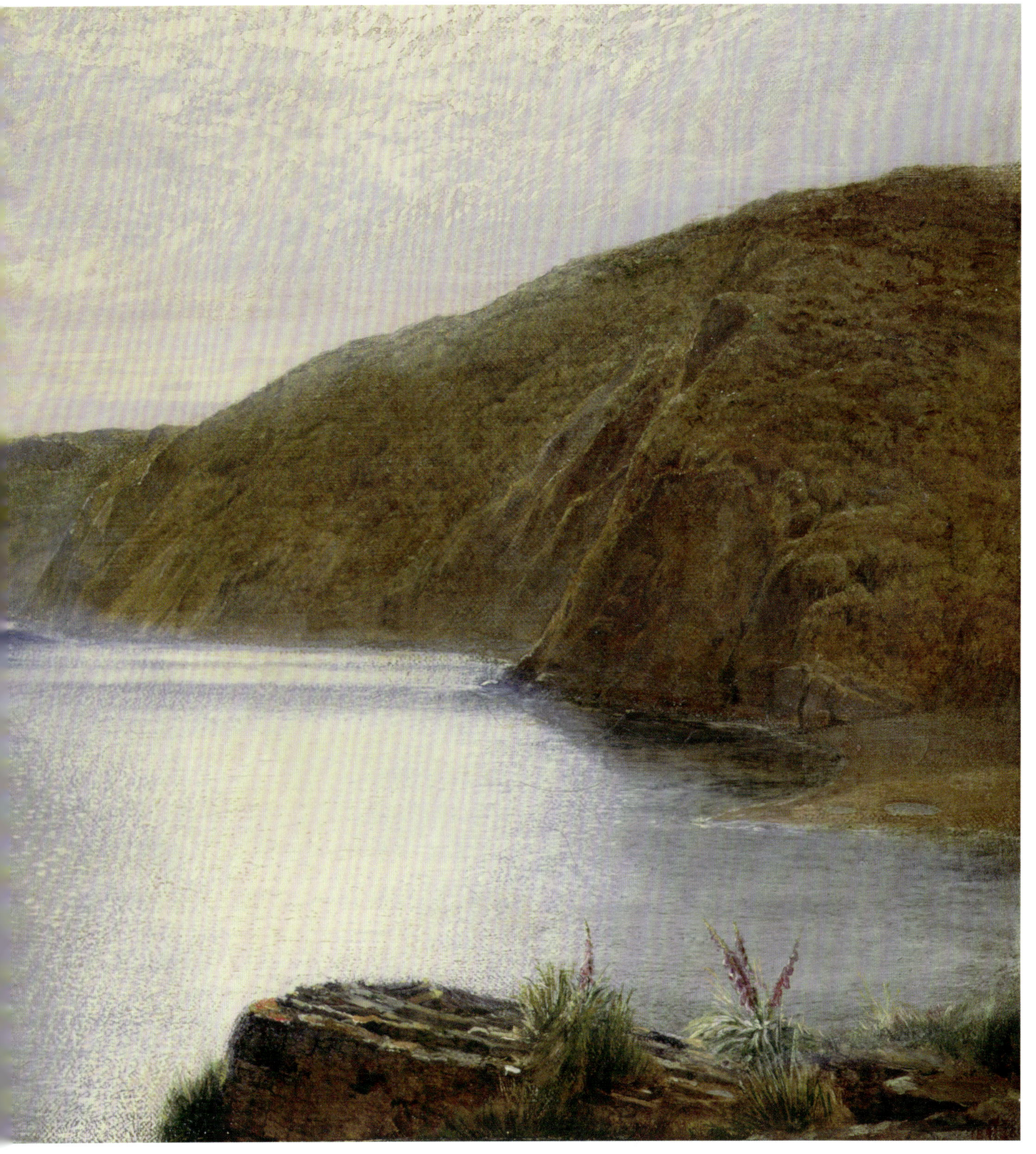

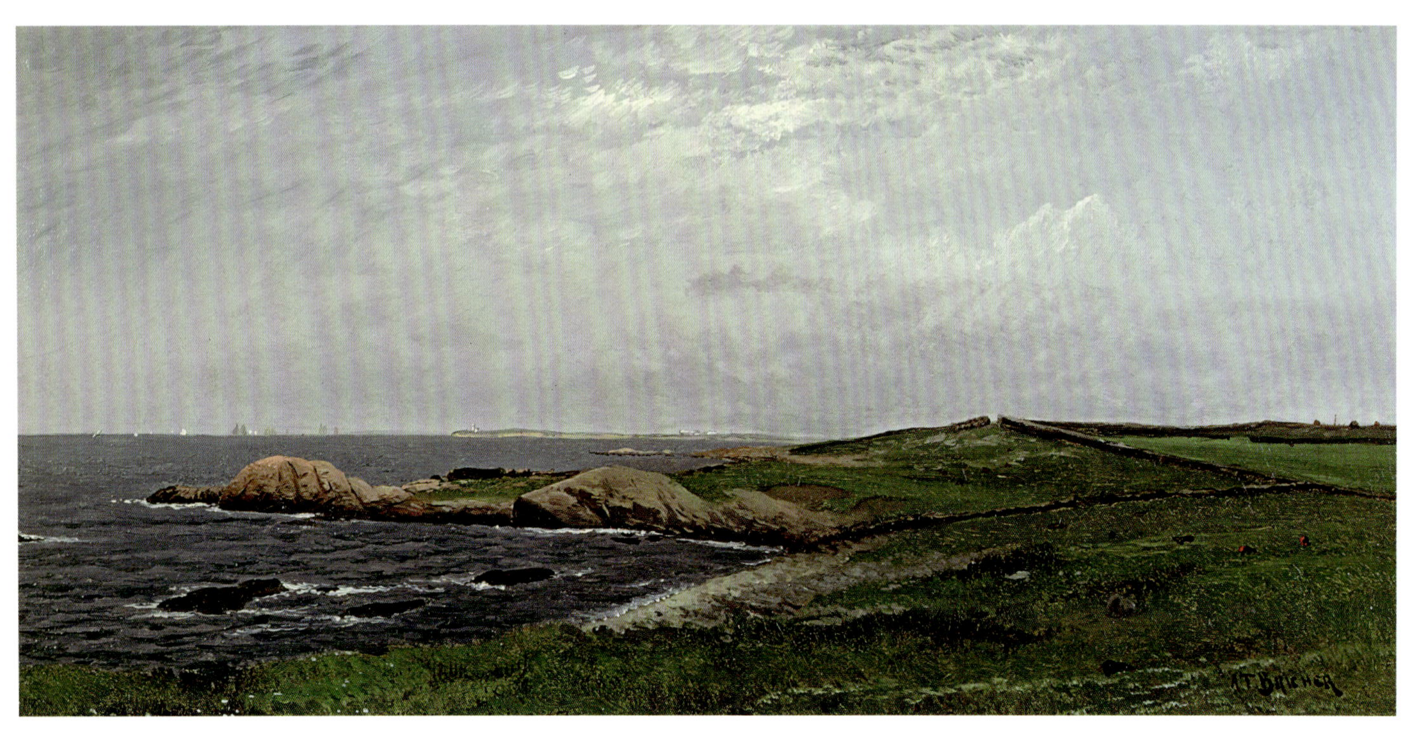

Alfred Thompson Bricher (1837–1908)

New England Coast

Côte de Nouvelle-Angleterre

Küste in Neuengland

Costa de Nueva Inglaterra

Costa na Nova Inglaterra

De kust van New England

n. d., Oil on canvas/Huile sur toile, Private collection

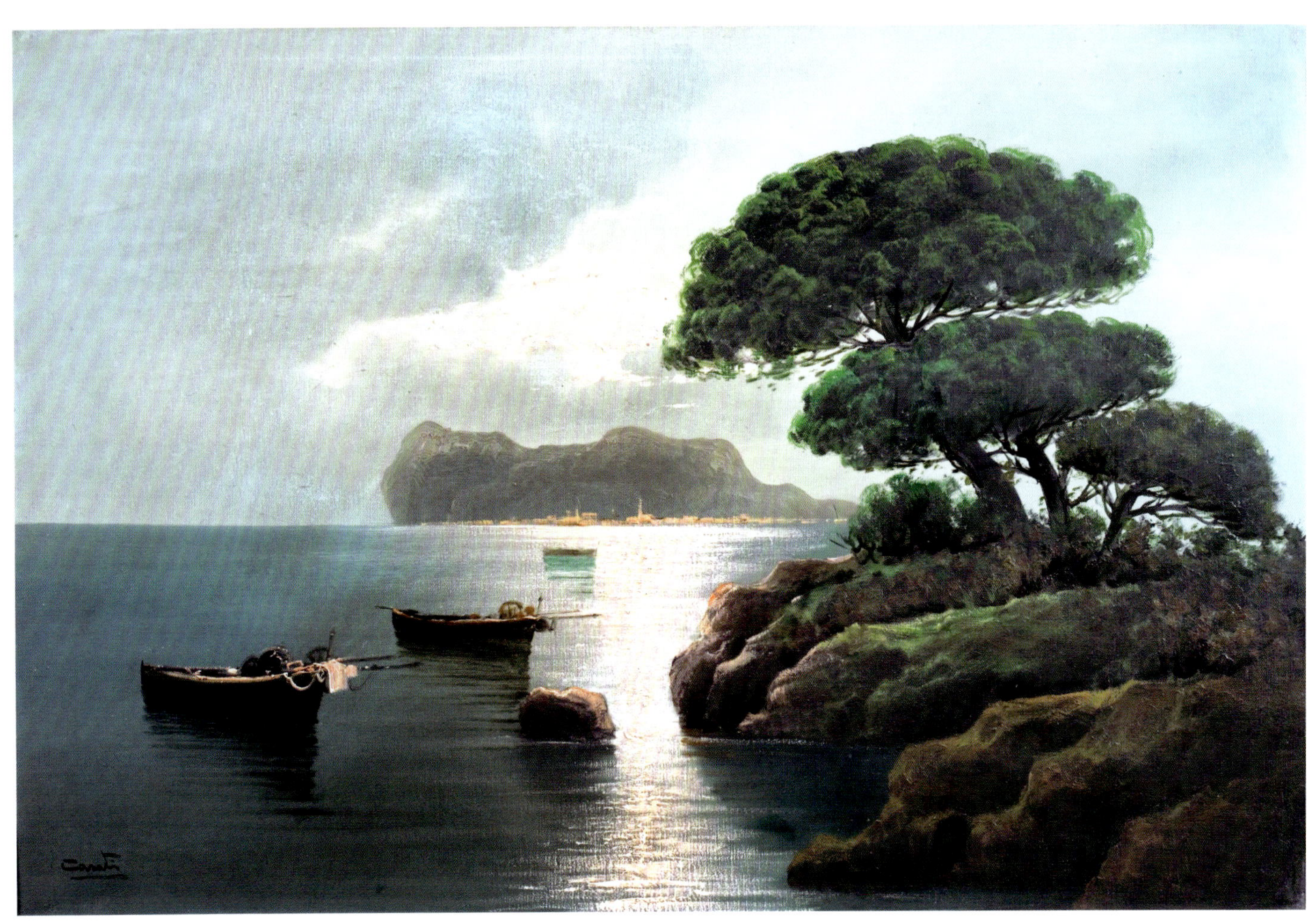

Italian school/École italienne

Seascape

Paysage de mer

Seestück

Pieza marina

Marinha

Zeegezicht

n. d., Oil on canvas/Huile sur toile, 61,4 × 92,2 cm, Shipley Art Gallery, Gateshead

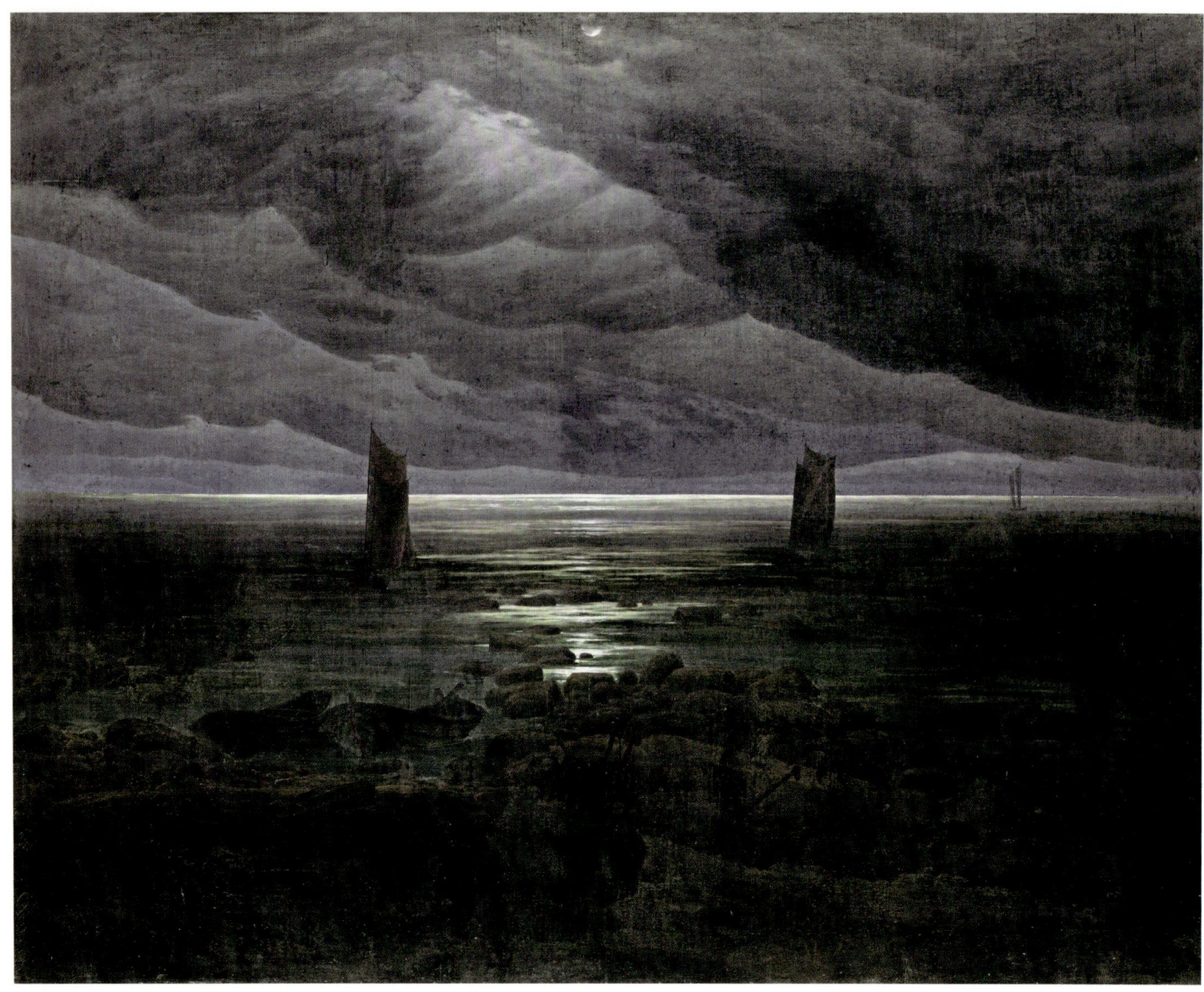

Caspar David Friedrich (1774–1840)

Sea Shore in Moonlight

Rivage par clair de lune

Meeresufer im Mondschein

Orilla del mar bajo la luz de la luna

Litoral ao luar

Kust bij maanlicht

c. 1835/36, Oil on canvas/Huile sur toile, 134 × 169,2 cm, Kunsthalle, Hamburg

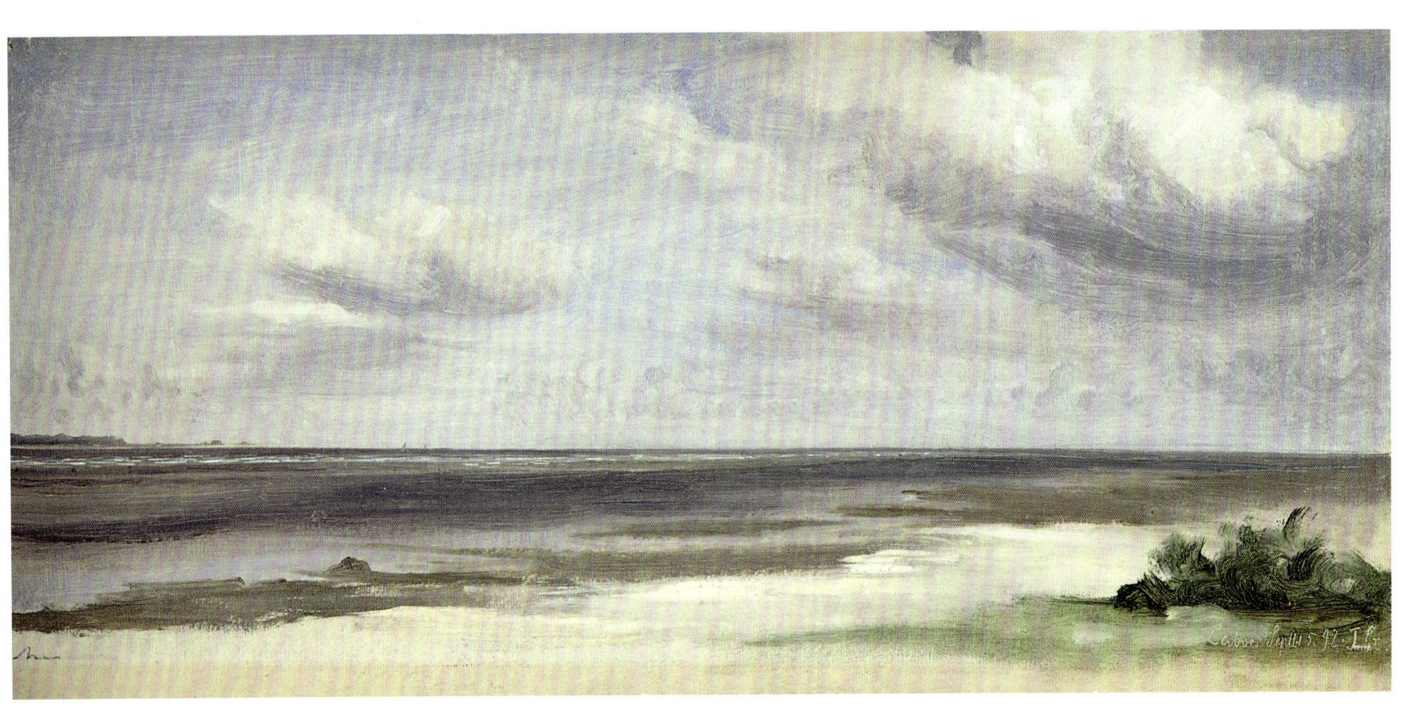

Jacob Gensler (1808–45)

A Beach on the Baltic Sea at Laboe

Plage de la Mer baltique à Laboe

Strand an der Ostsee bei Laboe

Playa en el Mar Báltico en Laboe

Praia no mar Báltico em Laboe

Strand aan de Oostzee bij Laboe

1842, Watercolor on paper/Aquarelle sur papier, 21,4 × 46,3 cm, Kunsthalle, Hamburg

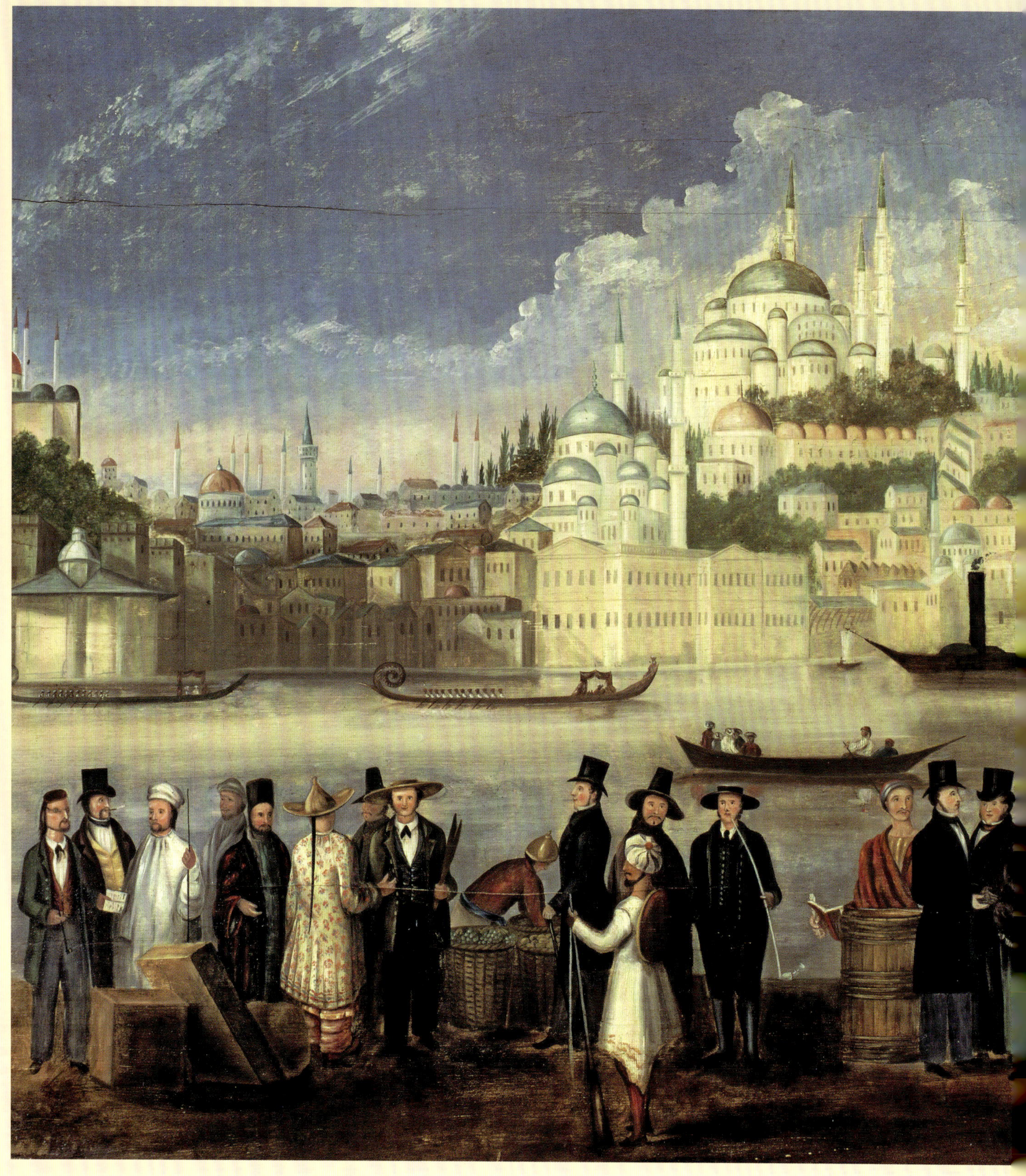

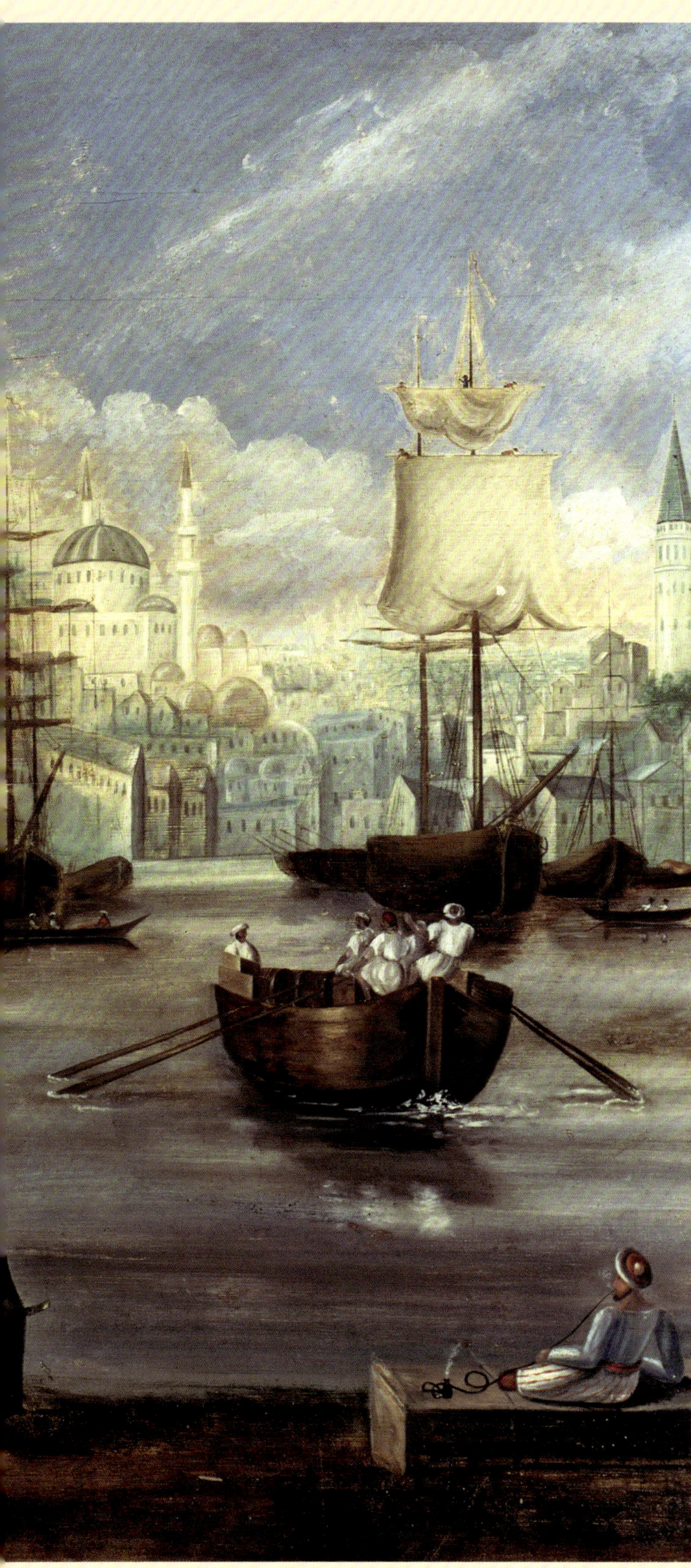

English school/École anglaise
On the Bosporus, Istanbul
Sur le Bosphore, Istanbul
Am Bosporus bei Istanbul
El Bósforo en Estambul
No Bósforo em Istambul
Aan de Bosporus bij Istanboel

19th century/XIXᵉ siècle, Oil on canvas/Huile sur toile, Atkinson Art Gallery, Southport

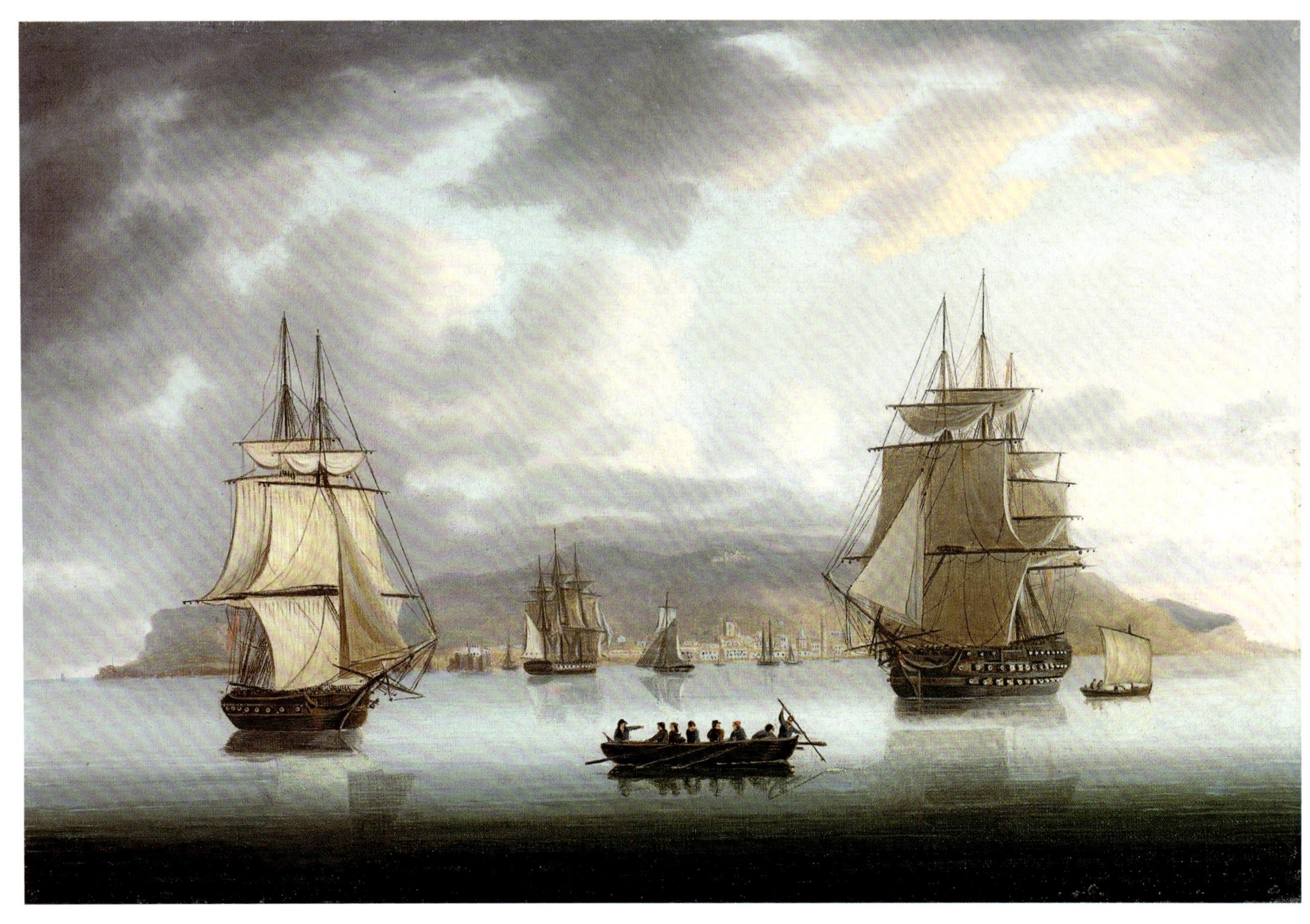

Thomas Buttersworth (1768–1842)

Funchal Roadstead, *HMS Blenheim* with *Greyhound* and *Harrier,* Outward Bound

Rade de Funchal, *HMS Blenheim* avec *Greyhound* et *Harrier,* voyage aller

Britische Schiffe vor der Reede von Funchal

Barcos ingleses en la rada de Funchal

Navios britânicos ao largo do porto do Funchal

Britse schepen op de rede van Funchal

1805, Oil on canvas/Huile sur toile, 29,9 × 43,8 cm, Private collection

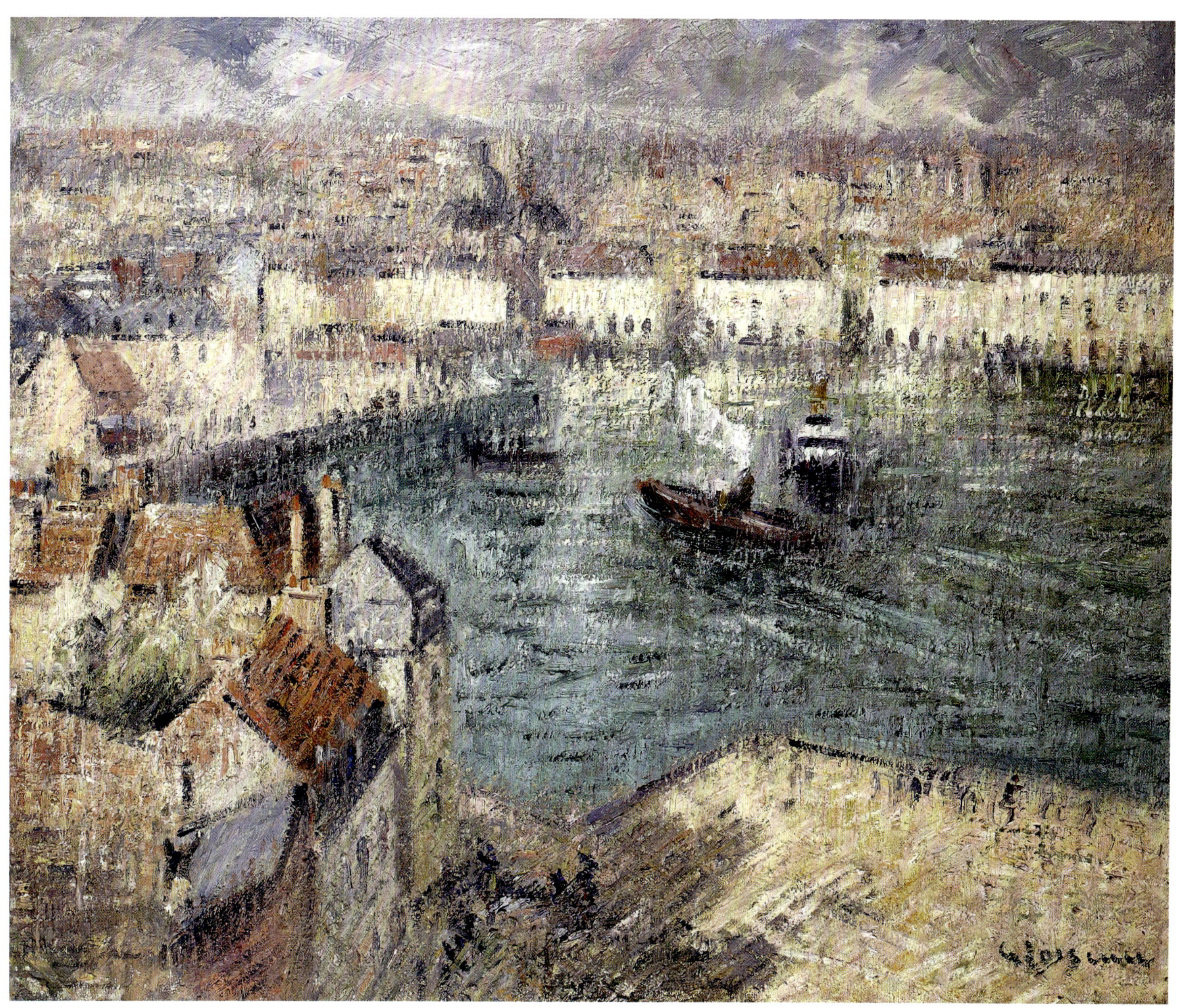

Gustave Loiseau (1865–1935)

Dieppe

1929, Oil on canvas/Huile sur toile, 60,3 × 73,6 cm, Private collection

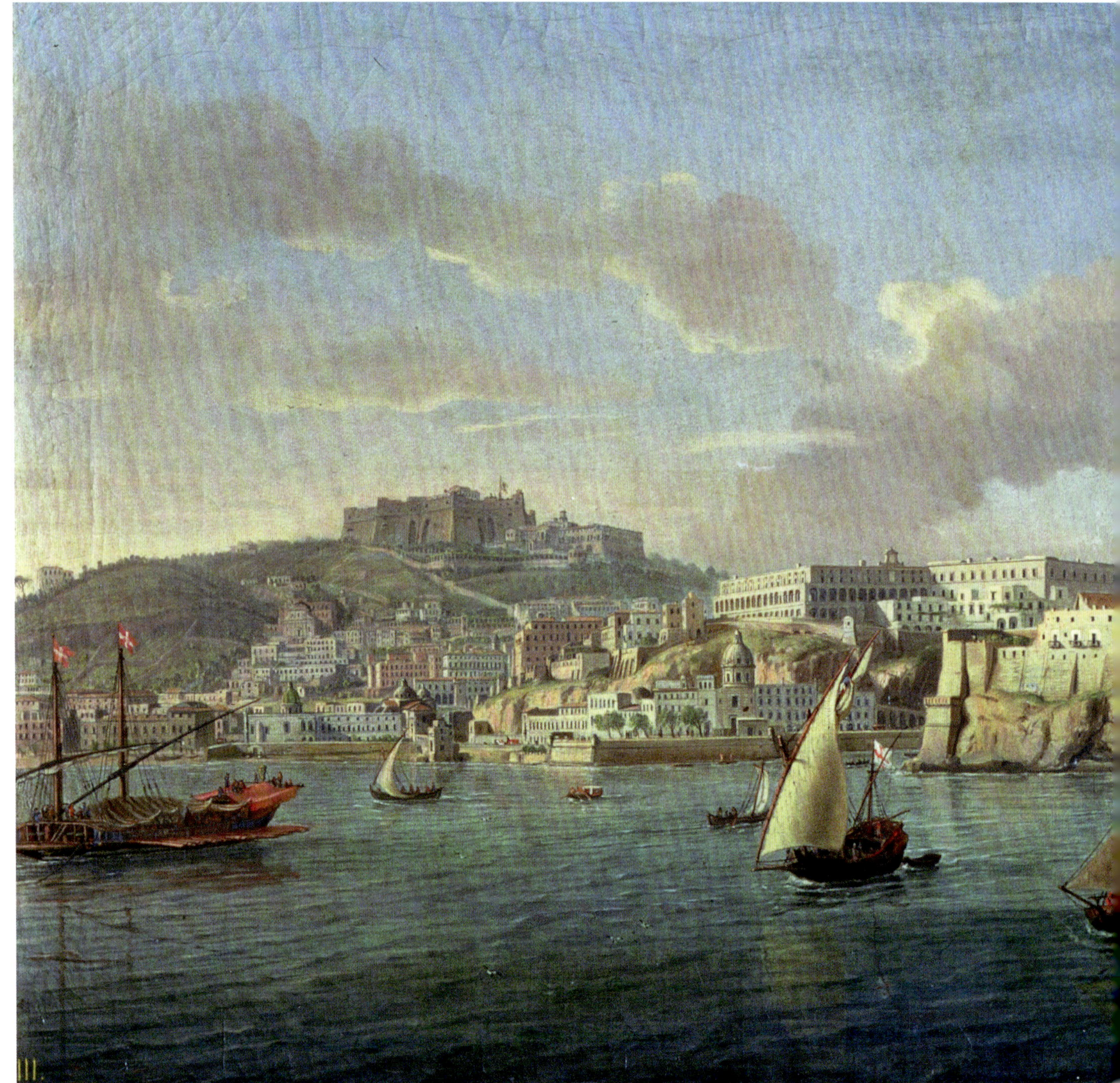

Gaspar van Wittel (1653–1736)

View of Naples

n. d., Oil on panel/Huile sur bois, 48,5 × 102,7 cm, Palazzo Pitti, Firenze

Gaspar van Wittel (also known as Gaspare Vanvitelli) was born in Utrecht but went to Italy in his early 20s, where he became an extremely productive painter of vedute (landscapes). This view of Naples reveals van Wittel's interest in topographically exact representations.

Vue de Naples

Gaspar van Wittel (également connu sous le nom de Gaspare Vanvitelli) est né à Utrecht mais partit en Italie dans la vingtaine, où il devint un peintre extrêmement productif de vedute (paysages). Cette vue de Naples révèle l'intérêt de van Wittel pour des représentations topographiquement exactes.

Blick auf Neapel

Gaspar van Wittel (auch bekannt als Gaspare Vanvitelli), in Utrecht geboren, ging schon mit Anfang 20 nach Italien, wo er zu einem äußerst produktiven Maler von Veduten wurde. Diese Ansicht von Neapel offenbart van Wittels Interesse an topographisch exakten Darstellungen.

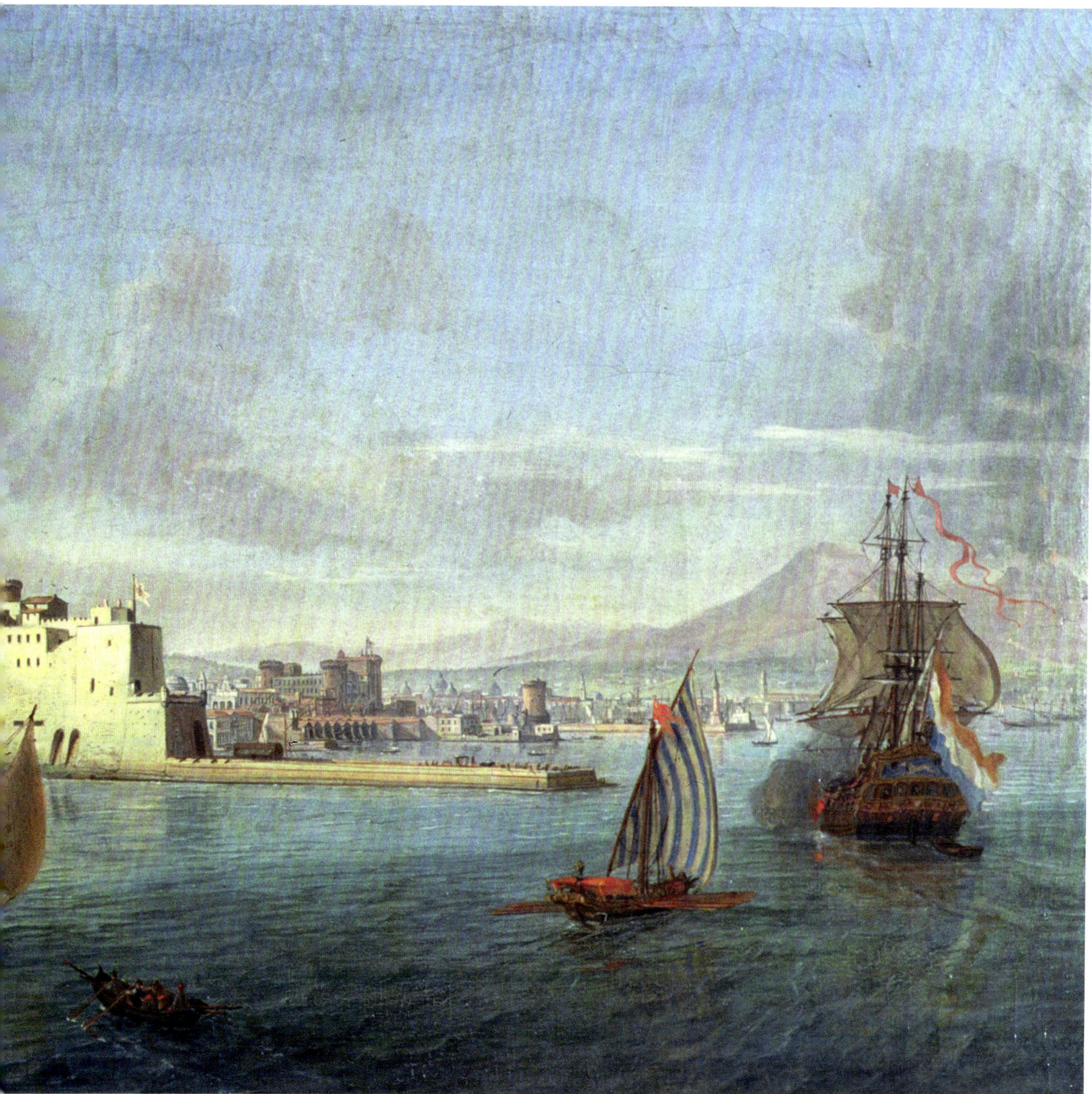

Vista de Nápoles

Gaspar van Wittel (también conocido como Gaspare Vanvitelli), nacido en Utrecht, viajó ya con unos 20 años a Italia, donde se convirtió en un prolífico pintor de vedute. Esta vista de Nápoles revela el interés de van Wittel por las representaciones topográficamente exactas.

Vista de Nápoles

Gaspar van Wittel (também conhecido como Gaspare Vanvitelli), nascido em Utrecht, foi para a Itália logo que ele completou 20 anos, onde ele se tornaria um prolífico pintor de vedutas. Esta vista de Nápoles revela o interesse de van Wittel por representações topograficamente precisas.

Gezicht op Napels

De in Utrecht geboren Gaspar van Wittel (ook bekend als Gaspare Vanvitelli) trok reeds als 20-jarige naar Italië, waar hij een zeer productieve schilder van vedute (weidse stadsgezichten) werd. Dit panorama van Napels getuigt van Van Wittels aandacht voor de topografische nauwkeurigheid van zijn werken.

Johan Barthold Jongkind (1819–91)

Dordrecht

1873, Oil on canvas/Huile sur toile, Private collection

Johan Barthold Jongkind, born in Lattrop, was a pupil of Paris-based maritime painter Eugène Isabey, who later helped his pupil get commissions. Psychologically unstable and later struggling with heavy drinking, his seascapes are particularly noteworthy for the influence they exerted on Boudin and Monet. Monet even said that Jongkind had "opened a door" for him.

Johan Barthold Jongkind, né à Lattrop, était un élève du peintre de mer Eugène Isabey, basé à Paris, qui l'aida ensuite à obtenir des commandes. Psychologiquement instable et luttant plus tard contre la consommation excessive, ses paysages marins sont particulièrement remarquables pour l'influence qu'ils ont exercée sur Boudin et Monet. Monet déclara même que Jongkind lui avait « ouvert une porte ».

Johan Barthold Jongkind, geboren in Lattrop, wurde in Paris Schüler des Marinemalers Eugène Isabey, der ihm auch half, an Aufträge zu kommen. Psychisch labil und später mit schweren Alkoholproblemen kämpfend, übte er vor allem mit seinen Seestücken großen Einfluss auf Maler wie Boudin und Monet aus, der über Jongkind sagte, dass dieser ihm „eine Tür geöffnet" habe.

Johan Barthold Jongkind, nacido en Lattrop, se convirtió en París en alumno del pintor de marinas Eugène Isabey, que también le ayudó a conseguir encargos. Era mentalmente inestable y más tarde tuvo que luchar con graves problemas con el alcohol, ejerció gran influencia, sobre todo con sus paisajes marinos, en pintores como Boudin y Monet, el cual dijo acerca de Jongkind, que éste le había "abierto una puerta".

Johan Barthold Jongkind, nascido em Lattrop, foi em París aluno do pintor de marinhas Eugène Isabey, que também o ajudou a conseguir encomendas. Mentalmente instável, e se debatendo mais tarde com problemas graves de álcool, ele exerceu, especialmente com suas marinhas, grande influência sobre pintores como Boudin e Monet, que revelaria, a respeito de Jongkind, que ele lhe havia "aberto uma porta".

De in Lattrop geboren Johan Barthold Jongkind werd in Parijs een leerling van de maritieme schilder Eugène Isabey, die hem ook aan opdrachten hielp. De psychisch labiele en later alcoholische Jongkind zou vooral met zijn zeegezichten grote invloed uitoefenen op schilders als Boudin en op Monet, die over Jongkind zei dat deze voor hem "een deur had geopend".

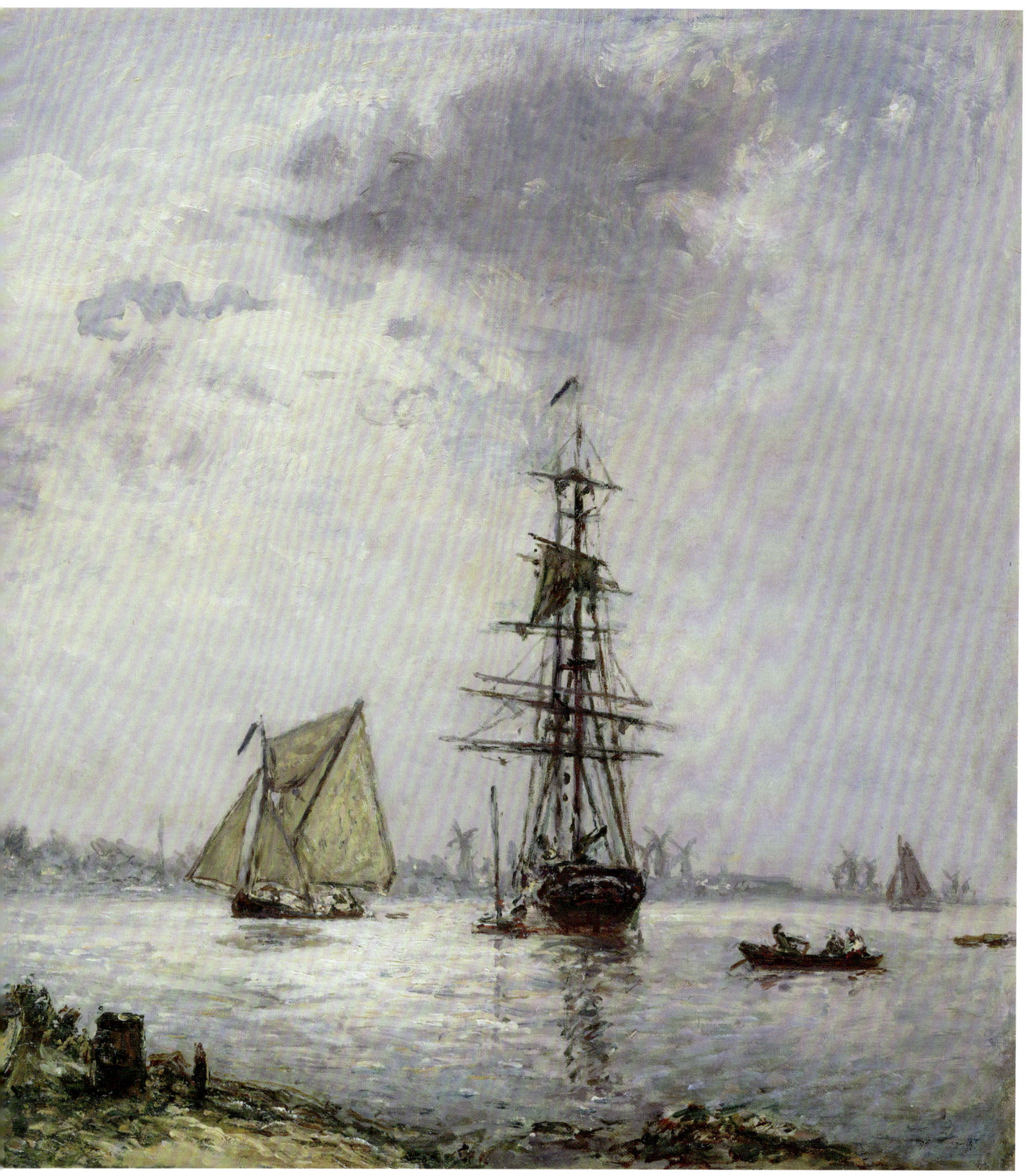

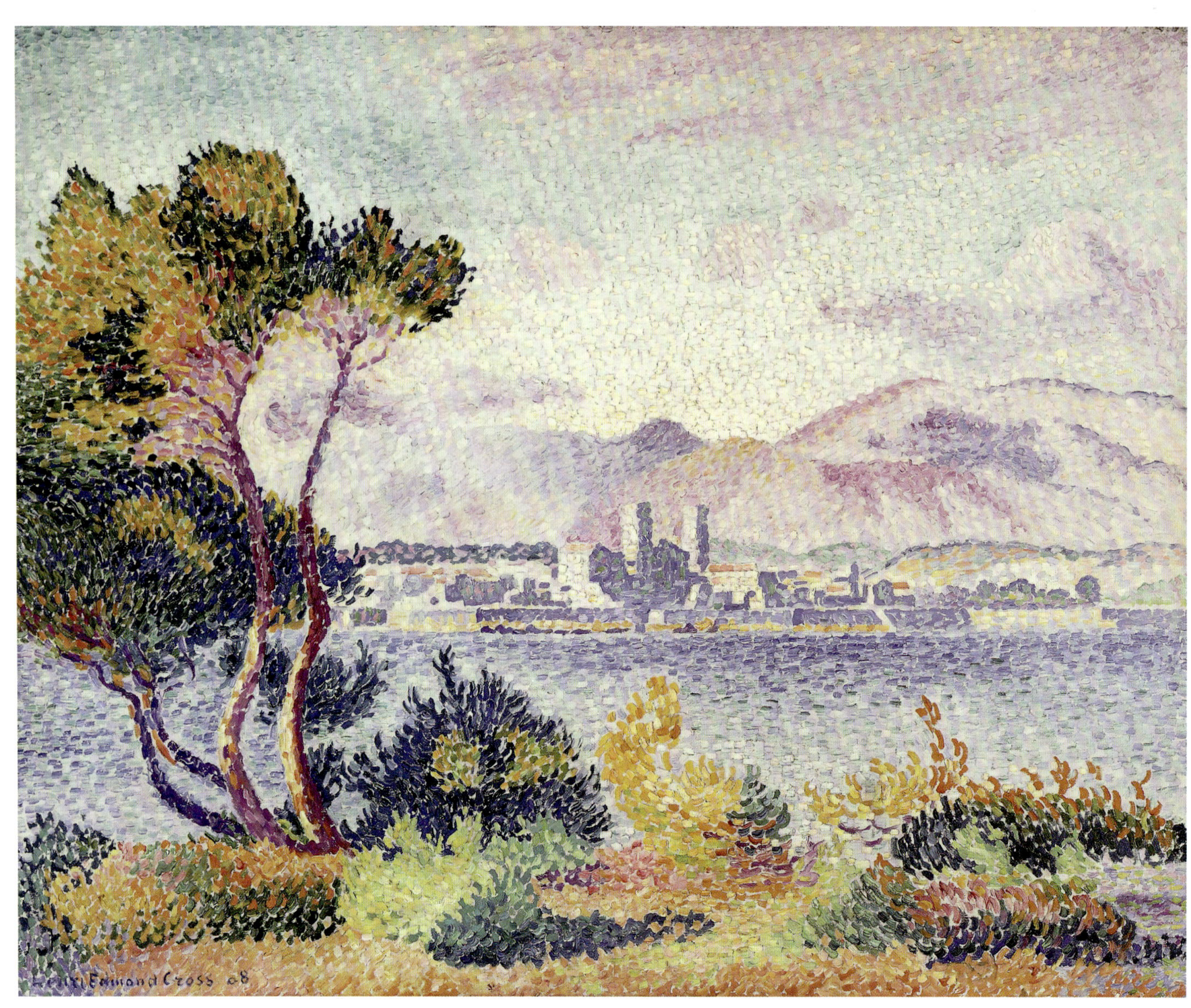

Henri-Edmond Cross (1856–1910)

Antibes, Afternoon

Antibes, effet d'après-midi

Antibes, Nachmittag

Antibes, tarde

Antibes, tarde

Antibes, namiddag

1908, Oil on canvas/Huile sur toile, 81 × 100 cm, Private collection

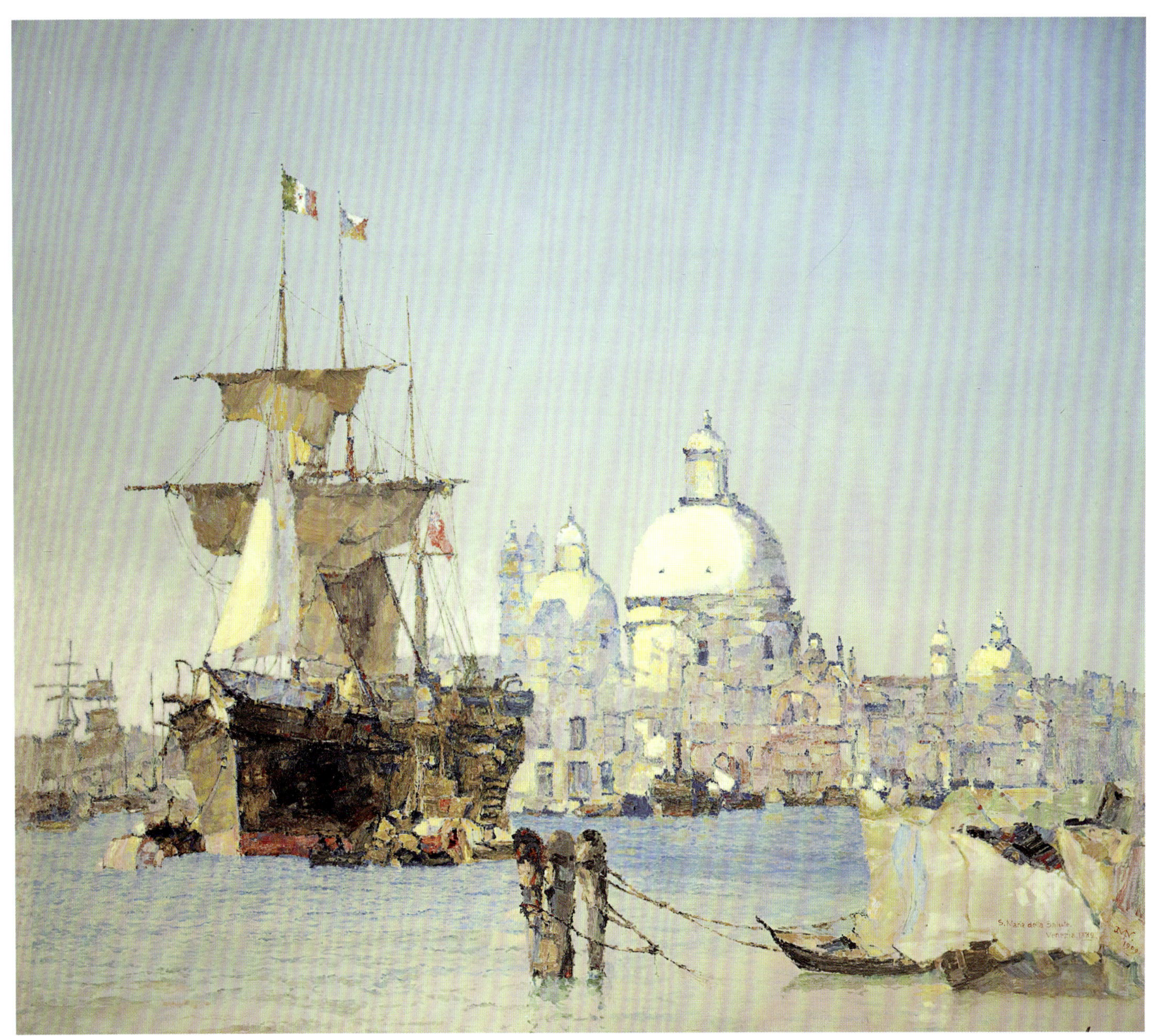

John Miller Nicholson (1840–1913)

Santa Maria della Salute, Venice

Santa Maria della Salute, Venise

Santa Maria della Salute, Venedig

Santa Maria della Salute, Venecia

Santa Maria della Salute, Veneza

Santa Maria della Salute, Venetië

1909, Oil on canvas/Huile sur toile, 70 × 83 cm, Manx Museum, Douglas

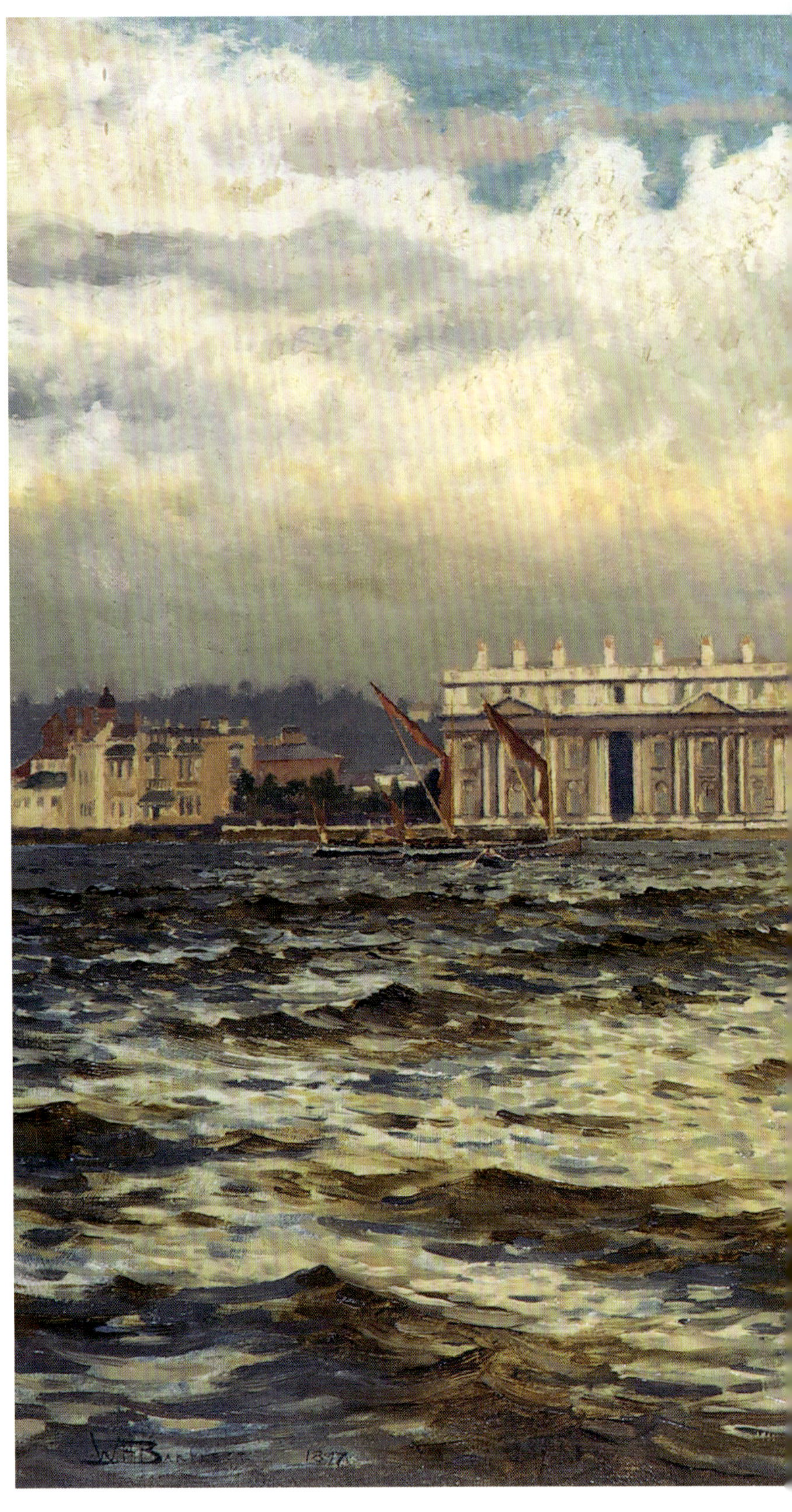

William Henry Bartlett (1858–1932)
Off Greenwich, London
Au large de Greenwich, Londres
Auf der Themse vor Greenwich
El Támesis delante de Greenwich
No Tamisa, ao largo de Greenwich
Op de Theems bij Greenwich
1897, Oil on canvas/Huile sur toile, Touchstones Rochdale, Rochdale

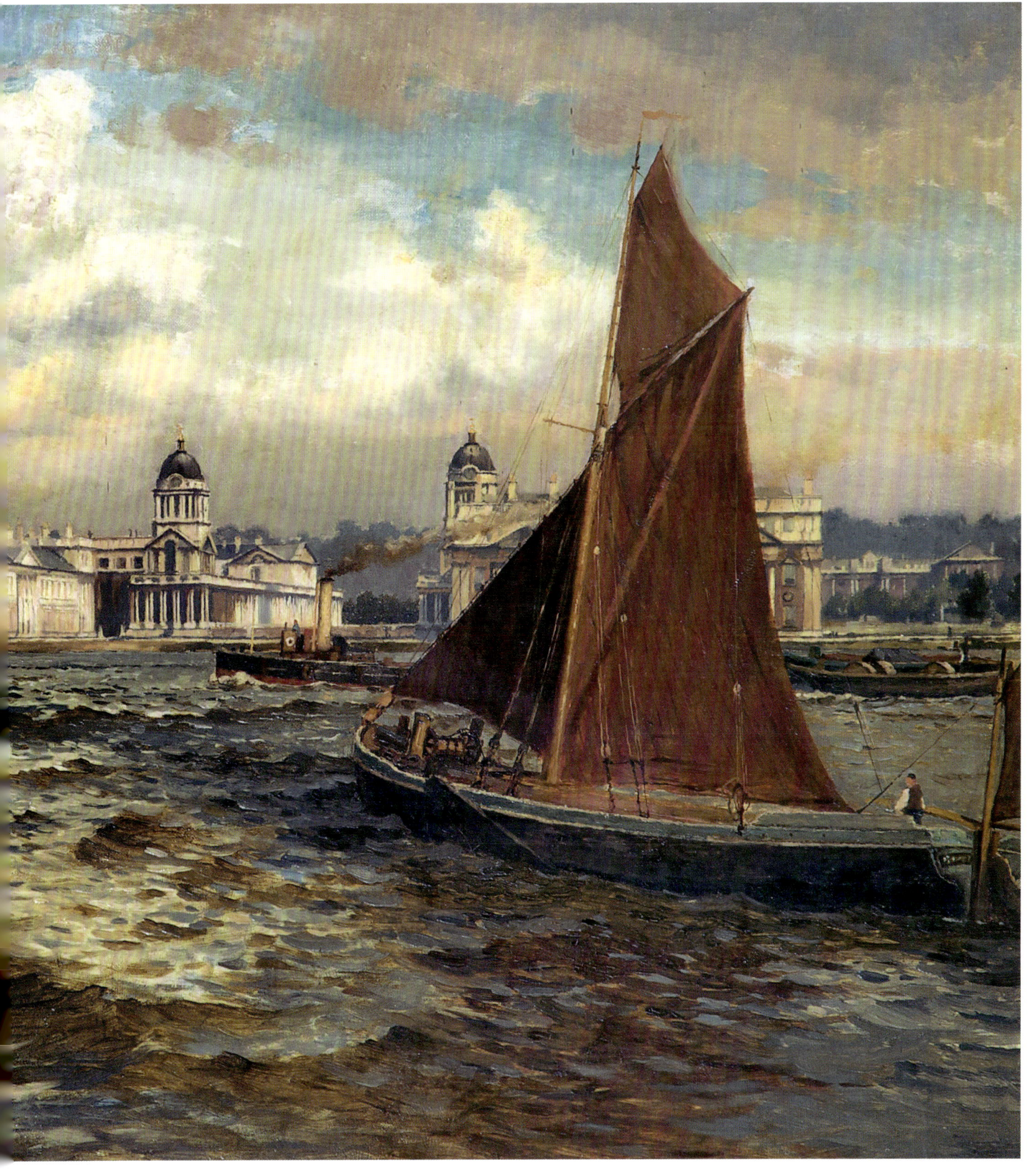

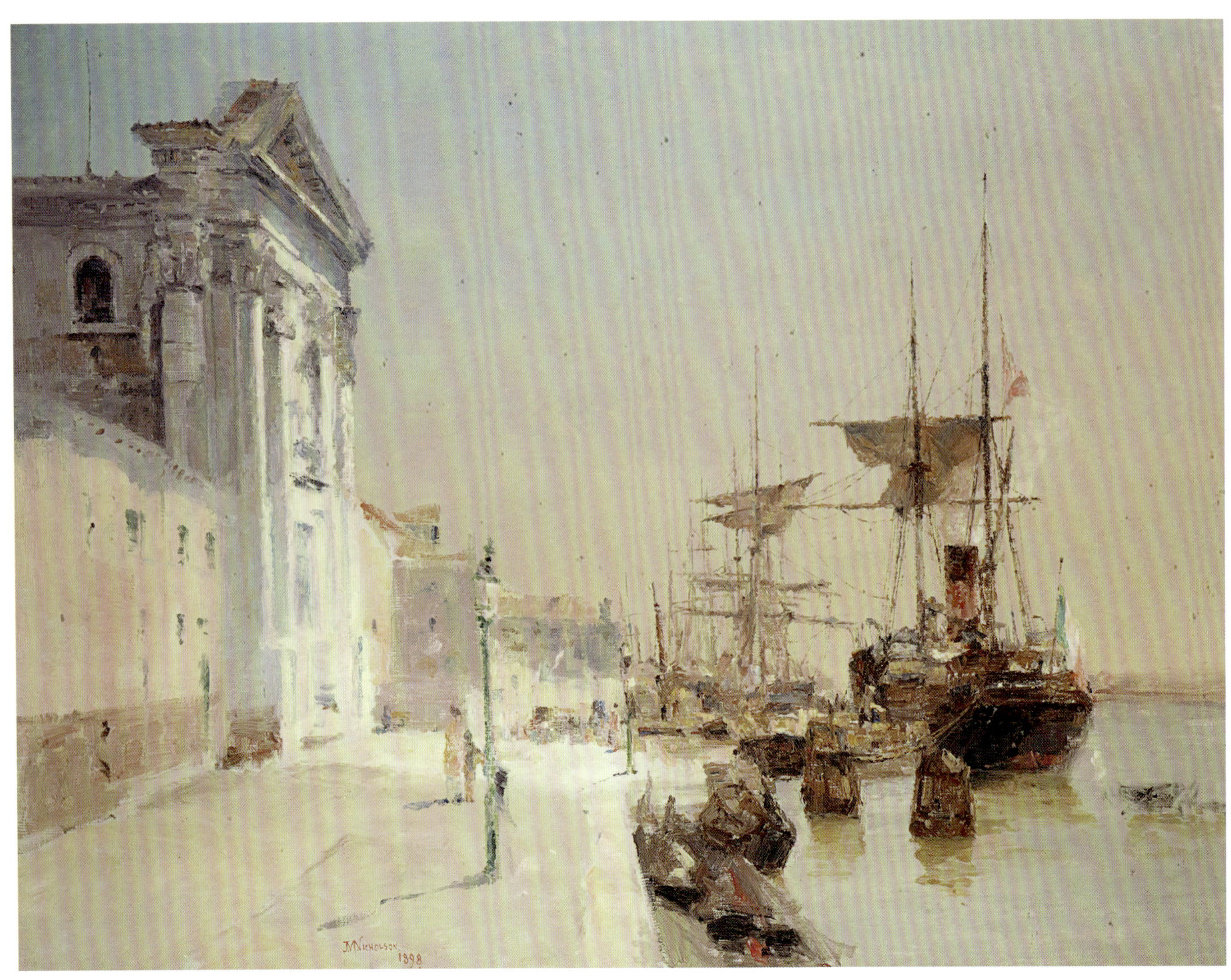

John Miller Nicholson (1840–1913)

A Quay Scene, Venice

Scène de quai, Venise

Szene am Kai, Venedig

Escena en el muelle, Venecia

Cena no cais, Veneza

Kadescène, Venetië

1898, Oil on canvas/Huile sur toile, 48 × 75 cm, Manx Museum, Douglas

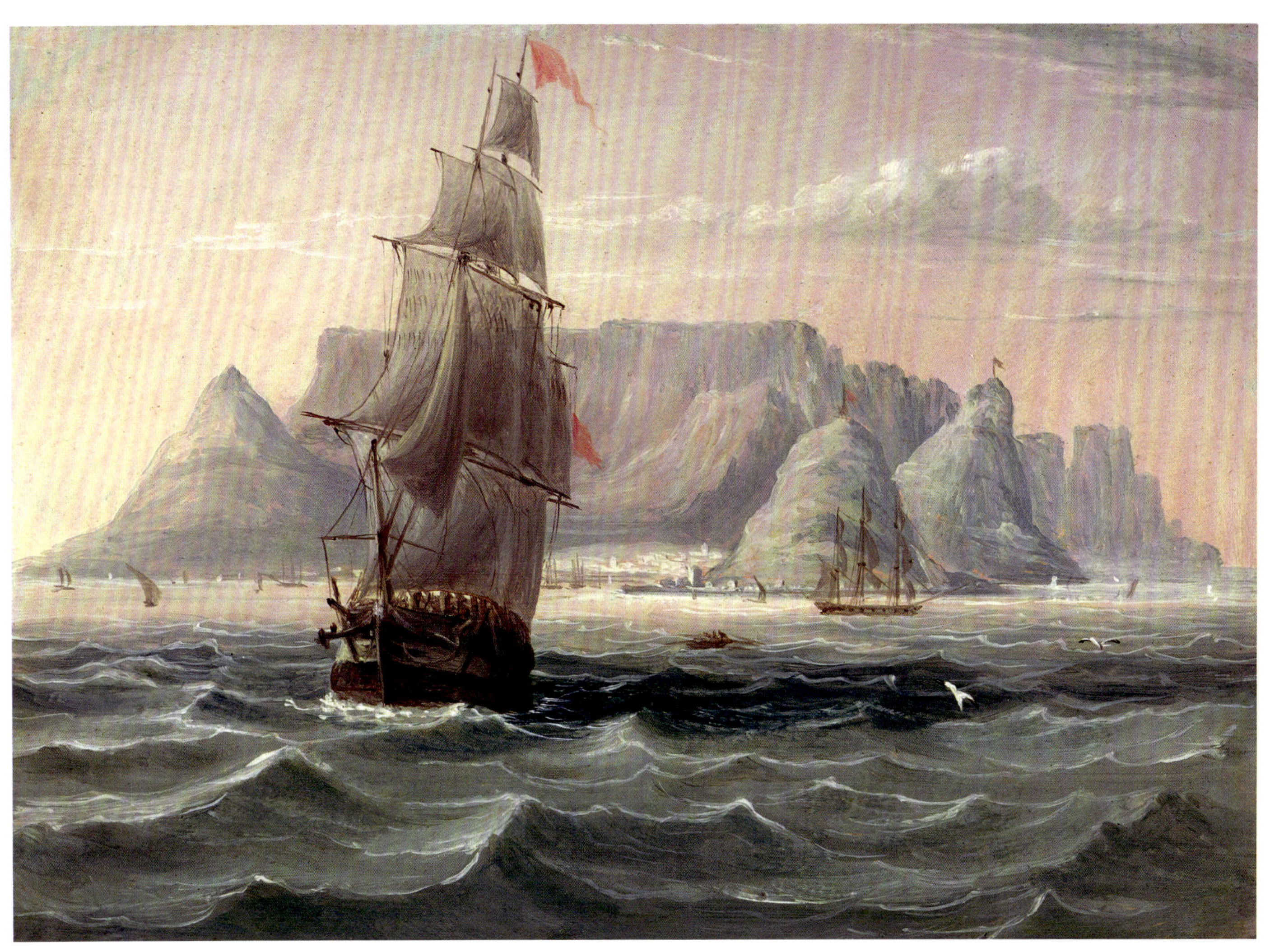

English school/École anglaise

Table Mountain, Cape Town from the Sea

Montagne de la Table, Le Cap, de la mer

Tafelberg, Kapstadt

Montaña de la Mesa, Ciudad del Cabo

Montanha da Mesa, Cidade do Cabo

Tafelberg, Kaapstad

1820, Oil on cardboard/Huile sur carton, Private collection

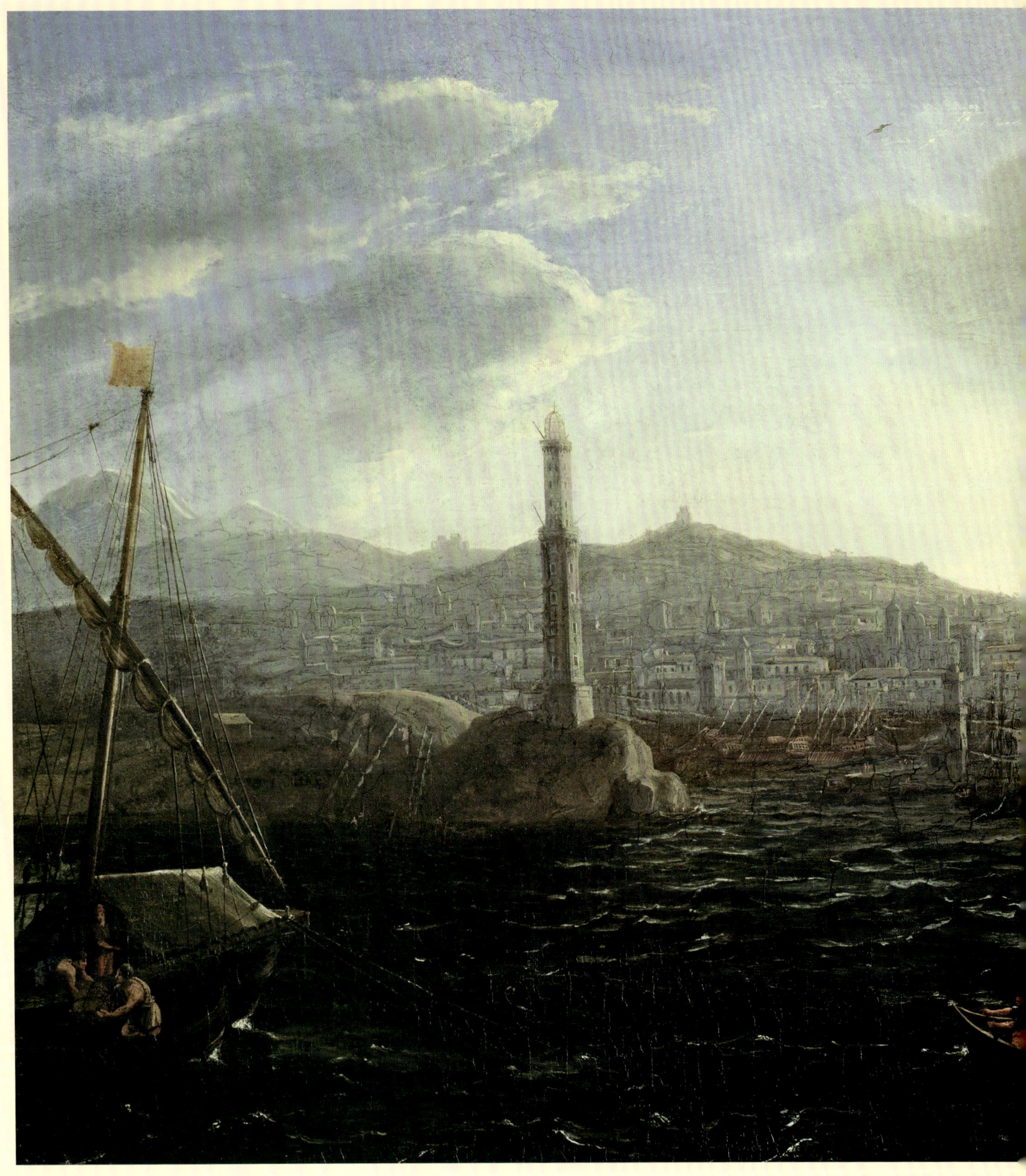

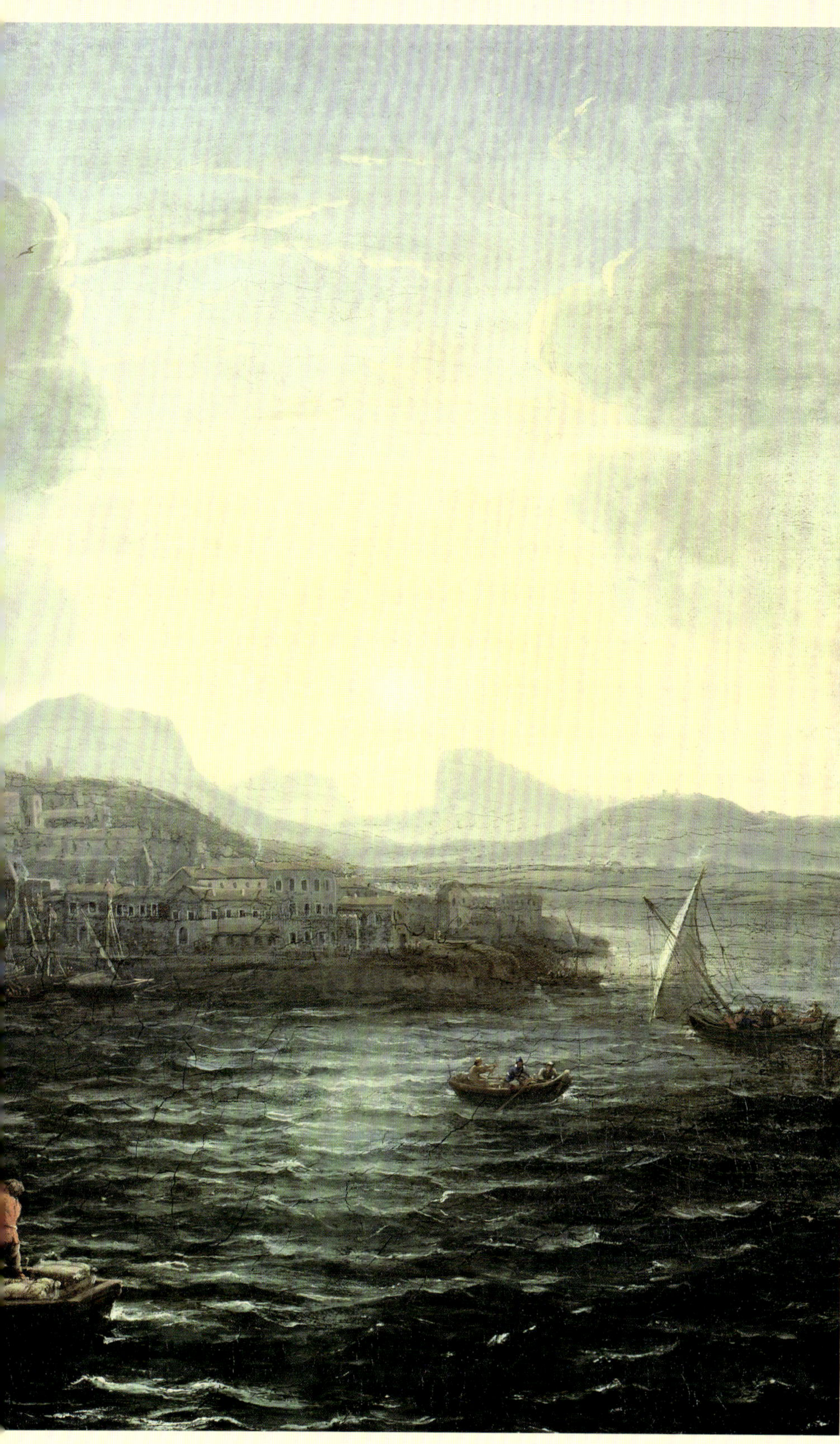

Claude Lorrain (1600–82)

The Port of Genoa, Sea View

Le Port de Gênes, vu de la mer

Blick vom Meer auf den Hafen von Genua

Vista del mar en el puerto de Génova

Vista do mar no porto de Gênova

Gezicht vanaf zee op de haven van Genua

c. 1627–29, Oil on canvas/Huile sur toile,
64 × 101 cm, Musée du Louvre, Paris

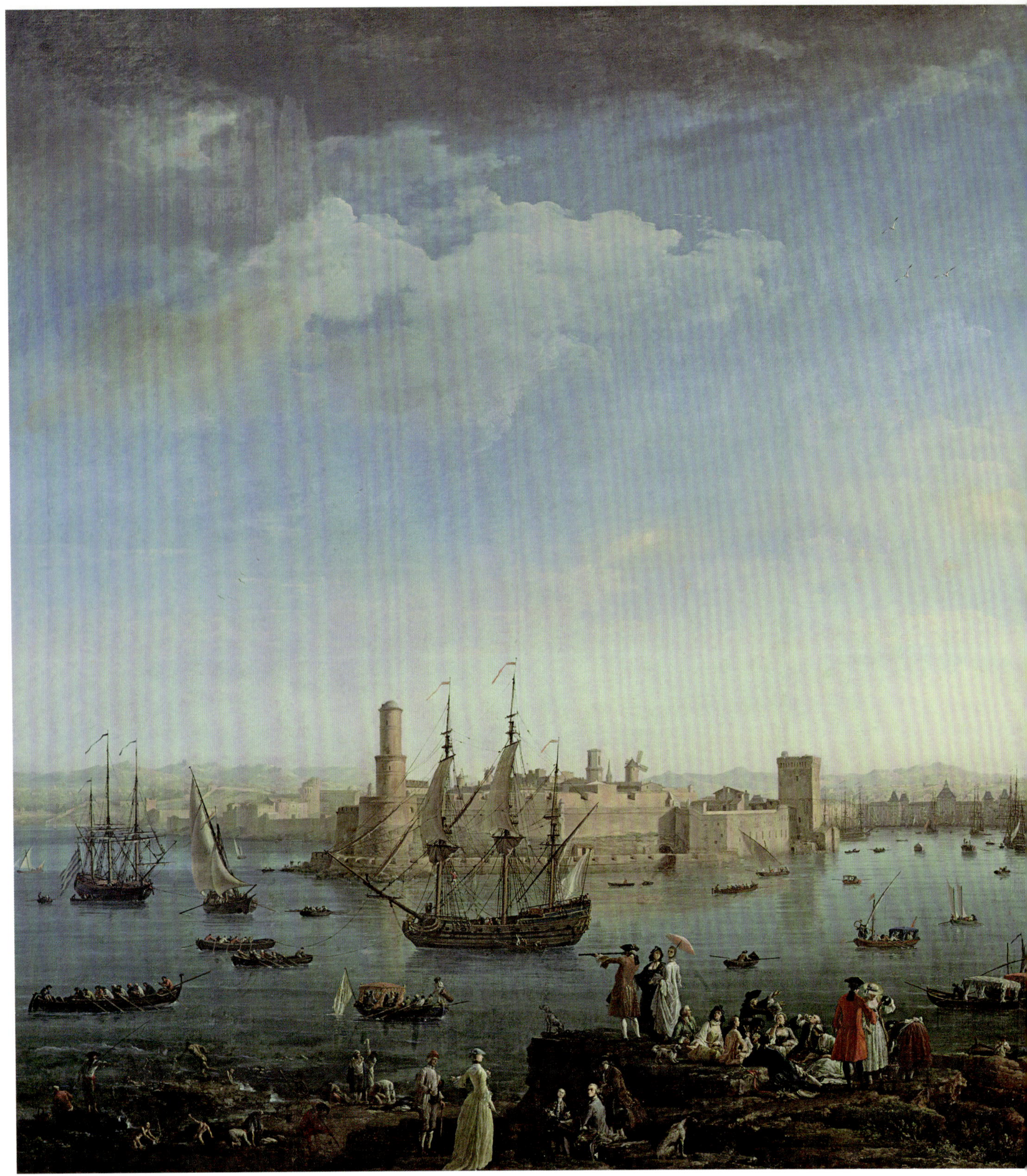

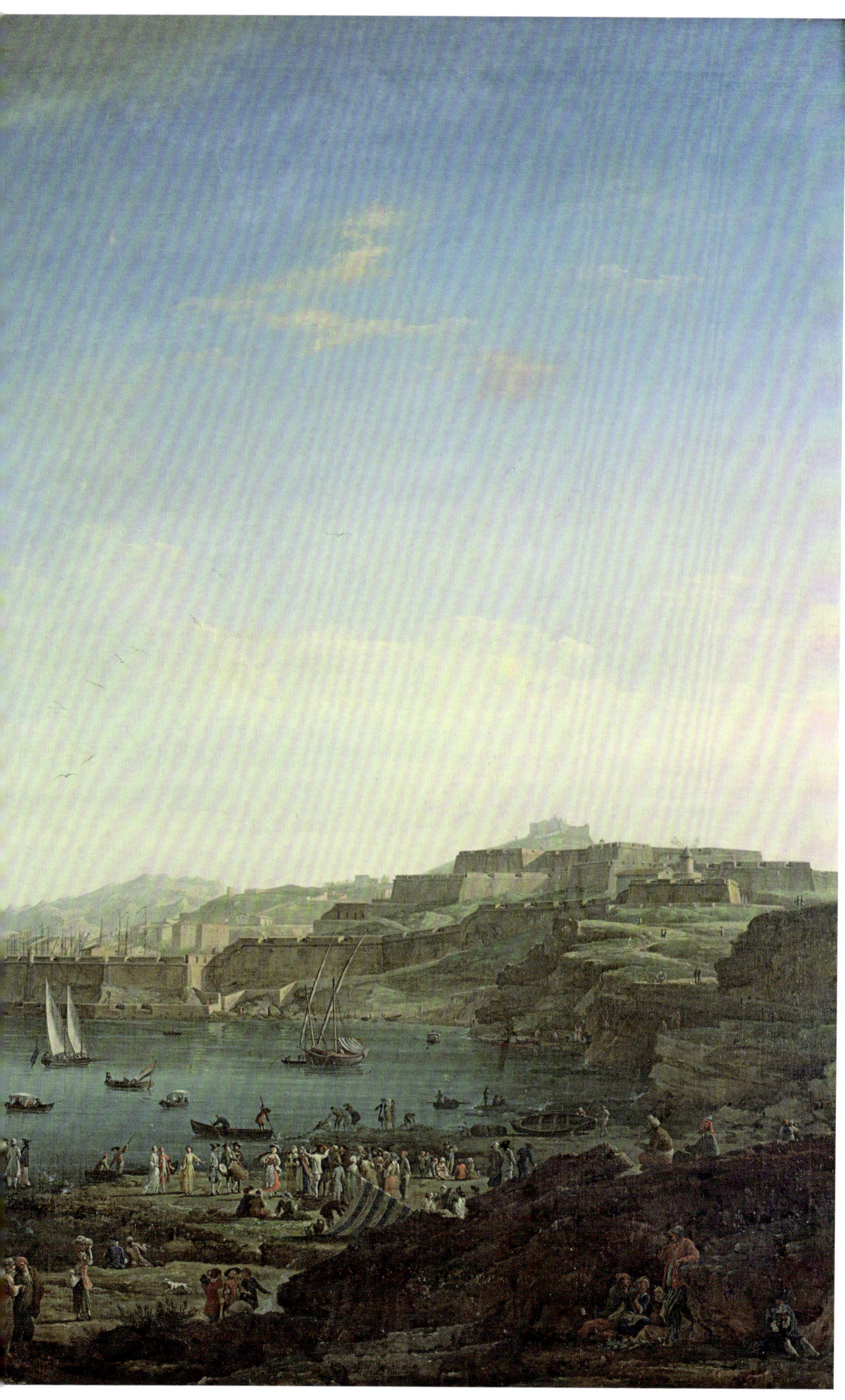

The Entrance to the Port of Marseille

Entrée du port de Marseille

Hafeneinfahrt von Marseille

Entrada en el puerto de Marsella

Chegada de Marselha

Havenmond van Marseille

1754, Oil on canvas/Huile sur toile,
165 × 263 cm, Musée du Louvre, Paris

*Claude Joseph Vernet, born in Avignon, came from
a family of painters from the South of France. After
training under his father and then several stays in Italy,
he settled in Paris in the mid-18th century. Some of his
most important clients included not only the French king,
but also English nobility who appreciated his works.*

*Claude Joseph Vernet, né à Avignon, est issu d'une
famille de peintres du sud de la France. Après
s'être entraîné avec son père et après plusieurs
séjours en Italie, il s'installa à Paris au milieu du
XVIIIᵉ siècle. Certains de ses clients les plus importants
comptaient non seulement le roi français, mais aussi
la noblesse anglaise qui appréciait ses œuvres.*

*Der in Avignon geborene Claude Joseph Vernet stammte
aus einer südfranzösischen Malerfamilie. Nach der
Ausbildung – unter anderem durch seinen Vater und
mehrerer Italienaufenthalte – ließ er sich Mitte des
18. Jahrhunderts in Paris nieder. Zu seinen wichtigsten
Auftraggebern gehörte nicht nur der französische
König, auch englische Adlige schätzten seine Werke.*

*Claude Joseph Vernet, nacido en Avignon, provenía
de una familia de pintores del sur de Francia.
Después de formarse – incluyendo entre otros a su
padre y varias estancias en Italia – se estableció
en el siglo XVIII en París. Sus principales clientes
incluían no sólo al rey de Francia, sino también a
los aristócratas ingleses, que apreciaban sus obras.*

*Nascido em Avinhão, Claude Joseph Vernet era oriundo
de uma família de pintores do sul da França. Após seu
treinamento – entre outras pessoas, por seu pai, e várias
permanências na Itália, ele se estabeleceu em meados
do século XVIII em Paris. Seus principais clientes
foram não somente o rei da França, mas também os
aristocratas ingleses, que apreciavam suas obras.*

*De in Avignon geboren Claude Joseph Vernet stamde
uit een Zuid-Franse schildersfamilie. Na zijn opleiding
– onder anderen door zijn vader en op meerdere reizen
naar Italië – vestigde hij zich halverwege de achttiende
eeuw in Parijs. Tot zijn belangrijkste opdrachtgevers
behoorden Franse koningen en Engelse aristocraten.*

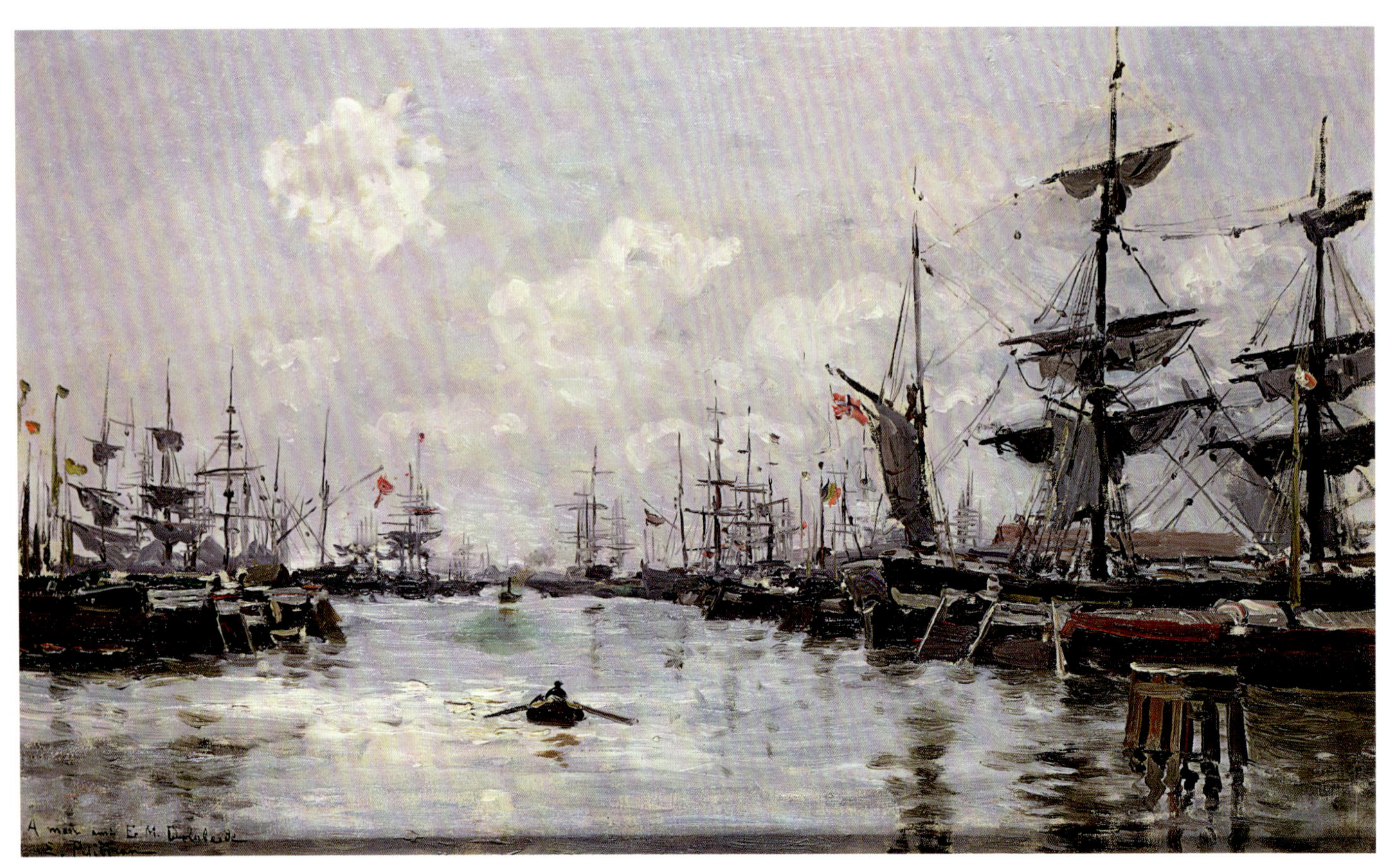

Edmond Petitjean (1844–1925)

The Port

Le Port

Der Hafen

El puerto

O Porto

De haven

n. d., Oil on canvas mounted on wood/Huile sur toile montée sur du bois, 29 × 48 cm, Private collection

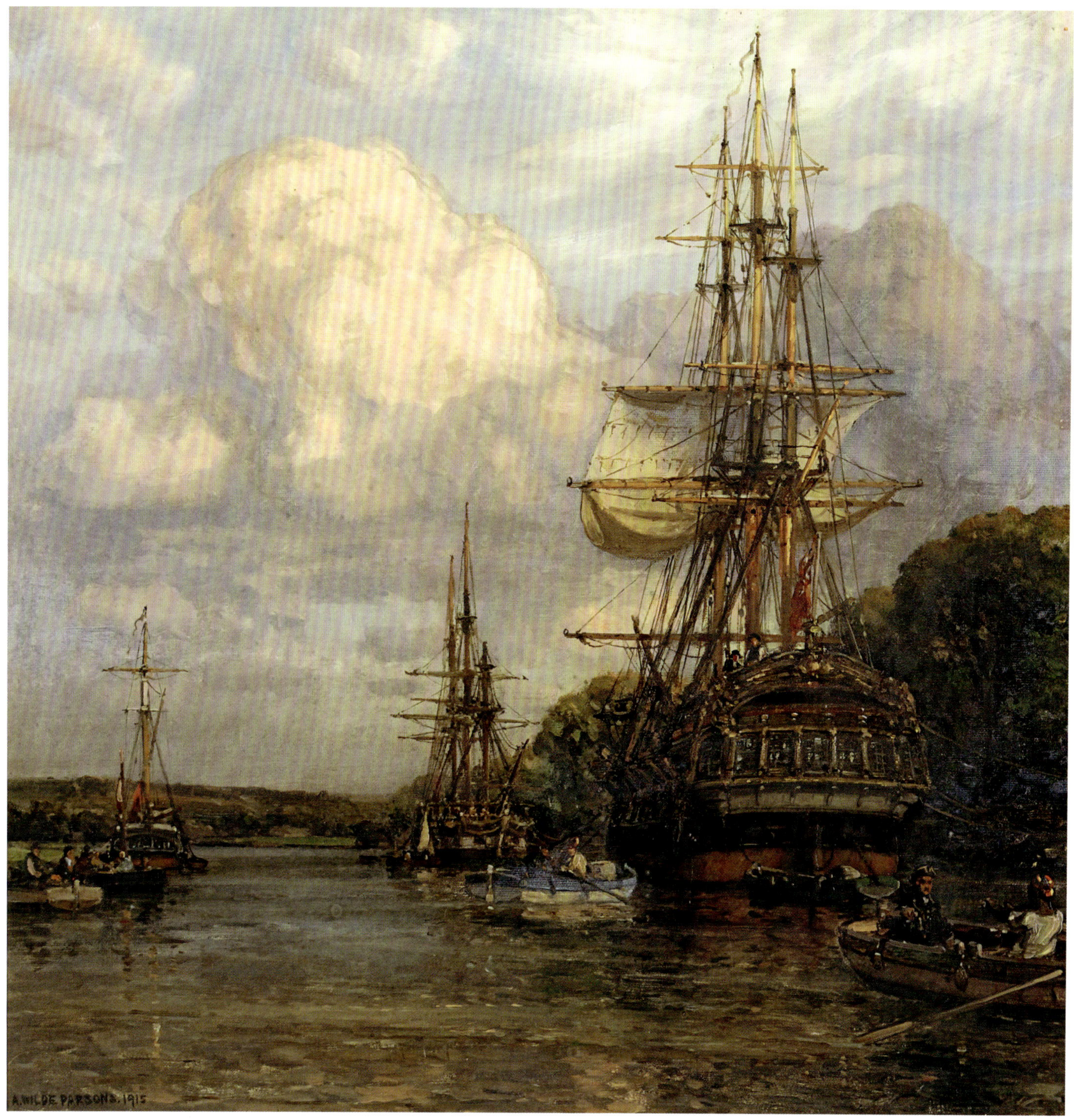

Arthur Wilde Parsons (1854–1931)

Privateers, tied up at Hung Road, Bristol

Kaperschiffe, an der Hung Road von Bristol festgemacht

Corsários, atracados em Hung Road de Bristol

Corsaires, attachés à Hung Road, Bristol

Buque corsario, amarrado en Hung Road, Bristol

Kaperschepen aangemeerd in Hungroad, Bristol

1915, Oil on canvas/Huile sur toile, 59,5 × 59,5 cm, Bristol Museum and Art Gallery, Bristol

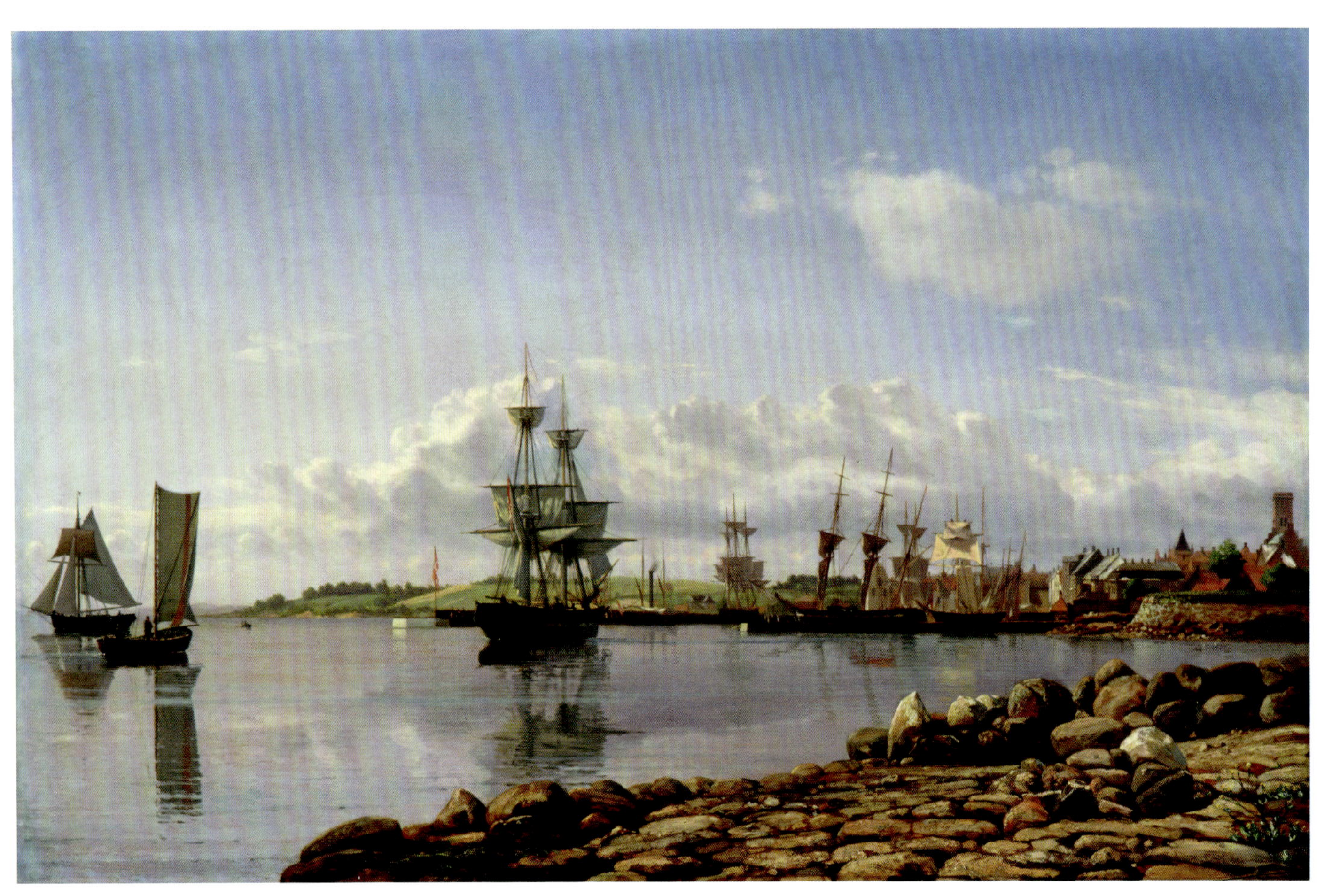

Carl Frederik Emanuel Larsen (1823–59); Carl Johan Neumann (1833–99)

Shipping off a Baltic Port

Expédition au large d'un port baltique

Schiffe vor einem Hafen an der Ostsee

Barcos delante de un puerto en el Mar Báltico

Navios ao largo de um porto no mar Báltico

Schepen voor een haven aan de Oostzee

n. d., Oil on canvas/Huile sur toile, 56 × 86,3 cm, Private collection

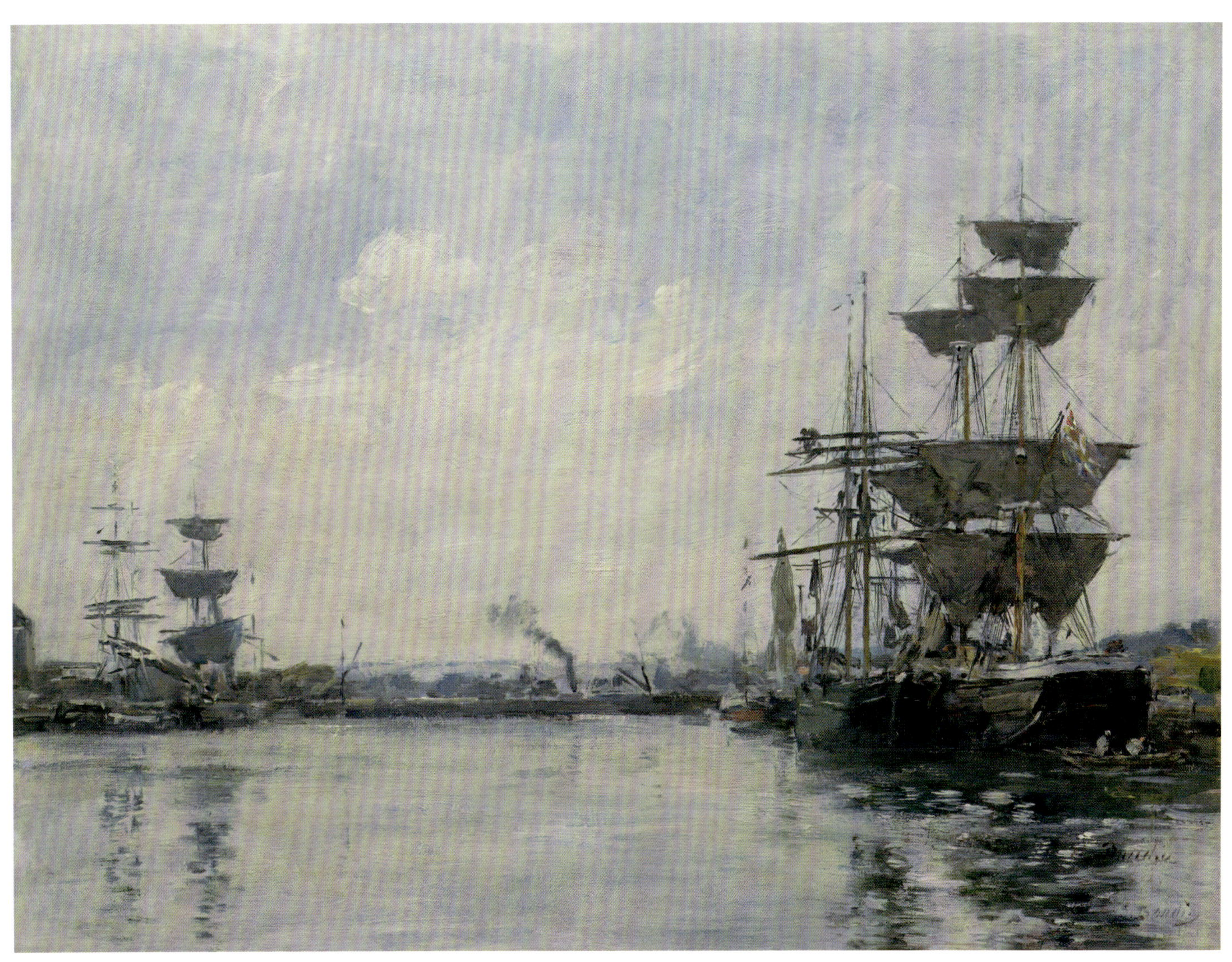

Eugène Louis Boudin (1824–98)

Le Havre, Ships in a Harbour Basin

Bateaux dans le port du Havre

Le Havre, Schiffe im Hafenbecken

Le Havre, barcos en zona portuaria

Le Havre, navios na doca

Le Havre, schepen in de haven

n. d., Oil on canvas/Huile sur toile, 31 × 41 cm, Private collection

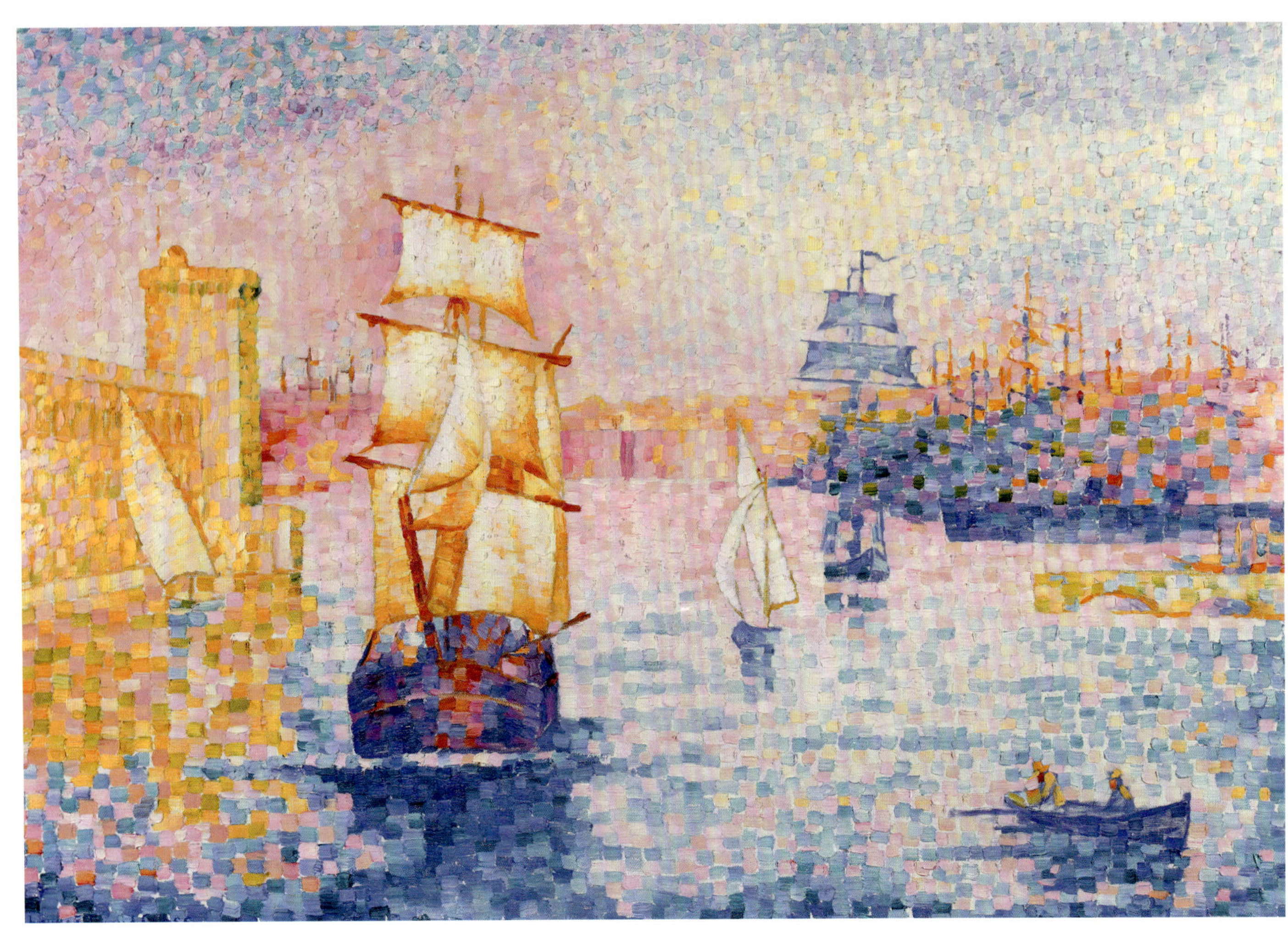

Henri-Edmond Cross (1856–1910)

Port of Marseille

Le Port de Marseille

Hafen von Marseille

Puerto de Marsella

Porto de Marselha

De haven van Marseille

c. 1899, Oil on canvas/Huile sur toile, 65 × 92 cm, Private collection

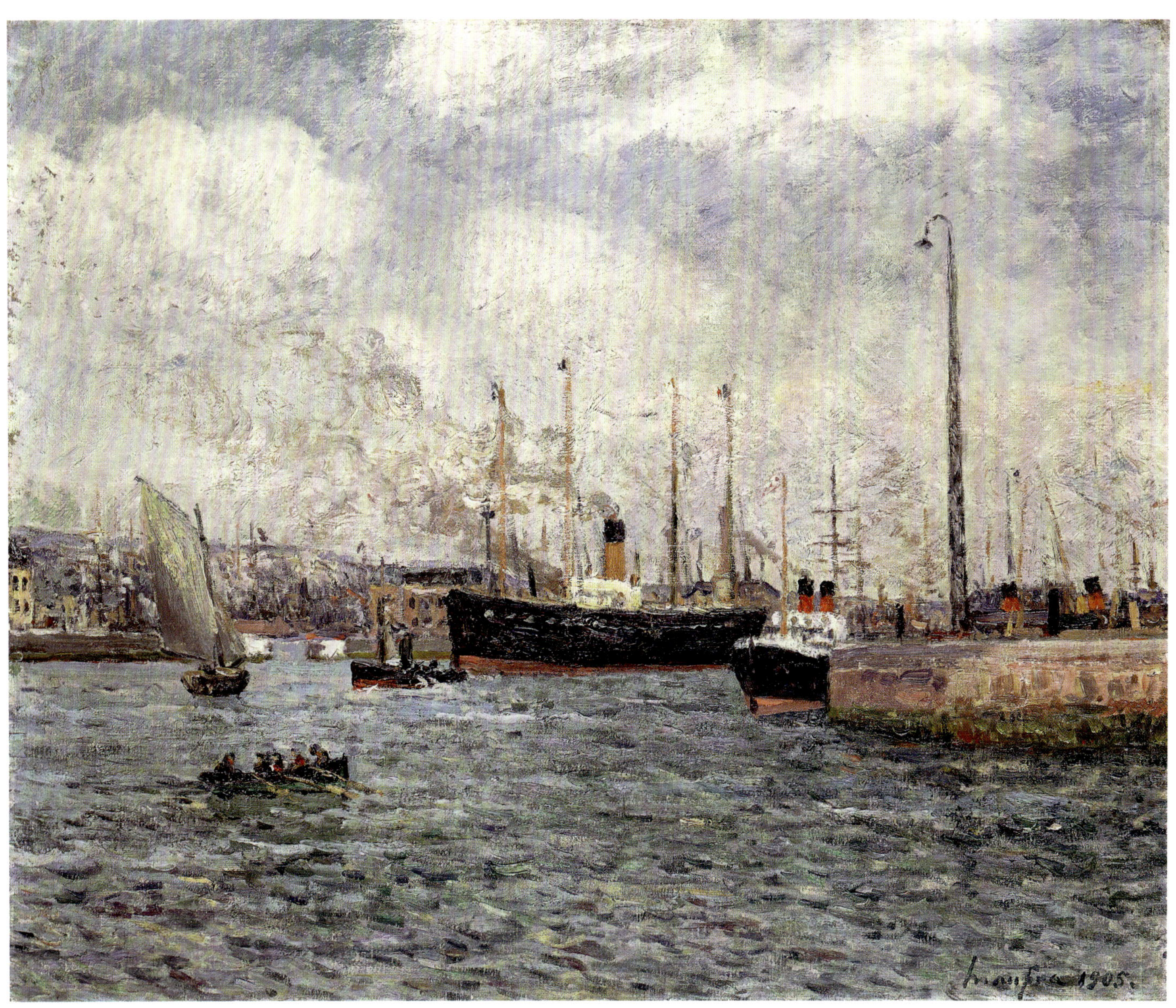

Maxime Maufra (1861–1918)

The Port of Le Havre

Le Port du Havre

Der Hafen von Le Havre

El puerto de Le Havre

O porto de Le Havre

De haven van Le Havre

1905, Oil on canvas/Huile sur toile, 61,5 × 73 cm, Private collection

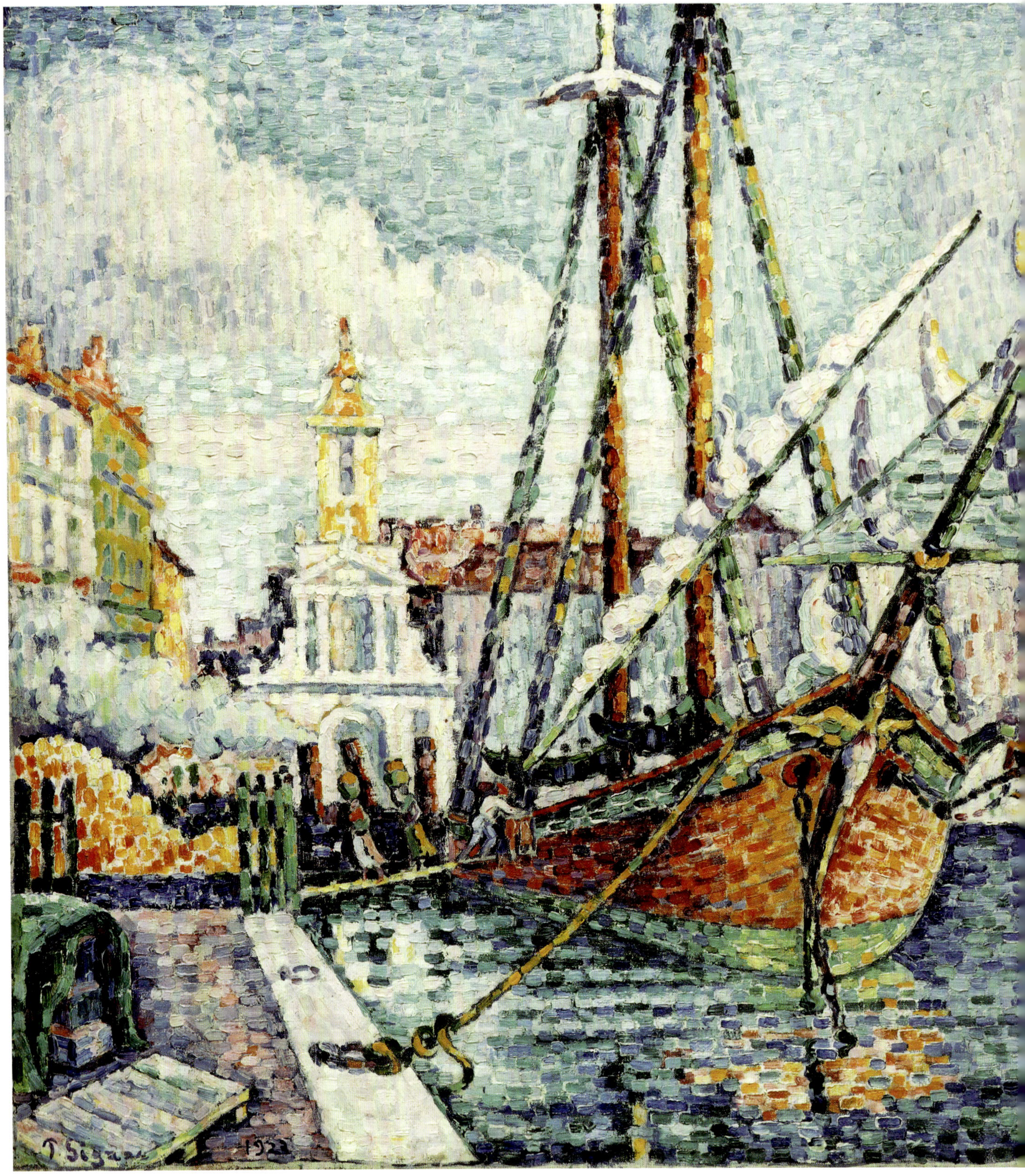

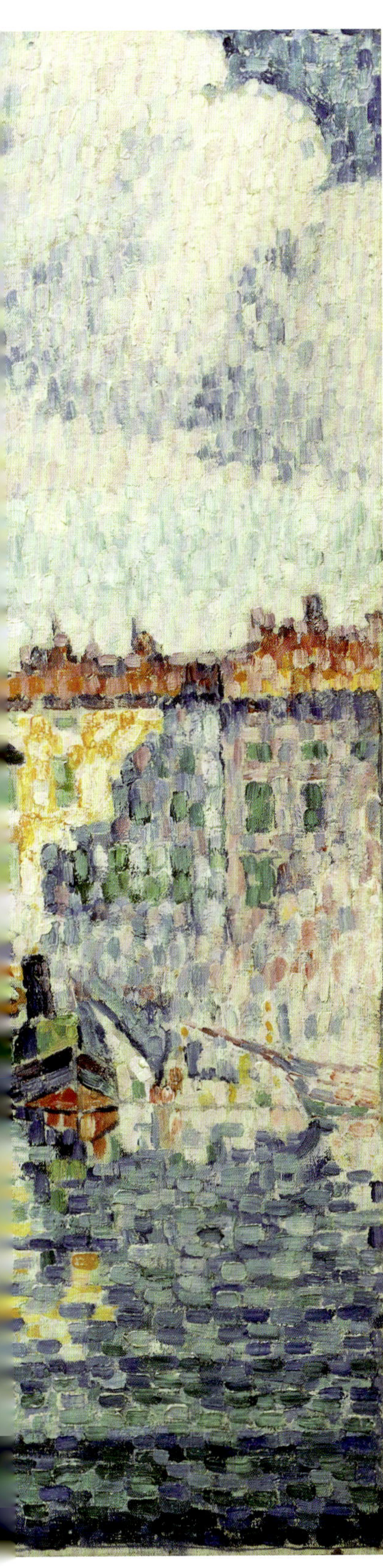

The Port of Saint-Tropez

Le Port de Saint-Tropez

Der Hafen von Saint-Tropez

El puerto de Saint-Tropez

O porto de Saint-Tropez

De haven van Saint-Tropez

1923, Oil on canvas/Huile sur toile, 59,7 × 73 cm, Private collection

Among all the French painters of the 19th century and not just among the Impressionists, Paul Signac was undoubtedly the one with the most intimate connection to the sea and seafaring. Not only his countless marine images, but also the fact that he was the owner of eight boats during his lifetime, including the last, a small fish logger, which he named La Ville de Honolulu.

Parmi tous les peintres français du XIXᵉ siècle, et pas uniquement les impressionnistes, Paul Signac était sans aucun doute celui qui avait le lien le plus intime avec la mer et la navigation. Non seulement de par ses innombrables images marines, mais aussi du fait qu'il fut propriétaire de huit bateaux durant sa vie, dont le dernier, un petit bateau de pêche, baptisé La Ville de Honolulu.

Unter allen französischen Malern des 19. Jahrhunderts, nicht nur unter den Impressionisten, war Paul Signac zweifellos derjenige mit der innigsten Verbindung zum Meer und der Seefahrt. Davon zeugen nicht nur seine zahllosen Marinebilder, sondern auch der Umstand, dass er im Laufe seines Lebens selbst Besitzer von acht Booten war, von denen das letzte, ein kleiner Fischlogger, den Namen La Ville de Honolulu *trug.*

De entre todos los pintores franceses del siglo XIX, no sólo entre los impresionistas, Paul Signac fue, sin duda, el que tuvo la conexión más íntima con el mar y la navegación. Esto lo prueban no sólo sus innumerables imágenes marinas, sino también el hecho de que tuvo ocho barcos a lo largo de su vida, el último de los cuales fue un pequeño lugre pesquero al que llamó La Ville de Honolulu.

Entre todos os pintores franceses do século XIX, não só entre os impressionistas, Paul Signac foi, sem dúvida, aquele que tinha uma conexão mais íntima com o mar e a navegação. Não somente seus numerosos quadros de marinhas testemunham isso, mas também o fato de ele ter sido, ao longo de sua vida, o proprietário de oito barcos, o último dos quais, um pequeno barco de pesca, recebeu o nome La Ville de Honolulu.

Van alle Franse schilders van de negentiende eeuw, en niet alleen onder de impressionisten, was Paul Signac de kunstenaar die de innigste band met de zee en de scheepvaart had. Daarvan getuigen niet alleen talloze maritieme werken, maar ook het feit dat hij in de loop van zijn leven zelf acht boten bezat, waarvan de laatste, een kleine vissersboot, de naam La ville de Honolulu *droeg.*

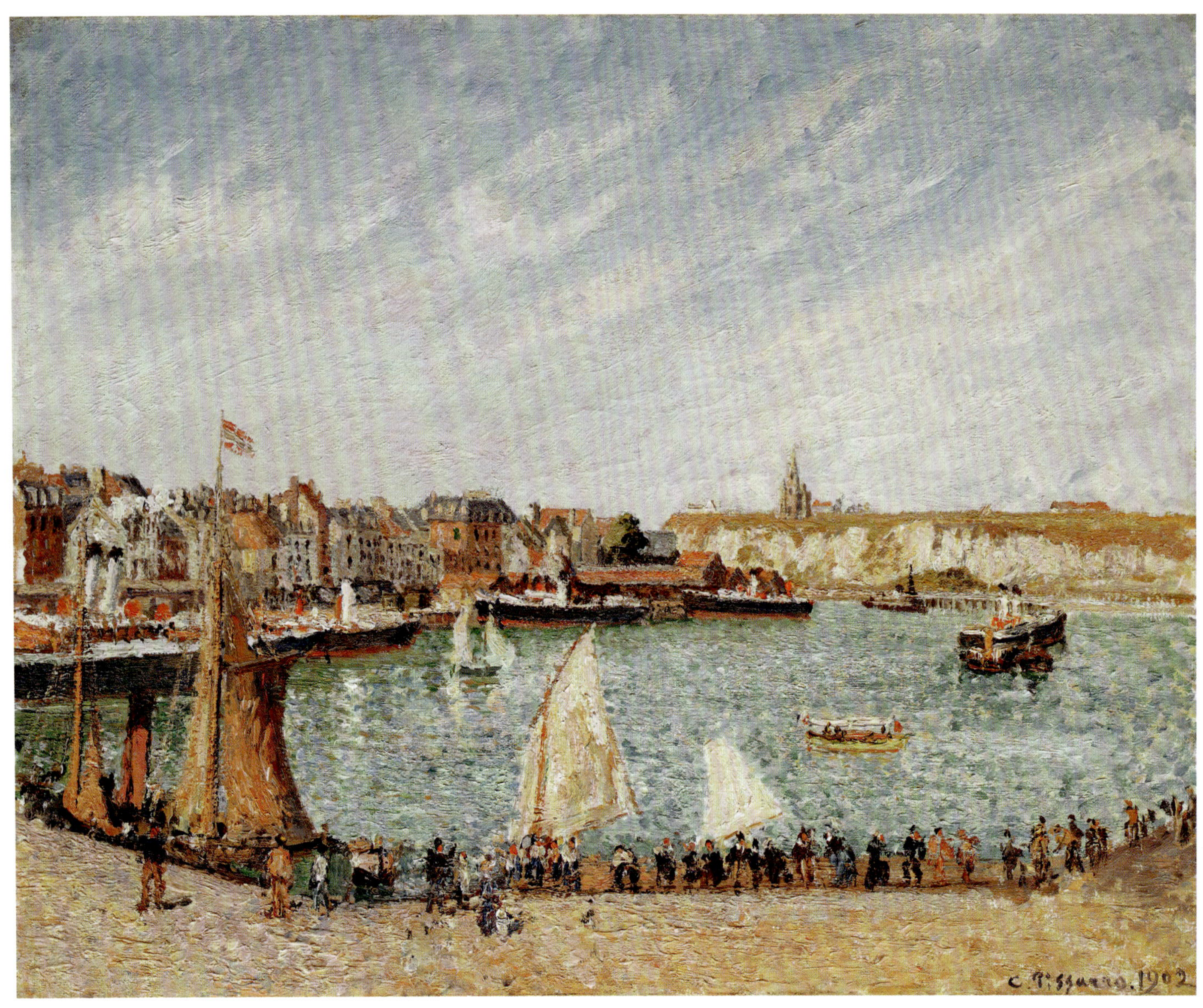

Camille Pissarro (1830–1903)

The Afternoon Sun, Outer Part of Dieppe

L'Avant-port de Dieppe, après-midi, temps lumineux

Nachmittagssonne am Hafen von Dieppe

Sol de la tarde en el puerto de Dieppe

Sol da tarde no porto de Dieppe

Namiddagzon in de haven van Dieppe

1902, Oil on canvas/Huile sur toile, 66 × 81,3 cm, Private collection

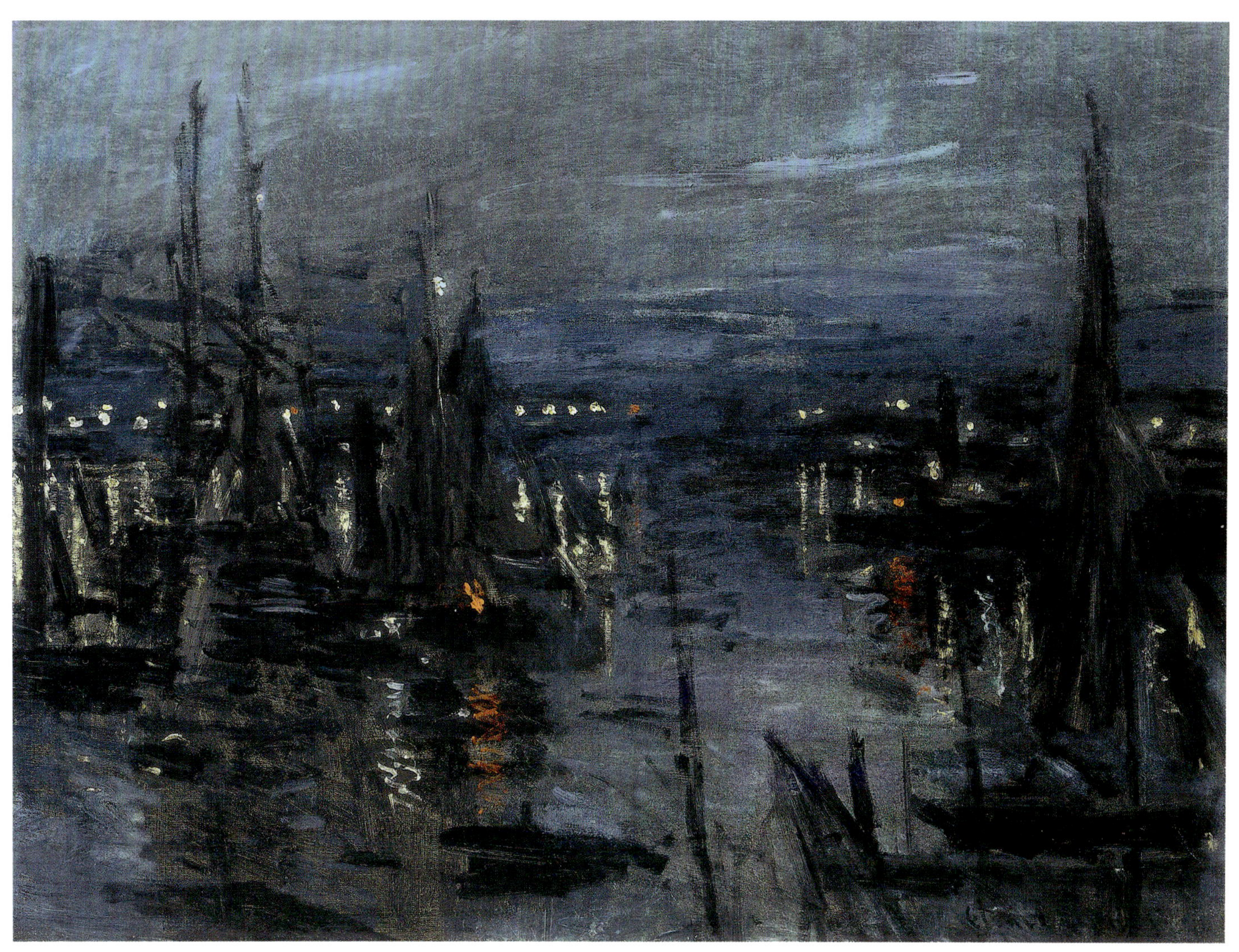

Claude Monet (1840–1926)

The Port of Le Havre, Night Effect

Le Port du Havre, effet de nuit

Hafen von Le Havre, Nachteffekt

Puerto de Le Havre, efecto de noche

Porto de Le Havre, efeito noturno

De haven van Le Havre, nachteffect

1873, Oil on canvas/Huile sur toile, 60 × 81,3 cm, Private collection

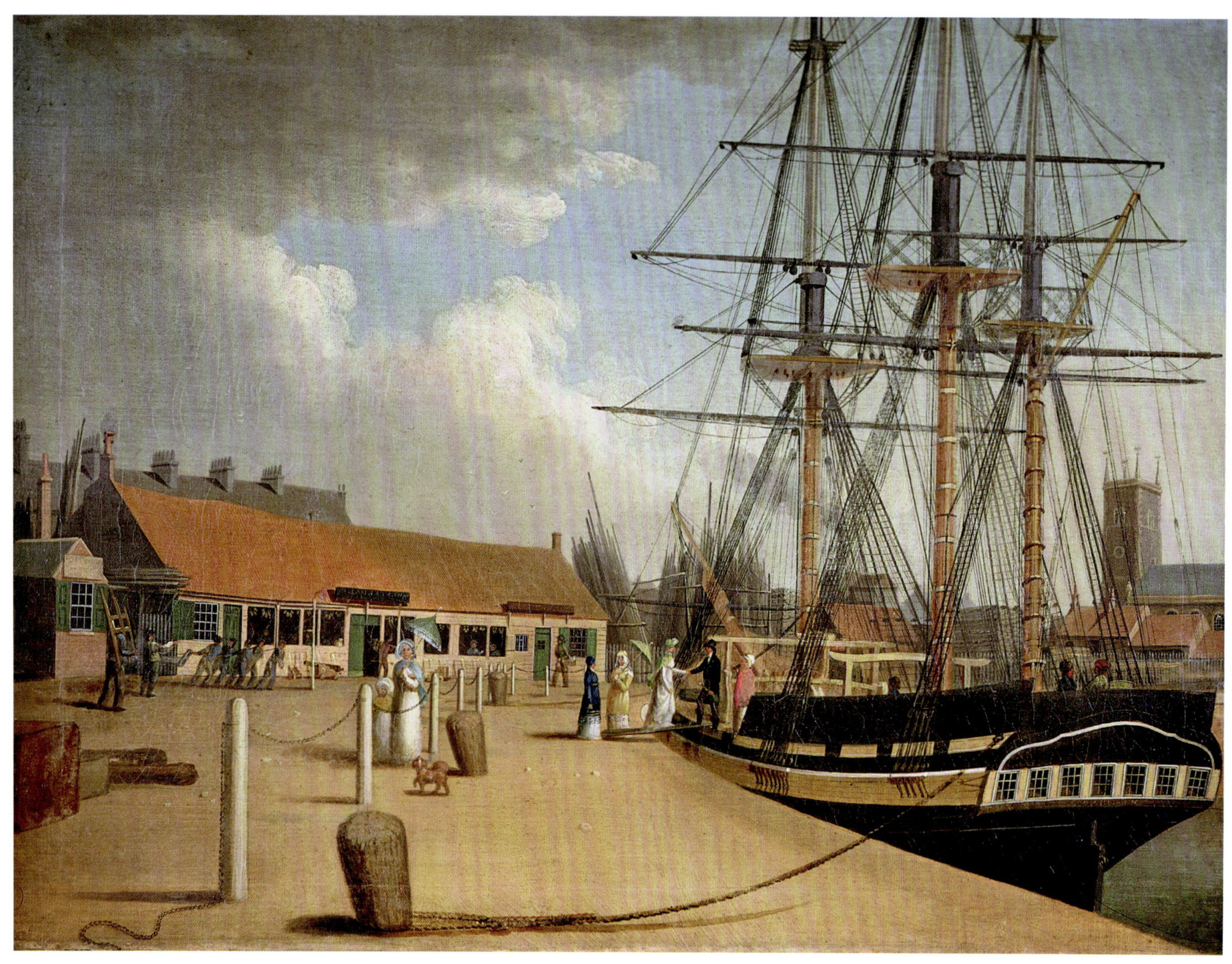

Robert Willoughby (1768–1843)

Westerdale's Yard and the Wellington from the New Dock

Le Port de Westerdale et le Wellington au nouveau quai

Westerdale's Yard und die Wellington vom New Dock aus gesehen

Westerdale's Yard y el Wellington desde el New Dock

Westerdale's Yard e o Wellington vistos de New Dock

Westerdale's Yard en de Wellington aan de New Dock

c. 1820, Oil on canvas/Huile sur toile, 61,7 × 82,9 cm, Ferens Art Gallery, Hull

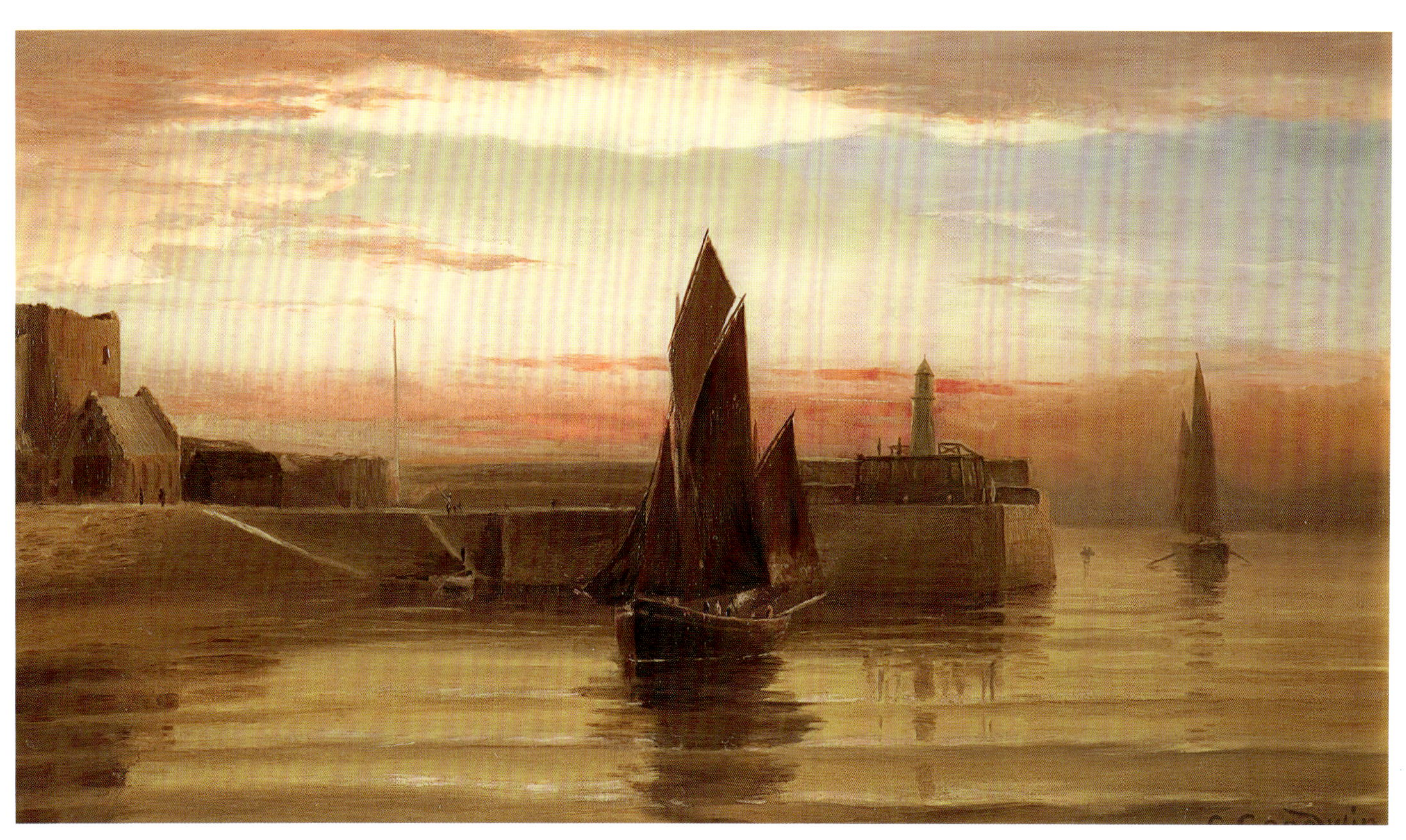

George Goodwin (1851–1922)

Lugger entering Peel Harbour

Lougre entrant au port de Peel

Ein Logger fährt in Peel Harbour ein

Lugre entrando en el puerto de Peel

Um Logger entra em Peel Harbour

Een logger loopt de haven van Peel binnen

1891, Oil on canvas/Huile sur toile, 29 × 56 cm, Manx Museum, Douglas

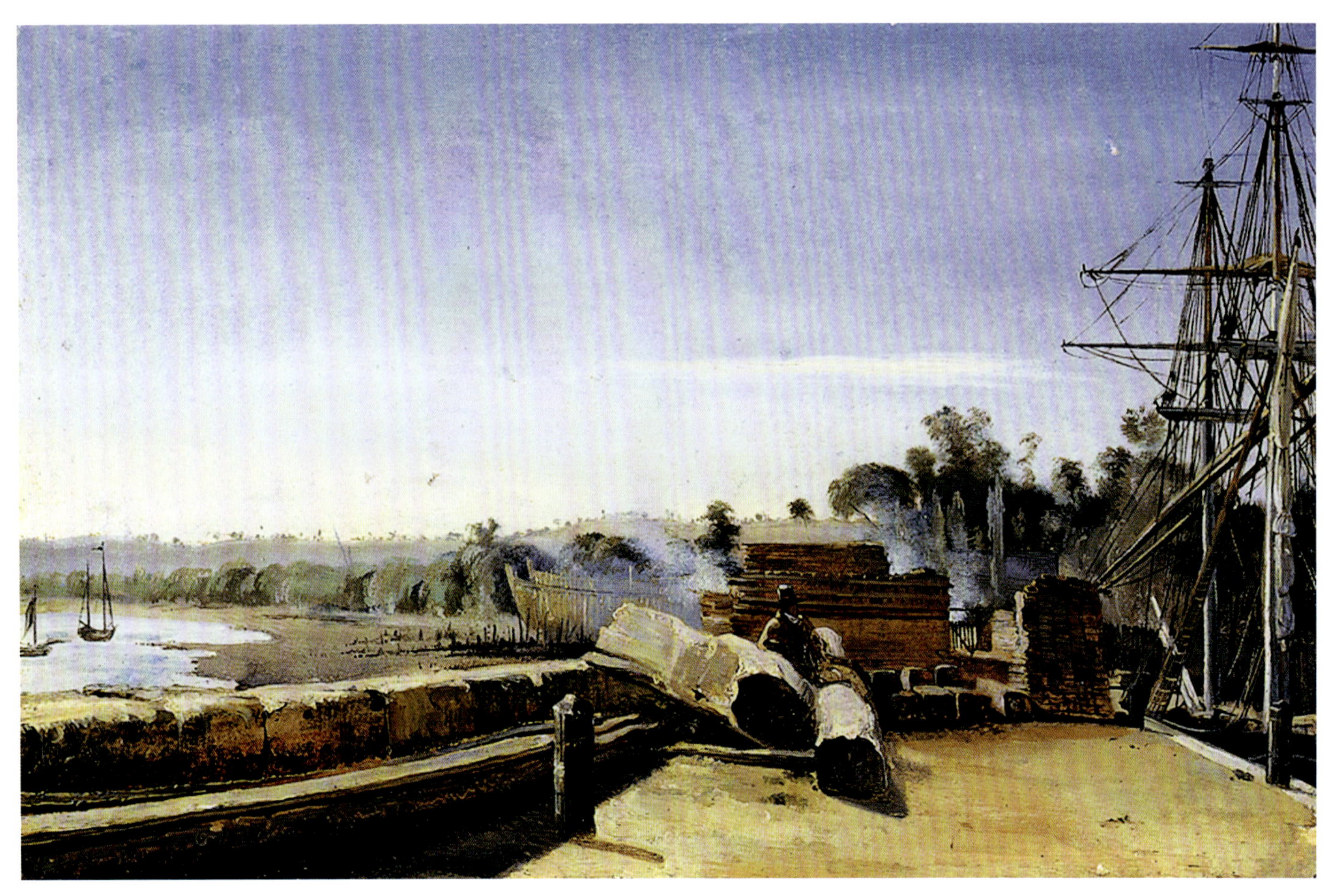

Jean-Baptiste Camille Corot (1796–1875)

Shipyard in Honfleur

Chantier naval à Honfleur

Werft in Honfleur

Astillero en Honfleur

Estaleiro em Honfleur

Werf in Honfleur

c. 1823, Oil on paper, 29,5 × 44 cm, Private collection

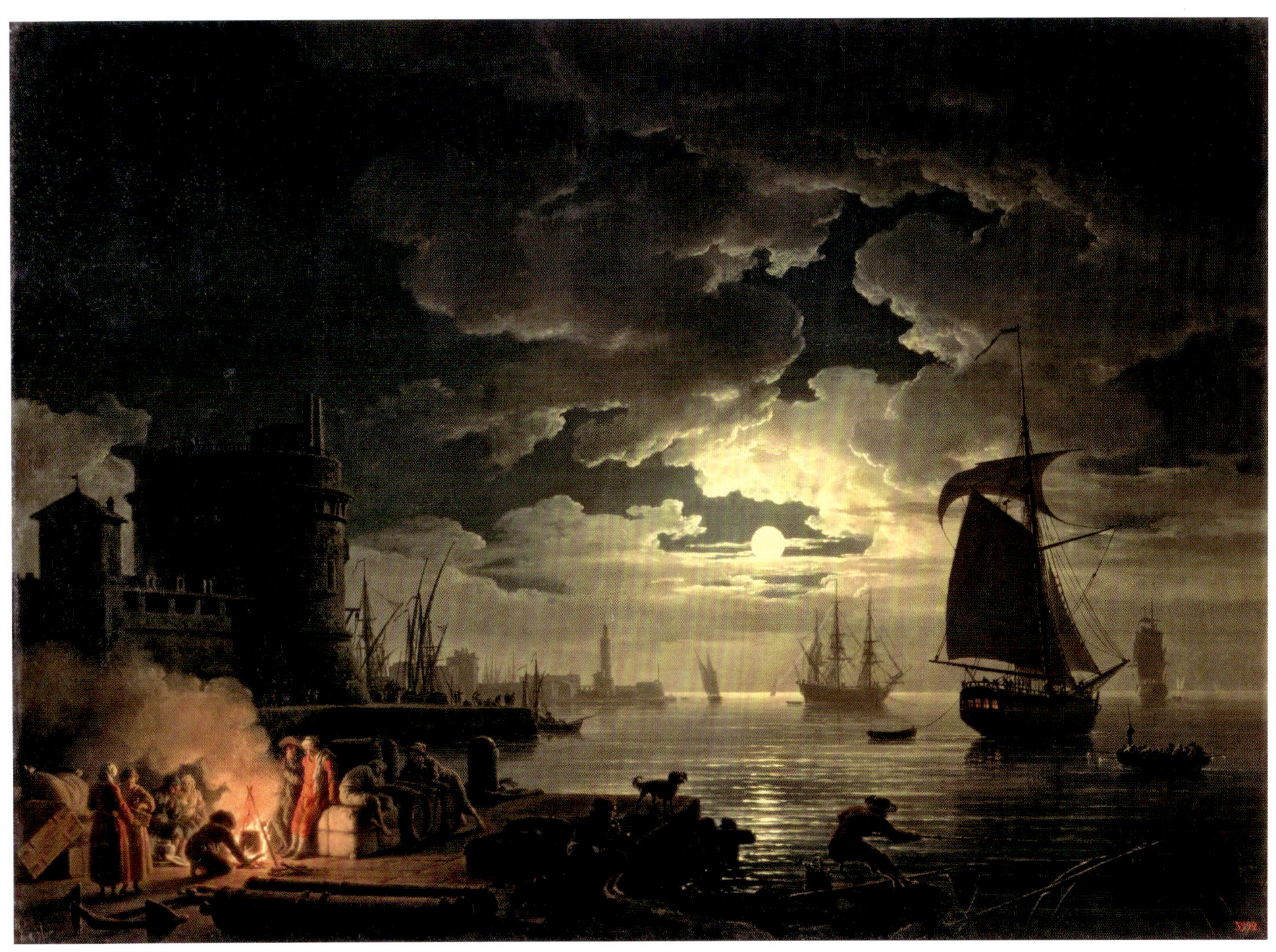

Claude Joseph Vernet (1714–89)

The Harbour of Palermo

Le Port de Palerme

Der Hafen von Palermo

El puerto de Palermo

O porto de Palermo

De haven van Palermo

1750, Oil on canvas/Huile sur toile, State Hermitage Museum, St. Petersburg

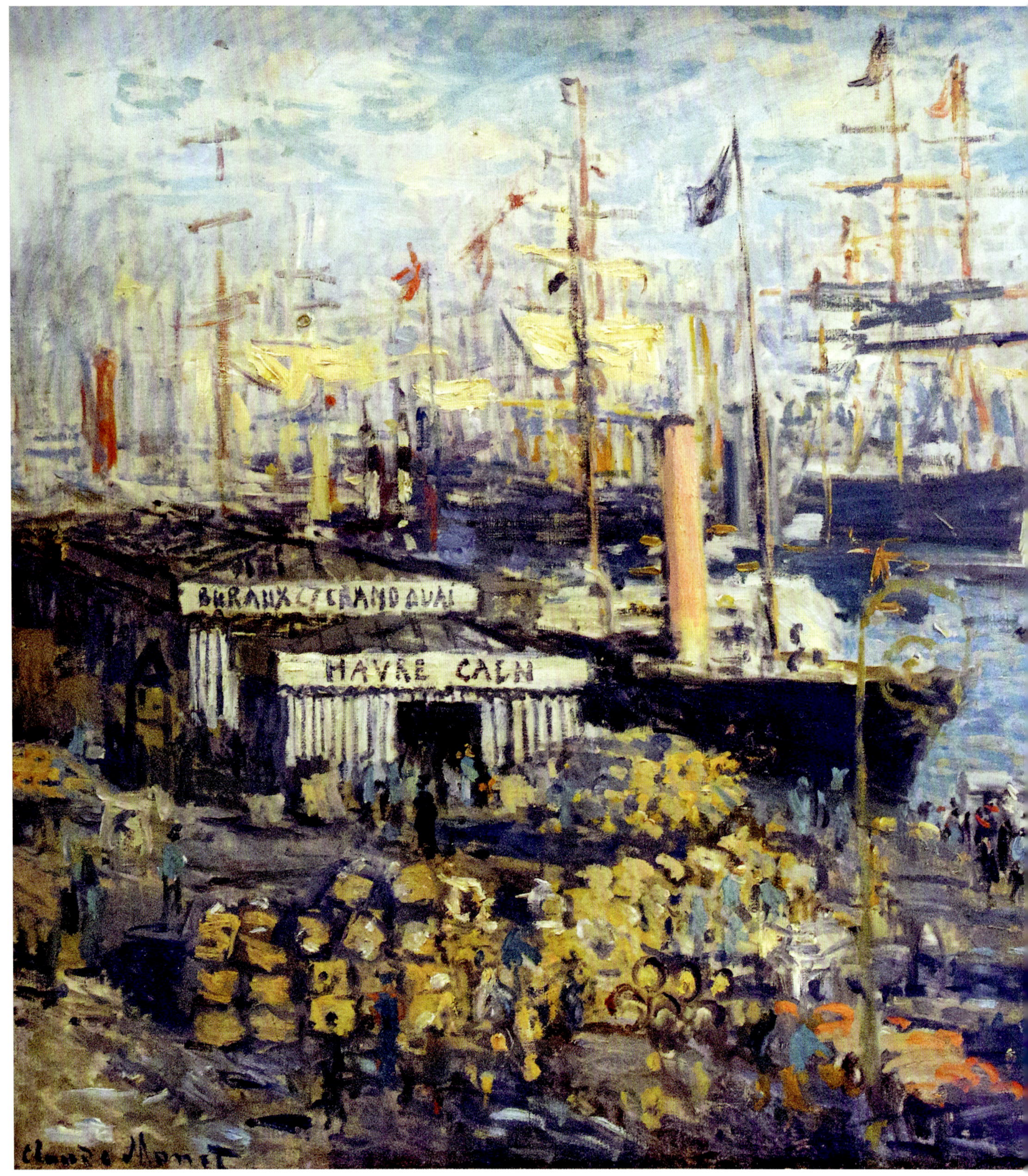

BUREAUX GRAND QUAI
HAVRE CAEN
Claude Monet

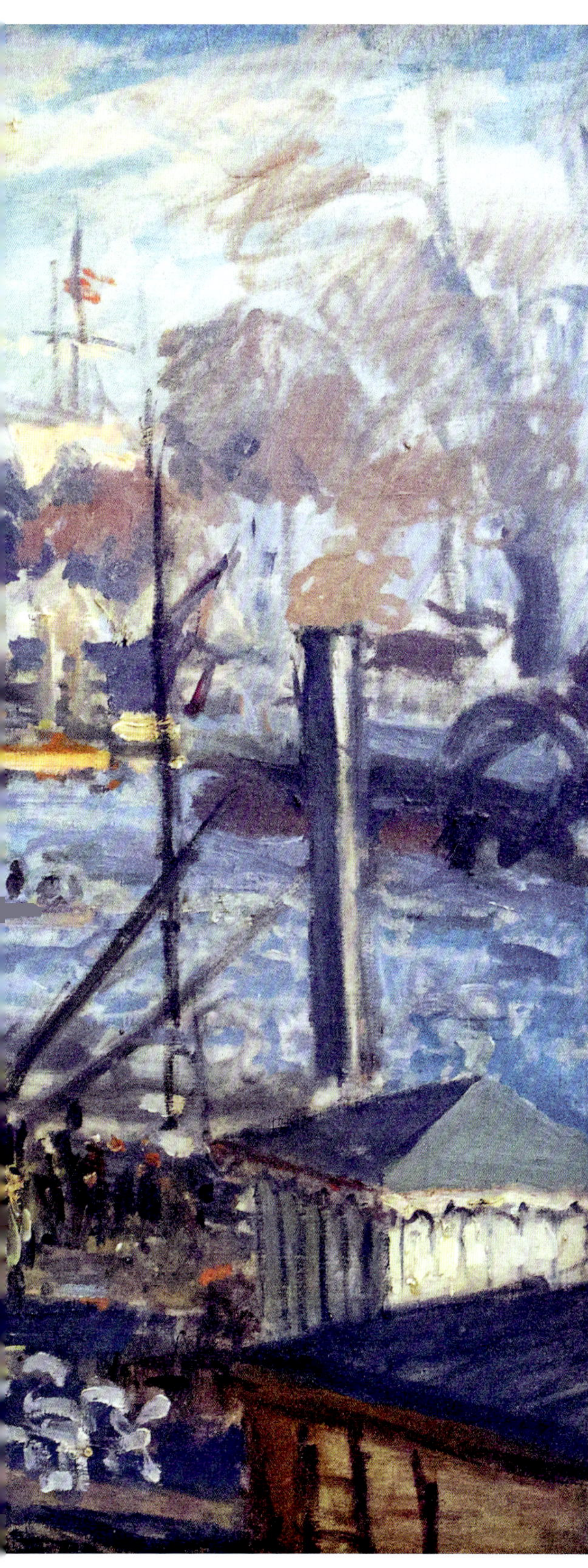

Claude Monet (1840–1926)

Grand Quay at Le Havre

Le Grand Quai au Havre

Der große Kai von Le Havre

El gran muelle de Le Havre

O grande cais de Le Havre

De grote kade van Le Havre

1874, Oil on canvas/Huile sur toile, 61 × 81 cm, State Hermitage Museum, St. Petersburg

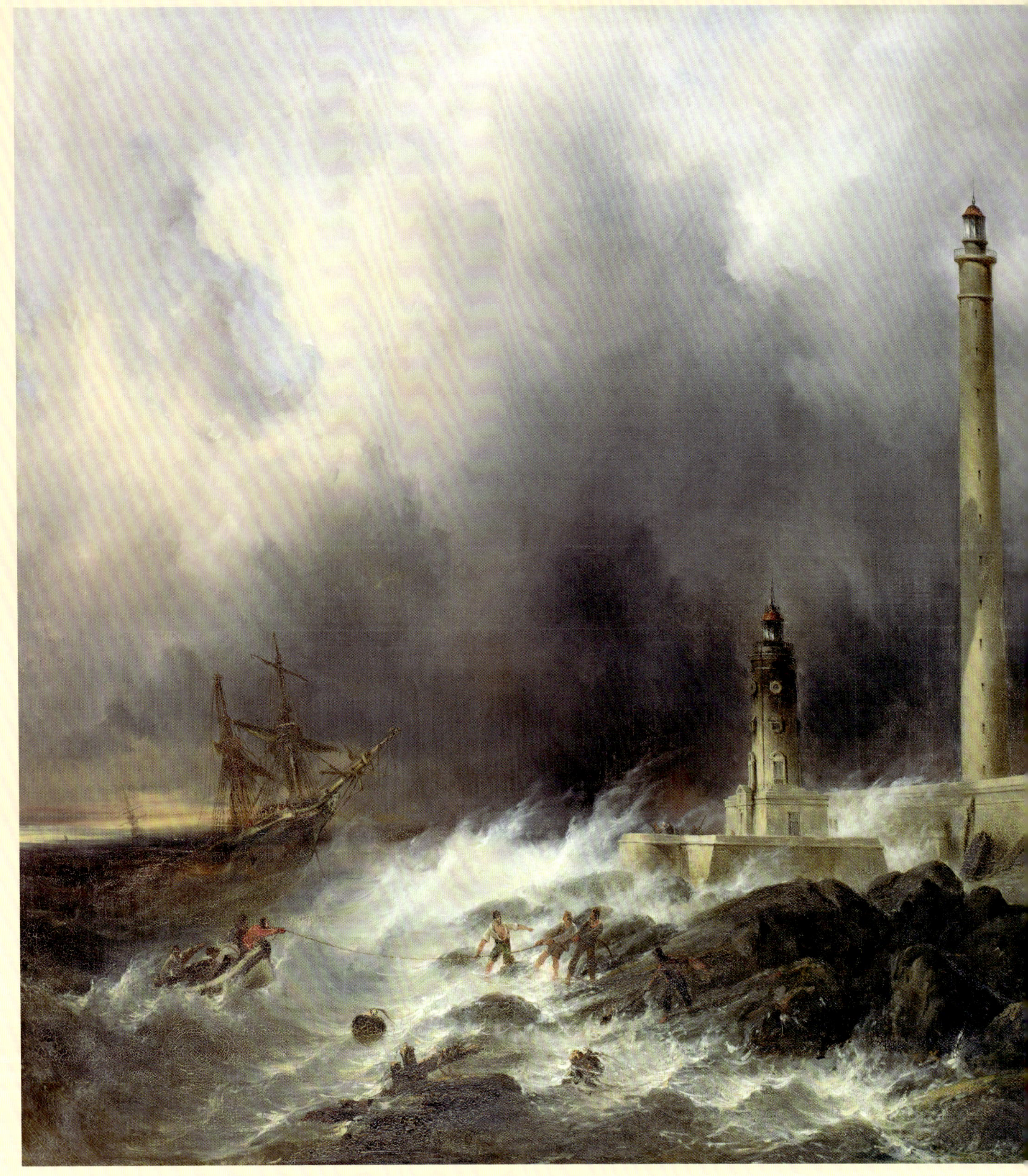

Lighthouses

Phares

Leuchttürme

Faros

Faróis

Vuurtorens

Jean-Louis Petit (1795–1876)

View of the Lighthouse at Gatteville

Vue d'un phare à Gatteville

Blick auf den Leuchtturm von Gatteville

Vista del faro de Gatteville

Vista do farol de Gatteville

Gezicht op de vuurtoren van Gatteville

1839, Oil on canvas/Huile sur toile, Musée d'Art Thomas Henry, Cherbourg

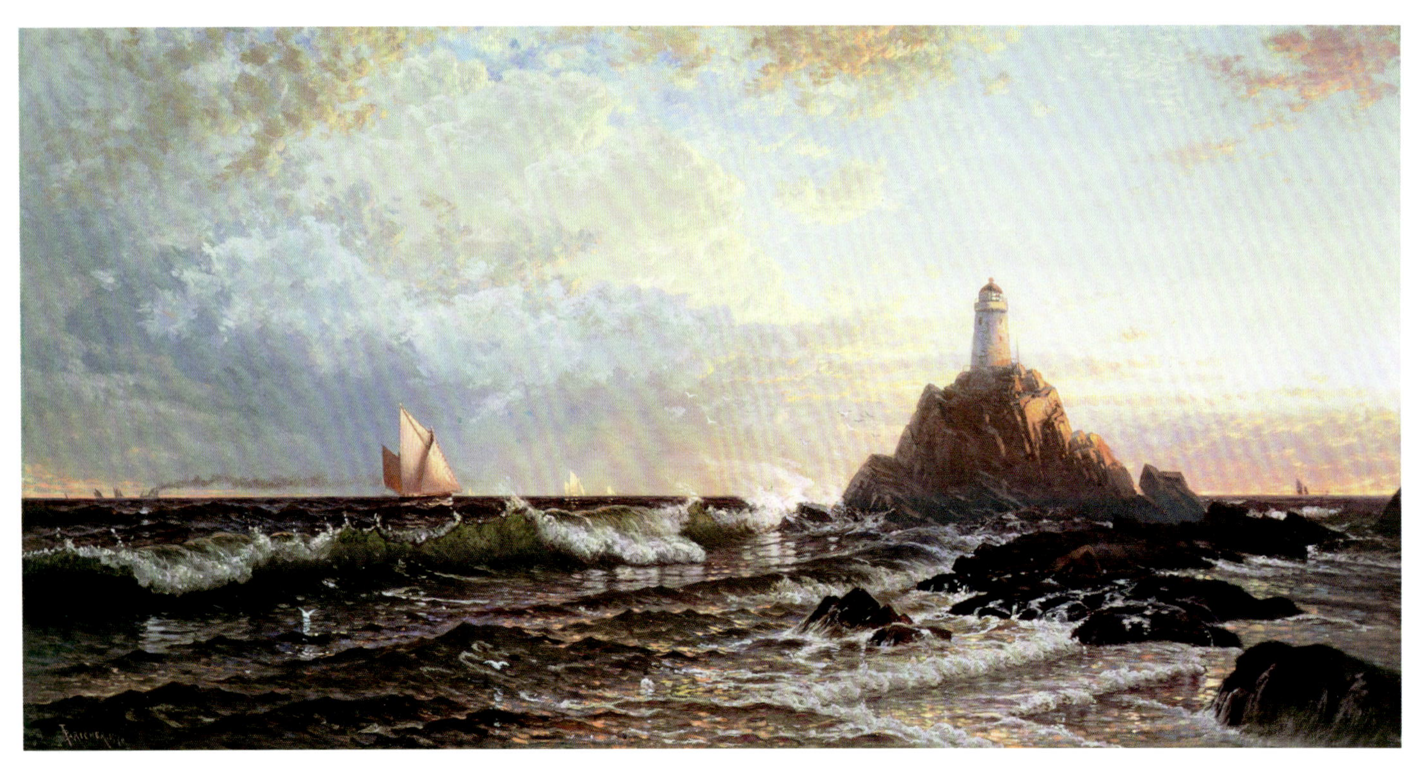

Alfred Thompson Bricher (1837–1908)

The Lighthouse

Le Phare

Der Leuchtturm

El faro

O Farol

De vuurtoren

n. d., Oil on canvas/Huile sur toile, Private collection

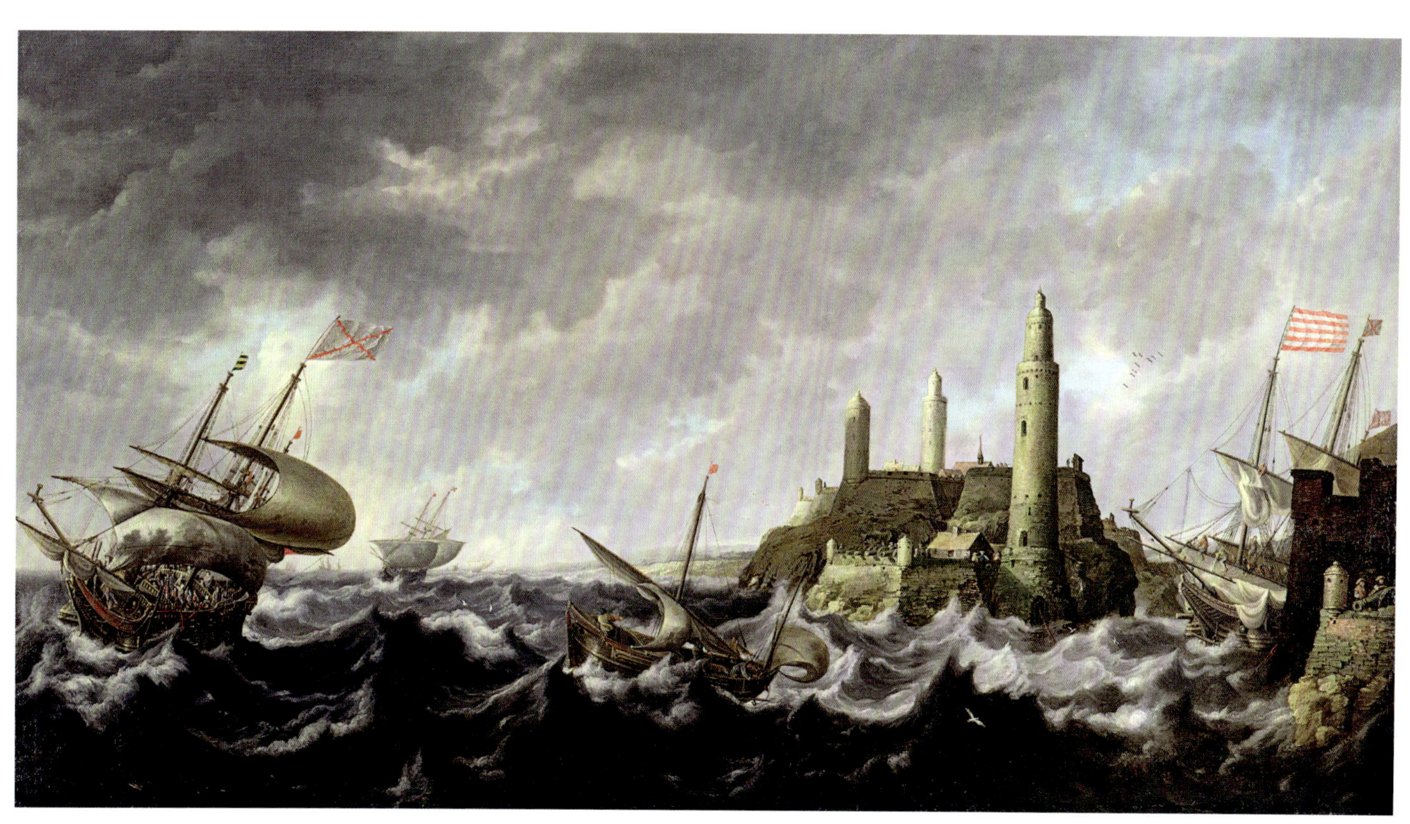

Bonaventura Peeters (1614–52)

Seascape with a Lighthouse

Paysage de mer avec phare

Meerespanorama mit Leuchtturm

Marina con faro

Paisagem marinha com farol

Zeegezicht met vuurtoren

n. d., Oil on canvas/Huile sur toile, 105,5 × 190,5 cm, Private collection

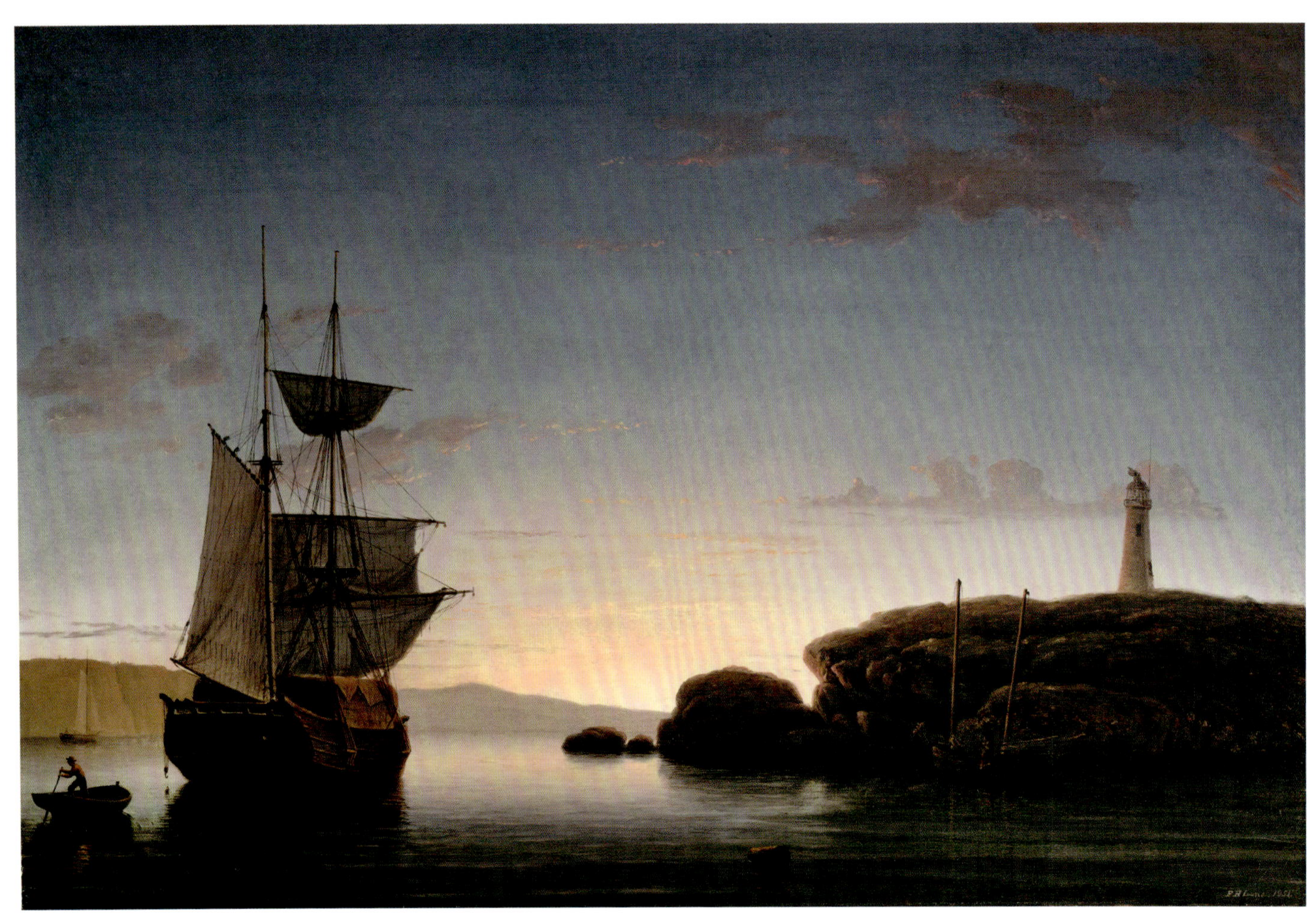

Fitz Henry Lane (1804–65)

Lighthouse at Camden, Maine

Phare à Camden, Main

Leuchtturm in Camden, Maine

Faro en Camden, Maine

Farol em Camden, Maine

Vuurtoren in Camden, Maine

1851, Oil on canvas/Huile sur toile, 58,4 × 86,4 cm, Yale Center for British Art, New Haven

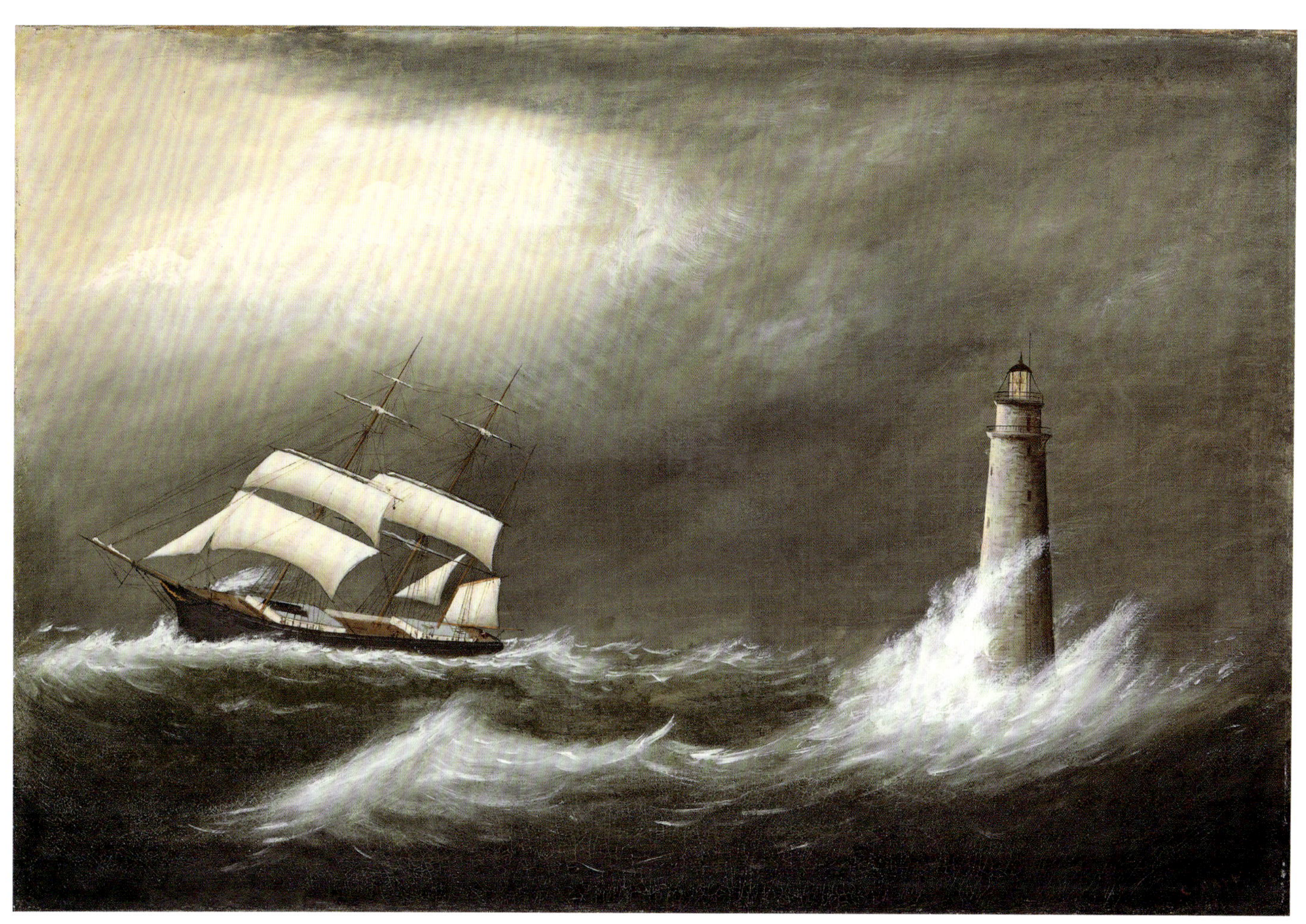

Clement Drew (1806–89)

Ships Passing Minot's Ledge Light

Bateaux passant devant le phare de Minot's Ledge

Schiffe passieren den Leuchtturm von Minot's Ledge

Barcos pasando el faro de Minot's Ledge

Navios passam o farol de Minot's Ledge

Schepen passeren de vuurtoren van Minot's Ledge

n. d., Oil on canvas/Huile sur toile, 50,8 × 76,2 cm, Private collection

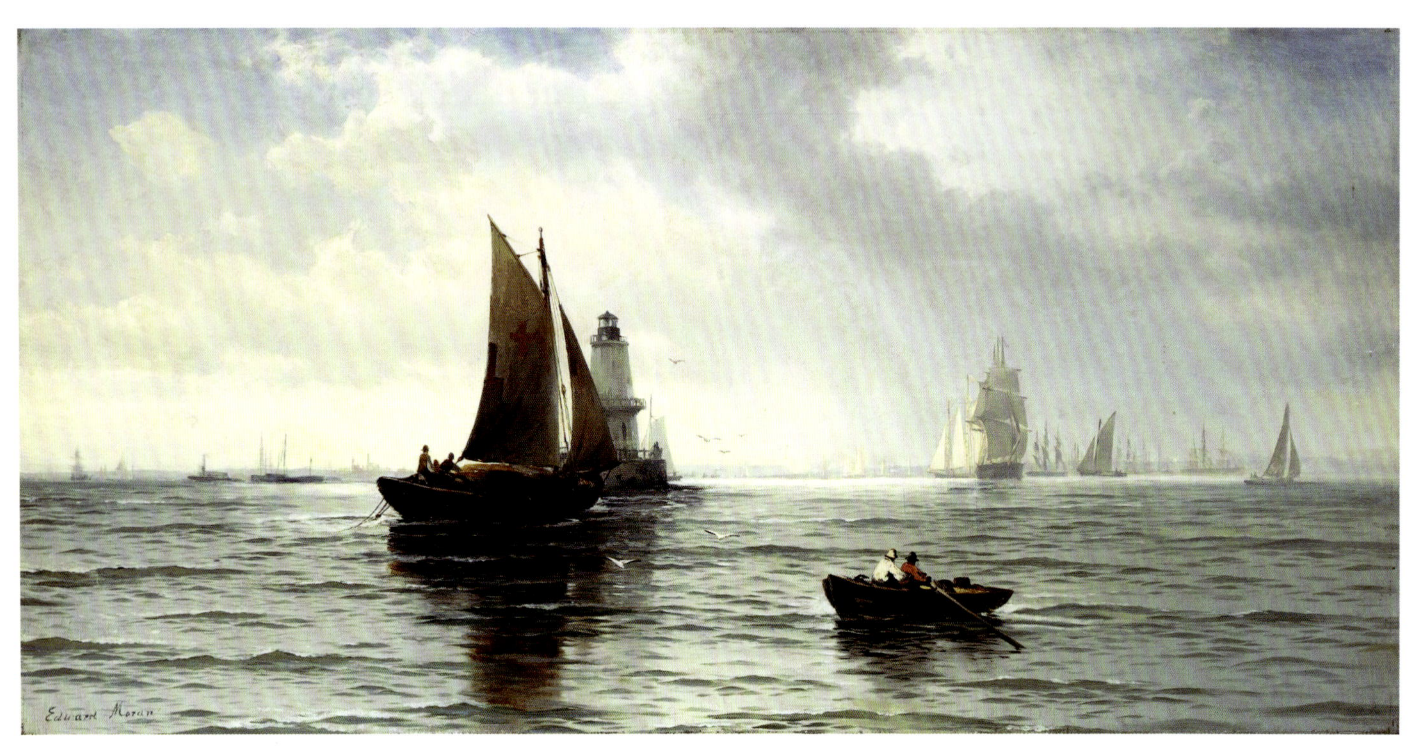

Edward Moran (1829–1901)

Around the Lighthouse

Autour du Phare

Um den Leuchtturm

Alrededor del faro

Em volta do farol

Rond de vuurtoren

n. d., Oil on canvas/Huile sur toile, 46,4 × 91,5 cm, Private collection

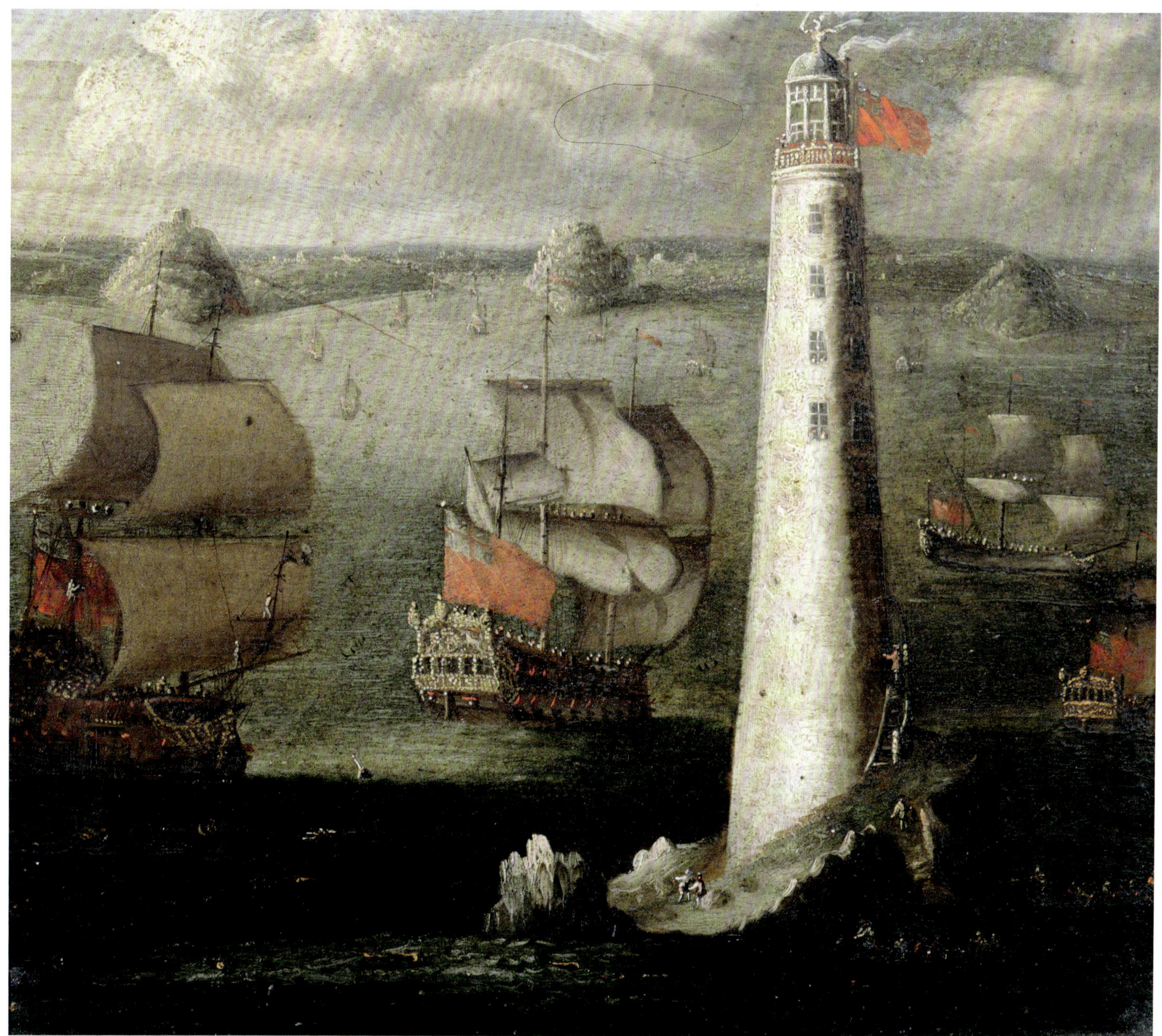

Isaac Sailmaker (c. 1633–1721)

Men o' War and Other Vessels before the Eddystone Lighthouse

Hommes à la guerre et autres embarcations devant le phare d'Eddystone

Kriegs- und andere Schiffe vor dem Eddystone-Leuchtturm

Barcos de guerra y otras embarcaciones delante del faro de Eddystone

Navios de guerra e outras embarcações ao largo do Farol de Eddystone

Oorlogsschepen en andere schepen bij de vuurtoren van Eddystone

n. d., Oil on canvas/Huile sur toile, Private collection

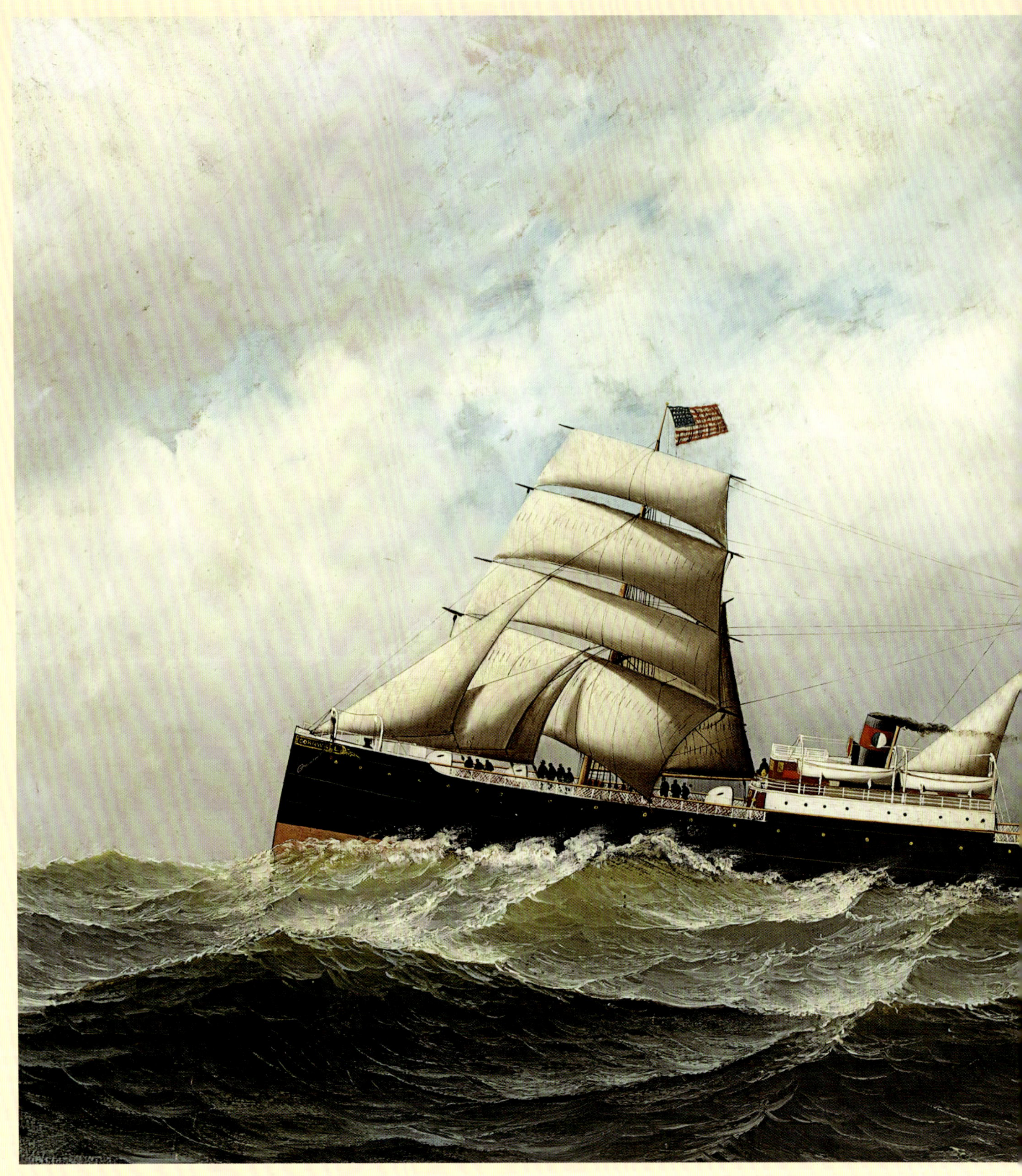

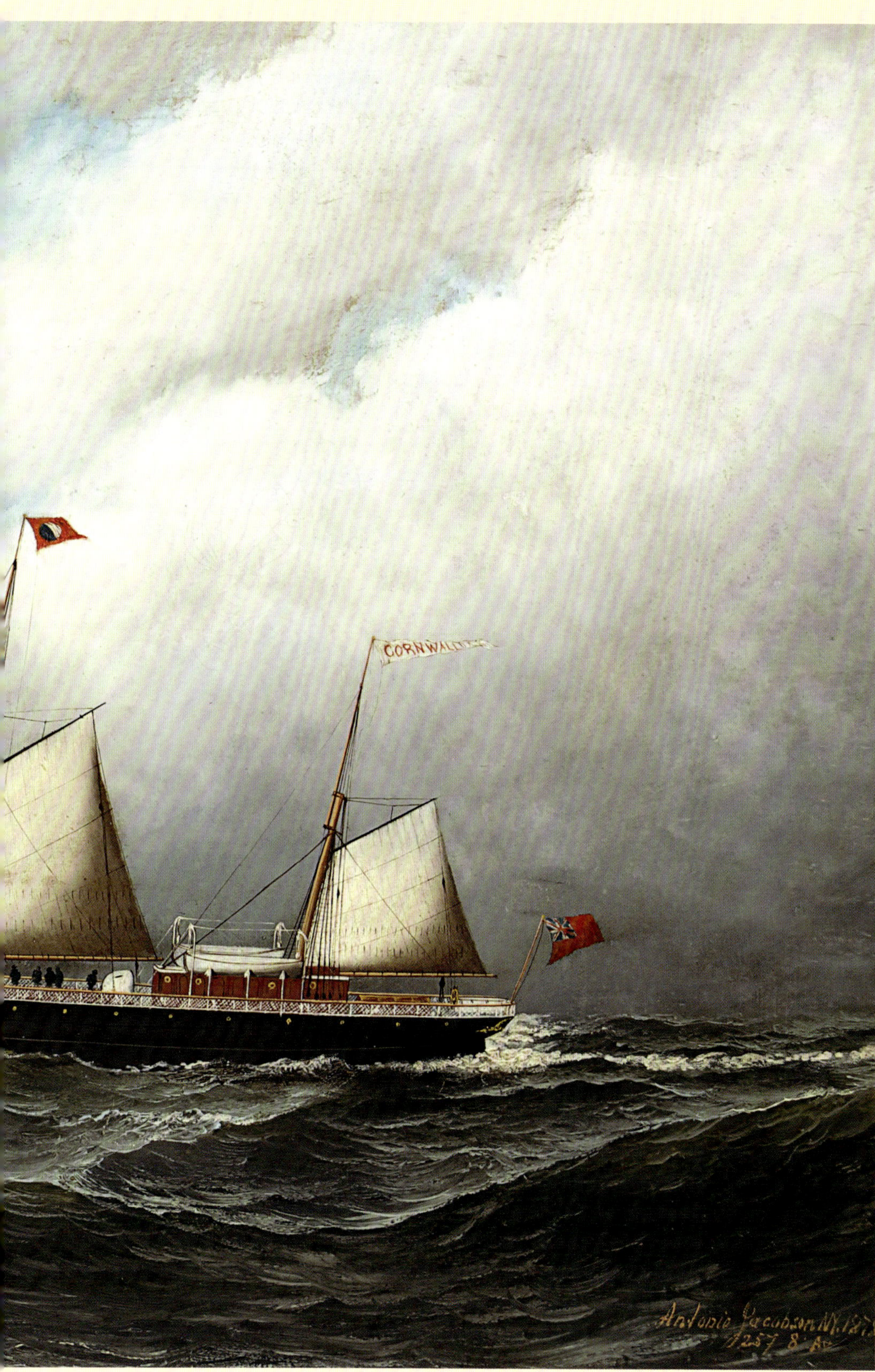

Antonio Jacobsen (1850–1921)

Steamship *Cornwall*

Bateau-vapeur *Cornwall*

Das Dampfschiff *Cornwall*

El barco de vapor *Cornwall*

O navio a vapor *Cornwall*

Het stoomschip *Cornwall*

1878, Oil on canvas/Huile sur toile, Bristol
Museum and Art Gallery, Bristol

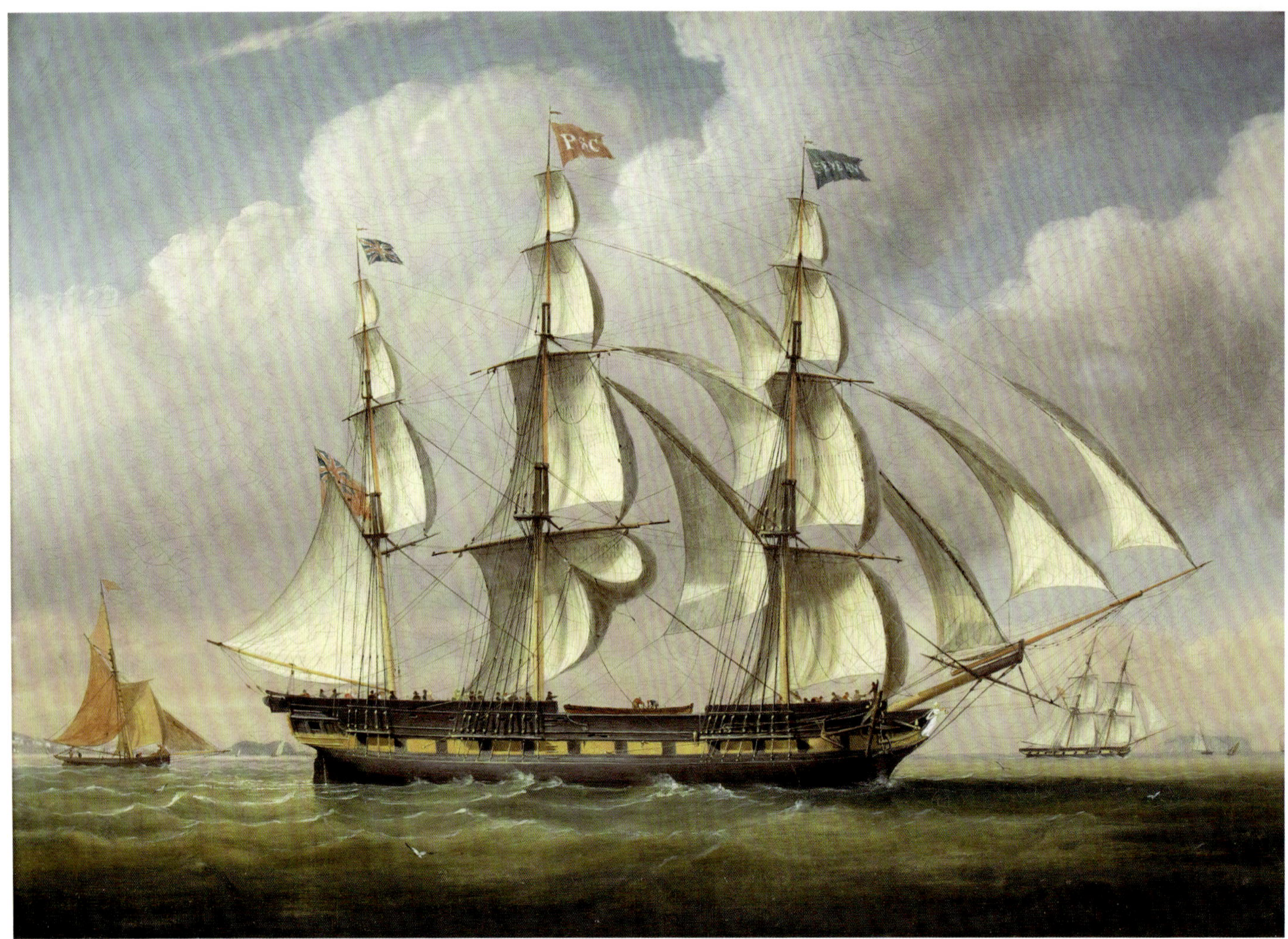

Joseph Walter (1783–1856)

The *Severn*

Le *Severn*

Die *Severn*

El *Severn*

O *Severn*

De *Severn*

c. 1835, Oil on canvas/Huile sur toile, 52 × 75 cm, Bristol Museum and Art Gallery, Bristol

Joseph Walter (1783–1856)

Three-masted Ship before the Wind

Navire à trois mâts face au vent

Dreimaster vor dem Wind

Buque de tres mástiles ante el viento

Navio em linha ao vento

Driemaster voor de wind

n. d., Oil on canvas/Huile sur toile, 82 x 69 cm, Bristol Museum an Art Gallery, Bristol

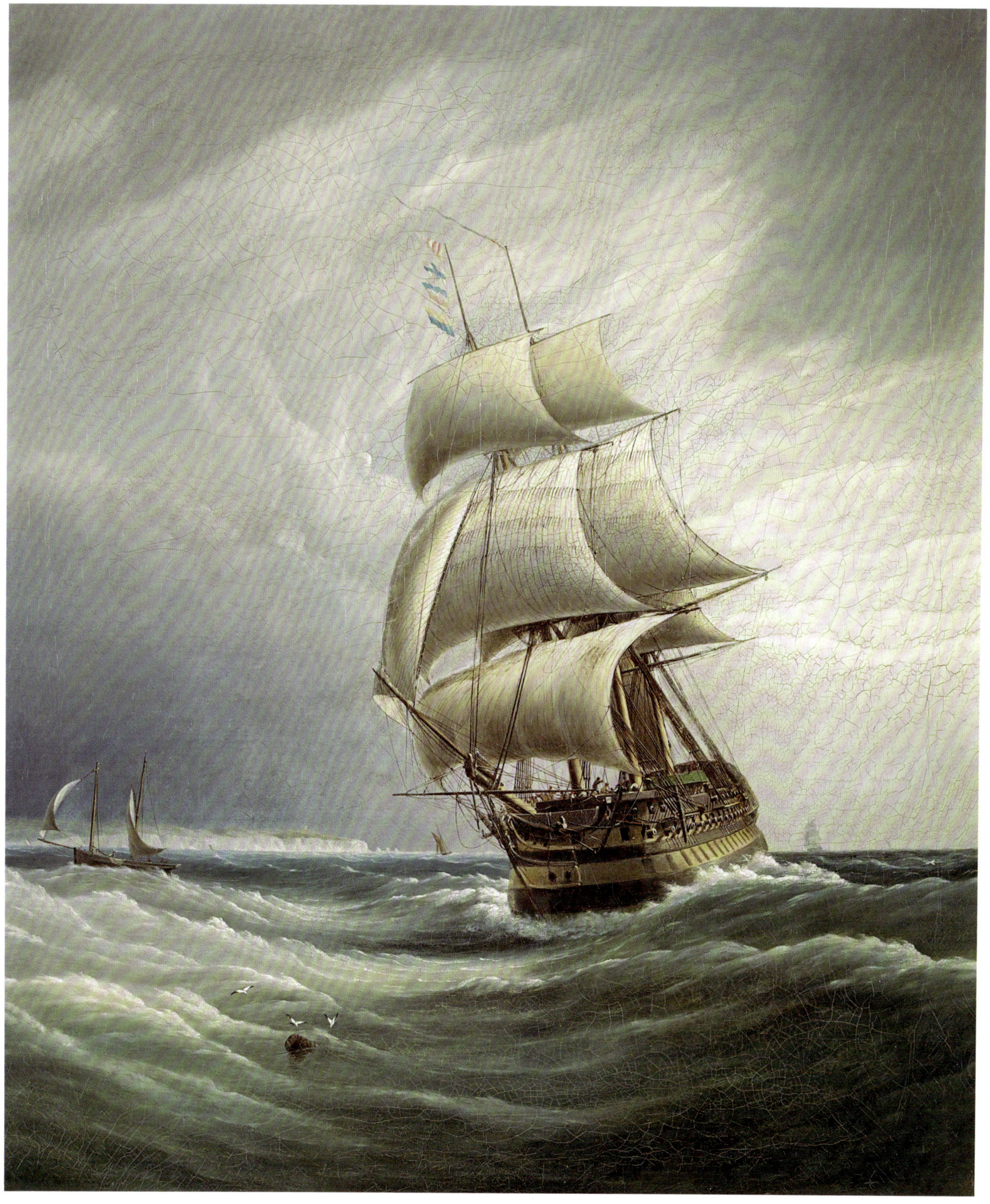

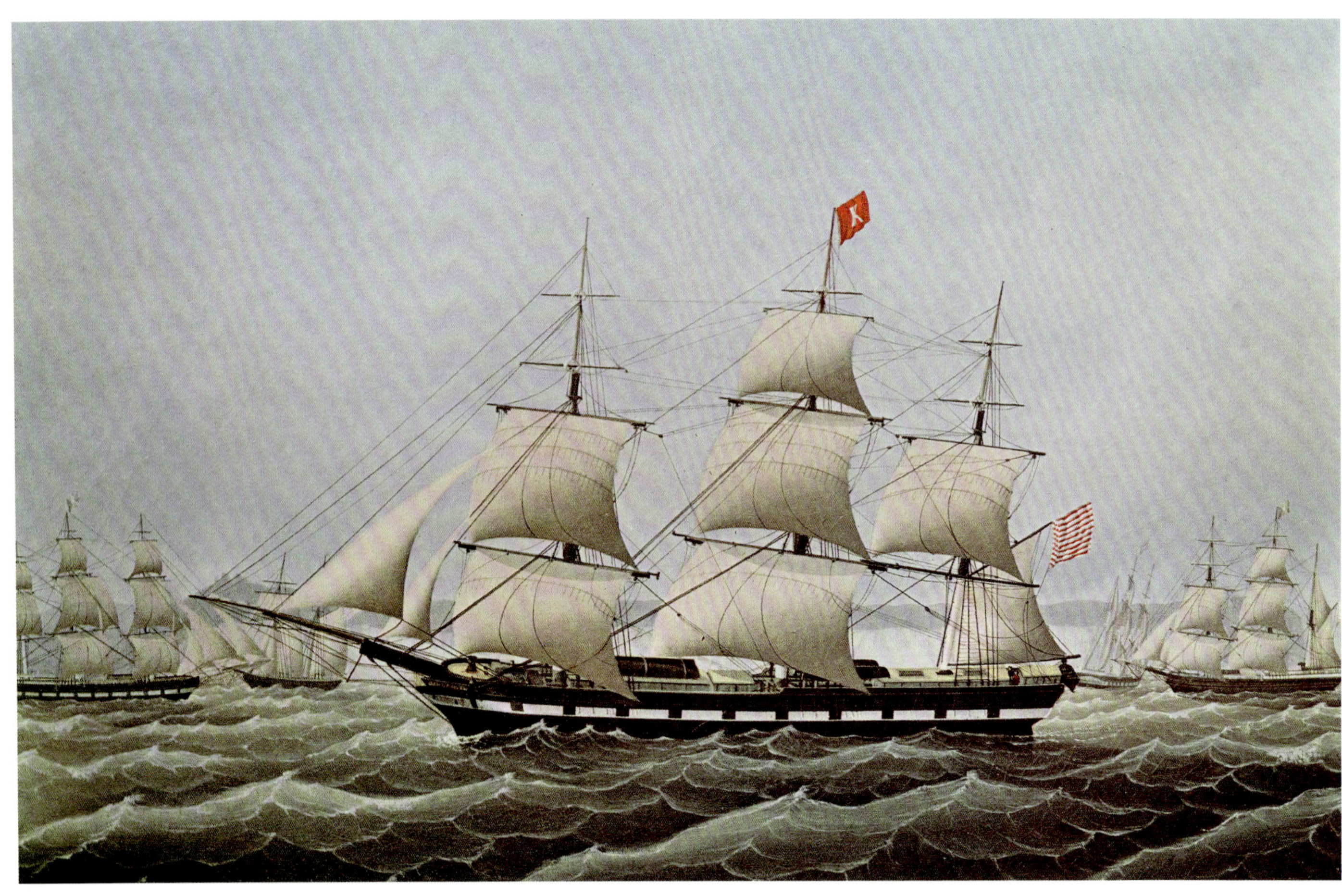

Anonymous

Full-rigged Ship *Bremerhaven*, ex-*Rochester*

Trois-mâts carré *Bremerhaven*, ex-*Rochester*

Das Vollschiff *Bremerhaven*, vormals *Rochester*

El *Bremerhaven* completamente equipado, antiguamente el *Rochester*

A fragata *Bremerhaven*, anteriormente *Rochester*

De *Bremerhaven*, voorheen de *Rochester*, onder vol zeil

n. d., Color lithography/Lithographie couleur, Private collection

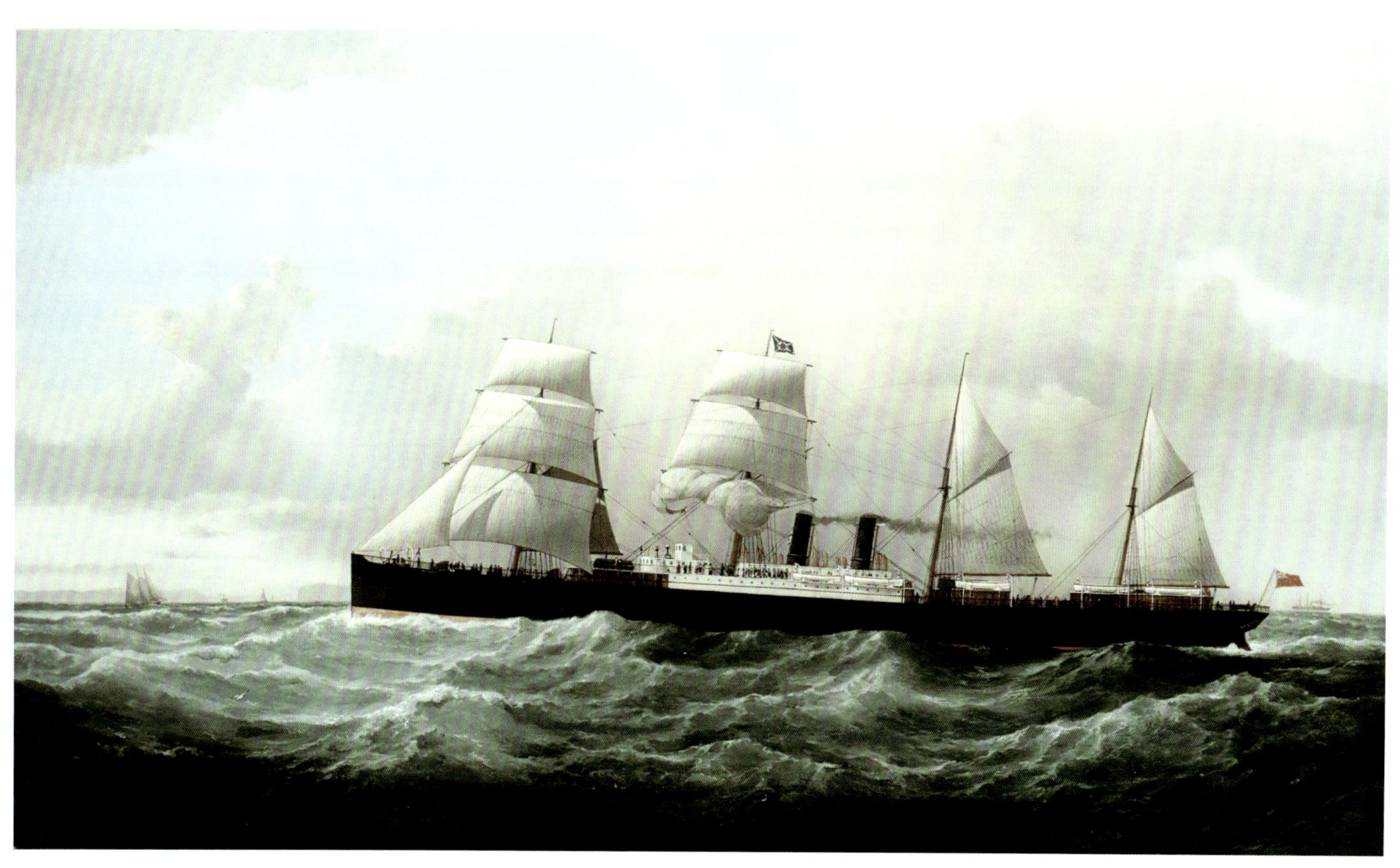

Samuel Walters (1811–82)

The *Orient* on the Clyde

L'*Orient* sur le Clyde

Die *Orient* auf dem Clyde

El *Orient* en el Clyde

O *Orient* no Clyde

De *Orient* op de Clyde

n. d., Oil on canvas/Huile sur toile, 92,1 × 154,9 cm, Private collection

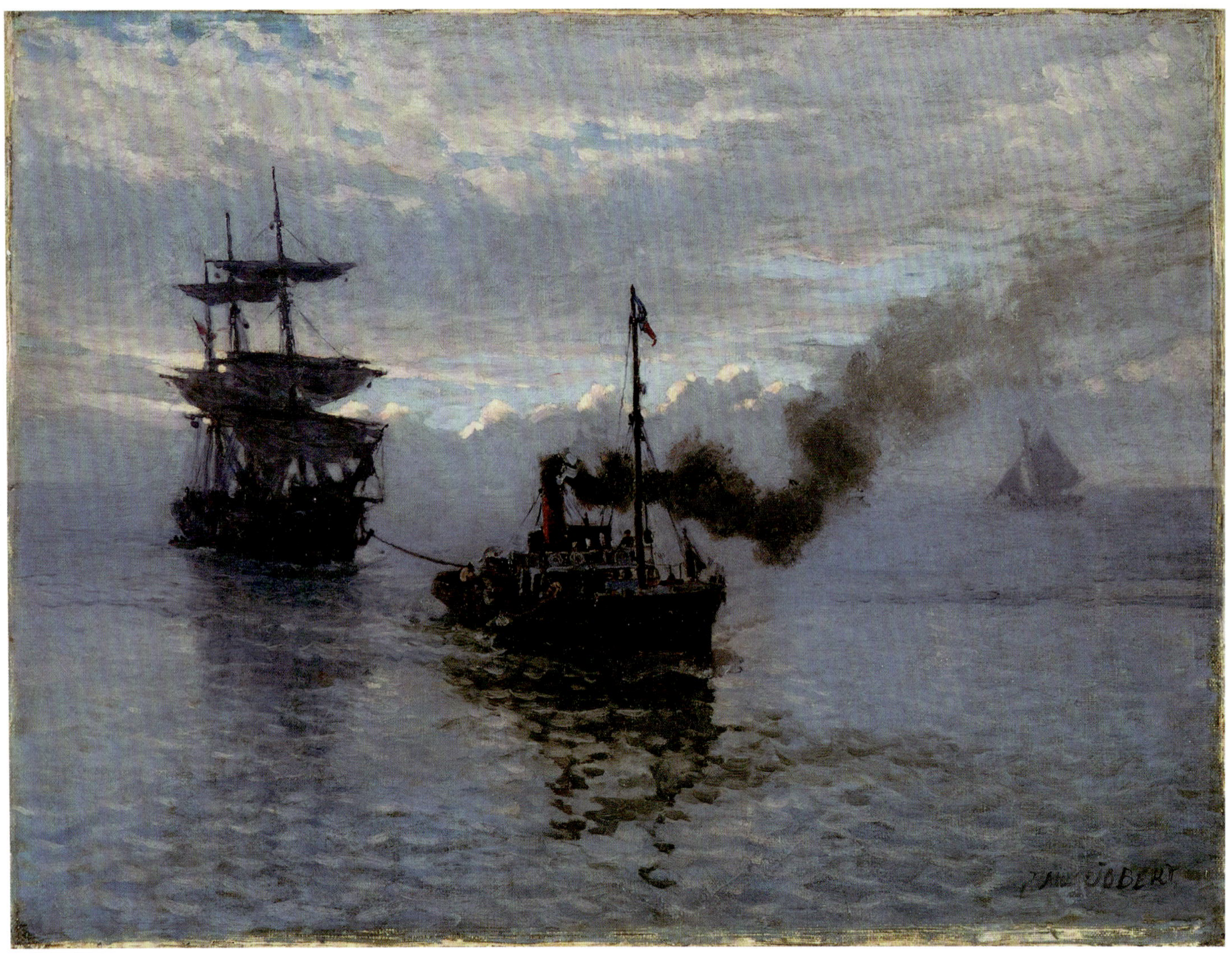

Paul Jobert (1863–1942)

Tug Towing a Three-Masted Ship

Bateau remorquant un navire à trois mâts

Schlepper mit Dreimaster im Schlepptau

Remolcador con buque de tres palos

Rebocador com navio em linha a reboque

Sleepboten nemen een driemaster op sleeptouw

n. d., Oil on canvas/Huile sur toile, 46,5 × 61 cm, The Beaney, Canterbury

Alejo Fernández (1475–1543)

Spanish Caravel *(detail from the* Virgin of Navigators *altarpiece)*

Caravelle espagnole *(détail du rétable de la* Vierge des Navigateurs*)*

Spanische Karavelle *(Detail des Altarbildes* Die Jungfrau der Seefahrer*)*

Caravela española *(detalle del Altar de la* Virgen de los Navegantes*)*

Caravela Espanhola *(detalhe do retábulo* A Virgem dos Navegantes*)*

Spaans karveel *(detail van het altaarstuk* De Maagd der Zeevaarders*)*

n. d., Oil on panel/Huile sur bois, Casa de Contratación, Sevilla

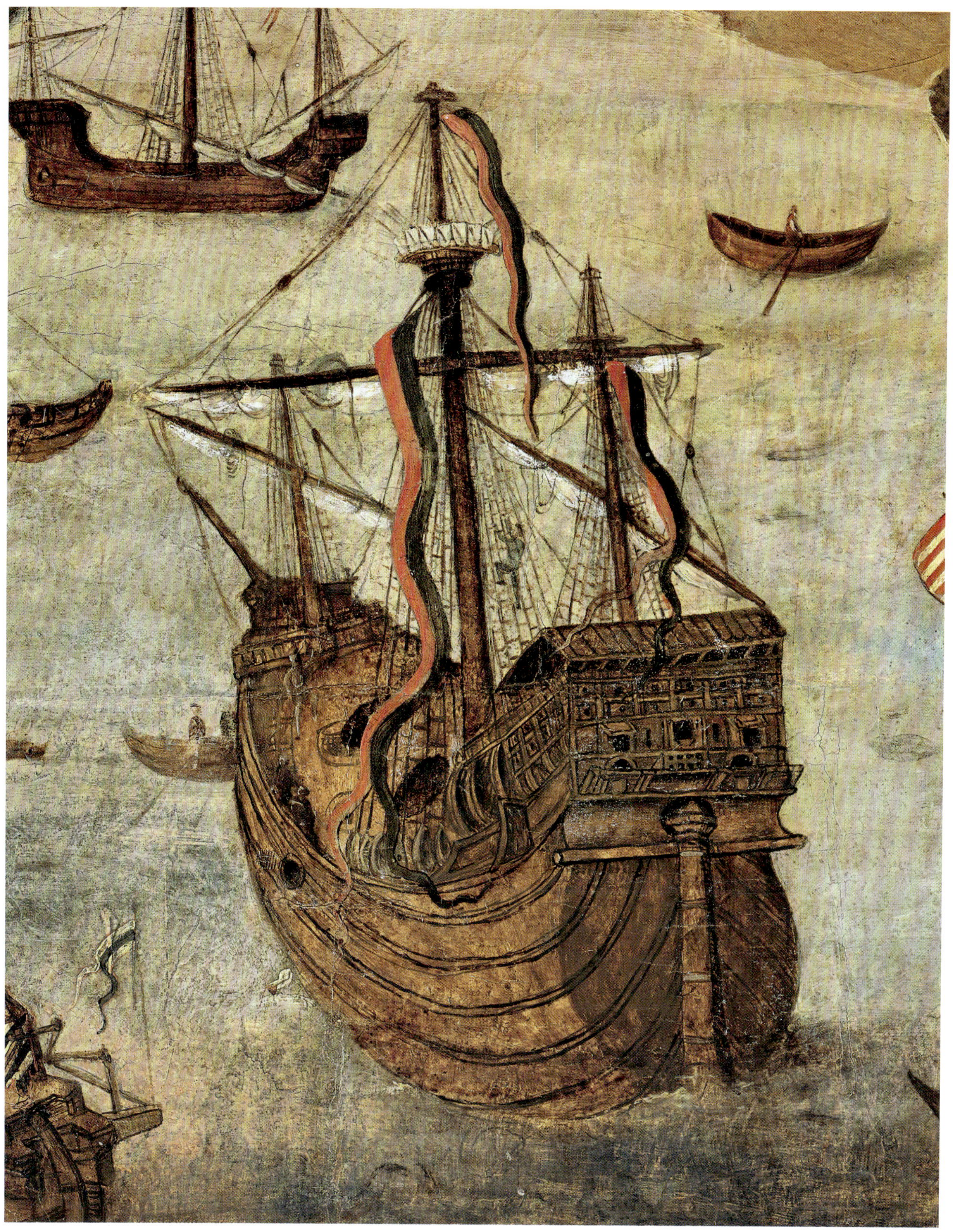

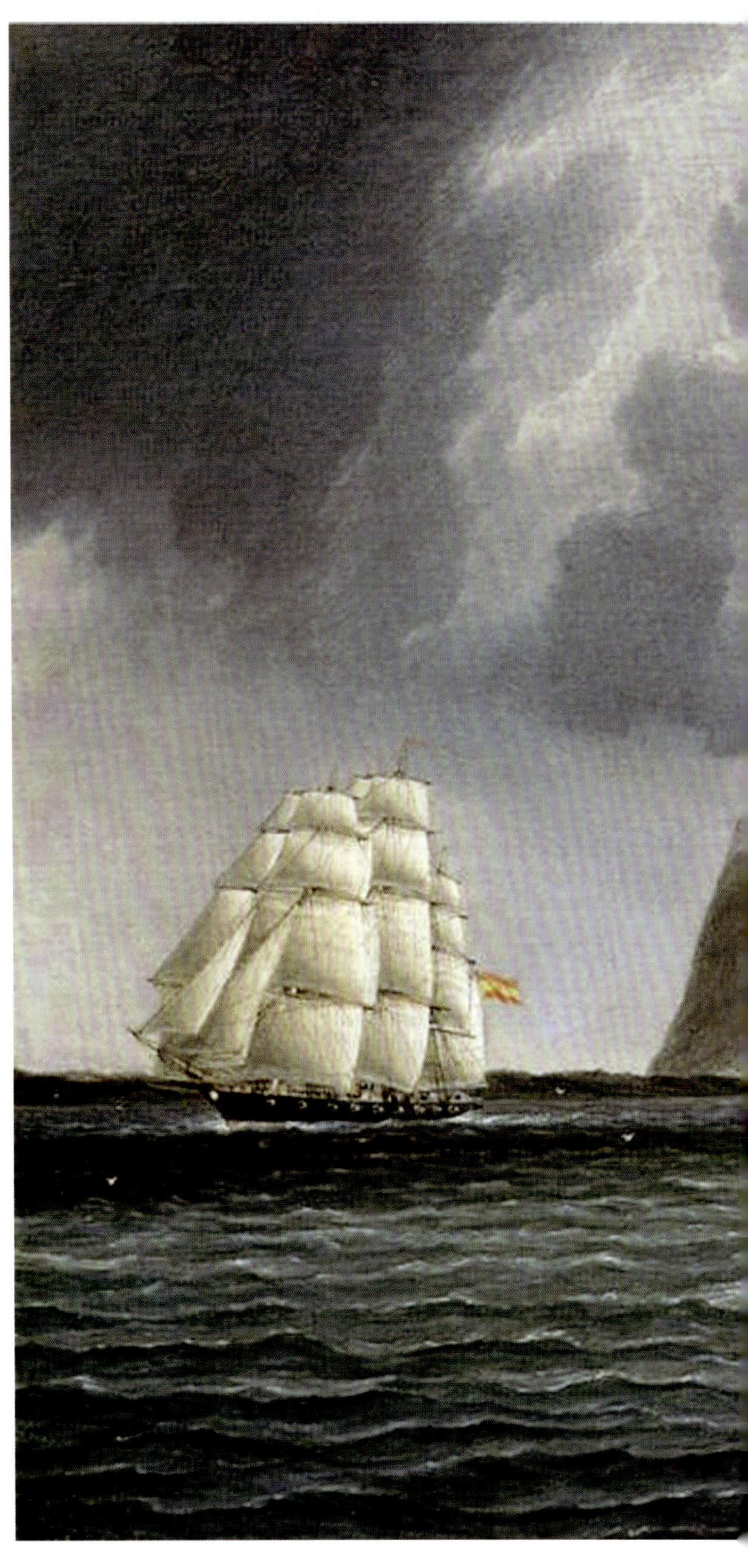

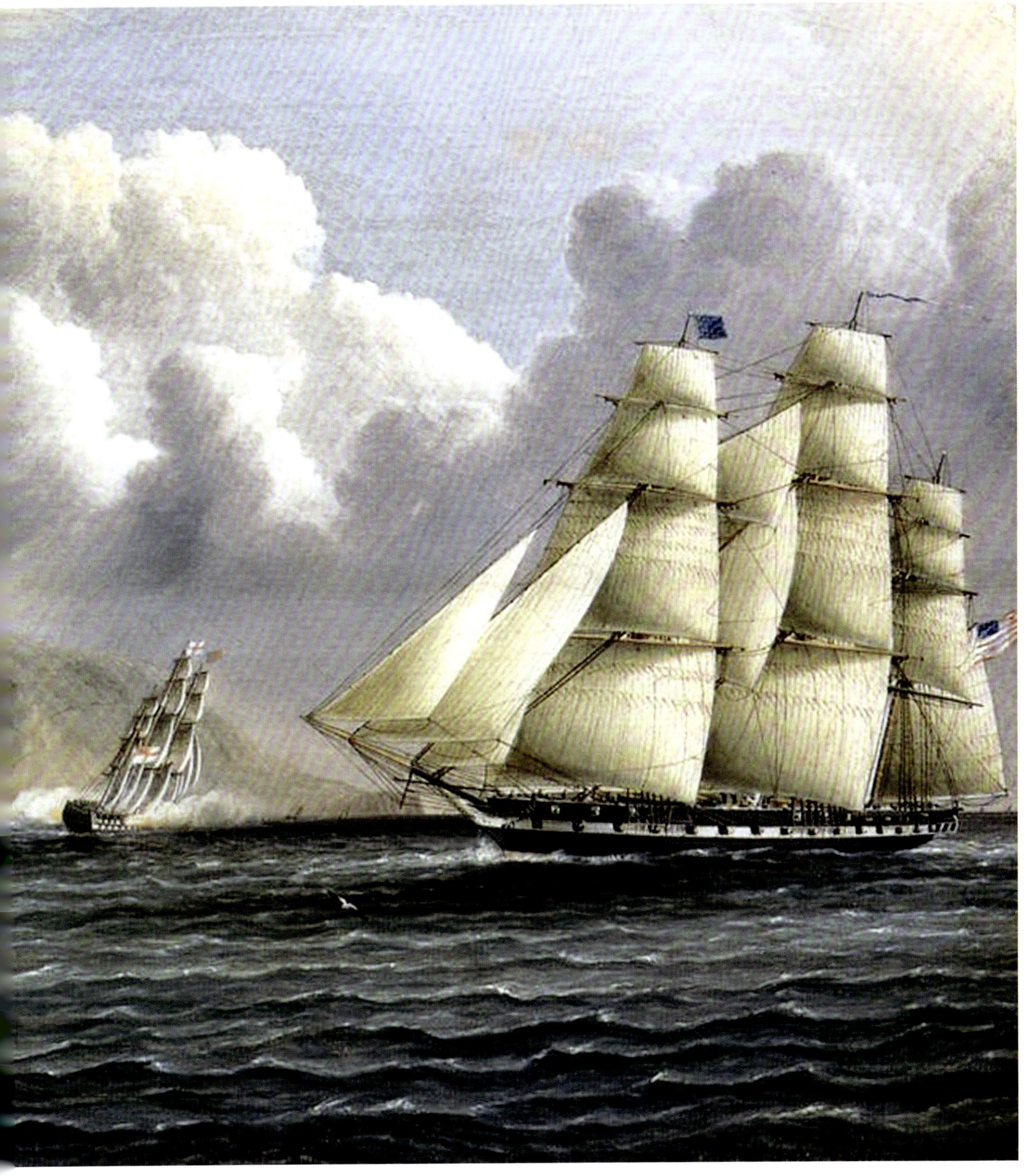

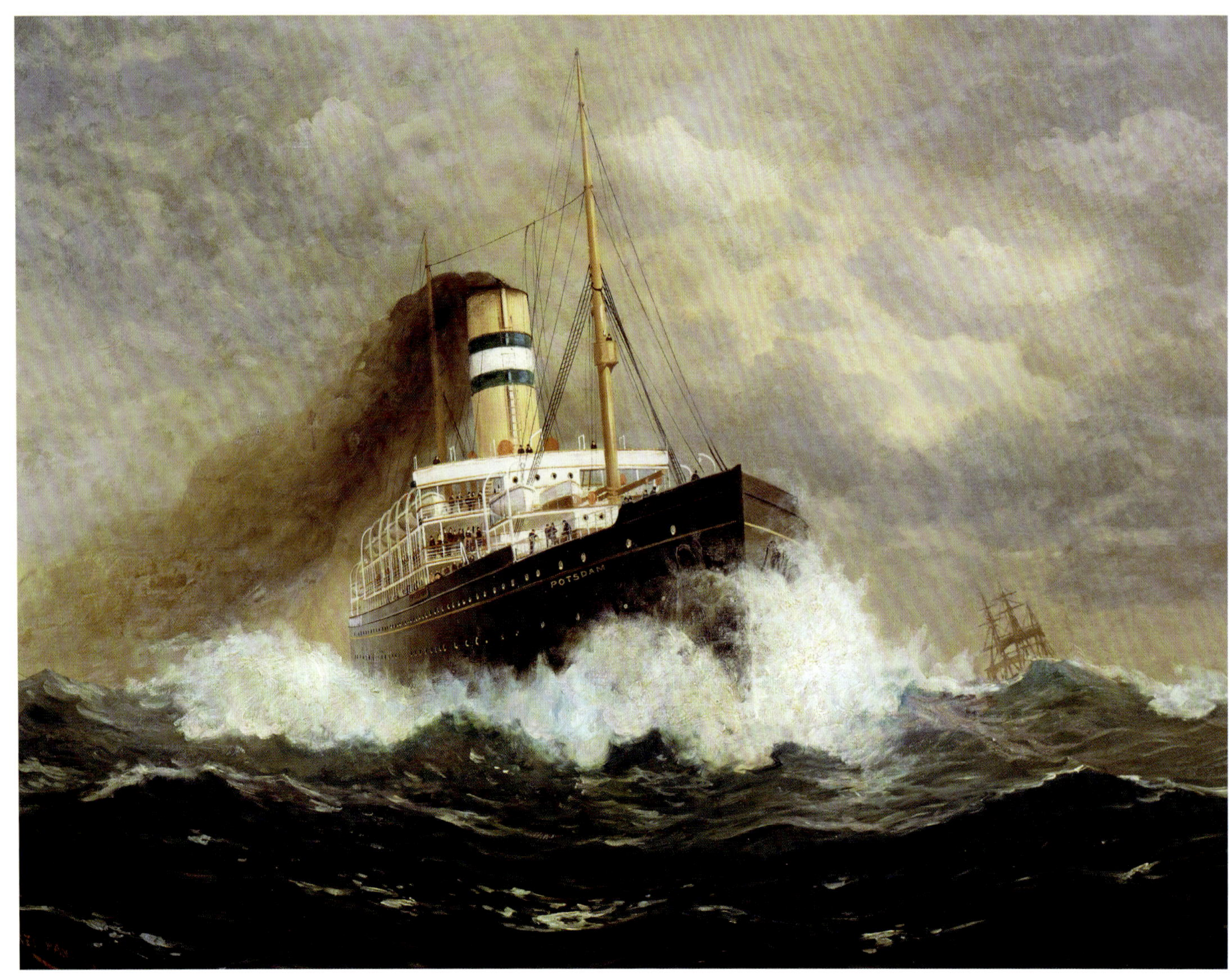

Fred Pansing (1844–1912)

The *Potsdam*

Le *Potsdam*

Passagierschiff *Potsdam*

Barco de pasajeros *Potsdam*

Navio de passageiros *Potsdam*

Het passagiersschip de *Potsdam*

20th century/xxe siècle, Oil on canvas/Huile sur toile, Private collection

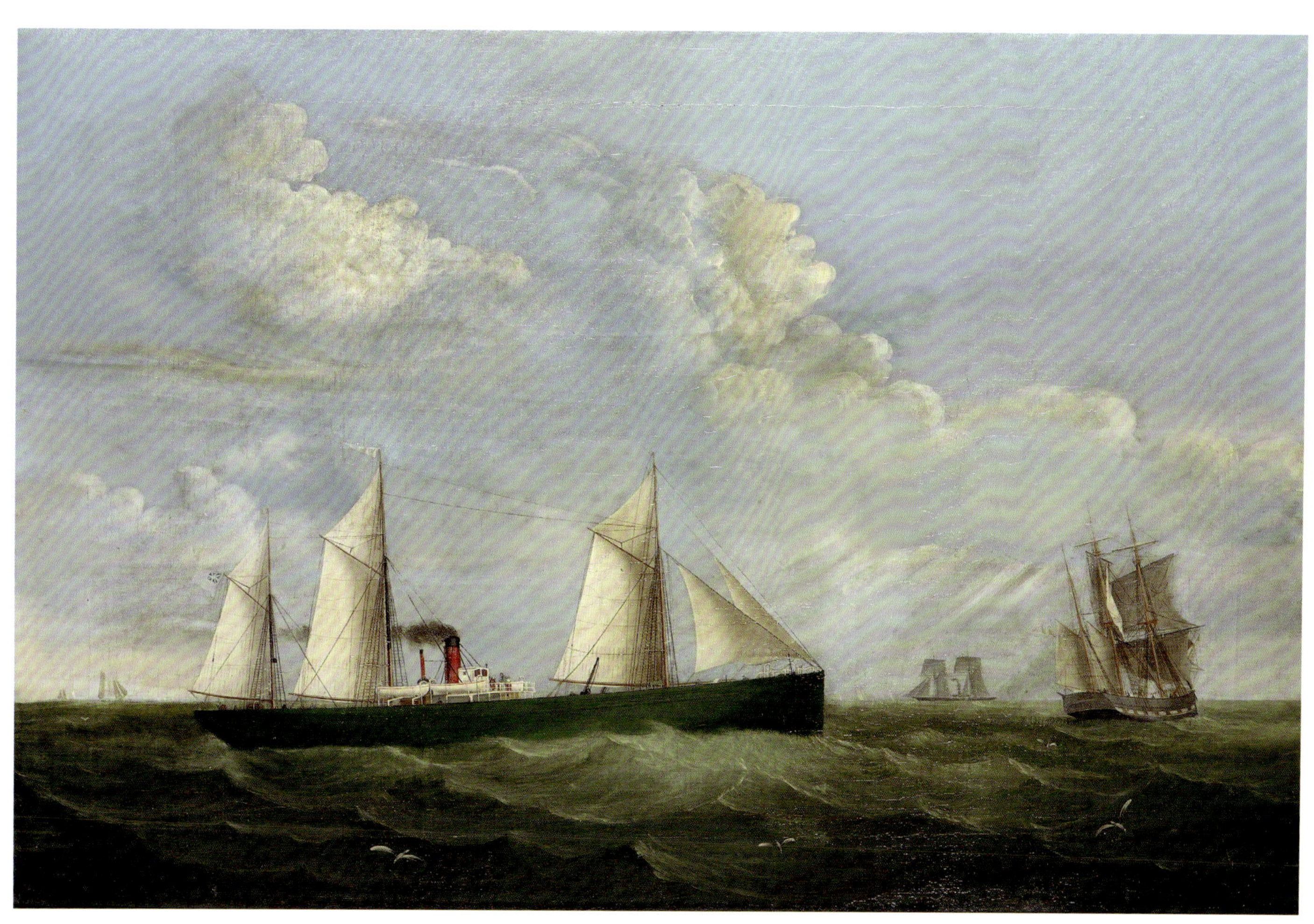

English school/École anglaise

S.S. *Juno*

S.S. *Juno*

Dampfschiff *Juno*

Barco de vapor *Juno*

Navio a vapor *Juno*

Het stoomschip *Juno*

19th century/XIXe siècle, Oil on canvas/Huile sur toile, 67x97 cm, Maritime Museum, Hull

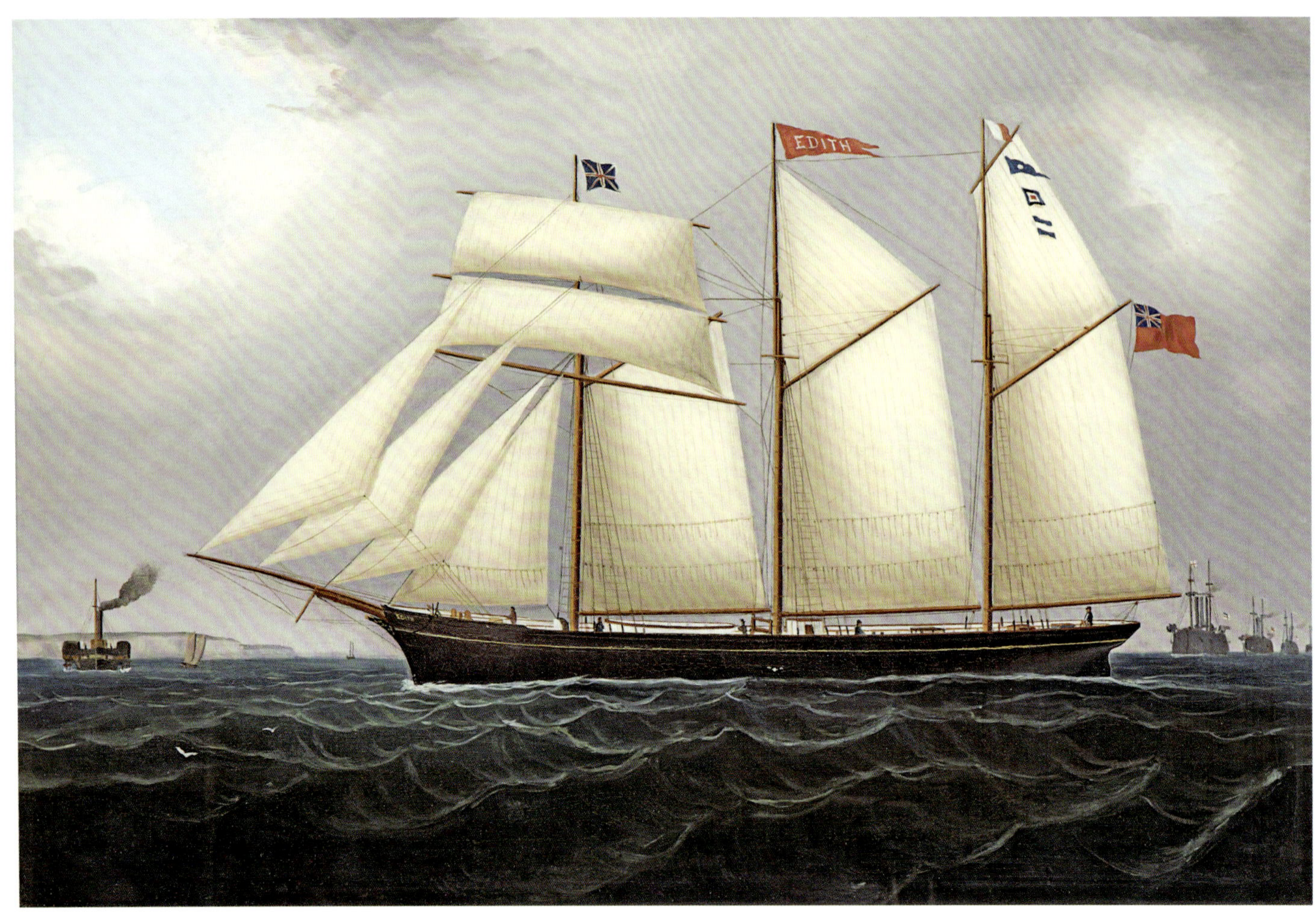

Thomas Chidgey (1855–1926)

The Schooner *Edith*

La Goélette *Edith*

Der Schoner *Edith*

La goleta *Edith*

A escuna *Edith*

De schoener *Edith*

1890–1900, Oil on canvas/Huile sur toile, 61 × 91,4 cm, Gloucester City Museum, Gloucester

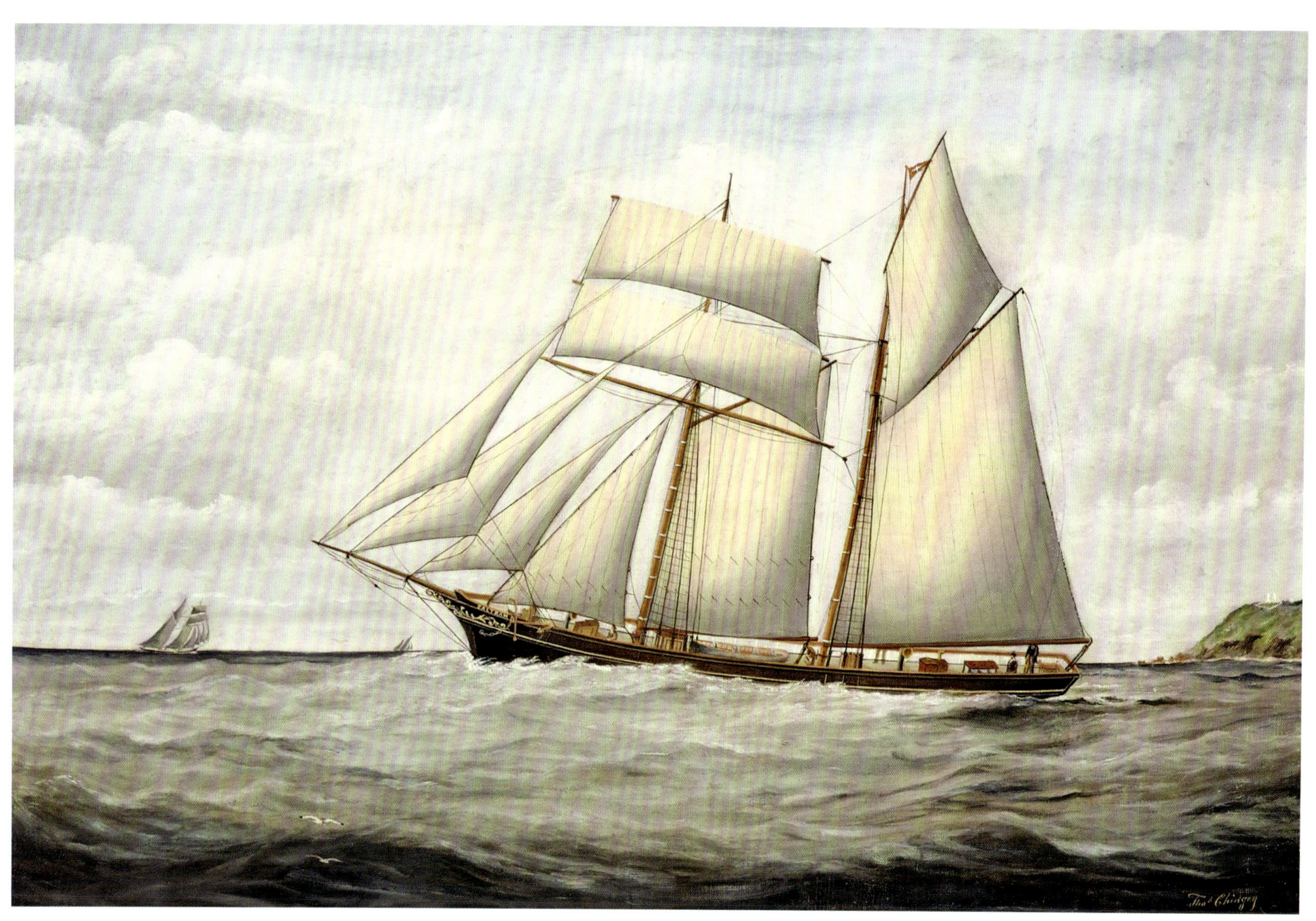

Thomas Chidgey (1855–1926)

The Schooner *Saltram*

La Goélette *Saltram*

Der Schoner *Saltram*

La goleta *Saltram*

A escuna *Saltram*

De schoener *Saltram*

1890–1900, Oil on canvas/Huile sur toile, 60,8 × 91,4 cm, Gloucester City Museum, Gloucester

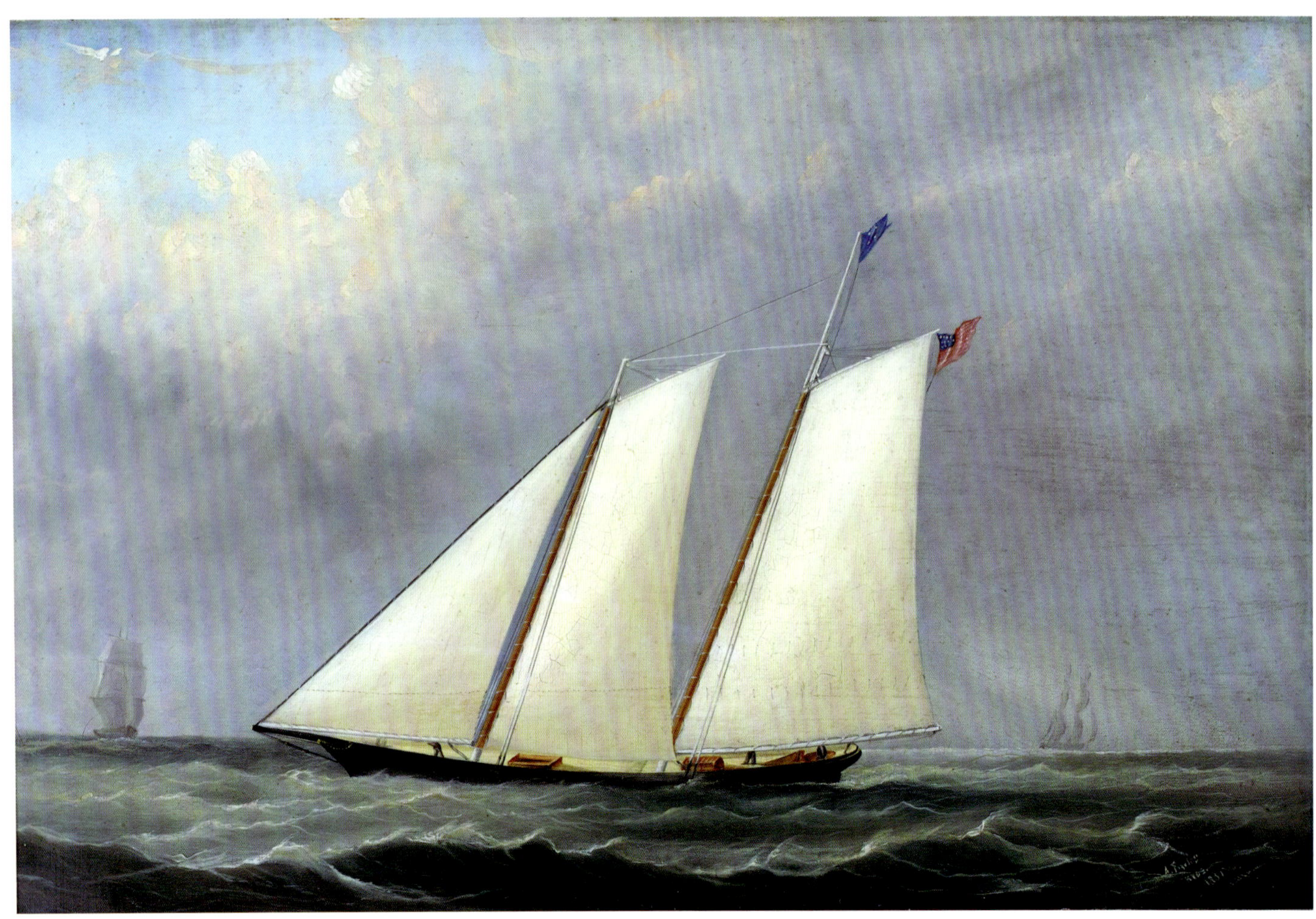

Arthur Wellington Fowles (c. 1815–83)

The Yacht *America*

Le Yacht *America*

Die Jacht *America*

El yate *America*

O iate *America*

Het jacht *America*

1851, Oil on canvas/Huile sur toile, 29,5 × 44 cm, The Holborne Museum of Art, Bath

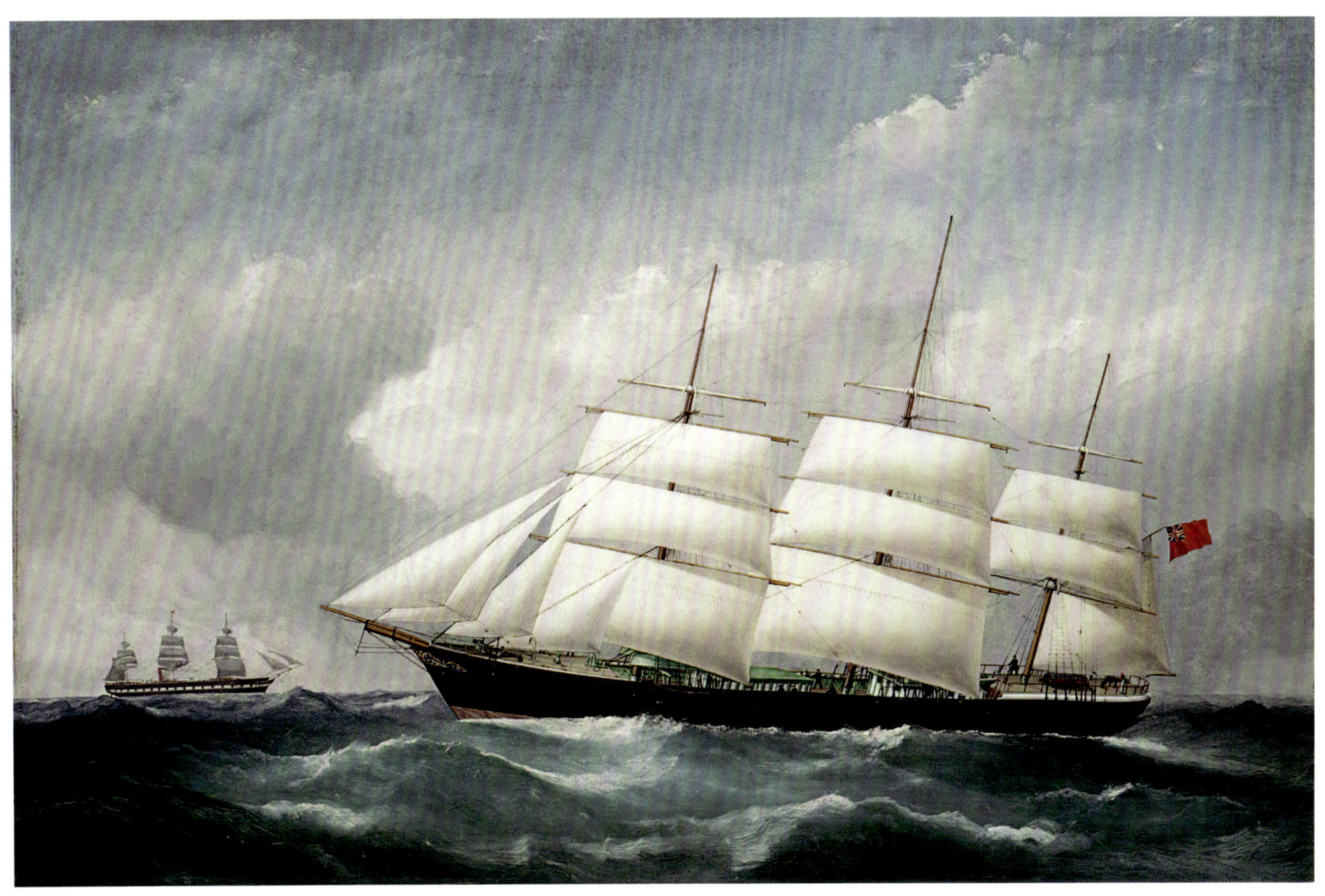

The Iron-Clad Barque *Ramsay*

Le barque *Ramsay*

Die mit Eisen gebaute Bark *Ramsay*

El bricbarca *Ramsay*, construido en hierro

O barque *Ramsay* construído com ferro

De van ijzer gebouwde bark *Ramsay*

1847, Oil on canvas/Huile sur toile, 61 × 92 cm, Manx Museum, Douglas

The Dutchman Willem van de Velde the Younger emigrated to England together with his father, who was also a painter, during the third English-Dutch War. He was asked to depict the English fleet and, to this day, he is regarded as the founder of English maritime painting.

Le Néerlandais Willem van de Velde le Jeune émigra en Angleterre avec son père, peintre également, pendant la Troisième Guerre anglo-néerlandaise. Il lui fut demandé de représenter la flotte anglaise et, à ce jour, il est considéré comme le fondateur de la peinture maritime anglaise.

Der Niederländer Willem van de Velde der Jüngere emigrierte während des dritten Englisch-Niederländischen Krieges gemeinsam mit seinem ebenfalls als Maler tätigen Vater nach England. Dort oblag ihm die repräsentative Darstellung der englischen Flotte. Bis heute gilt er damit als Begründer der englischen Marinemalerei.

El holandés Willem van de Velde el Joven emigró a Inglaterra junto a su padre, que aún ejercía de pintor, durante la tercera guerra anglo-holandesa. Allí fue responsable de la ilustración representativa de la flota inglesa. Por lo tanto, está considerado hasta la fecha como el fundador de la pintura marina inglesa.

O holandês Willem van de Velde, o Jovem, emigrou , para a Inglaterra durante a terceira guerra anglo-holandesa, juntamente com seu pai, que também era pintor. Lá, ele se dedicou à ilustração representativa da frota inglesa. Assim, ainda os dias de hoje ele é considerado o fundador da pintura marinha inglesa.

De Nederlander Willem van de Velde de Jongere emigreerde tijdens de Derde Engels-Nederlandse Oorlog samen met zijn eveneens als schilder werkende vader naar Engeland, waar hij tot taak kreeg de Engelse vloot op representatieve wijze uit te beelden. Tot op heden wordt hij als de grondlegger van de Engelse maritieme schilderkunst beschouwd.

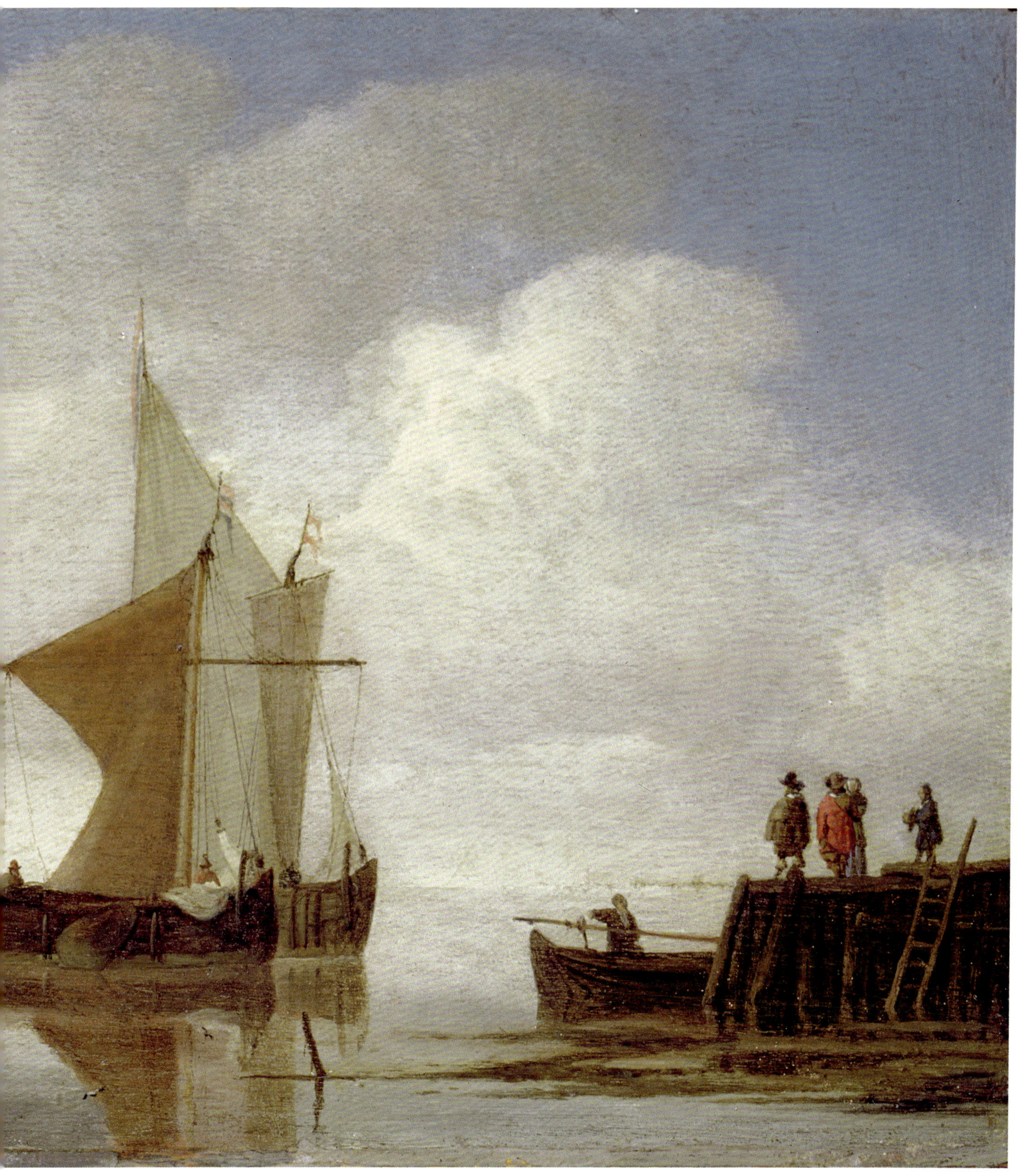

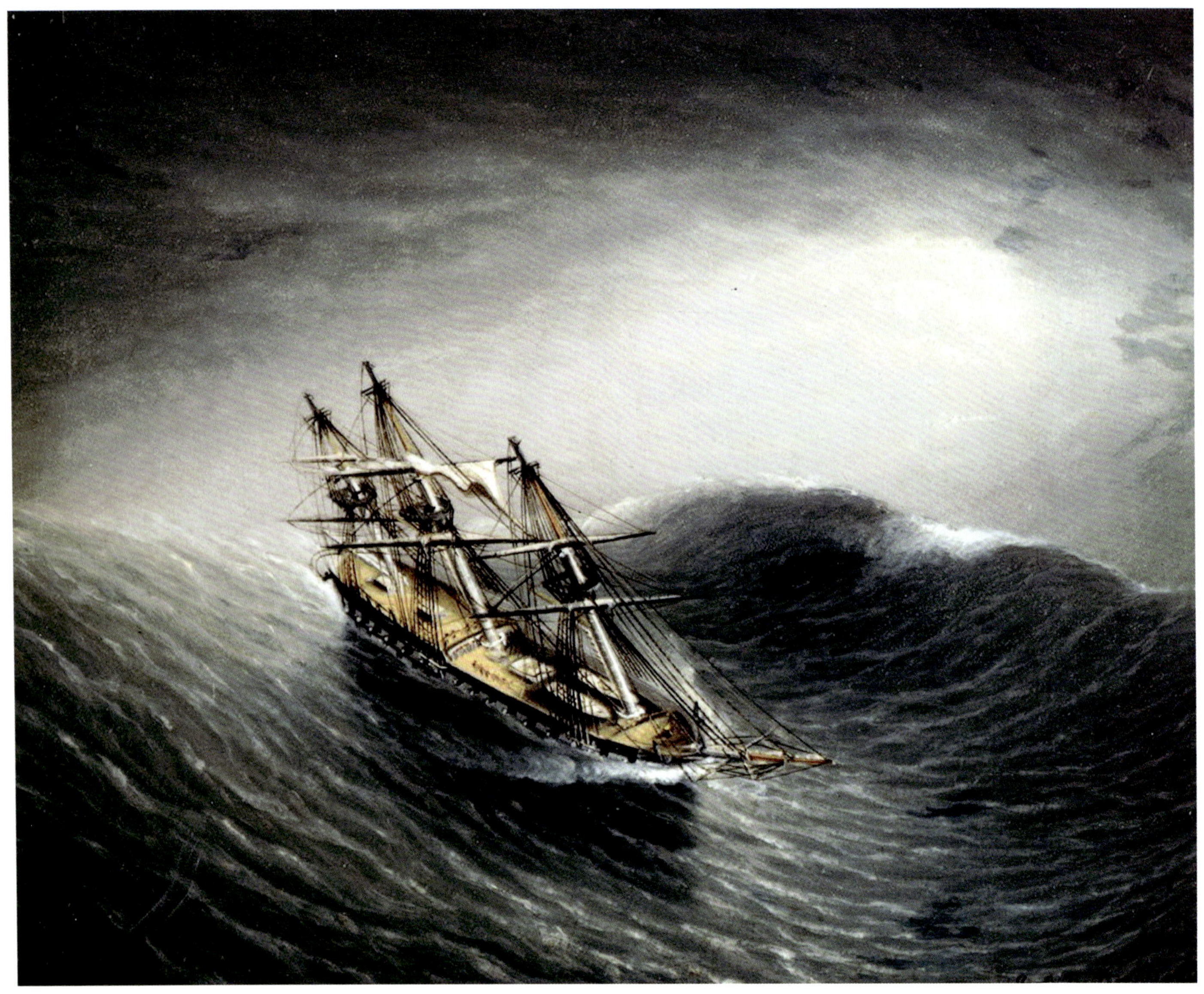

James E. Buttersworth (1817–94)

A Schooner in Heavy Sea

Une Goélette par mer forte

Ein Schoner in schwerer See

Una goleta en mar agitado

Uma escuna no mar agitado

Een schoener bij zware zee

n. d., Oil on canvas/Huile sur toile, 20,5 × 25,5 cm, Private collection

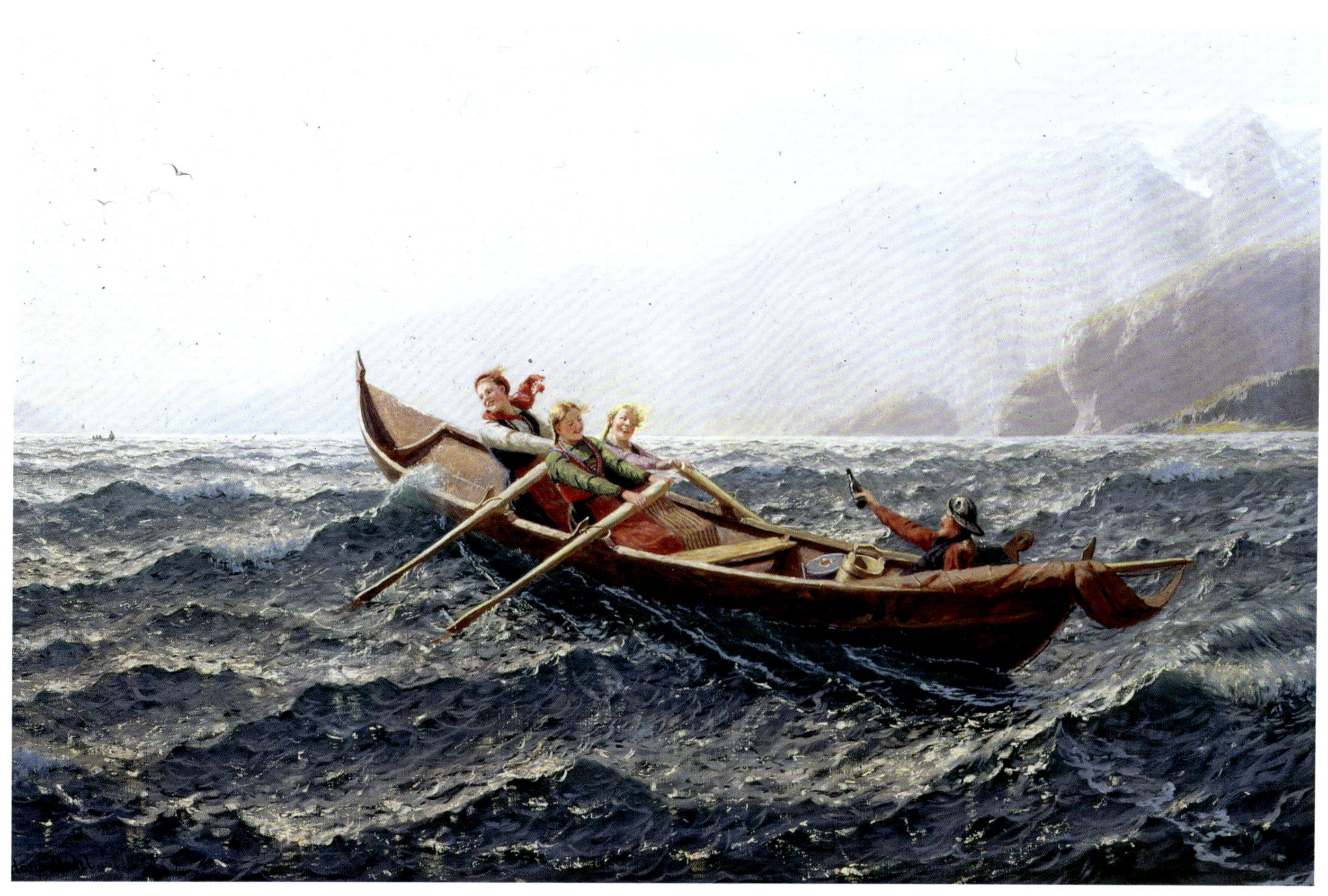

Hans Andreas Dahl (1881–1919)

People in a Rowing Boat

Personnes sur une chaloupe

Menschen in einem Ruderboot

Hombres en barco de remos

Pessoas em um barco a remo

Mensen in een roeiboot

n. d., Oil on canvas/Huile sur toile, 92 × 144 cm, Private collection

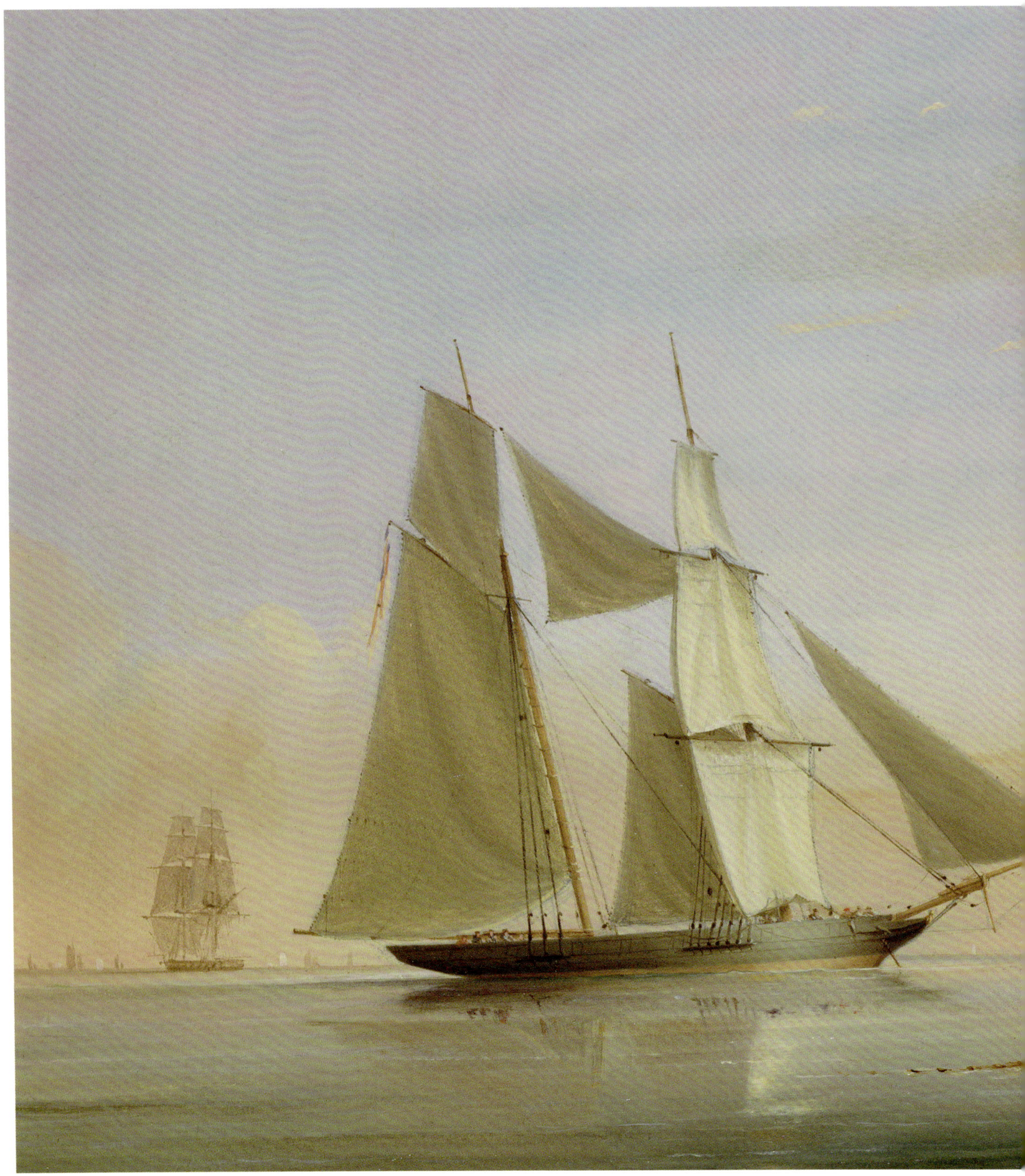

The *Kestral R.Y.S.*, Becalmed Off Shore

Le *Kestral R.Y.S.*, encalminé au large

Die Jacht *Kestral R.Y.S.*, bei Flaute nicht fern der Küste

El yate *Kestral R.Y.S.* en calma no lejos de la costa

O iate *Kestral R.Y.S.*, na calmaria, não muito longe da costa

Het jacht *Kestral R.Y.S.* bij windstilte voor de kust

n. d., Oil on canvas/Huile sur toile, 22,2 × 30 cm, Private collection

The Royal Yacht Squadron (RYS) is often considered the classiest yacht club in Great Britain. All the boats of the club members, whose clubhouse is located on the Isle of Wight, have the suffix of RYS, including the Kestral, painted here by Plymouth-born Nicholas Matthews Condy.

Le Royal Yacht Squadron (RYS) est souvent considéré comme le club de plaisance le plus chic de Grande-Bretagne. Tous les bateaux des membres du club, situé sur l'île de Wight, ont le suffixe de RYS, y compris le Kestral, peint ici par Nicholas Matthews Condy, originaire de Plymouth.

Der Jachtclub Royal Yacht Squadron (RYS) wird oft als honorigster Yachtclub Großbritanniens angesehen. Alle Boote der Mitglieder des Clubs, dessen Clubhaus sich auf der Isle of Wight befindet, führen den Zusatz RYS in ihren Namen, so auch die hier vom im südwestenglischen Plymouth geborenen Nicholas Matthews Condy gemalte Jacht Kestral.

Al Club de Yates Royal Yacht Squadron (RYS) se le considera a menudo como el más honorable club náutico de Gran Bretaña. Todos los barcos de los miembros del club, cuya sede se encuentra en la Isla de Wight, llevan adicionalmente las siglas RYS en sus nombres, por lo que el Kestral, el yate aquí representado por Nicholas Matthews Condy, nacido en la ciudad de Plymouth al sur de Inglaterra, también las lleva.

O yacht club Royal Yacht Squadron (RYS) é frequentemente considerado o yacht club com maior prestígio na Grã-Bretanha. Todos os barcos dos membros deste clube, cuja sede está localizada em Isle of Wight, juntam o prefixo RYS em seus nomes, tal como este iate Kestral, pintado por Nicholas Matthews Condy, nascido em Plymouth, no sudoeste da Inglaterra.

De jachtclub Royal Yacht Squadron (RYS) op het Isle of Wight wordt beschouwd als de meest prestigieuze watersportclub van Groot-Brittannië. Alle boten van de clubleden hebben de toevoeging "RYS" achter hun naam, zo ook het jacht Kestrel, dat door de in Plymouth in Zuidwest-Engeland geboren Nicholas Matthews Condy werd geschilderd.

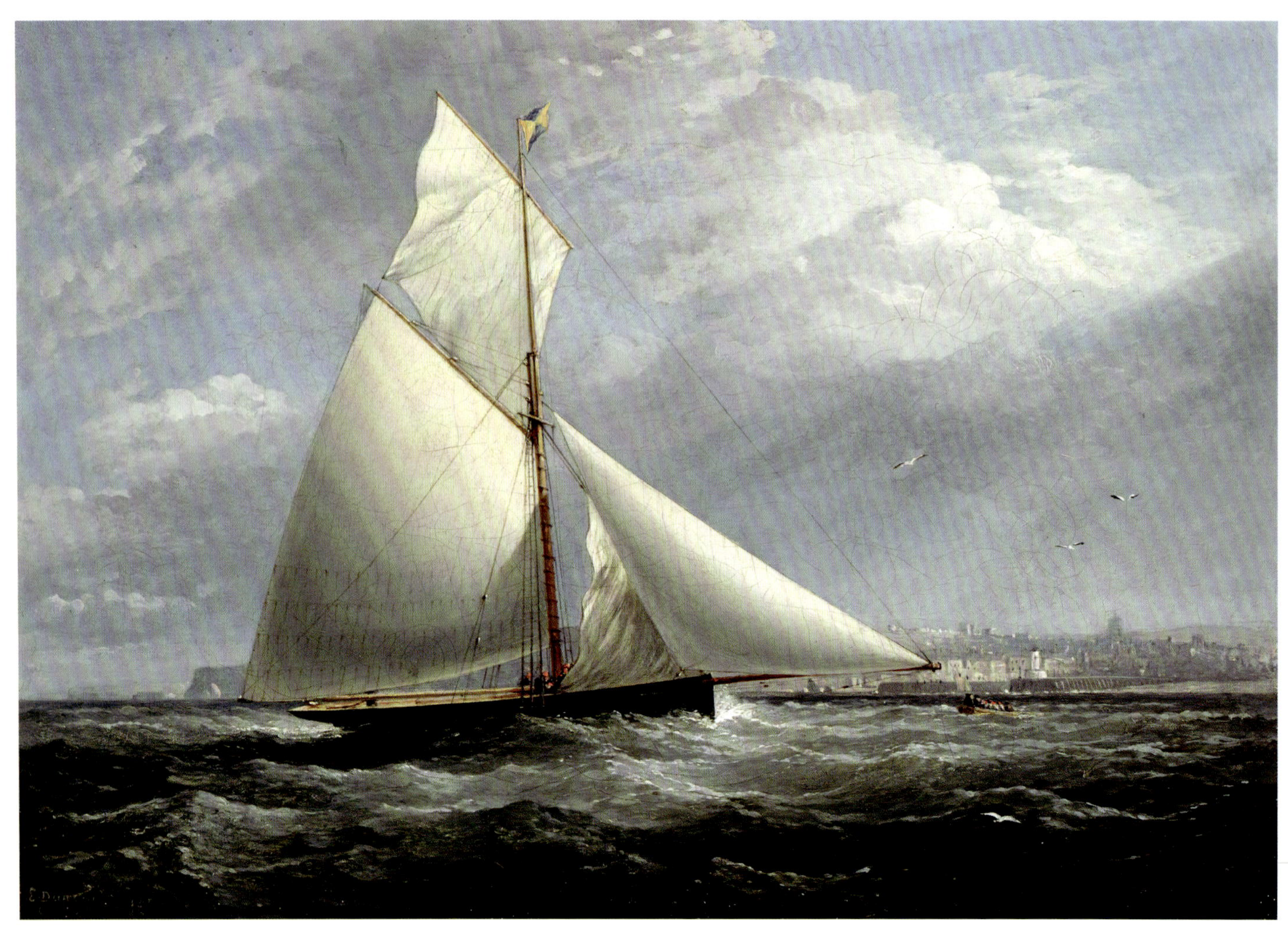

Edward Duncan (1803–82)

Off Ramsgate

Au large de Ramsgate

Vor Ramsgate

Ante la costa de Ramsgate

Ao largo de Ramsgate

Op de rede van Ramsgate

1853, Oil on canvas/Huile sur toile, 35,6 × 50,8 cm, Private collection

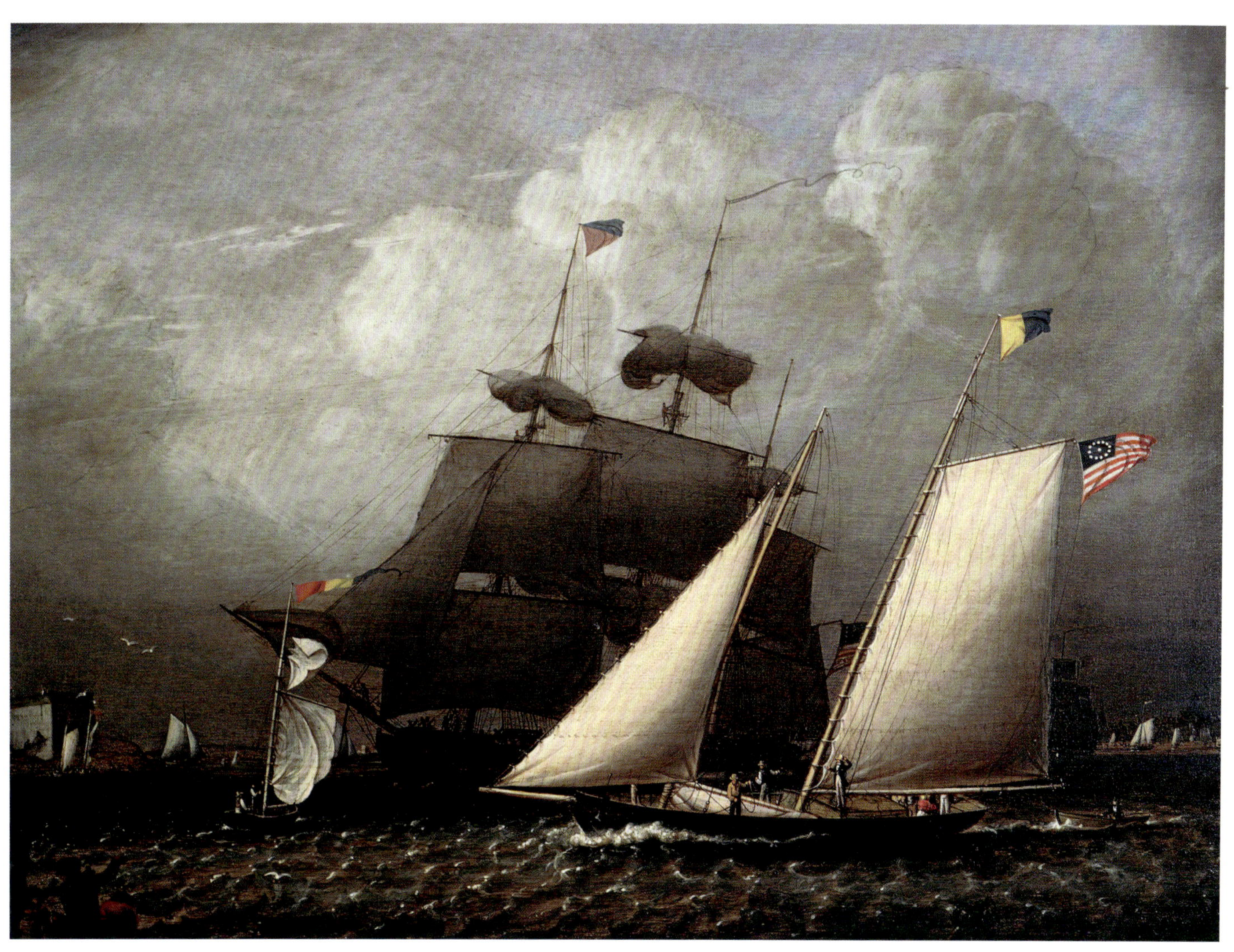

Robert Salmon (1775–1845)

The Dream, Pleasure Yacht

The Dream, bateau de plaisance

Vergnügungsjacht *The Dream*

Yate de placer *The Dream*

Iate de recreio *The Dream*

Het plezierjacht *The Dream*

1839, Oil on panel/Huile sur bois, 42 × 62,2 cm, Museo Thyssen-Bornemisza, Madrid

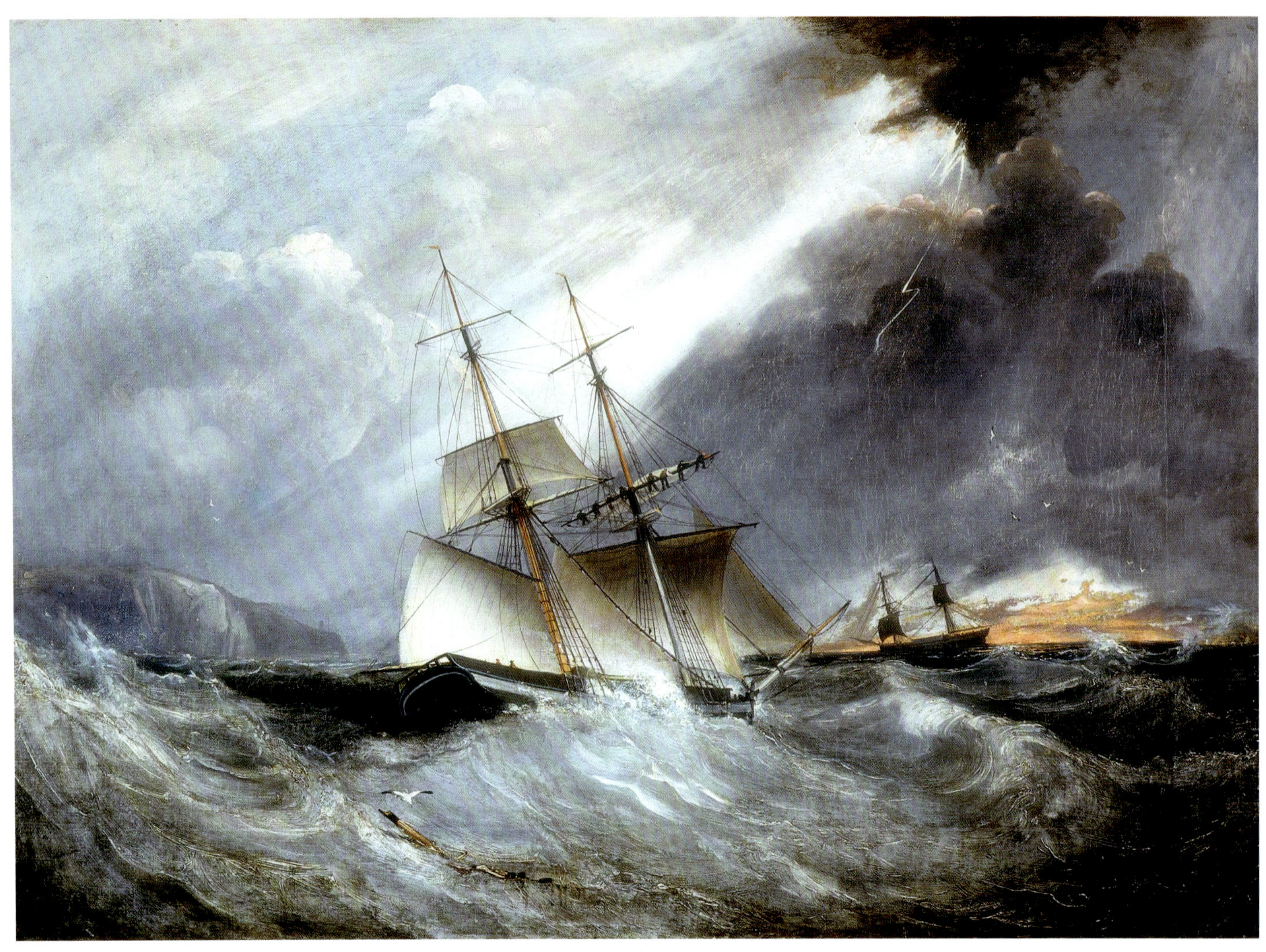

George Balmer (c. 1806–46)

The Brig *Hermaphrodite*

Le brigantin *Hermaphrodite*

Die Brigg *Hermaphrodite*

El bergantín *Hermaphrodite*

O brigue *Hermaphrodite*

De brik *Hermaphrodite*

1830, Oil on canvas/Huile sur toile, 63 × 89,6 cm, Laing Art Gallery, Newcastle-upon-Tyne

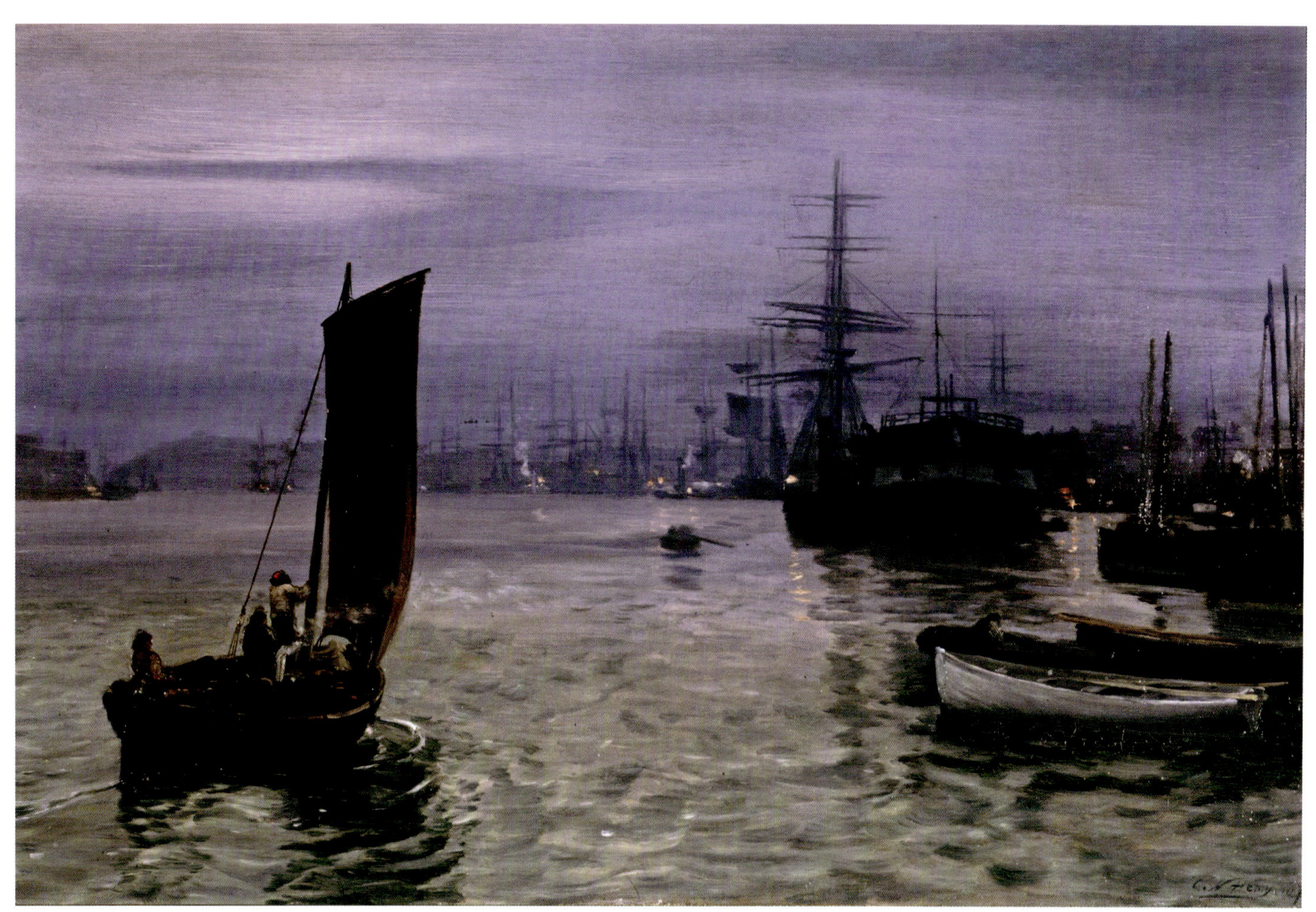

Charles Napier Hemy (1841–1917)

The Last Boat In

Le dernier bateau

Das letzte Boot läuft ein

El último barco

O último barco chega

Het laatste schip loopt binnen

n. d., Oil on canvas/Huile sur toile, 74,9 × 57 cm, South Shields Museum & Art Gallery, South Shields

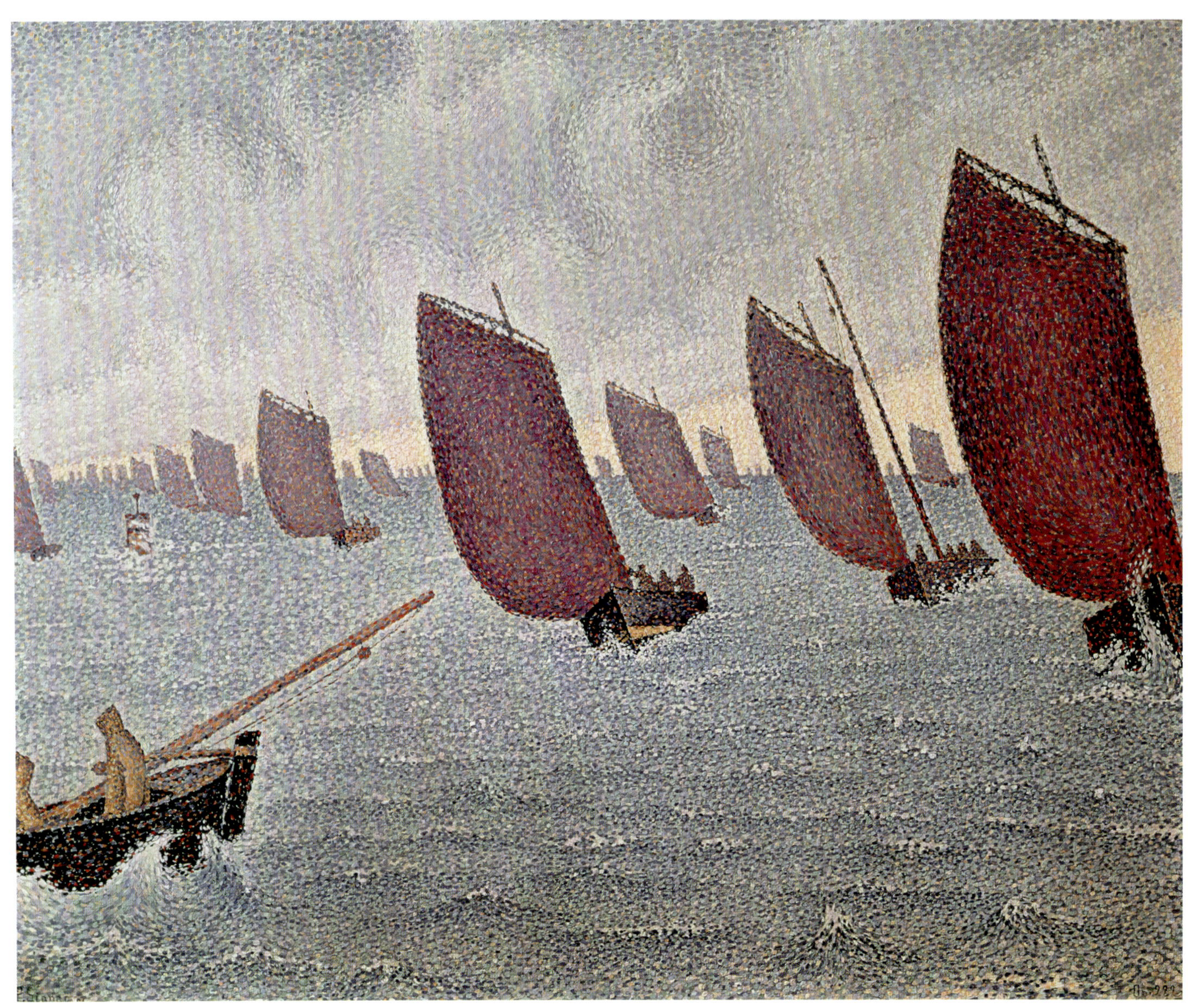

Paul Signac (1863–1935)

Breeze, Concarneau

Brise, Concarneau

Brise in Concarneau

Brisa en Concarneau

Brisa em Concarneau

Bries in Concarneau

1891, Oil on canvas/Huile sur toile, 66,5 × 82 cm, Private collection

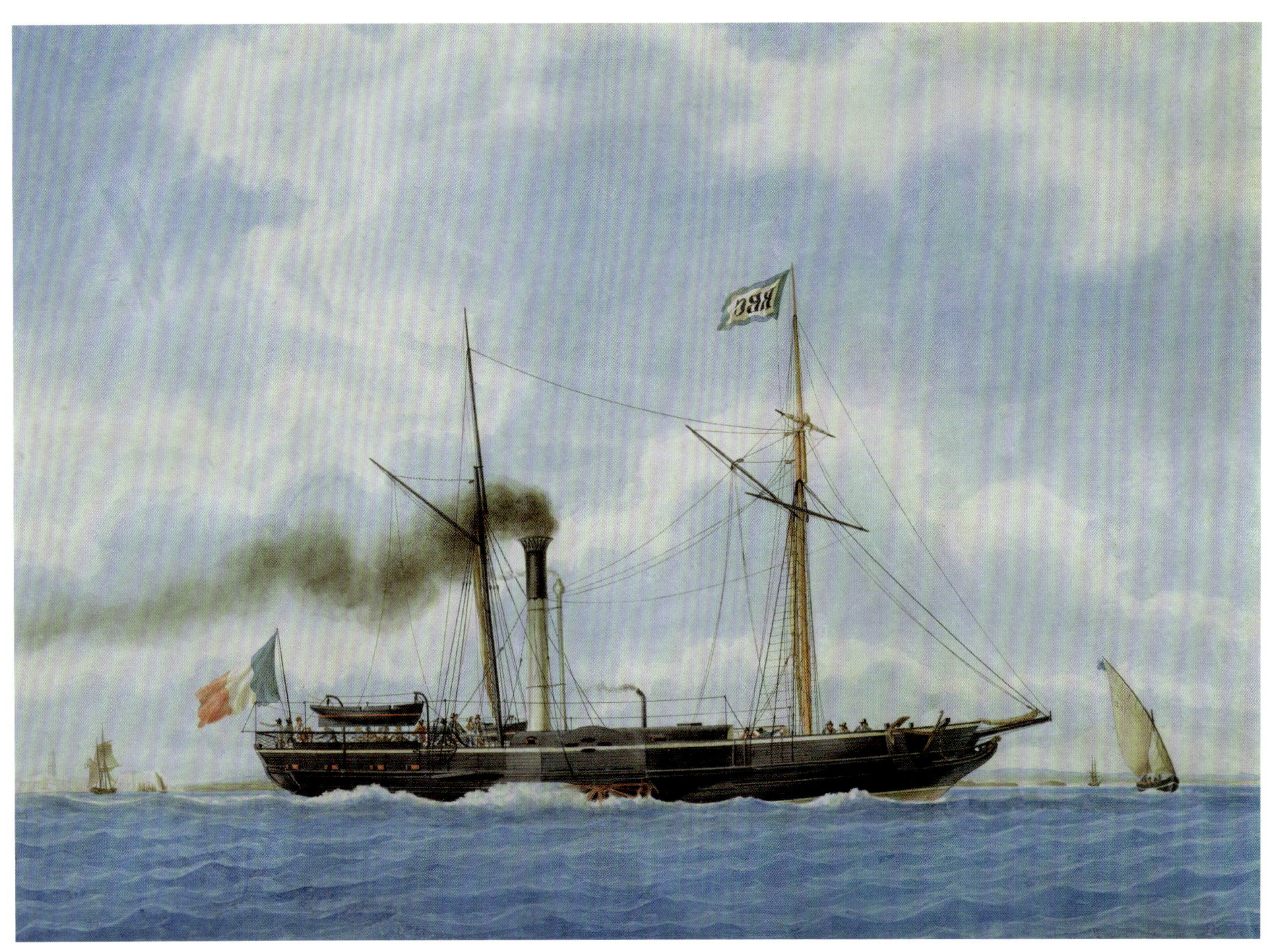

Antoine Roux (1765–1835)

Océan, the Ship of Captain Combes the Elder

Océan, le bateau du capitaine Combes l'Ancier

Die *Océan,* das Schiff Kapitän Combes des Älteren

Océan, el barco del capitán Combes el Viejo

Océan, o navio do capitão Combes, o Velho

Het stoomschip *Océan* van kapitein Combes de Oudere

n. d., Watercolor on paper/Aquarelle sur papier, Musée de la Marine, Marseille

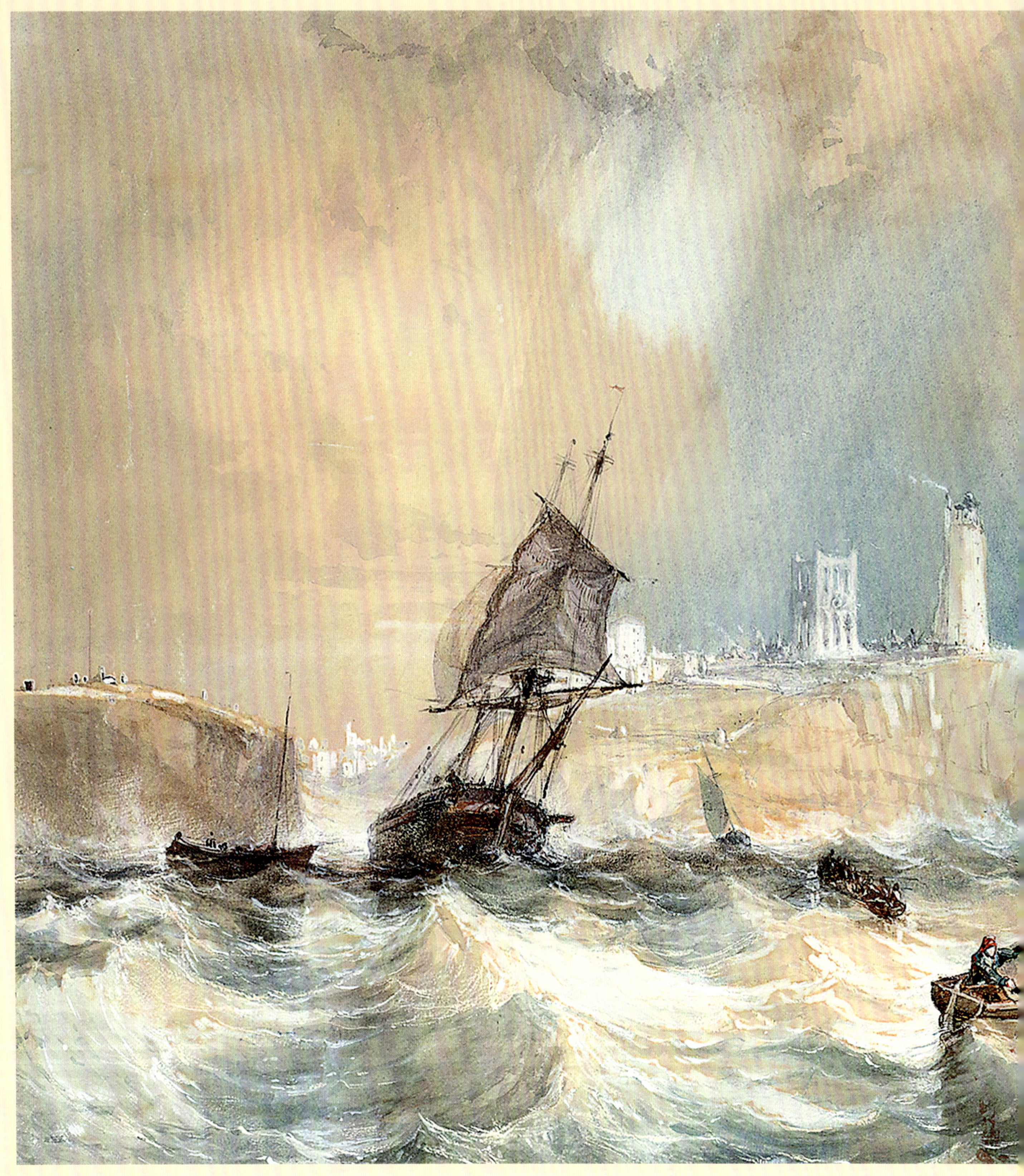

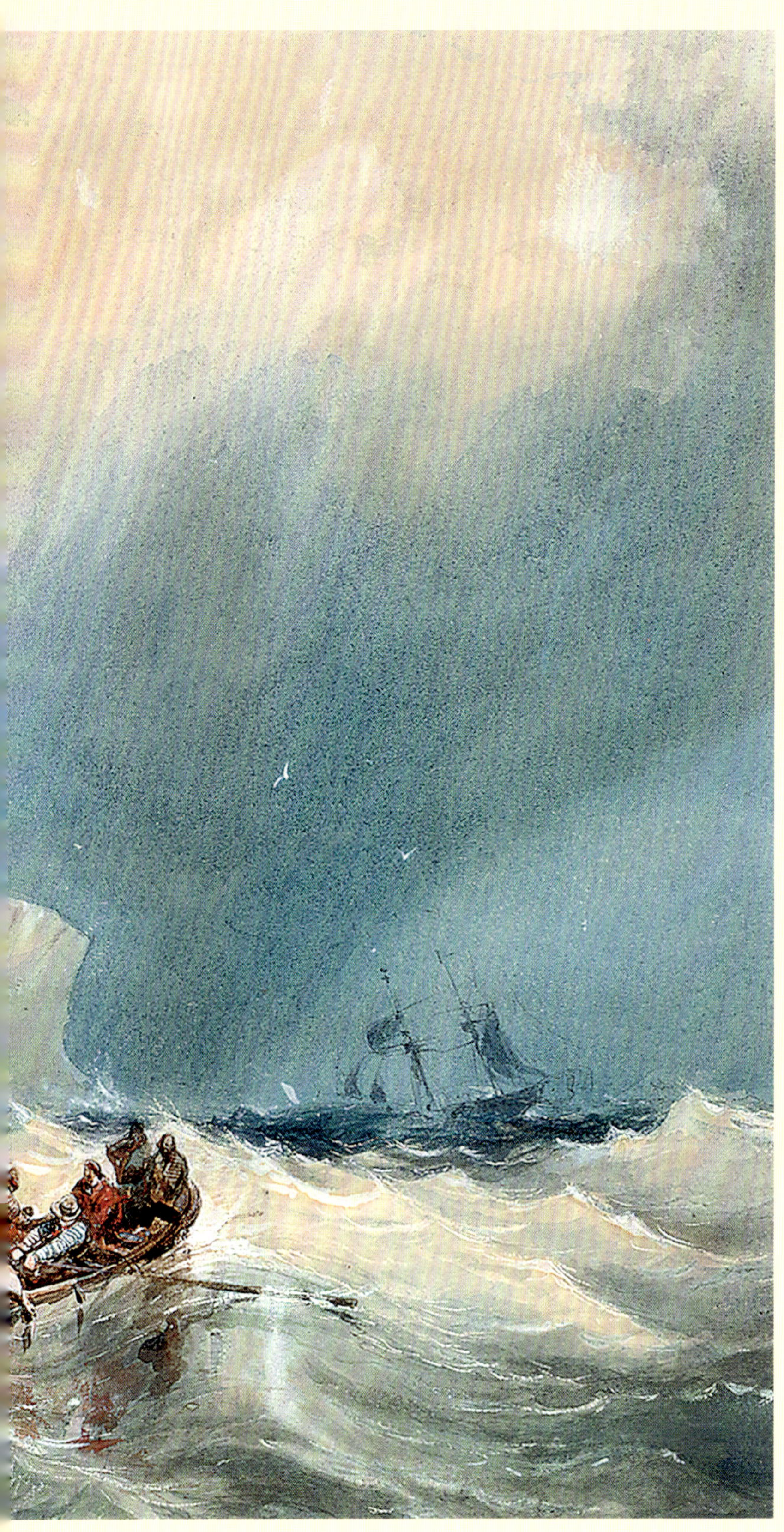

Fishermen, traders and smugglers

Pêcheurs, commerçants et contrebandiers

Fischer, Händler und Schmuggler

Pescadores, comerciantes y contrabandistas

Pescadores, comerciantes e contrabandistas

Vissers, kooplui en smokkelaars

John Wilson Carmichael (1800–68)
A Trading Brig Running Out of Tynemouth
Un brigantin de commerce au large de Tynemouth
Handelsbrigg aus Tynemouth auslaufend
Bergantín mercante saliendo de Tynemouth
Brigue mercante saindo de Tynemouth
Koopvaardijbrik loopt de haven van Tynemouth uit
n. d., Pencil, watercolor, and highlights on paper/Crayon, aquarelle
et rehauts sur papier, 43,2 × 63,5 cm, Private collection

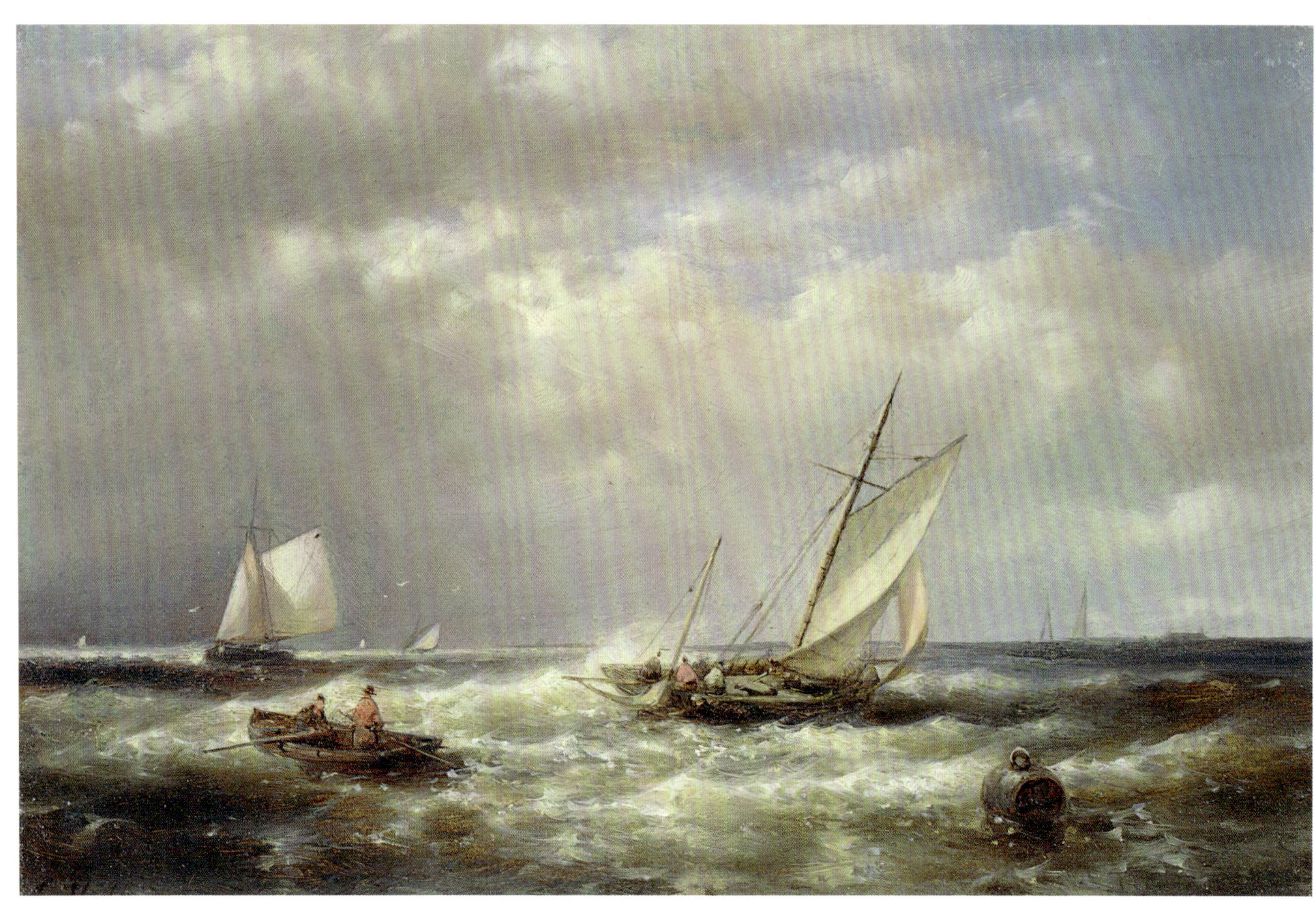

Abraham Hulk (1813–97)

Fishing Boats off the Coast

Bateaux de pêche au large

Fischerboote vor der Küste

Barcos pesqueros delante de la costa

Barcos de pesca ao largo da costa

Vissersboten voor de kust

n. d., Oil on panel/Huile sur bois, 15,2 × 20,3 cm, Private collection

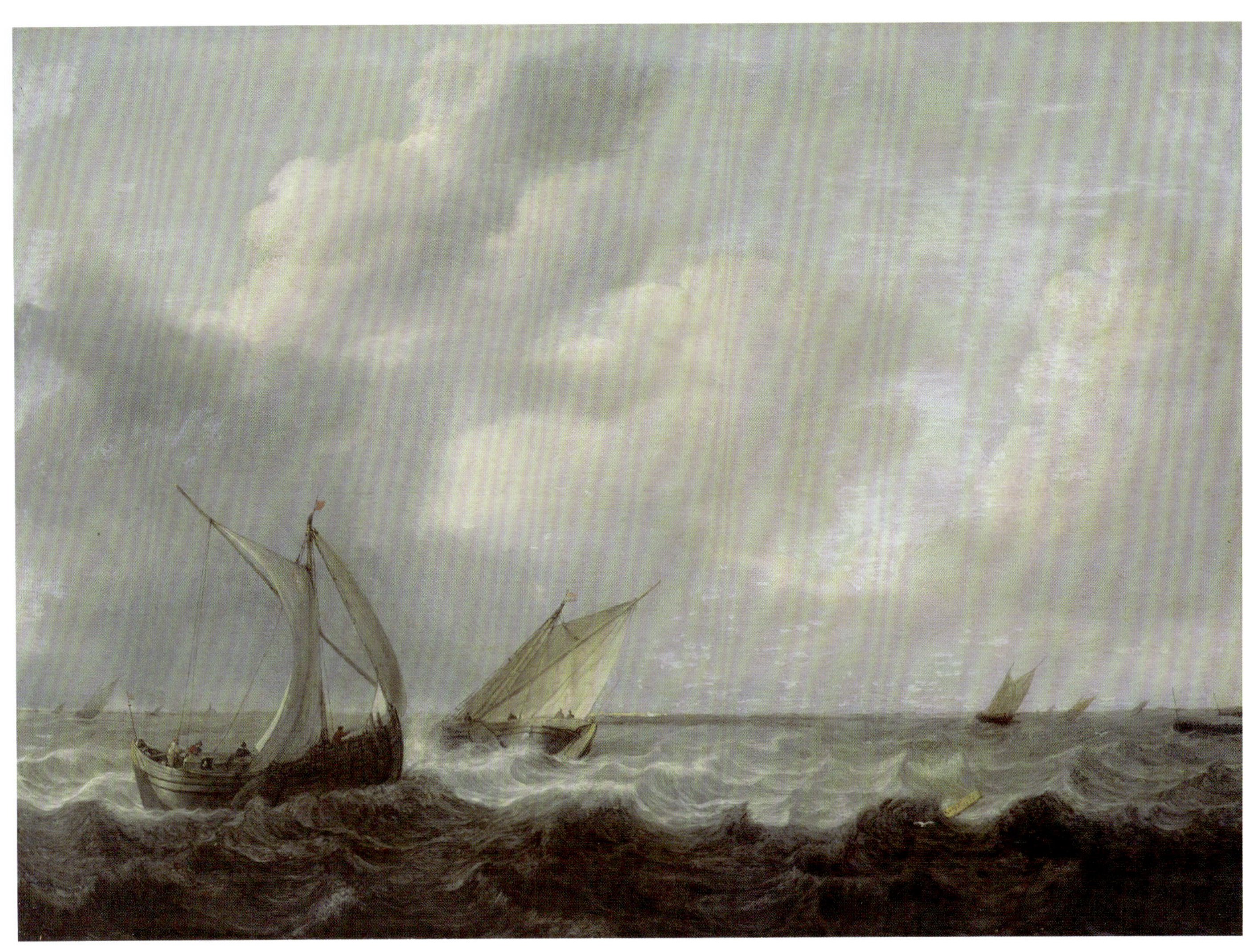

Hendrik Martensz Sorgh (c. 1611–70)

Fishing Boats in a Choppy Sea

Bateaux de pêche sur mer agitée

Fischerboote in unruhiger See

Barcos pesqueros en mar picado

Barcos de pesca em mar revolto

Vissersboten bij onrustige zee

1666, Oil on panel/Huile sur bois, 35,7 × 49,6 cm, Manchester Art Gallery, Manchester

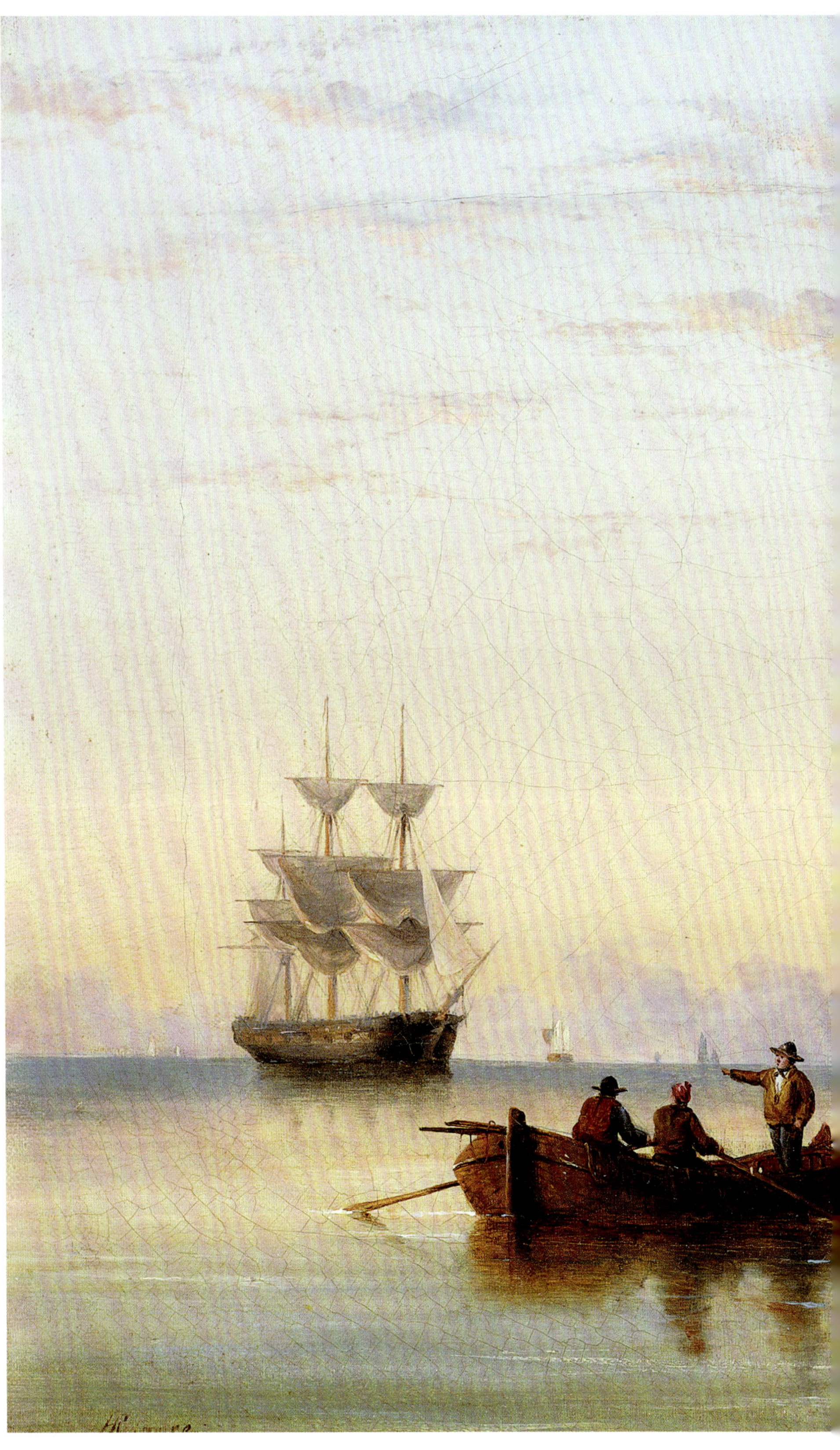

Henry Redmore (1820–87)

Fishing Boats and Other Vessels on
the Scheldt near Rotterdam

Bateaux de pêche et autres navires sur
l'Escaut, près de Rotterdam

Fischerboote und andere Wasserfahrzeuge
auf der Schelde nahe Rotterdam

Barco de pesca y otras embarcaciones en
el río Escalda cerca de Rotterdam

Barcos de pesca e outras embarcações
no Escalda, perto de Roterdã

Vissersboten en andere vaartuigen op de Schelde

1852, Oil on canvas/Huile sur toile,
31,1 × 91,4 cm, Private collection

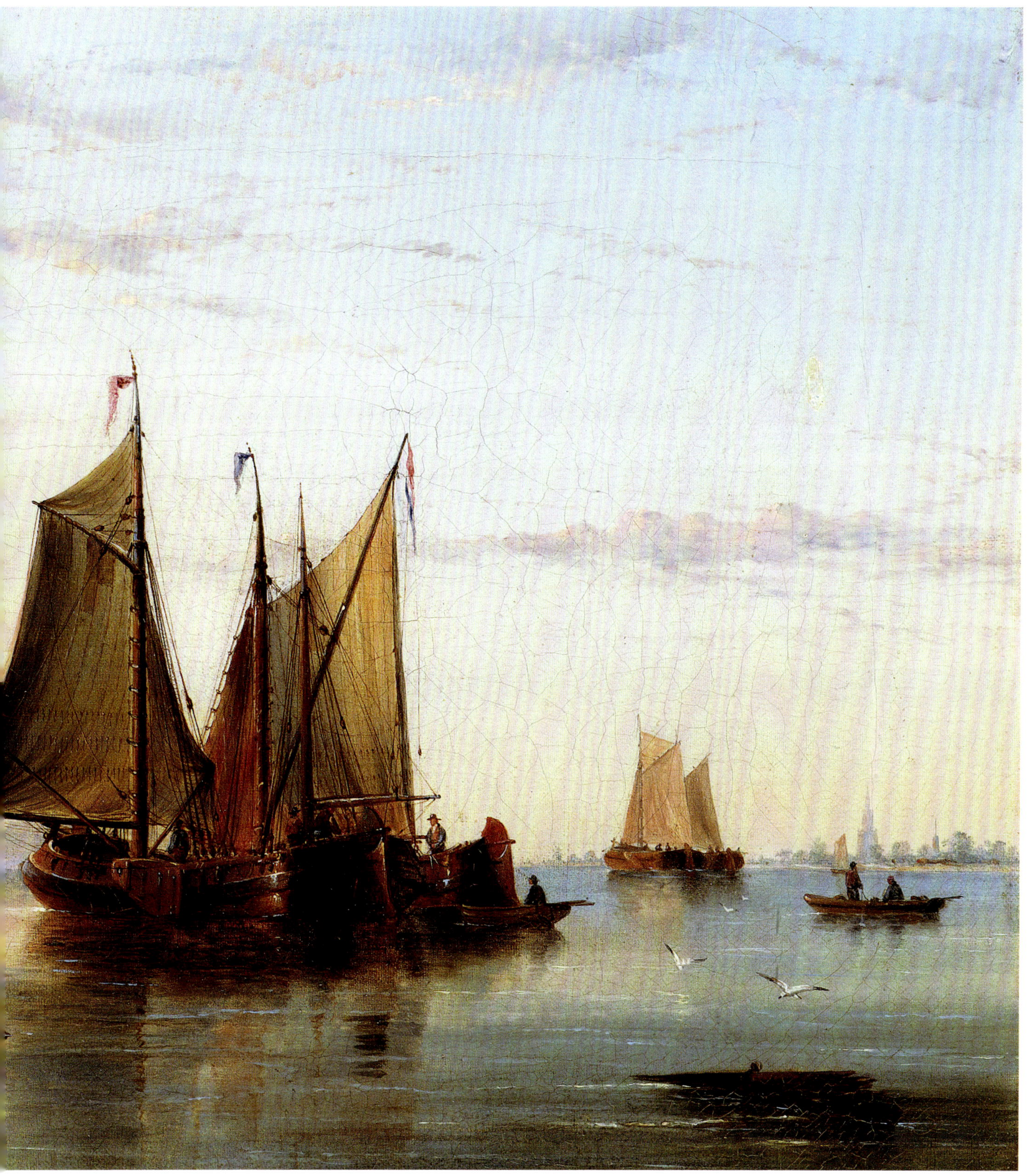

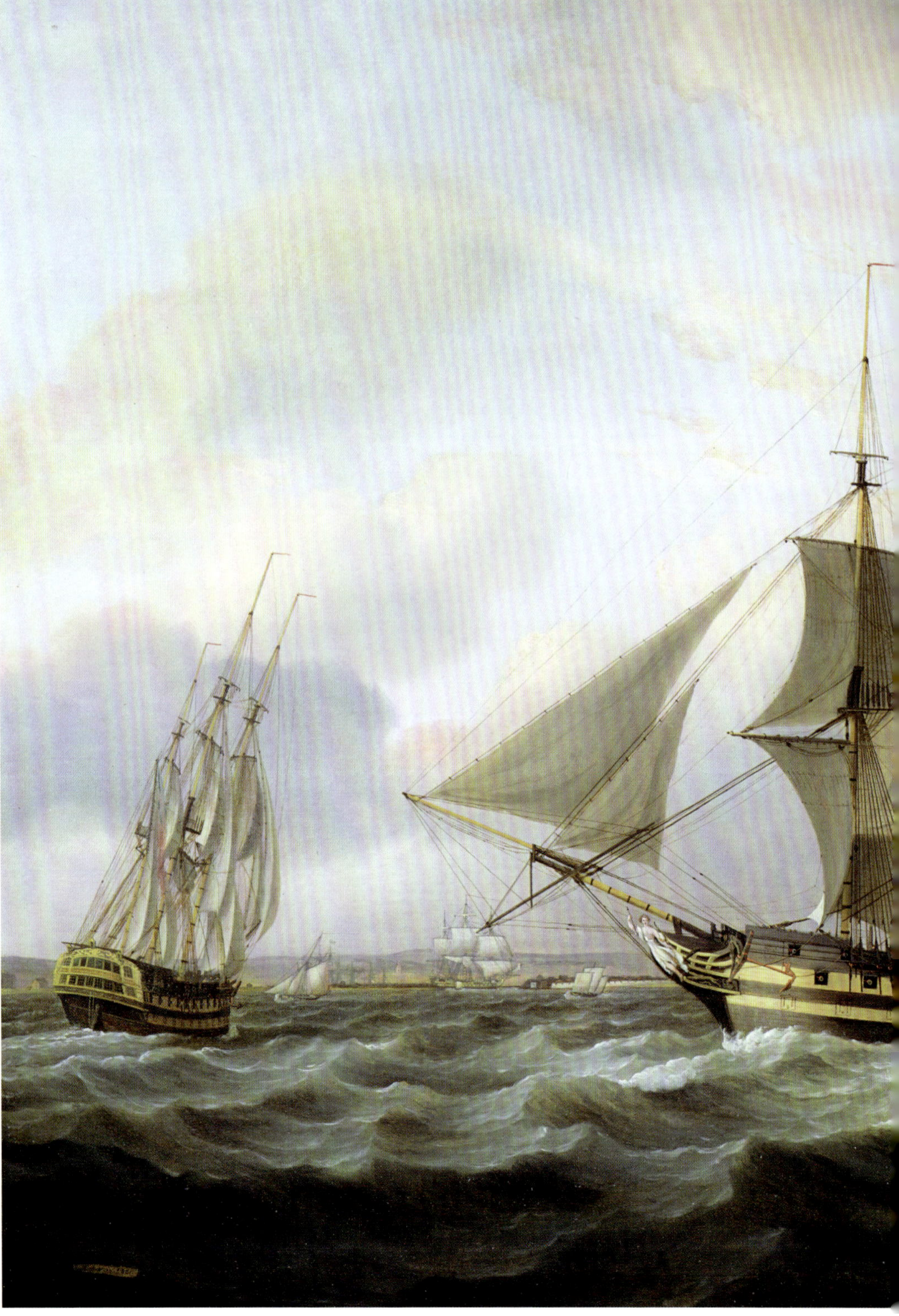

The East India Company's Ship *Belvedere*,
Captain Charles Christie, Commander

Le Navire *Belvedere* de la Compagnie
des Indes orientales, le capitaine
Charles Christie, commandant

Die im Dienste der East India
Company stehende *Belvedere*

El honorable *Belvedere* de la Compañía
de las Indias Orientales

O *Belvedere*, ao serviço da Companhia
das Índias Orientais

De *Belvedere* in dienst van de
East India Company

1800, Oil on canvas/Huile sur toile,
83,8 × 144,8 cm, Private collection

*The Belvedere, painted here by Englishman
Thomas Luny, weighed 988 tons, making it one
of the larger ships of the East India Company.
Built in 1791 in Itchenor, West Sussex, it was
removed from service just fifteen years later
and then only used for another three years
as a merchant vessel in the Caribbean.*

*Le Belvedere, peint ici par l'anglais Thomas Luny,
pesait 988 tonnes, ce qui en fit l'un des plus grands
navires de la Compagnie des Indes orientales.
Construit en 1791 à Itchenor, dans le Sussex de
l'Ouest, il fut retiré du service quinze ans plus tard
à peine, puis utilisé durant trois autres années
comme navire marchand dans les Caraïbes.*

*Der hier vom Engländer Thomas Luny gemalten
Belvedere, die mit ihren 988 Registertonnen zu
den größeren Schiffen der East India Company
gehörte, war nur ein relativ kurzes Schiffsleben
beschieden. 1787 in Itchenor, West Sussex
gebaut, schied es nach nur 15 Jahren wieder aus
dem Dienst aus und wurde danach noch drei
Jahre im Handel mit der Karibik eingesetzt.*

*Este Belvedere, pintado por el inglés Thomas
Luny, que pertenecía con sus 988 toneladas
a los barcos más grandes de la Compañía de
las Indias Orientales, tuvo una vida sencilla y
relativamente corta. Construido en Itchenor,
West Sussex, en 1787, se retiró después de 15
años fuera de servicio, y luego fue utilizado
durante tres años en el comercio con el Caribe.*

*Aqui pintado pelo pintor inglês Thomas Luny,
o Belvedere, que com suas 988 toneladas foi
um dos maiores navios da Companhia das
Índias Orientais, teve uma vida de navegação
relativamente curta. Construído em Itchenor,
West Sussex, em 1787, deixou de navegar após
somente 15 anos, e foi depois ainda utilizado
durante três anos, no comércio com o Caribe.*

*De hier door de Engelsman Thomas Luny
geschilderde Belvedere, die met 988 registerton
tot de grotere schepen van de East India
Company behoorde, was geen lang leven
op zee beschoren. Het in 1787 in Itchenor,
West Sussex, van stapel gelopen schip werd
na slechts vijftien jaar verkocht, waarna
het nog drie jaar als koopvaardijschip op de
route naar het Caribisch gebied diende.*

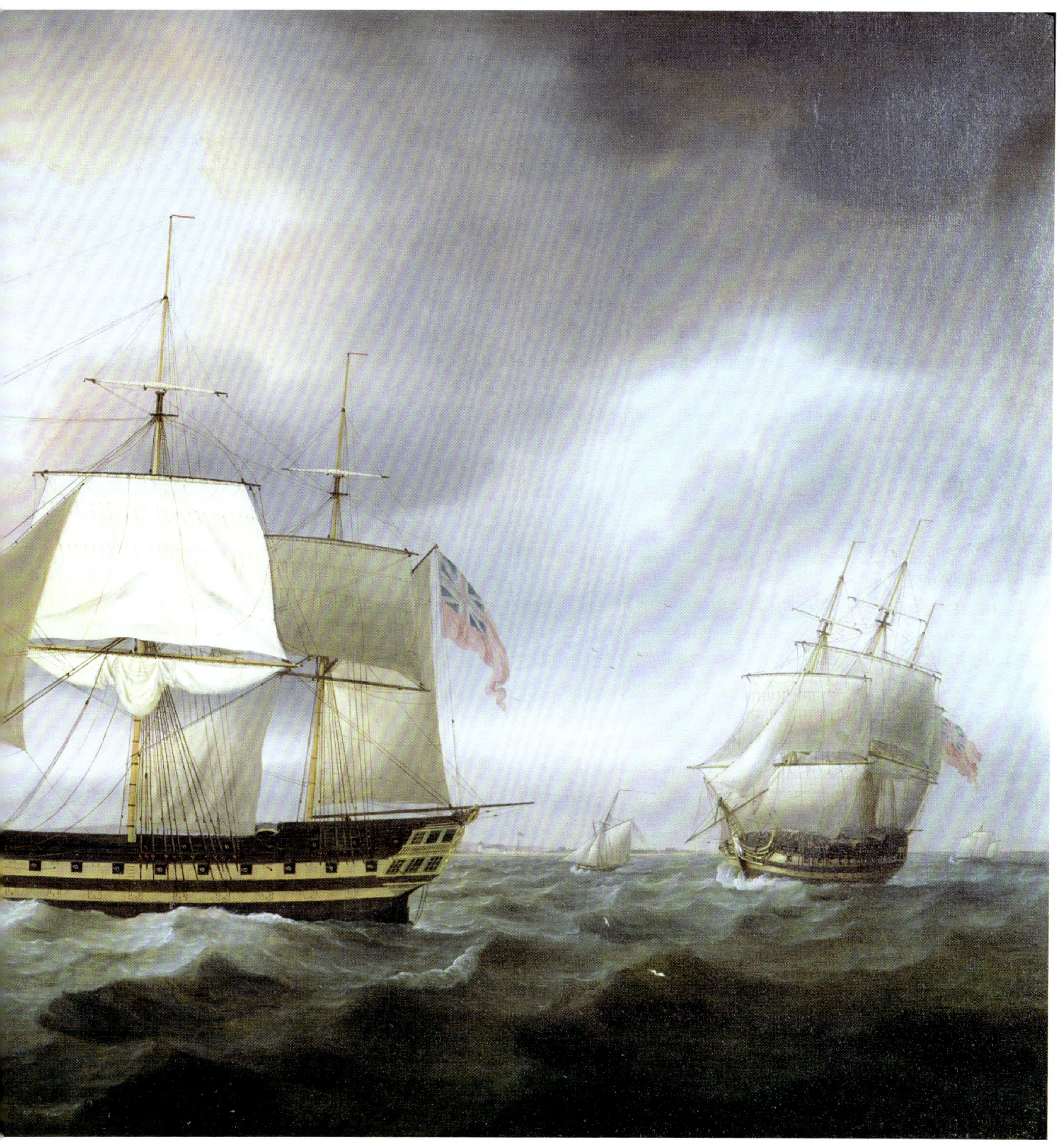

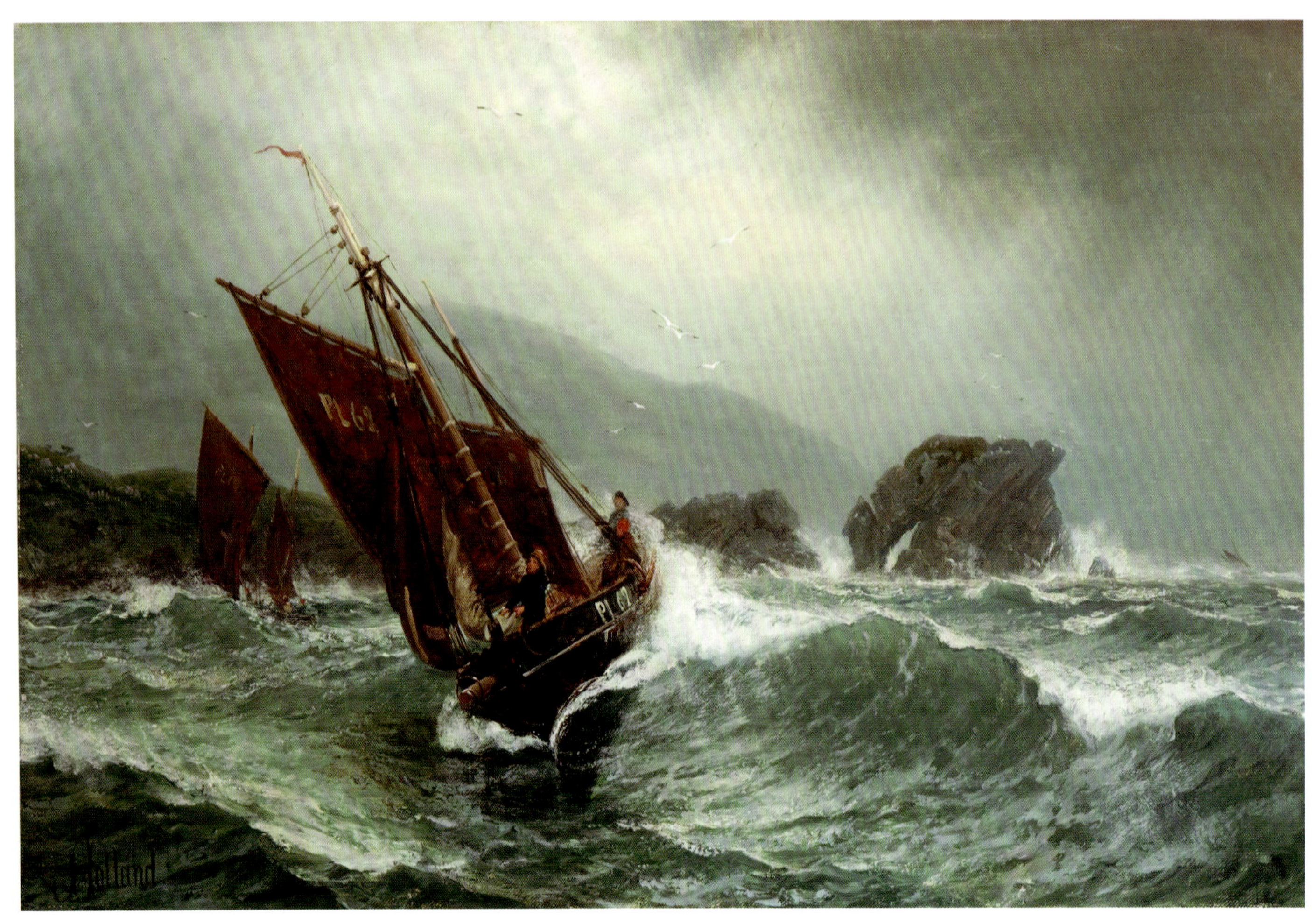

John Holland (1857–1920)

Peel Fishing Boats

Bateaux de pêche de Peel

Fischerboote aus Peel auf der Isle of Man

Barcos pesqueros en Peel, Isla de Man

Barcos de pesca de Peel, na Ilha de Man

Vissersboten uit Peel op het eiland Man

n. d., Oil on canvas/Huile sur toile, 35 × 61 cm, Manx Museum, Douglas

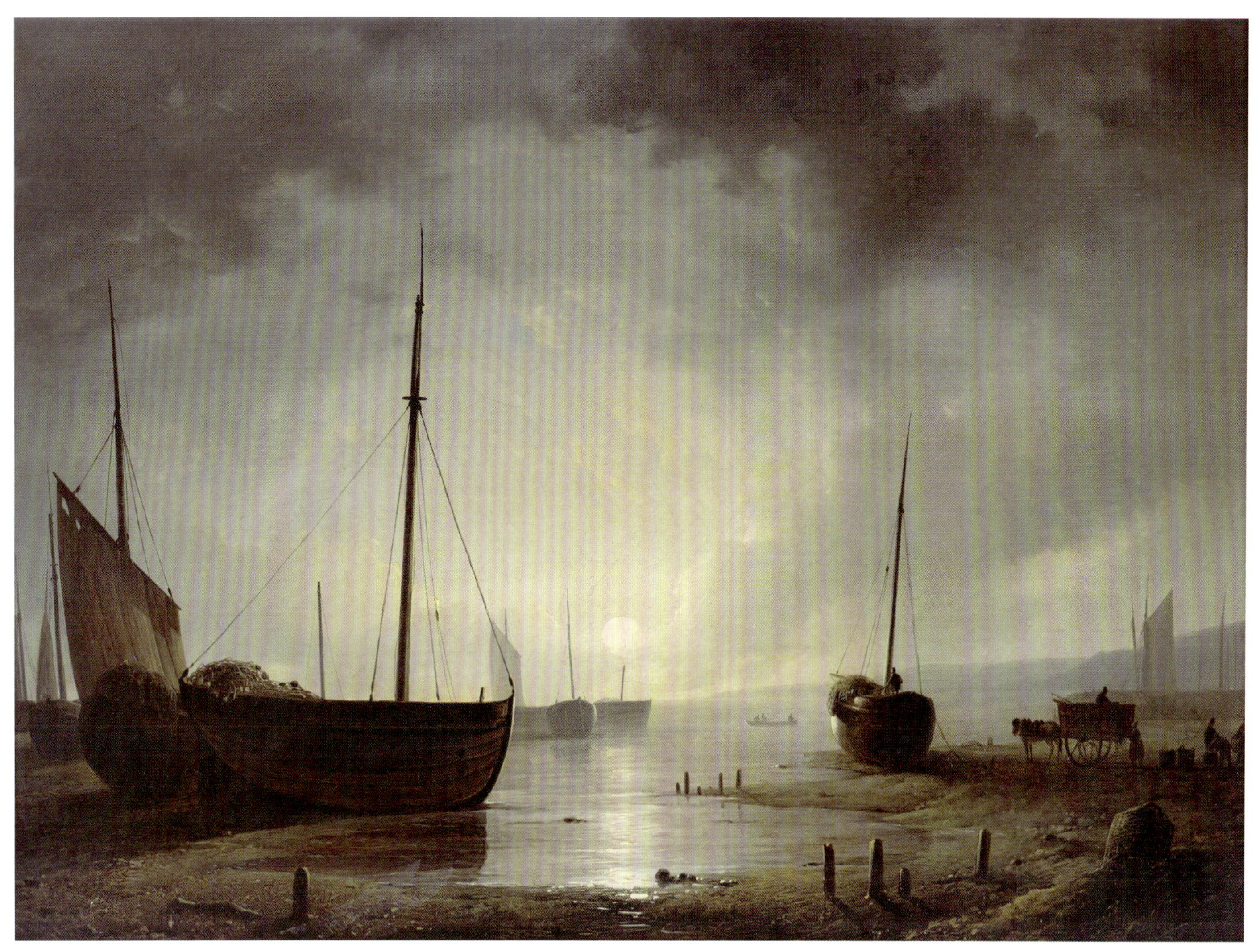

Remigius van Haanen (1812–94)

Beached Fishing Boats by Moonlight

Bateaux de pêche échoués au clair de lune

Gestrandete Fischerboote im Mondschein

Barcos pesqueros varados bajo la luz de la luna

Barcos de pesca encalhados no luar

Gestrande vissersboten bij maanlicht

n. d., Oil on canvas/Huile sur toile, 42 × 57 cm, Private collection

Not much is known about the painter of this nighttime seascape, Thomas Buttersworth, born on the Isle of Wight. The ship portraits he made seem to have been largely commissioned and he did not exhibit many of them during his lifetime.

On ne sait pas grand-chose du peintre de ce paysage marin nocturne, Thomas Buttersworth, né sur l'île de Wight. Les portraits de navires qu'il réalisa semblent avoir été largement commandés et très peu furent exposés durant sa vie.

Über den Maler dieser nächtlichen Szene auf dem Meer, den auf der Isle of Wight geborenen Thomas Buttersworth, ist nicht viel bekannt. Die von ihm angefertigten Schiffsporträts scheinen zum größten Teil Auftragswerke gewesen zu sein, so dass zu seinen Lebzeiten nicht viel von ihm ausgestellt wurde.

No se sabe mucho acerca del pintor de esta escena marina nocturna, Thomas Buttersworth nacido en la Isla de Wight. Los retratos de embarcaciones parecen ser el grueso de sus encargos, de modo que no se sabe más acerca de su vida ni de lo que hizo.

Não se sabe muito sobre Wight Thomas Buttersworth, nascido na Ilha de Wight, e o pintor desta cena marítima noturna. A maior parte das representações de navios pintadas por ele parecem ter sido obras encomendadas, de maneira que durante sua vida não foram expostas muitas obras dele.

Over de schilder van dit nachtelijke zeegezicht, de op het eiland Wight geboren Thomas Buttersworth, is weinig bekend. Zijn scheepsportretten lijken grotendeels werken in opdracht te zijn geweest, zodat er tijdens het leven van deze schilder weinig werk van hem werd geëxposeerd.

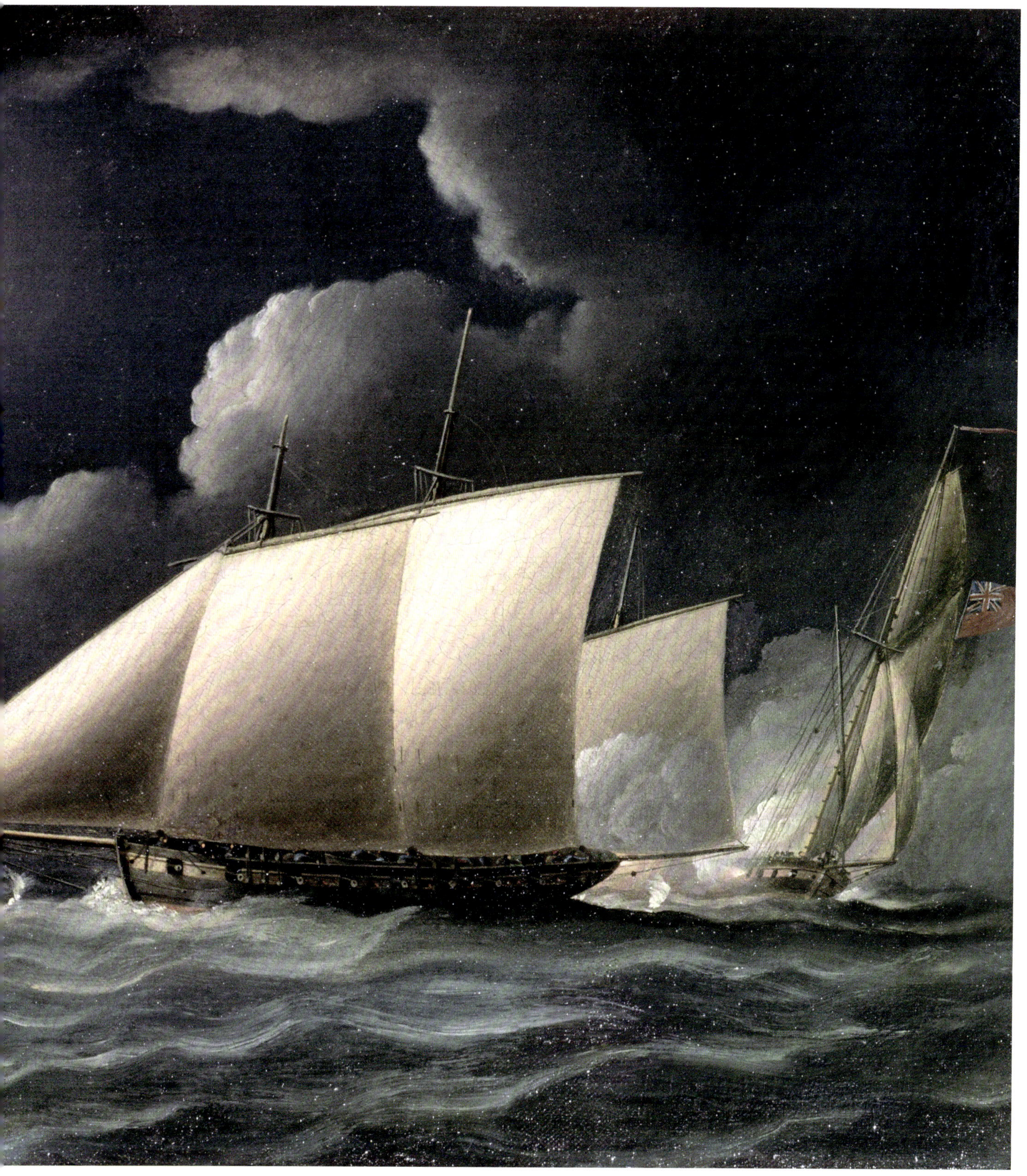

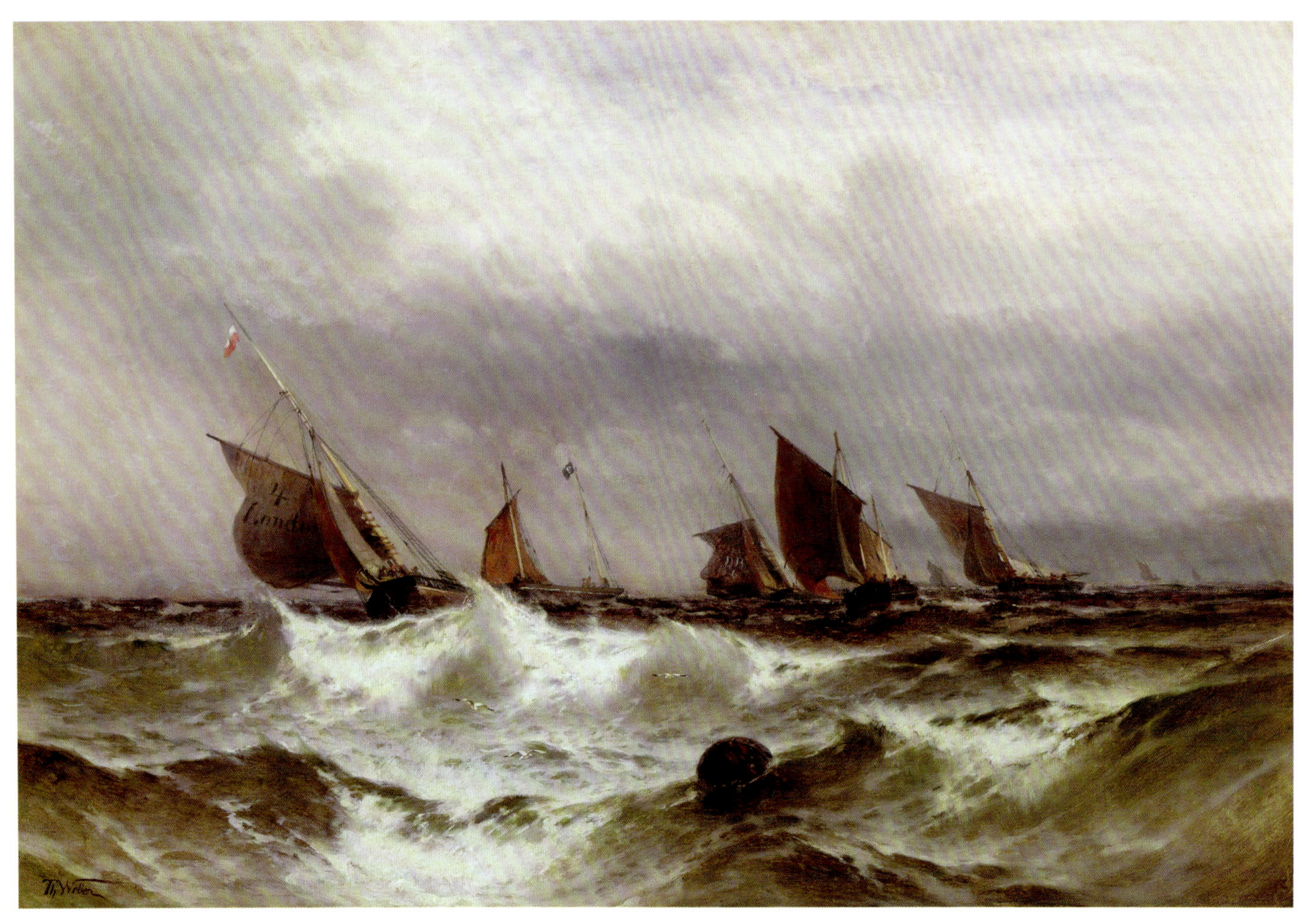

Theodore Weber (1838–1907)

Dover Pilot and Fishing Boats

Pilote de Douvres et bateaux de pêche

Ein Lotse in Dover und Fischerboote

Barco controlador en Dover y pesqueros

Um piloto em Dover e barcos de pesca

Een loods uit Dover met vissersboten

n. d., Oil on canvas/Huile sur toile, 60,9 × 91,4 cm, Royal Holloway, University of London, Egham

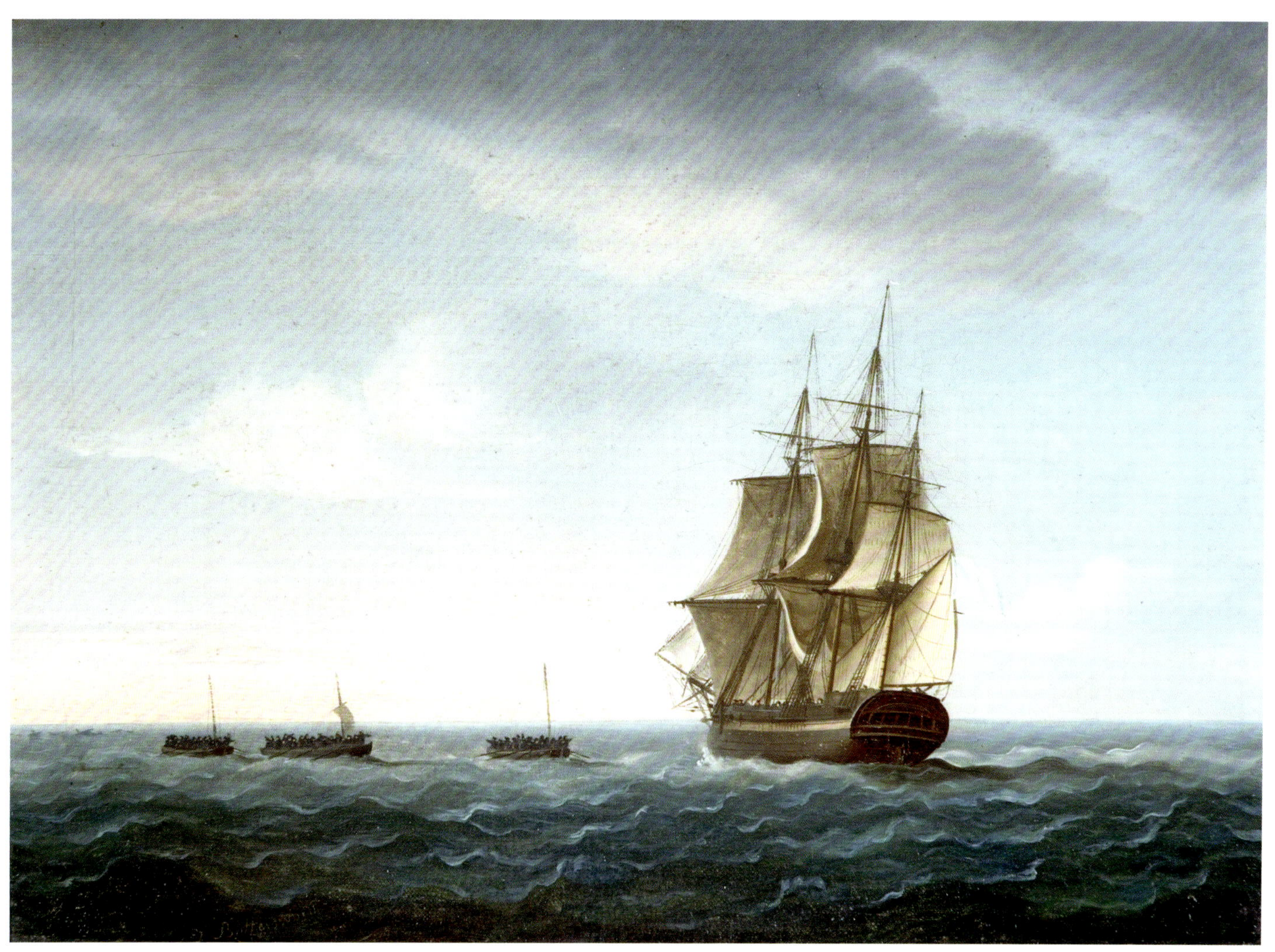

Thomas Buttersworth (1768–1842)

Rescue of the *Guardian's* Crew by a French Merchant Ship

Sauvetage de l'équipage du *Guardian* par un navire marchand français

Die Rettung der Crew des Schiffes *Guardian* durch ein französisches Handelsschiff

Rescate de la tripulación del *Guardian* por un barco mercante francés

O resgate da tripulação do navio *Guardian* por um navio mercante francês

Redding van de bemanning van de *Guardian* door een Frans koopvaardijschip

n. d., Oil on canvas/Huile sur toile, 30 × 42,6 cm, Shipley Art Gallery, Gateshead

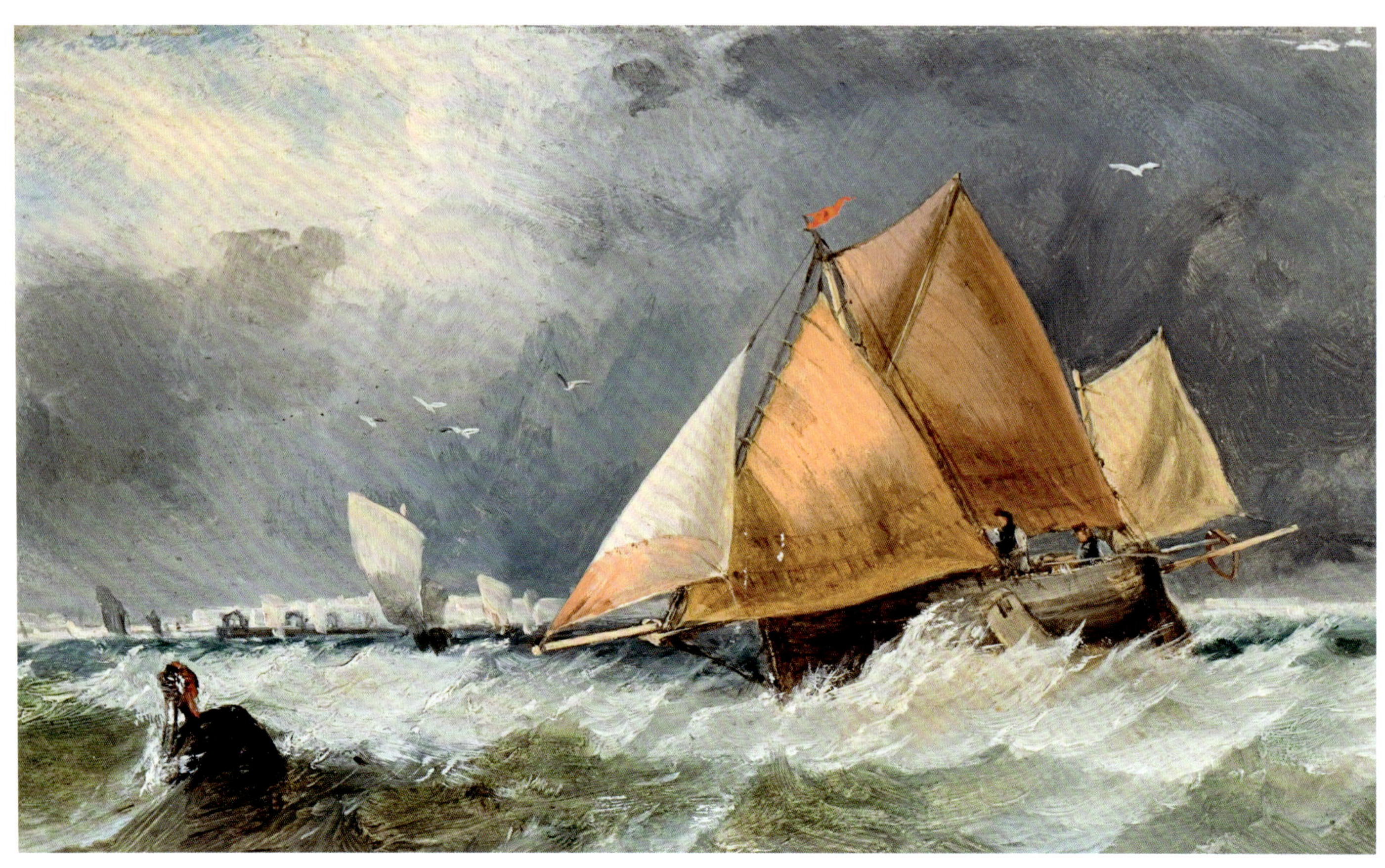

Richard Beavis (1824–96)

Fishing Boats, Brighton

Bateaux de pêche, Brighton

Fischerboote in Brighton

Barcos pesqueros en Brighton

Barcos de pesca em Brighton

Vissersboten in Brighton

n. d., Oil on canvas/Huile sur toile, 14,3 × 24,5 cm, Laing Art Gallery, Newcastle-upon-Tyne

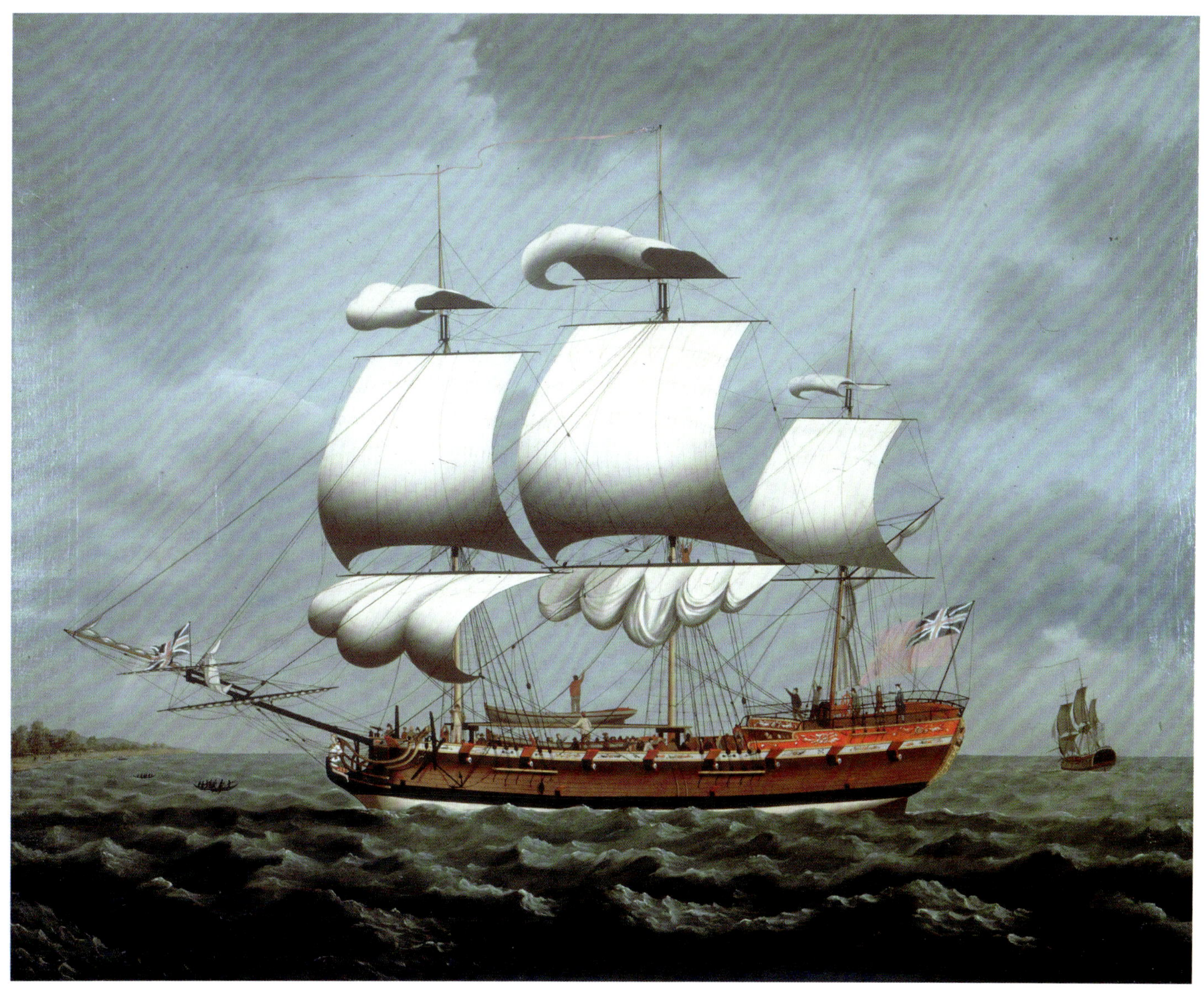

William Jackson (1730–1803)

A Liverpool Slave Ship

Bateau négrier de Liverpool

Ein Liverpooler Sklavenschiff

Barco de esclavos de Liverpool

Um navio negreiro de Liverpool

Een slavenschip uit Liverpool

c. 1780, Oil on canvas/Huile sur toile, 102 × 127 cm, Walker Art Gallery, Liverpool

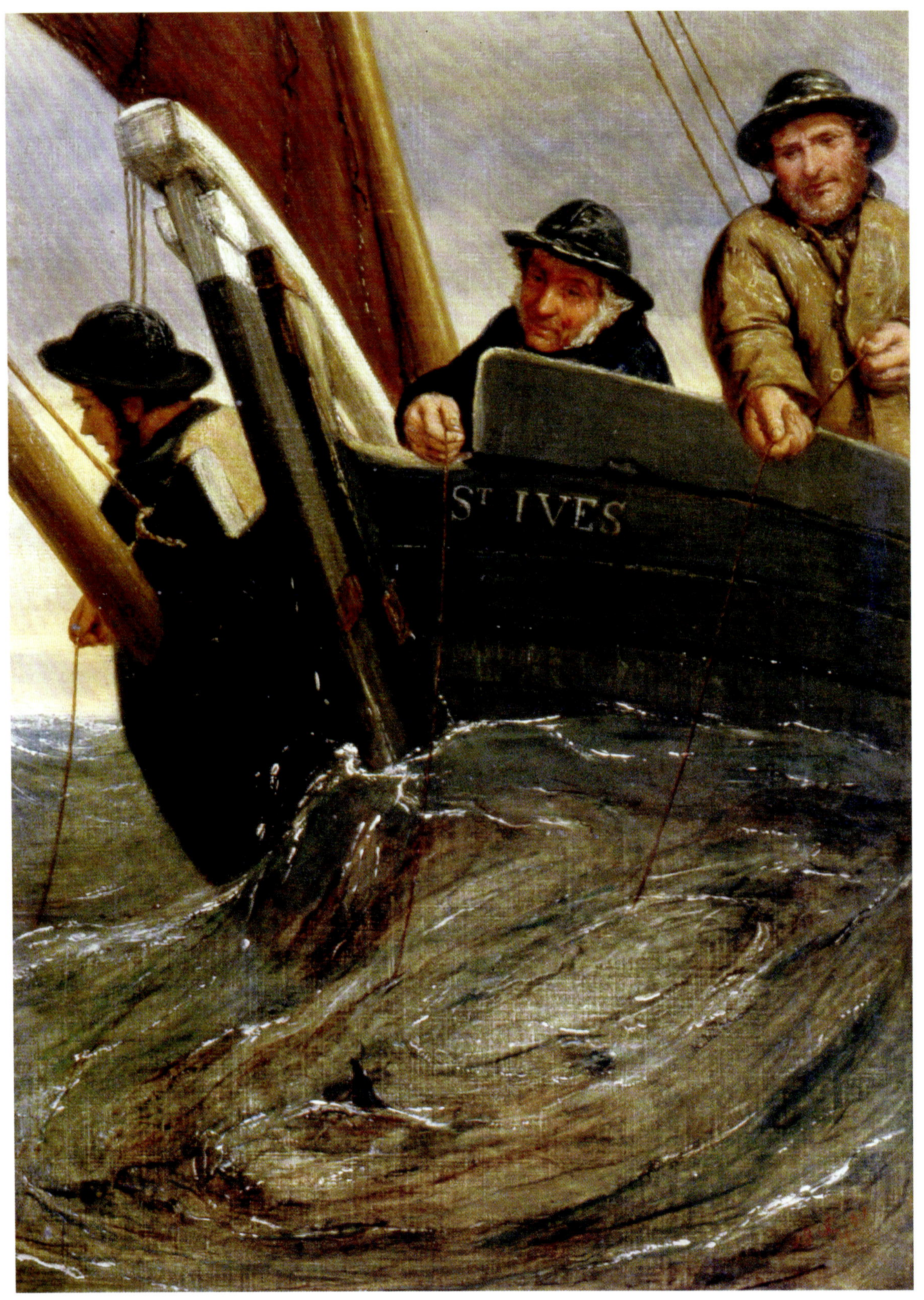

*James Clarke Hook
(1819–1907)*

Deep-Sea Fishing

Pêche hauturière

Hochseefischerei

Pesca en alta mar

Pesca de alto mar

Hoogzeevissers

1861, Oil on canvas/Huile sur
toile, Royal Pavilion, Brighton

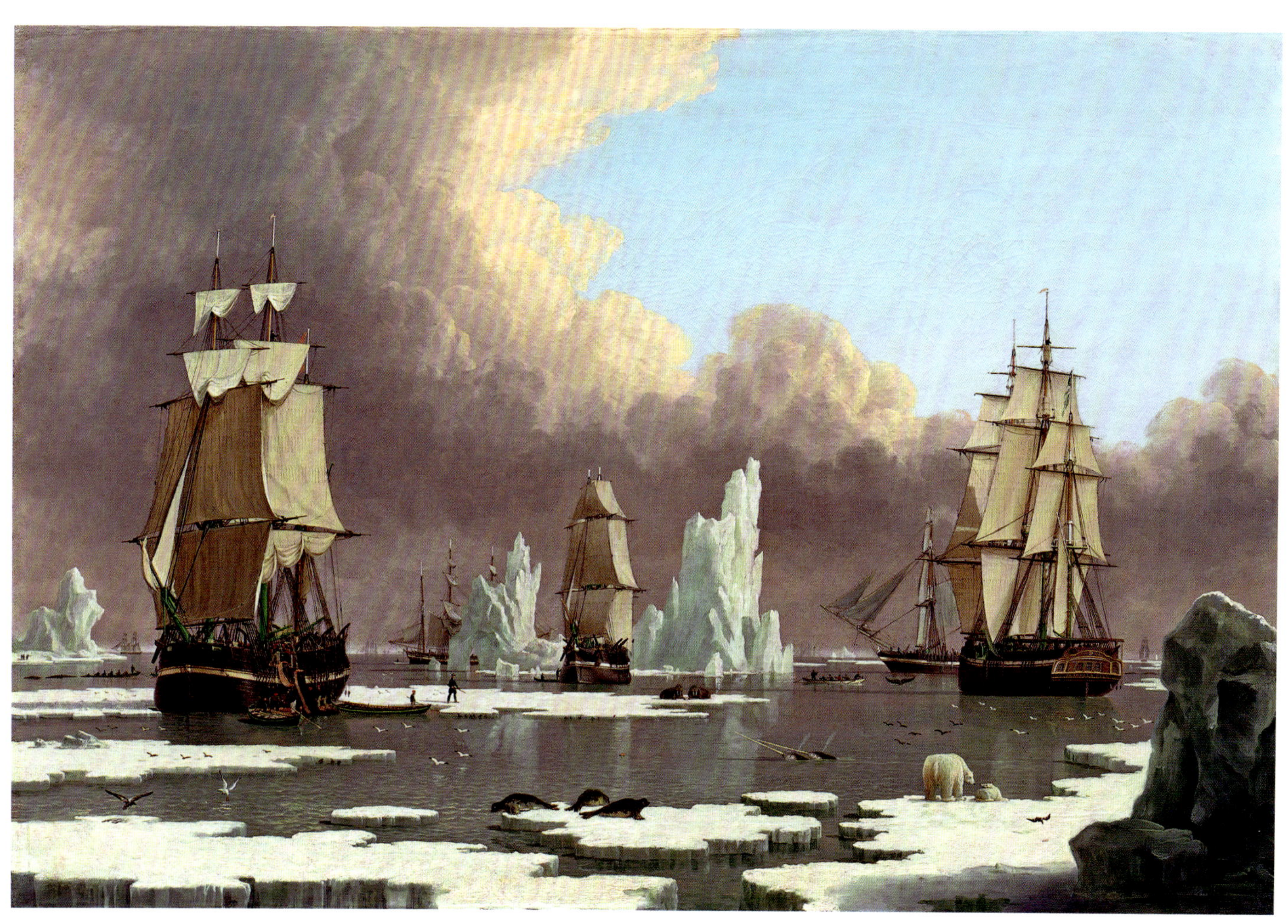

John Ward (1798–1849)

The Northern Whale Fishery, The *Swan* and The *Isabella*

Pêche à la baleine nordique, le *Swan* et l'*Isabella*

Die Walfänger *Swan* und *Isabella*

Los balleneros *Swan* e *Isabella*

Os baleeiros *Swan* e *Isabella*

De walvisvaarders *Swan* en *Isabella*

c. 1840, Oil on canvas/Huile sur toile, 48,9 × 71,8 cm, National Gallery of Art, Washington

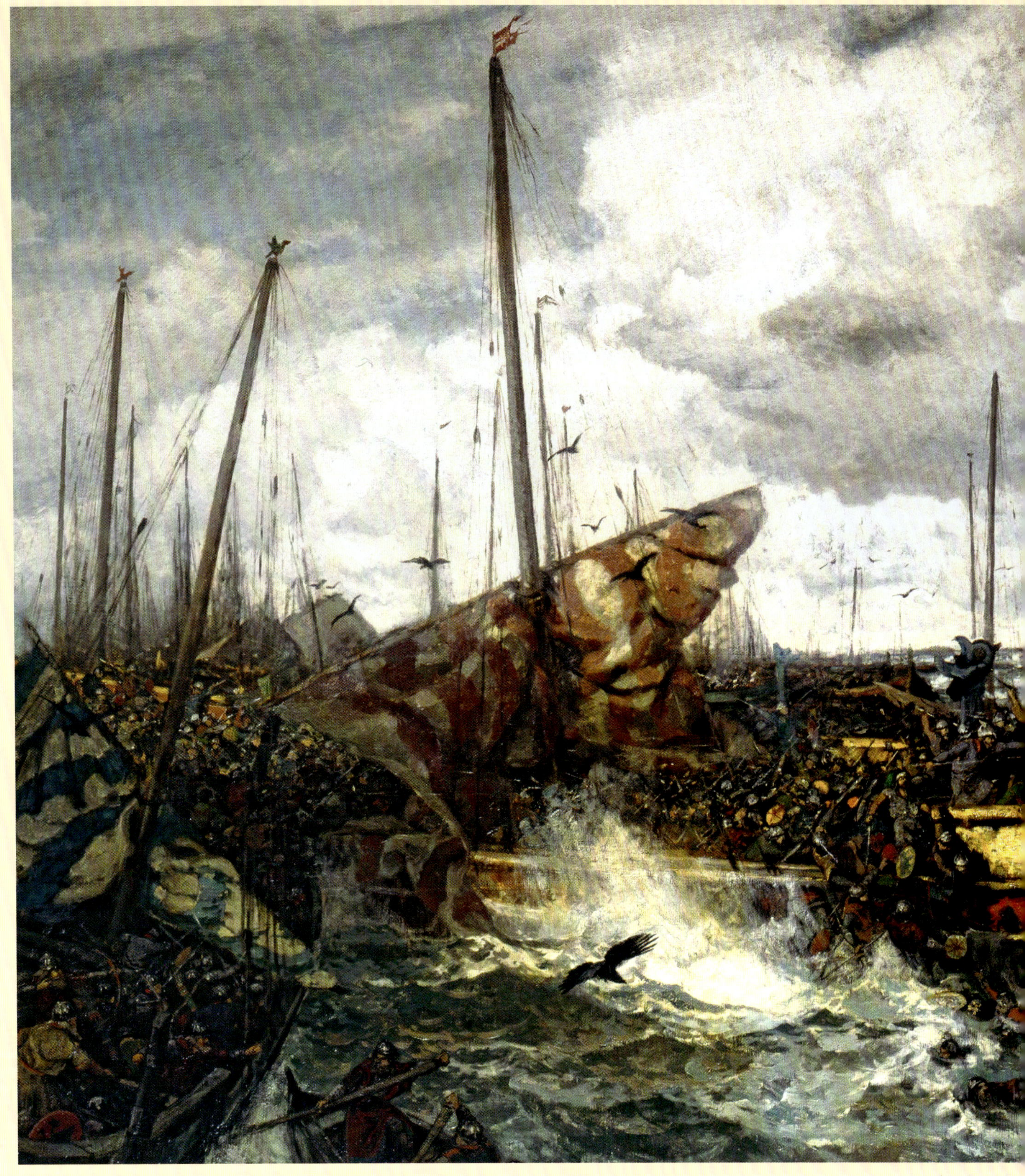

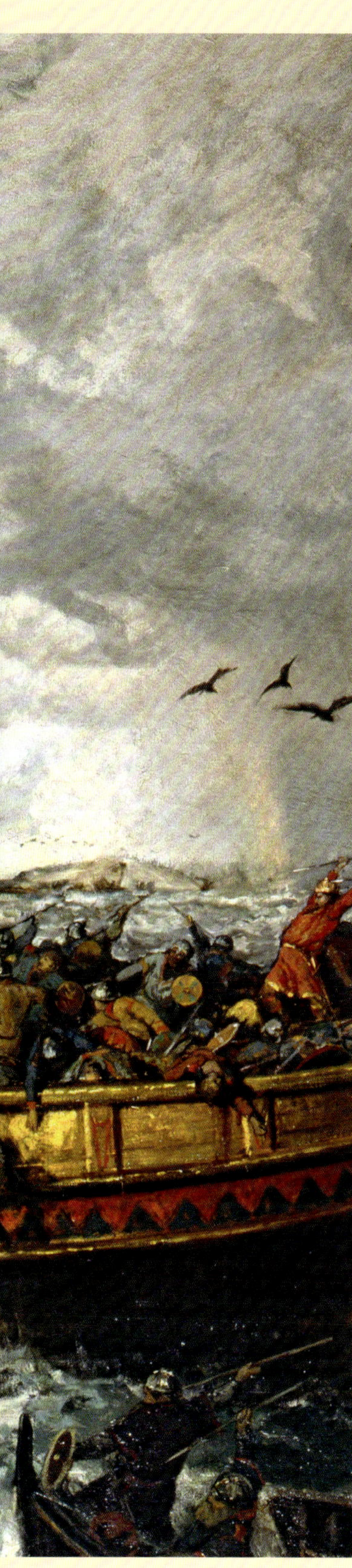

Navies and pirates

Marines et pirates

Krieger und Piraten

Guerreros y piratas

Guerreiros e piratas

Oorlog en piraterij

Otto Ludvig Sinding (1842–1909)
The Battle at Svolder
Bataille à Svolder
Die Schlacht bei Svolder
La batalla de Svolder
A batalha de Svolder
De Zeeslag bij Svolder
c. 1883/84, Oil on canvas/Huile sur toile, 175 × 350 cm, Private collection

Vice Admiral Parker's Action with the
Dutch Fleet on the Doggerbank

Action du vice-amiral Parker avec la
flotte hollandaise sur le Dogger Bank

Das Manöver des Vize-Admirals Parker
während der Schlacht auf der Doggerbank

La maniobra del vicealmirante Parker
durante la batalla en el Doggerbank

A manobra do Vice-Almirante Parker
durante a batalha de Dogger Bank

De manoeuvre van viceadmiraal Parker
tijdens de Zeeslag bij de Doggersbank

1781, Oil on panel/Huile sur bois, Private collection

*The Doggerbank is an extensive sandbank running
only a few meters below the surface of the sea.
It is considered the north-western boundary
between the North Sea and the Atlantic. The
Battle of Doggerbank took place here in August,
where the British fought against the Dutch who
were supplying the rebels with weapons and
munitions during the American Revolution.*

*Le Dogger Bank est un grand banc situé à
quelques mètres seulement sous le niveau de
la mer. Il est considéré comme la limite nord-
ouest entre la mer du Nord et l'Atlantique. La
Bataille de Dogger Bank eut lieu au mois d'août,
où les Britanniques affrontèrent les Hollandais
qui fournissaient aux rebelles des armes et des
munitions pendant la Révolution américaine.*

*Die Doggerbank ist eine ausgedehnte, teilweise
nur wenige Meter unter der Meeresoberfläche
verlaufende Sandbank, die als nordwestliche
Begrenzung der Nordsee gegenüber dem
Atlantik gilt. Hier fand im August die nach
ihr benannte Schlacht statt, in der die
Engländer einmal mehr gegen die Niederländer
kämpften, in diesem Fall, weil letztere die
nach Unabhängigkeit strebenden Amerikaner
mit Waffen und Munition unterstützten.*

*El Doggerbank es un extenso banco de arena,
a veces desarrollado sólo unos pocos metros
por debajo de la superficie del mar, que se
considera el límite noroeste del Mar del Norte
sobre el Océano Atlántico. Aquí tuvo lugar en
agosto la batalla que lleva su mismo nombre,
en la que los británicos lucharon una vez más
contra los holandeses, a los que en este caso, les
apoyaron los norteamericanos de mentalidad
independiente mediante armas y municiones.*

*O Doggerbank, um banco de areia extenso que
se prolonga às vezes somente alguns metros sob
a superfície do mar, é considerado como uma
demarcação do noroeste do Mar do Norte em
relação ao Atlântico. Aí se realizou em Agosto
a batalha com o mesmo nome, na qual os
britânicos batalharam mais uma vez contra
os holandeses, nesse caso, porque estes últimos
haviam apoiado com armas e munições os
americanos, que lutavam por sua independência.*

*De Doggersbank is een uitgestrekte zandplaat in de
Noordzee die op sommige plekken slechts vijftien
meter onder de zeespiegel ligt. Hier vond op 5
augustus 1781 tijdens de Vierde Engels-Nederlandse
Oorlog de Zeeslag van de Doggersbank
plaats, in dit geval omdat de Republiek der
Nederlanden het onafhankelijkheidsstreven
van de VS met wapens en munitie steunde.*

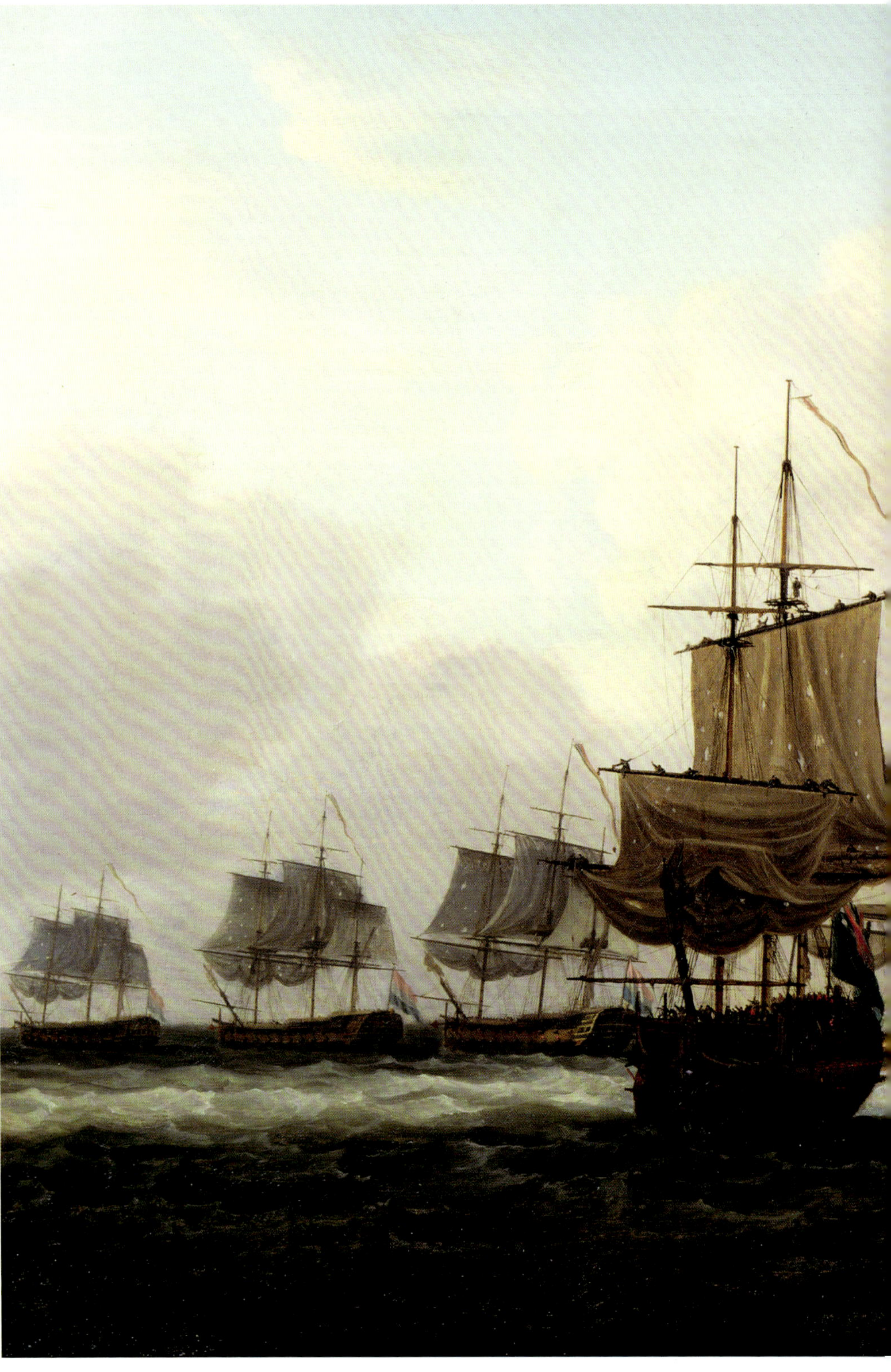

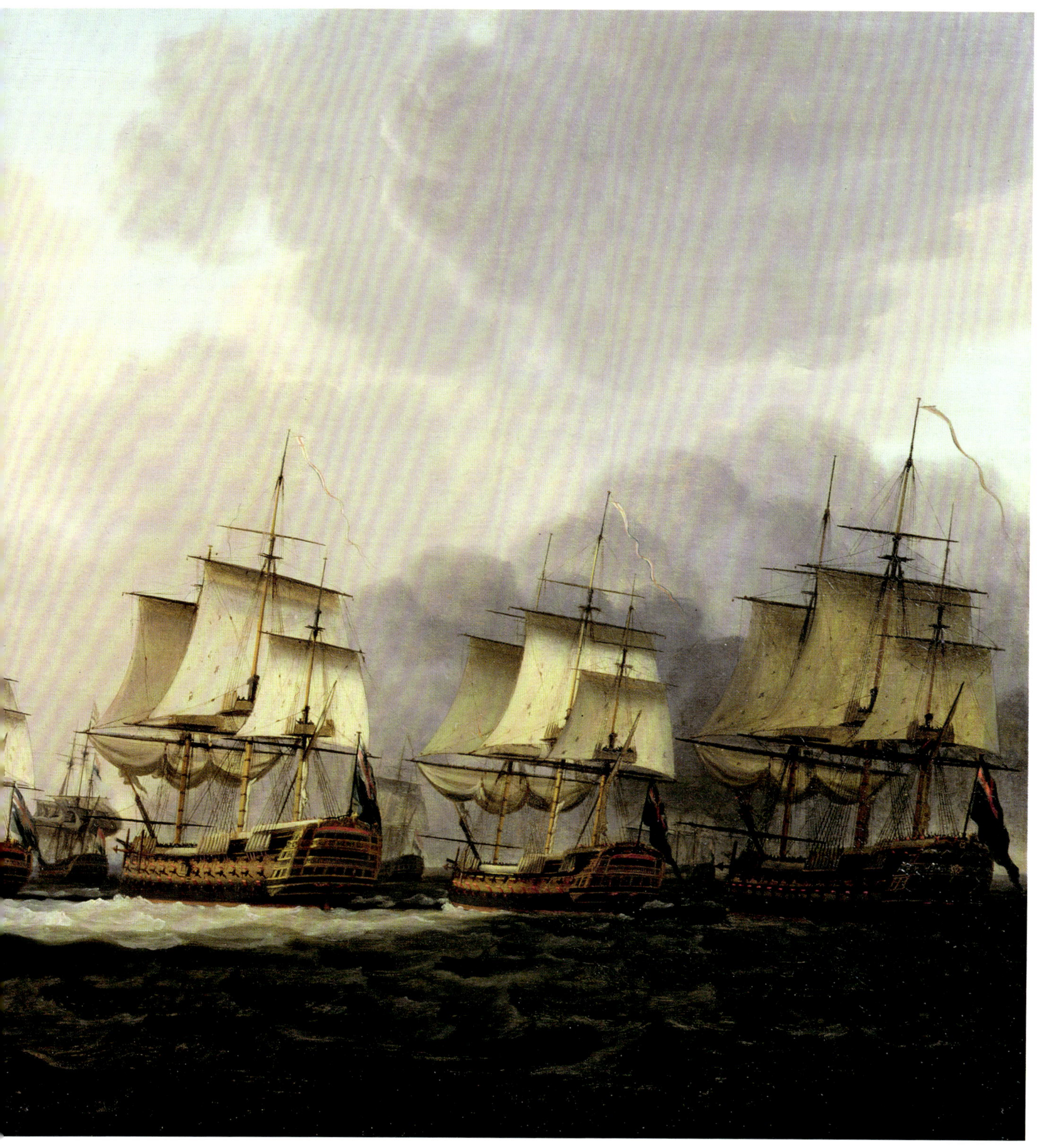

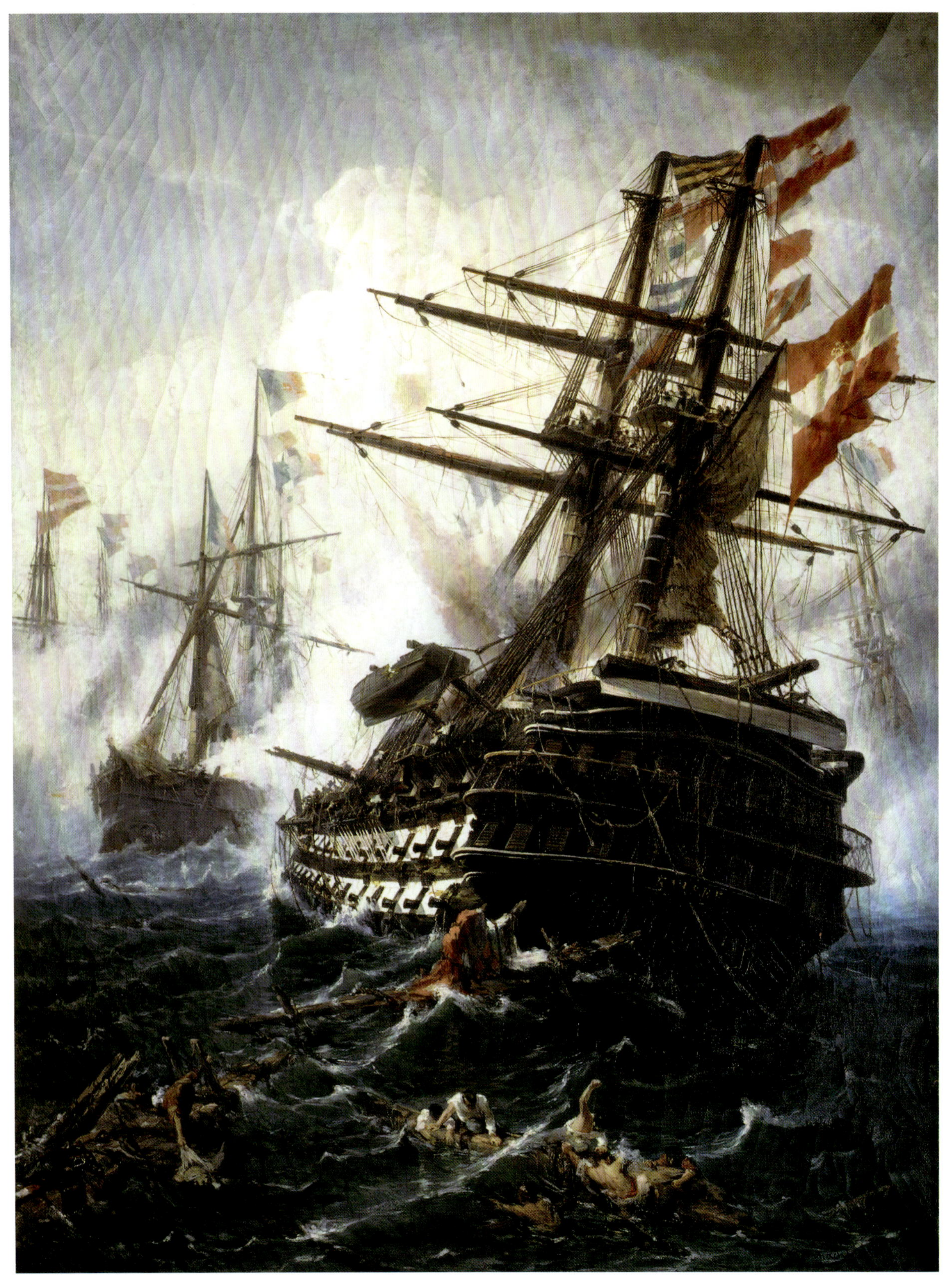

Constantin Volonakis (1837–1907)

The Emperor's Ship During the Battle of Lissa, 1866

Le Navire de l'Empereur lors de la bataille de Lissa, 1866

Das kaiserliche Schiff während der Schlacht von Lissa, 1866

El barco imperial durante la batalla de Lissa, 1866

O navio imperial durante a batalha de Lissa, 1866

Het keizerlijke schip tijdens de Zeeslag bij Lissa in 1866

1868, Oil on canvas/ Huile sur toile, 164 × 127 cm, Belvedere, Wien

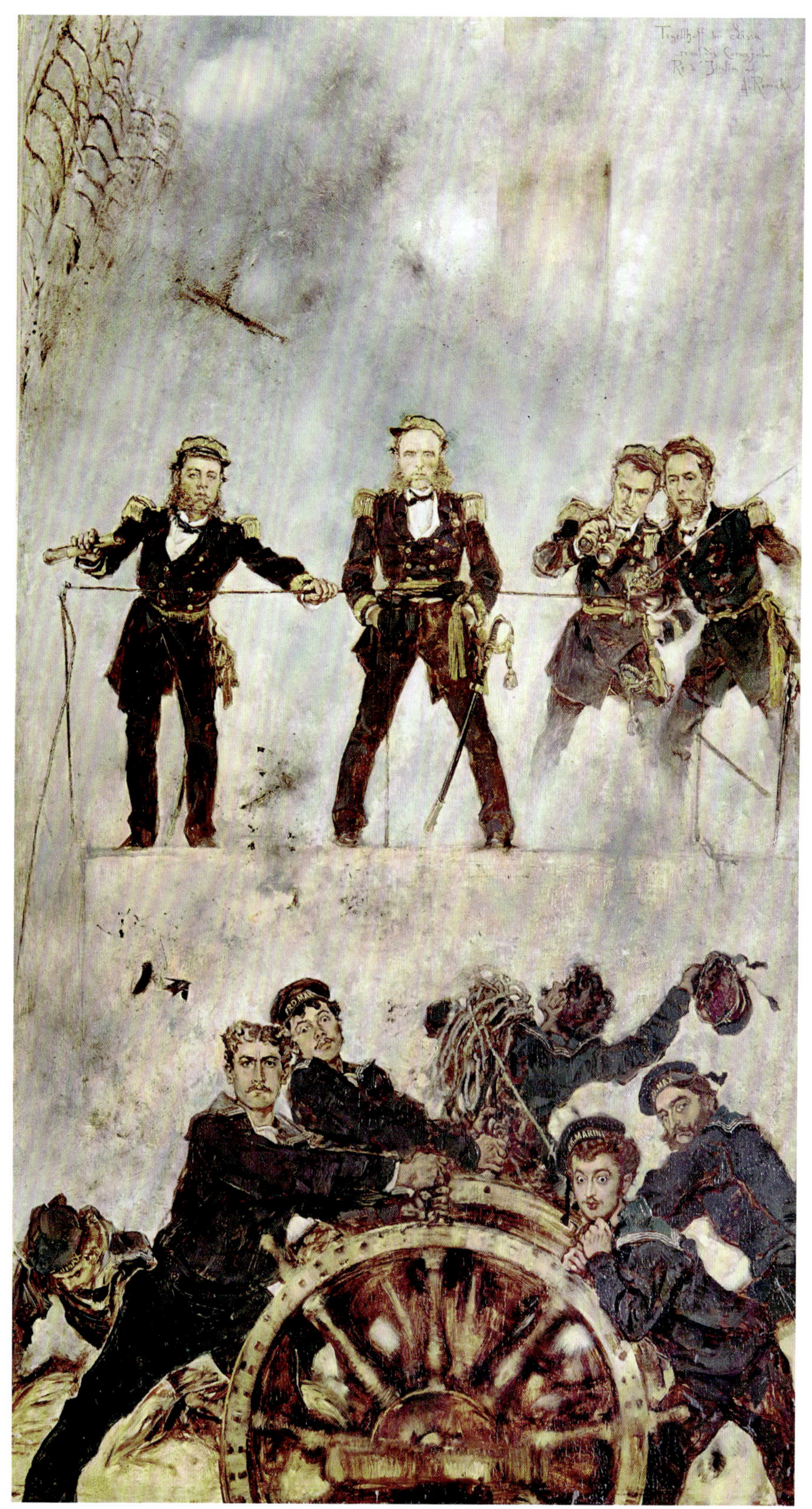

Anton Romako (1832–89)
Tegetthoff at the Battle of Lissa I
Tegetthoff pendant la bataille navale de Lissa I
Tegetthoff in der Seeschlacht von Lissa I
Tegetthoff en la batalla naval de Lissa I
Tegetthoff na batalha de Lissa I
Tegetthoff in de slag bij Lissa I
1878–80, Oil on panel/Huile sur bois, 82 × 110 cm, Belvedere, Wien

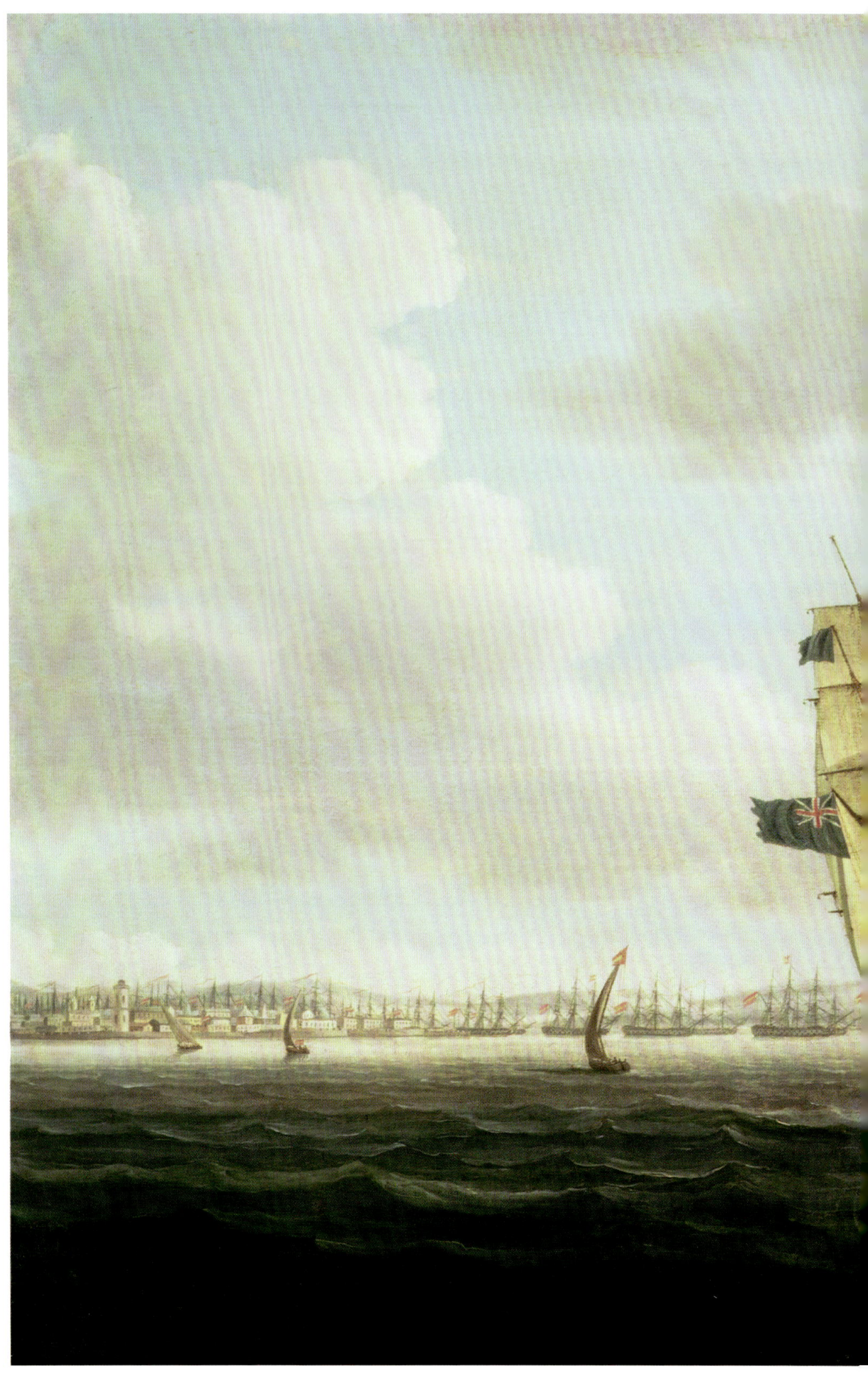

Thomas Buttersworth (1768–1842)

Nelson on the *Theseus* with Inshore
Squadron off Cádiz, July 1797

Nelson sur le *Theseus* avec l'Escadron
côtier au large de Cadix, juillet 1797

Nelson auf der *Theseus* mit dem
Küstengeschwader vor Cádiz, Juli 1797

Nelson en el *Theseus* con el escuadrón
de costa delante de Cádiz, julio 1797

Nelson no *Theseus* com esquadra costeira
ao largo de Cádis, julho de 1797

Nelson op de *Theseus* met een kusteskader
voor de rede van Cádiz in juli 1797

n. d., Oil on canvas/Huile sur toile, Private collection

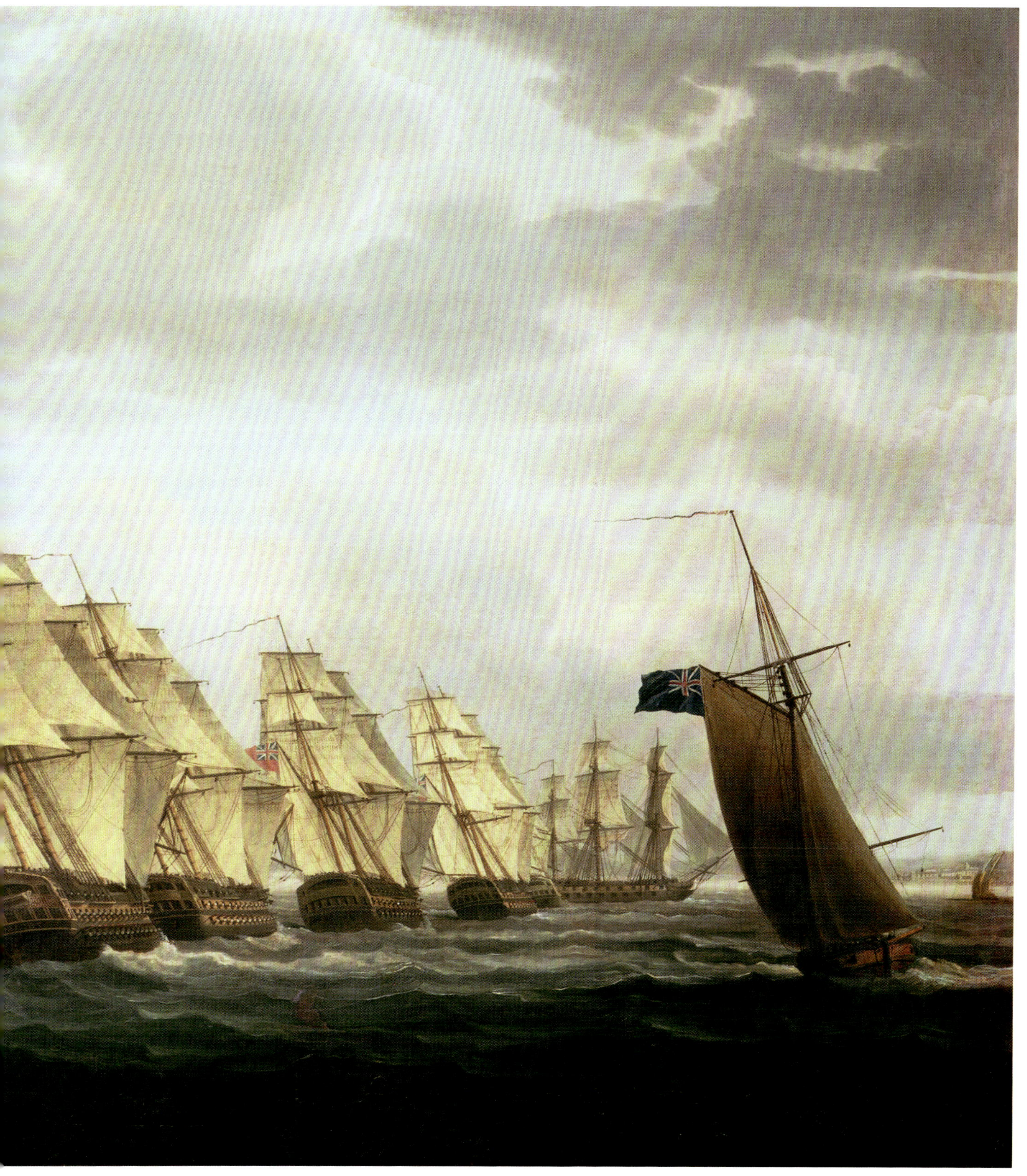

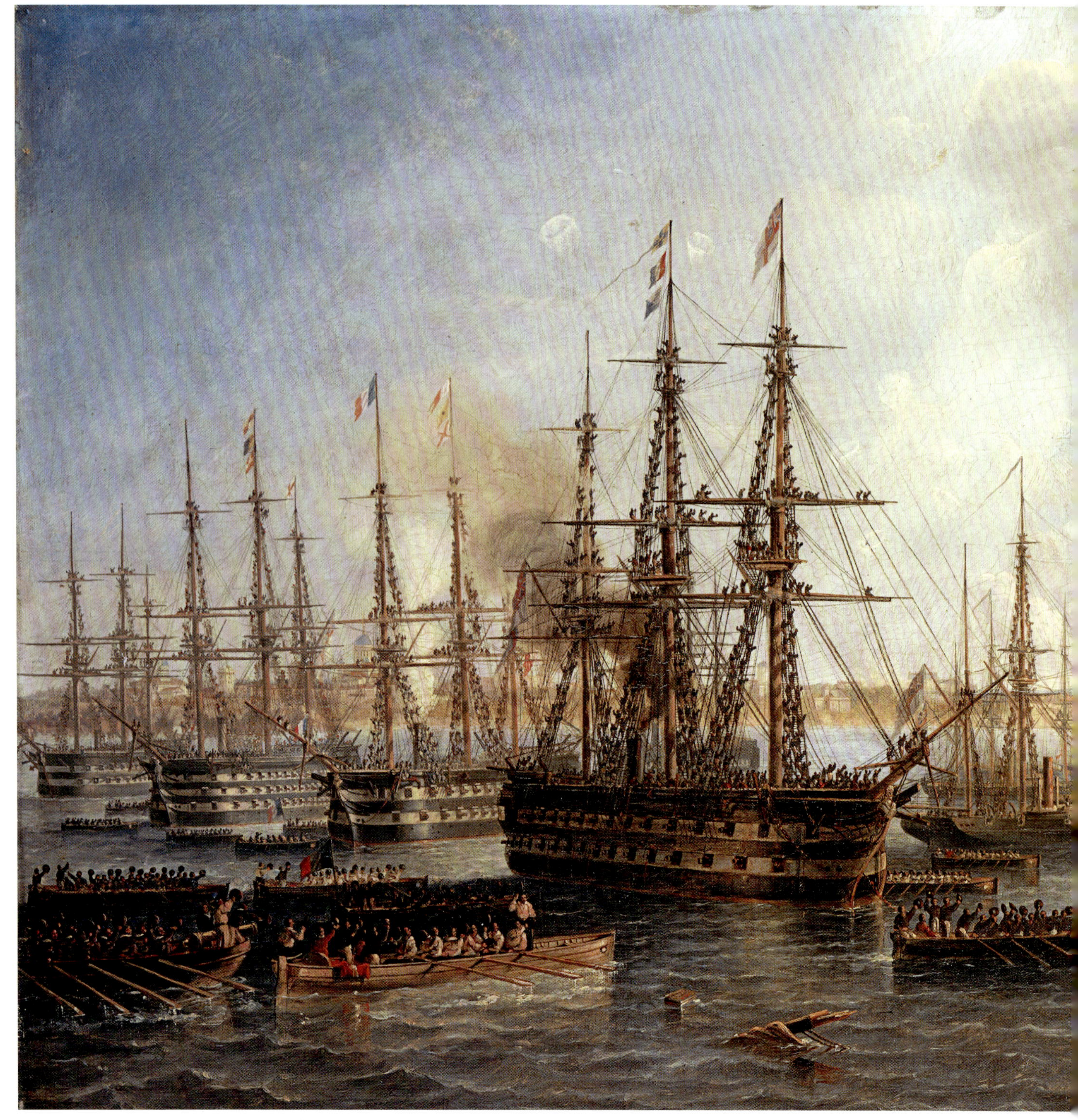

John Wilson Carmichael (1800–68)

The Bombardment of Sveaborg, 5 August 1855

Le bombardement de Sveaborg, 5 août 1855

Das Bombardement von Sveaborg im Jahr 1855

El bombardeo de Sveaborg 1855

O bombardeamento de Sveaborg em 1855

Het bombardement van Sveaborg in 1855

1856, Oil on canvas/Huile sur toile, 53,5 × 106,7 cm, Private collection

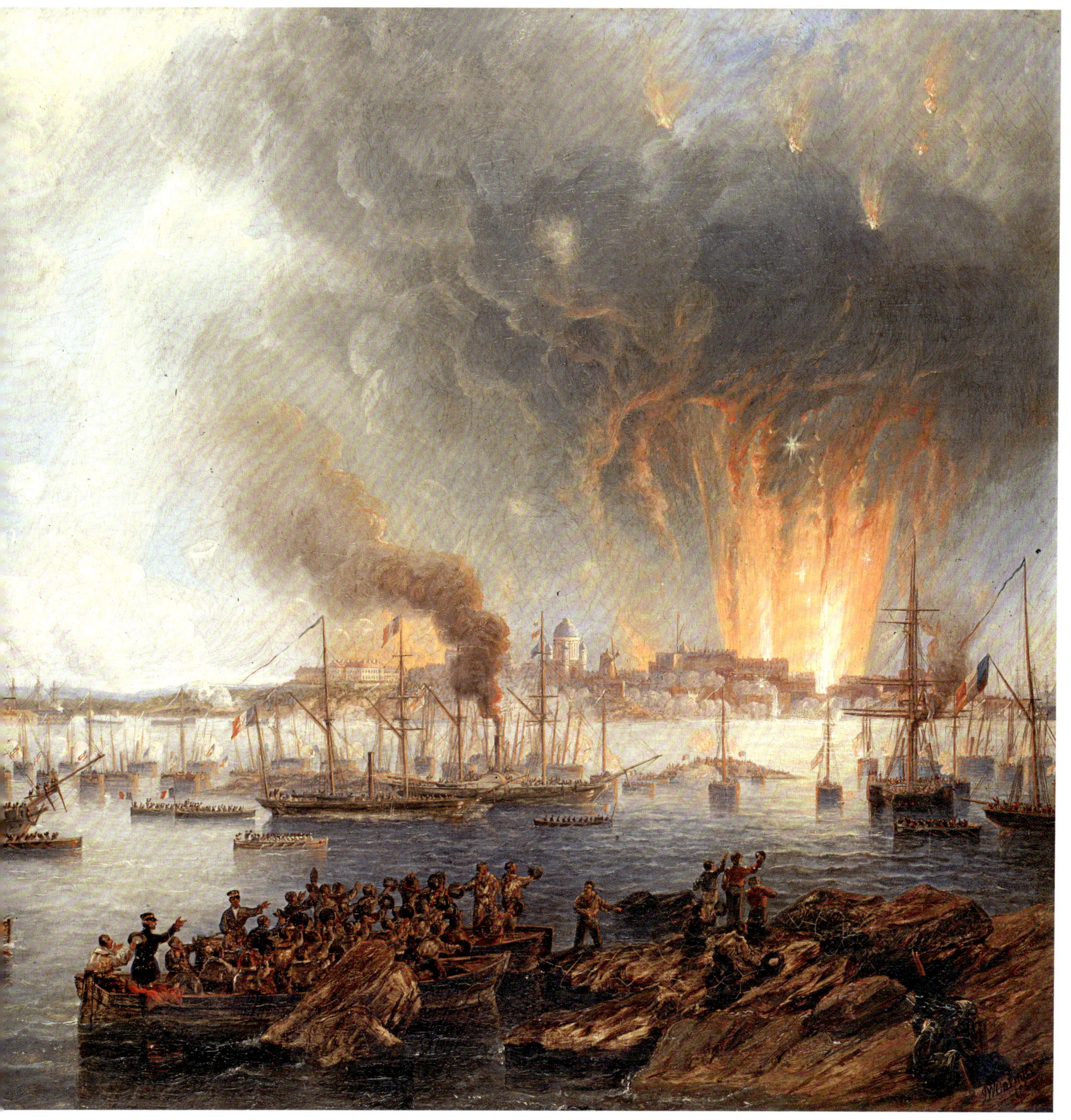

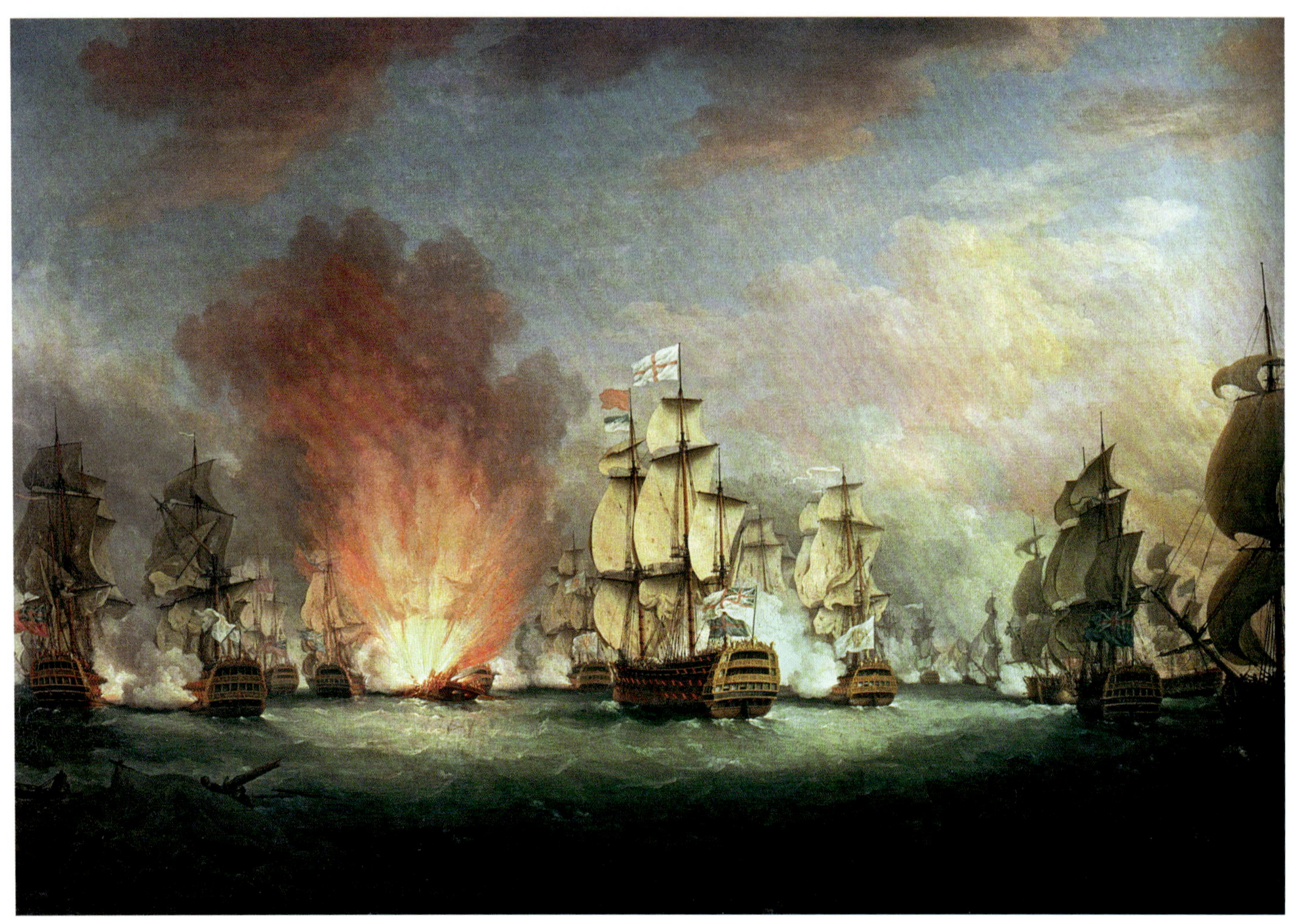

Richard Paton (1717–91)

The Moonlight Battle: The Battle of Cape St. Vincent, 16 January 1780

Bataille au clair de lune : la Bataille du cap Saint-Vincent, 16 janvier 1780

Gefecht im Mondlicht: Die Schlacht bei Kap St. Vincent, 16. Januar 1780

Batalla a la luz de la luna: la batalla del Cabo de San Vicente, 16 de enero de 1780

Batalha ao luar: A batalha do Cabo de São Vicente, 16 de janeiro de 1780

Gevecht bij maanlicht: de Zeeslag bij Kaap Sint-Vincent op 16 januari 1780

n. d., Oil on canvas/Huile sur toile, 101,6 × 147,3 cm, National Maritime Museum, London

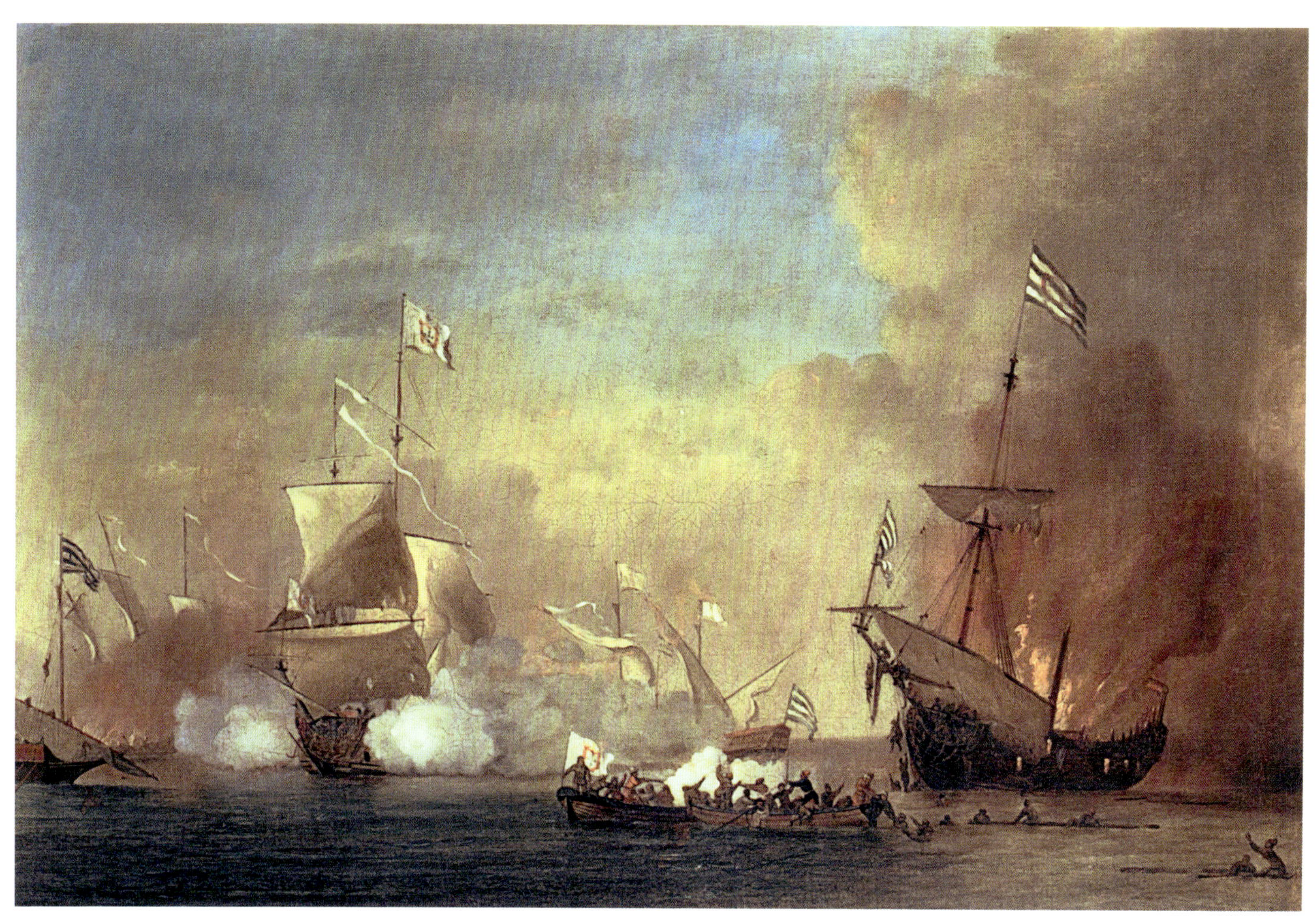

Willem van de Velde d. J. (1633–1707)

Barbary Pirates Attacking a Spanish Ship

Barbares pirates attaquant un navire espagnol

Barbaresken-Korsaren greifen ein spanisches Schiff an

Piratas bárbaros atacando a un barco español

Piratas de Barbaria atacam um navio espanhol

Barbarijse zeerovers vallen een Spaans schip aan

n. d., Oil on canvas/Huile sur toile, 77,5 × 106,7 cm, Private collection

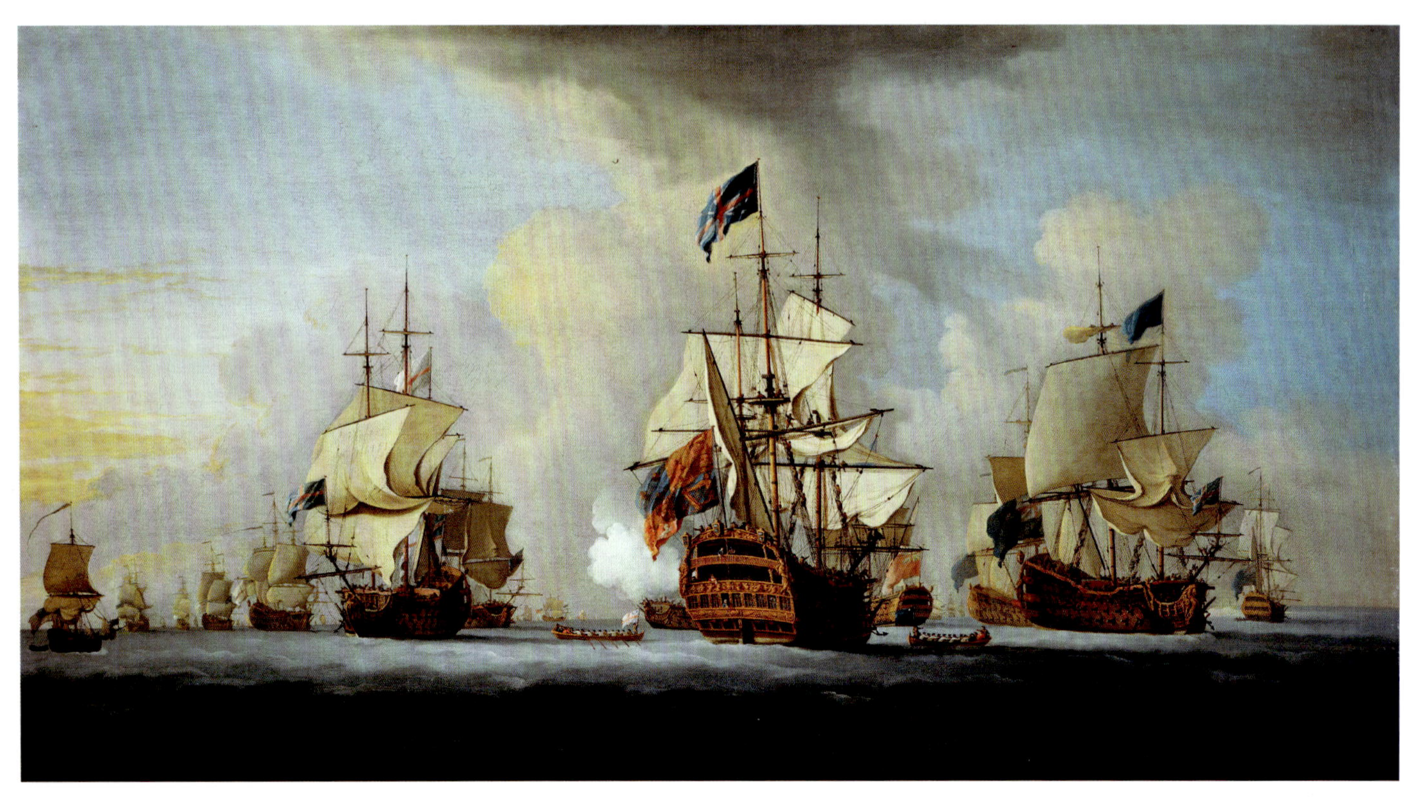

Peter Monamy (1681–1749)

The English Fleet at Anchor

La Flotte anglaise à l'ancre

Die englische Flotte vor Anker

La flota inglesa anclada

A frota inglesa fundeada

De Britse vloot voor anker

n. d., Oil on canvas/Huile sur toile, 83,7 × 155 cm, Private collection

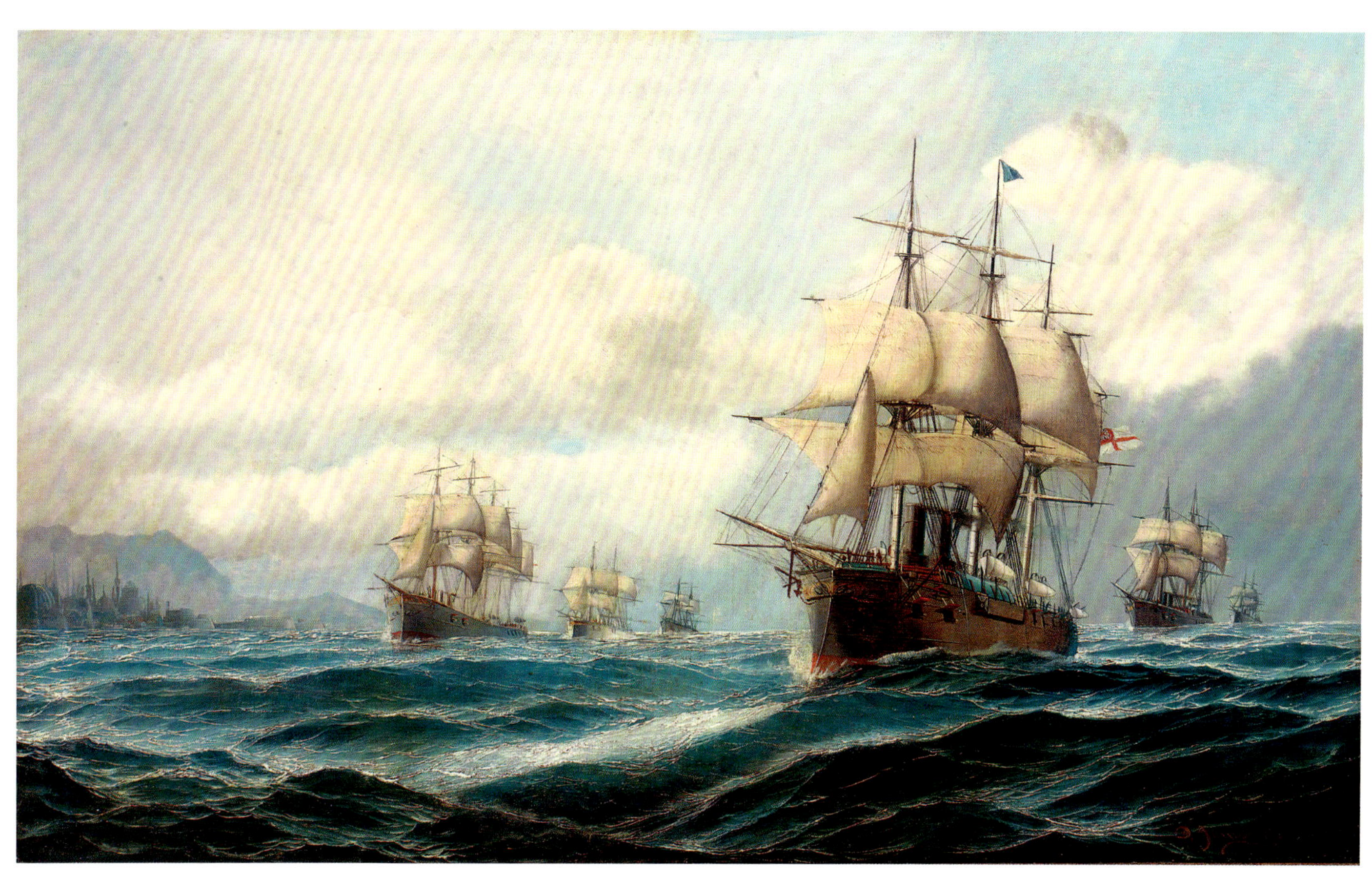

David James (1853–1904)

Vice Admiral Phipps Hornby's Squadron

L'Escadron du vice-amiral Phipps Hornby

Das Geschwader des Vize-Admiral Phipps Hornby

El escuadrón del vicealmirante Phipps Hornby

A esquadra do Vice-Almirante Phipps Hornby

Het eskader van viceadmiraal Phipps Hornby

n. d., Oil on canvas/Huile sur toile, 76,3 × 127 cm, Private collection

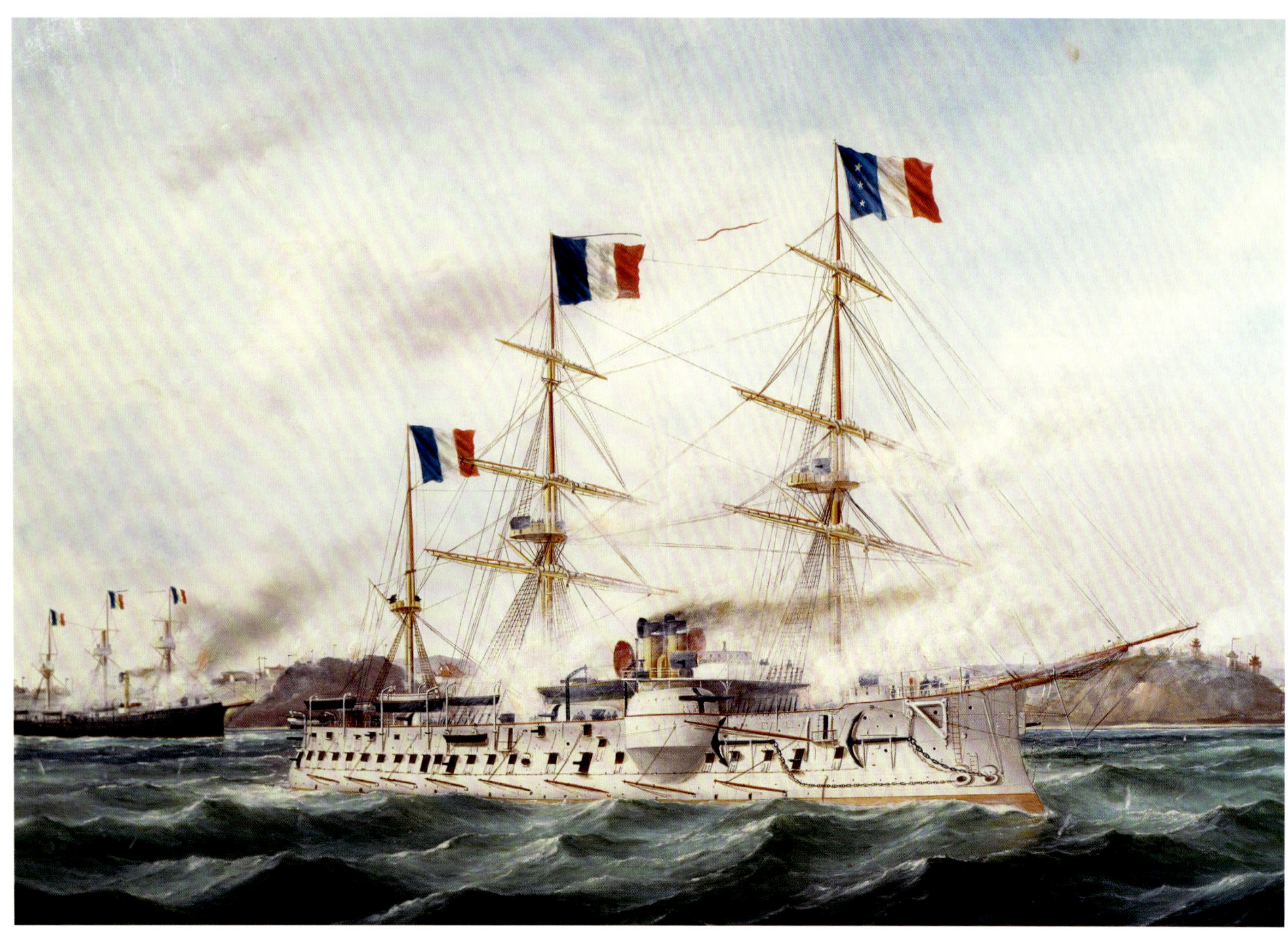

Anonymous

Courbet's Navy Squadron Capturing Makung, 1884

L'Escadron de marine de Courbet capturant Magong, 1884

Das Geschwader Admiral Courbets nimmt Magong ein, 1884

El escuadrón del almirante Courbet tomando Magong, 1884

Esquadra naval do Almirante Courbet em Ma-Kung, 1884

Het eskader van admiraal Courbet neemt Magong in 1884

19th century/XIXᵉ siècle, Oil on canvas/Huile sur toile, Musée de la Marine, Paris

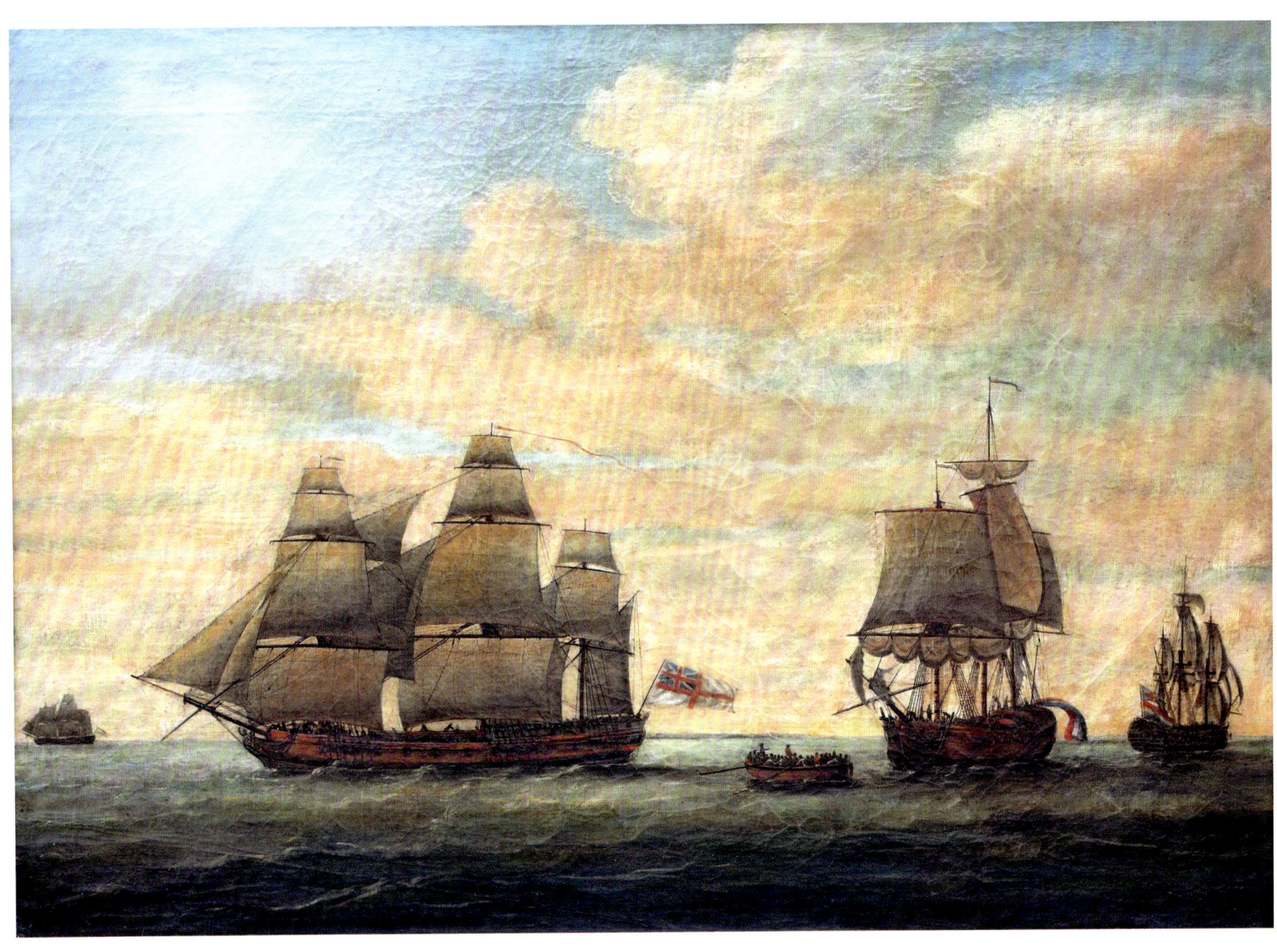

Francis Holman (1729–84)

HMS Hyaena, Capturing Three Dutch West Indiamen off the Island of St Eustace, August 1781

HMS Hyaena, capturant trois Indiens de l'Ouest néerlandais au large de l'île de St-Eustache, août 1781

Ihrer Majestät Schiff *Hyaena*, drei niederländische Westindiensegler vor der Insel Sint Eustatius stellend

El barco de Su Majestad, *Hyaena*, capturando tres barcos holandeses de la Compañía de las Indias Occidentales delante de la Isla de Santa Eustasia

O navo de Sua Majestade *Hyaena*, três veleiros das Antilhas holandesas ao largo da ilha de Sint Eustatius

HMS Hyaena houdt drie Nederlandse westindiëvaarders aan bij het eiland Sint-Eustatius

1782, Oil on canvas/Huile sur toile, 74,3 × 124,5 cm, Private collection

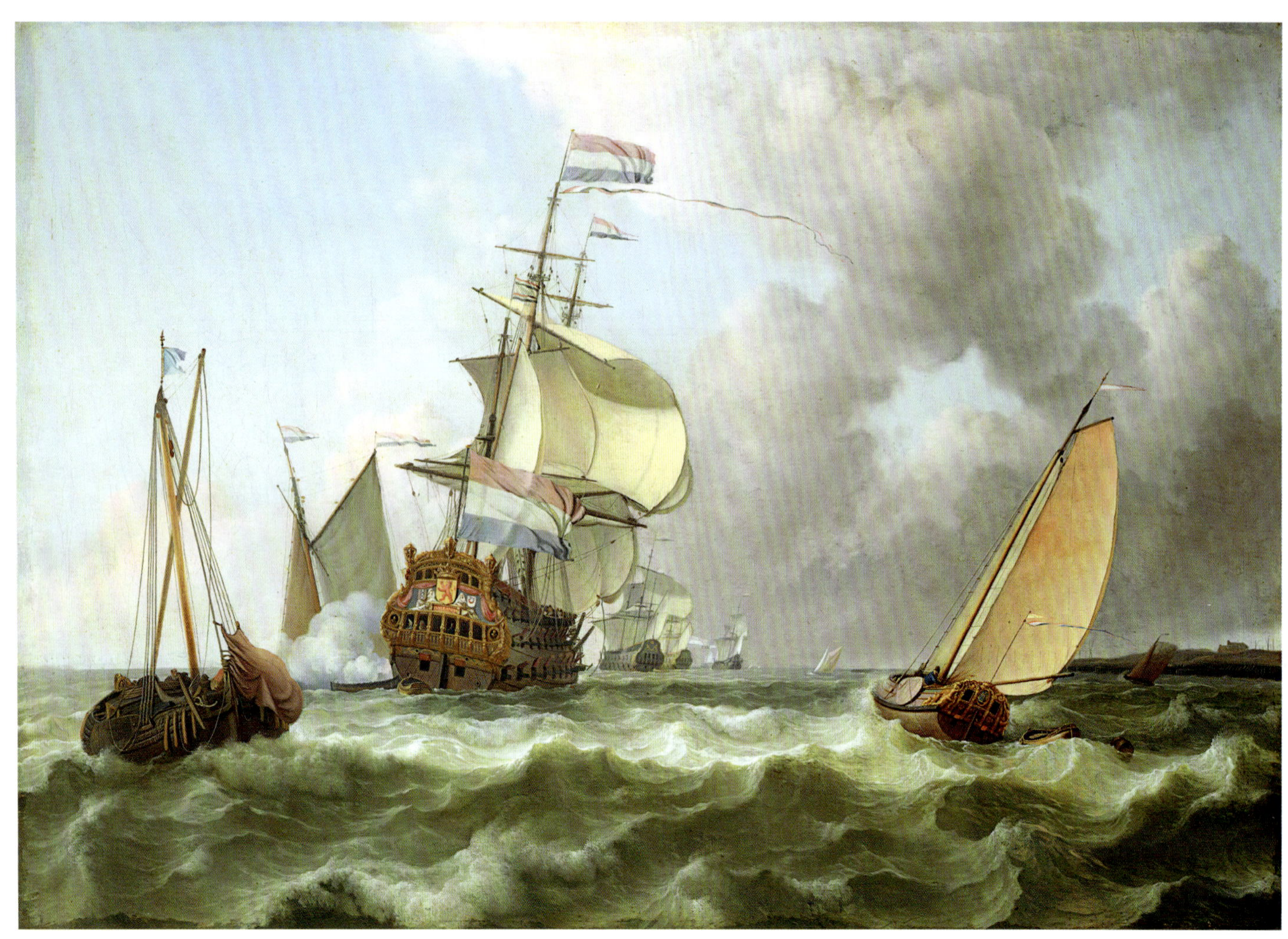

Ludolf Backhuysen (1630–1708)

The Warship *Hollandia* in Full Sail

Le Bâtiment de guerre *Hollandia* en pleine voile

Das Kriegsschiff *Hollandia* unter vollen Segeln

El buque de guerra *Hollandia* a toda vela

O navio de guerra *Hollandia* sob a vela cheia

Het oorlogsschip *Hollandia* onder vol zeil

n. d., Oil on canvas/Huile sur toile, 68,6 × 95,2 cm, Lotherton Hall, Leeds

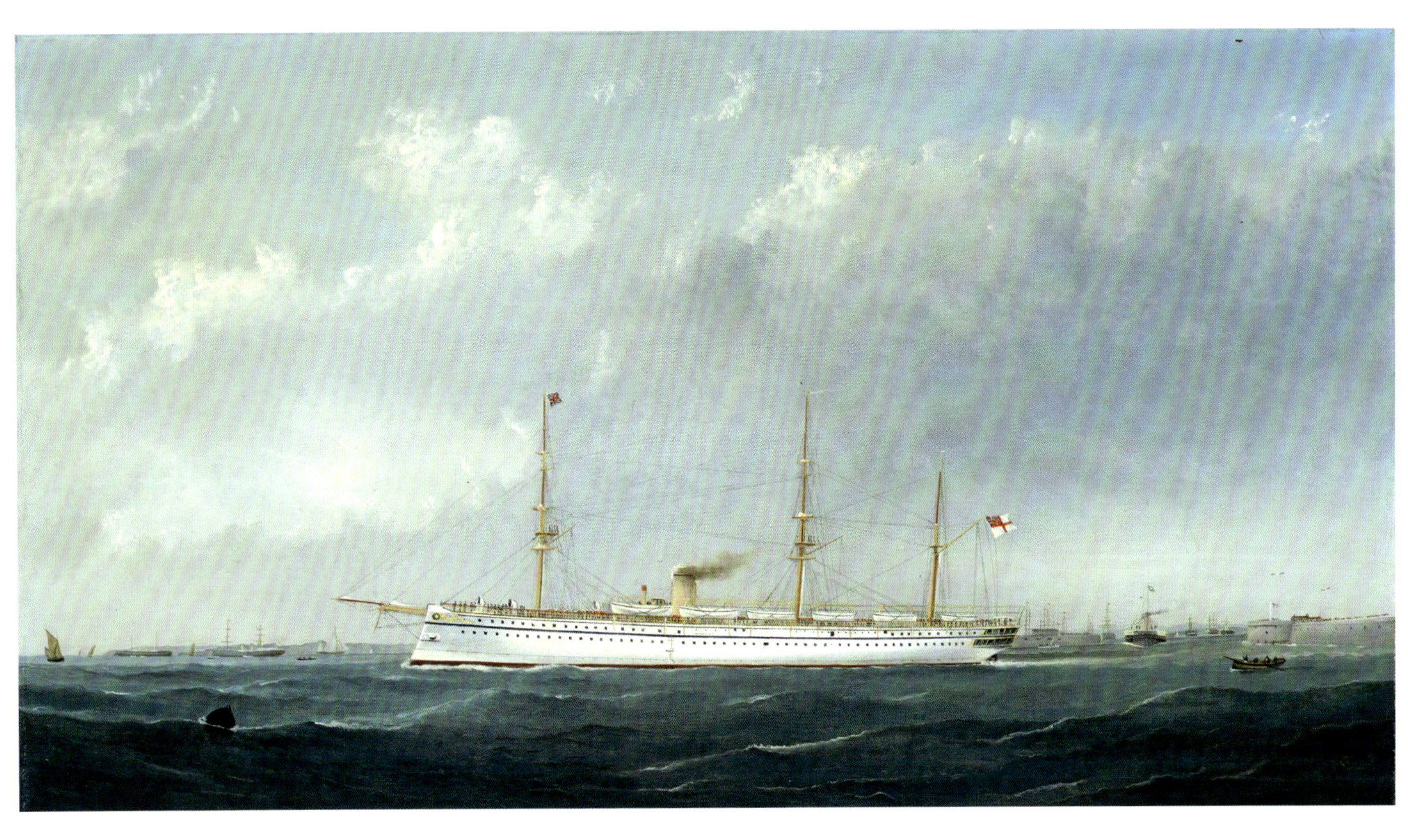

George Mears (fl. 1870–95)

The Troop Ship *Euphrates* Leaving Harbour

Le Navire de la troupe *Euphrates* quittant le port

Der Truppentransporter *Euphrates* verlässt den Hafen

El barco militar *Euphrates* dejando puerto

O transportador de tropas *Euphrates* deixando o porto

Het troepentransportschip *Euphrates* loopt uit

c. 1870, Oil on canvas/Huile sur toile, National Army Museum, London

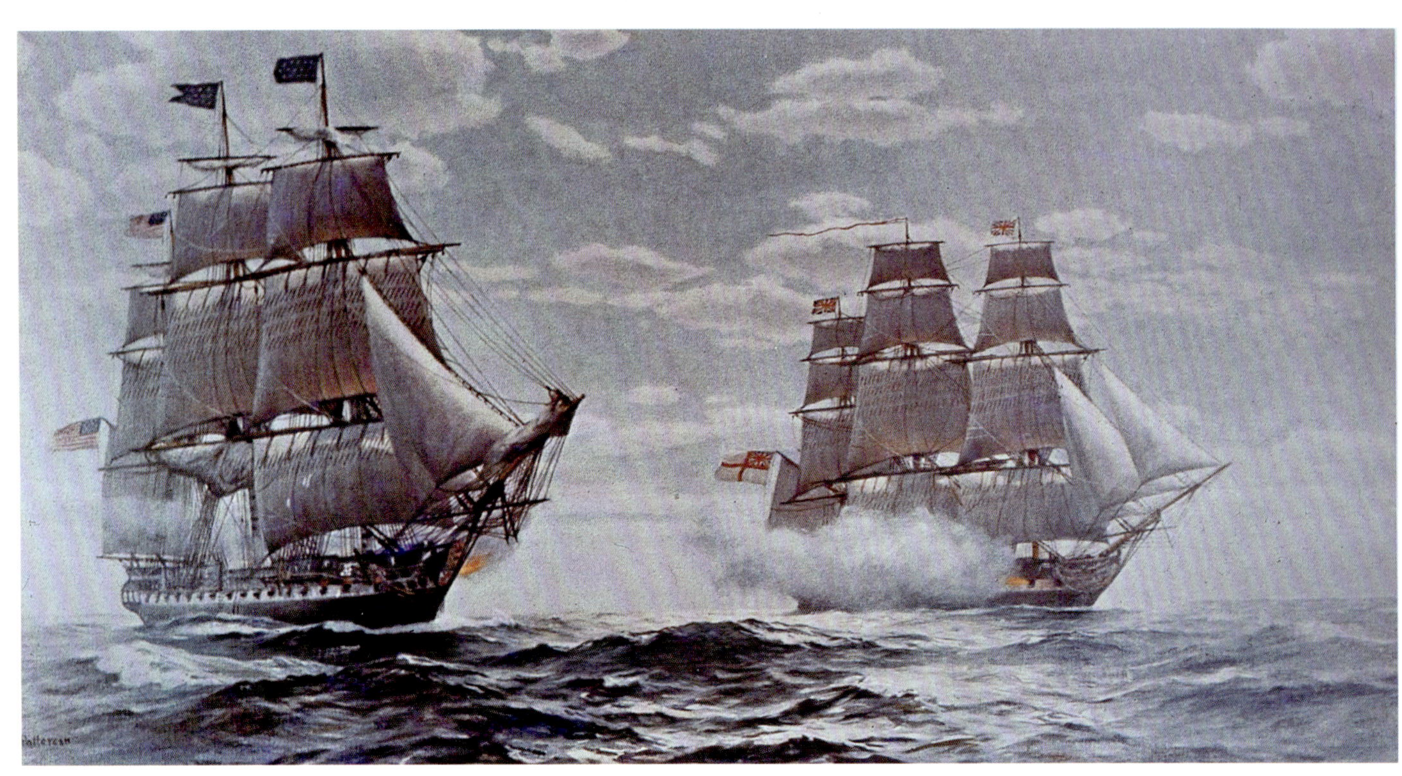

Charles Robert Patterson (1774–1833)

USS Constitution and *HMS Java*

USS Constitution et *HMS Java*

Die *USS Constitution* und die *HMS Java*

El *USS Constitution* y el *HMS Java*

O *USS Constitution* e o *HMS Java*

De *USS Constitution* en de *HMS Java*

n. d., Oil on canvas/Huile sur toile, Private collection

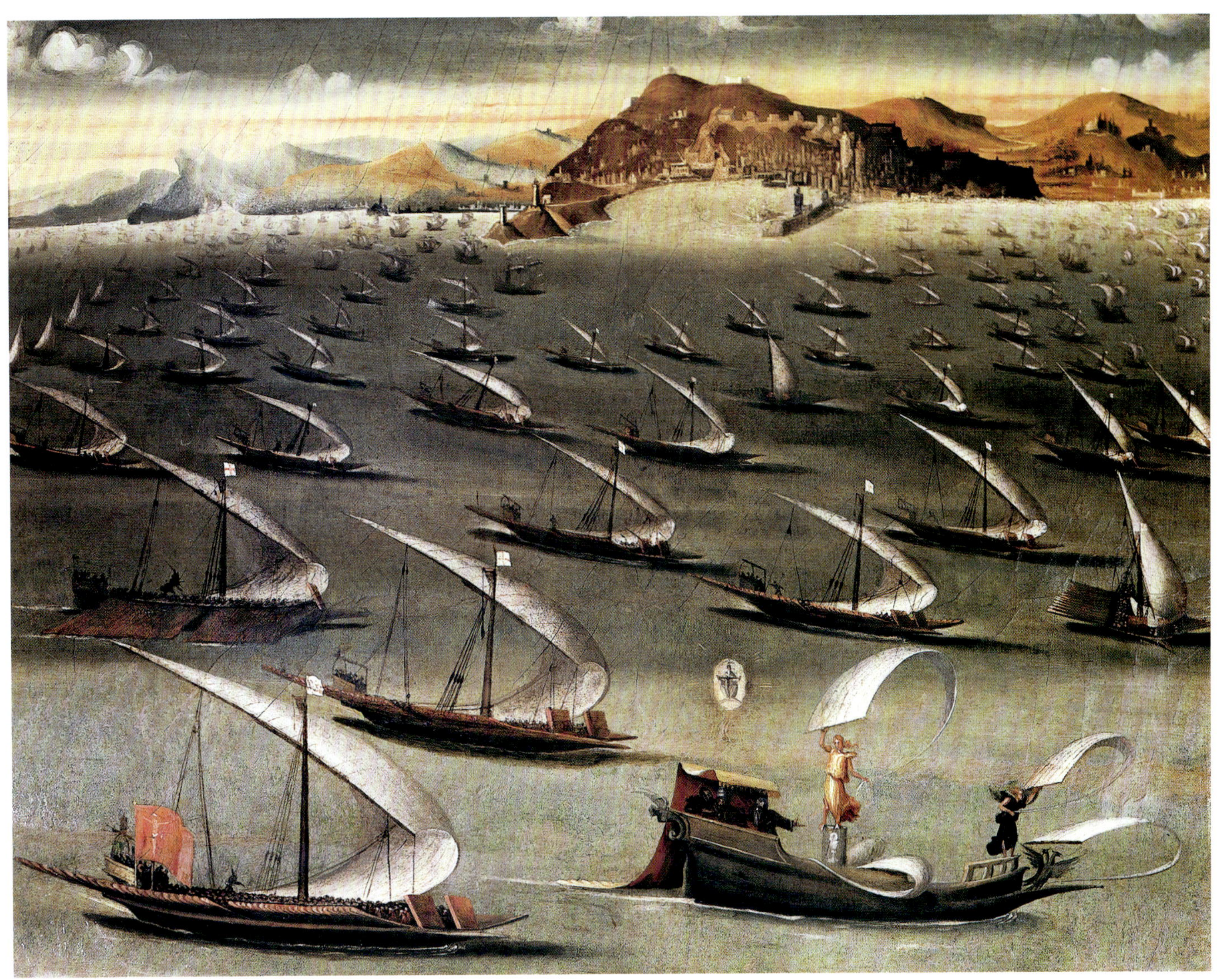

Anonymous

Returning from Nice, Charles V, Paul III, and Andrea Doria, 1538

De retour de Nice, Charles V, Paul III et Andrea Doria, 1538

Karl V., Paul III. und Andrea Doria auf dem Rückweg von Nizza, 1538

Carlos V, Pablo III y Andrea Doria a su regreso de Niza, 1538

Charles V, Paul III e Andrea Doria no retorno de Nice, 1538

Karl V, Paulus III en Andrea Doria op de terugweg vanuit Nice, 1538

16th century/XVIe siècle, Oil on canvas/Huile sur toile, Private collection

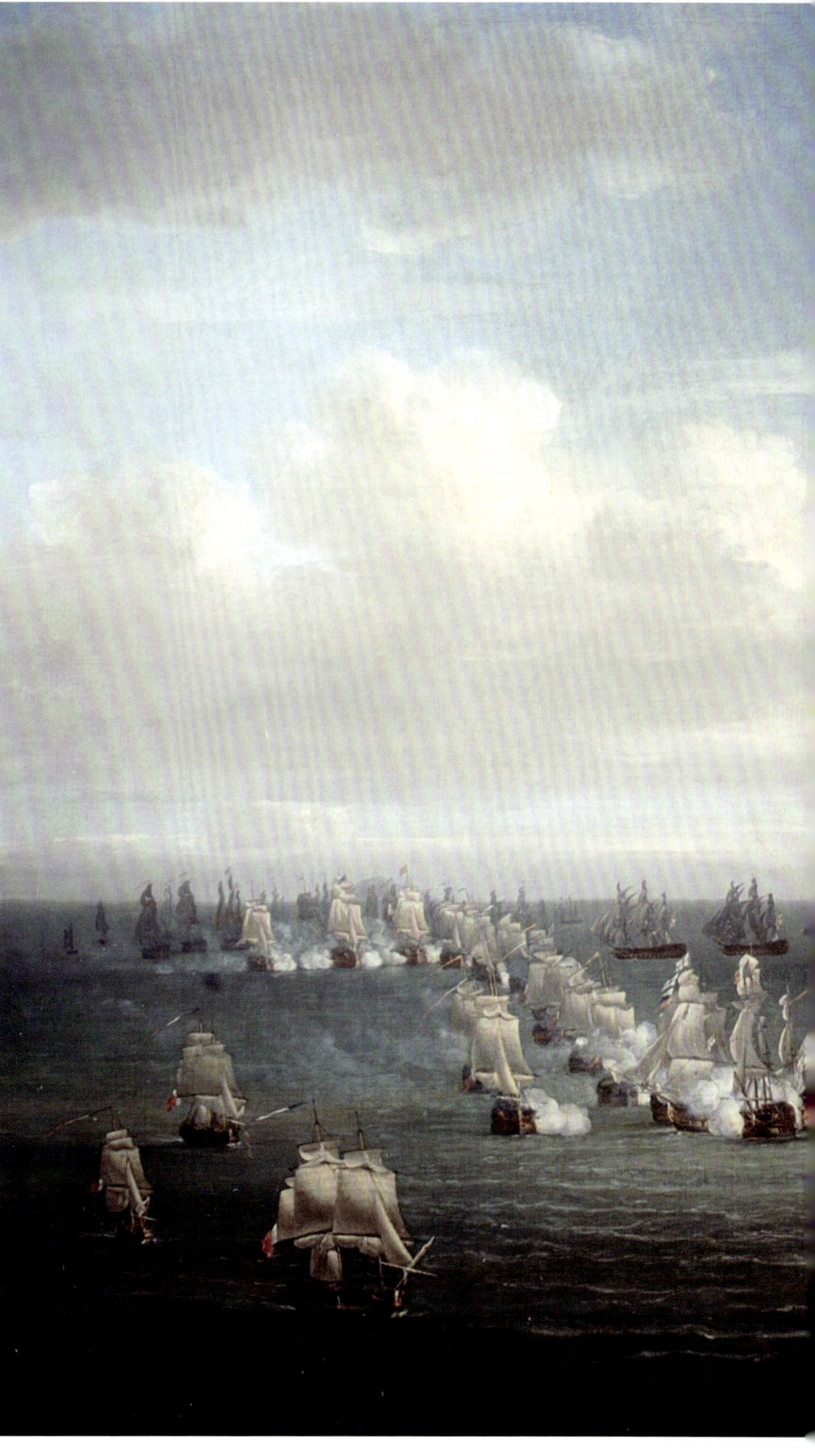

Nicholas Pocock (1741–1821)

The Battle of Trafalgar

La Bataille de Trafalgar

Die Schlacht von Trafalgar

La Batalla de Trafalgar

A batalha de Trafalgar

De Zeeslag bij Trafalgar

n. d., Oil on canvas/Huile sur toile, National
Museum of the Royal Navy, Portsmouth

*Nicholas Pocock made a name for himself as a painter of sea
battles. Already as a young man, he worked on merchant ships and
acquired his artistic skills by illustrating his journals with drawings.
The battle off the southern Spanish Cape Trafalgar, in which the
British won against the united fleet of the French and Spaniards, is
still regarded as a decisive turning point in the Napoleonic Wars.*

*Nicholas Pocock se fit connaître en tant que peintre de batailles
en mer. Jeune homme déjà, il travailla sur des navires marchands
et acquit ses compétences artistiques en illustrant ses journaux
avec des dessins. La bataille au large du Cap de Trafalgar, au
sud de l'Espagne, lors de laquelle les Britanniques vainquirent la
flotte unie des Français et des Espagnols, est encore considérée
comme un tournant décisif dans les guerres napoléoniennes.*

*Nicholas Pocock hat sich vor allem als Maler von Seeschlachten
einen Namen gemacht. Schon als junger Mann arbeitete er
auf Handelsschiffen und erwarb sich seine künstlerischen
Fertigkeiten, indem er seine Reisetagebücher mit Zeichnungen
bebilderte. Die Schlacht vor dem südspanischen Kap Trafalgar,
bei der die Engländer gegen die vereinte Flotte der Franzosen
und Spanier gewannen, gilt bis heute als entscheidender
Wendepunkt im internationalen Machtgefüge.*

*Nicholas Pocock se forjó un nombre como pintor de batallas. Ya
de joven trabajó en buques mercantes y obtuvo sus habilidades
artísticas a partir de sus diarios de viaje ilustrados con dibujos.
La batalla del Cabo de Trafalgar, al sur de España, en la que
los ingleses ganaron a la flota combinada de los franceses
y españoles, sigue siendo considerada como un punto de
inflexión decisivo en la estructura de poder internacional.*

*Nicholas Pocock ganhou acima de tudo reputação como um pintor
de batalhas navais. Desde muito jovem, ele trabalhou em navios
mercantes, e adquiriu suas habilidades artísticas ilustrando seus
diários de viagem com desenhos. A batalha ao largo do Cabo
Trafalgar, no sul da Espanha, na qual os Ingleses venceram a frota
aliada de Franceses e Espanhóis, ainda é considerada como um
ponto de viragem decisivo na estrutura de poder internacional.*

*Nicholas Pocock maakte naam als schilder van zeeslagen.
Als jongeman werkte hij op koopvaardijschepen en maakte
hij zich zijn artistieke vaardigheden eigen door zijn
reisdagboeken met tekeningen te verrijken. De zeeslag voor
de kust van de Zuid-Spaanse Kaap Trafalgar, waarbij de
Engelsen een verenigde vloot van Fransen en Spanjaarden
overwonnen, wordt gezien als een beslissend keerpunt in
de machtsbalans tussen de Europese grootmachten.*

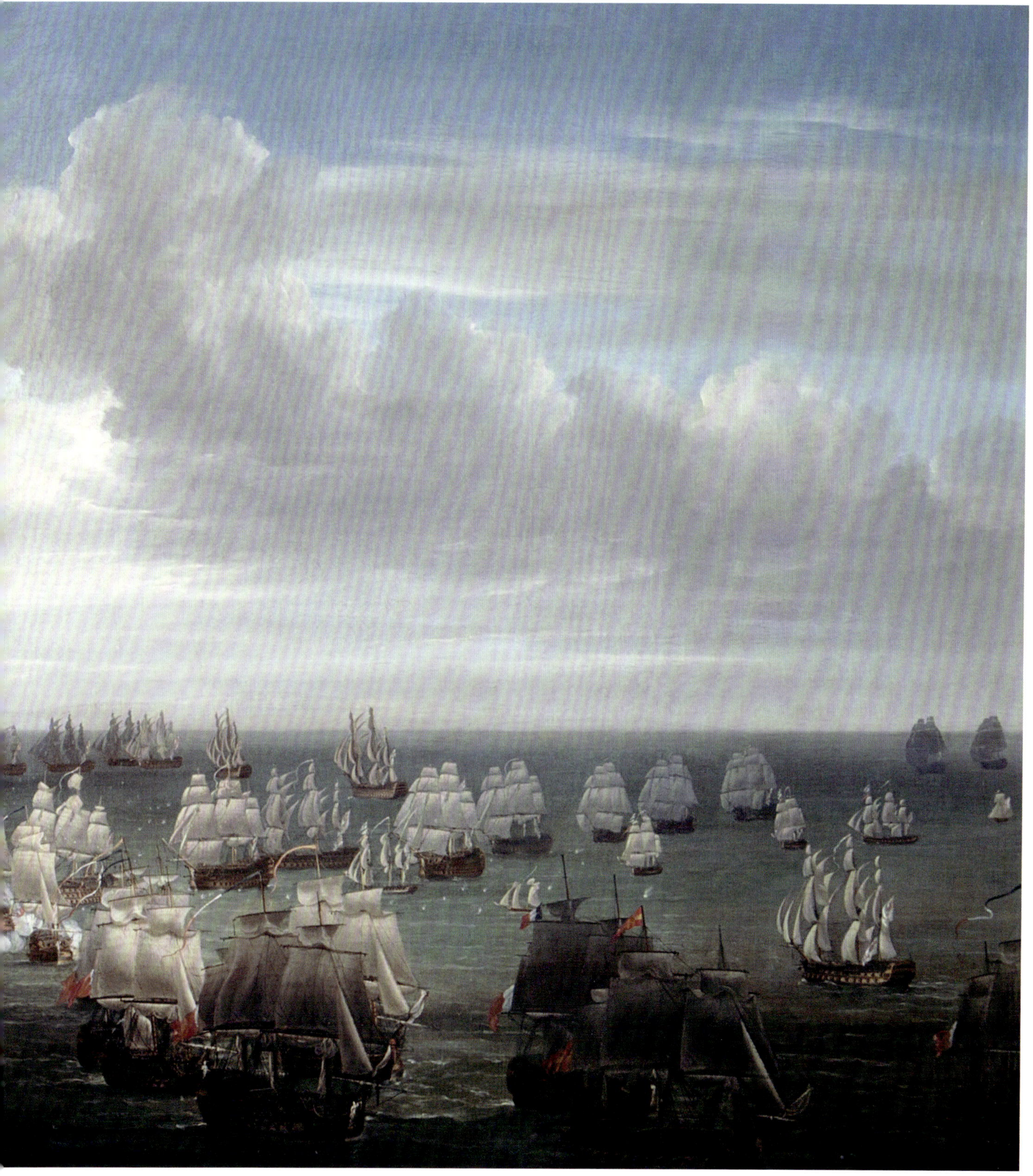

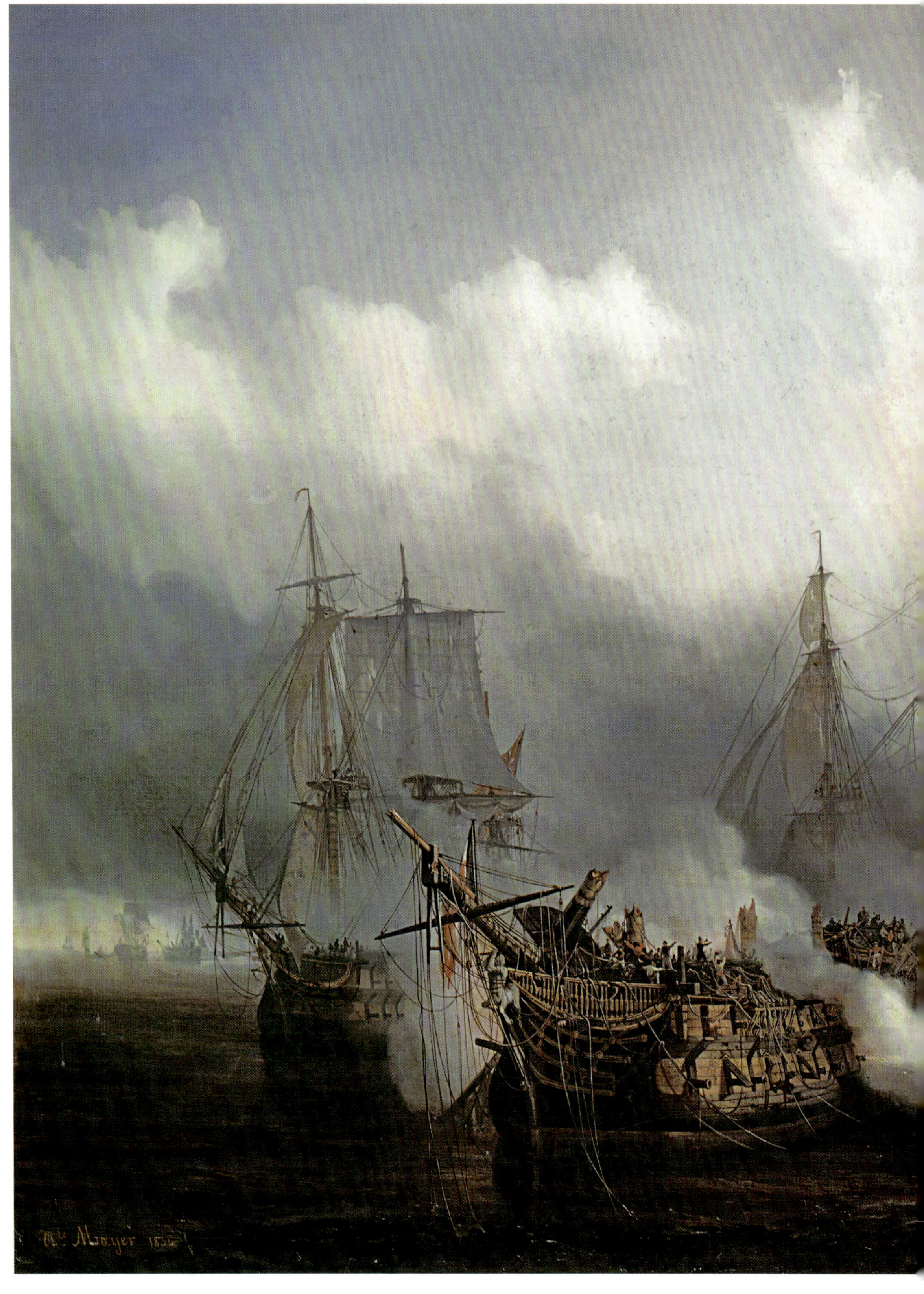

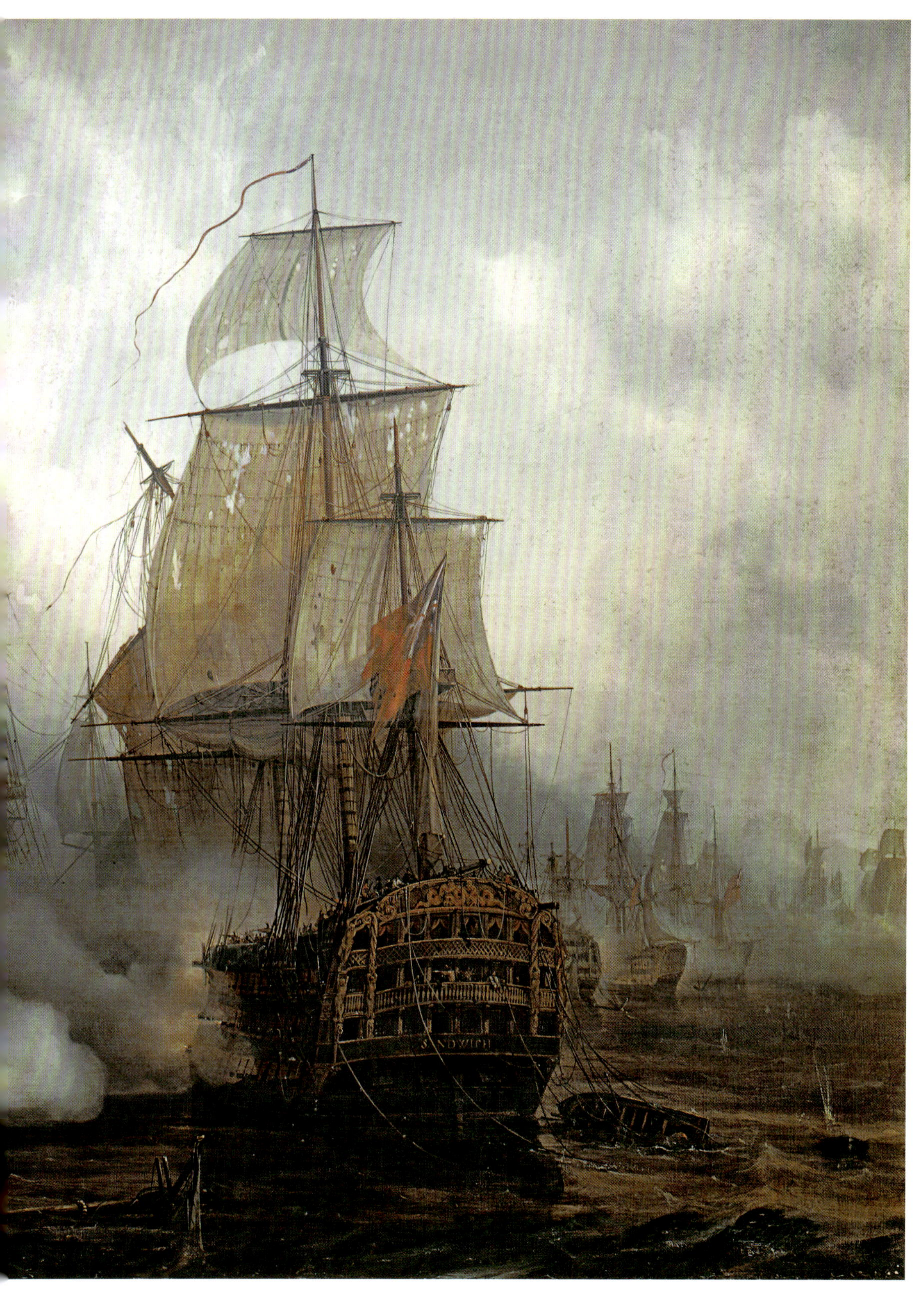

Auguste Étienne François Mayer (1805–90)

The *Redoutable* in the Battle of Trafalgar, 21 October 1805

Le *Redoutable* lors de la Bataille de Trafalgar, 21 octobre 1805

Die *Redoutable* in der Schlacht von Trafalgar, 21. Oktober 1805

El *Redoutable* en la Batalla de Gibraltar, 21 de octubre de 1805

O *Redoutable* na Batalha de Trafalgar, 21 de outubro de 1805

De *Redoutable* in de slag Zeeslag bij Trafalgar op 21 oktober 1805

1836, Oil on canvas/Huile sur toile, 105 × 162 cm, Musée de la Marine, Paris

215

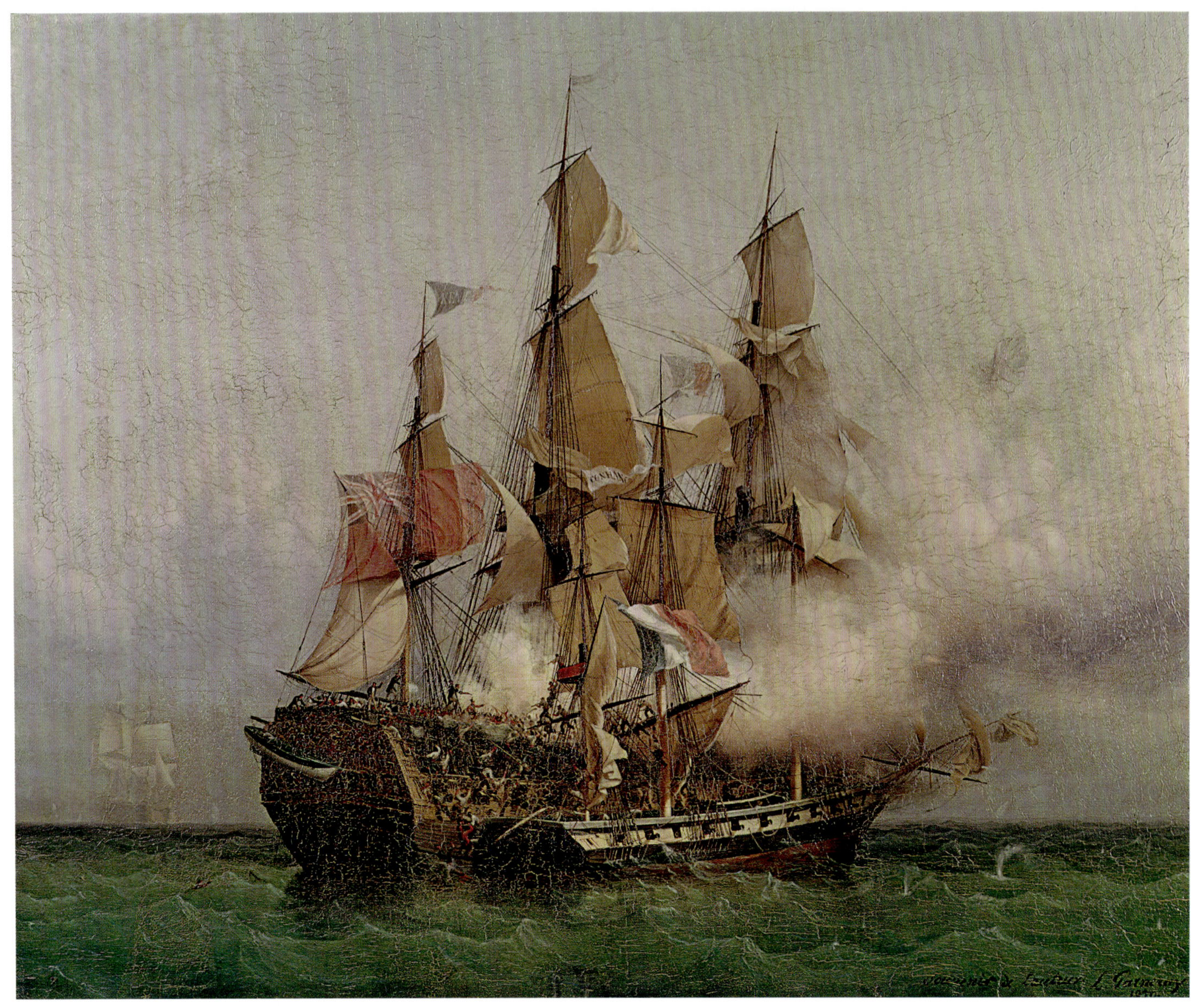

Ambroise-Louis Garneray (1783–1857)

The Taking of the Kent by Robert Surcouf in the Gulf of Bengal

La Prise du Kent par Robert Surcouf dans le golfe du Bengale

Die Kaperung der Kent durch Robert Surcouf im Golf von Bengalen, am 7. Oktober 1800

La toma del Kent por Robert Surcouf en el Golfo de Bengala el 7 de octubre de 1800

O seqüestro de Kent por Robert Surcouf no Golfo de Bengala, em 7 de outubro de 1800

De entering van de Kent door Robert Surcouf in de Golf van Bengalen op 7 oktober 1800

1850, Oil on canvas/Huile sur toile, Musée de l'Histoire de la Ville, Saint-Malo

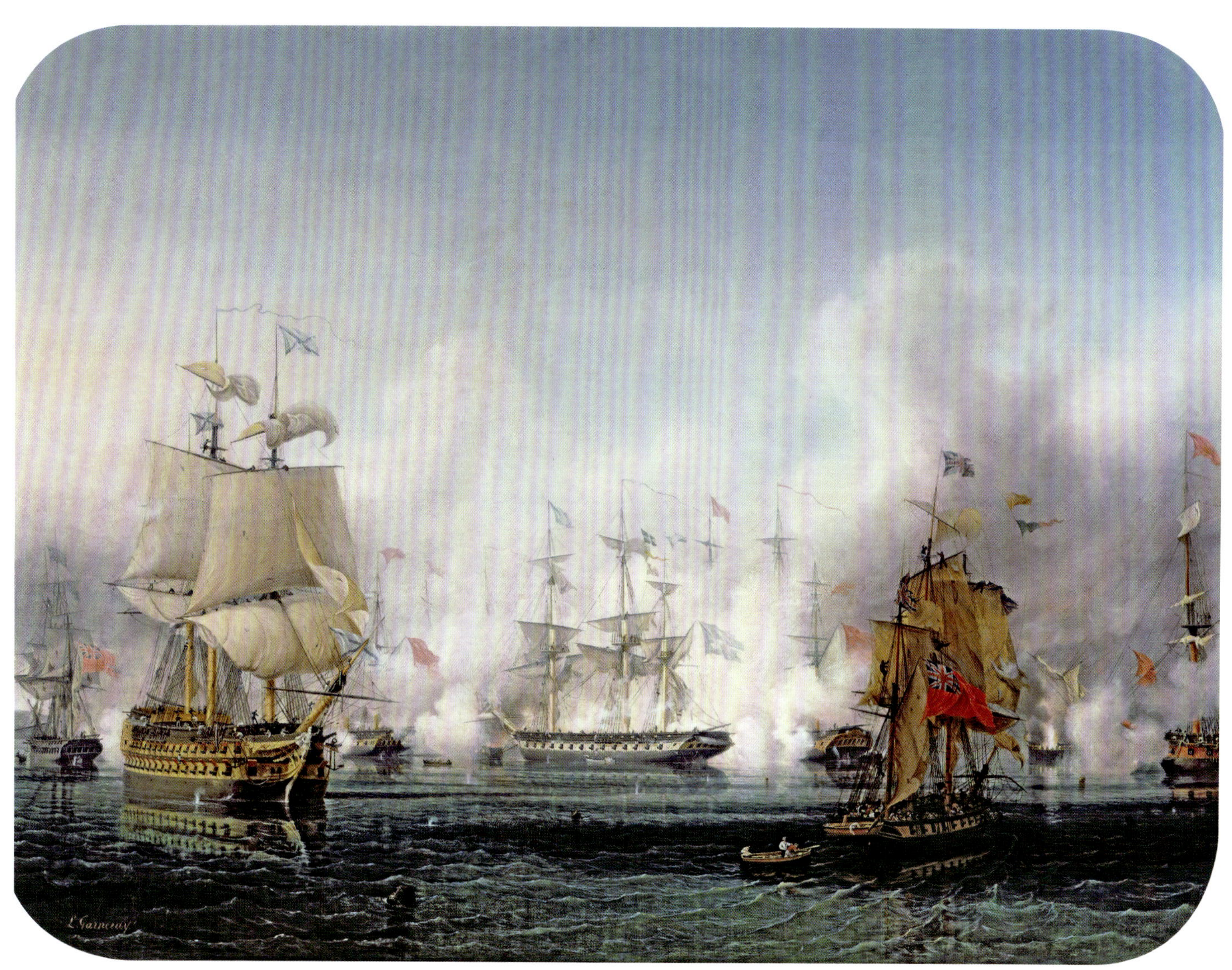

Ambroise-Louis Garneray (1783–1857)

Episode of the Battle of Navarino, 20 October 1827

Épisode de la Bataille de Navarin, 20 octobre 1827

Episode der Schlacht von Navarino, 20. Oktober 1827

Episodio de la Batalla de Navarino, 20 de octubre de 1827

Episódio da batalha de Navarino, 20 de outubro de 1827

Episode uit de Zeeslag bij Navarino op 20 oktober 1827

c. 1853, Oil on canvas/Huile sur toile, 147 × 196 cm, Musée des Beaux-Arts, Nantes

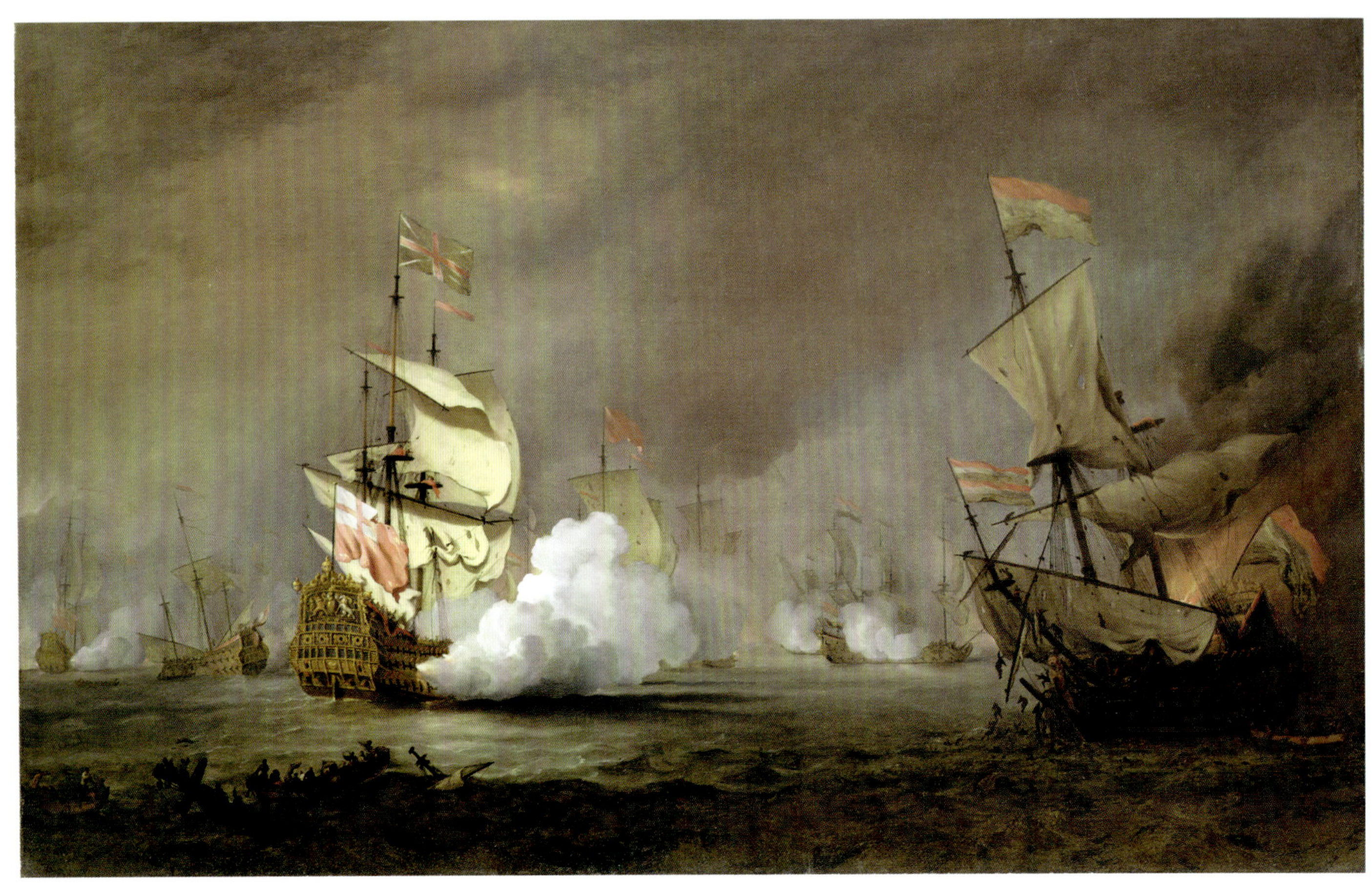

Willem van de Velde d. J. (1633–1707)

Sea Battle of the Anglo-Dutch Wars

Bataille navale anglo-néerlandaise

Seeschlacht während der englisch-niederländischen Kriege

Batalla durante la guerra inglesa-holandesa

Batalha durante as guerras anglo-holandesas

Zeeslag tijdens de Engels-Nederlandse oorlogen

c. 1700, Oil on canvas/Huile sur toile, 116,2 × 184,2 cm, Yale Center for British Art, New Haven

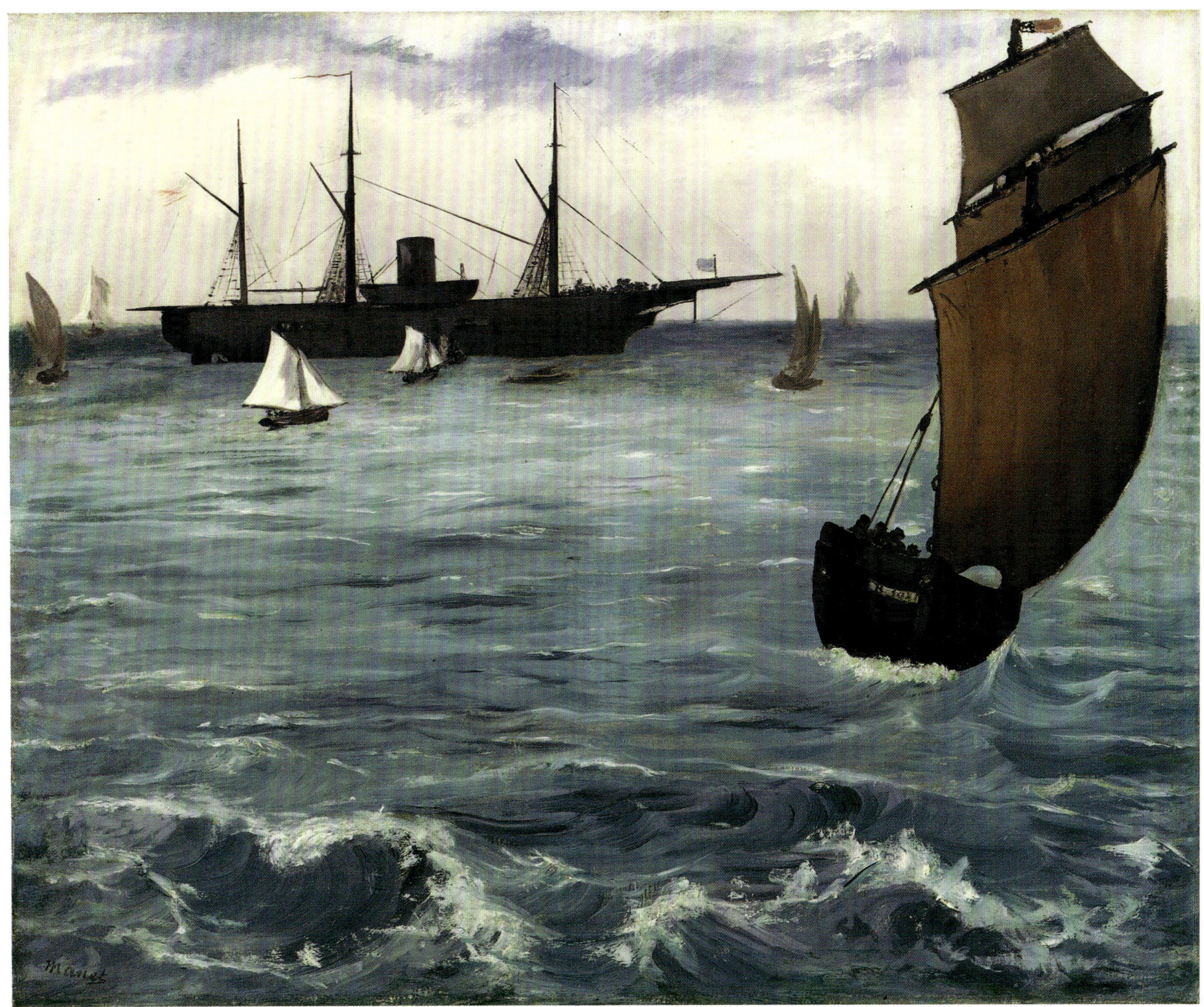

Édouard Manet (1832–83)

The *Kearsage* at Boulogne

Le *Kearsage* à Boulogne

Die *Kearsage* in Boulogne

El *Kearsage* en Boulogne

O *Kearsage* em Boulogne

De *Kearsage* in Boulogne

1864, Oil on canvas/Huile sur toile, 81,6 × 100 cm, Metropolitan Museum of Art, New York

**Vice Admiral Sir George Anson's
Victory off Cape Finisterre**

La Victoire du vice-amiral Sir George
Anson au large du cap Finisterre

Vize-Admiral Sir George Ansons
Sieg vor Kap Finisterre

Victoria del vicealmirante Sir George
Ansons delante del Cabo de Finisterre

Vitória do Vice-almirante Sir George
Ansons, ao largo do Cabo Finisterra

De zege van viceadmiraal sir George
Anson voor Kaap Finisterre

1749, Oil on canvas/Huile sur toile, 101,6 × 179,1 cm,
Yale Center for British Art, New Haven

*The eight-year War of the Austrian Succession
was fought over who would take over the
Habsburg throne of Emperor Charles VI. His
daughter Maria Theresia, having won the war,
would go on to govern the country until her death
and retain most of the Habsburg possessions. Here
we see one of the most important sea battles of the
war in April 1747 off Cape Finisterre in Galicia.*

*La guerre de la Succession d'Autriche, qui dura
huit ans, eut lieu pour savoir qui prendrait le
trône des Habsbourg de l'empereur Charles VI.
Sa fille, Maria Theresia, ayant remporté la
guerre, continua à gouverner le pays jusqu'à sa
mort et à conserver la plupart des possessions de
Habsbourg. Nous observons ici l'une des batailles
maritimes les plus importantes de la guerre en
avril 1747, au large du cap Finisterre en Galice.*

*Im acht Jahre dauernden Österreichischen
Erbfolgekrieg ging es um die Nachfolge Karls VI.,
dessen Tochter Maria Theresia nach erfolgreichem
Bestehen des Krieges bis zu ihrem Tod das
Land regieren und die meisten habsburgischen
Besitzungen behaupten sollte. Hier sehen wir
eine der wichtigsten Seeschlachten des Krieges im
April 1747 vor dem galicischen Kap Finisterre.*

*En la Guerra de Sucesión de Austria, que
duró ocho años, se llevó a cabo la sucesión de
Carlos VI, cuya hija María Teresa, después de
pasar con éxito la guerra, gobernó el país hasta su
muerte y mantuvo la mayoría de las posesiones
de los Habsburgo. Aquí vemos una de las más
importantes batallas navales de la guerra en
abril de 1747 delante del cabo gallego Finisterre.*

*Na Guerra de Sucessão Austríaca que durou
oito anos esteve em causa a sucessão de
Carlos VI, cuja filha Maria Theresia, após a
vitória na guerra, governaria o país até sua
morte, mantendo a maioria das possessões dos
Habsburgos. Aqui vemos uma das batalhas
navais mais importantes da guerra, em abril
1747, ao largo do Cabo Finisterra, da Galiza.*

*De aanleiding voor de acht jaar durende
Oostenrijkse Successieoorlog was de opvolging
van Karel VI, wiens dochter Maria Theresia na de
succesvolle afsluiting van de oorlog tot aan haar
dood over het uitgestrekte Habsburgse Rijk zou
regeren. Hier uitgebeeld is een van de belangrijkste
zeeslagen van de oorlog, die in april 1747 voor
de Galicische Kaap Finisterre plaatsvond.*

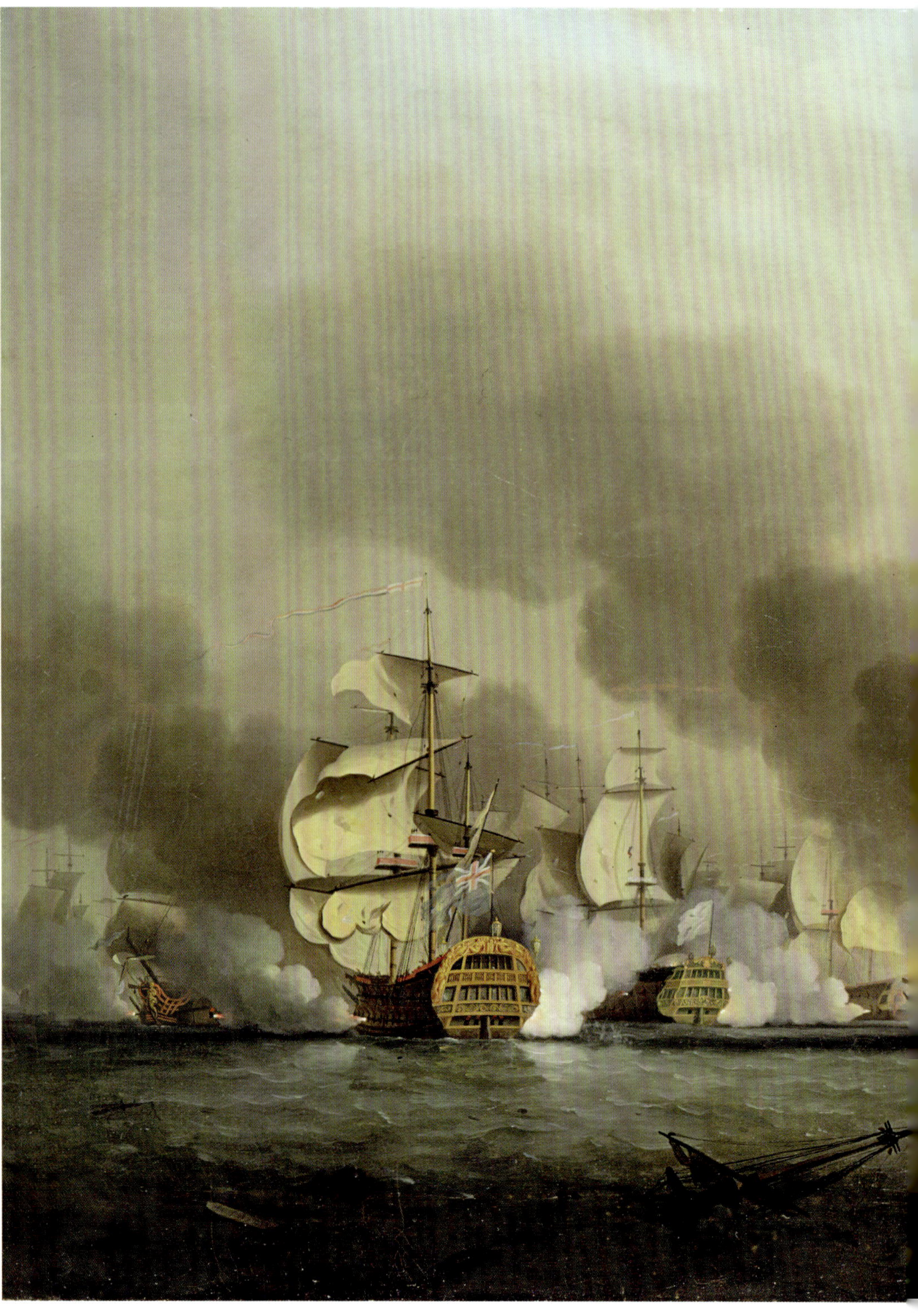

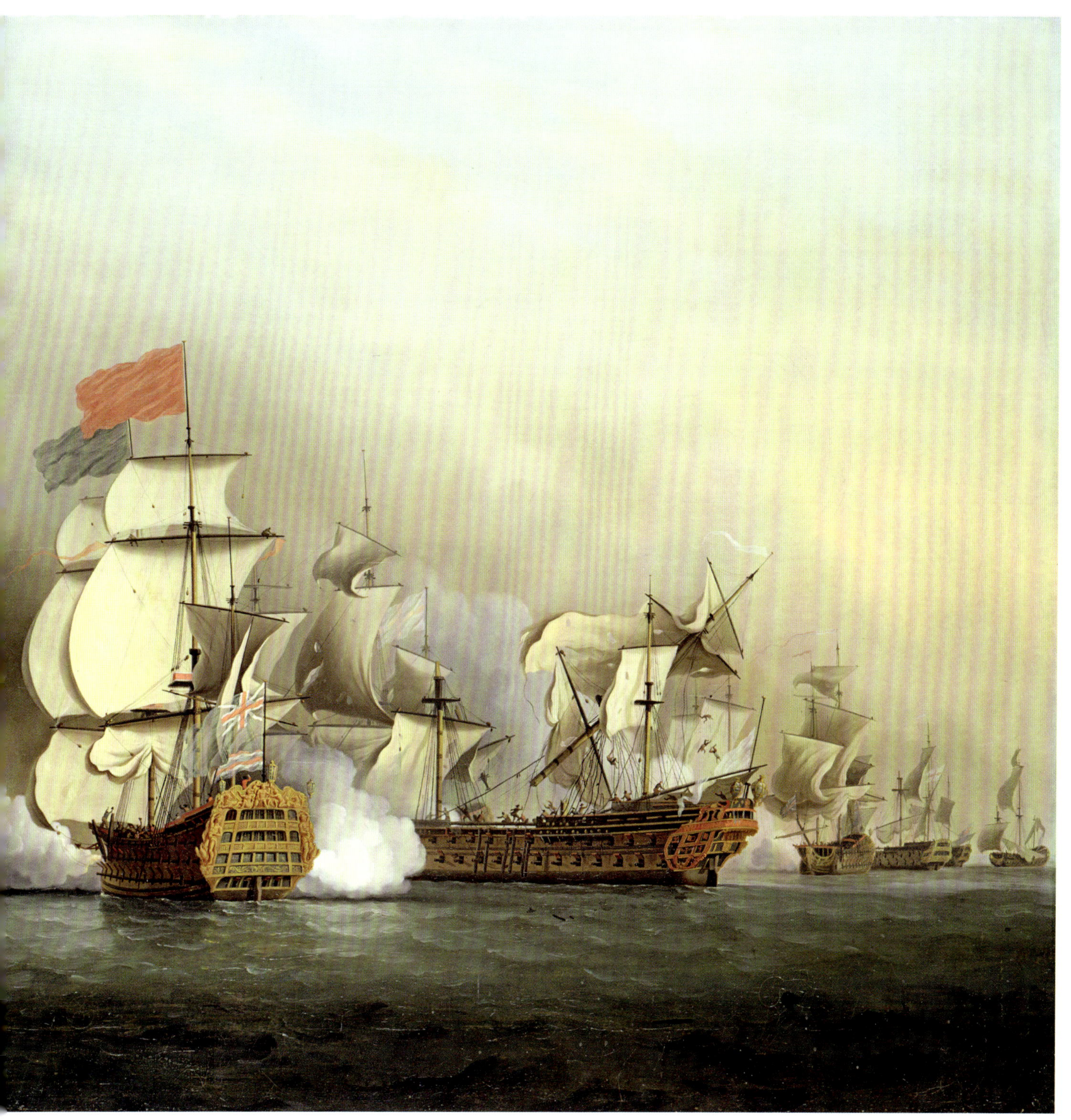

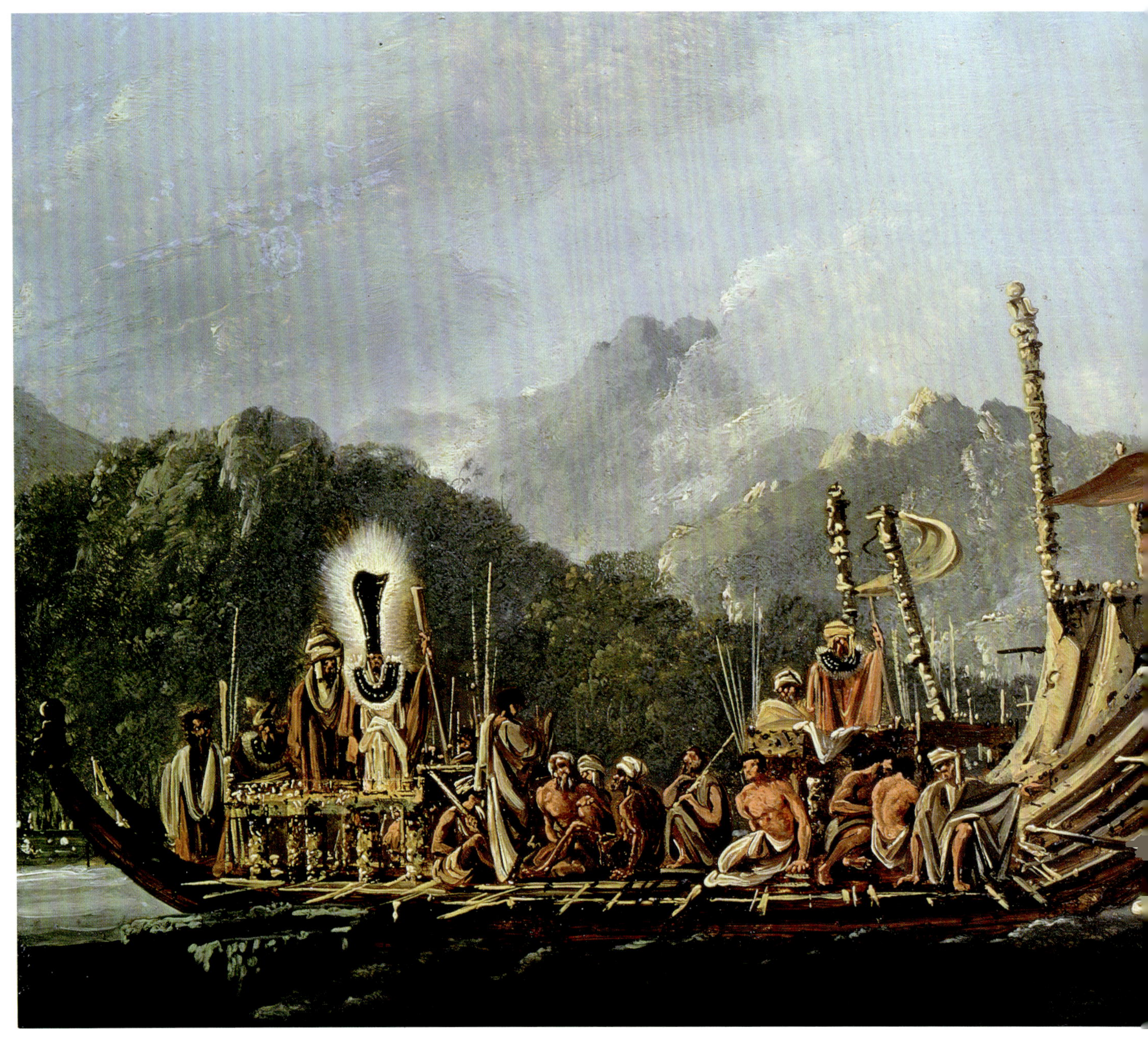

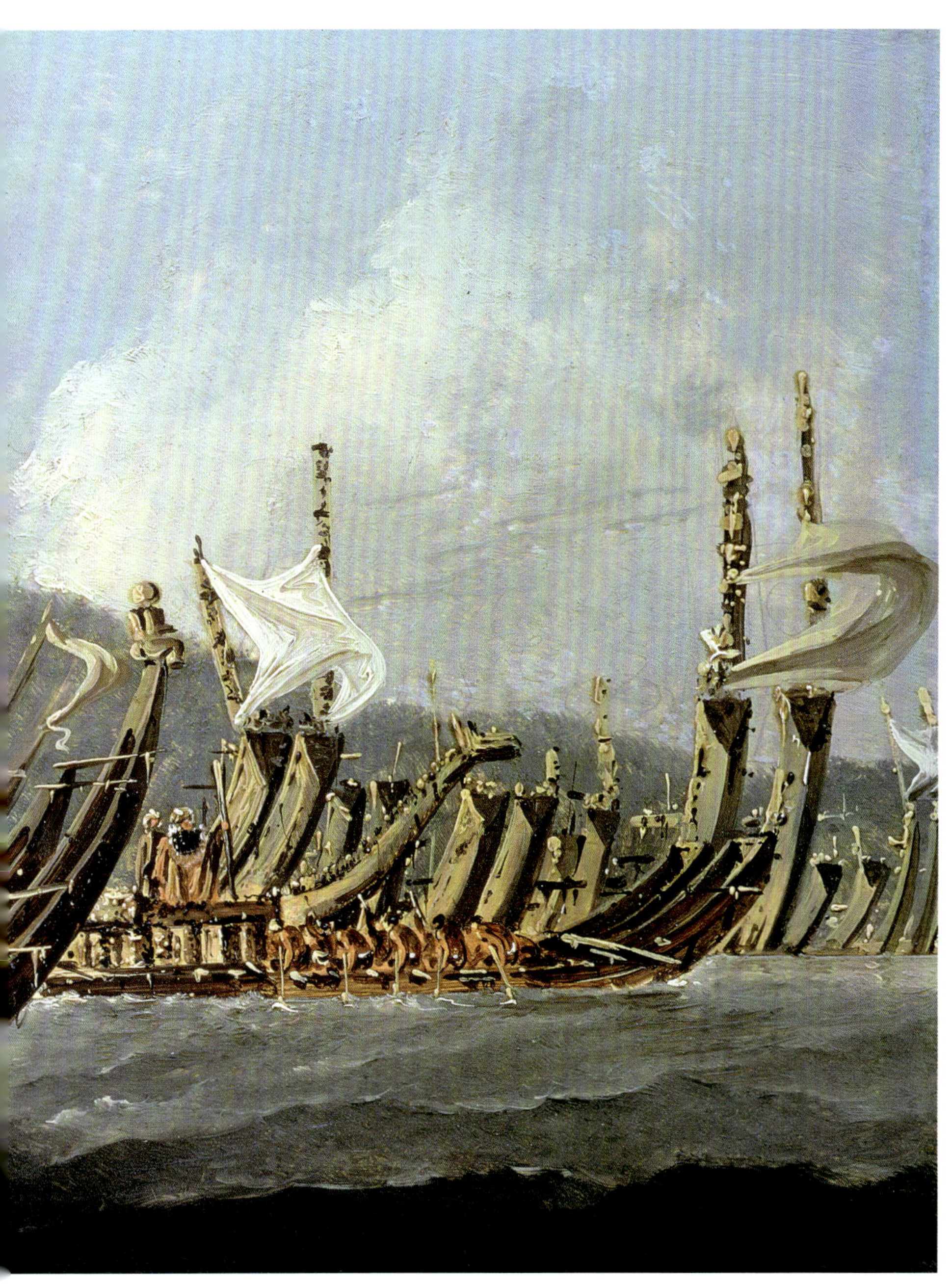

The name of London-born William Hodges is still associated with the trips of Captain James Cook on the Resolution, with which Cook made his second journey around the world. The resulting sketches of Tahiti and many other islands of the South Seas helped him to earn commissions for paintings from the British Admiralty. Prints based on these pictures also achieved great popularity.

Le nom de William Hodges, né à Londres, est toujours associé aux voyages du capitaine James Cook sur le navire Résolution, avec lequel Cook fit son deuxième voyage à travers le monde. Les croquis résultant de Tahiti et de nombreuses autres îles des mers du Sud l'aidèrent à recevoir des commandes de peintures de la part de l'Amirauté britannique. Les impressions basées sur ces images ont également rencontré un grand succès.

Der Name des in London geborenen William Hodges ist bis heute vor allem mit den Fahrten des Captain James Cook auf dem Schiff Resolution verbunden, den er auf dessen zweiter Reise um die Welt begleitete. Die dabei entstandenen Skizzen von Tahiti und vielen anderen Inseln der Südsee dienten ihm später, um im Auftrag der britischen Admiralität Gemälde anzufertigen. Auch nach diesen Bildern entstandene Drucke erreichten eine große Popularität.

El nombre de William Hodges, nacido en Londres, todavía se asocia hoy día principalmente con los viajes del Capitán James Cook en el barco Resolution, que le acompañó en su segundo viaje alrededor del mundo. Los bocetos desarrollados sobre esto en Tahití y otras islas de los mares del sur le sirvieron más tarde para prepararse para las pinturas del Almirantazgo británico. También los grabados hechos a partir de estos cuadros alcanzaron una gran popularidad.

O nome de William Hodges, nascido em Londres, ainda é até hoje principalmente associado com as viagens do Captain James Cook no navio Resolution, a quem ele acompanhou em sua segunda viagem à volta do mundo. Os esboços que ele então criou do Taiti, e outras ilhas dos Mares do Sul, serviram-lhe mais tarde para se preparar para as pinturas encomendadas pelo Almirantado britânico. Mesmo as estampas criadas com base nesses quadros alcançariam uma grande popularidade.

De in Londen geboren William Hodges wordt tot op heden in één adem genoemd met de zeereizen van kapitein James Cook met het schip Resolution, waarop Hodges meevoer. De schetsen die hij tijdens Cooks tweede reis om de wereld maakte, van Tahiti en tallozе andere eilanden in de Stille Zuidzee, werkte hij later in opdracht van de Britse Admiraliteit uit tot schilderijen. De naar deze schilderijen vervaardigde prenten werden enorm populair.

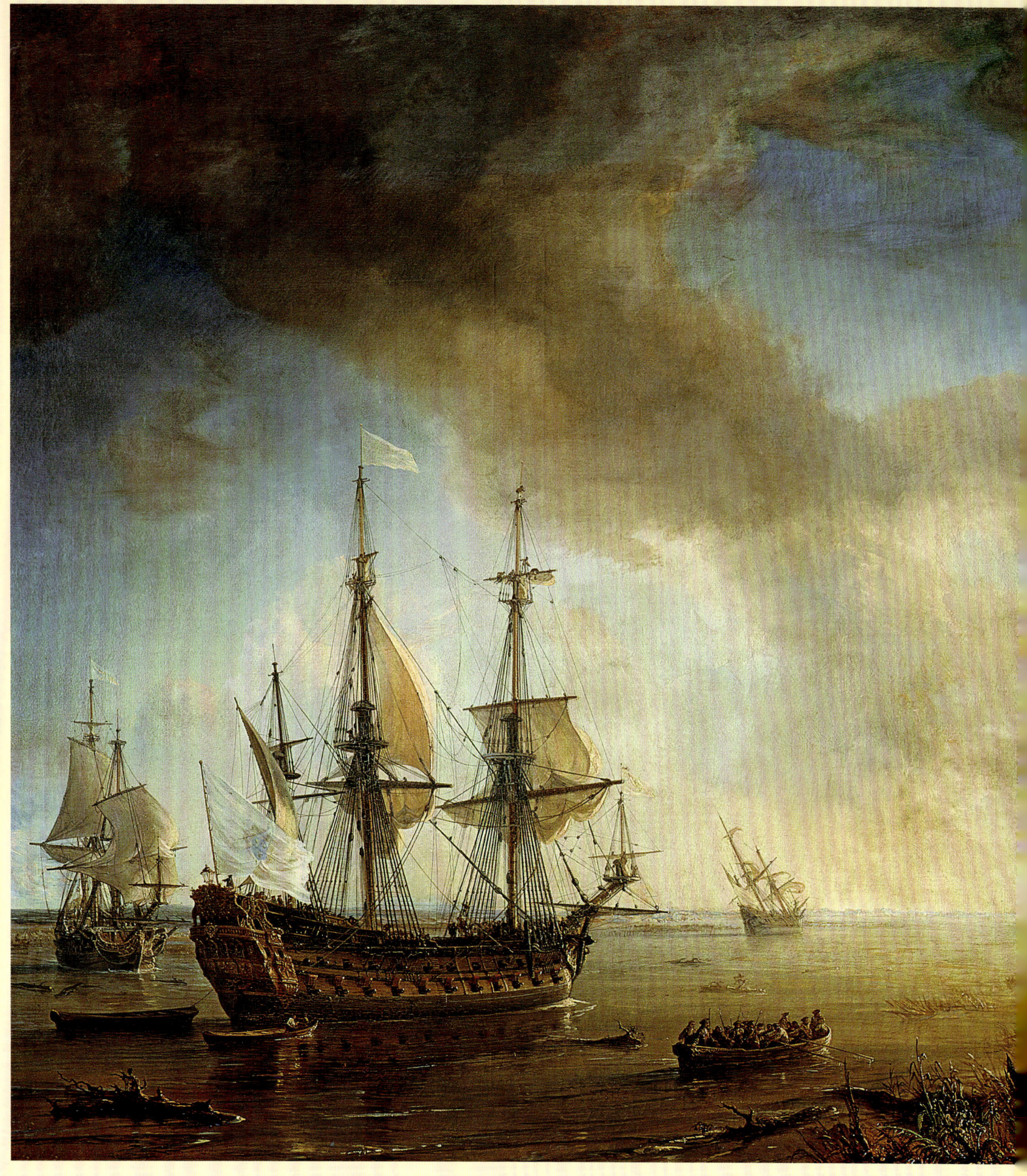

Explorers and emigrants

Explorateurs et émigrants

Entdecker und Auswanderer

Exploradores y emigrantes

Exploradores e emigrados

Ontdekkingen en emigratie

Jean Antoine Théodore Gudin (1802–80)

Expedition of Robert Cavalier de la Salle in Louisiana, 1684

Expédition de Robert Cavalier de la Salle en Louisiane, 1684

Die Expedition Robert Cavalier de la Salles nach Louisiana im Jahr 1684

La expedición de Robert Cavalier de la Salle a Louisiana en el año 1684

A expedição de Robert Cavalier de la Salles para Louisiana, em 1684

De expeditie van Robert Cavalier de la Salle naar Louisiana in het jaar 1684

1844, Oil on canvas/Huile sur toile, 167 × 228 cm, Château de Versailles, Versailles

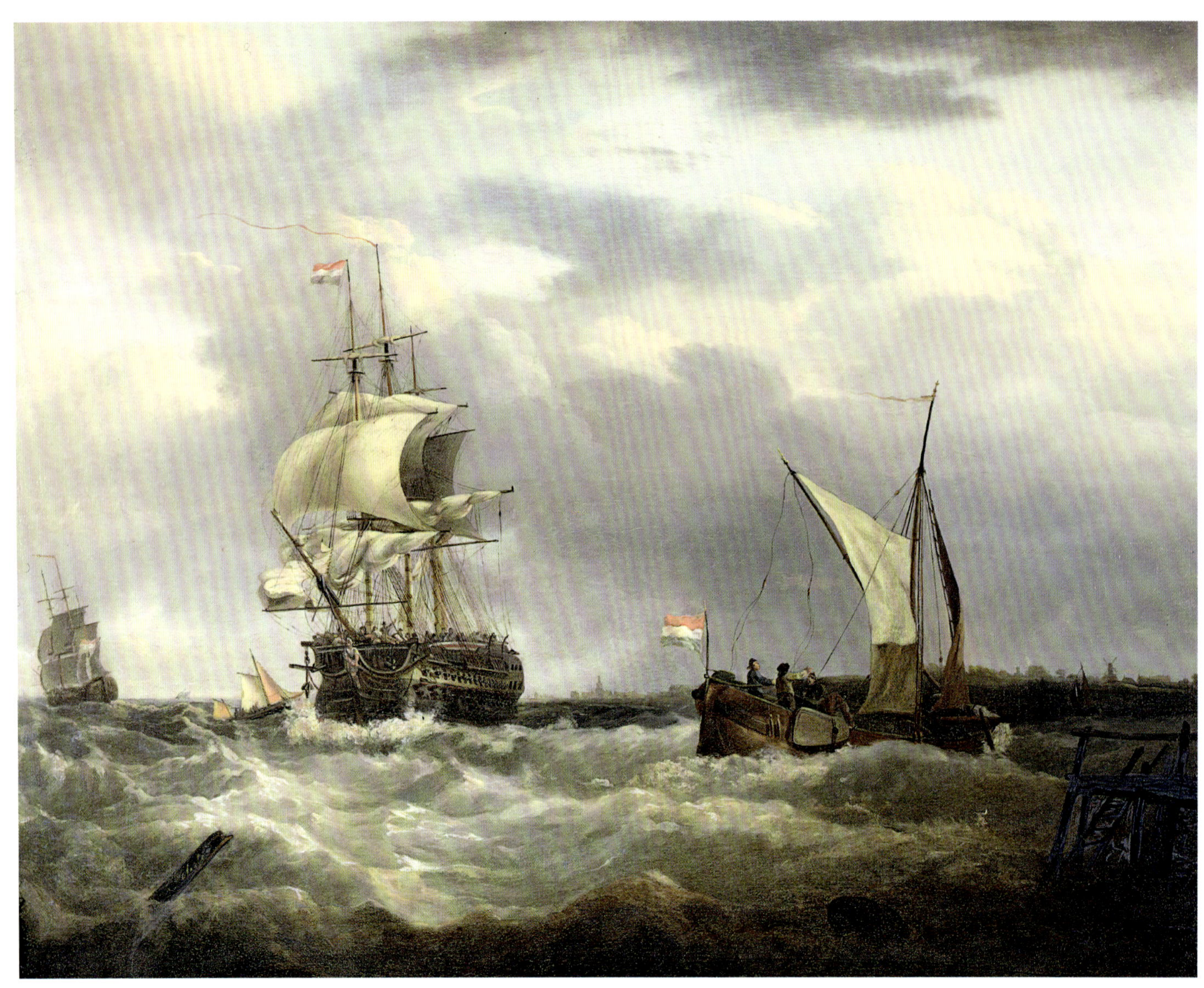

George Webster (1797–1832)

Dutch Emigrant Ship Dropping the Pilot and Leaving Her Homeland Astern

Le Navire émigrant néerlandais abandonnant le capitaine et quittant sa patrie

Lotse verlässt ein niederländisches Auswandererschiff, das sein Heimatland hinter sich lässt.

Patrullero abandona a barco emigrante holandés que deja su patria tras de sí

Piloto deixa um navio de emigrantes holandeses deixando sua terra natal para trás.

Een loods verlaat een Nederlands emigrantenschip dat het vaderland achter zich laat

n. d., Oil on canvas/Huile sur toile, 63,5 × 76,2 cm, Private collection

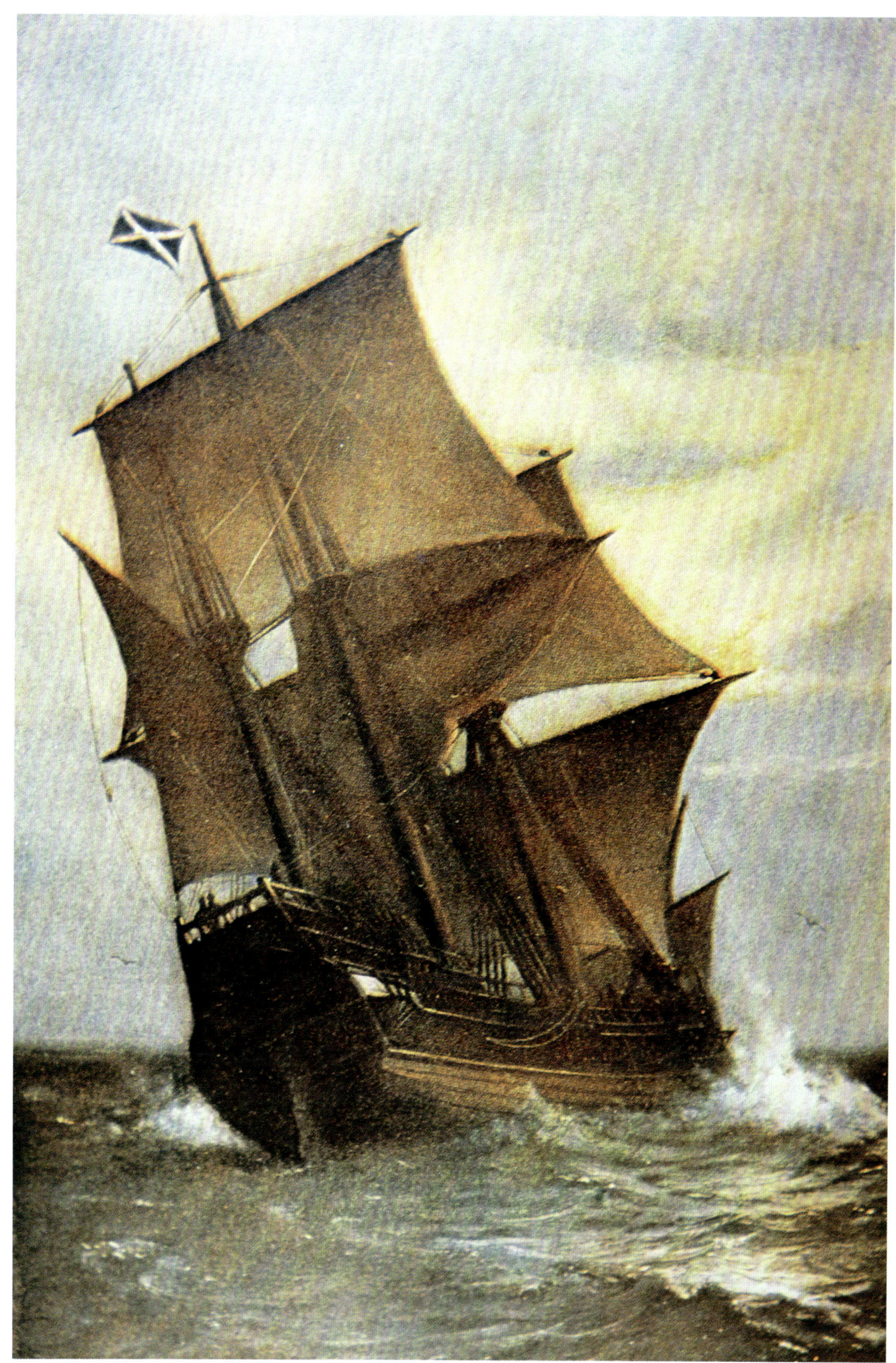

Marshall Johnson (c. 1850–1921)

The *Mayflower* carrying the
Pilgrim Fathers Across the
Atlantic to America in 1620

Le *Mayflower* emmenant les
pères pèlerins sur l'Atlantique
vers l'Amérique en 1620

Die *Mayflower* bringt die Pilgerväter
1620 über den Atlantik nach Amerika

El *Mayflower* lleva a los padres
peregrinos a través del Atlántico
a América en 1620

O *Mayflower* leva os Pilgrim Fathers em
1620 através do Atlântico para a América

De *Mayflower* waarmee de Pelgrimvaders
in 1620 over de Atlantische
Oceaan naar Amerika varen

n. d., Oil on canvas/Huile sur
toile, Private collection

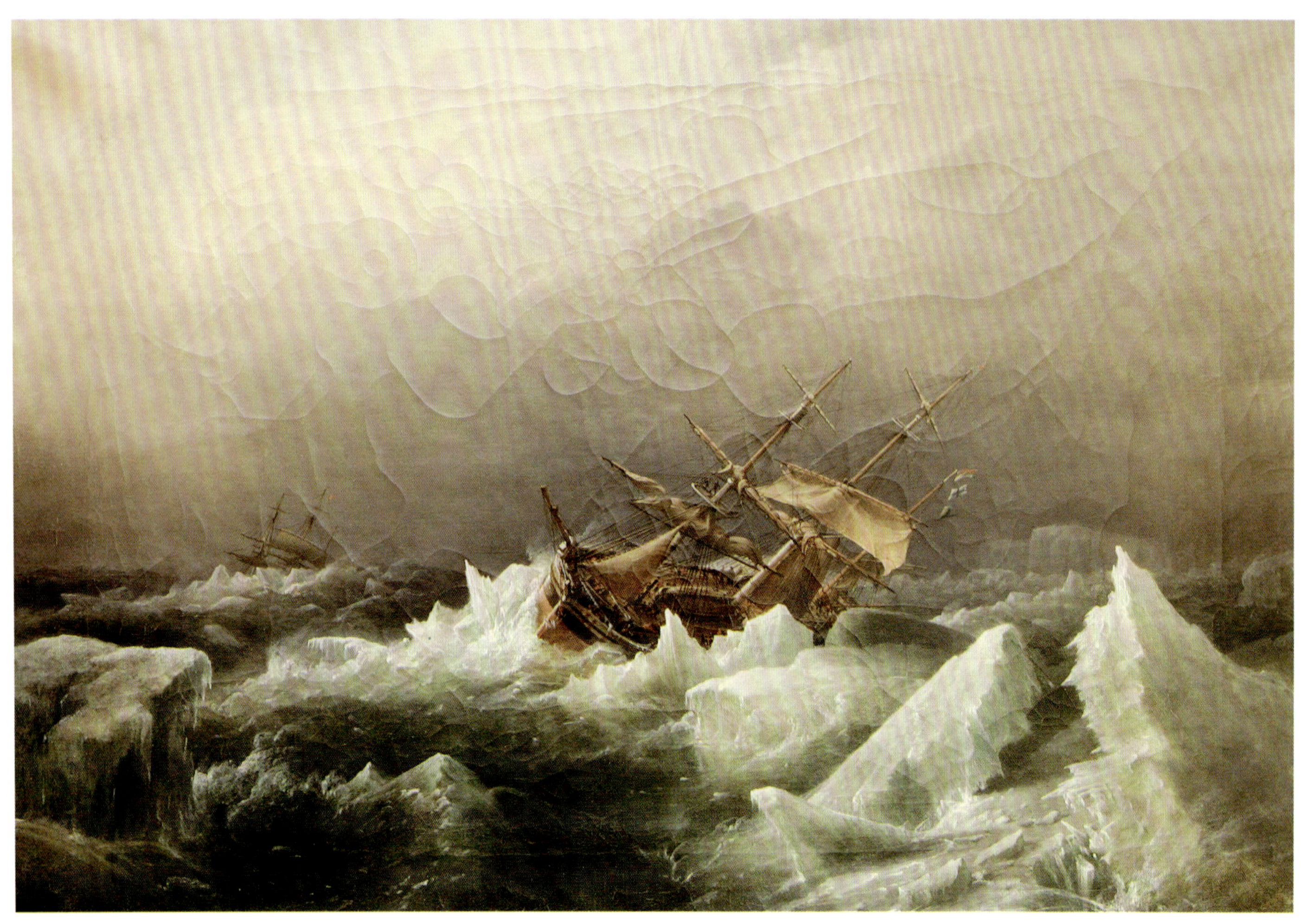

Richard Bridges Beechey (1808–95)

HMS Erebus and *HMS Terror*: Gale in the Pack, 20 January 1842

HMS Erebus et *HMS Terror*: Tempête, 20 janvier 1842

HMS Erebus und *HMS Terror*: Sturm im Packeis, 20. Januar 1842

HMS Erebus y *HMS Terror*: vendaval en el hielo, 20 de enero de 1842

HMS Erebus e *HMS Terror*: Tempestade no banco de gelo, 20 de janeiro de 1842

HMS Erebus en *HMS Terror*: Storm in het pakijs, 20 januari 1842

1863, Oil on canvas/Huile sur toile, 62 × 90 cm, Scott Polar Research Institute, Cambridge

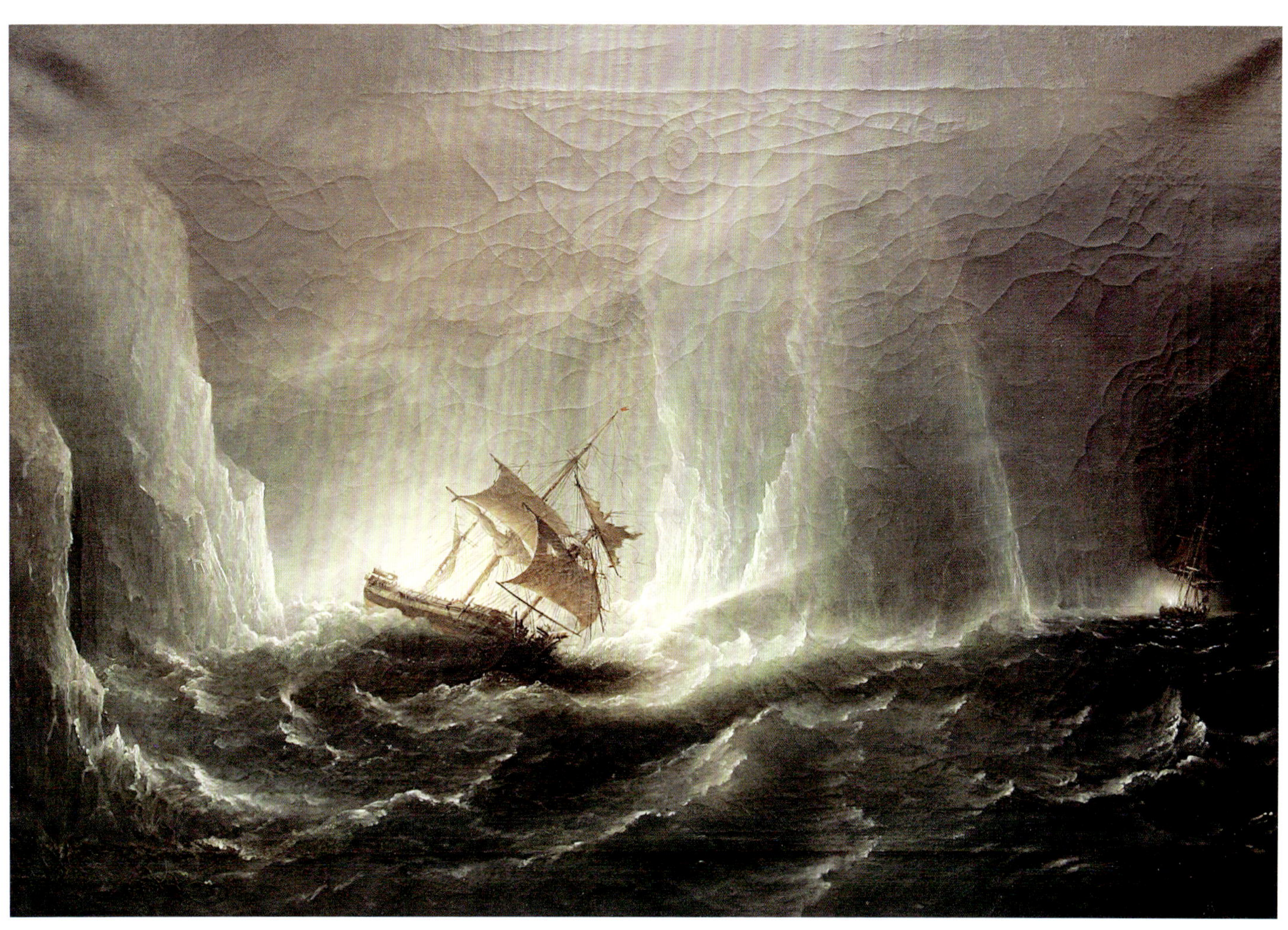

HMS Erebus and *HMS Terror:* Escape from the Bergs, 13 March 1842

HMS Erebus et *HMS Terror* fuyant les icebergs, 13 mars 1842

HMS Erebus und *HMS Terror:* Rettung aus den Eisbergen, 13. März 1842

HMS Erebus y *HMS Terror:* rescate en las montañas de hielo, 13 de marzo de 1842

HMS Erebus e *HMS Terror:* Resgate dos icebergs, 13 de março de 1842

HMS Erebus en *HMS Terror:* Redding uit de ijbergen, 13 maart 1842

1863, Oil on canvas/Huile sur toile, 62 × 90 cm, Scott Polar Research Institute, Cambridge

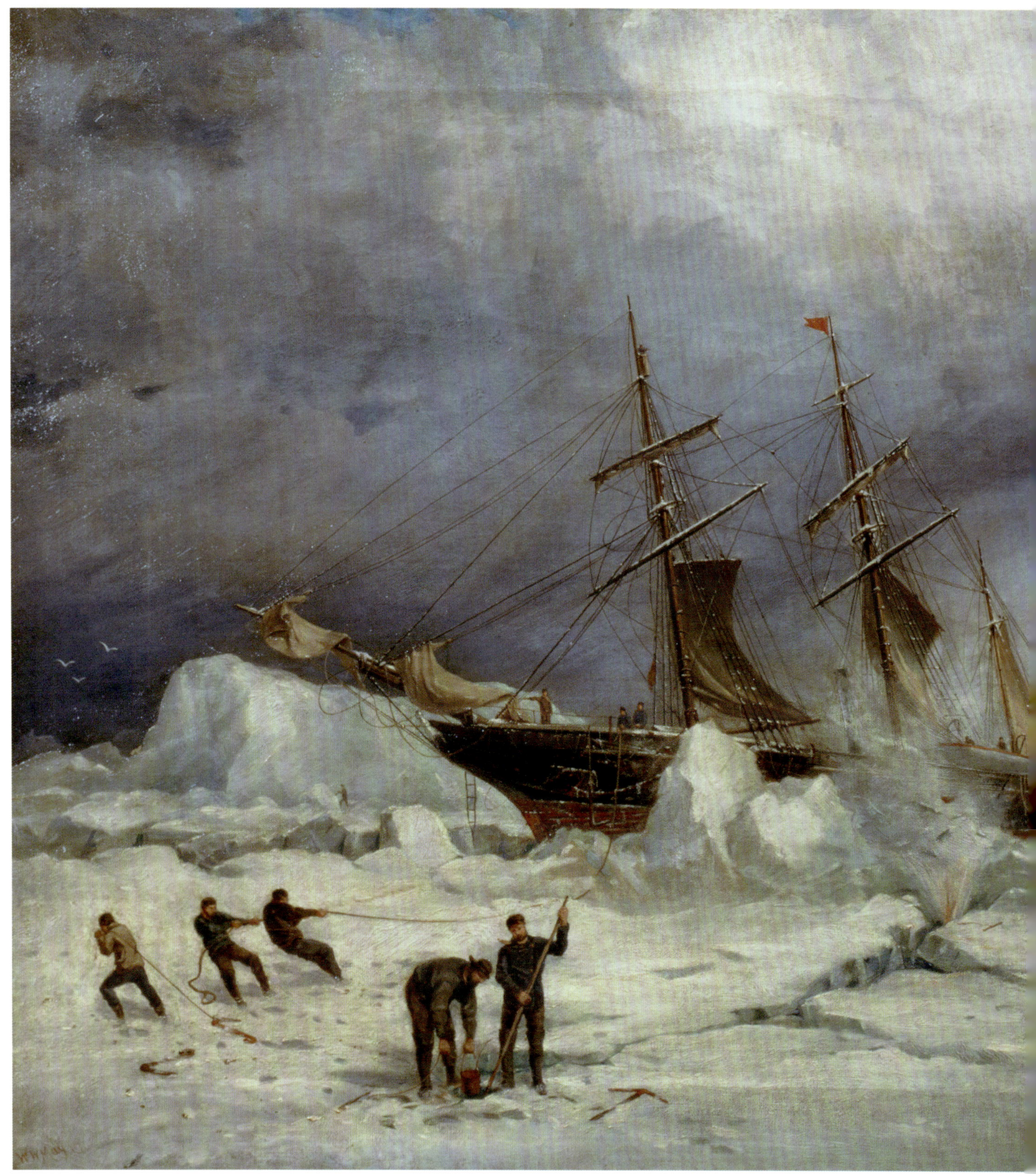

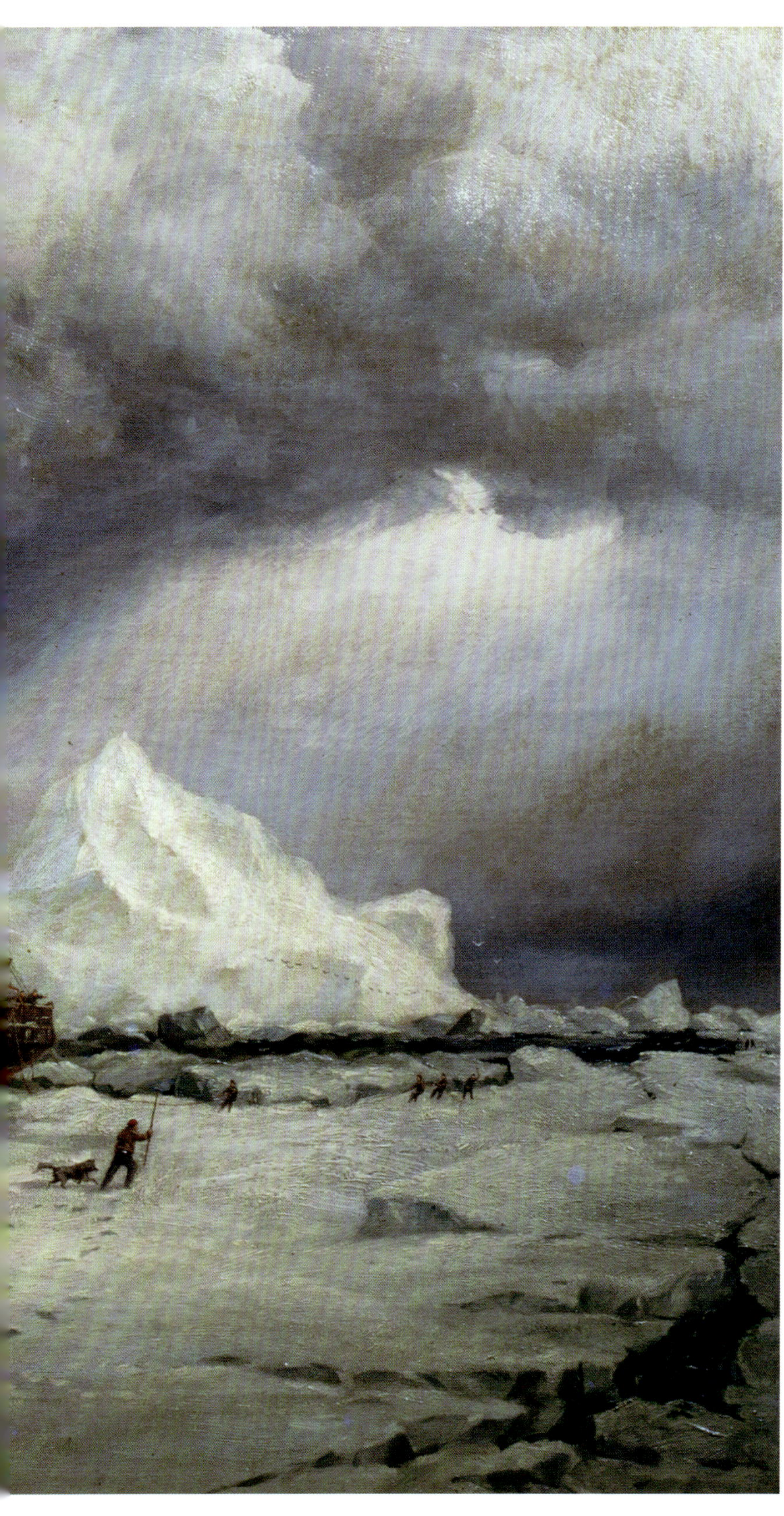

The *Pandora* Nipped in the Pack in Melville Bay, 24 July 1876

Le *Pandora* coincé dans la banquise de la baie de Melville, 24 juillet 1876

Die *Pandora* im Packeis der Melville Bay gefangen, 24. Juli 1876

El *Pandora* en el hielo de Melville Bay, 24 de julio de 1876

O *Pandora* preso no banco de gelo da Melville Bay, 24 de julho de 1876

De *Pandora*, vastzittend in het pakijs van de Melvillebaai, 24 juli 1876

c. 1877, Oil on canvas/Huile sur toile, Royal Geographical Society, London

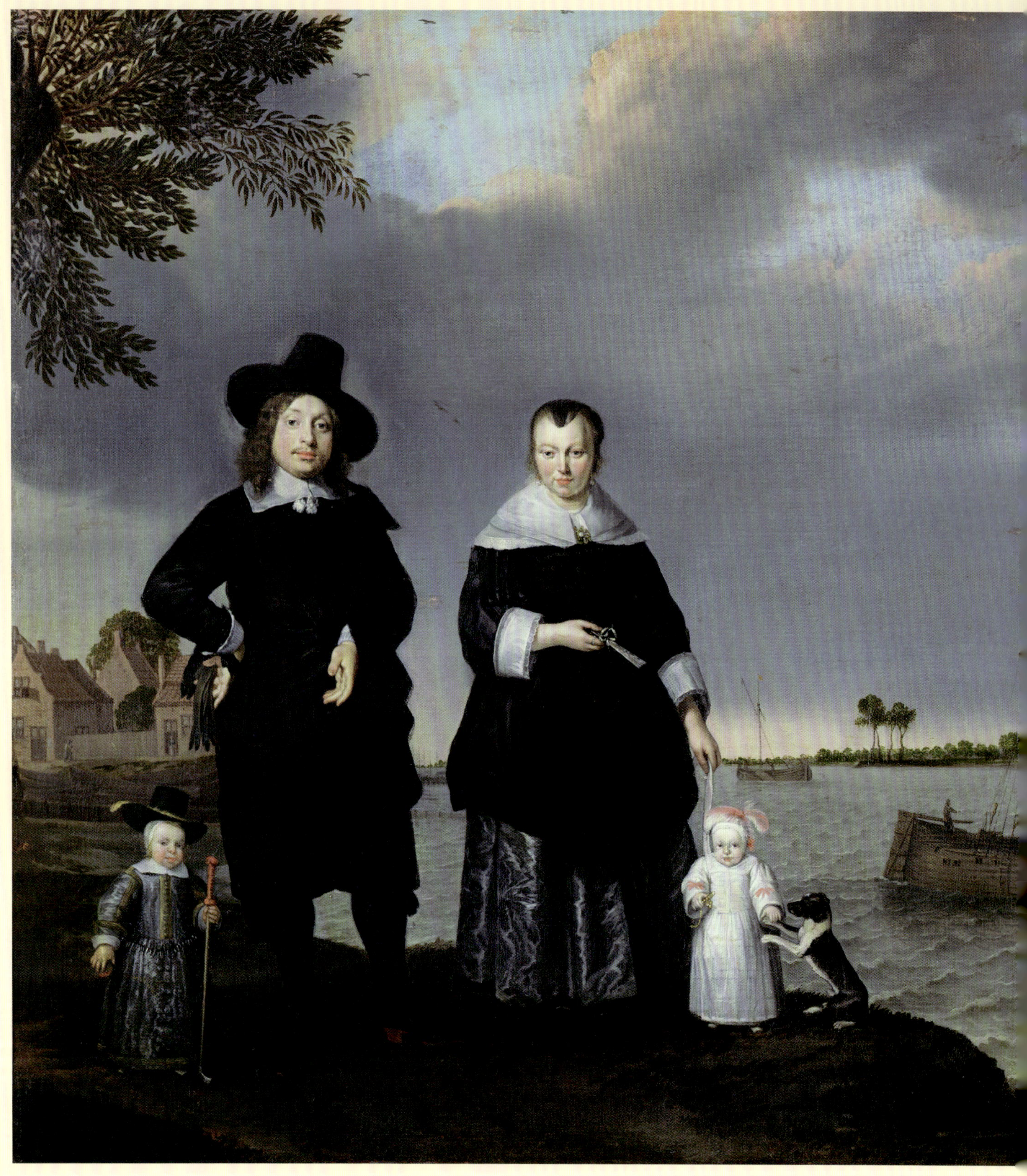

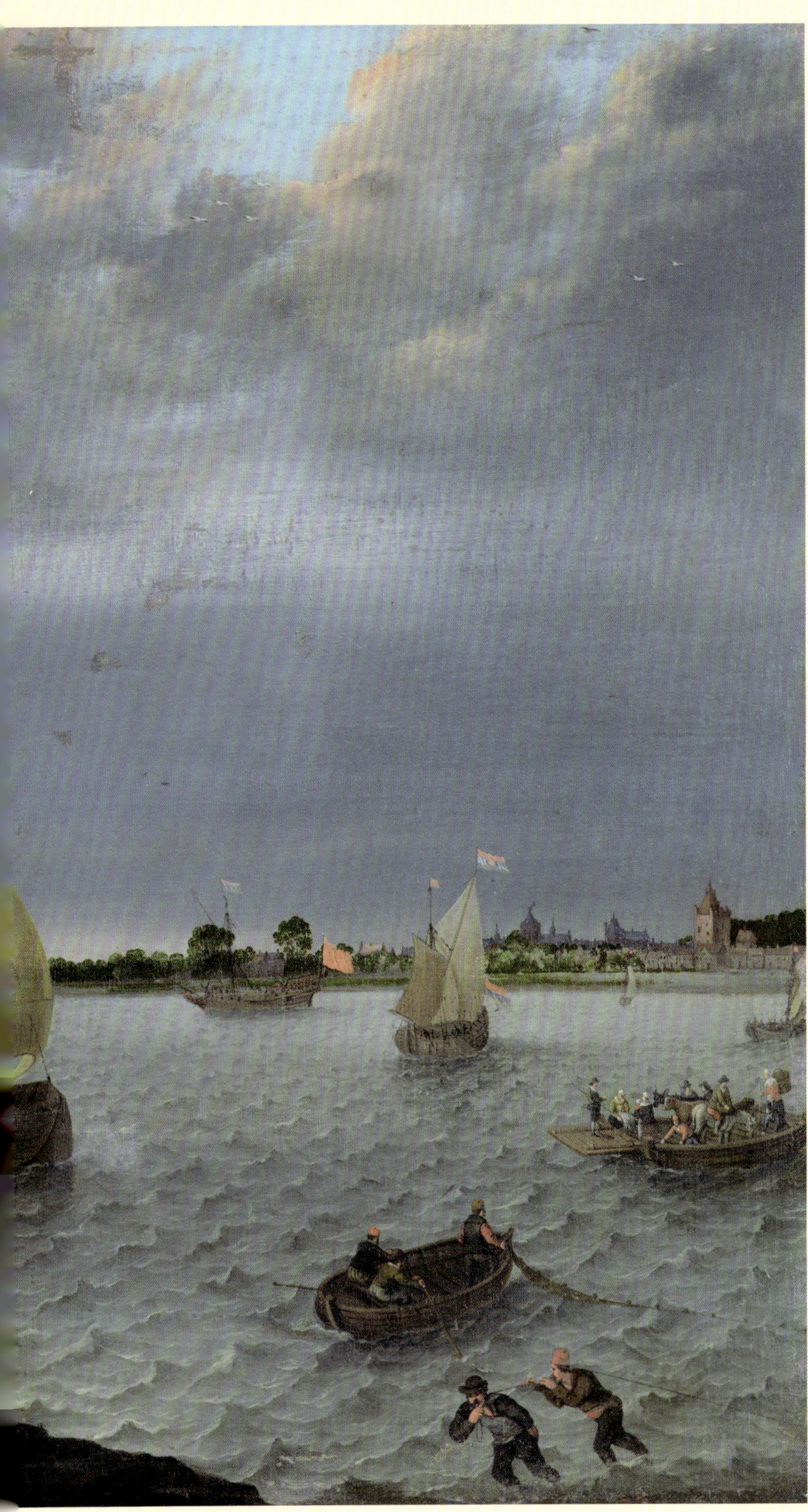

Abraham Willaerts (c. 1603–69)
A Ship Owner and His Family
Un propriétaire de bateau et sa famille
Ein Schiffsbesitzer und seine Familie
Propietario de barco y su familia
Um proprietário de navio e sua família
Scheepseigenaar en zijn gezin
1650, Oil on canvas/Huile sur toile, 85,5 × 130,5 cm,
Musée des Beaux-Arts, Valenciennes

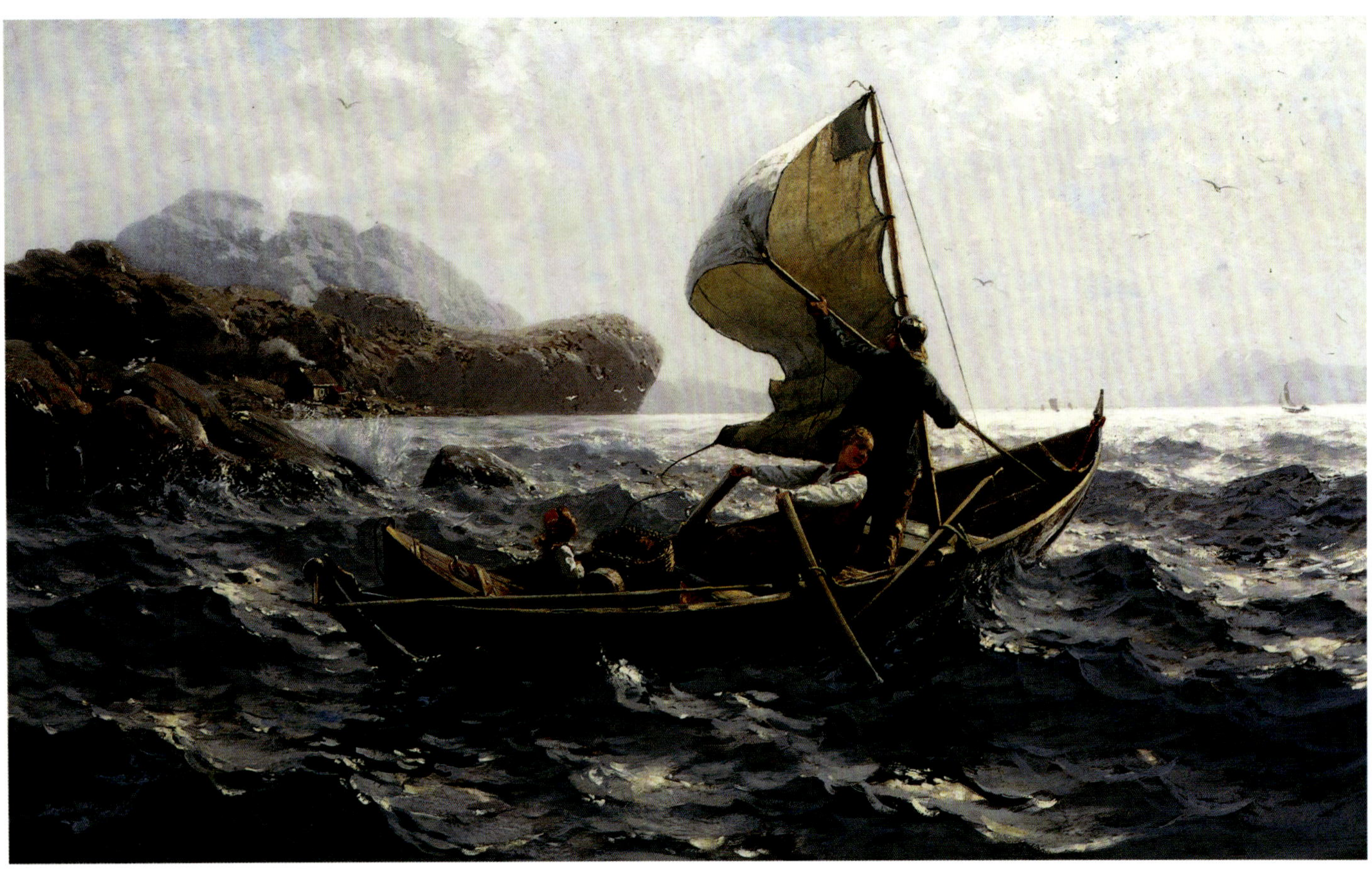

Hans Andreas Dahl (1881–1919)

Woman, Man, and Child in an Oselver

Femme, homme et enfant dans un oselvar

Frau, Mann und Kind in einem Oselver

Mujer, hombre y niño en un oselver

Mulher, homem e criança em um Oselver

Vrouw, man en kind in een oselvar (Noorse roeiboot)

n. d., Oil on canvas/Huile sur toile, 97x157 cm, Private collection

Thomas Alexander Ferguson Graham (1840–1906)

Two Women Seated on Deck

Deux femmes sur le pont

Zwei Frauen sitzen an Deck

Dos mujeres sentadas en cubierta

Duas mulheres sentadas no convés

Twee vrouwen zitten aan dek

n. d., Oil on canvas/Huile sur toile, 35 × 30 cm, Ashmolean Museum, Oxford

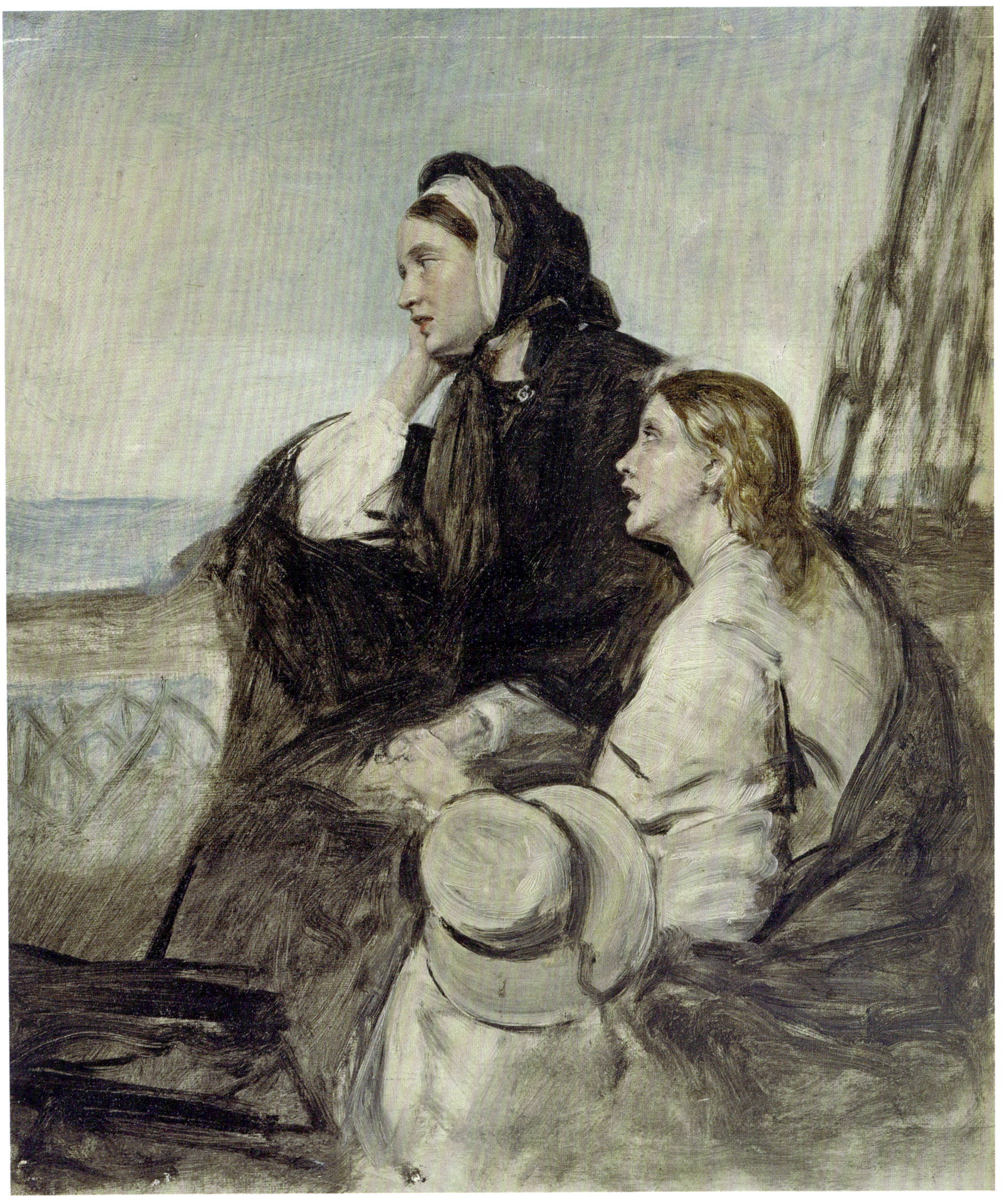

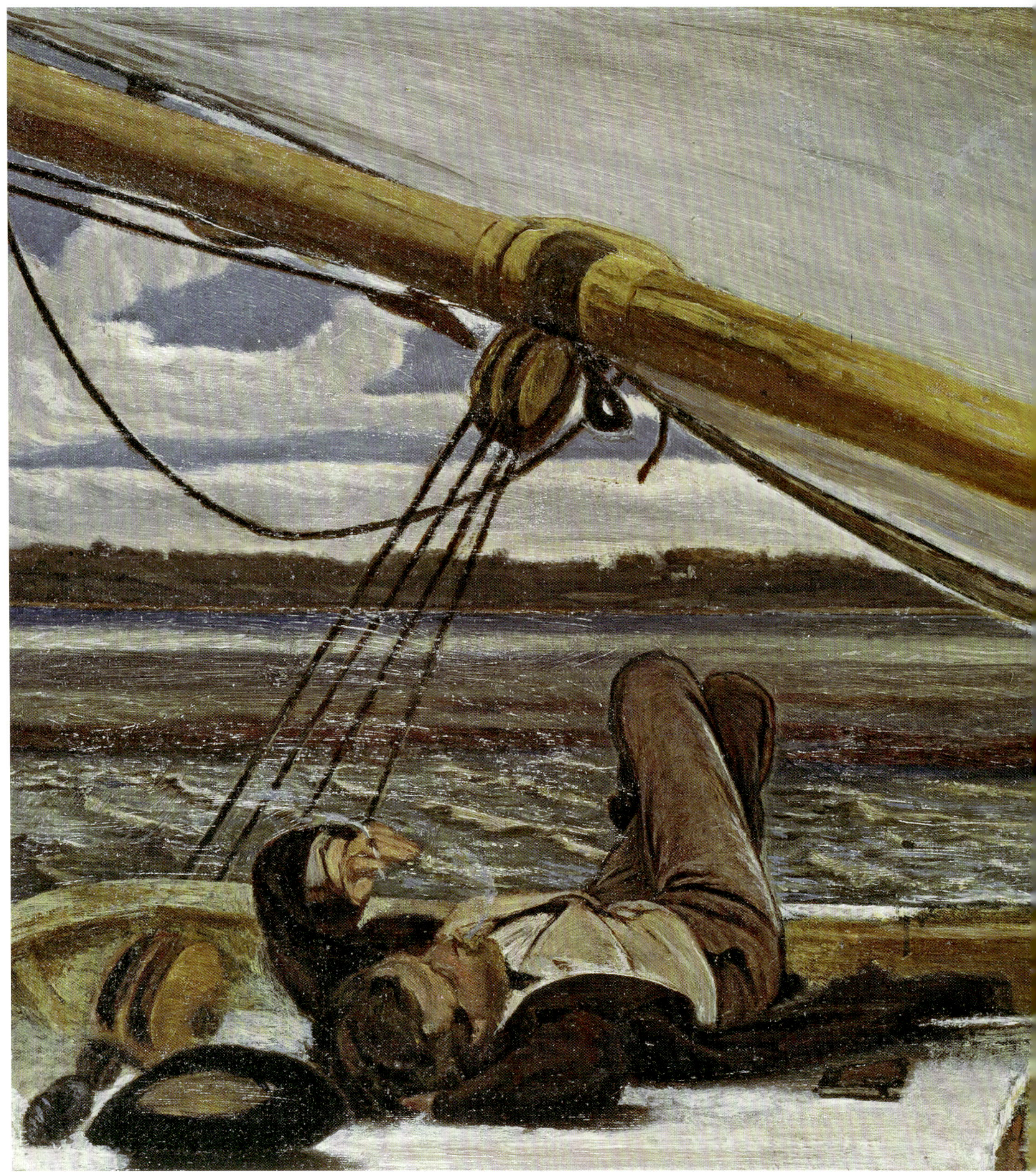

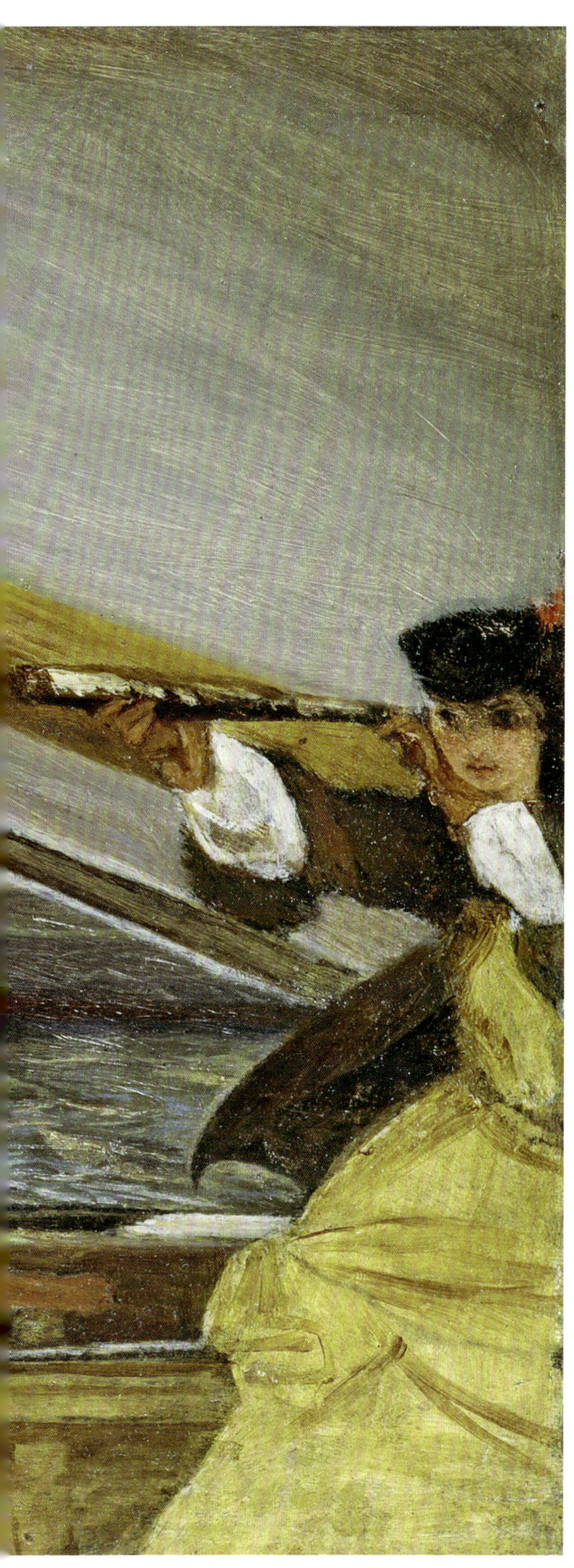

Outward Bound

En partance

Das Auslaufen

Zarpando

A largada

Het uitlopen

19th century/XIXᵉ siècle, Oil on canvas/Huile sur toile, 17 × 23 cm, Ashmolean Museum, Oxford

Augustus Leopold Egg was anything but an obvious maritime painter. Instead, he was known for precisely observed scenes from everyday life in Victorian England. Here we see a scene on the deck of a sailing ship, setting sail with two people on board. The waves in the background indicate a light breeze and the light tells us that the sun is shining. Even if we do not know anything else about the people, we can sense the relaxed atmosphere on board.

Augustus Leopold Egg était tout sauf un peintre de mer évident. Il était plutôt connu pour les scènes précisément observées de la vie quotidienne dans l'Angleterre victorienne. Nous observons ici une scène sur le pont d'un voilier, avec deux personnes à bord. Les vagues en arrière-plan indiquent une brise légère et la lumière montre le beau temps. Même si nous ne connaissons rien d'autre sur les personnes, nous ressentons une ambiance détendue à bord.

Augustus Leopold Egg war alles andere als ein ausgewiesener Marinemaler. Bekannt war er stattdessen für präzise beobachtete Szenen aus dem viktorianischen Alltag. Hier sehen wir eine Szene an Deck eines Segelschiffs, das mit zwei Menschen an Bord ausläuft. Die Wellenbewegungen im Hintergrund deuten auf eine leichte Brise, das Licht auf einen sonnigen Tag. Auch wenn wir sonst nichts über die Personen wissen, spüren wir die entspannte Atmosphäre.

Augustus Leopold Egg era de todo menos un respetado pintor de marinas. En vez de esto, era conocido por precisas escenas del modo de vida victoriano. Aquí vemos una escena en la cubierta de un barco de vela que se hace a la mar con dos personas a bordo. Las ondulaciones del mar en el fondo sugieren una ligera brisa, la luz en un día soleado. Incluso si no sabemos nada más acerca de las personas, sentimos el ambiente relajado.

Augustus Leopold Egg foi tudo menos um pintor de marinhas exilado. Ele ficou sim conhecido por cenas da vida vitoriana meticulosamente observadas. Aqui nós vemos uma cena no convés de um veleiro, culminando com duas pessoas a bordo. As ondulações no fundo sugerem uma ligeira brisa, a luz sugere um dia ensolarado. Mesmo que não soubermos mais nada sobre essas pessoas, sentimos o ambiente descontraído.

Augustus Leopold Egg was allesbehalve een schilder van typische zeestukken. In plaats daarvan maakte hij naam met taferelen uit het dagelijks leven van het Victoriaanse Engeland. Hier zien we een scène op het dek van een zeilboot, die met twee mensen aan boord uitloopt. De golfbewegingen op de achtergrond duiden op een lichte bries, het licht op een zonnige dag. Hoewel we niets over de afgebeelde personen weten, is de ontspannen sfeer voelbaar.

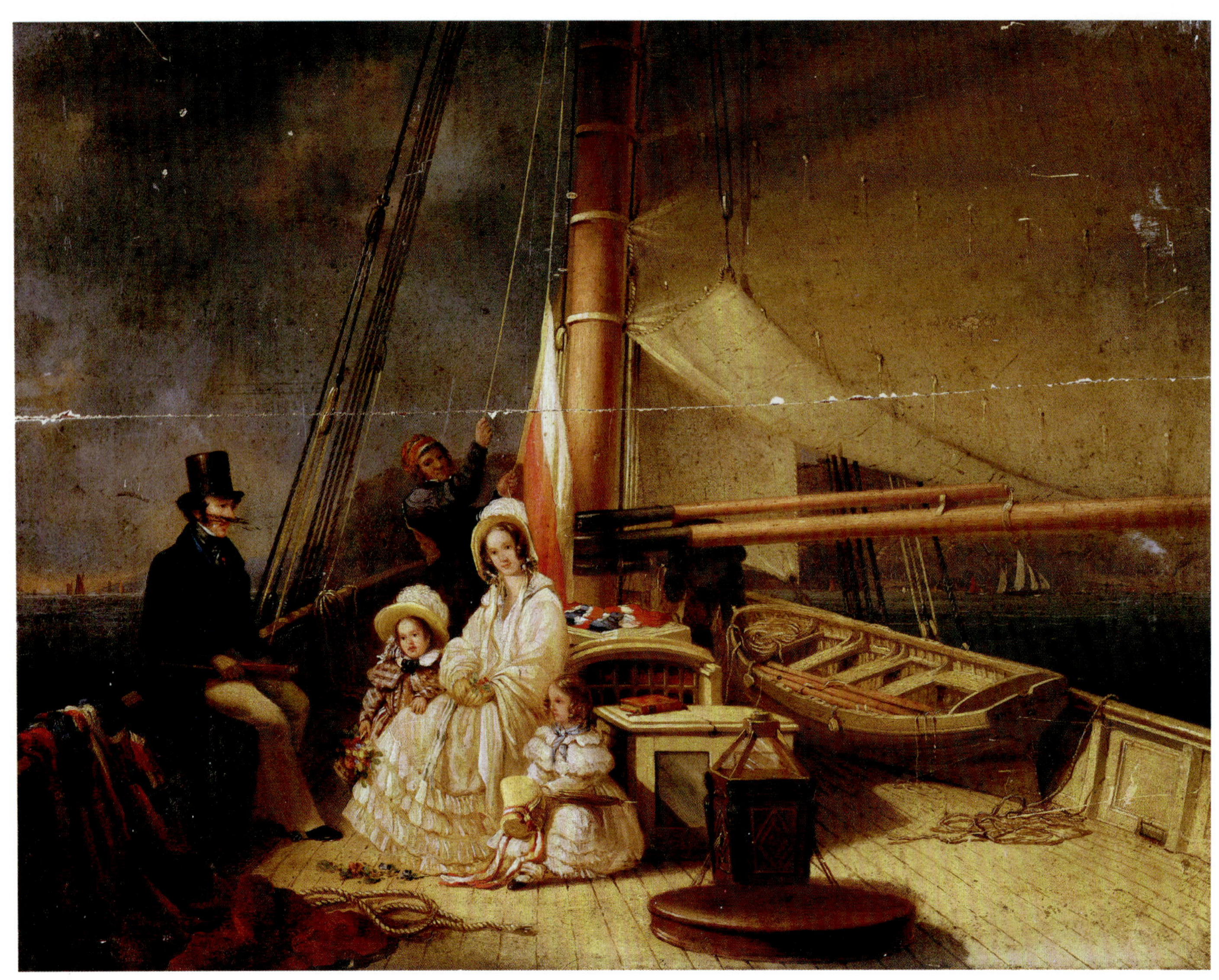

Nicholas Matthew Condy (1816–57)

The Yacht *The Guernsey* with Her Owner and His Family and Crew Aboard

Le Yacht *The Guernsey* avec son propriétaire, sa famille et l'équipage à bord

Mr. Ward und seine Familie an Bord seiner Jacht *The Guernsey*

El yate *The Guernsey* con su propietario y su familia y la tripulación a bordo

Sr. Ward e sua família a bordo de sua iate *The Guernsey*

Mr. Ward en zijn gezin aan boord van zijn jacht *The Guernsey*

c. 1840, Oil on panel/Huile sur bois, 35,5 × 45,7 cm, Private collection

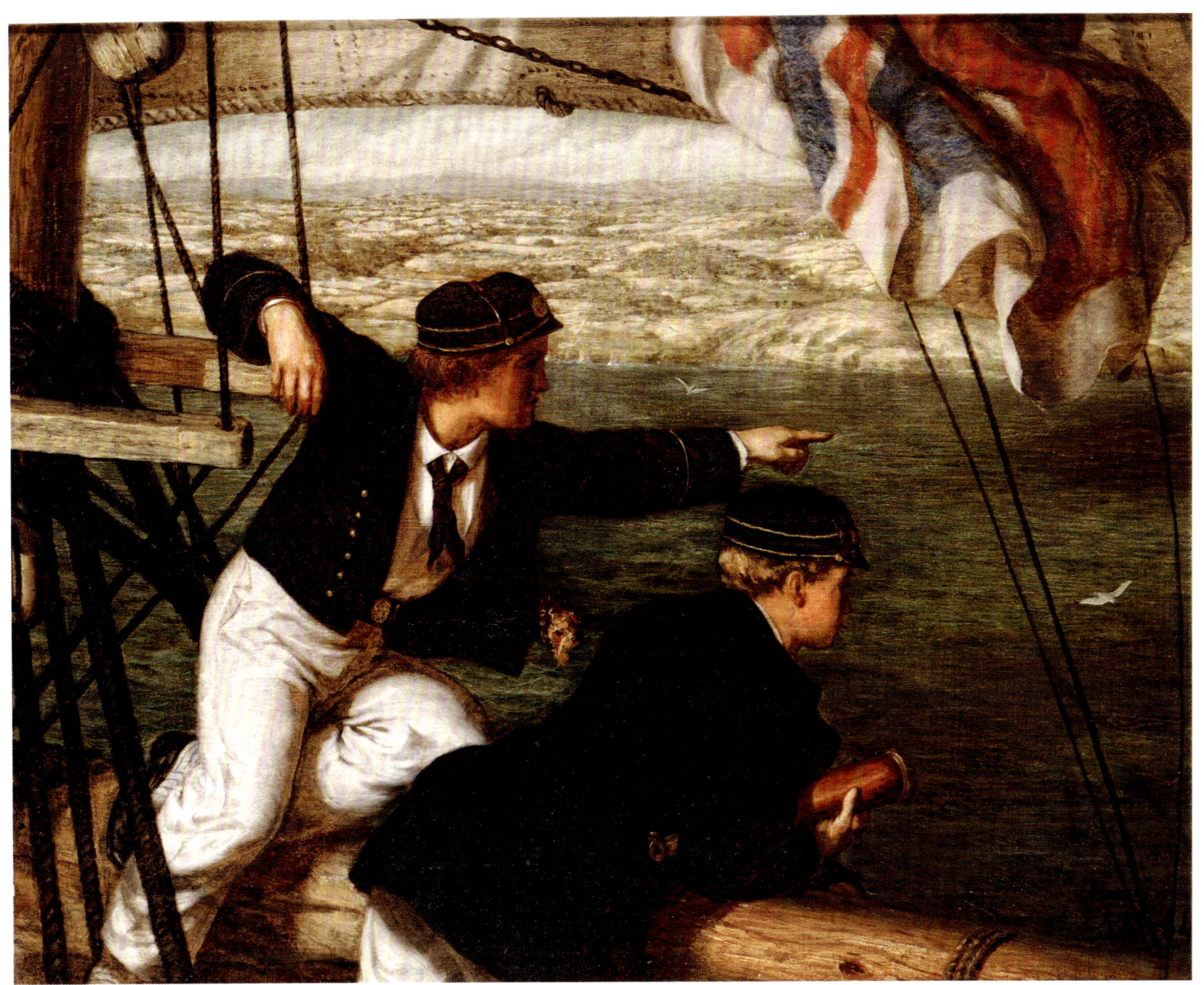

Philip Richard Morris (1836–1902)

Land ahoy!

Terre en vue !

Land ahoi!

¡Tierra a la vista!

Land ahoi!

Land Ahoy!

1864, Oil on canvas/Huile sur toile, 44,4 × 53,3 cm, Private collection

French school/
École de francaise

Lady on the Deck
of a Ship

Femme sur le pont
d'un bateau

Dame an Bord
eines Schiffes

Mujer a bordo
de un barco

Senhora a bordo
de um navio

Dame aan boord
van een schip

19th century/XIXᵉ siècle,
Oil on canvas/Huile
sur toile, 107 × 80 cm,
Private collection

Bernhard Axel Bendixen
(1810–77)

Portrait of a Young
Danish Naval

Portrait d'un jeune
officier naval danois

Porträt eines jungen
dänischen Marineoffiziers

Retrato de joven
marino danés

Retrato de um Jovem
Oficial da Marinha
Dinamarquesa

Portret van een jonge
Deense marine officier

1841, Oil on canvas/Huile
sur toile, 67 × 56,5 cm,
Kunsthalle Hamburg

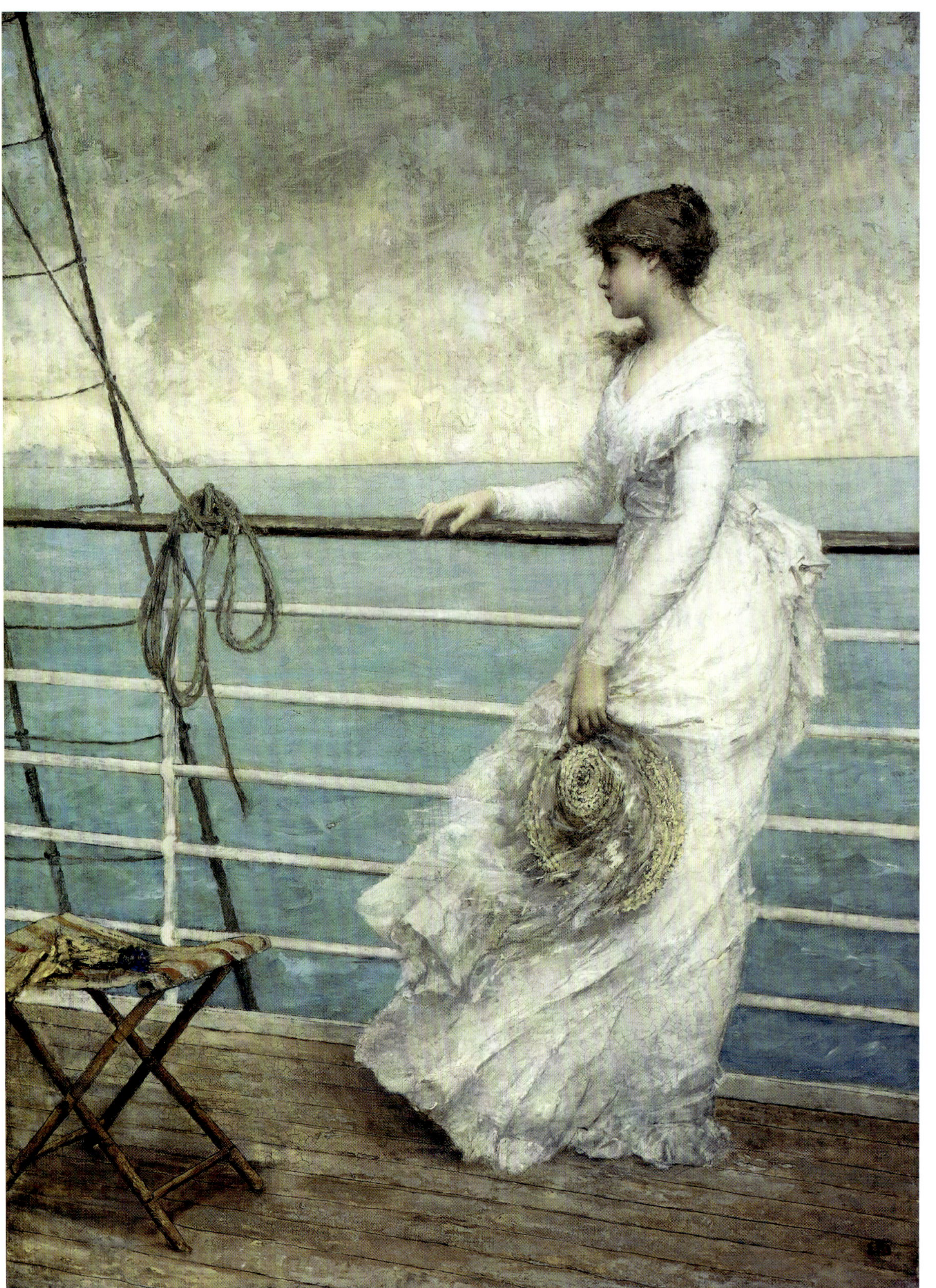

240

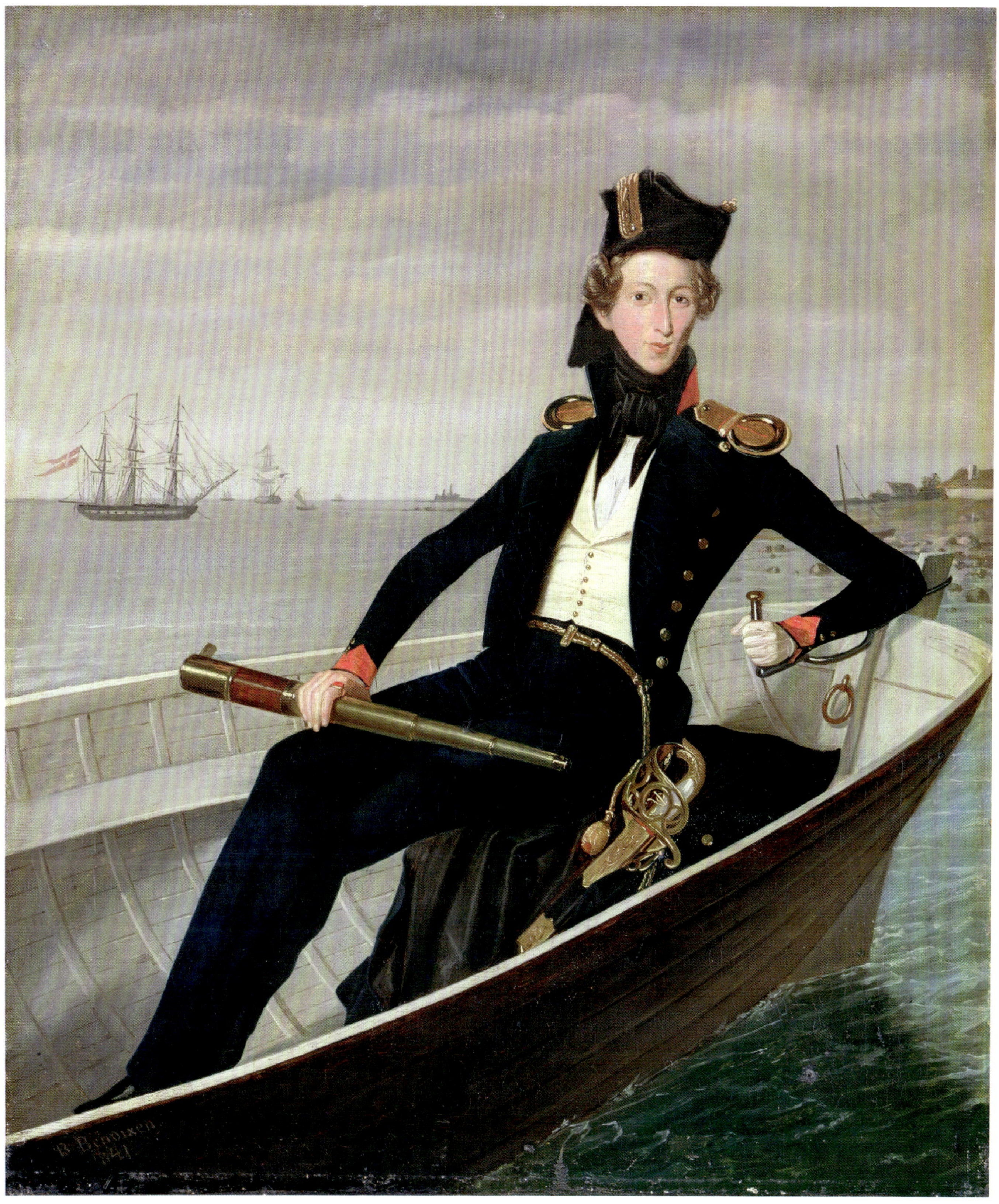

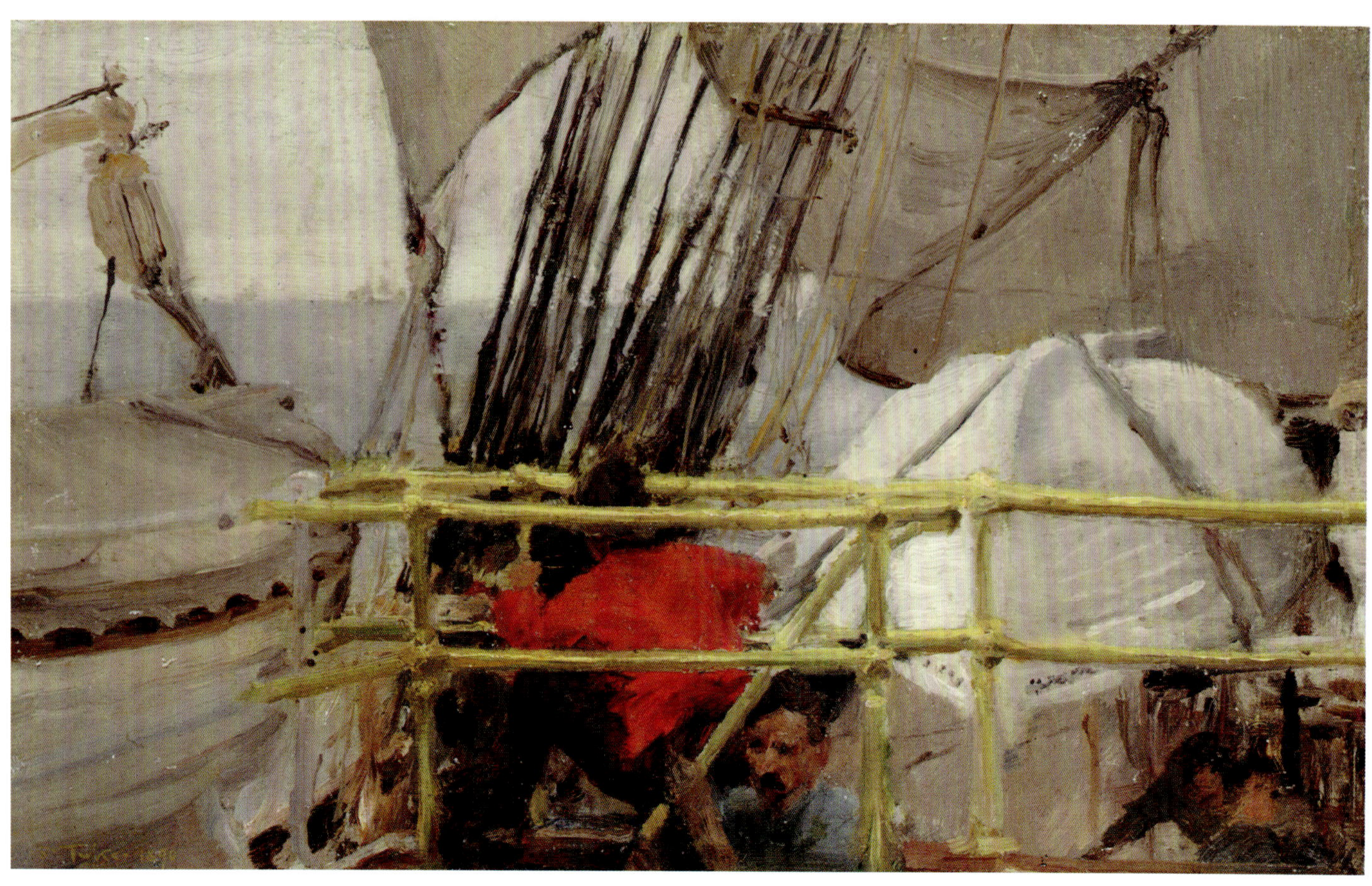

Henry Scott Tuke (1858–1929)

On Board the Sailing Ship *Roman Emperor*, June 1890

À bord du voilier *Roman Emperor*, juin 1890

An Bord des Segelschiffes *Roman Emperor*, Juni 1890

A bordo del barco de vela *Roman Emperor*, junio de 1890

A bordo do veleiro *Roman Emperor*, junho de 1890

Aan boord van het zeilschip *Roman Emperor*, juni 1890

1890, Oil on panel/Huile sur bois, 14 × 22,2 cm, Private collection

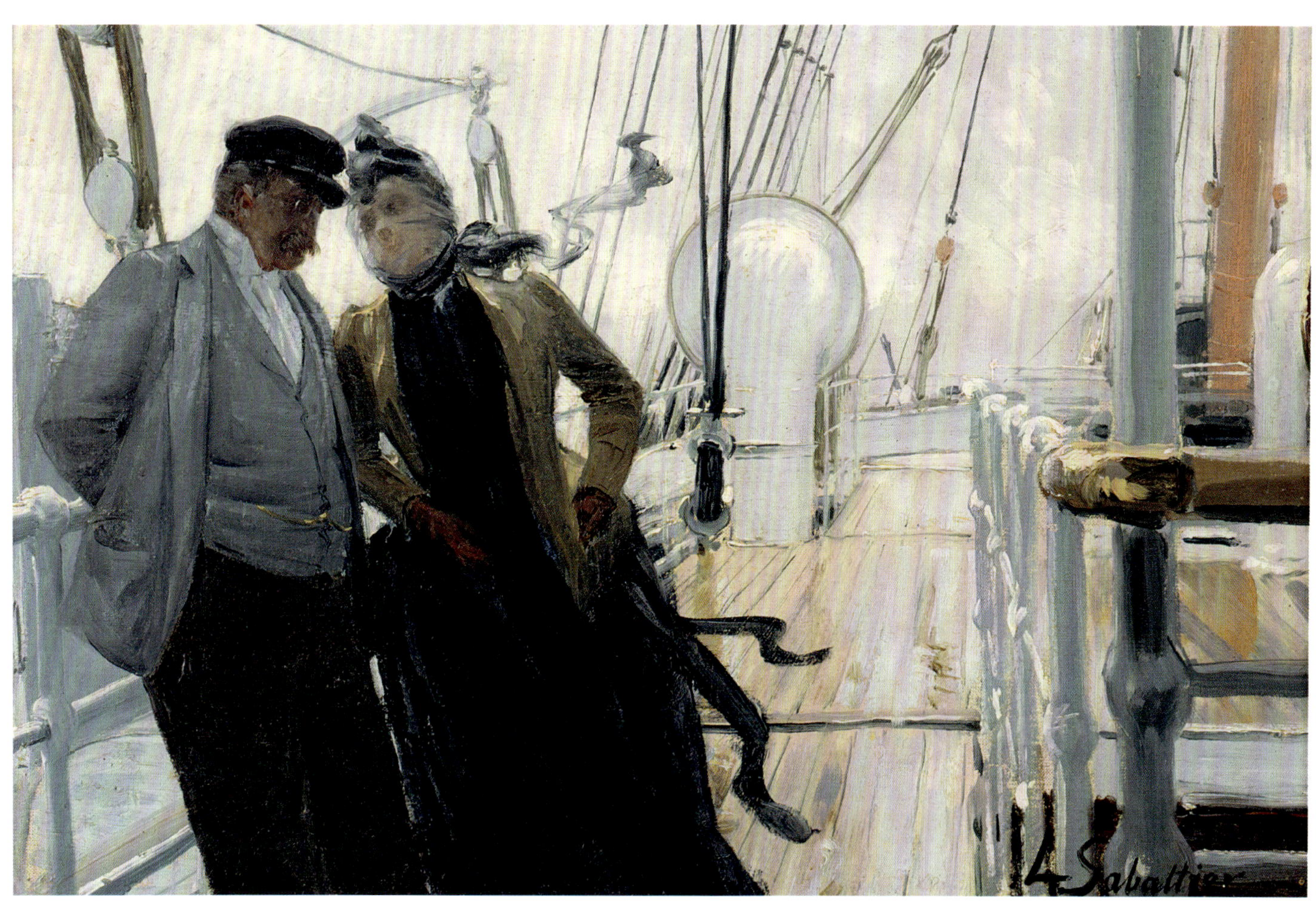

Louis Anet Sabatier

On Deck

Sur le pont

An Deck

En cubierta

No convés

Aan dek

19th century/XIXe siècle, Oil on canvas/Huile sur toile, 21,7 × 33 cm, Private collection

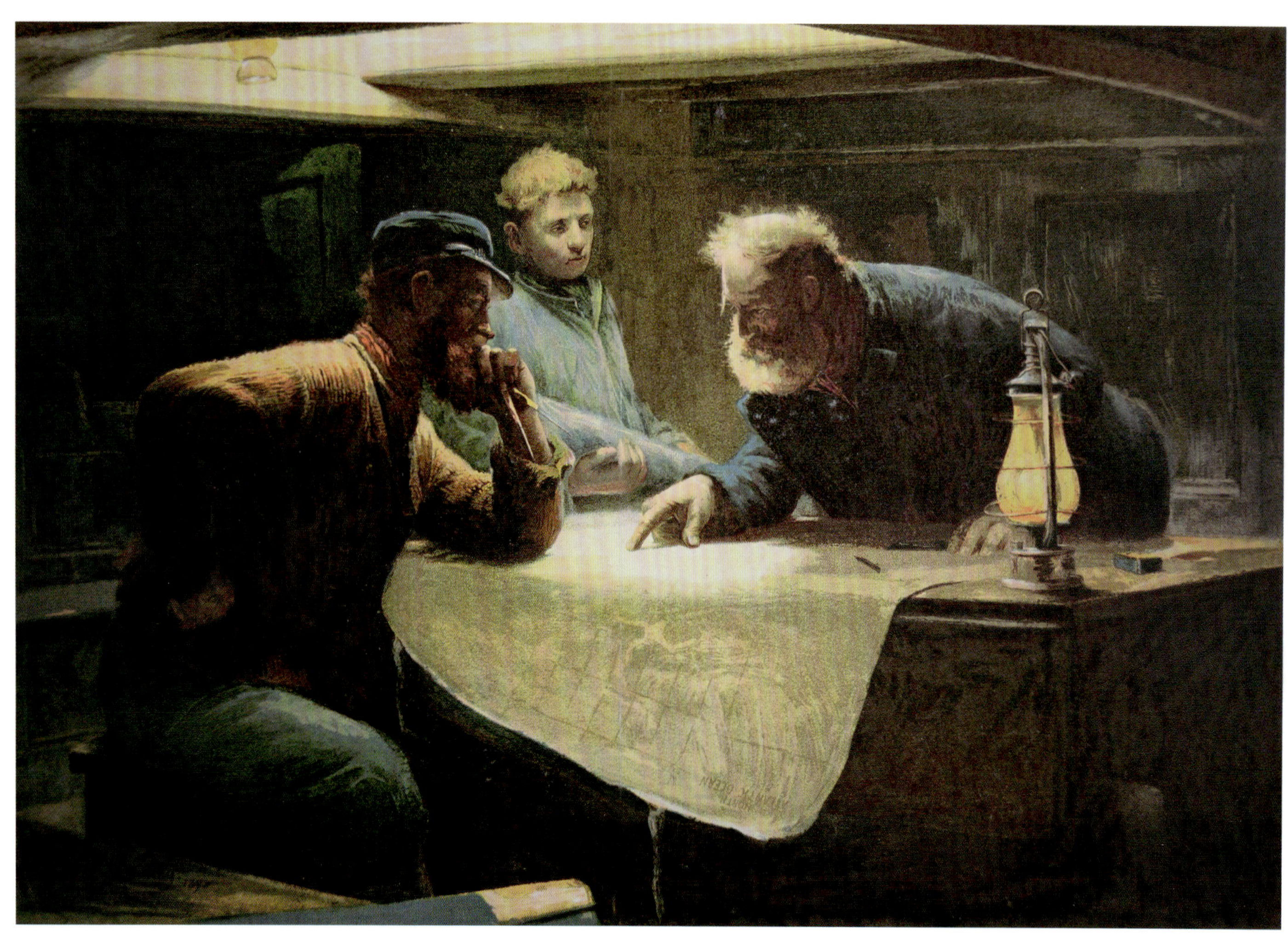

Albert Starling (1858–1947)

Out of their Reckoning

En pleine reconnaissance

Vom Kurs abgewichen

Desviados de la ruta

Desvio de rota

Naar hun berekening

1892, Oil on canvas/Huile sur toile, Private collection

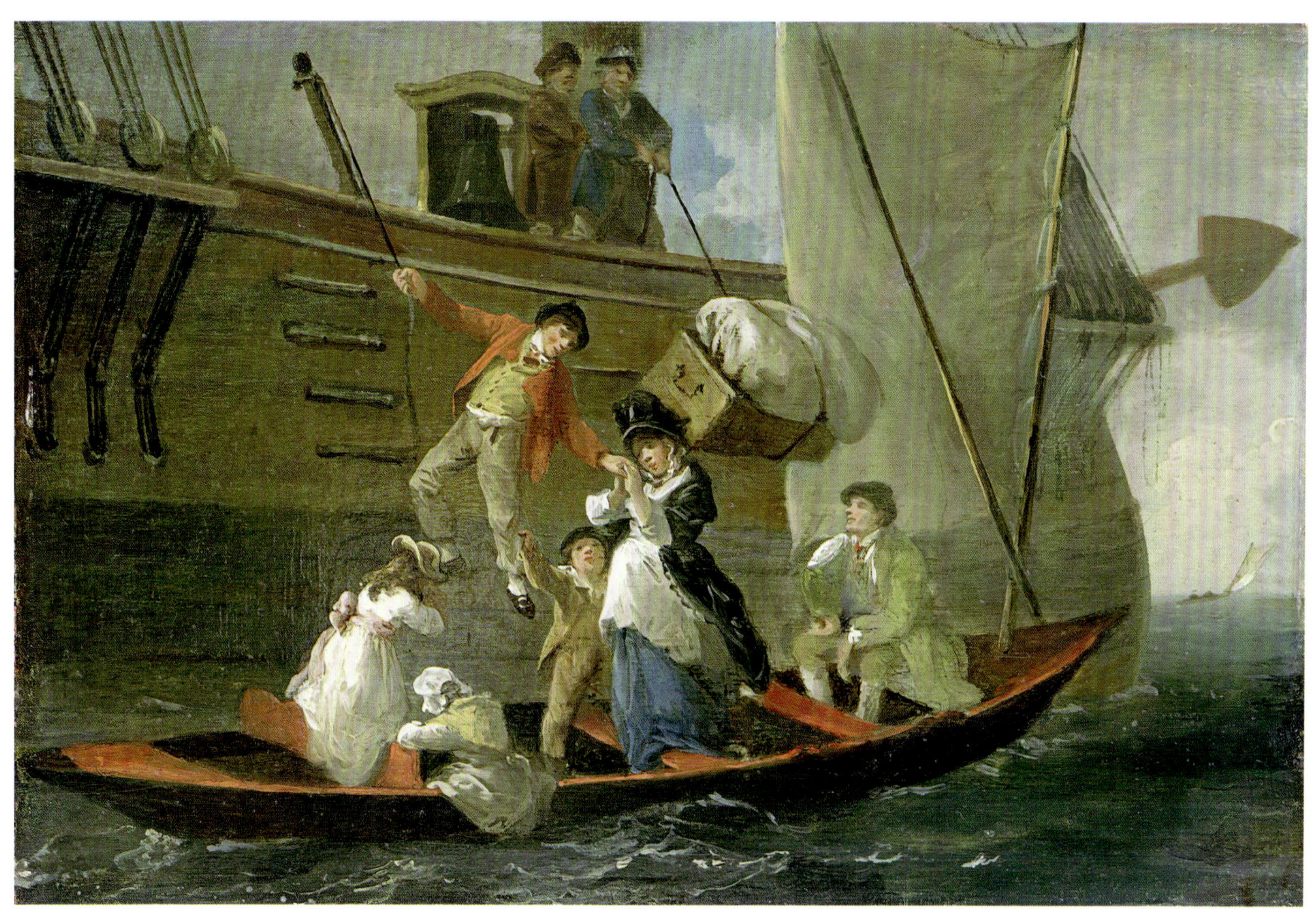

Julius Caesar Ibbetson (1759–1817)

A Married Sailor's Adieu

Adieu d'un marin marié

Abschied eines verheirateten Seemannes

Despedida de un marinero casado

Adeus de um marinheiro casado

Afscheid van de gehuwde zeeman

c. 1800, Oil on panel/Huile sur bois, 17,2 × 25,4 cm, Yale Center for British Art, New Haven

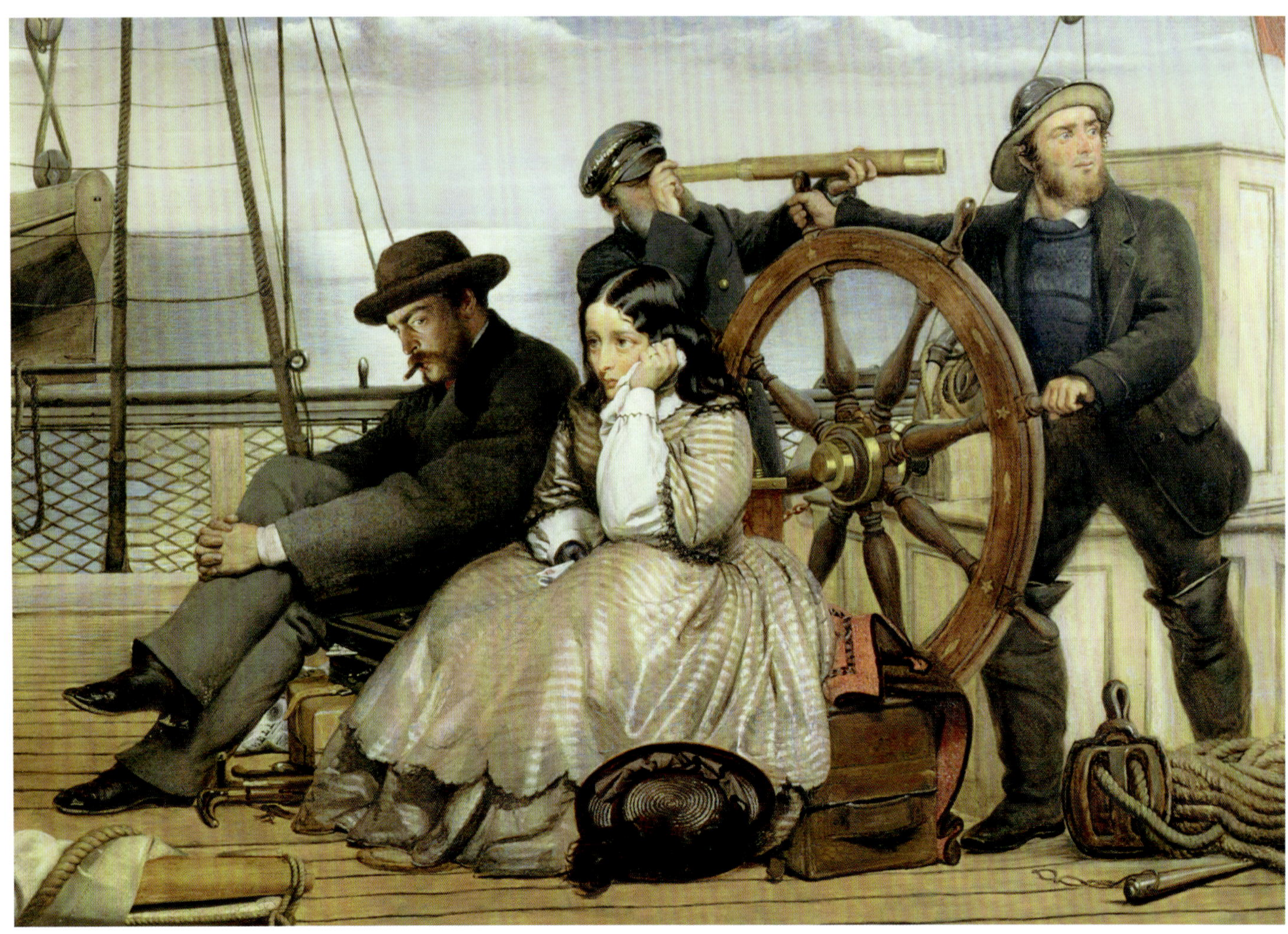

Henry Garland (1854–90)

The Escape

La Fuite

Die Flucht

La huida

A fuga

De vlucht

n. d., Oil on canvas/Huile sur toile, 69,8 × 100 cm, Private collection

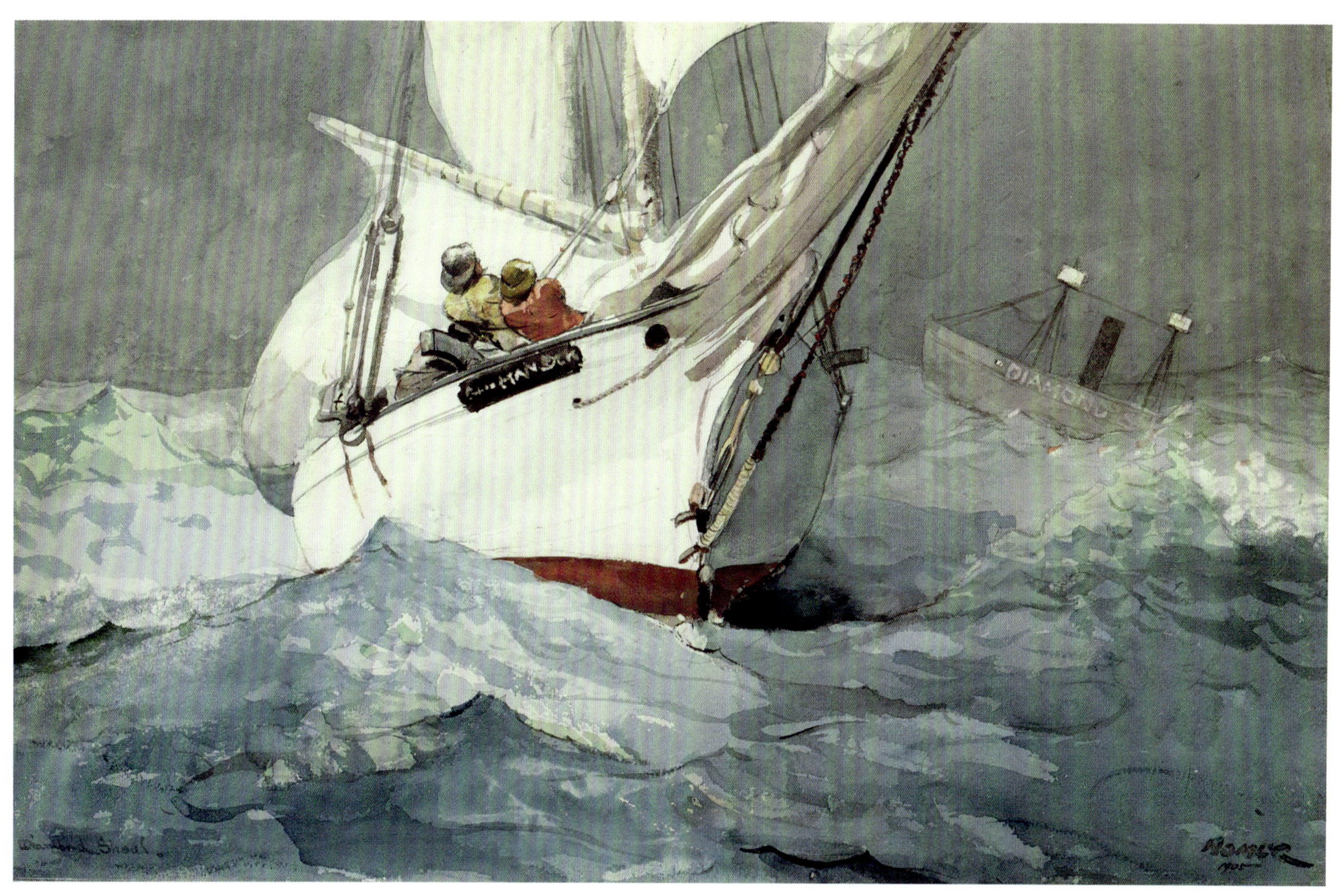

Winslow Homer (1836–1910)

Diamond Shoal

1905, Watercolor on paper/Aquarelle sur papier, Private collection

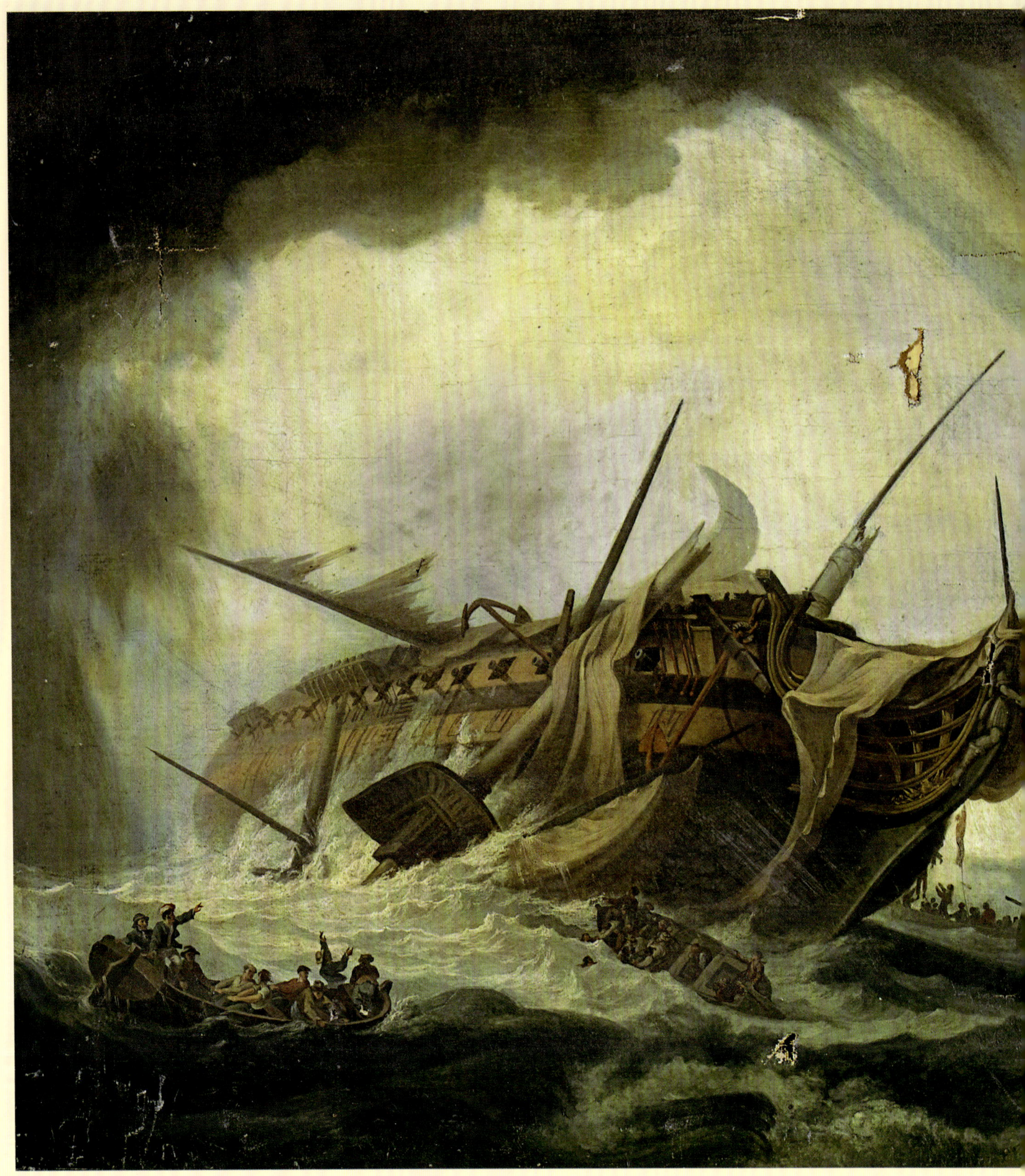

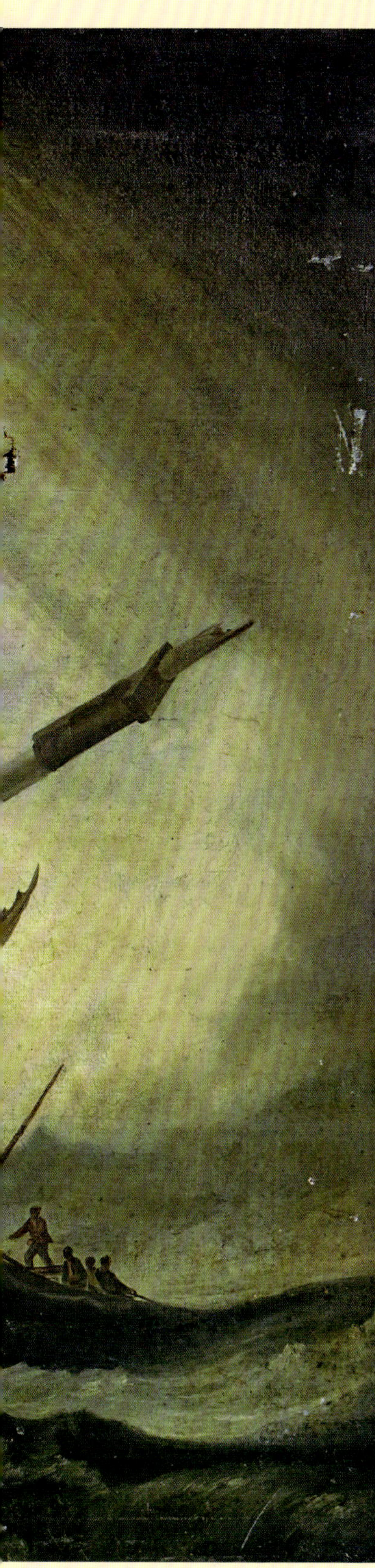

A wet grave

Une tombe humide

Das nasse Grab

La tumba húmeda

A sepultura úmida

Het zilte graf

Hermanus Koekkoek (1815–82)
Sinking Frigate
Naufrage d'une frégate
Sinkende Fregatte
Hundimiento de fragata
Fragata afundando
Zinkend fregat
n. d., Oil on canvas/Huile sur toile, Bristol Museum and Art Gallery, Bristol

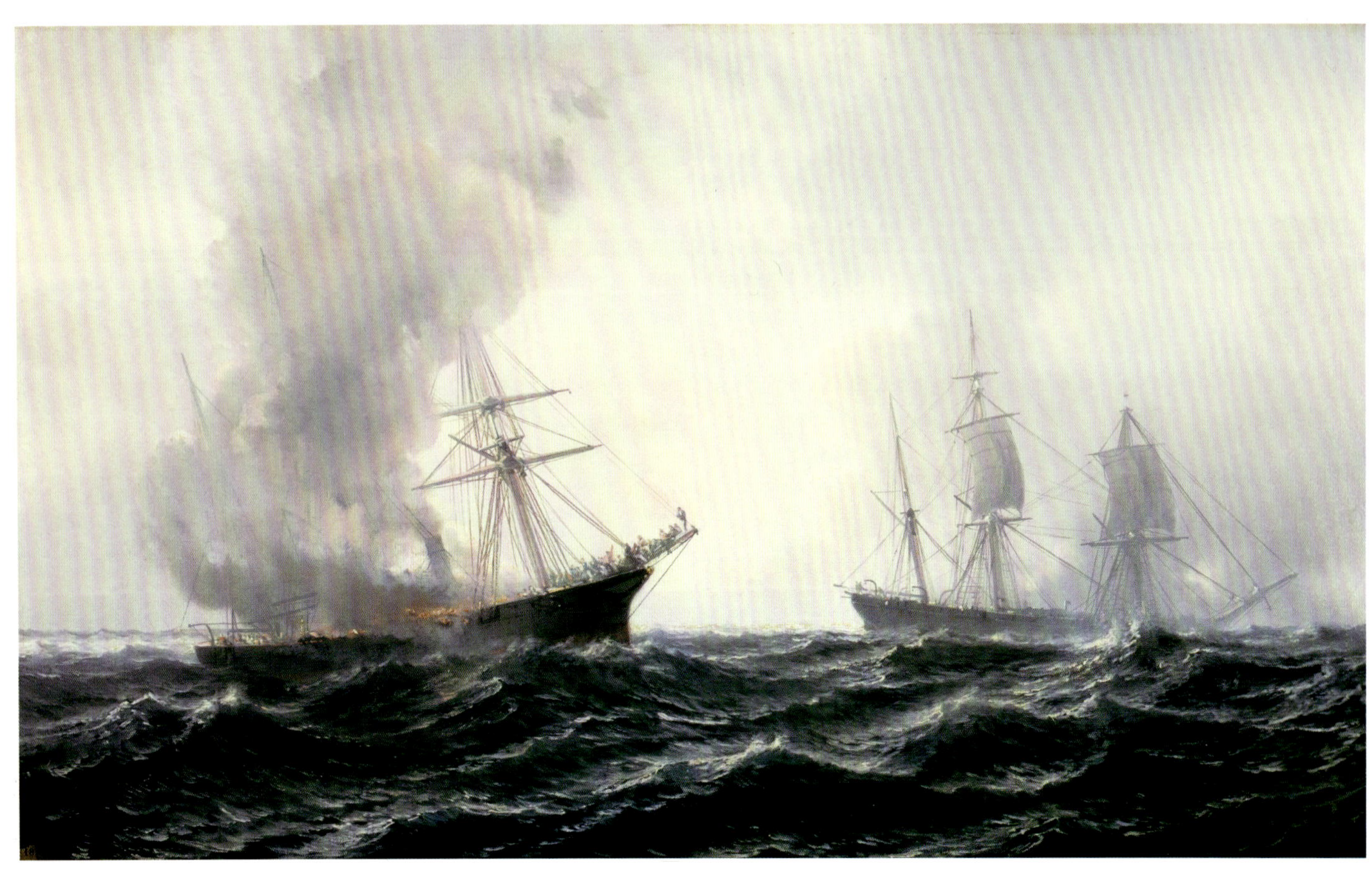

Jean-Baptiste Henri Durand-Brager (1814–79)

A Ship on Fire at Sea with Another Standing By

Navire en feu en pleine mer, un autre à côté

Brennendes Schiff auf dem Meer

Incendio de barco en el mar

Navio em chamas no mar

Brandend schip op zee

n. d., Oil on canvas/Huile sur toile, 48,3 × 81,1 cm, Bowes Museum, Barnard Castle

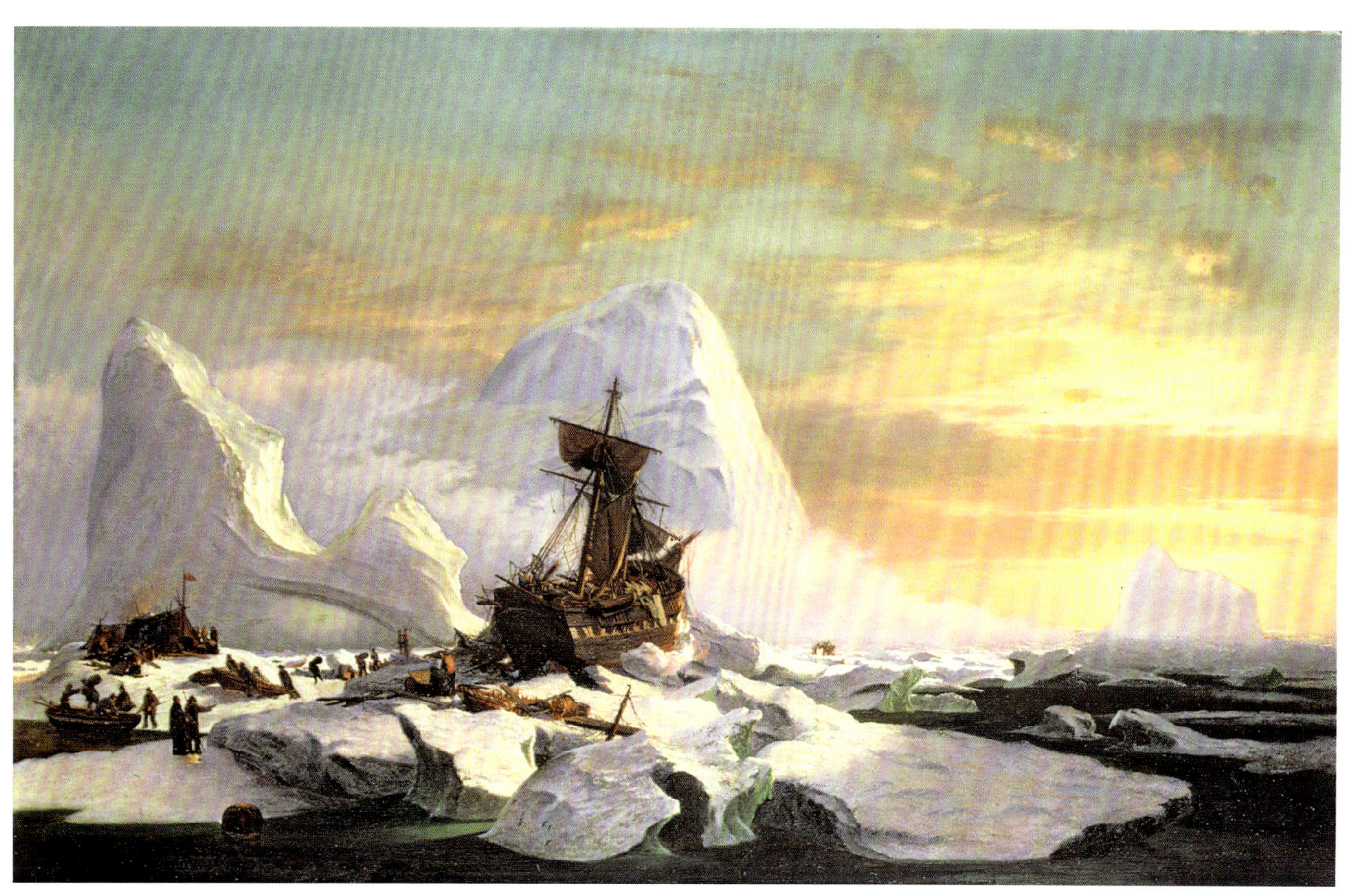

William Bradford (1823–92)

Crushed in the Ice

Échoué sur la glace

Vom Eis zerquetscht

Atrapado en el hielo

Esmagados por gelo

Door het ijs vermorzeld

n. d., Oil on canvas/Huile sur toile, Private collection

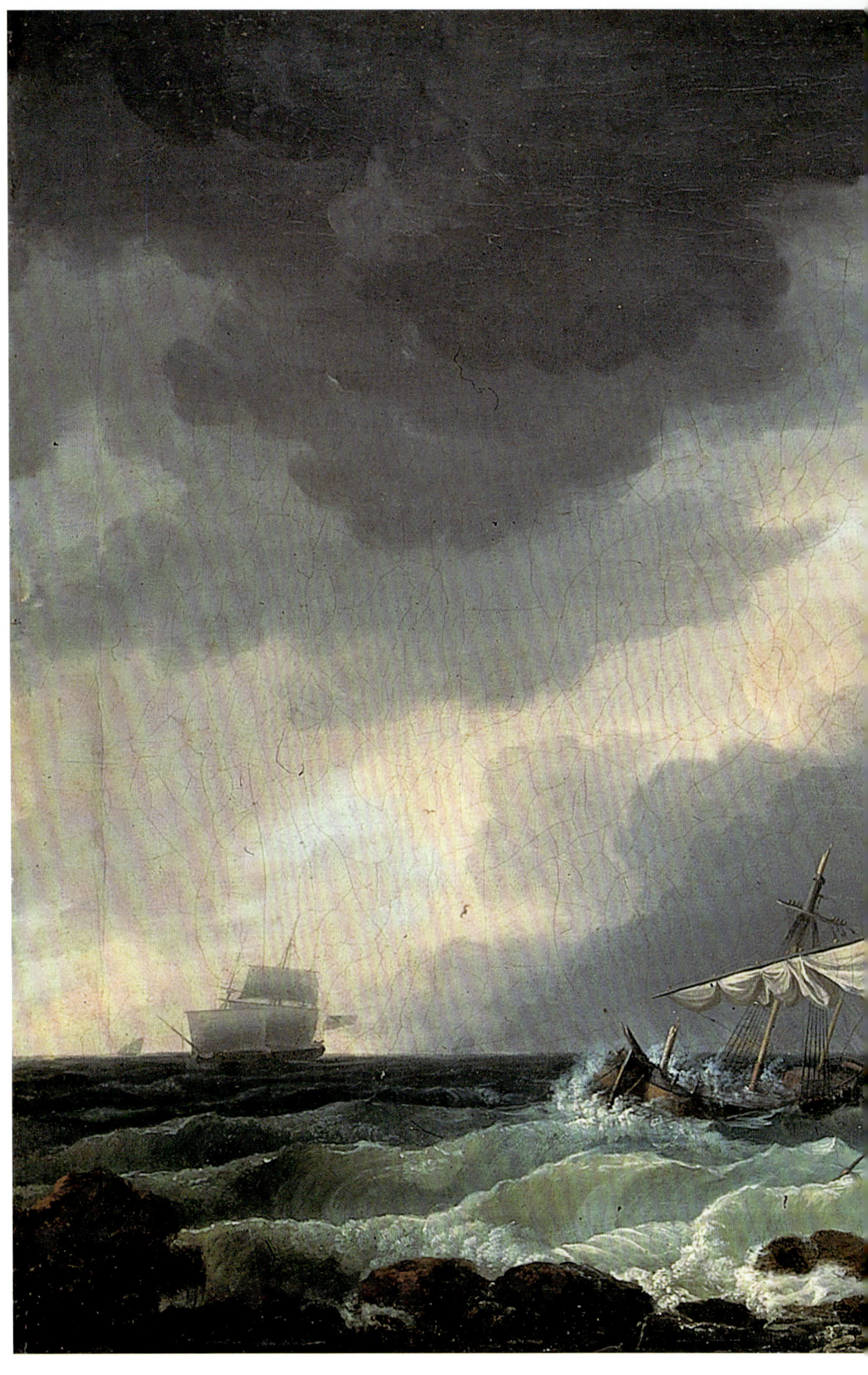

Dominic Serres (1722–93)

A Shipwreck off a Coast with Survivors
and Rescuers on a Beach

Un naufrage au large des côtes avec des
survivants et des sauveteurs sur une plage

Wrack vor der Küste, mit Überlebenden
und Rettern am Strand

Naufragio delante de la costa con
supervivientes y rescate en la playa

Naufrágio ao largo da costa, com
sobreviventes e equipes de resgate na praia

Scheepswrak voor de kust met
overlevenden en redders op het strand

n. d., Oil on canvas/Huile sur toile,
63,5 × 102,3 cm, Private collection

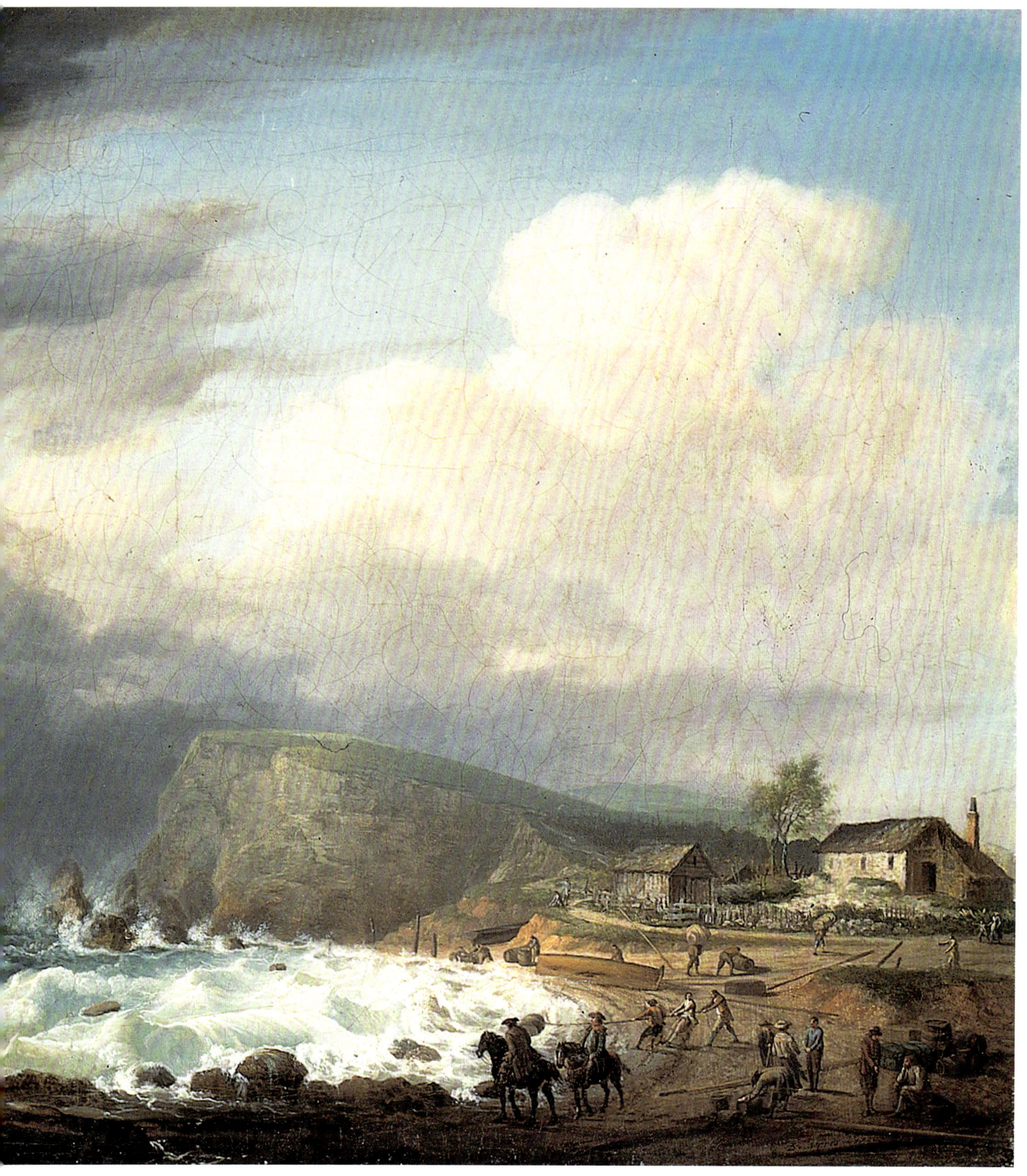

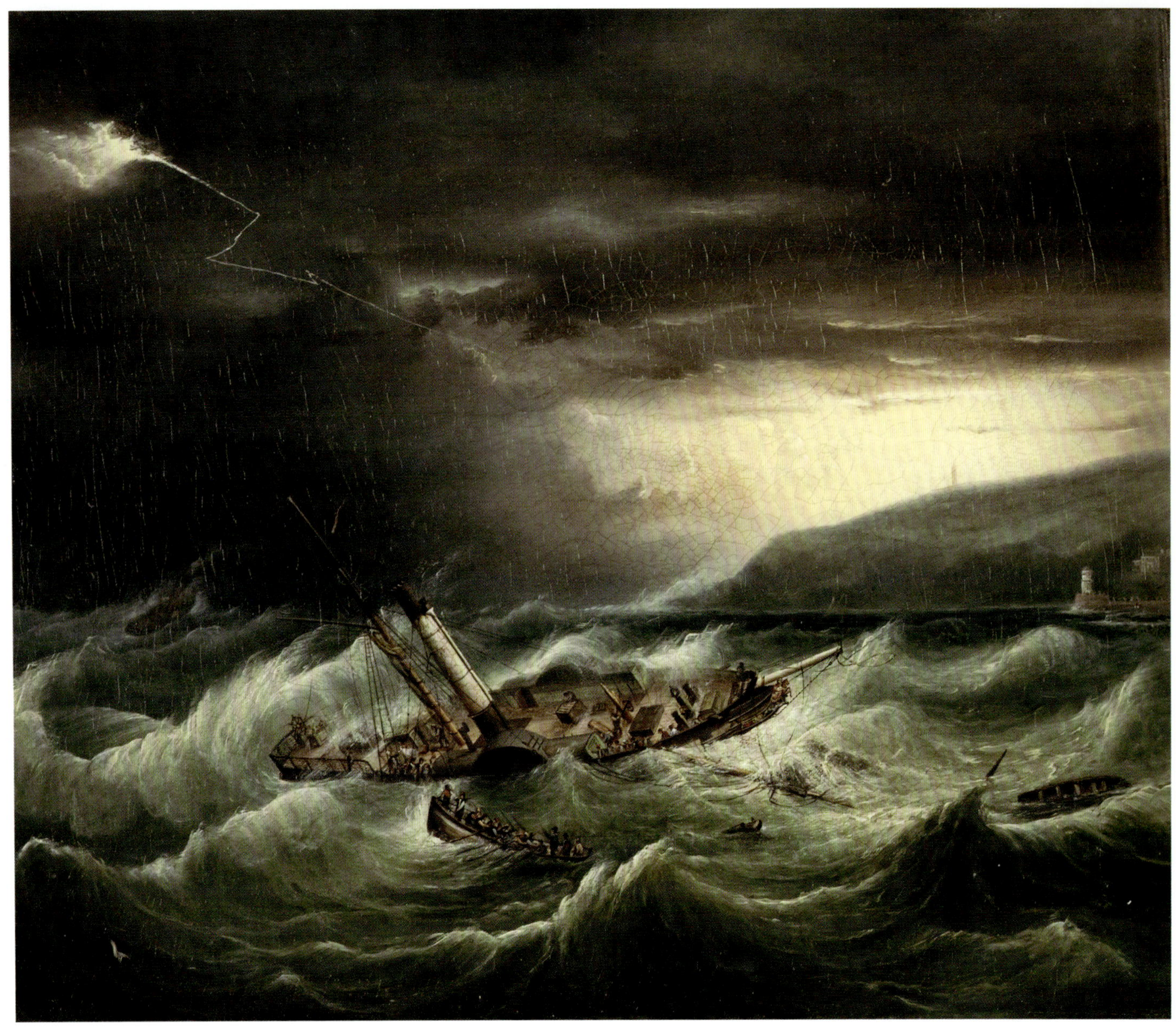

English school/École anglaise

The Wreck of the *Saint George*

Épave du *Saint George*

Das Wrack der *Saint George*

El naufragio del *Saint George*

O naufrágio do *Saint George*

Het wrak van de *Saint George*

1830, Oil on canvas/Huile sur toile, 40 × 49 cm, Manx Museum, Douglas

Ivan Aivazovsky (1817–1900)

Searching for Survivors

À la recherche des survivants

Die Suche nach Überlebenden

Búsqueda de supervivientes

A busca por sobreviventes

Het zoeken naar overlevenden

1863, Oil on canvas/Huile sur toile, 60,2 × 58,6 cm, Private collection

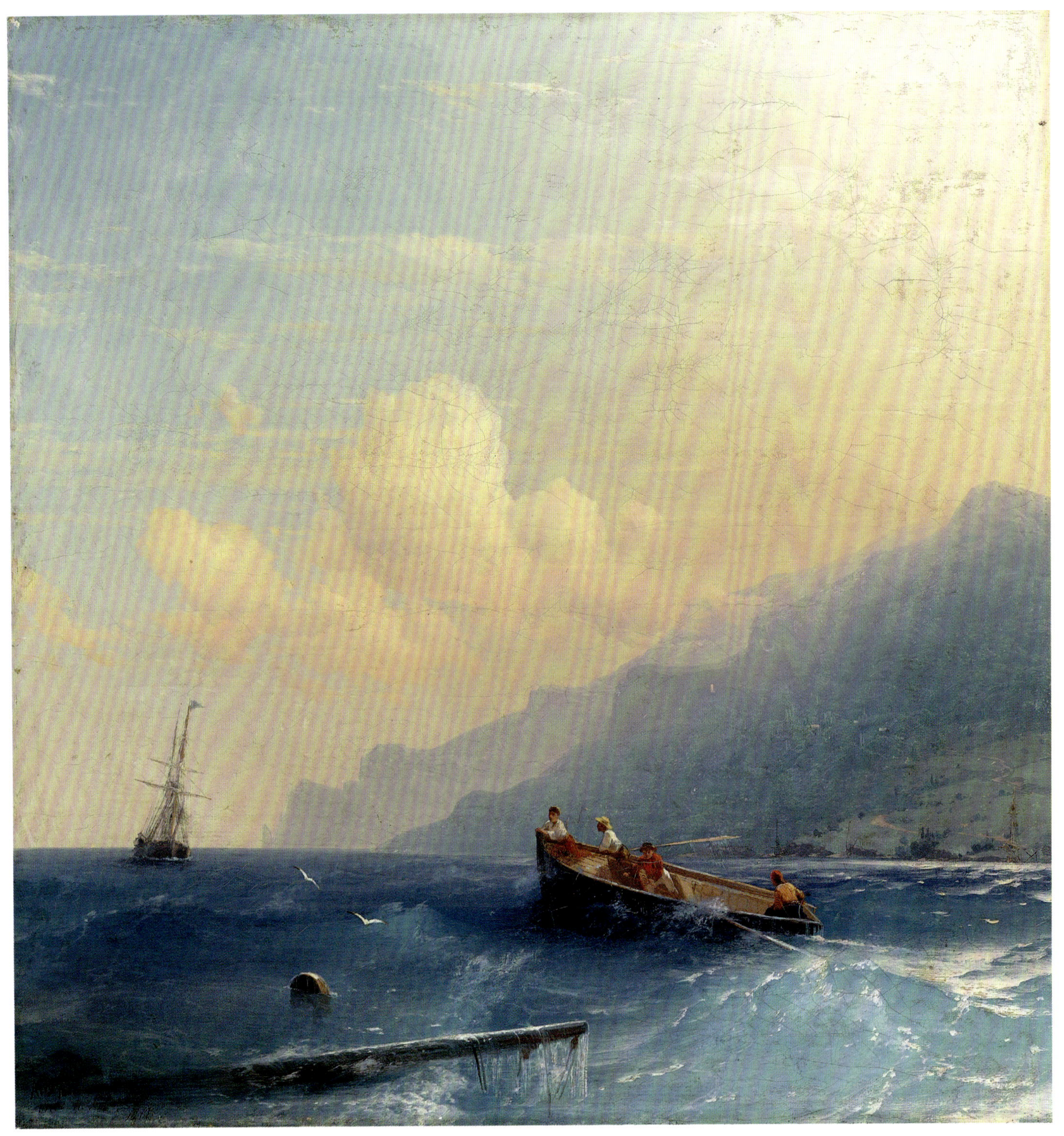

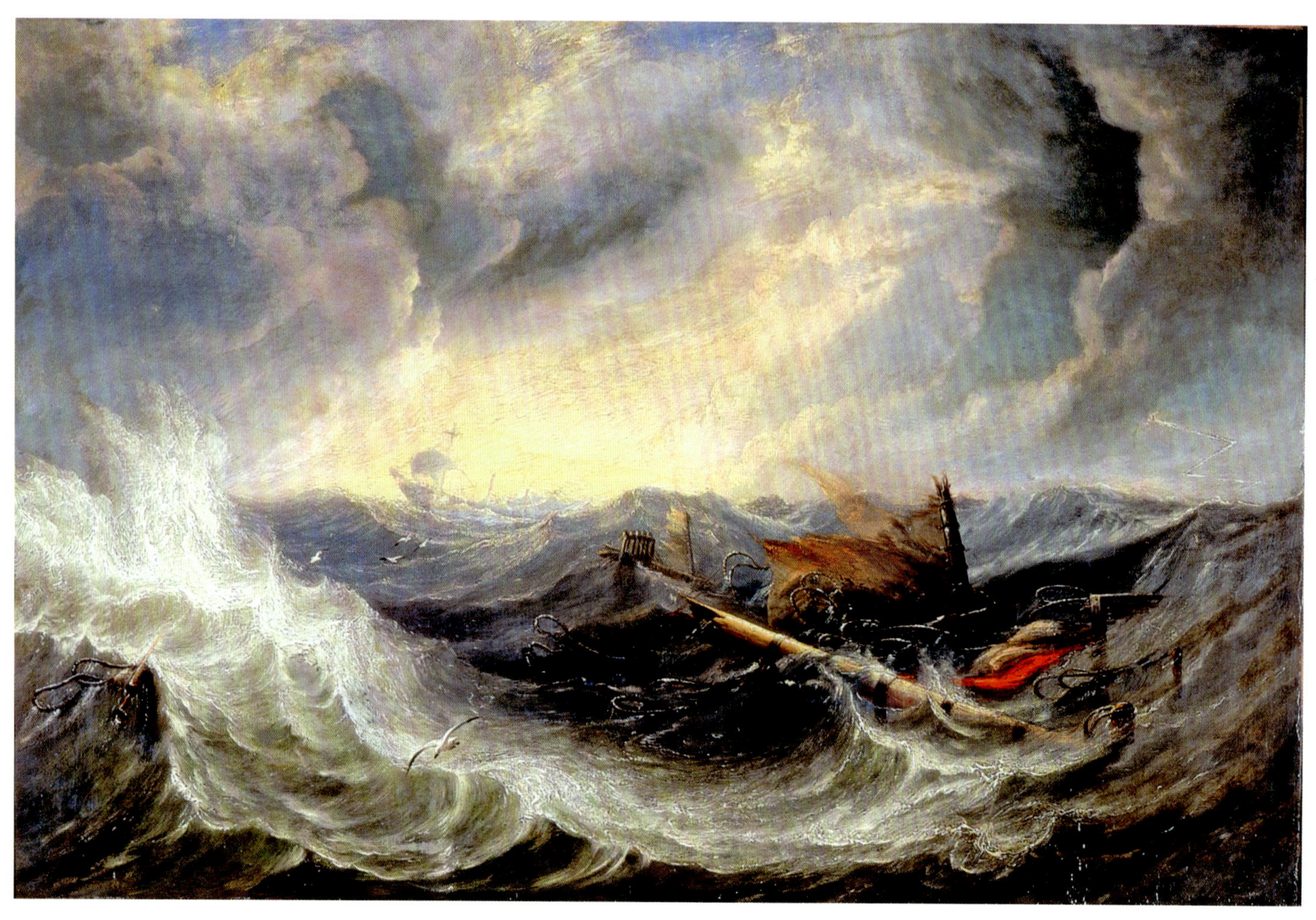

John Wilson Carmichael (1800–68)

Seascape with Wreckage

Paysage de mer avec épave

Meerespanorama mit Schiffswrack

Marina con naufragio

Paisagem marinha com naufrágio

Zeegezicht met scheepswrak

19th century/XIXᵉ siècle, Oil on canvas/Huile sur toile, 50,8 × 76,1 cm, Laing Art Gallery, Newcastle-upon-Tyne

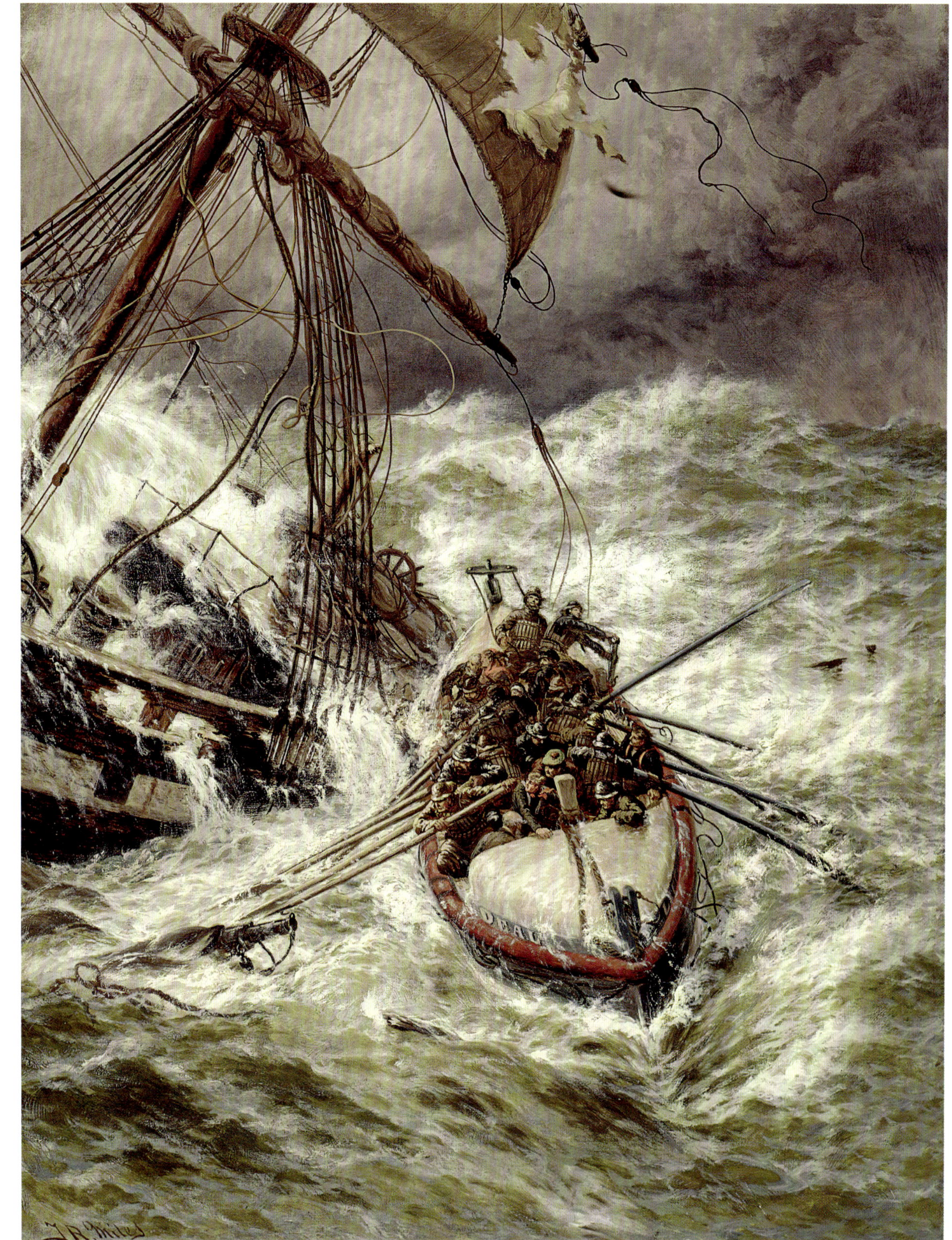

Thomas Rose Miles (1844–1916)

Saved

Sauvé

Gerettet

Salvados

Resgatado

Gered

n. d., Oil on canvas/
Huile sur toile,
91,4 × 71,2 cm,
Private collection

The *Ramillies* Water-Logg'd with Her Admiral and Crew Quitting the Deck

Le *Ramillies* avec son amiral et l'équipage quittant le pont

Die *Ramillies* voll Wasser gelaufen, mit ihrem Admiral und der Crew das Wrack verlassend

El *Ramillies* anegado con su almirante y tripulación dejando el naufragio

Afundamento do *Ramillies*, deixando o naufrágio com seu Almirante e tripulação

De volgelopen *Ramillies* terwijl haar admiraal en bemanning het wrak verlaten

1795, Aquatint/Aquatinte, Royal Naval Museum, Portsmouth

This work is one of four motifs with which Englishman Robert Dodd described the fate of the Ramillies. The ship was commissioned in 1763 and was used by the British in the American War of Independence until it sank twenty years later in a huge storm off the coast of Newfoundland.

Ce travail est l'un des quatre motifs avec lesquels l'Anglais Robert Dodd décrivit le sort des Ramillies. Le navire fut commandé en 1763 puis utilisé par les Britanniques dans la guerre d'indépendance américaine jusqu'à son naufrage vingt ans plus tard dans une énorme tempête au large de la côte de Terre-Neuve.

Das vorliegende Bild ist eines von vier Motiven, mit denen der Engländer Robert Dodd das Schicksal der Ramillies nachzeichnet. Das 1763 in Dienst gestellte Schiff wurde von den Briten im Amerikanischen Unabhängigkeitskrieg eingesetzt, bis es zwanzig Jahre später in einem gewaltigen Sturm vor der Küste Neufundlands sank.

La presente imagen es uno de los cuatro diseños con los que el inglés Robert Dodd describe el destino del Ramillies. La nave, en servicio en 1763, fue utilizada por los británicos en la Guerra de la Independencia americana, hasta que veinte años más tarde se hundió en una violenta tormenta frente a la costa de Terranova.

Este quadro é um de quatro temas com os quais o inglês Robert Dodd traça o destino do Ramillies. O navio, colocado ao serviço em 1763, foi usado pelos ingleses na Guerra Revolucionária Americana, até o seu afundamento vinte anos depois, em uma violenta tempestade na costa da Terra Nova.

Dit werk is een van de vier schilderijen waarin de Engelsman Robert Dodd het lot van de Ramillies heeft vastgelegd. Het in 1763 van stapel gelopen schip werd door de Britten in de Amerikaanse Onafhankelijkheidsoorlog ingezet, totdat het twintig jaar later bij zware storm voor de kust van Newfoundland zonk.

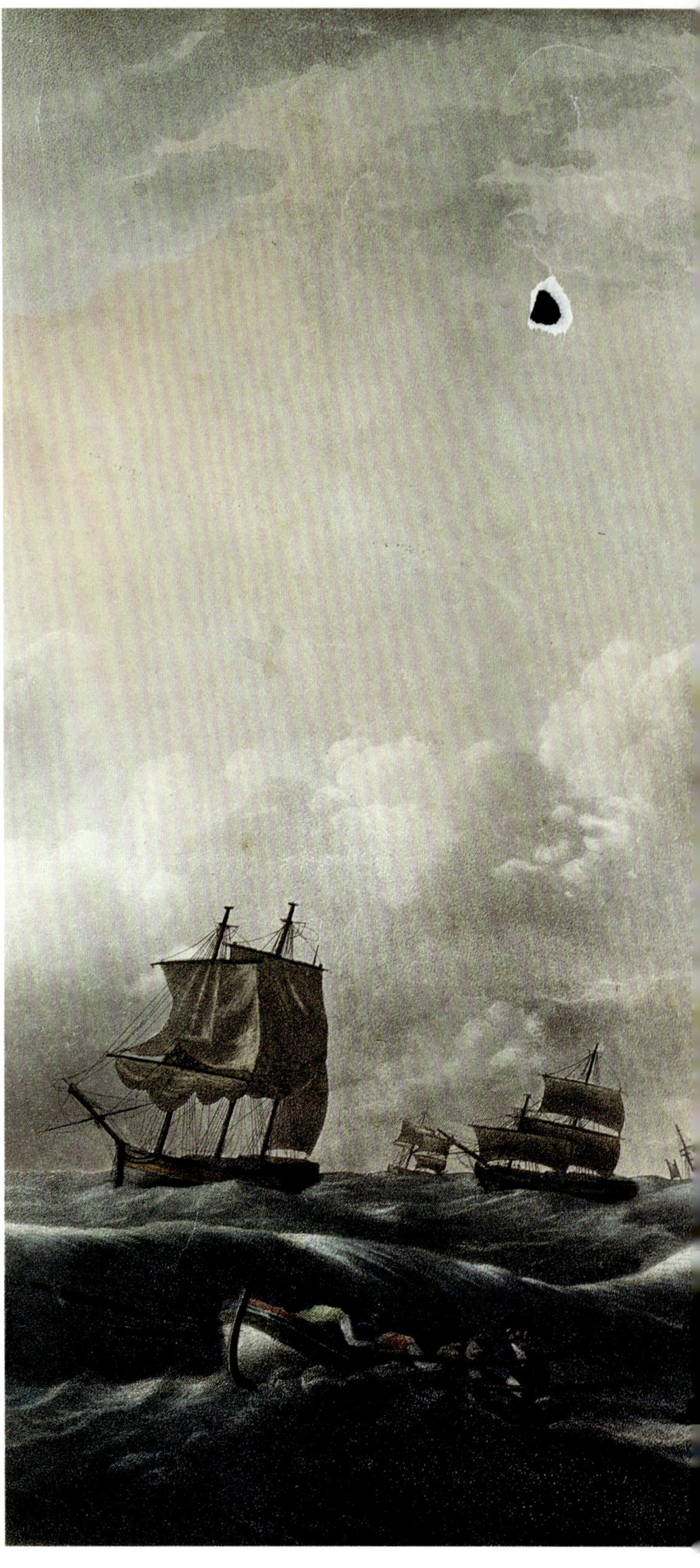

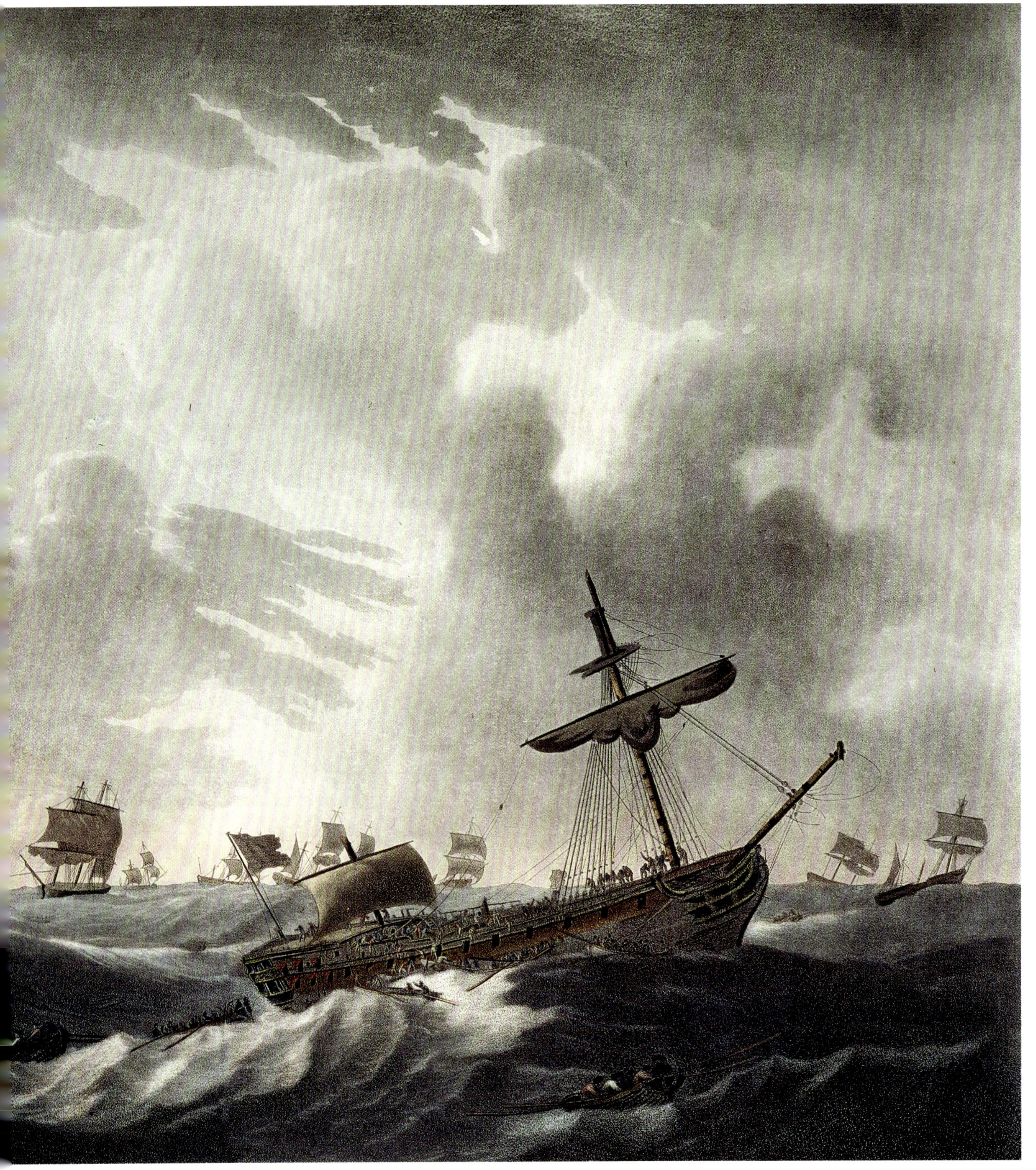

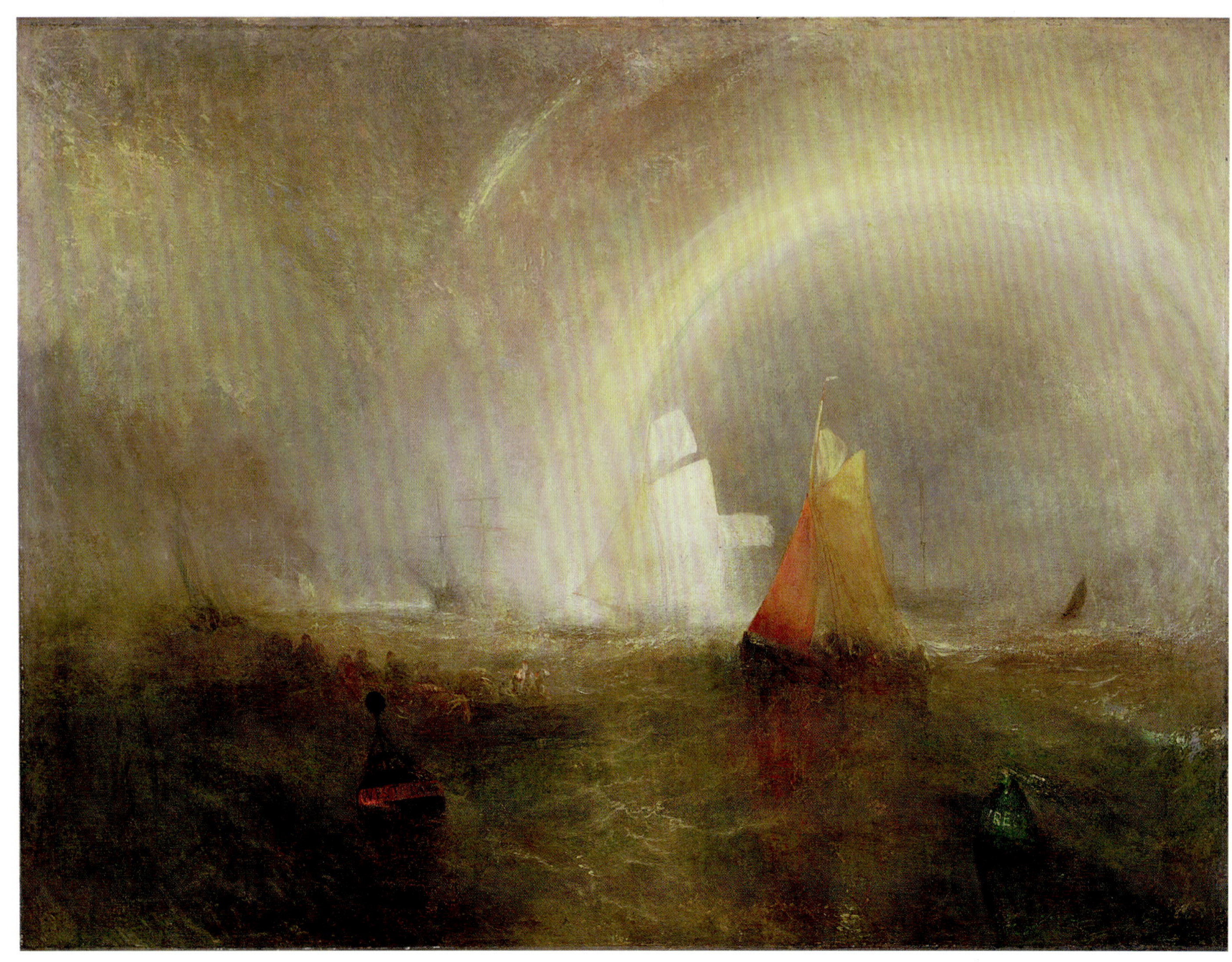

Joseph Mallord William Turner (1775–1851)

The Wreck Buoy

Bouée de l'épave

Die Wrackboje

La boya del naufragio

O Wrackboje

De wrakboei

1849, Oil on canvas/Huile sur toile, 92,7 × 123,2 cm, Walker Art Gallery, Liverpool

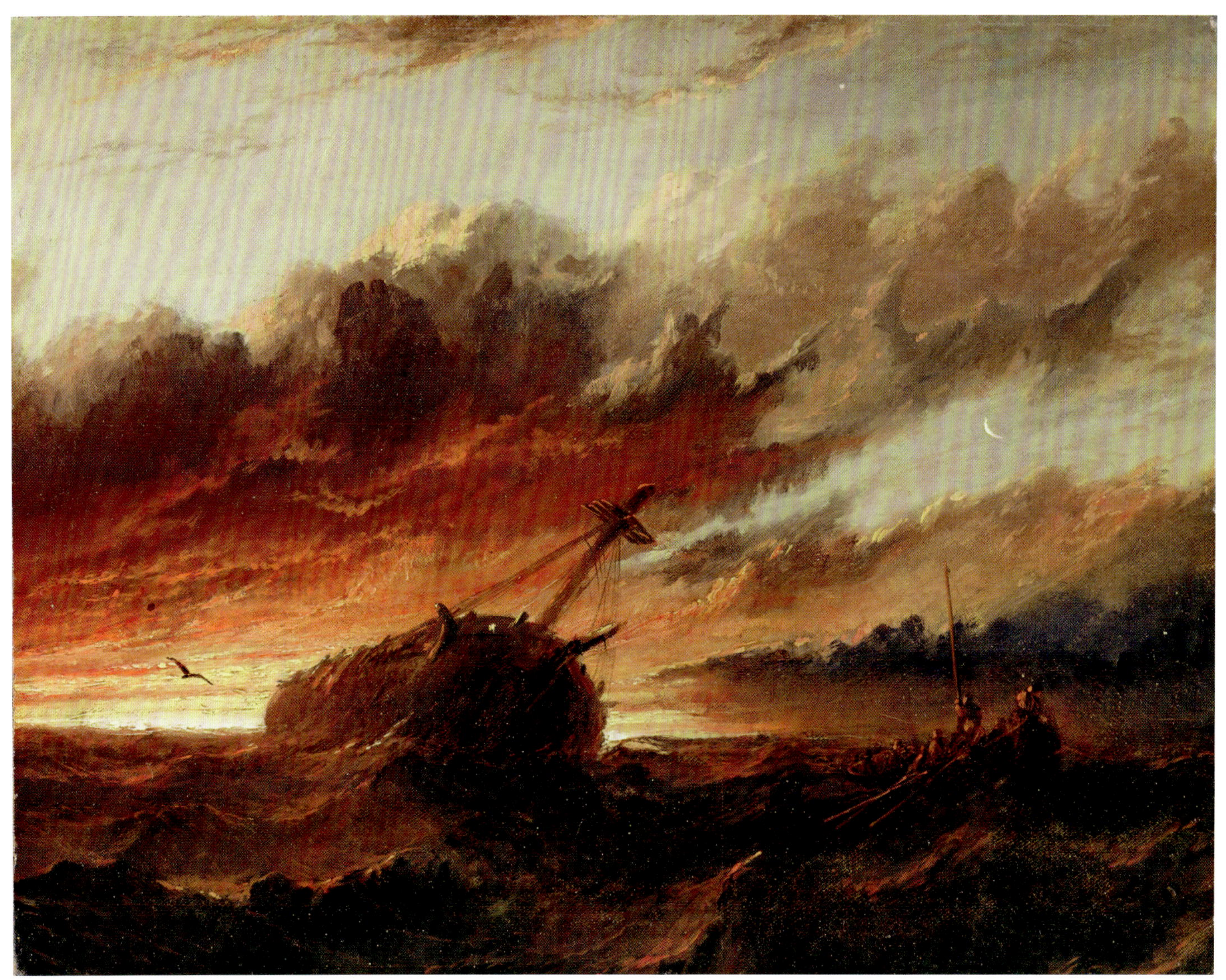

Francis Danby (1793–1861)

Shipwreck

Naufrage

Schiffswrack

Naufragio

Naufrágio

Scheepswrak

c. 1850, Oil on canvas/Huile sur toile, 31,7 × 40,5 cm, Yale Center for British Art, New Haven

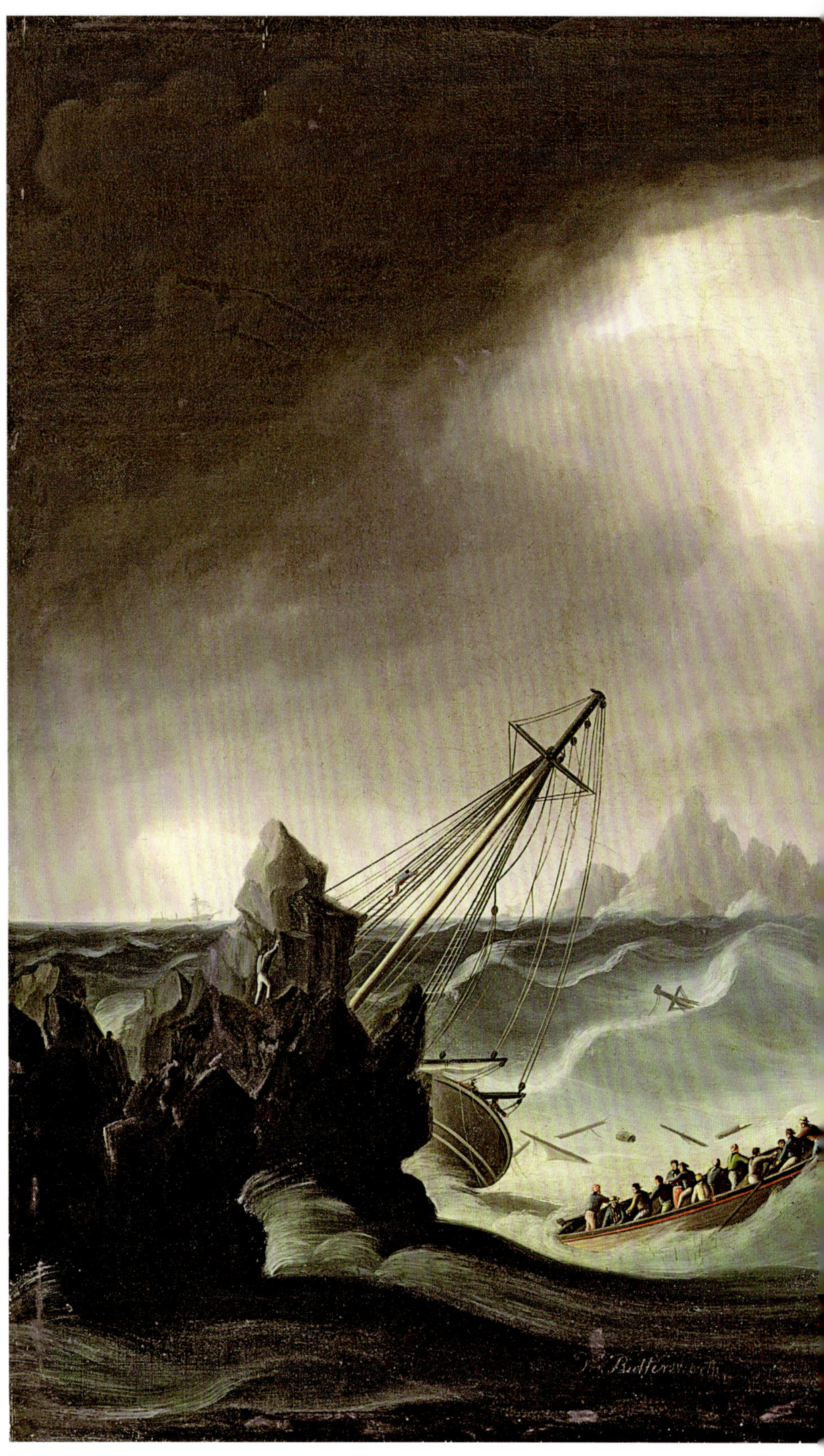

Thomas Buttersworth (1768–1842)

Shipwreck off a Rocky Coast

Naufrage au large d'une côte rocheuse

Schiffswrack vor einer felsigen Küste

Naufragio ante costa rocosa

Naufrágio ao largo de uma costa rochosa

Scheepswrak voor een rotskust

c. 1810, Oil on canvas/Huile sur toile, 59,1 × 89,5 cm,
Yale Center for British Art, New Haven

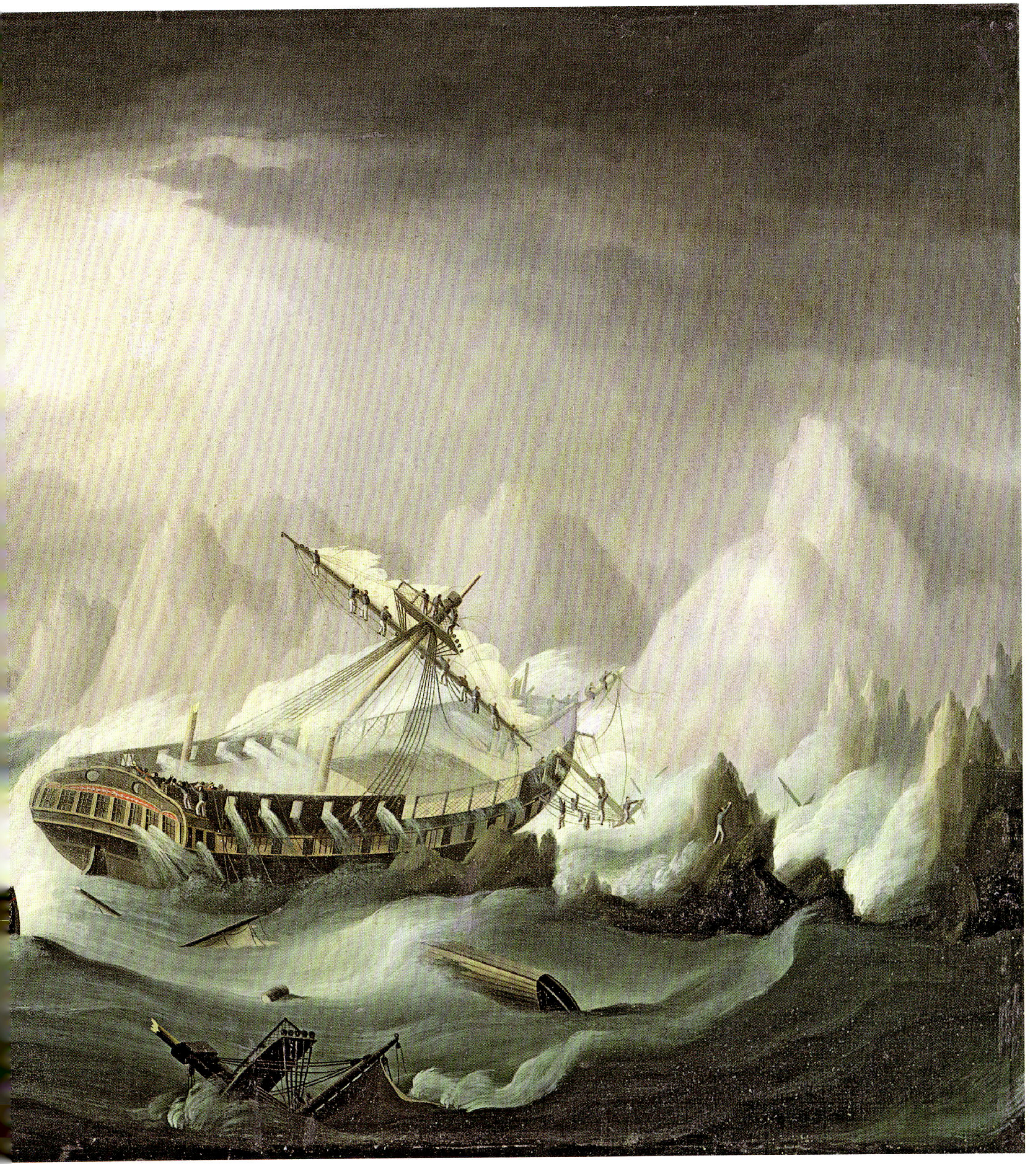

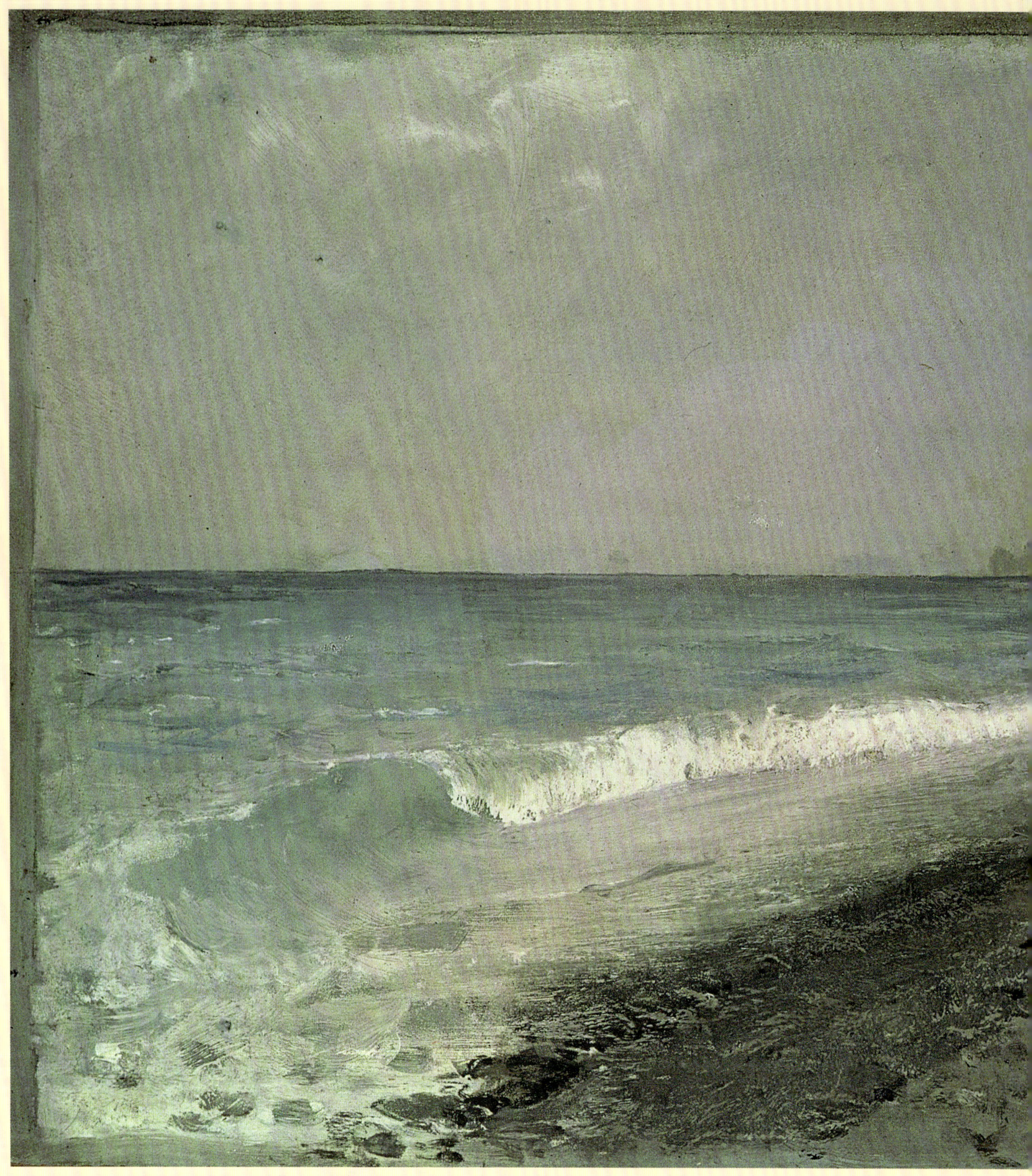

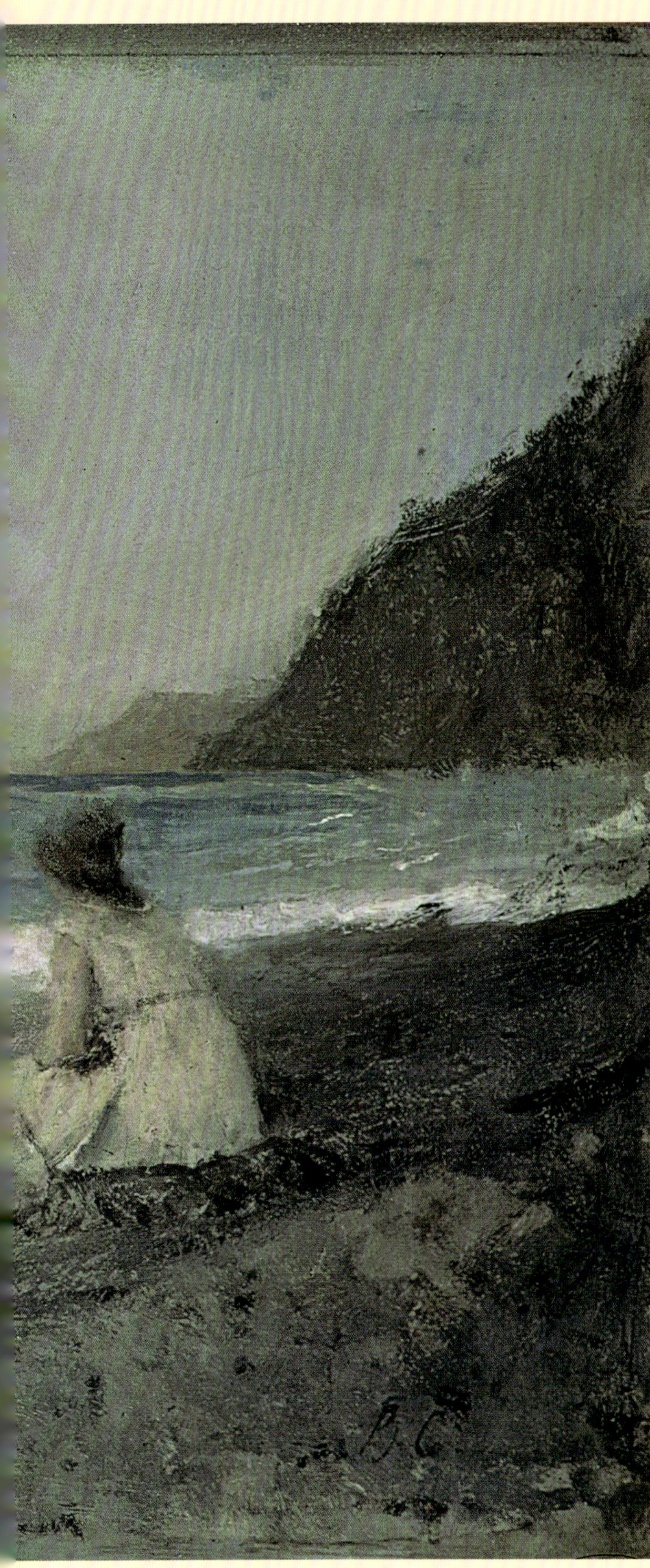

The sea as a symbol

La mer en tant que symbole

Das Meer als Symbol

El mar como símbolo

O mar como símbolo

De zee als symbool

Valentin Alexandrovitsch Serov (1865–1911)
Iphigenia at Tauris
Iphigénie en Tauride
Iphigenie auf Tauris
Iphigenie en Tauris
Ifigênia em Táurida
Iphigeneia in Tauris
1893, Oil on canvas/Huile sur toile, 94 × 134 cm, Brodsky Museum, St. Petersburg

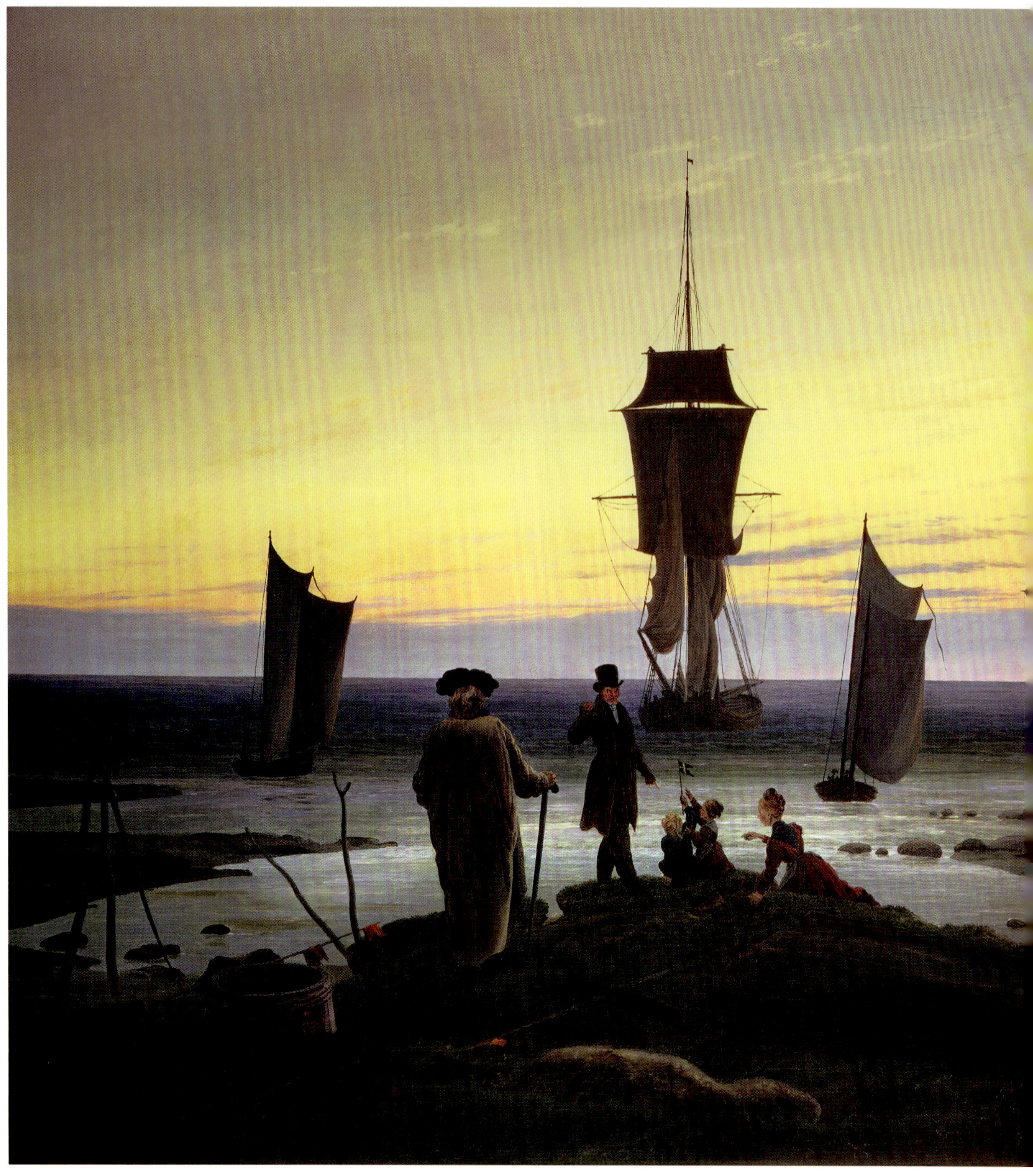

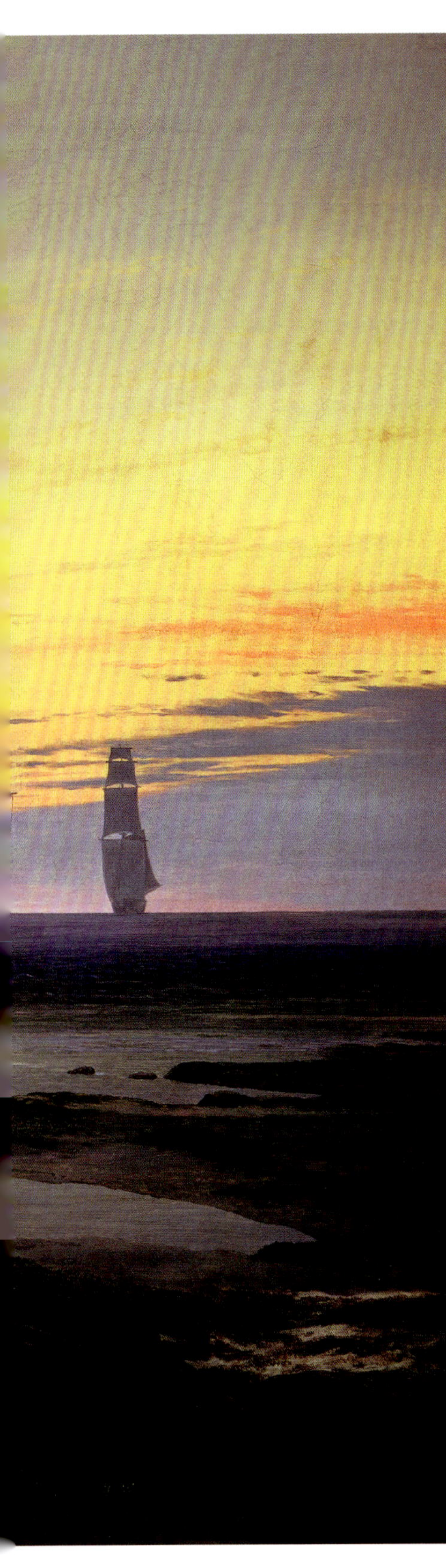

The Stages of Life

Les Âges de vie

Die Lebensstufen

Las etapas de la vida

As fases da vida

De levensfasen

c. 1835, Oil on canvas/Huile sur toile, 72,5 × 94 cm, Museum der Bildenden Künstle, Leipzig

The Stages of Life *is undoubtedly one of the most famous paintings by Romantic painter Caspar David Friedrich. The five ships heading for the coast correspond to the five people who are placed on a hill in the foreground and are symbolic of different ages.*

Les Âges de vie *est sans doute l'une des peintures les plus célèbres du peintre romantique Caspar David Friedrich. Les cinq navires qui se dirigent vers la côte correspondent aux cinq personnes qui sont placées sur une colline au premier plan et qui symbolisent les âges différents.*

Das Bild Die Lebensstufen *gehört zweifellos zu den berühmtesten Gemälden des Greifswalder Romantikers Caspar David Friedrich. Die fünf auf die Küste zusteuernden Schiffe korrespondieren mit den fünf Personen, die auf einer Anhöhe im Vordergrund platziert sind und symbolisch für unterschiedliche Lebensalter stehen.*

El cuadro Las etapas de la vida *es, sin duda, uno de los cuadros más famosos del romántico Caspar David Friedrich, nacido en Greifswald. Los cinco barcos que se dirigen a la costa corresponden a las cinco personas situadas en una colina en el primer plano y que representan simbólicamente una edad diferente.*

O quadro As fases da vida *é sem dúvida um dos mais famosos do pintor romântico Caspar David Friedrich, de Greifswald. Os cinco navios se dirigindo até a costa correspondem às cinco pessoas colocadas em uma colina, no primeiro plano, e representando simbolicamente diferentes idades.*

Die Lebensstufen *(De levensfasen) behoort ongetwijfeld tot de beroemdste werken van de uit Greifswald afkomstige romantische schilder Caspar David Friedrich. De vijf op de kust aansturende schepen staan voor de vijf personen die op een verhoging op de voorgrond zijn geplaatst en de verschillende fasen van het leven symboliseren.*

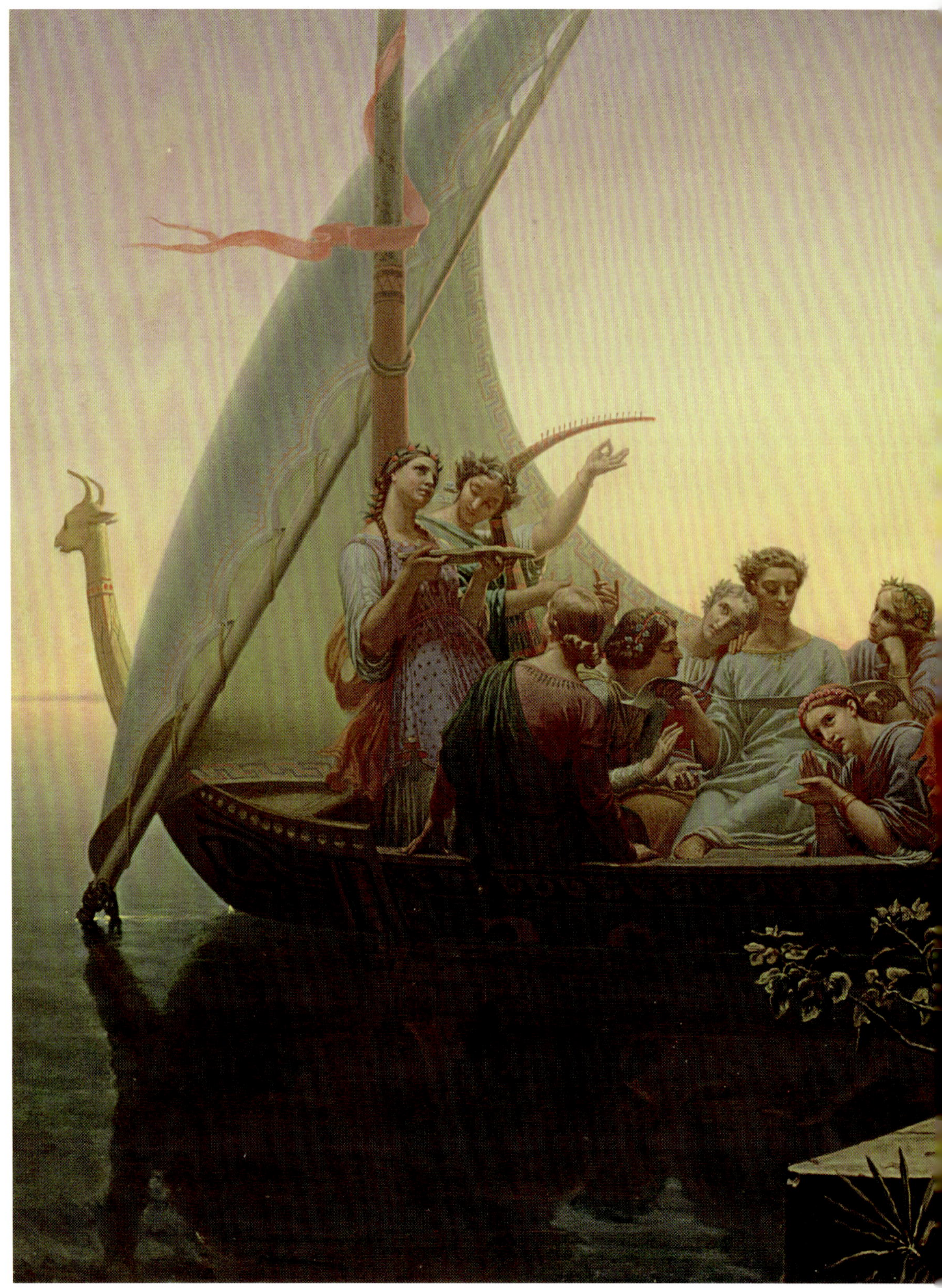

Charles Gleyre (1806–74)

The Evening *or* Lost Illusions

Le Soir *ou* Les illusions perdues

Der Abend *oder*
Verlorene Illusionen

Atardecer *o* Ilusiones perdidas

A Noite *ou* Ilusões Perdidas

De avond *of* Vervlogen illusies

1865–67, Oil on canvas/
Huile sur toile, 86,5 × 150,5 cm,
Walters Art Museum, Baltimore

This painting The Evening *is
also known as* Lost Illusions.
*It symbolizes the melancholy of
an elderly man, reflecting on his
youthful dream and illusions,
depicted as beautiful women
making music. Gleyre was
already over 60 years old at the
time he completed this piece.*

La peinture Le Soir *est également
connue sous le nom* Illusions
perdues. *Elle symbolise la
mélancolie d'un homme âgé,
reflétant ses rêves et ses illusions
de jeunesse, représentés comme
de belles femmes musiciennes.
Gleyre avait déjà plus de 60 ans
lorsqu'il acheva cette pièce.*

Das Gemälde Der Abend *ist auch
bekannt als* Verlorene Illusionen.
*Es symbolisiert die Melancholie
eines betagten Mannes – Gleyre war
zum Zeitpunkt der Fertigstellung
bereits über 60 Jahre alt – der
seinen jugendlichen Träumen
und Illusionen nachhängt,
im Bild als musizierende
Schönheiten dargestellt.*

El cuadro Atardecer *también se
conoce con el nombre de* Ilusiones
perdidas. *Simboliza la melancolía
de un hombre de edad avanzada
– Gleyre tenía ya más de 60 años
de edad en el momento de la
finalización del cuadro – que está
absorto en sus sueños e ilusiones
juveniles, representados en la
imagen como bellezas musicales.*

A pintura A Noite *também é
conhecida como* Ilusões perdidas.
*Ela simboliza a melancolia de um
homem idoso – Gleyre já tinha
mais de 60 anos de idade quando
o quadro foi finalizado – que se
entrega a seus sonhos e ilusões de
juventude, representados no quadro
como beldades tocando música.*

Het schilderij De avond *staat ook
wel bekend als* Vervlogen illusies.
*Het symboliseert de melancholie
van de man op leeftijd – Gleyre
was bij de voltooiing van dit werk
boven de zestig – die terugblikt
op de dromen en illusies van
zijn jeugd, hier uitgebeeld als
musicerende schoonheden.*

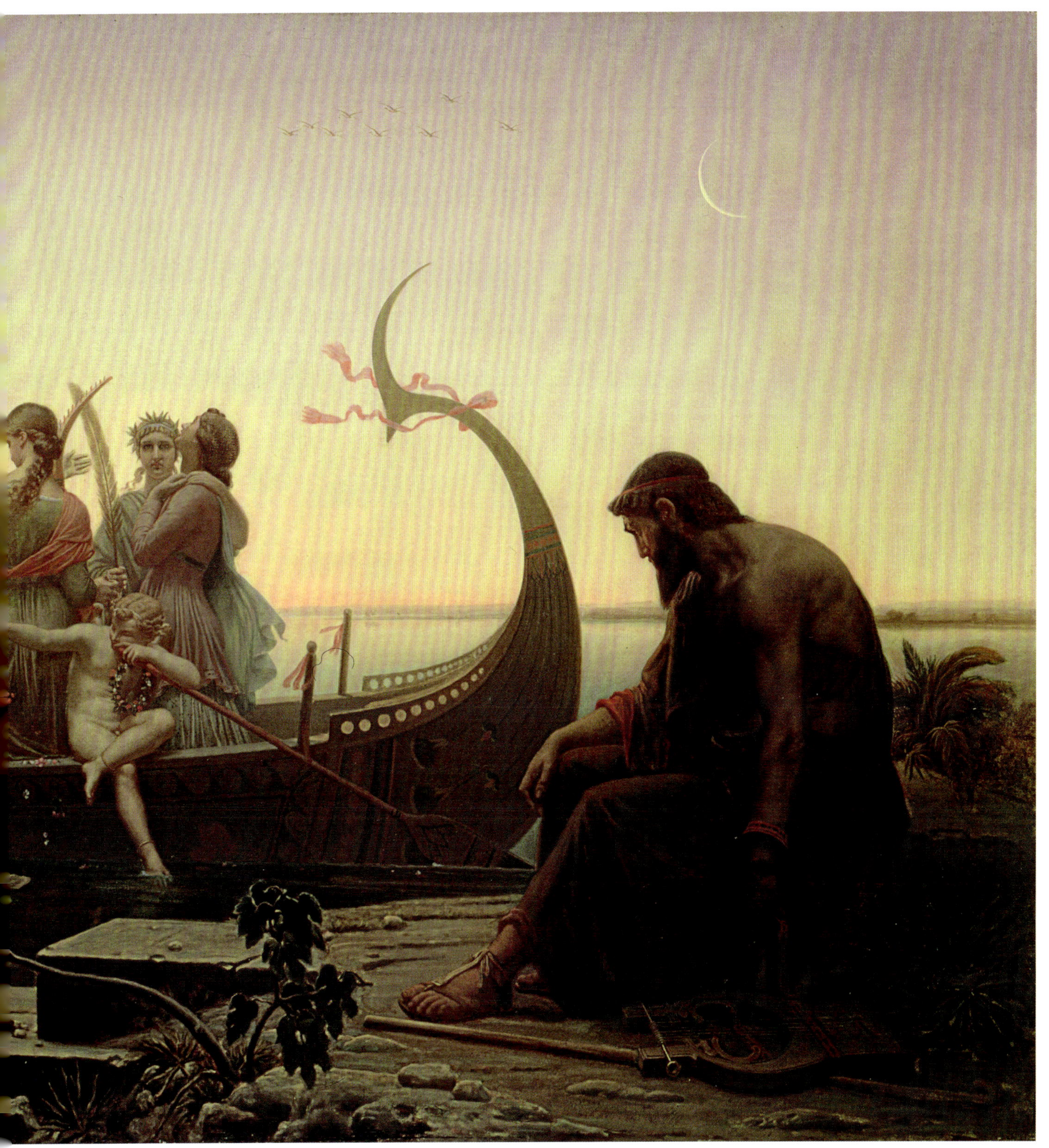

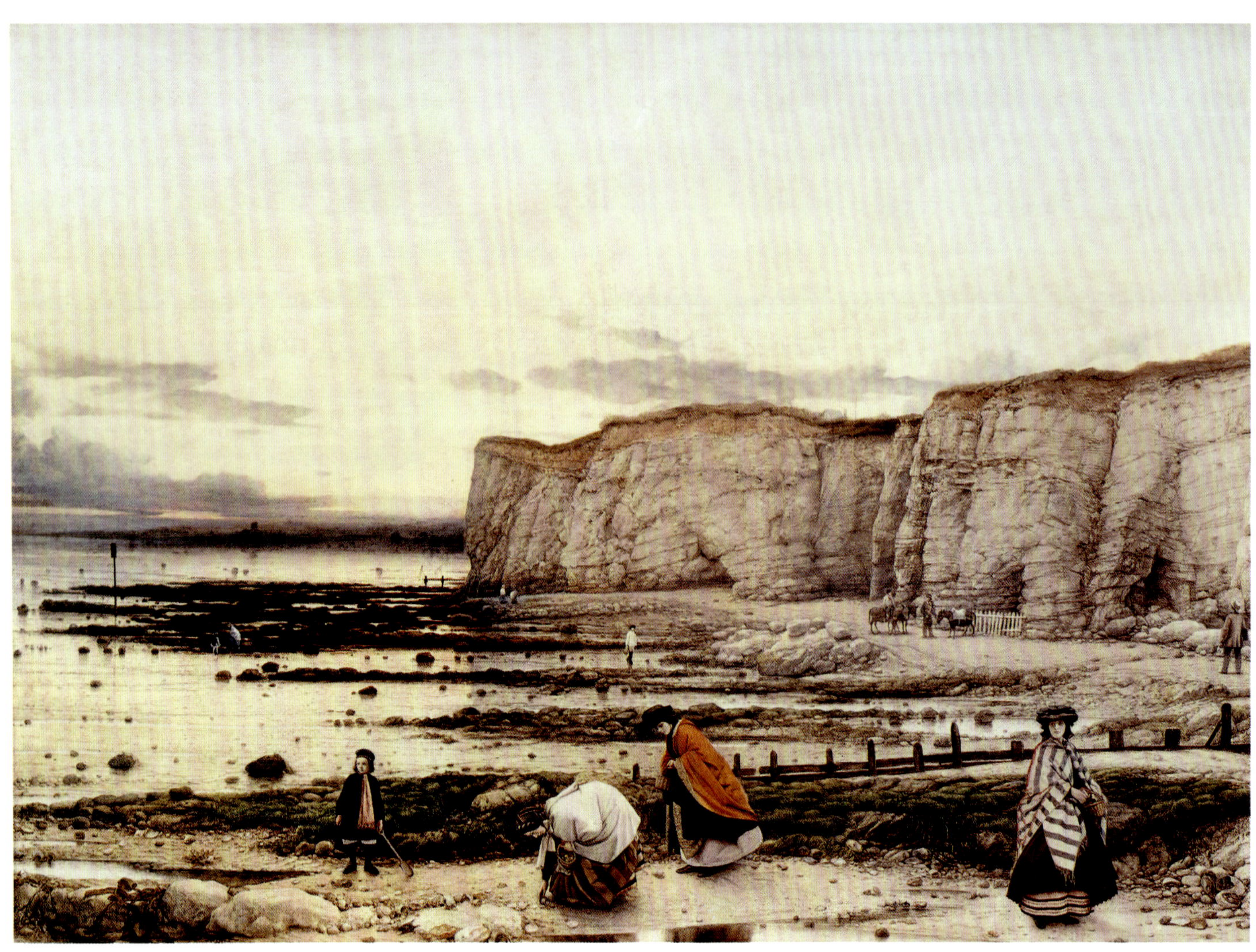

William Dyce (1806–64)

Pegwell Bay, Kent

Baie de Pegwell

Pegwell Bay

La bahía de Pegwell

Baía de Pegwel

Pegwell Bay

c. 1858, Oil on canvas/Huile sur toile, 63 × 89 cm, Tate Britain, London

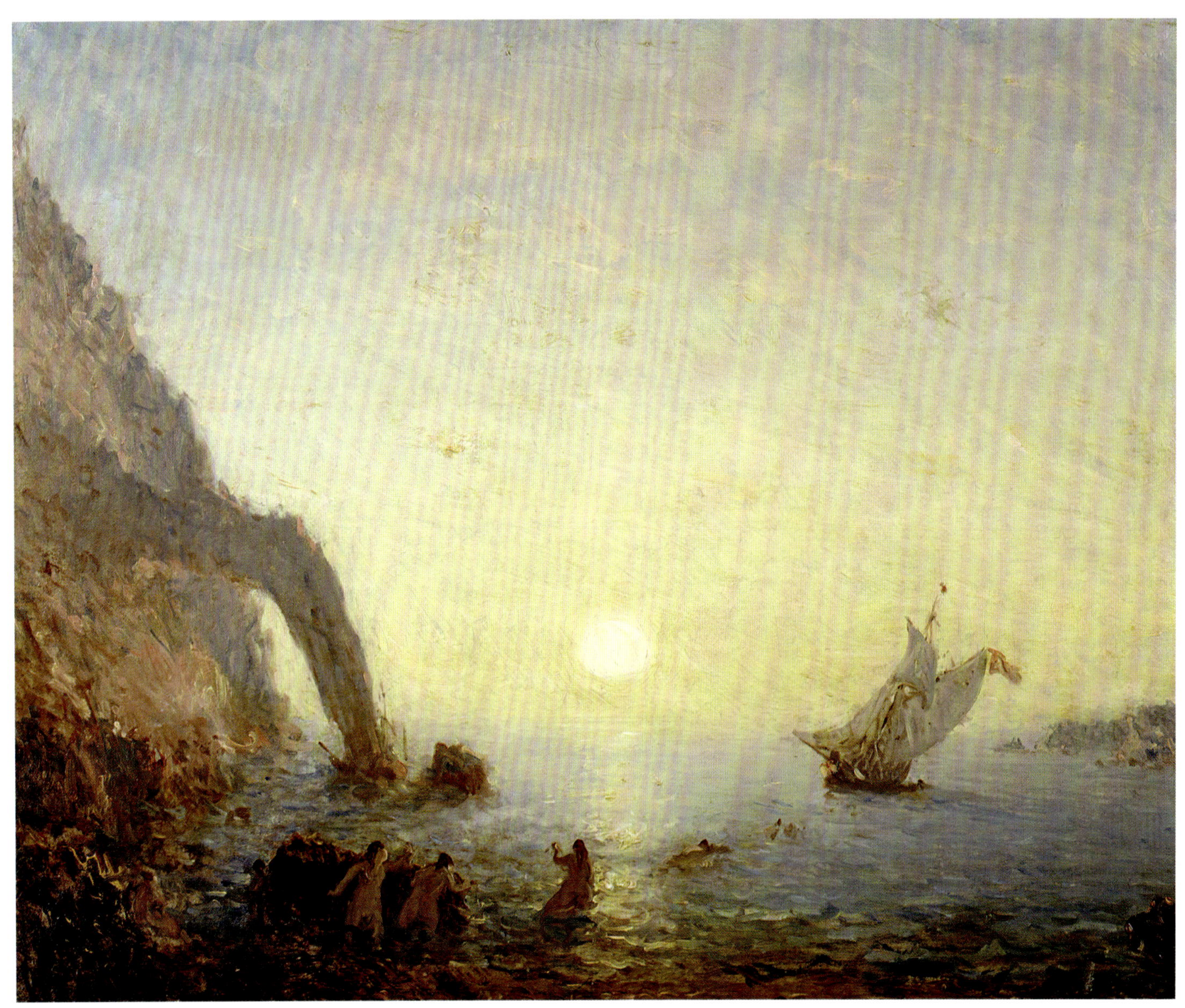

Felix Ziem (1821–1911)

The Call of the Sirens

L'appel des sirènes

Der Ruf der Sirenen

La llamada de las sirenas

O Canto das Sereias

De zang der Sirenen

19th century/XIXᵉ siècle, Oil on canvas/Huile sur toile, 49 × 60,3 cm, Private collection

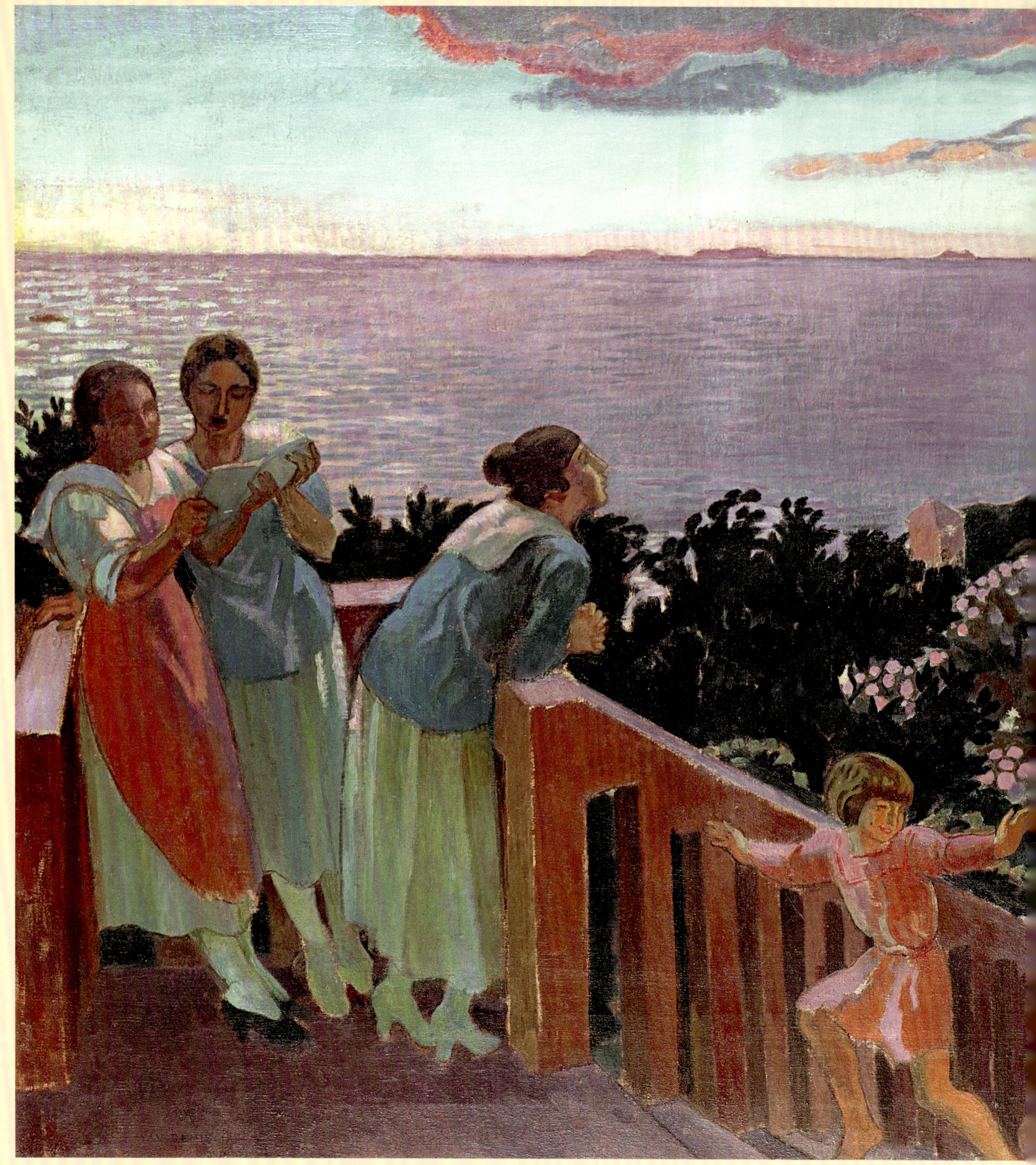

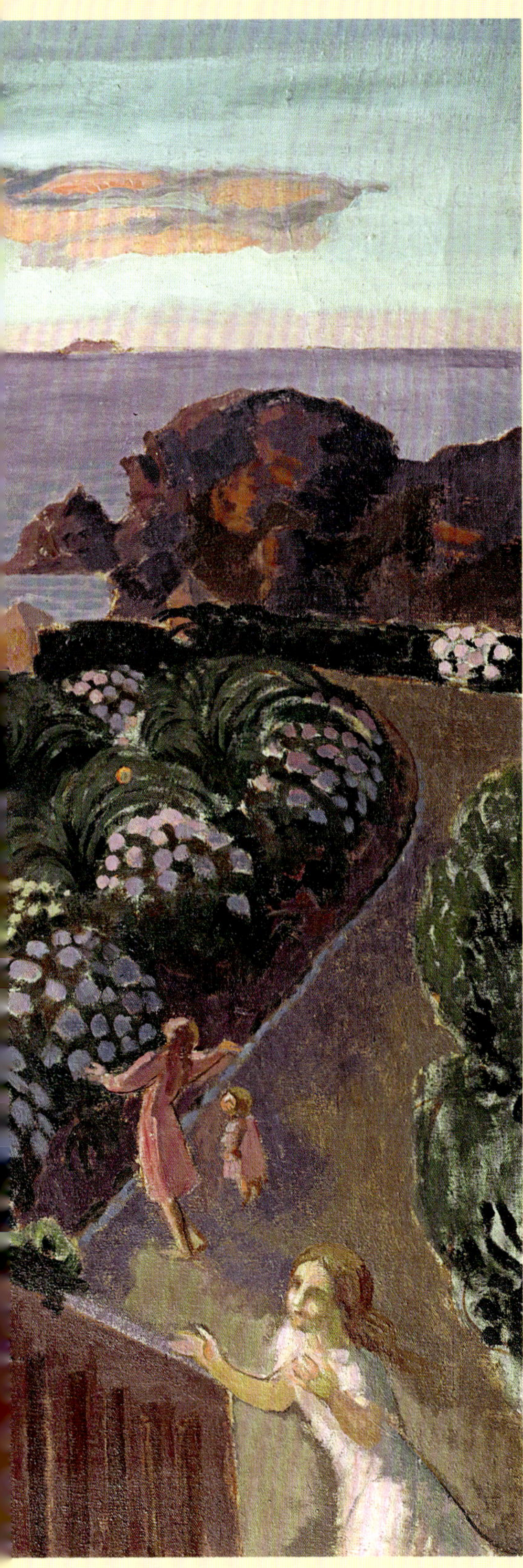

Maurice Denis (1870–1943)
Quiet on the Balcony
Silence au balcon
Ruhe auf dem Balkon
Balcón en Silencio
Descanso na varanda
Het balkon van villa Silencio
1918, Oil on canvas/Huile sur toile, 88 × 112 cm, Private collection

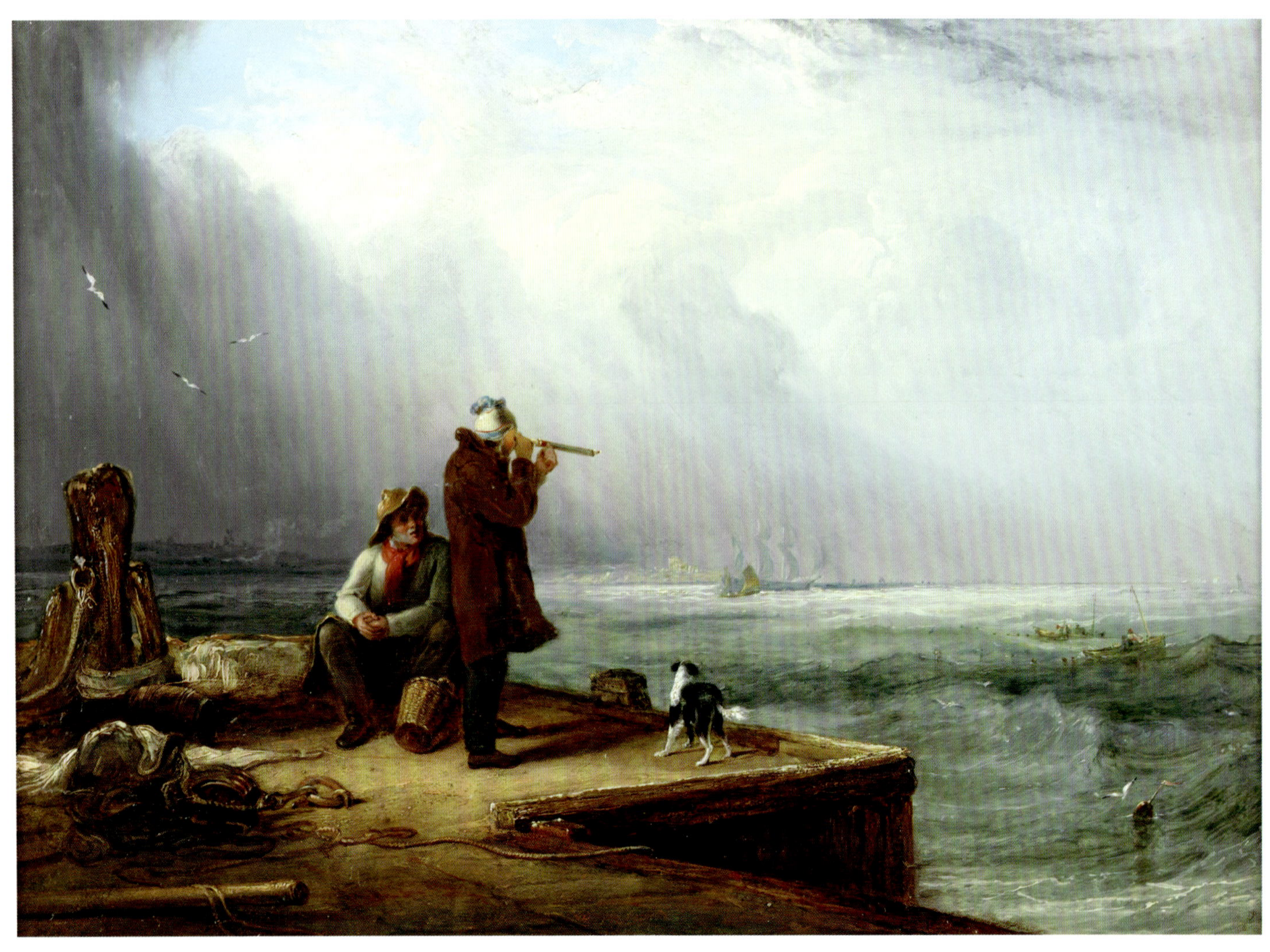

Henry Perlee Parker (1795–1873)

The Look Out, Shields Harbour

Surveillance, port de Shields

Der Ausguck, Shields Harbour

Puesto de observación, Shields Harbour

O Mirante, Shields Harbour

De uitkijk, Shields Harbour

1831, Oil on panel/Huile sur bois, 35,5 × 45,5 cm, Shipley Art Gallery, Gateshead

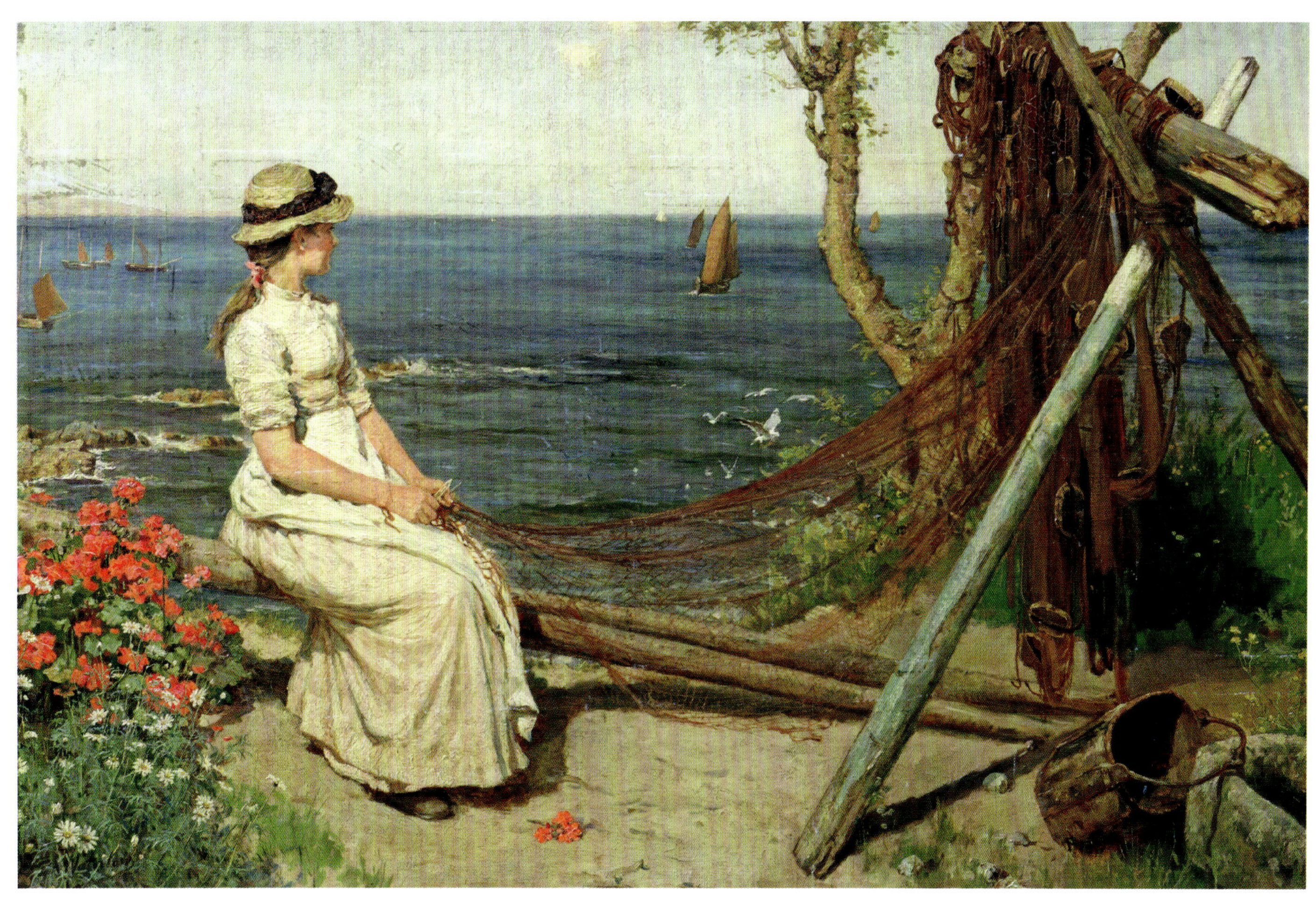

Ernest Albert Waterlow (1850–1919)

Mending the Nets, Newlyn, Cornwall

Réparation des filets

Ausbessern der Netze

Arreglando las redes

Emendando as redes

Het repareren van de visnetten

1882, Oil on canvas/Huile sur toile, 61,5 × 91 cm, Touchstones Rochdale, Rochdale

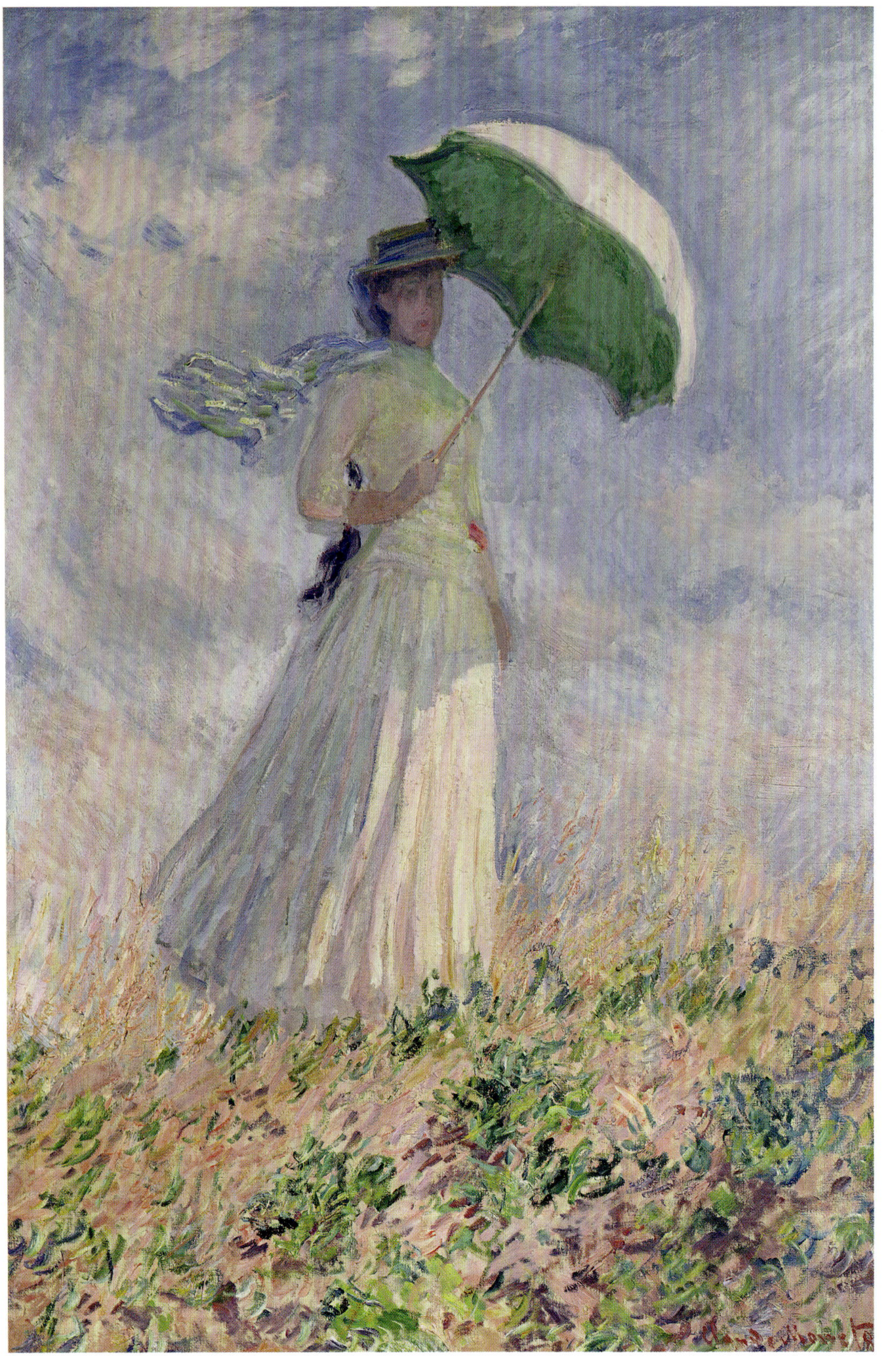

Claude Monet (1840–1926)

Woman with a Parasol

La Promenade

Frau mit Sonnenschirm

Mujer con sombrilla

Mulher com guarda-sol

Naar rechts gekeerde vrouw met parasol

1886, Oil on canvas/Huile sur toile,
131 × 88 cm, Musée d'Orsay, Paris

Monet's Lady with a Parasol *not only holds a special place in the work of the artist himself, but also in the entire history of art. For the first time, Monet paints the same subject at different times of the day to show the changing effects of the light. A procedure he would use a few years later in his two series* The Cathedral of Rouen *and the* Haystack.

La Promenade de Monet occupe non seulement une place particulière dans le travail de l'artiste lui-même, mais aussi dans toute l'histoire de l'art. Pour la première fois, Monet peint le même sujet à différents moments de la journée pour montrer les effets changeants de la lumière. Une procédure qu'il utilisera quelques années plus tard dans ses deux séries La Cathédrale de Rouen *et* La Meule de foin.

Monets Dame mit Sonnenschirm *nimmt nicht nur im Werk des Künstlers selbst einen besonderen Platz ein, sondern in der gesamten Kunstgeschichte. Zum ersten Mal malt Monet hier dasselbe Sujet zu unterschiedlichen Tageszeiten, um die wechselnden Effekte des Lichts zu zeigen. Ein Verfahren, das er weniger Jahre später auch in den beiden Bildserien* Kathedrale von Rouen *und den* Heuhaufen *anwenden sollte.*

La Mujer con sombrilla *de Monet no sólo ocupa un lugar especial en la obra del propio artista, sino en toda la historia del arte. Por primera vez, Monet pinta aquí el mismo tema en diferentes momentos del día, para mostrar los efectos cambiantes de la luz. Un procedimiento que se utilizaría un par de años más tarde en las dos series de imágenes de* La Catedral de Rouen *y de los* Almiares.

A Dama com guarda-sol, *de Monet, ocupa um lugar especial não somente na obra do próprio artista, mas em toda a história da arte. Pela primeira vez, Monet pinta aqui o mesmo assunto em diferentes momentos do dia, para mostrar os efeitos de mudança da luz. Um processo que ele usaria alguns anos mais tarde, também nas duas séries de quadros* Catedral de Rouen *e* Palheiros.

Monets Naar rechts gekeerde vrouw met parasol *neemt niet alleen in het oeuvre van de kunstenaar maar in de kunstgeschiedenis als geheel een bijzondere plaats in. Voor het eerst schilderde Monet hetzelfde object op verschillende tijdstippen van de dag, om de veranderlijke effecten van het licht vast te leggen – een procédé dat hij later zou herhalen in zijn beide series* De Kathedraal van Rouen *en* Hooibergen.

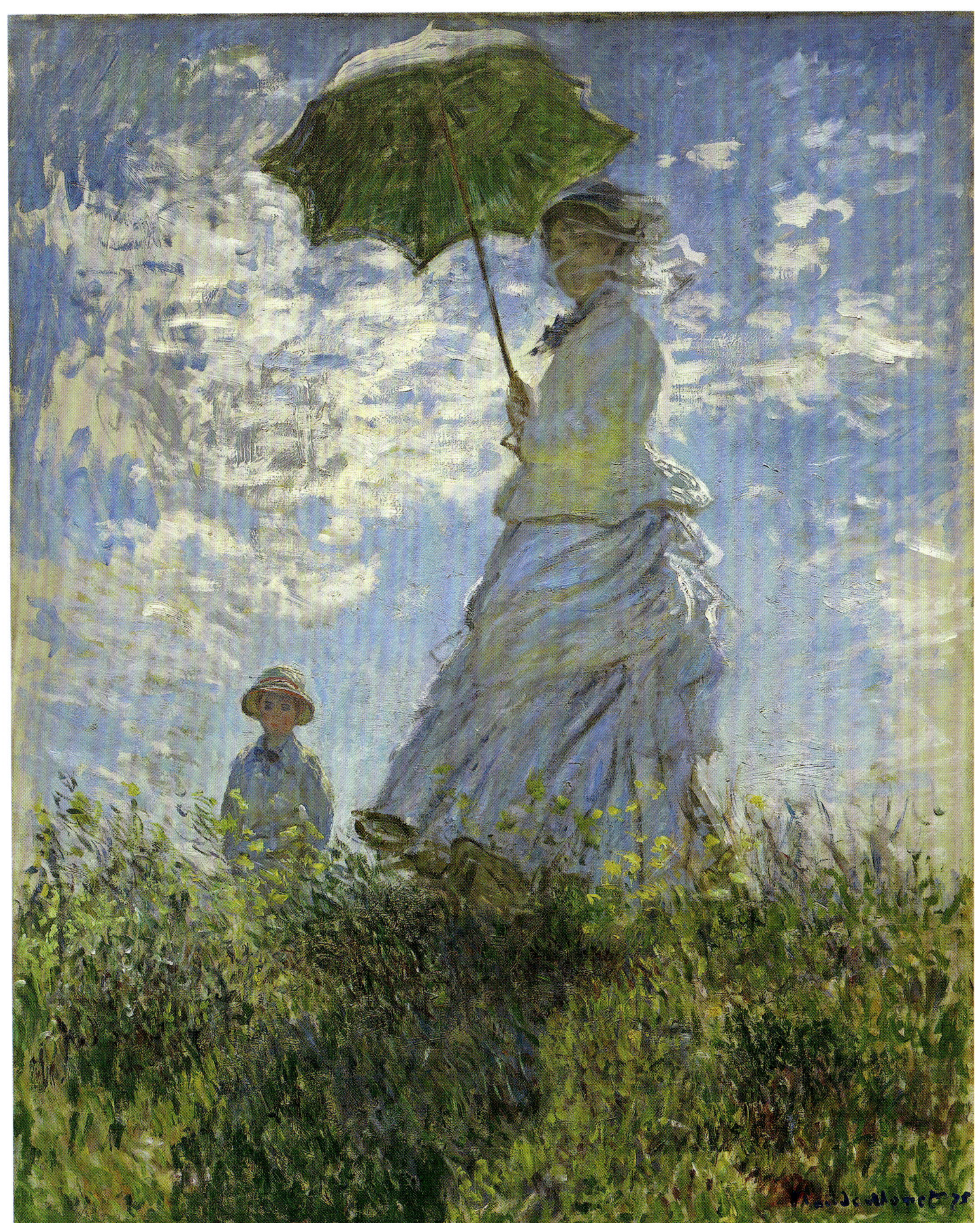

Claude Monet
(1840–1926)

Woman with a
Parasol—Madame
Monet and Her Son

La Promenade –
la femme à l'ombrelle

Der Spaziergang –
Frau mit Sonnenschirm,
Madame Monet
und ihr Sohn

El paseo– mujer con
sombrilla, Madame
Monet y su hijo

La passeggiata –
donna com
guarda-sol, la signora
Monet e suo figlio

Wandeling – vrouw
met parasol, Madame
Monet en haar zoon

1875, Oil on canvas/Huile
sur toile, 100 × 81 cm,
National Gallery of
Art, Washington

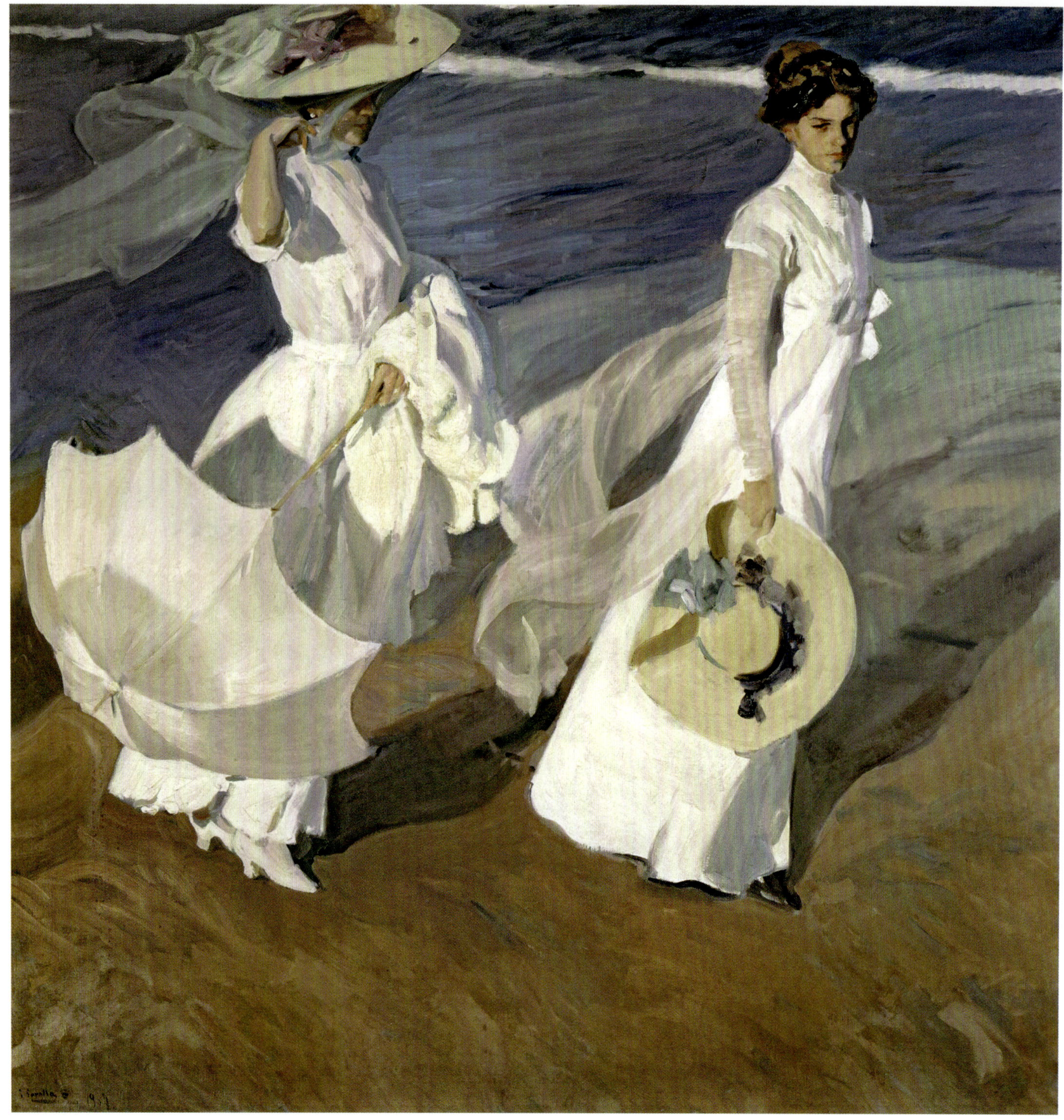

Joaquin Sorolla y Bastida (1863–1923)

Strolling Along the Seashore	Spaziergang an der Meeresküste	Passeio à beira-mar
Promenade le long de la plage	Paseo a orillas del mar	Wandeling langs de kust

1909, Oil on canvas/Huile sur toile, 205 × 200 cm, Museo Sorolla, Madrid

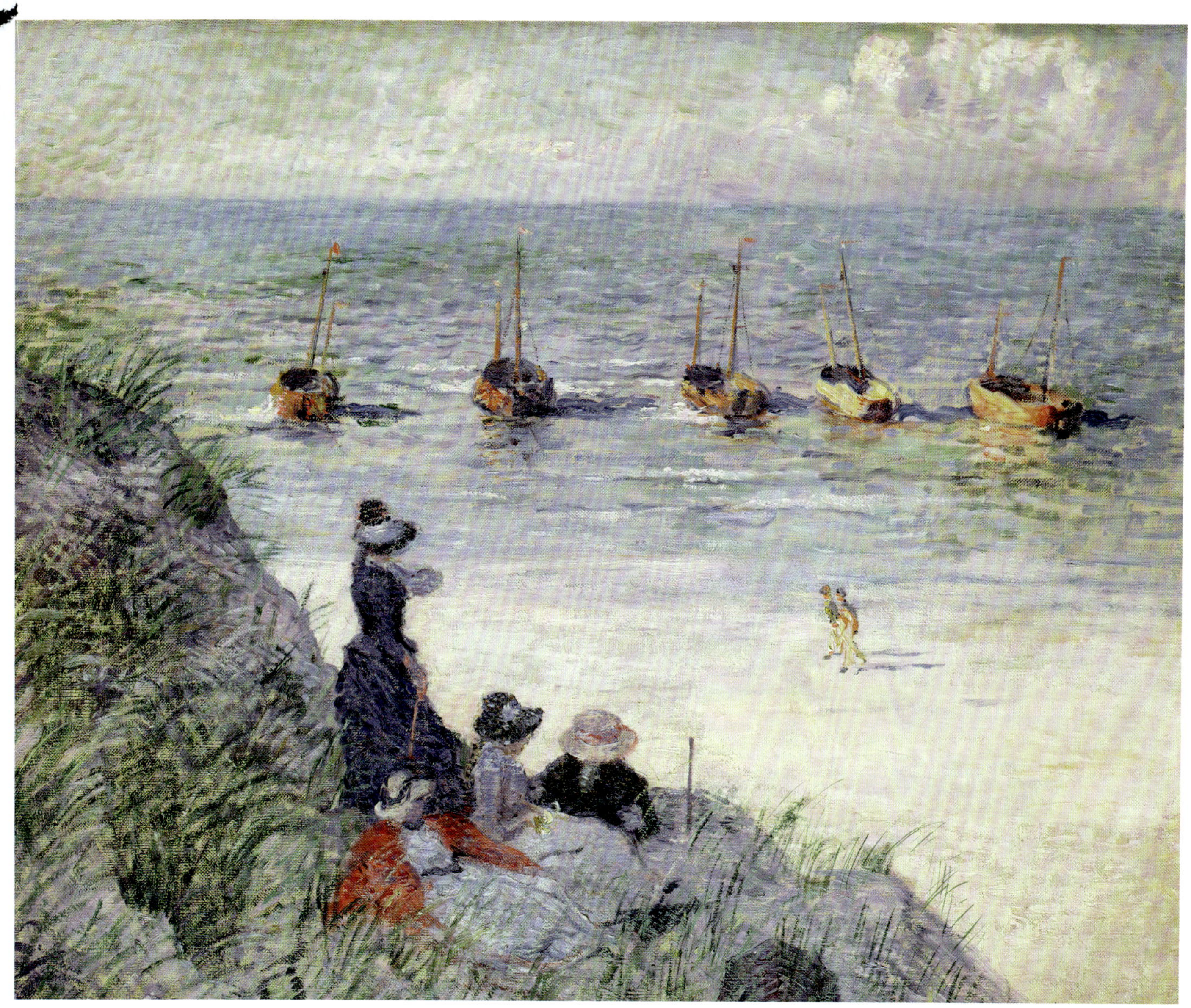

Théo van Rysselberghe (1862–1926)

On the Dunes, Heyst

Sur les dunes, Heyst

In den Dünen, Heyst

En las dunas, Heyst

Nas Dunas, Heyst

In de duinen bij Heyst

19th century/XIXᵉ siècle, Oil on canvas/Huile sur toile, Private collection

David Cordingly, *Ships and Seascapes: An Introduction to Maritime Prints, Drawings and Watercolours*, London 1997

Richard Johns, *Turner & the Sea*, London 2013

National Maritime Museum, *Concise Catalogue of Oil Paintings in the National Maritime Museum*, London 1988

James Taylor, *Marine Painting. Images of Sail, Sea and Shore*, London 1995

Aux couleurs de la mer (Catalogue de l'exposition, Musée d'Orsay), Paris 1999

Roberto Mussapi, *La mer en peinture*, Paris 2007

Ekhart Berckenhagen, *Schiffe – Häfen – Kontinente. Eine Kulturgeschichte der Seefahrt*, Berlin 1983

Jörgen Bracker, Peter Tamm (u. a. Hrsg.), *Maler der See. Marinemalerei in drei Jahrhunderten*, Herford 1980

Martin Faass (u. a. Hrsg.), *Seestücke. Von Caspar David Friedrich bis Emil Nolde*
(Ausst.-Kat., Kunsthalle Hamburg), München 2005

William Gaunt, *Das Schiff in der Malerei*, Bielefeld 1976

Thomas Habersatter (Hrsg.), *Schiff voraus. Marinemalerei des 14. bis 19. Jahrhunderts*
(Ausst.-Kat., Residenzgalerie Salzburg), Salzburg 2005

Brian Lavery, *Schiffe. 5000 Jahre Seefahrt*, Starnberg 2005

Boye Meyer-Friese, *Marinemalerei in Deutschland im 19. Jahrhundert*, Hamburg 1981

Helge Sieffert (Hrsg.), *Claude-Joseph Vernet (1714–1789)* (Ausst.-Kat. Neue Pinakothek), München 1997

Werner Timm, *Schiffe und ihre Schicksale. Maritime Ereignisbilder*, 2. Aufl., Bielefeld 1977